GW01606669

# REMAINS
# Historical and Literary
CONNECTED WITH
THE PALATINE COUNTIES OF
# Lancaster and Chester

Volume LVII – Third Series

MANCHESTER
2024

# Officers and Council Members of the Society 2022–2023

# Henry V and the Earldom of Chester, 1399–1422

Anne Curry

*General Editor: Tim Thornton*

MANCHESTER
2024

Published by The Chetham Society



A Catalogue Record for this book is available from the British Library.

ISSN 0080-0880

ISBN 978-1-7394679-0-6

Prepared by:

York Publishing Services Ltd
64 Hallfield Road
Layerthorpe
York YO31 7ZQ
Tel: 01904 431213

www.yps-publishing.co.uk

Printed and bound by:

Smith Settle
Gateway Drive
Yeadon
LS19 7XY
Tel: 0113 250 9201

www.smithsettle.com

# *Contents*

# *Foreword*

To explain this book I must indulge in an autobiographical reminiscence. When I started my BA in History at the University of Manchester in 1972 I was already quite committed to medieval history, the result, perhaps, of having a view of Lumley Castle from my bedroom window as I grew up in another 'Chester' – Chester-le-Street in County Durham. Experiences during my degree course made me all the more certain I wanted to be a medievalist. I was particularly inspired by a second-year course on English Rural Society 1250–1400, brilliantly taught by Ian Kershaw, but Ian's appointment to a post in twentieth-century history in the same department meant I had to switch from his proposed third-year Special Subject on English Monasteries in the Fourteenth Century to John Roskell's Reign of Henry V, where I was the only student. Those were certainly the days!

The University had a special arrangement for its graduates to take a one-year MA by research which customarily built upon the final year dissertation. I therefore gained funding to expand my work on the treaty of Troyes of 1420. But just as I was poised to begin, Ian alerted me to the researches of Paul Booth at the University of Liverpool on the financial administration of the earldom of Chester in the late thirteenth and fourteenth centuries. It took only one highly stimulating seminar led by Paul, along with encouragement from Ian, to persuade me that my MA should instead focus on the financial administration of that same earldom under Henry V as prince and king. This topic offered me the best of both worlds, as well as the exceptionally strong supervisory team of both Kershaw and Roskell. I have much reason to be grateful, since it was this research in social and economic history that gained me my first permanent academic post as a lecturer in that pathway ('Syllabus C' as it was curiously called) at the University of Reading in 1978.

Yet most people know me now as a historian of the Hundred Years' War. As the end of my Master's year approached I looked for a job and found one, as well as a husband, at what was then

Teesside Polytechnic, supporting Tony Pollard in his exploration of French sources on John Talbot, first earl of Shrewsbury and developing the doctoral project I had been assigned on how English captains formed their war retinues. That is where the work I had done earlier on the treaty of Troyes, supported also by Richard Davies's stimulating module on France and the Hundred Years' War, came back into play. And that's how I first came across muster rolls.

The rest, as they say, is history. Thousands of muster rolls later, including the many surviving not only for Henry V's campaign of 1415, which marched me to Agincourt, but also for the garrisons of Lancastrian Normandy, led me, with the encouragement of my external doctoral supervisor Christopher Allmand, to the Anglo-French specialism for which I am now known. Professor Roskell had been disappointed at my decision to drop Troyes for Cheshire. So I am sure he would feel vindicated by the fact that I was on the comité scientifique for a major exhibition in Troyes to commemorate the treaty of 1420 and that I have now published a number of articles on that very subject.

Life comes full circle. Here I am back in Cheshire, but still in Henry V territory. I have become increasingly fascinated by Henry at home and abroad, writing a short biography for Penguin Monarchs, editing a collection on his funeral and commemoration in Westminster Abbey, and creating an online edition of his Norman rolls. I was delighted to be invited by Tim Thornton to revisit my MA thesis for the Chetham Society, not least as a few years ago I'd started to look at Henry's lands, as prince, as a whole. Furthermore, when studying English armies in France, I'd found a good number of Cheshire soldiers, some of whom had first grabbed my attention through the study of the chamberlain of Chester's accounts for my MA.

In preparing this book, it has been a pleasure to reconnect with Paul Booth whose advice now, as during my MA, has been both useful and inspiring. Thanks also to Tim Thornton for his support in seeing the book through the press, and to his daughter Carys and Elizabeth Berry for turning the blurry third carbon copy of a 1977 thesis into word-processed pages on which I could base my new text. Dorothy Clayton, then starting her doctorate on mid fifteenth-century Cheshire, gave much encouragement as did Brian Harris, then editor of the newly revived VCH for Cheshire. And, of course, a special thanks to Ian Kershaw for the initial idea and for his unflagging interest in my career ever since. Whilst taking the MA, I was generously supported by the historian Decima Douie as well as by the Theodora Bosanquet Bursary of the British Federation of Women Graduates. Another pioneering woman – Dorothea Oschinsky – kindly invited me to her home in deepest Wirral and shared her wisdom on medieval accounting techniques.

I was also inspired by the thesis of Margaret Sharp on the earldom of Chester 1237 to 1399, which had gained a doctorate from the University of Manchester in 1925. Here we come full circle again since the history teacher who inspired me in Chester-le-Street, Cecil Patterson, who just happened to be my next door neighbour as well, was at the same university at the same time and reminisced about being taught by Margaret Sharp's father, the renowned medievalist Professor T. F. Tout.[1] I have a dog-eared copy of the medieval volume of Tout's *An Advanced History of Great Britain from the Earliest Times to the Death of Queen Victoria*, written for Longman's Historical Series for Schools in 1906, which belonged to my great aunt, then a pupil teacher, and subsequently to my mother in the late 1930s. I read there a pencil annotation – 'first part of Hundred Years' War. Learn Notes'. Such interconnections and continuities generate very special memories for me in preparing this book.

**Anne Curry**

1 See also Tom Sharp, 'Reflections on My Grandfather, The Historian T. F. Tout', in Caroline M. Barron and Joel T. Rosenthal (eds), *Thomas Frederick Tout (1855–1929): Refashioning History for the Twentieth Century*, (London: University of London Press, 2019), pp. 297–311.

# *Abbreviations*

| | |
|---|---|
| *36 DKR* | *The Thirty-Sixth Annual Report of the Deputy Keeper of the Public Records* (London: HMSO, 1875), Appendix II: No. 1 – Welsh Records: Calendar of Recognizance Rolls of the Palatinate of Chester. From the Earliest Period to the End of the Reign of Henry IV. |
| *37 DKR* | *The Thirty-Seventh Annual Report of the Deputy Keeper of the Public Records* (London: HMSO, 1876), Appendix II: No. 1 – Welsh Records: Calendar of Recognizance Rolls of the Palatinate of Chester, from the Beginning of the Reign of Henry V. to the End of the Reign of Henry VII. |
| Booth, *Financial Admin.* | P. H.W. Booth, *The Financial Administration of the Lordship and County of Chester, 1272–1377*, Chetham Society, 3rd Ser., 28 (1981). |
| CALS | Chester, Cheshire Archives and Local Studies. |
| *CCR* | *Calendar of the Close Rolls.* |
| *CPR* | *Calendar of the Patent Rolls.* |
| Dodgson, *Place Names* | J. McN. Dodgson, *The Place-Names of Cheshire*, 4 vols, English Place-Name Society, 44, 45, 46 and 47 (1970–2). |
| *EcHR* | *Economic History Review.* |

JRRIL — Manchester, John Rylands Research Institute and Library

Ormerod, *Cheshire* — G. Ormerod, *The History of the County Palatine and City of Chester*, 2nd edn, ed. T. Helsby (3 vols, London: George Routledge & Sons, 1882).

*PPC* — *Proceedings and Ordinances of the Privy Council of England*, ed. N. Harris Nicolas, 7 vols (London: Record Commission, 1834–7).

*PROME* — *The Parliament Rolls of Medieval England, 1275–1504*, ed. C. Given-Wilson *et al.*, 16 vols (Woodbridge: Boydell; London: National Archives, 2005).

Sharp, 'Earldom and County of Chester' — M. Sharp, 'Contributions to the History of the Earldom and County of Chester, 1237–1399, Historical, Topographical and Administrative, with a Study of the Household of Edward the Black Prince and its Relations with Cheshire', unpublished PhD thesis (University of Manchester, 1925).

*THSLC* — *Transactions of the Historic Society of Lancashire and Cheshire.*

TNA — Kew, The National Archives of the U.K.

# *List of tables*

## *List of figures*

# *Note on terminology*

Nomenclature is difficult since the period from 1399 to 1422 includes tenure by a prince of Wales and then a king. 'Prince' and 'king' are used when referring to a specific individual. When comparisons are being drawn with earlier royal earls, whether princes or kings, and where generalities are being stated for the whole period, then 'earl' is used.

The term 'burgus' has been preferred to the modern term 'borough' because of the complex status of those Cheshire towns which are called 'burgus' in the documents of the period.

The accounting year ran from Michaelmas to Michaelmas (29 September). Following the practice of other historians using such financial records,[1] I have dated the accounts by the Michaelmas at which they terminated. So, for example, the account for Michaelmas 1416 to Michaelmas 1417 is referred to as the account of 1417.

In the layout of accounts in Appendix II, for the sake of simplicity, the change in accounting practices discussed in Chapter 2 has not been taken into consideration. The sums given in Appendix II are as found in the original accounts and therefore any errors in totals are from the period.

As far as measurements are concerned, I have quoted acreages as they are stated in the documents. The Cheshire acre was larger than the statute acre, it was measured by the 24-foot perch rather than the 16½-foot perch.[2]

Money values are given throughout in the form used in the period, £ (pounds), s. (shillings) and d. (pennies). There were 20 shillings in each pound and 12 pennies in each shilling.

1 J. Titow, *English Rural Society 1200–1350* (London: Allen and Unwin, 1969), pp. 27–8.

2 D. Sylvester, 'The Open Fields', *THSLC*, 108 (1956), 27–8.

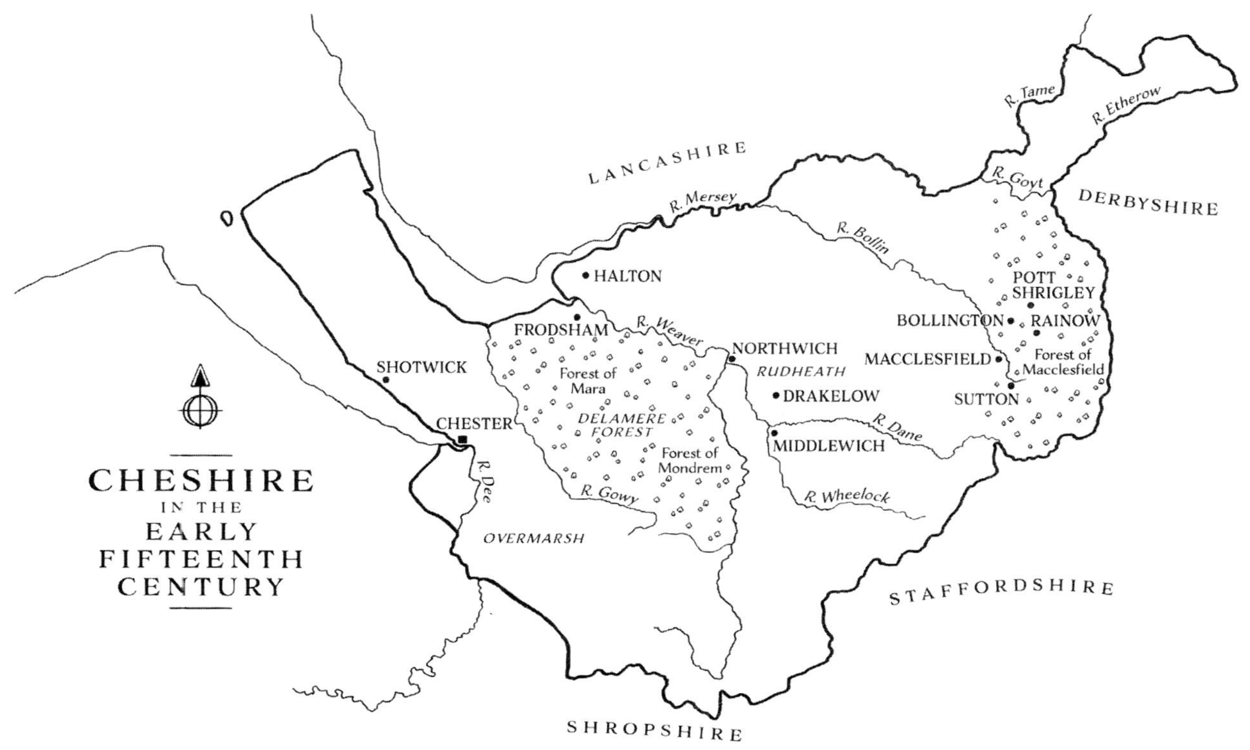
LANCASHIRE
R. Tame
R. Etherow
R. Mersey
R. Goyt
DERBYSHIRE
R. Bollin
HALTON
POTT SHRIGLEY
BOLLINGTON
RAINOW
FRODSHAM
R. Weaver
NORTHWICH
RUDHEATH
MACCLESFIELD
Forest of Macclesfield
SHOTWICK
Forest of Mara
DRAKELOW
SUTTON
CHESTER
DELAMERE FOREST
R. Dane
MIDDLEWICH
Forest of Mondrem
R. Dee
R. Gowy
R. Wheelock
OVERMARSH
STAFFORDSHIRE
SHROPSHIRE
CHESHIRE
IN THE
EARLY
FIFTEENTH
CENTURY

# *Introduction*

On Wednesday 15 October 1399, King Henry IV, sitting on his throne in the presence of the Lords and Commons in parliament at Westminster:

> placed a coronet on the head of his eldest son and placed a golden ring on his finger, and put a golden staff into his hand, and then kissed him, and gave him his charter on such matters. And thus he made him prince of Wales, duke of Cornwall and earl of Chester, and then caused him to be led, thus arrayed, by the duke of York, uncle to the king, to the seat ordained and assigned to him in parliament by reason of the aforesaid principality.[1]

By such means was the thirteen-year-old Prince Henry, the future King Henry V, formally admitted to his new titles which were traditionally held by the eldest son of the king. The principality of Wales had first been accorded to Edward of Caernarvon, son of Edward I, in 1301, and the duchy of Cornwall to Edward of Woodstock (the 'Black Prince'), eldest son of Edward III, in 1337. The link of the earldom of Chester to the heir to the throne had been forged a century earlier through a grant in 1254 by Henry III to his eldest son, the Lord Edward, the future Edward I, although the title of earl of Chester was not formally borne by a royal heir apparent until 1301.[2]

1 PROME, viii. 33. The duke of York was Edmund of Langley (d. 1402), fourth son of Edward III, who had been appointed keeper of the realm by Richard II on 1 June 1399 as the king set out for campaign in Ireland. York had come to an arrangement with Bolingbroke at Berkeley on 27 July 1399 (D. Biggs, *Three Armies in Britain: The Irish Campaign of Richard II and the Usurpation of Henry IV, 1397–99* (Leiden and Boston: Brill, 2006), pp. 145–7). For the charter of creation of Prince Henry's appanage, see *Calendar of Charter Rolls Edward III - Henry V, vol. 5 (1341-1417)*, pp. 384-7, with the full text in Reports from the Lords Committees touching the Dignity of a Peer (London: n.p., 1829), pp. 126-30

2 The first royal earl of Chester was therefore the future Edward II (b.

The formal according of all three titles to Prince Henry in October 1399, and the subsequent transfer to him of their appurtenant lands, was an essential symbol of, and stage in, the establishment of a new Lancastrian dynasty. The prince's father, Henry Bolingbroke, only son of Edward III's third son, John of Gaunt, duke of Lancaster (d. 1399), had become king only two weeks earlier. Whilst it was reported that Richard II had abdicated and had even indicated his personal approval for his cousin to replace him on the throne, the reality of the situation was that Henry IV was a usurper. For his eldest son, the transformation from 'the young lord Henry', as he had been known up to this point, to royal heir apparent had been truly remarkable. Cheshire featured in this transformation right from the start.

Bolingbroke had been sent into exile by Richard II in 1398 and was subsequently refused admittance to his ducal inheritance after Gaunt's death on 3 February 1399. In May of that same year, Richard II had taken the young lord Henry with him on campaign to Ireland, dubbing him a knight during the

1284) to whom his father Edward I granted the earldom as well as all royal lands in Wales on 7 Feb 1301 at a parliament held at Lincoln (*Calendar of the Charter Rolls, 1300–26* (London: HMSO, 1908), p. 6). It is likely that Prince Edward was invested with the insignia of the prince of Wales at the parliament although there is no specific evidence for this, or for any ceremony of investment as earl (Seymour Phillips, *Edward II* (New Haven CT and London: Yale University Press, 2010), p. 85). The earldom of Chester was granted by Edward II to his son, the future Edward III, when the latter was only 11 days old (W. Mark Ormrod, *Edward III* (New Haven CT and London: Yale University Press, 2011), p. 8). Within three months of the birth of Edward III's eldest son, Edward of Woodstock, on 15 June 1330, half of the revenues of the royal earldom of Chester were diverted to the baby prince's support, with the full revenues being granted for his maintenance to his mother on 25 Feb 1331. On 18 Mar 1333, Edward was created earl of Chester but the revenues of the county were to continue to go to his mother whilst he remained in her household. On 28 Apr 1343 he was invested in parliament as prince of Wales: 'a coronet was placed on his head, a ring put on his finger and he was given a silver rod, "according to custom"' (R. Barber, *Edward, Prince of Wales and Aquitaine: A Biography of the Black Prince* (London, 1978, repr, Woodbridge: Boydell Press, 1996), pp. 16–19, 41).

expedition.[3] When Richard heard in early July that Bolingbroke had invaded England, he had the boy imprisoned in Trim castle.[4] The king himself hurried back to England, landing at Milford Haven and moving northwards towards Cheshire which in recent years had become his 'inner citadel'.[5]

Richard's special relationship with the county, which he held in person as heir following the death of the Black Prince and also throughout his own reign as king since he had no heir of his body,[6] was made clear by his elevation of it to the status of a principality on 25 September 1397. This principality was intended, as with the earldom, to remain in the hands of the king or a male heir of his body.[7] The preamble to the statute of creation emphasised Richard's love and affection for the county, noting that he had held it briefly as heir to his grandfather and that it had been held by his royal progenitors before him. He expressed his hope that it would, in time, be held by his own son, God willing.[8] The terms of the creation of the principality confirmed the existing liberties of the county, in other words the special palatinate status which preserved its separate legal administration and lack

3 *La prinse et mort du roy Richart d'Angleterre, based on British Library MS Harley 1319, and Other Works by Jean Creton*, ed. and trans. Lorna A. Finlay, Camden Society, 5th ser., 65 (2023), p. 55

4 C. T. Allmand, *Henry V* (London: Methuen, 1992), p. 13.

5 The expression is that of T. F. Tout, *Chapters in Medieval Administrative History*, iv (Manchester: Manchester University Press, 1930), p. 59

6 The nine-year-old son Richard was acknowledged by Edward III as earl of Chester immediately after his father's death on 8 June 1376. He was brought to parliament on 25 June where the Commons petitioned that he should be styled prince of Wales but were told that as the decision lay with the king, who was absent. Richard was invested as prince of Wales and duke of Cornwall on 20 Nov 1376 (Ormrod, *Edward III*, pp. 559, 565).

7 R. R. Davies, 'Richard II and the Principality of Chester, 1397–9', in F. R. H. Du Boulay and Caroline M. Barron (eds), *The Reign of Richard II: Essays in Honour of May McKisack* (London: Athlone Press, 1971), pp. 256–79. For an alternative perspective, placing less emphasis on personal royal initiative, see Tim Thornton, 'Cheshire: The Inner Citadel of Richard II's Kingdom?' in Gwilym Dodd (ed.), *The Reign of Richard II* (Stroud: Tempus, 2000), pp. 85–96.

8 *PROME*, vii. 355–6.

of parliamentary representation. In addition, the king merged adjoining areas into the new principality 'for the ease, concord and tranquillity of his lieges therein', and also to create a larger apanage for a potential royal heir. But a strong motive behind Richard's creation of the principality of Chester was to exploit the seizure into royal hands of the landholdings of Richard, earl of Arundel, whom the king had had executed four days earlier, on 21 September 1397.[9]

We can assume that Richard was also motivated by the support which Cheshire men had given to his father, the Black Prince, who had held the county for almost forty years, drawing not only upon its revenues but also its manpower for his military campaigns.[10] Cheshire men had served Richard himself well in his conflict with some of his nobility, not least at the battle of Radcot Bridge in 1387.[11] His final triumph against his enemies at the parliament of September 1397 was achieved through Cheshire military support: in mid-July the king had ordered the sheriff of the county to raise 2,000 archers and to bring them to London.[12] Thereafter Richard maintained a personal bodyguard of Cheshire men in his household.[13]

9 Flintshire, Bromfield and Yale, Chirk and Chirkland, Oswestry, and various other castles and lordships in Shropshire, as well as the reversion of Clun then held by the duke of York, which had been held by the earls of Arundel.

10 P. H. W. Booth, *The Financial Administration of the Lordship and County of Chester 1272–1377*, Chetham Society, 3rd ser., 28 (1981), passim; P. J. Morgan, *War and Society in Medieval Cheshire, 1277–1403*, Chetham Society, 3rd ser., 34 (1987), chapter 3.

11 As noted by the Dieulacres Chronicle, in M. V. Clarke and V. H. Galbraith, 'The Deposition of Richard II', *Bulletin of the John Rylands Library*, 14 (1930), 125–81, at p. 168. In Dec 1398, 4,000 marks was sent to the county for the royal treasury for relief of those who had suffered at the battle (CHES 2/73, m 6 (7), *36 DKR*, p. 312).

12 Morgan, *War and Society*, p. 199, citing CHES 2/70, m7d (3), *36 DKR*, p. 98. On 24 Aug the under-sheriff, William Bagot, had been ordered to proclaim that all knights and esquires holding Richard's livery of the stag should assemble at Kingston-upon-Thames on 15 Sept to ride with the king towards London (CHES 2/70, m7d (5), *36 DKR*, p. 98). Parliament opened at Westminster on 17 Sept.

13 Morgan, *War and Society*, pp. 199–201; J. L. Gillespie, 'Richard II's Cheshire Archers', *THSLC*, 125 (1974), 1–39.

As we have seen, on his return from Ireland in July 1399, Richard made for Cheshire as speedily as he could. Bolingbroke also had the good sense to move towards the county quickly and got there first, thereby thwarting Richard's hopes of raising military support. Entering the county from the south-east in the first week of August, Henry entered Chester on 9 August.[14] By this point Richard had reached Conway but was tricked into meeting Henry at the castle of Flint (an area which lay administratively within the principality of Chester) on 16 August. From that point onwards, Richard was Henry's prisoner. Henry led him to Chester from which writs were sent out on 19 August in Richard's name for a parliament to meet at Westminster on 30 September.[15] Shortly afterwards, Richard accompanied Henry to London and was despatched to the Tower around 1 September. By the end of the month he had been deposed.

Henry IV was crowned in Westminster Abbey on 13 October with his eldest son carrying the sword of justice at the ceremony.[16] When precisely the now Prince Henry returned to England and which of these events he witnessed remains uncertain. But we know that during his stay at Chester, Bolingbroke commissioned Henry Dryhurst, a Chester merchant, to bring his son back from Ireland. The subsequent payment to Dryhurst confirms that the prince returned to England via Chester along with the furnishings of Richard's chapel.[17]

14 SC 6/774/10, mm. 2d, 3d, cited in Chris Given-Wilson, *Henry IV* (New Haven CT and London: Yale University Press, 2016), p. 133 n. 67.

15 *CCR 1396–9*, pp. 520–1.

16 Allmand, *Henry V*, p. 16; *The Chronicle of Adam Usk 1377–1421*, ed. C. Given-Wilson (Oxford: Clarendon Press, 1997), pp. 71–3.

17 E 404/16/394, calendared in *Issues of the Exchequer: Being a Collection of Payments made out of His Majesty's Revenue, from King Henry III to King Henry VI Inclusive*, ed. Frederick Devon, Record Commission (London: John Murray, 1837), p. 281. Dryhurst is described there as 'of West Chester'. He had been involved in a dispute over a prise of wine near Southampton in 1390 (CHES 2/62, m 1d (10), *36 DKR*, p. 158). See also A. Curry, 'The Making of a Prince: The Finances of "the Young Lord Henry", 1386–1400', in Gwilym Dodd (ed.), *Henry V: New Interpretations* (Woodbridge: York Medieval Press, 2013), pp. 11–33, at p. 22.

The events of the autumn of 1399 were remarkable at the time and have engaged historians ever since. From the perspective of the history of Cheshire, they occupy a very special place. With the arrival of a new dynasty, there was a direct princely, as opposed to royal, lord – an earl of Chester who was also a prince of Wales and a duke of Cornwall – for the first time for twenty-two years. The income of all the parts of the prince's appanage and responsibility for its governance were transferred to Prince Henry on 8 November.[18] On 10 November, a writ was sent by the prince to the chamberlain of Chester to levy all arrears in the county as well as in Flintshire (customarily administered alongside Cheshire) and North Wales.[19] The earldom of Chester remained with Henry as prince from October 1399 to his accession to the throne on 21 March 1413, and thereafter as king until his death on 31 August 1422, a period of almost 23 years.

This present study focuses on the revenues which Henry received from the county. Whilst we shall consider income from the taxation which Henry as prince and king levied in the county, as well as on income from the activities of the sheriff and escheator, the principal focus is on the lands which he held directly – his 'demesne lands'.[20] We shall define such lands more precisely later in this introduction as well as outlining the rich survival of archives on which we have been able draw.

There can be no doubt that the county was firmly part of the crown's assets, whether in the hands of prince or king – taking the period from 1301 to 1547 as a whole, the county was for

18 *CPR 1399–1401*, pp. 61, 373. Announcement was ordered in Chester on 12 Nov that the king had granted the principality of Wales to his son and that all courts and offices should be held and money collected in his name (CHES 2/74, m 1 (3), *36 DKR*, p. 100). See also R. A. Griffiths, 'Wales and the Marches', in S. B. Chrimes, C. D. Ross and R. A. Griffiths (eds), *Fifteenth Century England 1399–1509* (Manchester: Manchester University Press, 1972), pp. 145–72, at p. 147.

19 CHES 2/74, m 1(4), *36 DKR*, p. 100.

20 Hence the title of my MA thesis, 'The Demesne of the County Palatine of Chester in the Early Fifteenth Century'.

more than half the time in the hands of the king as earl. As such, it demonstrated many of the features of other royal lands, such as in offering opportunities for the exercise of patronage as well as financial income. Indeed, for the royal demesne as a whole, patronage was often more important than profit.[21] Yet legally speaking, the king never held any demesne lands as king within the county: any benefits he enjoyed were by virtue of his being earl of Chester.[22]

The demesnes in Cheshire never conformed with the traditional lines of control by the royal exchequer as did other parts of the royal demesne, even when in the hands of the king himself.[23] The county stood as a self-contained unit with a well-established administration and with the nature of a virtually unchangeable institution, the tenure of which could never be in dispute since the earldom was inalienable from the crown, whether vested in the heir apparent or else the king himself. Here it contrasted with other seigneurial estates where there was possibility of escheat for lack of an heir or seizure owing to political embroilment.

The individuality of the county was certainly enhanced by the survival of its institutions – especially its separate justiciar and county court as well as its own chamberlain and exchequer – but its cherished independence was bureaucratic and social rather than constitutional. Richard's creation of a principality had been too short-lived to generate any major changes. The county was 'in general, subject to English statute law', and the appointment of officials 'often reflected national political developments'.[24]

21 B. P. Wolffe, *The Royal Demesne in English History: The Crown Estate in the Governance of the Realm from the Conquest to 1509* (London: Allen and Unwin, 1971), pp. 63–5; B. P. Wolffe, 'The Management of English Royal Estates under the Yorkist Kings', *English Historical Review*, 71 (1956), 20.

22 Sharp, 'Earldom and County of Chester', p. 424.

23 J. R. Lander, *Crown and Nobility, 1450–1509* (London: Edward Arnold, 1976), pp. 40–4.

24 B. E. Harris, 'The Palatinate 1301–1547', in B. E. Harris (ed.), *The Victoria History of the Counties of England: A History of the County of Chester*, ii (Oxford: Oxford University Press for the University of

On the face of it, the earldom of Chester was the least valuable of all of the heir apparent's possessions. In a valor drawn up shortly after the Black Prince's death in 1376, for instance, the valuation given to the earldom, including the lordship of Macclesfield, was £1,252.[25] By contrast, North Wales was worth £3,041, South Wales £1,830, the lands of the duchy of Cornwall in Devon and Cornwall over £2,250, and the 'foreign manors' of the duchy outside the south-west £922.

There can be no doubt, however, that the dramatic events of 1399–1400 gave Cheshire considerable importance in the establishment of the new regime given the close links which Richard II had forged with the county. The charges against Richard twice mentioned the use he had made of the support of Cheshire men against his political enemies. The picture portrayed was hardly flattering, his 'great multitude of evildoers from the county', being deemed responsible for rape, murder and pillage, which Richard had done nothing to punish. Indeed he had continued to 'favour the same people in their evil deeds, trusting in them and their protection against all others of his realm'.[26] Ending his principality of Chester was immediate and straightforward. There was no special act needed to dismantle it: its demise was simply part of the abolition of all of the acts of Richard II's parliament of September 1397 in Henry IV's first parliament at the petition of the Commons on 15 October.[27] The order of the entries on the parliament roll suggests that this had happened before the creation on the same day of the prince as prince of Wales, duke of Cornwall and earl of Chester. From the start, therefore, Prince Henry ruled the traditional palatinate county.

London Institute of Historical Research, 1979), p. 10. Subsequent pages provide the best succinct account of county-level officials and institutions.

25 C 47/9/57, summarised in Booth, *Financial Admin.*, pp. 173–5.

26 *PROME*, viii. 15, 16.

27 *PROME*, viii. 30–1. Even in the last month of Richard's reign after his capture, the Chester exchequer continued to use his title as 'prince of Chester', as for instance in an example dated 23 Sept (CHES 2/74, m 3, noted in Davies, 'Richard II and the Principality of Chester', p. 279).

At his creation as earl on 15 October 1399, Prince Henry was still a minor. The influence of his royal father was bound to be significant, at least at first, given the circumstances of the usurpation and Richard II's relationship with the county. Furthermore, there was a rising in Cheshire early in 1400, possibly connected with the Epiphany plot to kill the king.[28] Indeed, as Peter McNiven has pointed out, Cheshire was the only county in which Henry IV's triumphant advance had met with any real resistance.[29] Although the 1403 rebellion was a Percy rising in its leadership and main aims, in its lesser personnel it was very much a Cheshire rebellion since, of the 122 known participants, 95 were Cheshire men.[30] Not surprisingly, their actions triggered the imposition of a large collective fine on the county. In the early years of the new regime, the prince and his father had to balance suppression with conciliation in order to secure their position in the county. This is revealed in the personnel chosen to administer the prince's lands, as discussed in Chapter 1.

Geoffrey Barraclough suggested that the 'revolution' of 1399 should have presented an opportunity to level Cheshire with the rest of the kingdom. That it did not was because of the rebellion in Wales led by Owain Glyndŵr which broke out in September 1400.[31] The border status of Cheshire had always been a key factor in the attitudes of its royal and princely earls. Once Wales had been subdued, and the royal principality created, at the turn of the fourteenth century, the earldom of Chester had become rather a subordinate part of the great

28 Peter McNiven, 'The Cheshire Rising of 1400', *Bulletin of the John Rylands Library*, 52 (1970), 375–96.

29 P. McNiven, 'Rebellion and Disaffection in the North of England 1403–1408', unpublished MA thesis (University of Manchester, 1967), p. 43.

30 Peter McNiven, 'The Men of Cheshire and the Rebellion of 1403', *THSLC*, 129 (1979), 1–2.

31 Geoffrey Barraclough, 'The Earldom and County Palatine of Chester', *THSLC*, 103 (1951), 41, 43. For the outline of events see R. R. Davies, *The Revolt of Owain Glyn Dŵr* (Oxford: Oxford University Press, 1995).

appanage which was the endowment of the prince of Wales, with a growing tendency for the latter's administration to be centralised in London. But when Wales again became a centre of revolt in the early years of the fifteenth century, Cheshire, as a marcher region, once more came into prominence in its own right, both militarily and within the financial administration of the prince of Wales's lands as a whole.

Chester was to be an important headquarters of Prince Henry as the king's lieutenant in the conduct of the war,[32] even though he was only rarely present in the county in person.[33] In 1404, the chamberlain of the county, John Trevor, bishop of St Asaph, defected to Glyndŵr. Even before this stage of the revolt, the majority of the prince's lands in his principality of Wales and Flintshire had fallen easily into the hands of the rebels and Henry was unable to collect income from them. This prompted considerably greater emphasis on his revenues from Cheshire which were diverted to support military costs in Wales. As a result, we can detect an unusual level of pressure to increase his revenues in Cheshire and therefore to administer his resources there in the most efficient way to maximise ready income. We can see this not only in modifications to the forms and practices of financial administration but also in changing policies towards sources of income and categories of expenditure. This is explored in Chapter 2 through the study of changes in accounting methods and a review of the valuations drawn up to guide the prince's administration in the early stages of the Welsh wars. It is also seen through discussion in Chapter 3 of the various sources of income derived from the demesnes, and in Chapter 5 through changing patterns of expenditure on

32 J. Gwynfor-Jones, 'Government and the Welsh Community: The North East Borderland in the Fifteenth Century', in H. Hearder and H. R. Loyn (eds), *British Government and Administration: Studies presented to S. B. Chrimes* (Cardiff: University of Wales Press, 1974), pp. 55–68, at p. 59.

33 For the presence of Prince Henry in the county see pp. 43-4. Richard II was in Chester in July 1387 and Feb 1399 (Nigel Saul, *Richard II* (New Haven CT and London: Yale University Press, 1997), pp. 471, 474).

annuities and policies towards the granting out of manors. In Chapter 6, landed income is compared with income from other sources in the county, including taxation which was levied after direct negotiation between the earl and county community given that Cheshire lay outside parliamentary arrangements for lay taxation.

In Chapter 7 we aim to pull these various themes together to assess the place of Henry's earldom within the wider context of his lands as prince and, after his accession as king, within the royal demesne as a whole. This chapter also considers the contribution of Cheshire to the military activities for which Henry V is most famous, as prince in his Welsh campaigns and as king in France. The earldom had proved vital to Henry as prince during the Welsh wars but after his accession as king, it was a small part of a much larger royal demesne which also included the great duchy of Lancaster. By studying the county over the whole of Henry's tenure of it – both as prince and king – we are able to trace and measure the effects of changing contexts and priorities. We can also consider the degree to which the earldom was assimilated within the royal demesne as a whole when it was held by the king, bearing in mind the fact that after the accession of Henry V in 1413 it remained in royal hands for over forty years, until the endowment of Edward, prince of Wales in 1454.

## The demesne lands of the earl

In this study, 'demesne' is considered here in its widest possible sense to signify the lands, rights and profits which appertained to the earl, where administrative control lay in his hands and where he enjoyed the resulting revenues. 'Estate' would perhaps be a more modern expression although that term tends to over emphasise the purely landed interest as opposed to income from a wide variety of sources, such as court fines and taxation. Contemporaries would have used such terms as 'dominium' ('lordship'), with an emphasis upon such lordship in all its aspects and without drawing clear distinctions between landed and non-landed revenue. The income of an estate, whether from landed or non-landed sources would be seen as an integrated whole. By this period, the earl enjoyed little direct income from agriculture. Instead, agricultural resources were leased out for a money payment. ('Put to farm' is the common expression used but this is not to be confused with the modern agricultural meaning.) The lord's interest was therefore predominantly financial even if some resources might be put out on an annual basis through what we today would call competitive tender.

What is to be considered here, then, is the nature and diversity of the earl's manors and sources of income, although fuller details are provided especially in Chapter 3. Awareness of the previous history of each location is helpful in order to explain developments within the period. Past practice was a powerful influence upon current policy. In this respect, the studies of Margaret Sharp and Paul Booth on the financial interests and administrations of the royal and princely earls in the fourteenth century provide vital background and comparative information for the present study.[34]

In the city of Chester, the earl received revenues from four main sources. The sheriff of the city accounted for the fee farm of the city and for miscellaneous rents and profits. The escheator of the city, who was also the mayor, accounted for those escheats arising solely within civic limits. At the castle, the outer bailey was defended by a ditch sufficiently wide to afford space for a garden. This garden of Chester Castle was a source of income, being regularly put to farm, although the keepership was used for patronage purposes and the actual use of the garden is uncertain.[35] The earl also possessed fulling and grinding mills on the River Dee within the city, as well as a fishery there.

34 Sharp, 'Earldom and County of Chester; P. H. W. Booth, 'The Financial Administration of the Lordship and County of Chester 1272–1377', unpublished MA thesis (University of Liverpool, 1974); idem, *Financial Admin.*

35 R. H. Morris, *Chester in the Plantagenet and Tudor Reigns* (Chester: printed for the author, 1893), p. 99. The garden is not mentioned in the discussion of the castle in H. M. Colvin (ed.), *The History of the King's Works* (6 vols, London: HMSO, 1963–82), ii. 607–12.

There were three units which we could roughly describe as traditional rural/agricultural manors, namely Frodsham, Shotwick and Drakelow. Although at Frodsham a *burgus* lay within the limits of the manor,[36] the principal sources of income derived from rents of tenants in the subsidiary hamlets of Overton, Netherton, Woodhouses and Mickledale,[37] and from piecemeal leases of the lands previously directly cultivated by the lord, with subsidiary income from courts, fisheries and the port of Frodsham. The whole lordship, including the *burgus*, was accounted as one unit at this time. Later, the manor area was separated from the township. The manor lay to the south of the township as well as between the township and the sea.[38] From 1385 until Michaelmas 1408, the manor was in the hands of Radegonde Béchet, dame de Morthemer, who was of Poitevin origin, for no render. Thenceforward, it remained in the hands of the earl for the rest of the period.

At Shotwick, the earl held the manor, park and castle. The latter had lost its importance in the later fourteenth century but the manor was valuable when the royal park was associated with it.[39] The tenants of the manor held land in Shotwick and also in Little Saughall, 1⅔ miles to the south-east. The earl also held woodland in Little Saughall.[40] For the greater part of the

36 Sharp, 'Earldom and County of Chester', p. 361; Ormerod, *Cheshire*, ii. 46. On the lordship in general, see W. Beamont, *An Account of the Ancient Town of Frodsham, in Cheshire* (Warrington: Percival Pearse, 1881); P. H. W. Booth and J. Philip Dodd, 'The Manor and Fields of Frodsham', *THSLC*, 128 (1978), 27-57. For further discussion of burgage tenure there see below Chapter 4. See Note on terminology for the use of the term 'burgus'.

37 Dodgson, *Place Names*, iii. 230.

38 The distribution is clear on the nineteenth-century tithe award (CALS, E.D.T. 162/1+2) and on the first edition 6" Ordnance Survey map OS XXIV.

39 The Black Prince had stayed in the castle in 1353 but by that time the place had no garrison and there is very little evidence of any repairs carried out after 1371 (*The King's Works*, ii. 834; Sharp, 'Earldom and County of Chester', pp. 349–50; R. Stewart-Brown, 'The Royal Manor and Park of Shotwick', *THSLC*, 64 (1912), 82–142.

40 Dodgson, *Place Names*, iv. 205. Lands formerly belonging to Guy de

thirteenth and fourteenth centuries, the manor was in the hands of the earl, although there were occasional grants to others.[41] From 27 April 1403 to Michaelmas 1407, the manor was leased to Richard Moston, but the park was kept in the earl's hands and sales of wood were accounted for.[42] From 28 April 1410, William Porter held the manor for life for no render, but the earl still maintained his rights in the park.[43]

The manor of Drakelow had been created out of the waste of Rudheath by the Black Prince in the mid-fourteenth century.[44] About 4,000 acres may have been recovered and this new land cast for administrative purposes into the mould of a traditional manor with demesne and tenant land but no labour services imposed. It was at first directly controlled by the escheator as the centre of a bloc of demesnes consisting of this manor, Northwich, Shotwick, Middlewich, Frodsham and Overmarsh. This experiment failed, and the prince's rights at the new manor never became well-established. For the remainder of the Black Prince's life, Drakelow was one of the worst places for the collection of arrears of rent, Delamere Forest being the other. In the early fifteenth century, the situation was much as it had been in the reign of Richard II. The manor of Drakelow and lordship of Rudheath were kept in the earl's hands and accounted together under one bailiff. The demesnes were leased out en bloc, and the majority of income derived from the rents of tenants on the heath.[45] Most of this income was expended as

Provence were accounted. Hugh Russell as occupier paid £4 in 1400 (SC 6/791/1, m 3d). John Goodfelowe was granted custody for no render, backdated to 18 Nov 1399 (SC 6/791/3, m 3d), which he seems to have enjoyed until 1413 (SC 6/792/10, m 4d).

41 Sharp, 'Earldom and County of Chester', p. 419.

42 SC 6/791/3, m 3; SC 6, 792/3, m 3.

43 CHES 2/82, m5d (2) (3), *36 DKR*, p. 387. The grant was extended to cover the lifetime of his wife also on 20 Apr 1412 (CHES 2/84, m 4d (7), *36 DKR*, p. 387).

44 The boundaries of Rudheath are described in the *Ledger Book of Vale Royal Abbey*, ed. John Brownbill, RSLC, 68 (1914), pp. 142–4. See also Dodgson, *Place Names*, i. 11–13. For the creation of Drakelow, see Booth, *Financial Admin.*, p. 128.

45 Sharp, 'Earldom and County of Chester', p. 397.

annuities.

Overmarsh, or King's Marsh, had also been recovered from the waste in the mid-fourteenth century but this recovery had not even been as successful as that carried out at Rudheath. Eight-hundred acres of newly recovered land were deemed worthless in 1349–50.[46] The area had been administered jointly with Drakelow in 1349 but was kept separate from 1353.[47] In the later fourteenth century, the marsh tended to be leased out on a short-term basis for little financial return.[48] In May 1399, it was taken to farm by John de Fulford and John Kettull of Stratton for three years at £24 per annum,[49] but from March 1400 it was in the hands of Richard Colfox for no render. Colfox had already held an earlier grant of the moor in December 1395. In 1400 he also held an annual rent of £7 6s. 8d. arising out of the moor, which had previously been held by John Holland.[50] Colfox's involvement in the Lollard rising of 1414 led to his imprisonment in the Tower of London and loss of lands. He was subsequently pardoned but there is some problem over whether he was restored to his full rights at Overmarsh.[51]

The earl also held two of the salt wiches, Northwich and Middlewich, towns which had some claims to borough status but which were not fully incorporated in this period.[52] In the fourteenth century, Middlewich was most commonly farmed out. On 16 August 1389 it had been granted to Richard II's favourite William Bagot, for life for no render.[53] This grant was revoked at Richard's deposition, and the town remained in the

46 SC 6/801/4, m 1 cited in P. H. W. Booth, 'The Financial Administration of the Lordship and County of Chester 1272–1377', unpublished MA thesis (University of Liverpool, 1974), p. 205.

47 Sharp, 'Earldom and County of Chester', p. 407.

48 See, for instance, the several entries noted in *36 DKR*, p. 271.

49 CHES 2/73, m 6d (7), *36 DKR*, p. 394.

50 1395: CHES 2/69, m 2 (7), m3d (1), *36 DKR*, p. 117. 1400: CHES 2/73, m 3d (1, 2), *36 DKR*, p. 394. J. H. Wylie and W. T. Waugh, *The Reign of Henry the Fifth*, 3 vols (Cambridge: Cambridge University Press, 1914–29), i. 272; CHES 2/88, m 5 (5), *37 DKR*, p. 159.

51 See below pp. 243-4.

52 Sharp, 'Earldom and County of Chester', p. 376.

53 CHES 2/61, m 3d (4), *36 DKR*, p. 17.

direct control of the royal earl for the whole of the period under review. In 1380, Northwich had been granted for no render to Richard II's half-brother John Holland, earl of Huntingdon and duke of Exeter.[54] He appears to have leased the town to a local man, Richard Winnington, in 1385,[55] and then exchanged properties elsewhere with the king so that by 1399 the town was once more in royal hands.[56] Holland was executed for his involvement in the Epiphany plot of 1400. Thenceforward the town remained in the hands of Prince Henry until 1411 when it was leased to Laurence Merbury for ten years.[57] Merbury held the lease until Michaelmas 1413.[58] In 1416, the town was leased to Peter de Dutton for six years.[59] He held the lease until 12 May 1418.[60] From 12 May 1418, Northwich was 'restored' to Holland's widow Elizabeth and son John jnr and held by them for the rest of the period.[61] Most of the revenue in both Middlewich and Northwich derived from seigneurial monopolies concerned with the salt industry and from courts held there. Middlewich was the more valuable of the two towns throughout this period as well as the more prominent: the Northwich hundred and town eyres, for instance, were actually held at Middlewich.

The earl had originally held three forest areas in demesne, Wirral, Delamere (i.e. Mara and Mondrem in the medieval spelling), and Macclesfield. Wirral had been disafforested in the fourteenth century and the earl now derived no profits from it.[62] The ancient forest of Mara and Mondrem included all the

54 *CPR 1377–81*, p. 539.

55 CHES 2/69, m 11d (9), *36 DKR*, p. 531.

56 SC 6/790/10, m 2d. The exchange was dated 15 Jan 1398 (*CPR 1396–9*, p. 467.)

57 SC 6/792/8, m 2d; CHES 2/83, m 2 (4, 5), *36 DKR*, p. 366.

58 Until 1405 the accounts noted this reason as to why there were no profits but from that year onwards this explanation was omitted (SC 6/792/10, m 3d).

59 SC 6/793/4, m 4d; CHES 2/89, m 1 (1), *36 DKR*, p. 566.

60 SC 6/793/7, m 4d. This lease as well as the earlier one to Merbury and an earlier abortive lease are discussed in detail in Chapter 5.

61 SC 6/793/7, m 4d. For fuller discussion of the complex problem of tenure by the Hollands both before and after 1399, see Chapter 5.

62 SC 6/791/10, m 1d. P. H. W. Booth, 'The Last Week in the Life of

hundred of Eddisbury and certain townships in the hundred of Nantwich.[63] There was no manorial organisation here but twenty-six townships (out of sixty-two in the forest) paid a rent in the form of frithmote and there were other profits deriving from the exercise of forest jurisdiction. Frodsham *burgus* and its attendant vills were described as 'within the liberties of the earl of Chester as lord within the boundaries of the forest' ('infra libertates domini comitis cestrie infra metas foreste predicte') but did not pay frithmote.

Macclesfield Forest formed part of the lordship of Macclesfield, an enclave within the county the distinctive character of which was emphasised by the several occasions on which it was granted out to the queens as dower.[64] Thus it had at times a relatively separate and distinctive administration, although in this period it was reasonably well assimilated with the rest of the county. The lordship was a complex union of hundred, *burgus*, and forest.[65] The earl held the hundred directly, meaning simply that he took the profits of the hundred court and other franchises, these being accounted for by the bailiffs of the hundred rather than by the sheriff of the county, as was the case with the other hundreds.[66] Rents and profits in the *burgus* appertained to the earl. Over the forest, which was the most valuable part of the lordship, he exercised quasi-manorial organisation as well as forest jurisdiction. From the early thirteenth century, the earl also had a park at Macclesfield

Edward the Black Prince', in Hannah Skoda, Patrick Lantschner and R. L. J. Shaw (eds), *Contact and Exchange in Later Medieval Europe: Essays in Honour of Malcolm Vale* (Woodbridge: Boydell Press, 2012), pp. 221–45.

63 Dodgson, *Place Names*, i. 8; Ormerod, *Cheshire*, ii. 107; B. C. Husain, 'Delamere Forest in Later Mediaeval Times', *THSLC*, 107 (1955), 25.

64 For examples in the period 1272–1377, see Booth, *Financial Admin.*, pp. 94–5 and Sharp, 'Earldom and County of Chester', pp. 314–15.

65 Booth, *Financial Admin.*, pp. 95–6; Sharp, 'Earldom and County of Chester', p. 304; Ormerod, *Cheshire*, iii. 538; J. P. Earwaker, *East Cheshire: Past and Present; or A History of the Hundred of Macclesfield, in the County Palatine of Chester*, 2 vols (London: printed for the author, 1877–80), ii. 5.

66 Sharp, 'Earldom and County of Chester', p. 315.

which had been used as a royal stud in the thirteenth and fourteenth centuries.[67] In the early fifteenth century, there were four accounting units at Macclesfield, the hundred, *burgus*, forest and park, the latter now no longer a stud. Anne of Bohemia, queen of England, held the lordship from 1389,[68] but after her death in June 1394, Richard II kept the lordship in his own hands.[69] Through our period it remained in the earl's hands. It was not granted to Henry IV's queen, Joan of Navarre, as it could have been, but it was assigned in dower to Queen Catherine after the death of Henry V.[70]

## Sources

Annual financial accounts preserved in The National Archives form the basis of this study, the financial year running from Michaelmas to Michaelmas.[71] We can draw on three sets of accounts which arise out of the different levels and responsibilities within the structures of the earldom.

First, there are the accounts of the chamberlain of the county which reflect the upper level of administration based at the exchequer of Chester in the castle. The chamberlain's accounts deal with county-level business: income such as the issues of the seal and expenditure such as alms, annuities, repairs to and maintenance of buildings and wages of officials and soldiers.

67 Sharp, 'Earldom and County of Chester', p. 324.

68 CHES 2/64, m 4 (3), *36 DKR*, p. 311.

69 In Aug 1394, Richard appointed commissioners to survey the lordship and dispose of it as seemed best for the king's profit (*CPR 1391–6*, p. 520). These commissioners were to report damages and to restore order and had the power to appoint new officers, but we can detect nothing of their operations (Sharp, 'Earldom and County of Chester', p. 315).

70 7 Nov 1422: *CPR 1422–9*, p. 17; 20 Oct 1423: *CPR 1422–9*, p. 166; *PROME*, x. 46.

71 Until 1854, the records of the palatinate of Chester were held in Chester Castle but were subsequently moved to the newly established Public Record Office in Chancery Lane, London (Booth, *Financial Admin.*, pp. 11–12). All were moved to The National Archives at Kew in 1997.

The chamberlain accounted for funds paid to him by the sheriff and the escheator of the county and by the second-tier officials, each of whom was based at and responsible for the income and expenditure of one of the earl's demesnes. Between 1399 and 1422, the chamberlain also received revenues generated from Macclesfield since that lordship was in the hands of the earl. When it was held by a queen, its local receiver accounted directly to her receiver-general.

The annual accounts of the officials of the four component units of Macclesfield were bound together and preserved separately. The annual accounts for the remaining parts of the earl's demesne – described in the PRO/TNA catalogues as 'Divers Ministers Accounts' – were bound together into a file. In all cases the format of the accounts followed standard royal exchequer practice where membranes were written on both sides, stitched together at the top and then rolled up for ease of storage.

There has been a tendency to write off late medieval accounts as being of little value in comparison with those of the high middle ages when lords had exploited their lands directly. The Cheshire accounts of our period reflect a rentier economy where lords relied on income from rents and leases of demesne lands. As a result they are 'fossilised', showing few differences year on year as well as containing little or nothing about agricultural practice. However, the increasing standardisation of the accounts also reflects a sophistication in accounting techniques whose roots can be traced back to the great elaboration of estate management in the thirteenth century.[72] A particular advantage of our Cheshire material is that there is a near continuous run of chamberlain's accounts as well as Divers Ministers and Macclesfield accounts. Any shortcomings in the information they afford is offset by the ability to view such changes as were made on a year-to-year basis. The accounts are as much administrative as financial documents. Many of our conclusions regarding policy towards the earl's lands and

72 R. H. Hilton, *Ministers' Accounts of the Warwickshire Estates of the Duke of Clarence, 1479–80*, Dugdale Society, 21 (1952), p. xi.

revenues must necessarily be the result of deduction from its effects upon county and demesne administration.

At least two copies were made of each account. One, marked 'originale', was, until 1854, kept at Chester but after its transfer to the PRO was classed within the Welsh Records. The other, marked 'duplicate', was kept at Westminster and subsequently included within the Ancient Miscellanea of the Queen's Remembrancer.[73] For the most part, the copies are identical save for marginal 'pointing' and marginal calculations by the auditors and officials of the earl's central financial administration. Where two accounts survive for the same year, the fairer copy has been used, with a check against the other copy where necessary.[74]

There are two 'valors' (periodic valuations) which are relevant to this study. The first is of the county alone, for the year 1402–3.[75] The second, undated but from the same early part of the reign of Henry IV, is of all the lands held by Prince Henry, Cheshire included.[76] For the tenure of the county by the Black Prince, we are fortunate to have a surviving register of acts and other documents concerning his lands.[77] For Prince Henry, we can draw on miscellaneous survivals of transcripts, inquisitions,

73 Booth, *Financial Admin.*, p. 14. See, respectively, the two accounts for 1399–1400: SC 6/791/1 (marked *Cestr' originale*) and SC 6/791/2 (marked Queen's Remembrancer). By the late nineteenth century all copies had been placed within an artificial collection at the Public Record Office (PRO), S(pecial) C(ollection) 6. See *List and Index V: Special Collection 6: Ministers and Receivers' Accounts* (London: HMSO, 1894), pp. 116–22. For ten years of our period there are two chamberlain's accounts surviving. For ten years (but not the same ten) we have two ministers' accounts surviving. For eleven years we have two Macclesfield accounts surviving. Only for the ministers' accounts for 4–5 Henry IV are there three copies surviving: SC 6/791/7, 791/8 (fragmentary), and 791/9.

74 A list of the accounts used is provided in the bibliography.

75 SC 11/904, translated in Appendix V. Special Collection 11 was also an artificial class created at the PRO, grouping together documents which were surveys of lands and similar documents.

76 SC 11/862, translated in Appendix VI.

77 *Register of Edward the Black Prince Preserved in the Public Record Office*, 4 vols (London: HMSO, 1930–3). The third volume concerns Cheshire 1361–5.

petitions and warrants related to the administration of the county which were submitted from Chester to his central administration at Westminster.[78] There are also a number of documents emanating from the prince's household which can provide information about councillors and sometimes financial policy.[79]

The earldom had its own equivalent to the various rolls of the royal chancery, since it had its own seal under which letters could be issued. The Cheshire enrolments emanated from the exchequer of the county and have commonly been called 'recognizance rolls' because recognizances for debt were commonly the first entries on each roll.[80] This emphasises the close connection between the county chancery and exchequer.[81] Much material relating to the demesnes appears here – appointments, enrolments of leases, recognizances entered into by officials in respect of those of their accounts which were in arrears, etc. Not all such matters are so enrolled, however, and it is therefore important to use the enrolments in conjunction with the accounts otherwise errors are liable to occur.[82]

78 E 163/6/41.

79 These are catalogued within the artificial collection, Exchequer Accounts Various (E101), under 'Wardrobe and Household'. See *List and Index XXXV: Exchequer Accounts Various* (London: HMSO, 1900).

80 CHES 2. Where I have given references to these rolls I have given the original manuscript reference as well as the calendar reference from the *36 DKR* and *37 DKR*. For discussion, see Dorothy J. Clayton, *The Administration of the County Palatine of Chester 1442–1485*, Chetham Society, 3rd ser., 28 (1990), pp. 11–15.

81 Sharp, 'Earldom and County of Chester', pp. 156–7. See also M. Sharp, 'The Central Administrative System of Edward, the Black Prince', in T. F. T. Tout, *Chapters in Medieval Administrative History*, v (Manchester: Manchester University Press, 1930), p. 307.

82 See, for example, J. T. Driver, *Cheshire in the Later Middle Ages* (Chester: Cheshire Community Council, 1971), p. 50, where the author states 'in the reign of Richard II, the manor of Northwich was held by John Holland, earl of Huntingdon and duke of Exeter. The duke was attainted for treason in 1400, but the family managed to obtain restoration of its property. As overlords the Hollands leased the manor, and in 1410 Sir Laurence Merbury took out a lease for ten years'. Driver is incorrect. The Hollands did not obtain restoration

There are copious materials relating to judicial activity in the county as a whole. Those which are most useful for a study of the demesnes are the indictment rolls. Four survive for this period, each connected with various judicial processes and courts. For the reign of Henry IV, there is a complete roll of indictments taken before the justiciar at Chester which includes many cases arising in the demesne lands, as well as records of the Dee Mills Courts, and a roll of indictments of the eyre of justiciar in all of the hundreds excluding Macclesfield.[83] For the reign of his son, we have another roll of Chester indictments as well as a roll of indictments for the justices of eyre at Macclesfield.[84]

The accounts themselves offer a relatively impersonal view of the demesnes and their tenants. No rentals survive for this period, but we can draw on the records created for the lordship of Macclesfield in 1383–4.[85] It is from the manorial court rolls of the various parts of the demesne that we can glean a wealth of evidence bearing upon tenant life, economic rivalry, violence, etc.. Macclesfield court rolls survive for seventeen of the twenty-two years of this study.[86] Survivals of court rolls for the other demesnes are more sporadic,[87] but nonetheless they

until 1410 and so were not overlords then. If Driver had consulted only the *DKR* calendars of the recognizance rolls, as seems likely, it is easy to see how he arrived at this erroneous view. Not all annuities granted are noted in the recognizance rolls but can be traced in issues of the seal in the chamberlain's accounts.

83 CHES 25/10 and CHES 25/9 respectively.

84 CHES 25/11 and CHES 25/23 respectively.

85 SC 11/898.

86 SC 2/255/3 to 255/19, SC 2/155/88. For general discussion see Anne Curry, 'The Court Rolls of the Lordship of Macclesfield, 1345–1485', *Cheshire History*, 12 (1983), 5–10, and for Macclesfield, A. M. Tonkinson, *Macclesfield in the Later Fourteenth Century: Communities of Town and Forest*, Chetham Society, 3rd ser., 42 (1999), pp. 44–6.

87 Shotwick 9–11 Henry IV (SC 2/156/13); Frodsham 1–2 Henry V (SC 2/155/83); Middlewich 1–2 Henry V (SC 2/156/3); Northwich 1–2 Henry V (SC 2/156/11). It may not be a coincidence that three rolls survive for the first year of the reign of Henry V given the king's proven interest in law and order after his accession (see E. Powell, *Kingship, Law and Society: Criminal Justice in the Reign of Henry V* (Oxford: Clarendon Press, 1989). The Middlewich court roll in the

provide a vivid picture of the demesnes as well as furnishing much evidence on how administration, as exemplified in the accounts, worked in practice, through, for instance, indictments for illegal hunting and wood cutting in the forests.

Unfortunately, only the court rolls for Macclesfield and Shotwick provide details on tenure. Elsewhere, such rolls are mainly taken up by litigation between tenants. The different kinds of evidence afforded by the court rolls is useful in revealing yet again the differences between the units and demonstrating the degree of seigneurial control. Those manors where there is chiefly tenant litigation demonstrate a highly developed society and community of the vill, largely independent of seigneurial control: those where tenurial obligations and transactions are recorded often show more seigneurial control over tenure and peasant activity in general. This is discussed in more detail in Chapter 4.

Where tenure was by copy of court roll, the entries on the manorial court rolls are complemented in some cases by survival of the copy which was given to the individual it concerned. Such survivals are random, preserved because of the interest of a particular family in certain tenements, although this in itself can be significant in identifying leading tenants of the manor who were the most precocious in record keeping and in emphasizing their rights.[88] The most interesting example of surviving family papers is the cartulary of John de Macclesfield – his compilation of documents relevant to his holdings and transactions.[89] Private collections often also contain miscellaneous material of interest but it cannot be claimed that a thoroughgoing survey has been made of such collections. On the whole, concentration has

TNA is now incomplete. The missing membrane which covers June to Aug 1414 is abstracted in *A Middlewich Chartulary*, ed. Joan Varley, 2 vols, Chetham Society, 105, 108 (with James Tait) (1941–4), i. 209.

88 For the purposes of this study, various collections in Cheshire Archives and Local Studies, the John Rylands Research Institute and Library University of Manchester, and Keele University have been examined.

89 BL, Cotton MS Cleopatra D VI; J. L. C. Bruel, 'An Edition of the John de Macclesfield Cartulary', unpublished PhD thesis (University of London, 1969).

been directed to 'official' documentation, but all the survivals offer great potential for further study.[90]

90 In this respect the study of Michael Bennett, *Community, Class and Careerism: Cheshire and Lancashire Society in the Age of Sir Gawain and the Green Knight* (Cambridge: Cambridge University Press, 1983) is extremely valuable, not least for the study of the Cheshire gentry of this period who are little considered in the present work. For the potential of the recognizance rolls in particular, see Clayton, *Administration of the County Palatine*, where they are put to excellent use for the period from 1442 to 1485.

CHAPTER I

# *The Administration of the Demesne*

Although we are concerned in this chapter principally with the administration of the lands held directly by the earl in Cheshire, this aspect cannot be seen in isolation from the control of the county as a whole. In the earldom of Chester, as in the duchy of Cornwall, there was no separate organization to deal with the manors.[1] The earl's officials exercised a wide range of functions, of which control of the demesne formed an important part. The administrative system developed under the Black Prince remained a model for the future.[2] There was a three-tier structure. The top tier comprised the control exercised from beyond the county by officials of the crown or the prince, including household officials, receivers-general, auditors and such like; the middle tier was made up of the county administration headed by the chamberlain, who was responsible for all financial matters, the justiciar, responsible for legal matters, the sheriff and the escheator, whose powers and responsibilities were much as in other counties; and the bottom tier consisted of local officials operating at the level of each unit, such as bailiffs, receivers, etc.

For the years from 1399 to 1422 it is not only structure and procedure which deserve attention but also changes of personnel. This is particularly important in assessing the impact of the usurpation of Henry IV. Given the young age of his son, the earl, the king's influence was likely to be substantial. It was to remain so over subsequent years because of the significance of Cheshire in the Welsh wars and as the epicentre of Hotspur's rebellion in 1403. The approach in this chapter is largely

1 J. Hatcher, *Rural Economy and Society in the Duchy of Cornwall 1300–1500* (Cambridge: Cambridge University Press, 1970), p. 43.

2 M. Sharp, 'The Central Administrative System of Edward, the Black Prince', in T. F. T. Tout, *Chapters in Medieval Administrative History*, v (Manchester, 1930), p. 400.

chronological, culminating in the contrasts and continuities which can be drawn between administration under Henry V as prince and king. Towards the end of the chapter we shall turn our attention to the local administration of the demesne lands of the earl.

## The deposition of Richard II and the creation of Prince Henry's earldom

The end of Richard II's regime and the imposition of that of the future Henry IV actually began in Cheshire even before the formal deposition of Richard. Henry Bolingbroke had arrived in Chester on 9 August 1399. Richard was brought from Flint to Chester on 16 August and lodged in the castle keep. On that very same day, John Trevor, bishop of St Asaph, was appointed during royal pleasure as chamberlain of Chester, Flintshire and North Wales, the appointment being enrolled at Chester in the enrolments (recognizance rolls) of the county as well as on the Patent Rolls.[3] This appointment was made in Richard II's name but was undoubtedly Bolingbroke's doing since the king had already lost any pretence of authority.

Trevor was appointed to replace the previous incumbent, Robert Parys, who had held office since 6 May 1394 as chamberlain of Chester as well as of North Wales, and who had had his functions as chamberlain of Chester extended in 1398 to reflect the larger extent of Richard's new principality.[4] On 29

3 CHES 2/73, m 9 (4), *36 DKR*, p. 99; *CPR 1396–9*, p. 591 ('teste rege'). This appointment is also given in his first chamberlain's account covering the year from Michaelmas 22 Richard II (1399) where it is followed by the appointment of Trevor as chamberlain, made by Prince Henry on 1 Nov 1399 (SC 6/774/11, m 6d).

4 Robert Parys's father, another Robert, had served as chamberlain of Chester under the Black Prince. Although the family had North Welsh origins, they had been settled in Cambridgeshire from the 1360s and Robert junior served as MP for that county in 1388. For his biography see J. S. Roskell, Linda Clark and Carole Rawcliffe (eds), *The House of Commons 1386–1421*, 4 vols (Stroud: Alan Sutton for the History of Parliament Trust, 1993), iv, 20–2.

July 1399, Roger Brescy, clerk of the chamberlain, had taken the seal of the principality, as well the old seal of the earldom, from the Exchequer at Chester Castle and handed them to Parys in the latter's house in Bridge Street. The relevant entry in the Chester enrolments indicates that Richard's justiciar of Chester, Thomas Holland, duke of Surrey, had ordered these seals to be taken by Parys to Richard in Wales.[5] We can assume that Parys set out from Chester soon after 29 July to seek out the king.[6] But the seals never reached Richard. A gloss to the entry of 29 July in the Chester enrolments indicates that instead they were handed over, presumably by Parys, when Richard and Henry were at Lichfield, en route from Chester to London, on 24 August.

The order concerning the seals is clear indication of how Richard had hoped to use his special relationship with Cheshire to fortify his position on his return from Ireland. A further indication is found in the king's appointment of John Montague, earl of Salisbury, as governor of the principality of Chester and North Wales. Although this is entered on the Chester enrolments under 19 July,[7] it is likely that the earl had already received his orders a week earlier when he was with the king in Dublin.[8] However, the earl had not been able to secure Cheshire and North Wales for Richard, being prevented from moving eastwards from his base at Conway, to which the king had made his way through Wales in the first weeks of August.[9]

5 CHES 2/73, m 1 (8), *36 DKR*, p. 376. Brescy's action had been in response to a request communicated via Parys's chaplain.

6 Biggs suggests that Parys left Chester with the seals on 5 Aug but this is a misreading of the date in the Chester enrolments of the Tuesday before St Peter ad Vincula (28 Jul) as the Tuesday *after* the feast (5 Aug). (D. Biggs, *Three Armies in Britain: The Irish Campaign of Richard II and the Usurpation of Henry IV, 1397–99* (Leiden and Boston: Brill, 2006), p. 223, n. 1).

7 CHES 2/73, m 1 (2, 3, 4, 5, 6), *36 DKR*, p. 99. The king is thought to have left Dublin on 17 July and to have landed at Milford Haven around 24 Jul.

8 Biggs, *Three Armies in Britain*, p. 221.

9 Biggs, *Three Armies in Britain*, pp. 223--5. Richard may have been at Conway on 2–3 Aug (ibid., p. 229) but Saul's itinerary places him

Henry Bolingbroke's swift march northwards from Bristol from late July was enough to outpace Richard and his would-be supporters in Cheshire. At least some of the latter decided on the wisdom of voluntary surrender to avoid a worse fate. The sheriff of the county, Sir Robert Legh, led a delegation from Chester, meeting Bolingbroke at Shrewsbury on 5 August and offering terms for the surrender of the city. Henry entered Chester with some ceremony on 9 August.[10] Sir Peter Legh, one of Richard's Cheshire retainers and bodyguard, had already been arrested in Chester by the sheriff, and was executed in the city at Henry's command on 12 August. Over the following weeks a number of Cheshire gentry made formal submission to Henry, described in the entries in the Chester enrolments as duke of Lancaster and steward of England.[11]

Immediately Henry had arrived in Chester, his men had seized large quantities of armaments from its castle as well as wine and salt stored there.[12] They caused much havoc elsewhere in the city and its hinterland in the days before Richard's surrender.[13]

there on 12–15 Aug (Nigel Saul, *Richard II* (New Haven CT and London: Yale University Press, 1997), pp. 413, 474. According to Jean Creton, Salisbury told the king at Conway that he had raised 40,000 troops but they defected, some to Duke Henry, and others even believed the king was already dead (*La prinse et mort du roy Richart d'Angleterre, based on British Library MS Harley 1319, and Other Works by Jean Creton*, ed. and trans. Lorna A. Finlay, Camden Society, 5th ser., 65 (2023), pp. 98–101).

10 Saul, *Richard II*, p. 412.

11 For instance, John de Legh of Booths submitted by 20 Aug, giving sureties from himself, Sir John Stanley and Sir Robert de Legh for his good behaviour (CHES 2/73, m 7 (2), *36 DKR*, p. 292).

12 SC 6/774/10, m 2d, 3d. At their arrival, the garrison had been around 30 men-at-arms and archers (P. J. Morgan, *War and Society in Medieval Cheshire, 1277–1403*, Chetham Society, 3rd ser., 34 (1987), p. 203 citing SC 6/774 10, m 2d.

13 Morgan, *War and Society*, p. 204. In addition, around 12 Aug Henry was able to conduct a lightening raid on Holt castle, thereby gaining control of the treasure which Richard had stored there: Christopher Given-Wilson, *Henry IV* (New Haven CT and London: Yale University Press, 2016), p. 134. At least some of the £43,964 held there was seized and used by Henry to pay his troops (ibid., pp. 139, 175).

The appointment of Trevor as chamberlain on 16 August, the very first day Richard was in Chester, gave Henry access not only to any cash held in the Chester exchequer but also to all of the resources in the county administered by the chamberlain. Equally important, it prevented Richard accessing such resources. Trevor's period of accounting began without delay on the day of his appointment. His first chamberlain's account shows income and expenditure for the rest of the twenty-third year of Richard's reign to Michaelmas (29 September 1399), and then from that date to Michaelmas in the first year of Henry IV (29 September 1400).[14] Such evidence demonstrates an important point on financial administration. There might be significant political changes but the collection and spending of revenues emanating from lands and rights continued without disruption.

The choice as chamberlain of John Trevor, who had been bishop of St Asaph since 1394, is not easy to explain.[15] He was certainly of Welsh ancestry, perhaps hailing from Llandudno – he later received compensation for lands lost in Flintshire although Adam Usk described him as being 'of Powis'. He was related to another John Trevor who had been bishop of St Asaph between 1346 and 1357. He was Oxford-educated, had served as papal chaplain and auditor of causes from 1390, and also as precentor of Wells Cathedral between 1386 and 1392. Whilst there is no evidence of strong Lancastrian links before 1399, he had served on a commission with John of Gaunt in 1398 concerning infractions of the truce with Scotland.

Trevor was the only Welshman to hold a bishopric at the turn of the century, his Welsh origins perhaps helping the Lancastrians to counter Richard's cause in those key days of

14 SC 6/774/11, m 1. See also SC 6/774/12, view of account of Trevor for the period 16 Aug 1399 to 22 Mar 1400.

15 For his biography, which includes full references to the activities noted here, see R. G. Davies, 'The Episcopate in England and Wales 1375–1443', unpublished PhD thesis (University of Manchester, 1974), iii, pp. cclxxxvii–ccxc. See also J. Tait and R. R. Davies, 'John Trevor [Siôn Trefor] (d. 1410/1412), bishop of St Asaph, *Oxford Dictionary of National Biography*, 27726. See also Davies, *Revolt of Owain Glyn Dŵr*, pp. 9–10, 59.

August 1399. His appointment as chamberlain of Chester, Flintshire and North Wales at Bolingbroke's behest in August 1399 indicates that he was deemed a trustworthy ally. This is confirmed by the fact he was chosen to read the sentence of deposition of Richard on 30 September.[16]

On 1 November 1399 he was appointed chamberlain of Chester, Flint and Caernarvon by the prince of Wales.[17] This appointment was recited at the end of Trevor's first account as chamberlain and was made by the prince in London at the wish of his father and with the consent of his own council.[18] By 10 December, however, Robert Parys had been reinstated as chamberlain of North Wales,[19] and can be seen to have subsequently been a member of the prince's council.[20] Subsequently we find Trevor serving on Henry IV's expedition to Scotland in 1400 and also acting as lieutenant in North Wales in the absence of the prince in early 1402 and again in 1403. He was also with the prince at the battle of Shrewsbury.

The removal of Richard's chamberlain of Chester in August 1399 is paralleled by what happened in the case of the justiciar of the county. Richard's last justiciar of Chester was one of his favourites, William le Scrope, earl of Wiltshire, who had been appointed in January 1398 but had his powers

16 The *Chronicle of Adam Usk 1377-1421,* ed. C. Given-Wilson (Oxford: Clarendon Press, 1997) pp. 68–9. Walsingham also mentions him as a member of the six-strong commission which carried out the public sentence of deposition (*St Alban's Chronicle*, vol. II: *1394–1422. The* Chronica Maiora *of Thomas Walsingham*, ed. John Taylor, Wendy R. Childs and Leslie Watkiss (Oxford: Clarendon Press, 2011), pp. 202–3, 212–13), and claims that Henry IV subsequently sent him to Spain to explain Henry's title to the throne (pp. 278–9).

17 Initially he had been appointed on that same day chamberlain of Chester, Flint and North Wales CHES 2/74, m 16 (5), *36 DKR*, p. 9) but the second appointment made on the same day was for Chester, Flint and Carnarvon (CHES 2/74, m 1 (1), *36 DKR*, p. 9).

18 SC 6/774/11, m 6d.

19 *House of Commons 1386–1421*, iv. 21.

20 SC 6/774/11, m 3d (at Chester along with Sir Hugh Holes, the steward of the prince's lands, and ordering the purchase of grain to make bread for the royal army in Wales).

extended in July to cover the extended principality.[21] Scrope surrendered to Henry at Bristol on 29 July 1399 and was executed immediately. Although the enrolled appointment in the Cheshire enrolments of Sir Henry Percy (Hotspur), eldest son of the earl of Northumberland, is dated 29 October 1399, on which date he was given the office for life,[22] it seems that Hotspur was in office by, or shortly after, 20 August.[23] Hotspur had met Bolingbroke at Bridlington in late June, and a week later at Doncaster, along with his father the earl, made an oath to support him. The earl of Northumberland himself was sent by Henry to Richard at Conway in early August.

Since Hotspur was unlikely to be able to serve as justiciar in person, by 12 November deputies had been formally appointed, John de Knyghtley and William Swinburne.[24] Like his master, the Northumberland knight Swinburne had also been in office since the Lancastrian coup in Cheshire, being called vice-justiciar as early as 22 August.[25] In the first chamberlain's account he was compensated for his costs in holding certain knights and esquires in the castle of Chester and arranging their transfer to London at Henry's order.[26] We also know that Nicholas Rygby, a member of Bolingbroke's military retinue,

21 CHES 2/ 71, m 3 (2), n. 5 (1–7) *36 DKR*, pp. 426. His deputies were Hugh Holes and Robert Parys the chamberlain (CHES 2/71 m 3 (3), *36 DKR*, p. 426). For the vast amount of patronage given by Richard to William le Scrope in Wales and the marches see R. R. Davies, *The Revolt of Owain Glyn Dŵr* (Oxford: Oxford University Press, 1995), p. 81.

22 Along with Flintshire and North Wales (CHES 2/74, m 7 (4), *36 DKR*, p. 378).

23 The Chester enrolments include an entry of that date concerning sureties that James Darteys, imprisoned in the castle of Chester by command of Henry duke of Lancaster, would not escape but these were cancelled because Darteys was released on the duke's order addressed to Henry Percy, justice of Chester, and by Hotspur's warrant to Nicholas de Rygby, constable of the castle (CHES 2/72, m 7 (3), *36 DKR*, p. 136).

24 CHES 2/72, m 7d (4), *36 DKR*, p. 379.

25 CHES 2/74, m 1d (9), *36 DKR*, p. 462.

26 SC 6/774/12, m 1, cited in Morgan, *War and Society in Medieval Cheshire*, p. 204.

had temporarily assumed the constableship of Chester Castle following his master's arrival in the city.[27] On 24 October Hotspur was appointed for life as constable of Chester Castle and of the castles of Flint, Conway and Caernarvon,[28] but on 18 November 1399, a local knight, Sir William Venables, who had served as constable of Chester Castle before the usurpation, was restored to his post by the prince.[29]

Other changes of officeholders in the county are seen following the usurpation. In the last year of Richard II, Robert de Legh had been sheriff and Adam Kingsley escheator.[30] Henry IV appointed Sir John Massey of Puddington as sheriff from Michaelmas 1399,[31] testimony to the fact that even those who had served Richard might accommodate themselves with the new regime.[32] Similarly, Richard de Manley, who had held an annuity from Richard, was appointed escheator on 10 November 1399.[33] On 28 October 1399, Robert de Whitlegh, also the holder of a Ricardian annuity, was appointed as bailiff itinerant, and on 10 November, Matthew del Mere, also a Cheshire man, as attorney general.[34] On 20 November, Henry de Birteles, who had been appointed to hold the county court in October 1397, and Roger de Horton were appointed as sergeants-at-law. Roger had held this position since May 1396 having previously been justice of eyre at Macclesfield.[35] As can be seen, Henry IV was

27 CHES 2/72, m 7 (3), *36 DKR*, p. 136.
28 *CPR 1399–1401*, p. 158.
29 CHES 2/ 74, m 1 (8), *36 DKR*, p. 491. See CHES 2/71, m 7 (13), *36 DKR*, p. 490 for his service as constable in 1397–8.
30 SC 6/790/10, mm. 5, 7.
31 SC 6/791/1, m7.
32 Massey had been appointed steward of Hawarden in Oct 1397 (CHES 2/71, m 1 (9), *36 DKR*, p. 331).
33 CHES 2/74, m 1 (7), *36 DKR*, p. 323. For his annuity granted in Oct 1397, see CHES 2/71, m 19 d (4), *36 DKR*, p. 323.
34 CHES 2/74, m 9d (4), m 8 (5), *36 DKR*, p. 100. For Whitley's annuity of 1 July 1398 see CHES 2/71, m 36d (1), *36 DKR*, p. 522.
35 CHES 2/74, m 1 (9), m 7 (7), *36 DKR*, p. 100. For Birteles appointment in 1397, CHES 2/71, m4d (5), *36 DKR*, p. 361. For Horton, CHES 2/67, m 6d (11), CHES 2/69, m 11 (9), *36 DKR*, p. 249.

keen to keep local expertise in these executive and legal areas irrespective of any service connections to Richard's regime.

This was not the case where offices were instruments of patronage, as had been the case for Richard's beneficiaries, William de Becheton as 'equitator' of Delamere Forest, and William le Scrope, earl of Wiltshire as 'supervisor' of all the forests of the king in the county.[36] The Derbyshire knight, and Lancastrian supporter, Sir Thomas de Wendesley, was appointed for life by Henry IV on 13 October 1399 as master forester and equitator of the forests of Macclesfield and Delamere as well as steward of Macclesfield, with the prince confirming the appointment on 20 January 1400.[37] At the Dee Mills and fishery, the king's servant Henry Strangeways was appointed as keeper for life on 16 October 1399, replacing William Marshal. The latter was connected with Thomas Mowbray, earl of Norfolk, and had held the post since 1391.[38] This keepership was a lucrative post to which the new king was keen to nominate one of his own household.

The stewardship of Macclesfield was vacant at Henry's coming to the throne since it had been held by Sir Peter Legh who, as we have seen, had been executed during Bolingbroke's stay in Chester. Sir Peter had also been the lessee of Macclesfield park from the king. The park was now taken back into direct control and Hugh Hoby, another Lancastrian servant, appointed parker for life on 29 October 1399, the appointment being confirmed by the prince on 4 December.[39] Middlewich, too, was taken back into direct control from the hands of the favourite to whom Richard had granted it, William Bagot, who had been captured and sent for trial.[40] Henry Ravenscroft, who had previously served as sheriff of the county in 1396 after

36 SC 6/774/10, mm 4, 5.

37 *CPR 1399–1401*, p. 31; CHES 2/74, m 2d (6), *36 DKR*, p. 312.

38 *CPR 1399–1401*, p. 11; CHES 2/74, m 1d (3–5), *36 DKR*, p. 454. For Marshall's tenure see *36 DKR*, p. 326.

39 *CPR 1399–1401*, p. 41; CHES 2/74, m 8d (1), *36 DKR*, p. 235.

40 SC 6/790/10, m 3.

being under sheriff, acted as keeper from Michaelmas 1399.[41] He already had links with the town having acted as steward for Joan, Princess of Wales, in 1380 and receiver for the king in 1386.[42]

There were no changes in personnel in Shotwick, Frodsham and Northwich. At Drakelow, on 4 November 1399, Henry IV confirmed the life grant of the bailiwick of Rudheath to John Rose, which had been made in 1378.[43] But from 5 February 1400, the escheator of the county, Richard de Manley, was appointed as receiver of issues there, implying that Rose had died in the interim.[44]

There can be no doubt that both before and after his formal accession as king, all decisions concerning the county were made by Henry IV himself. Appointments were, by necessity, made by him before the county was formally granted to the prince in parliament on 15 October. There are therefore several early appointments enrolled on the patent rolls which were later confirmed by the prince, with the confirmations being also entered on the Chester enrolments. Some examples have already been given and others can be seen in Appendix I. Taking all the changes of personnel together, we can see that Henry IV had acted swiftly to take control of the county, both before and immediately after his accession. He had ensured that trusted supporters were introduced to the key offices, most notably of chamberlain and justiciar, and where posts were powerful instruments of patronage. Local men were left in post where they could be trusted. In reality, most of the actual administration at county and demesne level continued to be carried out by local men of lower rank. There is no sign in the chamberlain's and ministers' accounts of disruption in the collection of revenues

41 SC 6/791/1, m 4. Morgan, *War and Society*, p. 207, claims that Henry Ravenscroft was appointed steward of Northwich in 1399, citing Eaton Hall, Eaton Charter 389, but I have not found evidence of Ravenscroft in office at Northwich until 1413 (see Appendix I (i)).

42 *36 DKR*, p. 398.

43 *CPR 1399–1401*, p. 129. For the original grant see CHES 2/51, m 1 (4), *36 DKR*, p. 410.

44 SC 6/791/1, m 1d.

or in the administration of the demesnes as a result of the change of regime.

The impact of regime change is apparent, however, in terms of policy concerning the resources of the earldom, moved by a desire to ensure that Prince Henry would be able to draw as much income as possible from the lands of his appanage. Such a situation derived from the political circumstances of the usurpation. In Henry IV's first parliament of October 1399, the Commons had shown their concern about Richard II's tendency towards the alienation of royal lands to his favourites. As a result they petitioned that such lands should be resumed into royal hands, adding a request that this should also be done in the principality of Wales, Cornwall and Chester.[45]

The Commons also petitioned specifically that grants and alienations made by Richard II in Cheshire and in the principality of Wales should be revoked, otherwise it might be necessary for the prince to have assignment out of royal revenues, 'which would be a great charge on the king, on his kingdom and all the inhabitants thereof' ('qe serreit tres grant charge a nostre dit seigneur le roy de son roialme et de toute la communaltée d'icelle').[46] The royal response was that any who were unworthy recipients of grants should have their letters repealed. Usk suggests that it was the chamberlain John Trevor who spoke at the parliament against this petition, calling it rude and unjust, and claiming that it would encourage the king to be niggardly, which would be a disservice to kingship which is better served by a generous degree of largesse.[47] As we shall see in Chapter 5, there were indeed Ricardian supporters who had their annuities ended by the new regime. Yet, in practice, the sums spent on annuities in the earldom did not decrease. The need to reward supporters proved as pressing for the Lancastrians as it had for Richard II. In fact, there were many more 'officials' receiving

45 *PROME*, viii. 49.
46 *PROME*, viii. 68.
47 *Chronicle of Adam Usk*, pp. 82–3. The petition was put to the king and the lords, and John Trevor was present at the parliament (*PROME*, viii. 3, 68).

small fees under the Lancastrians, 'appointed' according to the dictates of patronage and the needs of the Welsh wars.[48]

That said, we can see evidence of early efforts to increase the new prince's income. There was an early move to restore demesne units to comital control, with only Frodsham being allowed to remain in the hands of Richard II's donee. Save for the less valuable units – Overmarsh, Saughall and Shotwick – which were soon leased, this remained the policy until later in this period. There was also a tightening up of administrative and financial control at the Dee grinding mills, and an abortive attempt at centralised control over Northwich and Drakelow.[49] This paralleled the policies pursued in the duchy of Cornwall at this point; at the accession of Henry IV many of the assessionable manors there were restored to the duchy and, with the influence of a parliament anxious to keep down royal expenses, it was established that in future only life interests could be granted out of the estate of the duchy.[50] We also see attempts to tighten centralised surveillance in the duchy after a slackening of control over demesne revenues under Richard II.[51]

An important change within the earldom of Chester was the resumption of the lordship of Macclesfield into the control of the chamberlain of Chester. From the death of Queen Anne in 1394, Richard II had kept the lordship in his own hands, so that its receiver accounted independently and rendered its issues directly to the king.[52] There was a considerable degree of disruption in the lordship at the time of the usurpation. In addition to the changes in personnel mentioned earlier, and the troubled state of the lordship because of frequent raids by the men of Derbyshire,[53] there was no income from either the mills

48 In North Wales too there were also many offices superfluous to actual needs (R. A. Griffiths, 'Patronage, Politics and the Principality of Wales 1413–61', in *British Government and Administration: Studies presented to S.B. Chrimes*, p. 72).

49 See below pp. 68, 163.

50 *PROME*, viii. 249–50; Hatcher, *Rural Economy*, pp. 7, 149.

51 Hatcher, *Rural Economy*, p. 7.

52 SC 6/805/14, m 3.

53 *CPR 1399–1401*, p. 83; SC 6/805/14, m 3.

or the park in 1399.[54] In the latter case, it was noted that Peter Legh, the previous farmer, had been executed as a rebel, and no one knew to whom the evidences concerning his account had devolved. John de Legh, the receiver, had also leased the demesne of the forest. He was removed from both the office and the lease in the first year of the new reign, but his outstanding debts were not resolved until 1405.[55]

The account for the lordship of Macclesfield for the year from Michaelmas 22 Richard II to 1 Henry IV is missing, which may in itself indicate further confusion and disruption. By 1401, however, the chamberlain was established as receiver of Macclesfield, for which office he received a supplementary fee, and the ministers of the lordship rendered their issues to him.[56] Thus, by that point, the hierarchical structure of the administration of the Black Prince had been re-established in its entirety now that the chamberlain was responsible once more for *all* the revenues of the county.[57]

At the parliament of October 1399, there were two further hostile Commons petitions concerning the county. The first asked that the large amounts of money which Richard had paid to his Cheshire bodyguard should be repaid,[58] presumably a reference to the 4,000 marks in compensation for their service at Radcot Bridge which had been paid out from the royal Exchequer in December 1398.[59] The king's reply was that, as they could not repay such a sum, he wished them to do him

54 SC 6/805/6, m 2d.

55 SC 6/805/14, m 3.

56 SC 6/805/7. When the lordship of Macclesfield was granted to Queen Catherine in 1422, William Troutbeck, the chamberlain of Chester, continued as receiver although its issues were paid to her and not to the king (SC 6/807/5).

57 After 1347, the chamberlain had been responsible for the issues of Macclesfield and after 1352 for those of the escheator, both of whom had previously accounted directly to the centre (Booth, *Financial Admin.*, p. 57). It should be noted, however, that the escheator did account directly to the household in certain years of the reign of Henry IV, as we shall see in Chapter 7.

58 *PROME*, viii. 63.

59 CHES 2/73, m 6 (7), *36 DKR*, p. 312.

service for a specified time at their own costs. It seems likely that such service was given in the campaign to Scotland which Henry led in July 1400.[60]

The second petition was put forward by the inhabitants of Shropshire, angry at raids launched by Cheshire men who had escaped punishment because Cheshire was a county palatine, and therefore, in the opinion of the Commons petitioners, 'a den of thieves' ('ut in spelunca latronum').[61] The request was that the county should lose its special status and be ruled under the common law of the land, or at least that offenders should be properly punished especially for offences committed outside their county. The king had no difficulty with the second proposal. If men were found guilty elsewhere and fled to Chester, the officials of that county were to arrest them and declare their goods forfeit. But no change was proposed for the special status of the county. And indeed it was fair to say that men from Shropshire, Staffordshire and Derbyshire were also troublemakers in their own right, carrying out raids into Cheshire during the upheaval of August 1399.[62] On 9 December 1399, the prince sent a writ to the sheriff of Chester on the matter, saying that since the last parliament the men of Cheshire had again been raiding these adjoining counties and returning with booty. Proclamations were ordered forbidding such practices.[63]

The petitions put forward at the first parliament of 1399 indicate that there was lingering suspicion of the county because of its previous close links with Richard II. Such suspicions proved correct in the first weeks of 1400 when there was a rising in Chester which seems to have been planned to coincide with the Epiphany plot against the king and his sons at Windsor.[64]

60 See below p. 303.

61 *PROME*, viii. 64–6.

62 As seen in a commission by Henry IV on 11 Nov 1399 to Thomas de Wendesley and others to investigate (*CPR 1399–1401*, p. 85).

63 CHES 2/74, m 3 (4), *36 DKR*, p. 100.

64 Peter McNiven, 'The Cheshire Rising of 1400', *Bulletin of the John Rylands Library*, 52 (1970), 386.

The garrison, of eight men-at-arms and 35 archers, under the chamberlain, the sheriff and the captain, Sir William Venables, held firm.[65] In early March, the main enquiry opened presided over by Hotspur as justiciar. On 25 May a general pardon was issued with 125 named exceptions, many of whom had had close connections with Richard II. The suing for pardons continued over the next year. [66] But this revolt had little impact on the financial administration of the demesnes. John de Legh of Booths was amongst those who needed to sue for pardon and pay a surety of £200. He temporarily lost his annuity from the rents payable at Sutton in Macclesfield Forest, a grant which had initially been made by Richard in 1397, and had his lands sequestrated.[67] It was regranted in July 1401 although under less generous conditions.[68]

Whilst ensuring that the main officials in the county were loyal outsiders, it is apparent that the new regime made efforts to gain and keep the support of the local gentry, despite the latter's previous, and even in some cases lingering, commitment to the Ricardian cause. Lancastrian policy is therefore best described as one both of conciliation and infiltration. It was motivated by both a sense of reality and fear of insecurity which moved Henry IV to seek to bend the county to his own will rather than breaking its back by a heavy-handed display of displeasure.

65 SC 6/774/13, m 3d, Morgan, *War and Society*, p. 205.

66 McNiven, 'Cheshire Rising of 1400', pp. 390–2.

67 On 3 June 1400, Thomas Sweetenham of Mobberley was appointed by the prince as collector of the rents of John de Legh of Booths' lands, then in the prince's hands (CHES 2/74, m 7d (7)).

68 McNiven, 'Cheshire Rising of 1400', p. 392. The grant of 1397 was for all profits of the rents as well as an annuity of 100s but the regrant in July 1401 was for rents up to 20 marks (£13 6s. 8d.) per annum, his being required to answer to the earl for any rent income above this (CHES 2/75, m 3 (10), *36 DKR*, p. 293. See also Keele University Library, Legh of Booths Charters 265, 266; SC 6/805/11, m 2d, /16, m 2d.

## The development of the prince's administration in the earldom

On 8 November 1399, Henry IV granted to Prince Henry all debts, arrears of debts, rents and fee farms due to the king within the principality of Wales, the duchy of Cornwall and earldom of Chester, which he had not yet granted to other persons.[69] The impact in Cheshire is revealed by two entries in the Chester enrolments. On 10 November, the prince ordered the chamberlain to levy all arrears and debts in Chester, Flint and North Wales.[70] Two days later the king informed all officials in the principality of Wales that he had granted the principality to his son.[71] On 15 November, the prince issued a warrant to the chamberlain for the repair of all castles, houses and mills in Cheshire, Flint and North Wales, after inspection by the sheriff, Sir John Massey of Puddington.[72]

Revenues therefore came to the prince, but his young age ensured the king's ongoing interest, as did the continuing political situation.[73] Although the king never visited Cheshire again after August 1399, the county still had a special importance for the new regime. Thus it was the king who responded on 11 November 1399 to a petition from the inhabitants of Macclesfield about the recent incursions and cattle rustling of men from Derbyshire and Staffordshire.[74] Chester's involvement in the revolt of 1400 was discussed by the royal council.[75]

69 *CPR 1399–1401*, p. 61; R. A. Griffiths, 'Wales and the Marches', in S. B. Chrimes, C. D. Ross and R. A. Griffiths (eds), *Fifteenth Century England 1399–1509* (Manchester: Manchester University Press, 1974), pp. 145–72, at p. 147.

70 CHES 2/74, m 1 (4), *36 DKR*, p. 100.

71 CHES 2/74, m 1 (3), *36 DKR*, p. 100. It is interesting that this act was placed on the Chester enrolments.

72 CHES 2/74, m 1 (2), *36 DKR*, p. 100.

73 Sharp, 'Earldom and County of Chester', pp. 46–7, suggested that the household of a royal son was rarely independent of the king's administration especially when it came to military matters.

74 *CPR 1399–1401*, p. 83.

75 See, for instance, *PPC*, vol. 1, pp. 109, 111–12.

The pardon for the 1400 revolt, with its listed exceptions, was issued by the king and enrolled on the Patent rolls. Five subsequent pardons, such as that to John de Legh of Booths, were also enrolled on the Patent rolls.[76] But the investigation and other pardons were handled in the county and recorded in the indictment rolls and Chester enrolments.[77] The participation of the troops from the county on Henry IV's expedition to Scotland in the summer of 1400 was also determined by the king, and may have been given without payment following the king's decision in the October 1399 parliament that the great largesse given by Richard II to his Cheshire bodyguard could best be repaid by service at their own cost.[78]

The Glyndŵr rebellion, which broke out in the autumn of 1400, reinforced the king's inclination to continue some supervision of his son's patrimony. Indeed, it was vital that he should do so if a united command was to be created and financed to crush the rebels in Wales. The direction of Cheshire revenues from 1403–4 to the support of the North Welsh garrisons, discussed in Chapter 7, seems have been made by royal or at least conciliar initiative.[79] The king's involvement was also to be expected when Hotspur's revolt in 1403 again made the county a matter of national concern rather than a local, domestic matter to which his son could be allowed to respond.[80] As in 1400, some pardons were issued by the king and enrolled on the Patent Rolls, even though it was the chamberlain, Sir John Stanley and other loyal members of the Cheshire gentry who were commanded by the prince to pardon 'all those rebels … who should be repentant'.[81] On 3 November, at the instance

76 *CPR 1399–1401*, p. 327 (10 July 1400).

77 *CPR 1399–1401*, pp. 285–6; McNiven, 'Cheshire Rising of 1400', pp. 390–1.

78 *PROME*, viii. 63. See below p. 303.

79 *PPC*, ii. 67. See below pp. 315-6.

80 Davies, *Revolt of Owain Glyn Dŵr*, p. 184.

81 Peter McNiven, 'The Men of Cheshire and the Rebellion of 1403', *THSLC*, 129 (1979), 22–3.

of the prince (or so the text reads), the king issued a general pardon to all his lieges in the county, with a separate pardon to the citizens of Chester, in return for a fine of 3,000 marks, the royal act also being enrolled on the Patent Rolls.[82] Initially the king wished that the fine should be paid to him, but on 29 August 1404 he granted its profit to the prince.[83]

The most obvious outcome of the 1403 revolt in terms of county administration was the ending of Hostpur's justiciarship. Hotspur had proclaimed his revolt in Chester on 9–10 July, but the chamberlain's account for 1402–3 indicates that his period of office was deemed to have ended on 1 July 1403.[84] A formal replacement was not made until 24 July, two days after the battle of Shrewsbury, when Gilbert, Lord Talbot (1383–1418) was appointed during royal pleasure rather than for life, as Hostpur had been. Talbot held lands in the south of the county and had already seen military service with the prince of Wales and was to be prominent in both the Welsh and French wars. Talbot held the office until his death at the siege of Rouen on 19 October 1418. His deputy, James del Holt, held the fort until Henry V's return from France in February 1421 when the king appointed his uncle Thomas Beaufort, duke of Exeter as justiciar.

It was probably through Talbot that Laurence Merbury, constable of Chester Castle from 1409, sheriff from 1411 to 1414 and lessee of the town of Northwich from 1411 to 1413, was introduced into the Cheshire administrative scene. Another casualty of the battle of Shrewsbury was Sir John Massey of Puddington, who had served as sheriff from 1399 to 1401, since he met his death in the royal army.[85] But Massey had already

82 *CPR 1401–5*, pp. 330–1. Nine individual pardons were also granted on this date (ibid.).

83 *CPR 1401–5*, p. 412, *PPC*, ii. 236.

84 SC 6/774/15, m 3.

85 The only other Cheshire man known to have died with the king was Sir John Calverley (McNiven, 'Men of Cheshire', p. 21). That said, a royal signet letter of 14 Jul 1403 to the town of Coventry claims that the king had received messages of support from Cheshire and Northumberland even though Hotspur had raised rebellion and passed through Cheshire into Wales trying to incite people to rise up

lost his office in the summer of 1401, probably because he had failed to hold Conway, of which he was constable.[86]

The embroilment of local gentry in the rebellion of 1403 had little impact upon demesne administration. In the few cases where officials were involved in the rebellion, they were initially penalised, but later returned to favour and functions.[87] Although the escheator was ordered initially to seize his lands,[88] John Done of Utkinton never lost his office as master forester of Delamere. The lands of John de Legh of Booths were also ordered to be seized,[89] but as in 1400 he again recovered his income from the town of Sutton and later served as sheriff of the county. John Kingsley of Nantwich is known to have approached the king for support in a petition to the prince's council for the restoration of an annuity and of the office of 'equitator' of Delamere Forest, both of which he had forfeited because of his involvement in Hotspur's rebellion in 1403.[90] He was not reappointed as 'equitator' of Delamere Forest but did secure restoration of his annuities in 1404.

The prince had been in the county in person on several occasions in the first years of the new reign. It is unclear how long he stayed in Chester after his return from Ireland, but he was certainly there again in April and October 1401, as well as in early 1402.[91] On the last occasion he had been ordered to return to London by 2 February and therefore appointed the earl of Stafford and Lord Grey of Ruthin as his lieutenants in the county, as well as John Trevor, the chamberlain, and John

(*Calendar of Signet Letters of Henry IV and Henry V*, ed. J. L. Kirby (London: HMSO, 1978), no. 930).

86 *Anglo-Norman Letters and Petitions from All Souls' MS 182*, ed. M. Dominica Legge, Anglo-Norman Text Society, 3 (Oxford, 1941), no. 247.

87 McNiven, 'Men of Cheshire', 23.

88 CHES 2/76, m 12(8), *36 DKR*, p. 155.

89 CHES 2/76 m 12 (6).

90 E 163/4/61 item 5.

91 James Hamilton Wylie, *History of England under Henry the Fourth*, 4 vols (London: Longmans, Green, 1884–98), i. 148, 191; *Anglo-Norman Letters and Petitions*, p. 313.

Massey the sheriff, and William Swinburne, the vice-justiciar.[92] The prince intended a further visit to the county in May 1405 and called a council to meet there on 27 May, but this plan was abandoned to meet the challenge of Archbishop Scrope.[93] Henry never visited the county again as prince or as king.

In the principality of Wales, the prince did not assume personal responsibility for more than routine business until 1405.[94] From that point, however, the king rarely assigned money for operations in the principality and hardly ever made appointments there.[95] It is difficult from the Cheshire sources to assess when the prince assumed complete freedom of action there. The pattern of the granting of annuities may confirm the turning point of 1405–6. We can also see evidence of the consultation of the prince in matters relating to financial administration. In May 1408, for instance, an allowance of the arrears of the escheator was made by order of the prince after he had discussed the matter personally with John Bonyngton, the auditor, at Westminster.[96] It is also apparent that the prince was behind the decision to support out-of-county sources to support the costs of troops which he chose to send to assist the duke of Burgundy in 1411.[97]

It is wholly apparent that the development of Prince Henry's administration in Cheshire is closely linked to the development of his household as a whole. A telling example is that of Hugh Holes. In the first year of the new reign, when the confusion at Macclesfield had been at its height, Hugh

92 CHES 2/75, m 5 (2), m 6 (7), m 7 (1), *36 DKR*, pp. 101–2.

93 Wylie, *Henry the Fourth*, ii. 173.

94 For royal interest see Griffiths, 'Patronage, Politics and the Principality of Wales 1413–61', p. 76, and idem, 'Wales and the Marches', p. 147.

95 R. A. Griffiths, *The Principality of Wales in the Later Middle Ages: The Structure and Personnel of Government*, 1: *South Wales 1277–1536*, Board of Celtic Studies, University of Wales, History and Law Ser., 26 (Cardiff: University of Wales Press, 1972), p. 31; E. F. Jacob, *The Fifteenth Century, 1399 to 1485* (Oxford: Clarendon Press, 1961), p. 102.

96 SC 6/792/3, m 8d.

97 SC 6/775/12, m 2d.

Holes had been temporarily installed as bailiff of the forest, and even perhaps of the whole lordship.[98] His appointment is significant as epitomising the move towards the introduction of both non-Cheshire officials and Cheshire men who had come to prominence in the central administration. Hugh Holes was, by origin, of Cheshire, with holdings in the city of Chester,[99] but he had come to prominence in the royal judiciary.[100] He then served as deputy-justiciar of the principalities of Chester and North Wales,[101] and was keeper of the garden of Chester Castle until his death in 1415.[102] After 1399, his service was predominantly outside the county. In 1400, he was steward of the prince's lands,[103] and it is presumably through this office that he became involved in the reorganization at Macclesfield. He was still a member of the prince's council in November 1405.[104]

The first Lancastrian steward of Macclesfield was Thomas de Wendesley (or Wensley), who had been appointed for life by the king on 13 October 1399, the appointment being confirmed by the prince of Wales on 20 January 1400.[105] He was chosen by the king, no doubt because of his experience as steward and constable of the duchy of Lancaster lands of the High Peak in Derbyshire from 1391.[106] He died in the king's service at the battle of Shrewsbury.

Wendesley may have remained in office until his death, although on 8 October 1401 Sir Hugh le Despencer, a

98 SC 6/805/14, m 2d.

99 CHES 2/89, m 1d (6), *37 DKR*, pp. 368–9; CHES 2/89, m 2d (1), *36 DKR*, pp. 370–1.

100 In Oct 1399, he was created justice de banco (CHES 2/71, m 39d (13, 14), *36 DKR*, p. 242). Later he frequently served as a trier of Gascon petitions in parliament (e.g. *PROME*, viii. 11, 160, 229, 328, 421).

101 1 Feb 1398, the justiciar at the time being William Scrope, earl of Wiltshire (CHES 2/71, m 3, *36 DKR*, p. 426 (3)).

102 SC 6/1303/1, m 3.

103 SC 6/774/11, m 3d.

104 E 163/6/41, item 22.

105 CHES 2/74, m 4 (7), *36 DKR*, p. 511.

106 *House of Commons 1386-1421*, iv 807–9.

Northamptonshire knight who was governor of the prince of Wales and who played a key role in the defence of North Wales, was appointed steward of Macclesfield for life.[107] However, Despencer seems to have held the office only briefly, perhaps dying as early as November 1401.[108] No new steward of Macclesfield is known until the appointment of Sir John Stanley (c. 1350–1414) for life on 13 September 1403. The fact that Stanley's appointment noted that he should enjoy the same fees as Wendesley had enjoyed suggests that Despencer had never actually taken up office.[109] In reality, the administration was dealt with by deputies, Robert and Reginald del Dounes for Wendesley and Sir Robert de Legh for Despencer.[110]

Sir John Stanley provides an excellent example of the combination of local and household service.[111] His family was based in Storeton in the Wirral. John himself had married the heiress to the Lathom and Knowsley estates in south-west Lancashire.[112] Although he had been justice *hac vice* of Chester in 1394,[113] he was prominent in the military service of Richard II, serving in both Irish campaigns. He submitted to Henry IV and continued in service in Ireland until 1402. He was then steward of Prince Henry's household from 1403 to 1405,[114] and steward of the royal household from February 1405 until November 1412.[115]

107 CHES 2/75, m 1 (4, 5), *36 DKR*, p. 145; Jacob, *Fifteenth Century*, pp. 45, 101; *Anglo-Norman Letters and Petitions*, no. 228.

108 *Anglo-Norman Letters and Petitions*, no. 215. Subsequently, although the exact date is uncertain, there was discussion in the royal council over the appointment of the prince's master, with Thomas Percy, earl of Worcester being chosen (*PPC*, i. 178).

109 CHES 2/77, m 2d (3), *36 DKR*, p. 446.

110 CHES 2/75, m 1 (6, 7), *36 DKR*, p. 145.

111 For his life see, M. J. Bennett's biography in the *Oxford Dictionary of National Biography*, article 26275.

112 Ormerod, *Cheshire*, ii. 411.

113 CHES 2/66, m 4 (4), m 5 (3), *36 DKR*, p. 444.

114 E 101/404/24, item 12; E 101/405/1.

115 F. M. Powicke and E. B. Fryde (eds), *Handbook of British Chronology* (2nd edn, London: Royal Historical Society, 1961), p. 75. For his later career in royal service see Wylie, *Henry the Fourth*, ii. 291–2.

When steward of the prince's household, Stanley was much employed as an intermediary between Cheshire and the prince's council, especially in the crucial days after the battle of Shrewsbury at which he was wounded, taking on responsibility for the defence of the city of Chester and for receiving Cheshire rebels back into obedience.[116] His appointment as steward of Macclesfield in September 1403, along with the offices of surveyor and master forester of the forests of Delamere and Macclesfield, must be seen in the context of this service. Interestingly too, on this occasion the appointment was first enrolled on the Chester enrolments and then a confirmation by the king enrolled on the Patent rolls, a reversal of the format used in 1399–1400 revealing the growing development of the prince's household and county administration.[117] Clearly, Stanley exercised much more influence in the county than his office as steward of Macclesfield might seem to allow.[118] His value lay not only in his proven ability and experience, but also in his acceptability to the king, the prince and the people of Cheshire. After his death early in 1414, his son, Sir John jnr, was quickly appointed to succeed him at Macclesfield.

Another member of the prince's household who gained office was his havener, Robert Castell, [119] who was appointed keeper of the Dee Mills from June 1401. He developed further connections in the Cheshire demesnes as steward of Northwich from 18 September 1403.[120] He also served Prince Henry as

116 CHES 2/76, m 11 (4), m 10d (4), *36 DKR*, p. 446. By this time he was clearly much more a royal servant than simply a Cheshire man (McNiven, 'Rebellion', p. 130).

117 *CPR 1401–5*, p. 400.

118 In July 1405, for instance, he wrote to Henry IV concerning rumours that Glyndwr was about to call a parliament at Harlech. Stanley was in touch with two prominent men of that county and had arranged to meet them again at the next county court of Chester to discover more information (*Royal and Historical Letters during the Reign of Henry IV*, ed. F. C. Hingeston, Rolls Ser., 18, 2 vols (London, 1860, 1965), ii. 76–8).

119 E 101/406/21, f. 34. This function may have motivated his appointment as keeper of the Dee Mills.

120 For the references to his appointments see Appendix I (g, l).

paymaster of troops involved in the Welsh wars,[121] and was clerk of the Marshalsea and officer of the household when he served in the Agincourt campaign.[122] Richard Moston, the lessee of Shotwick from 1401 to 1407, was clerk of the prince's pantry and butlery from 1401 to 1404.[123] Ralph Pope, bailiff of Drakelow from 1401 to 1408, was a yeoman of the prince's chamber.[124]

The Welsh wars placed considerable strains on the prince's position but it would seem unlikely that the decision of the chamberlain, John Trevor, to defect to Glyndŵr in the summer of 1404 had been anticipated.[125] The exact date of his defection is not known but the chamberlain's account for 1403–4 notes that his fee was not paid 'because he is a rebel so it is reported' ('quia rebellis est ut dicitur').[126] Trevor's action was significant enough to grab the attention of not only Adam Usk, who commented that Trevor 'abandoned the special friendship with the English which he had enjoyed and threw in his lot with Owen for both peace and war',[127] but also the criticism of the St Albans' chronicler, Thomas Walsingham: 'John Trevor, bishop of St Asaph, abandoned the court of the prince and, taking a retrograde step ('conversus retrorsum'), fled to Owain Glyndŵr[128]

Trevor was 'certainly known to Owain Glyndŵr: they came from the same district and the same background'.[129] Rees Davies suggests that Trevor's Welsh 'cultural and genealogical' leanings were the main impulse to his defection. In 1403 many of the inhabitants of his diocese had thrown their lot in with Glyndŵr

121 E 101/404/24, f. 15; E 101/405/1, m 7; SC 6/791/7, m 2d.
122 E 101/69/5/412 (indenture); N. H. Nicolas, *History of the Battle of Agincourt* (3rd edn, London: Johnson & Co., 1833), p. 377.
123 E 101/404/16, m 2–4. See also E101/404/23 and E 101/405/26.
124 *CPR 1401–5*, p. 53; *CCR 1413–19*, p. 380. See appendix I (i).
125 Davies, 'Episcopate in England and Wales 1375–1443', iii, p. ccxc.
126 SC 6/775/3, m 3.
127 *Chronicle of Adam Usk*, pp. 218–19.
128 Chronica Maiora *of Thomas Walsingham*, pp. 426–9.
129 Davies, *Revolt of Owain Glyn Dŵr*, p. 59.

and perhaps he felt he had no choice but to follow. Walsingham offers a rather more prosaic explanation, that Trevor had 'first complained that it was Prince Henry's fault that he had lost income, and though he had taken up residence in the prince's house by order of the king, he nevertheless lacked any financial income to pay for the essentials for which he and his retinue required funds'. Walsingham adds that the archbishop of Canterbury had offered both lodgings and expenses but Trevor chose to leave secretly 'and as an enemy now that he had joined an enemy, he was judged a public enemy of the realm'.[130]

Trevor went both to Scotland and France to raise support for Glyndŵr.[131] The latter had confirmed him in his see but, given Glyndŵr's pro-French stance, Trevor's defection also involved the transfer of his allegiance to the Avignon pope. This triggered the confiscation by the English crown of his temporalities in August 1405[132] and his translation by the Roman pope to the see of St Andrews *in extremis* in 1408. Even so, a new bishop of St Asaph was not consecrated until June 1411. By then it would seem that Trevor had died in Paris, although Usk claims he died in 1412 in Rome.

Trevor had taken a big gamble that the rebel cause would triumph. His decision may indeed reveal much about the difficulties facing the English at this point and not least the pressures placed on Cheshire revenues. A decision was taken around this point to divert Cheshire funds to support the defences of North Wales. Might it have been that Trevor was not happy with this strategy? We cannot know since no explanation for his actions is found within the records of the earldom itself. But the fact that both the justiciar and the chamberlain appointed at the choice of Henry Bolingbroke in 1399 chose to abandon the man who had appointed them emphasises the extremely challenging situations which the new dynasty continued to face. That said, a reading of the financial and

130 Chronica Maiora *of Thomas Walsingham*, pp. 428–9.

131 Davies, *Revolt of Owain Glyn Dŵr*, pp. 216, 188.

132 *Calendar of the Fine Rolls, 1399–1405* (London: HMSO, 1931), p. 247.

administrative records of Chester of this period gives no signs at all of any disruption to day-to-day business or to revenue collection. Whilst the chief officials might change, the lower ranking officers who did the work simply continued as normal.

Trevor's replacement as chamberlain was Thomas Barneby, a Yorkshireman. His accounting period was taken to be from Michaelmas 1404 but his letters of appointment, given in full at the end of this account, were dated at Coventry, a place often frequented by the prince, on 23 October.[133] It does not seem, however, that the appointment was entered on the Chester enrolments, which may reflect uncertainty, and even disruption, over Trevor's defection. Earlier, Barneby had served as Hotspur's receiver in Anglesey, the connection no doubt stemming from existing Yorkshire links with the Percies.[134] It is interesting to note that Thomas Carnyka, Prince Henry's receiver-general of 1412 and possibly earlier, had, like Barneby, come into the prince's service from the service of Hotspur.[135] In such cases, experience counted for more than politics, and it is another reminder of how administration, and administrators, continued even in the face of political clashes.

Barneby's career had begun as a customs official in Boston. A clerk in minor orders, he was installed in 1402 in the parsonage of Rothwell, a duchy of Lancaster manor a few miles south of Leeds. From February 1406, he was chamberlain of

133 SC 6/775/4, m 1, 6d. Also given on m 6d is a commission to Barneby, also dated at Coventry on 13 Nov, concerning the chamberlain's responsibility for ensuring repairs, paralleling that for Trevor on 15 Nov 1399.

134 R. A. Griffiths, 'The Glyndwr Rebellion in North Wales through the Eyes of an Englishman', *Bulletin of the Board of Celtic Studies*, 22 (1967), 154–67, which is also the source of the other biographical information given concerning Barneby. Davies, *Revolt of Glyn Dŵr*, p. 184, points out Hotspur had used him to whip up support for the Percy revolt in 1403.

135 *Issues of the Exchequer: Being a Collection of Payments made out of His Majesty's Revenue, from King Henry III to King Henry VI Inclusive*, ed. Frederick Devon, Record Commission (London: John Murray, 1837), p. 283, where Carnyka is described as clerk of Henry Percy. For his service as receiver-general, see SC 6/775/12, m 2d and E 163/6/41 passim. He is described as 'garderobarius' in 1413 (SC 6/775/14, m 2d).

North Wales as well as Chester, a sensible combination given the diversion of Cheshire revenues to support the defences of North Wales. He served in both posts until December 1412, but William Troutbeck was appointed on 1 November 1412 to replace him as chamberlain of Chester.[136] He was removed from his North Welsh office on 19 March 1414.[137] With respect to this latter office, this was most certainly the result of complaints of corruption from inhabitants of Anglesey, Caernarvon and Merioneth. Even so, he was trusted enough by Henry V to be appointed the latter's treasurer of Harfleur in early 1416 after the capture of the town, holding the post until the exchequer in the town was closed. Between 1423 and his death in 1427, he headed the financial administration of English Gascony.[138]

That Barneby was deployed in a number of different royal financial administrations is a sign of how Cheshire was integrated within the royal demesne as a whole. His successor, William Troutbeck, demonstrates the same phenomenon. Like Barneby, he had no existing connections with Cheshire but was brought in as an effective administrator. Troutbeck hailed from Westmorland.[139] In February 1423, he was appointed chancellor of the county palatine of Lancaster, a post he held probably until his death in 1444–5.[140] In 1437, his appointment as chamberlain of Chester, which had been during royal pleasure as for his immediate predecessors, was changed to an appointment for life, with reversion to his son John, to whom the office came on 10 August 1445.[141]

136 CHES 2/86, m 1 (1), *36 DKR*, p.104.

137 Griffiths, 'Glyndwr Rebellion in North Wales through the Eyes of an Englishman', p. 151.

138 Anne Curry, 'Henry V's Harfleur: A Study in Military Administration 1414–1422', in L. J. Andrew Villalon and Donald J. Kagay (eds), *The Hundred Years War (Part III): Further Considerations* (Leiden and Boston: Brill, 2013), pp. 259–84, at pp. 268, 280.

139 He originated in Westmorland. See J. Brownbill, 'The Troutbeck Family', *JCNWAS*, 28, part 2 (1929), 149–97.

140 Robert Somerville, *History of the Duchy of Lancaster*, 1: *1265–1603* (London: Duchy of Lancaster, 1953), p. 476.

141 CHES 2/109, m 9 (4), *37 DKR*, p. 718; CHES 2/118, m 8, *37 DKR*, p. 720.

There were other officials of Prince Henry with an interest in the county's financial administration, since from time to time they received monies from the county. As will be discussed in Chapter 7, we see payments made by the chamberlain to the prince's receiver-general, chamberlain and treasurer in the early years of Henry's principate. Money rendered directly by the escheator, rather than via the chamberlain of the county, was paid to the receiver-general from 1404 to 1406, and from 1408 to 1413 to the chamberlain. The treasurer of the prince's household, and indeed other household officials, was most closely involved when the prince or his officials were resident in the county. For instance, in 1401 Simon Bache, as treasurer of the household, purchased wheat and had it milled for the household which was then resident in Chester Castle, and John Spencer, the controller of the household in 1403, was also involved in such transactions.[142] The chancellor of the prince performed certain functions relating to the administration of his lands as a whole. In 1401, for instance, both he and the chamberlain of North Wales, Robert Parys, pursued negotiations concerning the expenses of the prince in the government of the principality, on behalf of the prince and his council, before the king and his council.[143]

Those officials who played the most prominent part in the administration of the demesne lands in Cheshire were the stewards of the prince's lands and the auditors. Hugh Holes, as steward in 1400, was involved in the reorganization of administration at Macclesfield, and also in the victualling of the household in Chester.[144] Thomas Tykhull's functions as

142 SC 6/774/13, m 2d, 774/15, m 2d.

143 SC 6/774/11, m 3d.

144 SC 6/774/11, m 3d. Save for the period from 1351 to 1361 when Sir John Wingfield was 'governor of the prince's business', The Black Prince had employed a chief steward for all his lands, whose role was that of a subordinate estate administrator, forming a link between London and the localities. In the fourteenth century his powers were much the same as those of the steward of the duchy of Lancaster in the fifteenth century, where he was to report to the council upon the state of the lands and the conduct of the local official so that any shortcomings could be remedied by the council. See also R. R. Davies,

steward ranged from sanctioning the appointment of demesne officials[145] to holding inquisitions into escheats,[146] to supervising the sale of corn at the Dee Mills,[147] as well as exercising general supervision.[148]

There is a far greater amount of information upon the function of the auditors, which is not surprising considering the fact that their contact with the demesne was placed upon a regular footing. The visit of the auditors was perhaps the chief connecting link between the earl's household and the local Cheshire administration.[149] As elsewhere,[150] the auditors played a prominent part in estate administration, and as delegates of the council, had general oversight of land and resources. By virtue of this, they had powers to lease at the yearly audit. As administrative supervisors of the officials whose account they inspected, they had power to make allowances and respites and to arrange for payment of debts by instalments. They were responsible for committing the sheriff of the county to prison for debt in 1406.[151]

In their persons, too, the auditors epitomised the unity of the prince's demesne, again reinforcing the fact that the earldom was part of a greater whole. John Bonyngton was also responsible for the audit of the accounts of the ministers

'Baronial Accounts, Incomes and Arrears in the Later Middle Ages', *EcHR*, 2nd ser., 21 (1960), 211–29, at p. 227.

145 CHES 2/78, m 6 (9), *36 DKR*, p. 399; the appointment of Henry de Ravenscroft as steward of Northwich in Sept 1406.

146 In 1408 an inquisition into an escheat in Macclesfield Forest was held in his presence in Macclesfield (E 163/6/41 items 2, 3).

147 SC 6/775/6, m 2d. He also ordered the purchase of victuals for the forthcoming visit of the council to Chester in 1410 (SC 6/775/11, m 2d).

148 He cancelled a recognizance in 1406 (CHES 2/78, m 5d (3), *36 DKR*, p. 213). A protection given to a man going to Wales in 1401 was issued under the Chester seal 'per quondam billam per consilium domini indorsatam sigillo senescalli domini signatam' (CHES 2/75, m 1d (2)).

149 Sharp, 'Earldom and County of Chester', p. 137.

150 Hatcher, *Rural Economy*, p. 46; Somerville, *History of the Duchy of Lancaster*, p. 106.

151 SC 6/792/1, m 6d.

in the prince's lordships in Yorkshire, Lincolnshire, Norfolk, Northamptonshire, Oxfordshire, Buckinghamshire and Bedfordshire. In addition, he audited accounts of certain of the prince's central financial officials – the receiver-general and the receiver of the great wardrobe in London.[152] In the reign of Henry V, it was usual for the same auditor to be responsible for the accounts of Cheshire, Cornwall, North and South Wales.[153] A further factor which facilitated assimilation into the royal demesne was the exchequer experience of these auditors. At least one of the two or three Cheshire auditors was a baron of the Exchequer, such as Richard Stokes or Roger Westwood.

During Henry's time as prince, however, the organ of government which demands our greatest attention is the prince's council. All the previously mentioned central officials, including the auditors, were answerable to the council, and generally constituted its executive arm. When the names of councillors are stated in matters relating to the Cheshire demesnes, they generally include the prince's chancellor, chamberlain, steward of lands and of the household, receiver-general, keeper of the wardrobe and of the secret treasury, as well as others with no specified function.[154] As in the fourteenth century, the council held overall control of the lordships and demesnes. Indeed, in the first half of this period, it appears to have exercised even greater control over estate administration than it had done under the Black Prince.[155] It had surveillance over both estate and household finances. It is clear from certain

152 CHES 2/77, m 7d, *36 DKR*, p. 453. He may also have audited accounts in the honour of Halton (SC 6/775/6, m 4).

153 *CPR 1413–16*, pp. 228, 247; *CPR 1413–16*, p. 338, *CPR 1416–22*, p. 117.

154 For instance, E 163/6/41, SC 6/792/2, m 11d. The auditors were probably co-opted to the council when the nature of its business demanded their presence.

155 Sharp considered that the council did actually exercise close scrutiny over the demesnes (Sharp, 'Earldom and County of Chester', p. 420). Booth noted that the Council met as a great council four times a year as an administrative court of appeal, receiver of petitions, high policy maker and, as far as Cheshire was concerned, occasional legislator. (Booth, *Financial Admin.*, pp. 75–6).

documents attached to the household account of 1404–5 that the administration and financial return of the prince's lands were regularly discussed by his council.[156]

Very little action during the principate was taken, save at the command of the council or with its consent. A proposal to lease the town of Northwich in 1403 (letters for which had already been issued under the Chester seal), had to be cancelled because it had been made without the knowledge of the prince and his council.[157] Leases in this period were most frequently sanctioned by them, and they also controlled the use of administration of the demesne in general. For instance, the lease of Shotwick to Richard Moston was made by their consent, just as the use of Shotwick park in 1401 for the pasturing of the prince's beasts for his larder was at their command. Moston later spent £3 6s. 8d. on repairs to the manor at their advice.[158] They are also seen endorsing the payment of wages to demesne officials.[159] A special surveillance was maintained by them over escheats.[160]

Officials in the county were responsible to them, and when the council was not present in the county, the usual method of control was for Cheshire business and petitions to be discussed by the council at Westminster, either with written contact with the relevant Cheshire officials, or by the presence of the latter in person before the council. An enquiry into the escheated manor of Ashton was conducted by county officials but the escheator, as was frequently the case, was ordered to send the relevant

156 E 101/404/16. They drew up a list in this year of ministers in other counties where the prince had lands who had not yet accounted. They discussed John Waterton's account as receiver of the duchy of Cornwall and, from the remainder of his account for Michaelmas 1403, estimated his profits for the following year (m 7). Certain other problems in Cornwall also merited attention. Another agenda for council business mentions aid to conventionary tenants in the duchy as well as, again, the matter of non-accounting ministers (m 12).

157 CHES 2/76, m 4d (4), *36 DKR*, p. 532.

158 SC 6/791/3, m 3, SC 6/791/5, m 3.

159 SC 6/792/1 m2.

160 This was also true in the fourteenth century (Sharp, 'Earldom and County of Chester', pp. 102–3). For instances of surveillance in this period see SC 6/792/2, m 11d and E 163/6/41.

documents to the prince's exchequer of receipt at Westminster, there to be examined by the council.[161] The mayor and escheator of the city of Chester appeared before the council during its stay in the county in 1408.[162] Henry de Birteles, then second sergeant at law in the county, appeared before the council at Westminster later in 1408 to discuss the escheated lands of Sir Richard Vernon.[163] Earlier in the year, an extent of Vernon's lands had been made before Thomas Tykhull and others of the council during their stay in the county.[164] In May of the same year, a copy of a rental of the lands in question was sent to the prince's council at Westminster.[165]

When the prince was based in the county, some of his council would be there with him, although some financial officials probably remained in London at his central exchequer and secretariat.[166] The council exercised executive control over the assignment of Cheshire revenues to Welsh defences in 1403–4, as is shown by the frequency of marginal notes such as 'loquendum cum consilio', written next to certain categories of income which were deemed to merit closer attention or increased exploitation. We can see, for instance, it was the council which ordered several assignments to Robert Parys as chamberlain at Caernarvon.[167] John Stanley, Peter de Melburn and Hugh Mortimer as members of the prince's council were in Chester shortly after the battle of Shrewsbury, principally to receive the men of the county back into the prince's grace: significantly, they were to report back to the king and his Great Council, then at Worcester.[168] Stanley, Mortimer and others of the council visited the county again in May 1405, and the

161 SC 6/792/2, m 11d.; The escheator was asked by letter for reasons for the seizure of the hospital of St Nicholas in Nantwich in Feb 1407 (E 163/6/41 item 17).

162 E 163/6/41 item 14.

163 E 163/6/41 item 2.

164 SC 6/792/5, m 9d.

165 E 163/6/41 item 22.

166 Wylie, *Henry the Fourth*, i. 214.

167 SC 6/774/14, m 4d.

168 E 101/405/1.

full council stayed in Chester for the months of March and April 1408 'for several items of difficult business concerning the prince' ('pro diversis arduis negotiis ipsum principem tangentibus').[169] A further visit of the council was expected in 1410. Victuals were purchased in anticipation, but these were wasted because the visit never took place.[170]

Undoubtedly, the prince relied more and more on the council as his role in national politics concentrated his interests elsewhere. As far as demesne administration is concerned, it was the council and the relevant estate officials who formulated policy and saw to its execution. This mirrored the situation under the Black Prince. His council had had a more significant influence on estate administration than the prince himself, as is seen from the greater quantity of conciliar warrants.[171] Whilst Prince Henry did not visit the county after 1402, at least he had been present on a few earlier occasions. The Black Prince never visited his earldom.

## The reign of Henry V – contrasts and continuities

Basically, the existing structure of administration was not changed by the accession of Henry V to the throne on 21 March 1413. Inevitably, there were some changes in function, especially in the higher echelons, but these did not follow the pattern of royal control in the thirteenth and fourteenth centuries. Following the example of Richard II, to all intents and purposes, the new king maintained the system whereby the chamberlain accounted for all issues, with supervision from crown officials with responsibility for the royal demesne.

Thomas Tykhull, previously steward of the prince's lands, was appointed chief steward of the king's lands in October 1413.[172] Other men who had served in various functions under the prince were also given offices in financial administration

169 SC 6/792/3, m 5d.
170 SC 6/775/11, m 2d.
171 Booth, *Financial Admin.*, pp. 76–7
172 *CPR 1413–16*, p. 107.

under the new king. Roger Leche was a councillor of the prince by 1407 and steward of the prince's household for the last six years of the principate.[173] In October 1407 he was also appointed sheriff of Flintshire and constable of Flint Castle.[174] He had earlier been controller of the household between 1403 and 1405. He was appointed keeper of the royal wardrobe on 31 October 1413. Hugh Mortimer served as the prince's chamberlain from around 1406 although he was a member of the prince's council from as early as 1403.[175] He became royal treasurer on 10 January 1416 but died within three months of appointment, being replaced by Leche from April to November in the same year.[176] Thomas More had been receiver-general of the prince in 1399 to 1400, having served Richard II as cofferer of the household from 1395 to 1398, and earlier as treasurer and receiver-general of Anne of Bohemia.[177] He became keeper of the royal wardrobe from 1401 to 1405, and was appointed to the same office from March to October 1413.[178] There was thus a considerable and unsurprising degree of continuity in personnel between Henry's financial administration as prince and as king, at least in the first years of the new reign.[179]

Early in Henry V's reign, a chest was purchased out of Cheshire revenues in which to lodge the duplicate rolls of the ministers' accounts from the period when the king had been prince of Wales. This chest was to be deposited in the Exchequer at Westminster so that these Cheshire evidences could be consulted by the royal council, if and when required.[180] This is a sign of centralisation. Whilst the prince's central officials

173 SC 6/792/3, m 5d, SC 6/775/11, m 3d.

174 CHES 2/80, m 3d (8), *36 DKR*, p. 284.

175 SC 6/775/6, m 2. For his role on council in 1403 see E 101/404/24, f. 12.

176 *Handbook of British Chronology*, pp. 79, 102.

177 Respectively, SC 6/791/1, m 11; *Handbook of British Chronology*, p. 79; SC 6/805/1, m 3, 805/5, m 4.

178 *Handbook of British Chronology*, p. 79.

179 For a similar observation deduced from Welsh evidence, see Griffiths, 'Patronage, Politics and the Principality of Wales', p. 76.

180 SC 6/1302/15, m 1d.

had been active in the county during the principate, there is no discernible evidence of their similar personal activity after the accession. Whilst the royal council as a whole maintained an interest – inquisitions, for instance, were occasionally taken at its insistence[181] – conciliar activity in the county was far diminished compared with the time of the prince. It does not seem Henry ever visited the county as king, although there has been a suggestion that he came in person linked to the mise of 1416.[182]

The business of the royal council was inevitably far wider and more diversified than that of Henry as a prince. The outcome was that responsibility for local estate administration was delegated to the lower levels of the administrative structure. It would seem there is no parallel in Cheshire during Henry V's reign to the increasing interference by the royal council and king in the duchy of Lancaster.[183] In 1417, duchy finances were brought under the control of the royal household. This never happened in Cheshire. In those years, between 1413 and 1422, in which the county contributed to royal finances, its issues, if not assigned at source, were delivered directly to the Exchequer of Receipt rather than directly to, or via, the royal household. Thus it was Exchequer officials who were instrumental in the financial administration of the county. An important aspect of their control was over the largest escheats arising in the county, which were dealt with by the royal treasurer and chancellor, and action concerning them was enrolled in the Patent rolls rather than in the Cheshire enrolments.[184] The Exchequer also exercised control over the collection of debts. The royal treasurer or his deputy authorised that certain debts should be paid in instalments.[185] In one example, authorisation was made at the instigation of James Strangeways who had graduated through the legal administration of the county to the national level. A

181 For instance, CHES 25/11, m 22.

182 See below p. 287 n. 44.

183 Somerville, *History of the Duchy of Lancaster*, pp. 189, 223; Davies, 'Baronial Accounts', p. 227.

184 See, for instance, *CPR 1416–22*, pp. 307, 309; *CPR 1416–22*, p. 249, and SC 6/1303/5, m 2.

185 SC 6/703/5, m 6d, 794/1, m 1 (which involved Strangeways).

similar situation is seen in the reign of Henry VI, when Ralph, lord Cromwell, as royal treasurer, ordered the chamberlain of Chester to pay sums due to certain mariners.[186]

A useful parallel can be drawn with the reign of Richard II; there was a similar central control by the Exchequer and by royal financial officials. Mandates from the treasurer of England were received in the county during Richard's reign. Certainly, in 1393, the fulling mill on the Dee had been put to farm by the Treasurer of England and others of the royal council.[187] In the time of Richard II, the county's revenues lay within the scope of the Exchequer.[188] The re-establishment of Exchequer control under Henry V is significant because it brought the county further into the general structure of royal demesne administration. Any danger of weaknesses associated with such control, given that the Exchequer had such an exceptionally wide remit, was mitigated by the increase in the powers and functions of the administration at a lower level, most notably of the auditors and of the chamberlain of the county. Such developments in financial administration parallel contemporary changes which have been detected in the other areas, which together had formed the appanage of the prince of Wales.[189]

The increase in the powers of the local Cheshire officials was hardly novel. In the later fourteenth century there was a detectable increase in the degree of independent action by resident officials, for instance as regards powers of leasing.[190] In

186 E 101/53/19.

187 SC 6/773/10, m 1.

188 Despite the fact that, according to Sharp and Wolffe, the county was never (officially at least) run in accordance with traditional Exchequer control over the royal demesne (Sharp, 'Earldom and County of Chester', p. 141, Wolffe, *Royal Demesne*, pp. 40–1).

189 For developments in South Wales, see Griffiths, *Principality of Wales*, i. 33–5, 42. In the duchy of Cornwall, firm moves were made in the fifteenth century towards the creation of a wholly separate administrative system for the duchy, culminating in the appointment of a receiver-general with functions akin to those of the chamberlain of Chester, during the reign of Henry VI (Hatcher, *Rural Economy*, p. 47).

190 Booth, *Financial Admin.*, p. 77.

particular, the chamberlain increased in importance. There were anticipations of a continuing development in this direction by the appointment of Thomas Barneby in 1404 and William Troutbeck in 1412, both of whom were estate administrators proper and not placemen.

Throughout the whole period, the chamberlain was by far the most important executive officer in the county, with general powers of surveillance over the demesnes and their local officials. He was responsible for the receipt and accounting of demesne issues, for paying out certain wages and annuities and foreign expenses, and for the supervision of capital investment and repairs.[191] Already he was involved in leases, but in very few instances before 1410 do we see him acting independently of the control of the prince's council. After this date, however, independent action was the rule rather than the exception, paving the way for what was the norm under Henry V as king.

Where the chamberlain did act in conjunction with other officials after 1410, these were local officials such as justiciar and escheator, or – as the sole representatives of central control – the auditors. For instance, in 1410, Barneby acted in conjunction with the escheator in leasing lands in Drakelow. In 1422, Troutbeck, the justiciar and auditors were called upon to examine the rental of the same manor.[192] In the reign of Henry V, we see the chamberlain making leases on his own authority, or with the added sanction of the auditors, often in cases which most certainly would have previously been the preserve of the prince's council. A good example is the deliberation and subsequent action in 1419 concerning the seizure of the township of Sutton when John de Legh of Booths had failed to pay his surplus rent. This was conducted by Troutbeck as chamberlain in consultation with the auditors.[193] Previously,

191 The chamberlain supervised repairs by virtue of briefs issued at the beginning of his tenure of office (SC 6/793/2, m 5). For a comparison with the responsibilities of the receiver-general of the duchy of Cornwall see Hatcher, *Rural Economy*, p. 44.

192 SC 6/792/6, m 1d; SC 6/794/2, m 2d.

193 SC 6/806/17, m 3.

a matter such as this would have most certainly been referred to the council. More leases began to be made at the annual audit in the county. This contrasts with the situation under the Black Prince where few leases were made at the audit because only the auditors and chamberlain were present.[194] A similar degree of collaboration between the chamberlain and auditors seems to have been common practice, however, under Richard II, a significant parallel with another period of royal rather than princely control.[195]

As we have seen, for most of the reign of Henry IV the prince's council had been closely involved in county administration, often by its actual physical presence in the county. Otherwise, communications between county officials and the prince and his council were conducted by means of messengers. For instance, in 1403, messengers were paid to carry letters to the king, the prince and the latter's council in London, Bristol, Hereford, Pontefract, Kenilworth and elsewhere.[196] Towards the end of the reign of Henry IV, however, it was the chamberlain who took on the itinerant role, frequently visiting the prince and later the king and his council, wherever they might chance to be. In 1414, Troutbeck was summoned to London, at the order of the king and council, with transcripts of various memoranda and evidences concerning the administration of Cheshire and Flintshire, in order to consult with the king on them.[197] Later in Henry's reign, Troutbeck regularly attended the great councils presided over by the Keeper of the Realm since the king was in France, such as that held at Winchester from April to June 1422. He was at the great council in London from October to December in the same year, following the king's death, and in January to February of 1423.[198] Again, this is demonstrative of an increase in the prominence of the chamberlain and another

194 Booth, 'Financial Administration', p. 74.
195 For example, CHES 2/70, m 1d (1), *36 DKR*, p. 319.
196 SC 6/774/15, m 6.
197 SC 6/1302/15, m 2d.
198 SC 6/1303/5, m 2d. See also E 101/620/24 for his expenses in travelling to London on several occasions under Henry VI.

indication of a relatively independent county administration when the earl was king.

Significantly, these changes began to appear after the proposed visit of the council to the county in 1410 had been called off. By this date, Cheshire had lost its recent importance bestowed by its role in the Welsh wars, and the prince's attentions had been wholly turned to national politics. The last three years of the reign of Henry IV sowed the seeds of changes which were to blossom under Henry V. The increased prominence of the chamberlain of Chester in national as well as local administration may have been due not only to changes in relative function but also to the person and capacities of the chamberlain from 1412, William Troutbeck. He was involved in the French expeditions and in various other national commissions.[199] He was also appointed Chancellor of the County Palatine of Lancaster in February 1423.[200]

It is worth noting, too, that John del Dedwood, vice-chamberlain of Chester in 1406, 1414 and again in 1439,[201] was a clerk in the Chancery of the County Palatine of Lancaster in 1438–9, and deputy Chancellor to Troutbeck from 1439 to 1440.[202] The duchy of Lancaster connections may be important as far as the administration of Cheshire is concerned, but one would need to pursue this study further into the reign of Henry VI to assess the impact of the dual function of such personnel.[203] Certainly, there is no parallel in Cheshire to the tightening up of duchy administration which occurred during the reign

199 Brownbill, 'Troutbeck Family', p. 150.

200 Somerville, *History of the Duchy of Lancaster*, p. 476. Note that Somerville overlooked the 1412 appointment as chamberlain of Chester and regarded the 1423 confirmation of office as the first appointment.

201 Respectively, CHES 2/78, m 5d (7), *36 DKR*, p. 335; CHES 25/11, m 3d; CHES 2/11, m 1 (6), *37 DKR*, p. 197.

202 Somerville, *History of the Duchy of Lancaster*, p. 477.

203 It is interesting that William Botiller, who was appointed chamberlain of South Wales in June 1421, was already an experienced duchy of Lancaster official although he had already served as a clerk in the prince's household in 1405 (Griffiths, *Principality of Wales*, i. 182).

of Henry V, nor, as we have seen, to crown interference, such as was experienced in the duchy. Obviously, some aspects of duchy administration, and possibly certain of its jurisdictional peculiarities, owed their inspiration to Cheshire precedents, but a reciprocal influence was certainly not experienced. The revenues of the duchy of Lancaster and of the palatinate of Chester were fulfilling very different functions in this period, so that the policy towards them, and the resultant administrative needs, were divergent.

There are no recorded attempts to extend the benefits of the duchy of Lancaster system to cover the other royal lands under Exchequer control until the reigns of Edward IV and Richard III. The existence of duchy estates in the lordship of Halton within the geographical county of Cheshire, however, is a connection which should be mentioned, not least in the light of the Lancastrian usurpation of 1399, since the new dynasty already had an interest in the county through its tenure of this lordship with its important castle. On the same day Bolingbroke had entered Chester, his troops had also ensured his authority in Halton.[204] Its administration and personnel were totally independent of the county although there was some confusion over spheres of authority. The sheriff of Chester, for instance, had wrongly taken amercements in the lordship in 1405.[205] The situation regarding taxation in Halton is puzzling. In 1353 the duke of Lancaster had been pardoned his contribution to the, then, mise for his lordship. In 1401, however, Halton was included in the assessment of the Cheshire mise, even though the chamberlain had to be respited £4 2s 1½d for the lordship because it was in the hands of the king. By 1403, the respite has risen to £20 8s 7¾d for two and a half years of ostensible non-payment of the contribution.[206] It appears that the lordship did not pay the contribution at this point but there is evidence that it did contribute to the mise in 1416.[207] Strangely too, 500

204 Morgan, *War and Society*, p. 207.
205 SC 6/791/10, m 5d.
206 SC 6/774/13, m 5d, 774/15, m 5d.
207 CHES 25/11, m 11.

marks were transferred from Cheshire revenues to the officials at Halton during the reign of Henry V on the order of the king.[208]

The increase in the powers of the chamberlain of Chester were accompanied by a contemporary increase in those of the auditors. During the reign of Henry IV, these officials had been very much under the scrutiny of the prince's council as a whole. In 1399, the terms of their appointment empowered them to make or refuse allowances at the audit on their own initiative but they were further ordered 'to certify clearly and fully to our council all your actions in this respect' ('ad consilium nostrum de toto facto vestro in hac parte distincte et aperte certificandum').[209] In July 1414, they were specifically allowed to place farms in Cheshire and North Wales to the king's advantage.[210] The powers allocated to the auditors appointed in October of the same year were considerably more extensive – full powers of charging and allowing, demising farms and selling casual profits.[211] This extension of powers is significant, coming as it does at a time when the central, princely, and later royal, council is retreating in its functions linked to demesne management.

The role of other county officials in demesne administration is sometimes clear cut, sometimes not, irrespective of whether the earl was prince or king. The escheator had control over escheats arising in the demesnes, as elsewhere, and he had further involvement since the mid-fourteenth century when he had become steward of the prince's courts in certain of the demesnes.[212] The justiciar (or in reality his deputy since the office was largely titular) was involved in legal matters concerning the demesnes, although separate justices of eyre were appointed for Macclesfield, and for Frodsham during the

208 The initial order to the chamberlain to pay the receivers of the castle and lordship of Halton 100 marks per annum in two instalments had been made in Dec 1413 (SC 6/776/4, m 2d.).

209 CHES 2/74, m 4 (4, 5), *36 DKR*, p. 453.

210 *CPR 1413–16*, p. 228.

211 *CPR 1413–16*, p. 247; CHES 2/88, m 3 (12), *36 DKR*, p. 632.

212 Booth, *Financial Admin.*, p. 54; Sharp, 'Earldom and County of Chester', p. 422.

time it was in the hands of Radegonde Béchet. The justiciar held special courts at the Dee Mills although it seems that the city officials were responsible for calling the jury.[213] The justiciar is occasionally seen acting in other aspects of demesne administration, including inquisitions into debts.[214] In 1410, the lease of the demesne at Macclesfield was made by him and the chamberlain. Twelve years later, in conjunction with the chamberlain and the auditors, the justiciar examined the rental of Drakelow.[215]

The sheriff of the county and other judicial officials were involved as their functions demanded, but usually in person. The bailiff itinerant assisted in the collection of fines arising on the demesnes.[216] The master carpenter was especially important in forest and park administration, both as regards the supervision of repairs and the sale of wood. He supervised both at Shotwick even when the manor was in the hands of Roger Moston.[217] Other men, whether discharging an official function or not, could be involved in demesne administration on an ad hoc basis. In 1407, for instance, Richard de Manley, the escheator, was accompanied by John del Dedwood, deputy chamberlain, and John Whetenhale in the re-leasing of atterminated tenements in Drakelow.[218]

Certainly, the county officials, and/or their deputies, acted together as an informal council based in Chester. Others could be called upon to give counsel when required. All examples of such co-option arise in the reign of Henry V.[219] We can suggest

213 Richard Bennett and J. Elton, *History of Corn Milling*, vol. 4: *Some Feudal Mills* (London, 1904, repr. Wakefield: EP Publishing, 1975), p. 66.

214 SC 6/805/7, m 1d, SC 6/805/14, m 2d.

215 SC 6/806/4, m 2d, SC 6/794/2, m 2d.

216 CHES 25/10, m 15d. Roger Horton, sergeant at law, was involved in an adjudication concerning the private lease of certain tenements in Northwich (HMC Leicester of Tabley, Charters and Deeds, Northwich B12).

217 SC 6/791/5, m 3, SC 6/791/7, m 3.

218 SC 6/792/3, m 1d.

219 SC 6/776/4, m 2d, SC 6/1303/1, m 2d, SC 6/1303/5, m 4d.

that there was an increasing formalisation and use of this local executive council under the chamberlain when external control diminished. All evidence, then, points to a rejuvenation of a more localised county administration after around 1410, and most especially, during the reign of Henry V. A self-contained county administration developed but this should certainly not be seen as independent of royal control. The landed interests of the earl had already been brought too far within the structure of the royal demesne in the earlier part of the period for any retrenchment now to occur. Under such administrators as Troutbeck, the process of assimilation continued, and indeed accelerated, not least as the death of Henry V in 1422 ushered in over thirty years where a king was earl of Chester.

## Local administration

Although there was no direct agricultural cultivation of the demesnes by the earl, there was still a multitude of important executive and administrative functions to be performed by local officials. Rents and fines were to be collected, repairs initiated and supervised, the most profitable use of lands and properties discovered and pursued, and local affairs regulated. In general, local administration followed the patterns laid down in the fourteenth century and earlier, both as regards personnel and functions.

First, each unit was administered as an entity in its own right. This had been the case since the failure of a scheme in the 1350s which planned that, in future, Rudheath, Middlewich, Northwich, Shotwick and Frodsham would be appurtenant to the newly created manor of Drakelow. This scheme was not carried through in full, although the Black Prince did manage to unify these manors into a loose knit unit by appointing the escheator of the county to be steward of them. [220] There was a similar attempt at unification, although on a much smaller scale, in the first two years of the reign of Henry IV.

220 Booth, 'Financial Administration', pp. 60–2, 206–7, Sharp, 'Earldom and County of Chester', pp. 381–2, 422, 427.

From 7 November 1399 to 20 June 1401, Richard de Manley accounted as receiver of Drakelow and Rudheath and receiver of Northwich, serving simultaneously as escheator in the county and steward of these two units.[221] This again proved an unsatisfactory arrangement, placing too heavy a burden upon the shoulders of one administrator. After June 1401, the two units were once again separately administered, with a bailiff, Ralph Pope, accounting as receiver of Drakelow,[222] although the escheator continued to act as steward there, and John de Legh as receiver and steward of Northwich.[223]

In general, the division of officials into those who fulfilled financial and those who fulfilled judicial functions was maintained. Thus in the Wiches, for instance, the steward held the courts but the chamberlain and catchpoles collected the fines and accounted for them. At Northwich, however, the responsibility for accounting lay with the steward until 1413 when the town officials took over and the steward's functions became once more exclusively judicial. This development had been anticipated during the tenure of the stewardship of Robert Castell between 1403 and 1409. Since he had many obligations elsewhere, his office at Northwich (and indeed as keeper of the Dee Mills) was performed by a local deputy who also served as chamberlain of the town.[224] Northwich is the exception to the administrative rule in several respects, possibly because of the Holland connection, which created an uncertainty in this period over future control of the town, a situation in which a permanent administrative structure was not able to develop.

Although the escheator for the county was steward of Drakelow throughout the period, this first quarter of the fifteenth century did not witness the retention of the fourteenth-century system in which the escheator was steward of all the demesnes save for Macclesfield. At Middlewich, Henry Ravenscroft was

221 SC 6/791/1, m 1d, m 2d.

222 SC 6/791/3, m 1.

223 SC 6/791/3, m 2d.

224 For the names of deputies at Northwich see Appendix I (l), and for the Dee Mills Appendix I (g).

steward throughout the period, but only held the escheatorship from 1412 to 1421.[225] Richard de Manley combined both offices at Northwich, in the first two years of the reign, as did Henry Ravenscroft in 1414. But in the following year, although Ravenscroft remained escheator, John Winnington, a member of a prominent Northwich family, acted as steward of the town. At Shotwick, manorial courts were held by the chamberlain of the county or his deputy.[226] Presumably this was the usual procedure at this time, and not just a temporary measure adopted in the period between the end of Richard Moston's lease with his death in 1408 and the grant to William Porter on 28 April 1410. The steward of Frodsham is never named. Macclesfield had its own specially appointed steward, a very prestigious office.

The move away from the dominance of the escheator as steward of the demesnes was probably motivated by the threat of the heavy burden which would then devolve upon one man. Certainly, the demesne stewards were fulfilling much wider functions than those primarily judicial. The demesne steward is seen in a general supervisory capacity, sanctioning repairs carried out on the initiative of the other officials,[227] certifying decayed rents, supporting claims of allowances from the accounting officials,[228] making leases on his own authority or in collaboration with the chamberlain of Chester,[229] and setting in motion procedures for the election of minor officials. The stewards at Macclesfield, for instance, or their deputies, were responsible for the regarders, verderers and foresters there. These minor officials were required to take oaths to the steward for the performance of their office.[230] Overall, the stewards acted as important intermediaries between central or county and local officials.

225 For references see the relevant sections of Appendix I.

226 SC 2/156/13, m 2, 3.

227 For instance, SC 6/791/10, m 4.

228 It was the steward at Macclesfield who was to be questioned on revenues from market tolls even though these were the responsibility of the catchpole (SC 6/805/14, m 1d).

229 For instance, SC 6/806/13, m 1d.

230 For examples, see CHES 2/77, m 2d (8), *36 DKR*, p. 313.

Otherwise, local administration was much as it had been in the fourteenth century, determined in the case of each unit by the differing nature of the sources of income and of the status of the unit.[231] In the city of Chester, at Middlewich, Northwich, and Macclesfield *burgus*, where there was actual or approximate urban status, there were yearly-elected officials, individually responsible for certain categories of income. The catchpole, for instance, was responsible for income from judicial fines.[232] By this time such offices may not have been restricted to burgesses, although certainly a few families tended to dominate them. Although there are several instances of men serving for more than one year, or in a different capacity on a later date, there would seem to have been a considerably large reserve of suitable people on which to draw, and there is no indication of reluctance to serve.

Where income was from more traditional agricultural sources, then responsibility for day-to-day management and for accounting was in the hands of an appointed bailiff (as in the cases of Drakelow and Frodsham) or of a reeve (as in the case of Shotwick). In the latter case, the obligation to perform the office of reeve derived from the tenurial obligations. However, in this period, the office was performed by a free tenant, and thus a wage had to be paid. In the case of Drakelow, virtually the sole duty of the bailiff was the collection of rents. Later in the century we find him described as bailiff and rent collector.[233] At Frodsham and Shotwick, such offices were held during pleasure, with a considerable degree of surveillance exercised by the chamberlain of the county, because the nature of the manorial income demanded continuing central control to assess the most profitable ways of exploiting the revenues.

Where income was stereotyped, such as in Macclesfield hundred, the accounting officials held their bailiwick in fee by service of grand serjeanty. During a minority of an heir, the

231 Booth, 'Financial Administration', pp. 24–6.

232 SC 2/156/3, m 1 (Middlewich); SC 6/810/15, m 1 (Northwich); C. Stella Davies, *A History of Macclesfield* (Manchester: Manchester University Press, 1961), p. 33.

233 CHES 2/117, m 1 (4), *37 DKR*, p. 513 (Nov 1446).

moiety of the bailiwick was farmed like any other escheat.[234] The two master foresterships were also held in fee, in Delamere by the Dones of Utkinton and in Macclesfield by the de Mottrams, until John de Mottram was replaced by John Savage. Certainly in Delamere, the master forester had few responsibilities because revenues were farmed to named individuals who themselves made payments to the chamberlain. In addition, sellers of moss and wood were employed. When the agistment was directly controlled, two approvers were paid. The subsidiary forest administration in both forests would protect the lord's rights therein. Indictments were said to be made by the rider (*equitator*) or master forester.[235] Owing to the manorial organization of Macclesfield Forest, the bailiff and master forester had much wider functions than his counterpart at Delamere. As regards manorial functions, he was an active executive official, but as regards the enforcement of forest rights, we may believe that he relied upon the foresters and other minor officials.

Although the parks were important sources of income and of jurisdiction, the parkerships tended to be patronage appointments made for life, and it is difficult to assess the extent to which the parkers actually performed their offices in person. There was, however, a house maintained for a parker at Shotwick, and in 1400–1 new locks were installed in its doors.[236] The parker at Shotwick gained further importance when the manor was granted to William Porter in 1410, for then the parker accounted directly to the earl for sales of wood within the park. Significantly, the earl retained the right to appoint the parker even when the manor was not in his hands.[237] There are some interesting examples of a clash of interests between the parker and the reeve at Shotwick, which may suggest that spheres of authority were not clearly delineated. The reeve was

234 SC 6/805/7, m 2.

235 For the workings of administration in the Wirral firest in the fourteenth century, see *Cheshire Forest Eyre Roll 1357. Part One: The Forest of Wirral*, ed. Phyllis M. Hill, J. Heery and members of the Ranulf Higden Society, RSLC, 151 (2015).

236 SC 6/774/13, m 1d.

237 Sharp, 'Earldom and County of Chester', p. 355.

responsible for the issues of pasturing within the park, and this was probably the reason for the conflict. In October 1408, for instance, a servant of the parker, John Brounwynd, had driven out certain animals agisted in the park without the knowledge and permission of the reeve.[238] On the other hand, Brounwynd may have been an objectionable character in himself, for he frequently came into conflict with the tenants of the manor. Not only did tenants claim that he was occupying land which belonged to the fishery leased by them, but we also find several recognizances guaranteeing good behaviour towards him. [239] Clashes of personality may have played a greater part in the day-to-day realities of estate administration than formalised documents would lead us to believe.

A similar situation is seen at the Dee grinding mills and fishery where, despite the importance of the issues, the keepership was generally vested for life in a merely titular official, for instance, Robert Castell, whose main duties lay in the prince's household. Admittedly, the major function of the keeper was one of supervision which could be adequately performed by a deputy, usually someone who lived in the city of Chester. The deputies of this period, John Hatton, Thomas Overton and Robert del Hope, were all citizens of Chester, and they or their relatives served as city officials. Interestingly, despite the fact that Hope was only a deputy, the terms of his appointment made him directly responsible to the chamberlain of Chester, both as regards issues and the policy to be followed on the sale of grain.[240] The actual milling was carried out by millers, salaried until June 1400.[241] The fishery was controlled by a fisherman. On certain occasions, when grain was required by the household of the lord, or for victualling garrisons, or when closer control over sale was demanded, ad hoc controllers of the mills were appointed.[242]

238 SC 2/156/13, m 2d.
239 SC 2/156/13, m 3; CHES 2/85, m 1d (7), *36 DKR*, p. 527.
240 CHES 2/82, m 1 (5), *36 DKR*, p. 504.
241 SC 6/791/1, m 5.
242 For instance, in 1407, 1408 and 1410, with appointments of John

The question of performance of office in person is important in several respects, namely with respect to the exercise of patronage, the payment of wages and the accountability of officials. Despite the stress on accountability, in this period, there was a considerable degree of delegation of authority to deputies. Indeed, it was often specifically stated at appointment that offices could be performed by deputies, as in the appointments of stewards at Macclesfield and of Hugh Hoby as parker of the same place. In such cases, we must assume that such deputies were paid out of the official's own wages but on a non-accountable basis.[243] As McFarlane notes, the end of demesne farming meant that fewer officials were required, yet the tendency was not for numbers to be reduced but for posts to be made honorary sinecures.[244] Now that there was little need for day-to-day surveillance, and the main duty of officials was one of collecting and accounting issues from well-established sources, offices could be granted out more for the sake of patronage than of efficient management. Appointments could be made of men who had little direct connection with a manor. The best example of this in Cheshire is the keepership of the garden of the castle. Hugh Holes was keeper of the garden of Chester from 1399 to 1416 and his son Thomas from 1417 to 1420, although they performed no function therein. This was clearly a patronage appointment since, although the earl received about four shillings per annum from the farm of the garden, he paid out £4 11s 3d to the keepers.[245]

Whetenhale and John del Dedwood (SC 6/792/2, m 5, SC 6/775/9, m 2d, SC 6/775/11, m 2d), and in 1416 with the appointment of John Huxley (SC 6/793/4, m 5).

243 This is also evidenced in the duchy of Cornwall (Hatcher, *Rural Economy*, p. 46).

244 *Nobility of Later Medieval England*, p. 216.

245 SC 6/791/1, m 2 to SC 6/793/5, m 1d for Hugh; SC 6/793/5, m 1d to SC 6/793/11, m 1d for Thomas. It was quite usual on the estates of Richard, duke of York, later in the century that many officials had no real connections with the manors. Their appointments were merely a way of providing them with income directly from the estates rather than by a disbursement through the central household (J. T. Rosenthal, 'The Estates and Finances of Richard, Duke of York', in

Unfortunately, it is sometimes very difficult, if not impossible, to discover whether an official was exercising his office in person or not. When a deputy is named, it is likely that he was in full executive control. In certain cases, however, documents suggest that an official was actually performing his office, when we know it to be impossible. Court cases are stated as being held before the justiciar when we know that Henry Percy, or Gilbert Talbot, or the duke of Exeter were most certainly involved in business elsewhere.[246] Accounts continued to be presented in the name of John Savage as bailiff of the forest and parker of Macclesfield park even in those years when he is known to have been overseas, such as on the campaign of 1415 which culminated in the battle of Agincourt.[247] His absences are not taken into consideration in the accounts. The chamberlain, William Troutbeck, also served on the Agincourt campaign.[248] Yet there is nothing in the Cheshire records to suggest his absence from the county, and, in general, we may believe the chamberlains to have been resident and personally active. The failure to mention such absences is surprising if only because it was surely important to know, for the sake of accountability and control of official behaviour, how the administration was actually being conducted.

It may appear from the above observations that real control over officials and their activities was non-existent. It is true that once direct exploitation was at an end, administration of the demesnes was considerably easier, with revenue collection often forming the single function of officials. However, adequate machinery did exist for the regulation of the activities of officials, as and when required. Far from being lucrative and

*Studies in Medieval and Renaissance History*, 2 (1965), 115–204, at p. 171). See also Hatcher, *Rural Economy*, p. 46.

246 Gilbert Talbot, for instance, was in constant attendance on the prince during 1404 and then involved in military activities in Wales. He served on the second French campaign in 1417, dying at Rouen in 1418.

247 SC 6/776/4, m 4d, E 403/31/316. From 1418 he was involved in the defence of Calais (E 101/70/3/631).

248 E 404/31/395.

trouble-free sinecures, certain offices were onerous and liable to give rise to conflict both with tenants and the central administration. Indeed, officials were often caught between the central administration anxious to exert the lord's rights in full and tenants who wished to preserve their own rights and protect their own pockets against the lord's demands. Roger Torfot, bailiff of Frodsham, for instance, was indicted at the county court of 16 June 1417 on several charges ranging from slandering certain tenants to occupying in the demesne to his own use without accounting for the profits. He had furthermore concealed rents from other demesnes owed to the lord, and had stolen crops belonging to the tenants under cover of his office ('colore officii sui'). Later that same year, he was indicted for breaking the enclosure of another tenant and for stealing oats growing there.[249] From these various charges, it would seem apparent that Torfot had antagonised not only his superiors in the lord's administration but also the tenants of the manor – a dangerous combination of offences which no doubt was the cause of his removal from office in 1420.

The citizens of Chester had been successful to some extent in their petition of 1397 when they complained of the extortion of the Dee millers. Richard II had then ordered that no more than the accustomed toll be taken for four years.[250] An enquiry held in 1400 emphasised the long-standing complaints of the citizens and led not only to the removal from office of the keeper, Henry Strangeways, but also to a reaffirmation of the lord's prerogatives, to the long-term detriment of the tenants.[251]

When tenants are found in opposition to the lord's administration, their criticism is seen to be directed against particularly odious officials or laying emphasis on certain

249 CHES 25/11, m 12d, 13.

250 CHES 2/71, m 9d (5), *36 DKR*, p. 98 Bennett and Elton, *Some Feudal Mills*, p. 69, quoting BL, Harley MS 2003, f. 857b.

251 The inquisition's findings are printed in Rupert H. Morris, *Chester in the Plantagenet and Tudor Reigns* (Chester: printed for the author, 1893), pp. 112–14. For further discussion see the relevant section in Chapter 3.

specific rights. There is no clear evidence of a hostile attitude towards the earl's administration and its personnel in general. There were no refusals to pay rent nor widespread revolts as elsewhere, but there are several instances of attacks upon officials whilst engaged in the pursuit of their duties. The catchpole of Northwich was attacked whilst trying to take a distraint, the bailiff of the hundred of Macclesfield likewise in 1411.[252] In September 1408, whilst on his way to Chester to render his account, Richard de Manley, as escheator, was attacked by a large band which included some gentry.[253] It is worth noting too that the tenants of Frodsham seem to have disliked the close control maintained over their activities. They attacked the earl's enclosures in the manor at one point.[254]

It has been suggested that lords may have had to countenance the nefarious practices of officials as a necessary evil.[255] But in Cheshire, officials were not allowed to feather their own nests at the lord's expense. Thomas Barneby was removed from office as chamberlain of North Wales on 19 March 1414, with tacit recognition that the charges of fraud and malpractices levied against him and investigated by a commission of inquiry were true.[256] Despite the fact that a rentier economy may have demanded less intimate control over local officials, a continuing emphasis was placed upon their administrative efficiency, possibly as one of the few criteria by which the success of estate administration could be judged now that economic trends were reduced to if not a minimal, then a lesser importance.[257]

252 SC 2/156/11, m 4, CHES 24/10, m 34d.

253 CHES 25/10, m 27d–28. See also the plan of Welsh rebels to ambush the chamberlain of North Wales as he travelled to Chester in 1408 (Davies, *Revolt of Owain Glyn Dŵr*, p. 125).

254 CHES 25/11, m 8.

255 A. J. Pollard, 'Estate Management in the Later Middle Ages: The Talbots and Whitchurch, 1383–1525', *EcHR*, 25 (1972), 560.

256 Griffiths, 'Glyndwr Rebellion in North Wales through the Eyes of an Englishman', 151–4.

257 See below pp. 101–2 for accounting officials arrested for failures in their duties. In the duchy of Lancaster, most of the reforming measures concentrated upon fraud, inefficiency and neglect by officials (Somerville, *History of the Duchy of Lancaster*, pp. 174, 189).

Charges against officials for fraud or maladministration were frequent. For instance, the bailiff of the hundred of Eddisbury was fined for extortion in 1406.[258] The keepers of the assize of ale at Macclesfield were fined for not presenting those who had broken the assize.[259] Henry Robinson of Burton was prosecuted in the manorial court of Shotwick for failing to fulfil his contract with the earl to repair the fence of the park.[260]

The most interesting case of failure of duty by a local official is that concerning John de Mottram, bailiff of the forest of Macclesfield from 1400 to 1413. His case demonstrates the degree of surveillance exercised by the central administration, the weaknesses of hereditary office when the official proved grossly unsuitable for the task, and the attraction of office to colleagues and rivals who were able to take advantage of his fall. At the beginning of the reign of Henry IV, de Mottram was already labouring under heavy arrears from his previous year in office, owing £34 4s. 3¾d. in 1401.[261] As keeper of the gaol of Macclesfield, he met with an equal lack of success, allowing a felon to escape in May 1401, so finding himself in prison in 1402, then being fined £8 which further added to his debt.[262] Such obvious maladministration led to his temporary removal from office in 1402. He was ordered to be delivered into the custody of the constable of Chester Castle at the next county court.[263] In the following year, his lands were seized by the prince and their revenues directed, in yearly instalments, to paying off his debt and the wages of his deputy, Reginald del Dounes, who was now having to exercise de Mottram's duties.[264] Stronger action was necessary by 1409, despite the seemingly regular payment of the instalments. In April 1409, de Mottram once again delivered his lands and offices into the

258 CHES 25/10, m 20d.
259 SC 2/255/18, m 4.
260 SC 2/156/13, m 2d.
261 SC 6/805/7, m 1.
262 SC 2/255/4, m 5, SC 6/805/9, m 2, SC 6/805/14, m 1d.
263 CHES 2/75, m 6d (10), *36 DKR*, p. 355.
264 SC 6/805/11, m 3.

prince's hands until he had paid off his debt which now stood at £37 10s. 1d.[265]

A private agreement with John Savage, who was now his deputy as steward, was in its teething stages, for Savage agreed to hold de Mottram's offices and lands in return for paying off the debt. This enabled the rate of repayment to be increased.[266] From 1410 to 1415, this total surrender of responsibility to Savage was formalised by a number of private agreements. On 30 May 1413, de Mottram granted Savage all his lands in the *burgus* and hundred of Macclesfield for eight years.[267] From Michaelmas 1413, Savage accounted in his own right as bailiff of the forest.[268] Two years later, on 1 June 1415, de Mottram had abdicated even his person to Savage; the former was to be allowed to live in the house next to the gaol, but Savage was to be responsible for the maintenance of him and his wife. He was to have lands to the value of £2 18s. 3½d. p.a., but these were to be inalienable, for he now held them of Savage in fee.[269] Other lands formerly belonging to de Mottram had, by 1415, come into the hands of John de Macclesfield, possibly through the latter's connections with John Savage.[270] It might be suspected that Savage had struck a bad bargain, which would prove a liability as far as both the repayment of arrears and the personal maintenance of de Mottram were concerned. In fact, Savage had acted very skilfully. Not only had he acquired a lucrative and prestigious office, but he was later able to so ingratiate himself with the comital administration as to secure a pardon for the debts he had undertaken to pay. On the account of 1416 it was noted that the king, by petition of the Commons in the

265 CHES 2/81, m 6d (7), *36 DKR*, p. 355.

266 CHES 2/81, m 6d (8), *36 DKR*, p. 355; CHES 2/83, m 1d (8), *36 DKR*, p. 422.

267 CALS, Cholmondeley MSS DCH R 22.

268 SC 6/806/6, m 2.

269 CALS, Cholmondeley MSS DCH R 22.

270 These included half a burgage and other lands in Sutton and Mottram. John de Macclesfield had already let these lands out at a profit of £2 8s. 8¾d. (BL, Cotton MS Cleopatra D VI, f. 201). For the connections between Savage and de Macclesfield see below p. 227.

parliament, had pardoned all fines and debts owed by Savage and his wife at the opening of the new reign, which included this £37 10s. 1d.[271]

This incident, and the career of John Savage as a whole, indicates the continuing attraction of holding office. For the right man, who was both willing and able, administrative office offered useful opportunities. Thus we see Savage in the late fourteenth century acquiring 'forestaria' in Macclesfield Forest, presumably various foresterships, and then penetrating the higher ranks of the forest and park administration as bailiff and parker and as deputy-steward to Sir John Stanley. From such beginnings, he also became prominent in military affairs later in the period. There seems to have been no lack of enthusiasm for office holding in the county as a whole. Despite its sometimes onerous responsibilities and low wages, there must have been adequate remuneration in social position and pecuniary benefits. There is little evidence in Cheshire, unlike Wales, that small local offices were regarded as tiresome obligations.[272] Duties were, with some inevitable exceptions, carried out as required, and administrative efficiency seems to have been adequate if not better.

271 SC 6/806/11, m 3. This was presumably by virtue of the general pardon at the Oct 1416 parliament (*PROME*, xi. 181–2).

272 Griffiths, 'Patronage, Politics and the Principality of Wales', p. 73.

CHAPTER 2

# *Financial Control*

## The form of account

As in the fourteenth century in Cheshire, and indeed as was the case throughout the medieval period in England and many other areas of Western Europe, accounts were based upon the charge and discharge principle.[1] The accountant stated what he ought to have received (the *charge*), which he then sought to reduce by payments he had made or by allowances for sums which he had been unable to collect (the *discharge*). Any sum which remained his liability (the *balance*) he might pay in part or in full to the next level in the hierarchy of the financial administration or to the lord directly. Such outpayments are called *liveries* (from the Latin term *liberationes*). Any *remainder* after the payment of liveries was carried forward as the *arrears* of the following year's account.[2]

The most notable aspect of the method of accounting within the county during this period was a significant change in the system which was introduced at Michaelmas 1402. At this point, the accounts of the lordship of Macclesfield and of the Cheshire demesnes and sheriff ceased to employ what historians have called the 'Winchester' form of account and henceforward adopted the 'Westminster' form.[3] The chamberlain's account followed suit the following year (the last year of John Trevor's period as chamberlain),[4] as did the escheator's account in the accounting year of 1404 to 1405.[5] It is interesting to note that, at the same time as each account changed its form, the method of writing the accounts also changed. From being written from

1 Double-entry bookkeeping was first recorded in Italy in 1494.
2 Booth, *Financial Admin.*, pp. 15–25.
3 The accounts of the first year where the Westminster form was employed are SC 6/805/11 and SC 6/791/6.
4 SC 6/775/3.
5 SC 6/791/10, m 6. The same escheator was in office from Sept 1403 to Mar 1407.

the head to the foot of each membrane, they were now written from head to foot on the recto but from foot to head of the dorse in order to make continuous reading. After the change from the Winchester to Westminster form, the accounts also appear much more orderly to the eye, with income and expenditure increasingly categorised. Before assessing the possible reasons for this change, let us refresh our minds about these two forms of account and of their previous use in the county.[6]

In the Winchester form, the categories of the account were treated thus:

RECEIPTS
EXPENSES
BALANCE (RECEIPTS MINUS EXPENSES)
ARREARS (i.e. REMAINDER of the previous year's account)
JOINT BALANCE ('SUMMA CONIUNCTA' = BALANCE + ARREARS)
LIVERIES
ALLOWANCES, RESPITES[7]
REMAINDER (which became the ARREARS of the next account)

In the Westminster form, the order was as follows:

ARREARS
RECEIPTS
TOTAL OF RECEIPTS AND ARREARS

6 What follows is derived primarily from *Walter of Henley and Other Treaties on Estate Management and Accounting*, ed. Dorothea Oschinsky (Oxford: Clarendon Press, 1971), p. 215, and eadem, 'Notes on the Editing and Interpretation of Estate Accounts', parts 1 and 2, *Archives*, 9 (1969–70), 84–9, 142–52.

7 Allowances were sums for which the accountant was completely exonerated. Respites were merely postponements of payment either to the following year or to a specific future date, for instance whilst pleas for allowance were still being made. For an example see SC 6/791/6, m 8.

EXPENSES
LIVERIES
TOTAL OF EXPENSES AND LIVERIES
BALANCE (TOTAL OF R&A MINUS TOTAL OF E&L)
ALLOWANCES, RESPITES
REMAINDER (WHICH BECOMES ARREARS OF FOLLOWING YEAR)

It can be seen that the two main differences between the Winchester and Westminster form lie in the treatment of arrears and liveries. In the Westminster form, arrears were added at the outset to the receipts to form a combined charge. In other words, arrears were treated as income that the accountant should have received. Liveries were also listed after expenses to form a combined discharge. The balance was struck by subtracting the combined discharge from the combined charge. In this Westminster form, liveries and expenses also tended to be deducted in a lump sum, whereas in the Winchester form they were often deducted from the balance item by item.[8]

The change from the Winchester to Westminster form occurred in the financial administration of all accounting units of the earldom of Chester, as we have noted, between 1402 and 1405. Both before and after the change, however, the chamberlain of Chester accounted in his accounts for the actual sums (liveries) which he had received from each of the demesnes. Change in accounting methods was nothing new. Before 1342, for instance, it had been the balance of each individual minister's account which had been transferred to the account of the chamberlain. This gave a misleading picture of the county's finances since it stated what the accounting

8 Booth, *Financial Admin.*, p. 21. This item-by-item method epitomises the idea of an established yearly charge which it is the accountant's task to reduce item by item as the auditors allow, rather than an established yearly expense automatically granted. Even after the change in accounting methods in the county, accounts of certain units were slow to develop this proper, totalled discharge. See for instance SC 6/792/3, m 3 and SC 6/792/5, m 2 (Shotwick).

officials *ought* to have received rather than what they actually had received; this method was feasible only when lordships and bailiwicks were farmed out in their entirety.[9]

The Westminster form of account had been used in the county's financial administration until 1347. Into the 1350s, a variation of the Winchester form was introduced and continued to be used until the change to the Westminster form in the early fifteenth century. There is an exception, however, in the accounts of the lordship of Macclesfield. Between 1347 and 1389, its accounts had employed the same Winchester form as the other Cheshire accounting units.[10] From 1389–90, however, arrears on the accounts of the lordship were placed at the head of the account and totalled with receipts as in a Westminster form, but liveries were not as yet classed as expenses.[11] The expenses were subtracted from the total of receipts and arrears to form the balance from which liveries were then subtracted, item by item. This change in form corresponds with the first year that the lordship was in the hands of Queen Anne, by exchange with the previous holder, Joan Mohun.[12] In the last account of Joan as holder of the manor, a valor was drawn up and appended to the account, and a roll of her personal debts established.[13] During the queen's subsequent tenure of Macclesfield, her Macclesfield officials were accountable to the Macclesfield receiver (John de Legh) who, in turn, accounted to her receiver-general and treasurer (Thomas More).[14] The fact that the Macclesfield officials were directly responsible to the

9 Booth, *Financial Admin.*, pp. 32–4.

10 See SC 6/804/11, the account for 1388–9, and previous accounts.

11 SC 6/804/12.

12 Joan Mohun (c. 1324–1404), daughter of Bartholemew de Burghersh and widow of Sir John de Mohun of Dunster (d. 1376), had been granted the lordship of Macclesfield on 5 June 1386 (CHES 2/57, m 6 (1) (2), *36 DKR*, p. 346). The exchange with the queen was made on 13 Nov 1389 or 1391 (CHES 2/64, m 4 (2), *36 DKR*, p. 311). In return Joan was given an annuity of £100 which the queen held from the mayor, commonalty and sheriffs of London.

13 SC 6/804/11, m 2d, m 3.

14 SC 6/805/1, m 3.

queen's central accounting official may explain the change in the form of these local accounts after the lordship came into the queen's hands.[15]

The use at Macclesfield of this partially Westminster form persisted after the death of Queen Anne in 1394, even though liveries from the lordship of Macclesfield were thenceforward made to the Chester chamberlain as well as to her former receiver.[16] The change to the Winchester form to bring Macclesfield into line with the other Cheshire accounts occurred in the account for 1398–9, which was audited in the first year of Henry IV's reign.[17] There were, in fact, no arrears or liveries that year.[18] However, a key statement occurs after the remainder in the accounts of the forest and of the hundred: 'for which he [i.e. the accounting official] must respond in the foot of the account of the following year' ('de quibus respondet in pede compoti sui de anno proxime sequente'). Unfortunately, no Macclesfield account survives for 1399–1400 so that we cannot know what form was used in that year. In the next extant account for 1400–1, the Macclesfield accounts follow the same Winchester form as the chamberlain's and ministers' accounts for the rest of the demesne lands of the county.[19] They underwent the same change in accounting from Winchester to Westminster forms at Michaelmas 1402.[20]

It has already been noted that the escheator's account did not change completely to the Westminster form until 1404–5. In the accounts of the two intervening years for 1402–3 and

15 It would be interesting to know whether the Westminster form was employed in lands held elsewhere by Queen Anne. Unfortunately, neither of the two accounts which I have been able to examine shed any light on this question, for neither includes a category of arrears (SC 6/1092/15, lands formerly of the queen in Northamptonshire in 1397, and SC 6/1294/3, subsidiary accounts and documents relating to the lands of Queen Anne, temp. Richard II).

16 SC 6/805/5, m 4.

17 SC 6/805/6.

18 This explains why John de Legh was called to account in 1405 for these years when he had been receiver (SC 6/805/14).

19 SC 6/805/7.

20 SC 6/805/11.

1403–4, arrears were added in after the balance had been established. [21] The change in format elsewhere in the county, however, had enough influence on the escheator's account in these two years to have liveries to be treated as expenses, with the result that the layout of these two accounts is as follows:

RECEIPTS
EXPENSES
LIVERIES
TOTAL OF EXPENSES AND LIVERIES
BALANCE
ARREARS
JOINT BALANCE
FURTHER LIVERIES
REMAINDER

Why should these escheator's accounts for 1402–3 and 1403–4 be different from the other accounts produced in the county when they were compiled by the same scribe and underwent the same audit? We can suggest that it was considered necessary to know the *current* potential value of the income from escheats untrammelled by the inclusion of arrears. We can see some further changes around this time in dealing with income from escheats which are potentially significant. Up to and including the account for 1401–2,[22] old and new escheats had been totalled separately, but this practice ceased from 1403 and both were totalled together. There was also a change in accountant at Michaelmas 1403, when Matthew del Mere was appointed as escheator.[23] Furthermore, in the account for 1402–3, there began a series of liveries directly from the escheator to the prince's receiver-general, bypassing the chamberlain.[24] It may be in this last point that explanation may be found of the delay in the escheator's accounts moving to the full Westminster form.

21 SC 6/791/6, m 8, and SC 6/791/7, m 7.
22 SC 6/791/5, m 7.
23 SC 6/791/6, m 8. See Appendix I (d).
24 SC 6/791/7, m 7. See pp. 307–8 and Table XIX.

It may appear strange to devote so much attention to the changes in accounting methods but they provide important insights into how the demesnes and their income were regarded at this key time for the earldom of Chester between 1402 and 1405, when its revenues were regarded as absolutely crucial for the support of the Welsh wars. The change from the Winchester to Westminster form at this stage cannot have been coincidental. It was a deliberate decision motivated by financial policies of the prince's advisors. At this point, when the prince was still under age and the Welsh wars were causing major pressures on resources, Henry IV had a strong interest in the administration of his son's estates. We can therefore suggest that this was also royal financial policy.

The most crucial element in financial administration was the treatment of the balance of the account. This balance could be liveried in the year due, in full or in part. If in part, then the remaining balance would be transferred to the next year's account as arrears.[25] In the Winchester form as used in the county up to the financial year 1401–2, the balance was struck simply by deducting expenses of the current year from receipts of the current year. It was therefore easy to see the profitability of that year. Arrears from the previous year were added in only after the balance was struck. By contrast, in the Westminster form, arrears from the previous year were treated as part of the income of the estate and therefore added to the receipts of the current year before any expenses of the current year were deducted.

Dorothea Oschinsky saw the Westminster form as a refinement, being brought into use on estates where lords considered demesne farming as a business enterprise.[26] In this scenario, arrears were treated as part of the income of the year because they included cash in hand – working capital – accumulated on the manor from the previous year and in the hands of the accountant, as well as debts which he was intending to collect since they were also part of the potential income of the estate. Such treatment of arrears as a real resource transformed

25 Oschinsky, 'Notes', p. 145.
26 Ibid., p. 148.

the money account from being not simply the balance sheet of the accountant but also the balance sheet of the manorial unit.

The central administrators of the prince's estate wished to have a clear idea of the total resources available. Yet this might appear to sit oddly with the increasing fossilization of sources of income in what was largely a rentier economy, such as we can see in Cheshire at this time. In this case, therefore, the change to the more refined Westminster form was not occasioned by a move towards direct exploitation but rather by the impact of the Welsh wars.

Arrears in Cheshire began to be regarded as cash in hand/working capital to pay for the Welsh wars and a vital supplement to the annual receipts. The wars had removed the possibility of income from the principality of Wales as well as Flintshire.[27] As a result, Cheshire revenues were increasingly directed to the costs of defence in North Wales. We see this in a valor of the county drawn up after the term of the 1402–3 account, based upon figures in that account, a document we shall discuss in more detail later in this chapter and which is presented in translation in Appendix V.[28] In this valor, the total income of the county was calculated as £798. 4s 0d. Out of this had to be paid not only the regular expenses of wages, annuities, etc., within the county but also £1,423 7s. 7d. for the wages of men-at-arms and archers holding the garrisons of North Wales against the rebels. It is apparent that such sums could not be met out of annual revenues alone. Hence arrears would need to be accounted as receipts and collected in full in order to help offset increased expenditure. Therefore the Westminster form was preferable as it made clear the cumulative total resources available for disbursement. Its introduction also needed to be accompanied by a move towards the rigorous collection of any outstanding arrears and a more intensive exploitation of resources. Both actions can be seen in the administration of the demesnes at the point the accounting form was changed and in the immediate years following.

27 See below pp. 312–13.

28 SC 11/904.

The change in accounting methods at this time was also made in order to bring the county in line with other estates held by the prince of Wales.[29] The accounts of the prince's household already used the Westminster form, as we see for the surviving accounts for 1401–2 and 1402–3.[30] Flintshire accounts for 1400–1 and 1401–2 used the Winchester form,[31] but adopted the Westminster form in the next account, which is hardly surprising given that the chamberlain of Chester was also chamberlain of Flint and North Wales.[32] We cannot prove categorically that the Westminster form was in use in North Wales. In the account of the prince's estates in North Wales covering Michaelmas 1401 to 9 December 1402, there were no arrears or liveries,[33] and there is then a gap in the records – no doubt caused by the disruption of the wars. But in the next surviving account covering the period February 1407 to February 1410, the full Westminster form was employed, as in Cheshire and Flint.[34] The same change in methods occurred in the duchy of Cornwall but about ten years later, it would seem. In the course of the early part of the reign of Henry V, the format of the duchy account changed from Winchester to Westminster, 'probably to bring it more into line with the established procedure in other parts of the royal estates', as John Hatcher suggests.[35]

29 It seems that the Westminster form was the most popular with landlords in the fifteenth century. See, for instance, J. L. Kirby, 'The Hungerford Family in the Later Middle Ages', unpublished MA dissertation (University of London, 1939), p.190. Note also that the estates of the honour of Halton, lands held of the duchy of Lancaster but within the geographical county of Chester, had consistently employed the Westminster form (Booth, 'Cheshire Estate Records', p. 8).

30 E 101/404/16, m 3, E 101/404/23, m 1.

31 SC 6/1190/9 and SC 6/1190/11.

32 SC 6/1191/1.

33 SC 6/1216/1. In fact there was a deficit (*superplusagium*) this year.

34 SC 6/1216/2. Thomas Barneby rendered this account as chamberlain of North Wales. He was also chamberlain of Chester and Flint at this time.

35 John Hatcher, *Rural Economy and Society in the Duchy of Cornwall*

The changes in accounting forms had their limitations. The Westminster form gave no ready view of the annual yield of manors. Moreover, the burdening of accounts with arrears, for which the officials were not personally responsible nor held liable to repay – since responsibility lay with the accountant in whose period of tenure they had been generated – could cause confusion.[36] But the current year's issues could be calculated even if, as often happened, the sum of current receipts was not even stated but placed within the total of receipts and arrears.[37]

## The mechanics of accounting

The change in the form of account was the most important aspect of financial administration in the county in this period. We shall now turn our attention to the less momentous but still highly important mechanics of the accounts. The accounts ran as usual from Michaelmas (technically the morrow of Michaelmas, 30 September) to Michaelmas (29 September)[38] save where a change in personnel necessitated more than one account in one year (as, for instance, at the Dee Mills in 1401),[39] or in the case of a 'view of account' ('visus compoti'), a special account drawn up as part of an inspection. Dating of accounts was customarily by regnal year. Some enrolments for the reign of Henry IV were dated by the year of Prince Henry's principate, but this did amount to a real difference since the prince had been created earl at his father's first parliament shortly after the coronation. Each unit was accounted separately. There was only

*1300–1500* (Cambridge: Cambridge University Press, 1970), pp. 49–50. Unfortunately, there is a gap in the extant accounts from 12–13 Henry IV (Duchy of Cornwall Record Office 41) to 3–4 Henry V (Duchy of Cornwall Record Office 42).

36 Hatcher, *Rural Economy*, p. 50.

37 For instance, SC 6/791/10, m 8, 792/5, m 5 and 792/6, m 5.

38 Booth, *Financial Admin.*, p. 45 n. 60.

39 Robert Castell replaced Henry Strangeways in July 1401 (Appendix 1(g)). Strangeways accounted from Michaelmas 1400 to 5 July 1401, and Castell from 5 July to Michaelmas 1401 (SC 6/791/3, mm 5 and 6).

one account per unit even where there were several accounting officials responsible for certain categories of income, as at the Wiches.[40]

Now that direct exploitation (i.e. cultivation of lands directly by the lord's officials) had come to an end, there were no stock and corn accounts entered upon the dorse of the money account as was customary practice where there was actual cultivation. The nearest we have to such documents are the occasional accounts of the quantities of grain and fish received in toll and sold at the Dee Mills which occur on the dorse of the money account of this unit in the first years of the period.[41] This was rather a redundant document since all grain and fish received was sold in the year, with the result there remained no surpluses to be recorded on the dorse of the following year's account. The practice came to an end with the move to the Westminster form.

A 'view of account' ('visus compoti') can be best described as 'the result of an inspection which might have taken place at the end of the year, twice yearly or more frequently'.[42] Four documents within the surviving accounts for this period are called 'visus compoti' but it is possible there were others which have not survived. The last account of the period for Macclesfield Forest and park with John Savage as bailiff and parker is termed 'visus compoti' although it covered the whole year, or at least until Henry V's death on 31 August 1422.[43] 'Visus' in this case may imply an account not drawn up by the accounting official in person. Savage was most likely serving with the king in France at this time. The account of John de Legh, drawn up in 1405 but which concerned debts owing from his time as receiver of Macclesfield under Richard II, is also termed 'visus compoti'.[44]

40 See above p. 68.
41 For instance, SC 6/790/10, m 4d, SC 6/791/3, m 5d.
42 Oschinsky, 'Notes', pp. 142–3.
43 SC 6/807/3, m 2 and m 3.
44 SC 6/805/14, m 3.

There are two extant 'views' appertaining to the office of chamberlain.[45] Both are in the same form as the full chamberlain's accounts but deal only with receipts and payments made in the period concerned. No arrears are accounted in the first example, which covers the period from 16 August 1399 to 22 March 1400.[46] But on the second, which covers the period from Michaelmas 1402 to 2 July 1403,[47] the remainder of the previous year's account was added in after the receipts had been totalled, and expenses were then subtracted. The positioning of arrears in this second view, therefore, foreshadows the change in accounting form in the full chamberlain's account. The survival of the two views is easily explained. The first reflects the confused state of affairs, especially with regard to accountability in the changeover from Ricardian to Lancastrian administration. The second was taken in a year when increasing interest was being shown in Cheshire revenues, so that they could be used to meet costs in the Welsh wars when the prince was unable to collect revenues from his principality.

The accounts which survive are fair copies written by the clerks and scribes of the Chester exchequer.[48] The Chester clerks remain anonymous but certainly, whoever drew up these accounts was well versed in Exchequer procedure.[49]

45 A mid-yearly view of the chamberlain's account may have been taken each year but not survived. According to Somerville, 'The view had less permanent interest and therefore less cause and chance of preservation' (Robert Somerville, *History of the Duchy of Lancaster*, 1: *1265–1603* (London: Duchy of Lancaster, 1953), p. 105). In the duchy the auditors were responsible for the view. Presumably this was also true for the Cheshire examples.

46 SC 6/774/12. Liveries to the Prince's receiver-general were not accounted on the 1400 view although some were certainly paid within its term, for instance, £353 6s. 8d. on 2 Feb 1400 (SC 6/774/11, m 3d).

47 SC 6/775/2.

48 In 1357, however, the clerks of the auditors were involved in writing the ministers' accounts (Booth, *Financial Admin.*, p. 15) and it is possible that in this period they were also responsible for making copies.

49 There is an example of the use of the Exchequer method of calculation

It was general practice here, as elsewhere in royal finance, to write up as much of the account as possible from the previous account before the information required specifically for the year in question was received. This proved a feasible method once many sources of income had become fossilised.[50] We see this in one of the chamberlain's accounts, which is an account in its initial form as compiled by the scribe. The names of officials and some stereotype sums are entered, but no demesne liveries are entered, nor any totals.[51]

The accounts were based upon a multiplicity of subsidiary documents and sub-accounts of which very few survive. This implies that local estate officials were literate, since, based on entries in the accounts, the normal method of recording transactions on the demesnes was by written bill, acquittance and indenture, rather than by wooden tally.[52] Each entry on the accounts required its accompanying warranties for payment and receipts witnessing that expenditure authorised by the voucher had reached the right pocket, although occasionally we find mention of acquitances and letters authorising allowances. In general, if such subsidiary documentation could not be shown, then payment or allowance could not take place.[53]

Most of the examples of subsidiary documentation which survive are from the early years of the reign of Henry VI but they would be no different from those in use earlier.[54] What is

using tabulated dots in the chamberlain's account for 1419–20 (SC 6/1303/3, m 2d).

50 Somerville, *History of the Duchy of Lancaster*, p. 105.

51 SC 6/775/15.

52 Anthony Steel, *The Receipt of the Exchequer, 1377–1485* (Cambridge: Cambridge University Press, 1954), p. 23.

53 On this system of bookkeeping see Booth, *Financial Admin.*, pp. 19–20, Somerville, *History of the Duchy of Lancaster*, p. 106, and Hatcher, *Rural Economy*, p. 50.

54 See a set of acquittances acknowledging receipt of alms, fees and annuities, 1425–9 (SC 6/1268/4), works accounts 1425–7 (E 101/545/25), and the expense account of the chamberlain whilst on business outside the county 1425–8 (E 101/620/24). It would be interesting to know why so many survive for these early years of Henry VI's reign. A roll of warrants also survives for 1428 (E 163/6/44).

immediately striking is the vast amount of detail supplied. On the expense account of the chamberlain, William Troutbeck, for 1425–8, for instance, we have full information upon location and living expenses – food at breakfast and in the evening, fodder, accommodation and light – as well as upon the purpose of the journey, its various stopovers and its duration.[55] Income from perquisites of court and from seigneurial monopolies also needed to be proved against the record of the courts. At Macclesfield it would seem that extracts of the court rolls were shown rather than the rolls themselves. To one of these is appended a repair account, since the auditors had to be assured of the accuracy and reasonableness of the cost of repairs.[56] A record of leases of lands and other resources was kept and checked off against entries in the accounts.[57]

Among the most interesting survivals are the accounts of the clerk of the chamberlain which are extant for several years under Richard II.[58] There are none surviving for this period although it is possible, if not likely, that they were still kept. Further discussion of these accounts is necessary because of their implications for the methods of day-to-day financial practice. I have scrutinised the last of these accounts, that of Roger Brescy as clerk, covering the period from 8 April to 15 July 1397.[59]

Interestingly, given that at this time the Winchester form of account was in general use in the county, here the arrears were entered at the head. Receipts were itemised on the front of the roll, giving the name of the person owing the sum, the date of receipt at the exchequer and the name of the person actually paying over the money to the clerk. For instance, all the money

There are similar survivals for the Caernarvon exchequer which dealt with principality revenues from North Wales (for instance, E 101/514/30).

55 E 101/620/24. This provides interesting material on the medieval diet, especially the many types of fish consumed in Lent.

56 SC 2/155/88, m 1, which is an extract of SC 2/255/10, m 4 (1413–14).

57 It is referred to in SC 6/806/8, m 3d and SC 6/793/11, m 5.

58 Sharp, 'Earldom and County of Chester', p. 149.

59 SC 6/774/7.

due from ministers in Flintshire was paid in by John Helegh, who held various offices in this county and seems to have acted as local receiver, even if unofficially.[60] Frequently, liveries were made by the servants or debtors of demesne officials. The tendency was for several liveries from one area or manor to be paid in on the same day, but apart from this there would not appear to be any particular or specific days on which liveries were made. With regard to liveries made out of demesne issues for instance, it is notable how many separate liveries were made, often of very small amounts. From these frequent and small payments, it would seem that cash was not kept in the hands of local officials. There would be no need for working capital to be kept in hand locally once direct exploitation had come to an end. There were, besides, few local expenses to be met. The dorse records expenses and liveries to the royal exchequer. Overall, the roll seems to be a fair copy, possibly compiled at the time of the audit from another book given as 'the book of receipts' (*Liber de Recepta*),[61] which was checked off against this roll at the audit.[62] Such compilations would do away with or facilitate the need to check off at the audit what must have been a considerable heap of bills, acquittances and indentures. Brescy's roll covers only four months, but runs to ten membranes with hundreds of entries, each of which would have needed its own ancillary documentation.

A further interesting point arises out of Brescy's roll concerning whether wages were actually paid to officials in full on the date due, or whether a method of assignment or payment in kind was used. For example, let us take the wages of Robert de Whitlegh, then bailiff itinerant. On the dorse of the roll, £1 14s. 0d. is duly accounted as paid to him for his wages from Michaelmas 1396 to 19 April 1397, 'retained in his

60 *36 DKR*, p. 229 passim.

61 SC 6/774/7, m 4.

62 Beside each entry in the roll is marked 'intr'. Sharp, 'Earldom and County of Chester' (p. 149), considered that this indicated its entering onto the chamberlain's account but there must surely have been an intervening stage where receipts were totalled by manor rather than by date.

hands as for the price of tree trunks of various oaks in Delamere Forest sold to him by Roger del Dedwood the seller of the same (£1 6s. 3d.) and from the price of various grains and malts of the issues of the Dee Mills sold to him by William Marshal clerk and approver there (4s.) and by the hands of Brescy from cash payments' ('in manibus suis obstupatis ut de precio corticis diversorum quercuum infra forestam de Mara sibi venditi per Rogerum del Dedwood venditorem eiusdem corticis (£1 6s. 3d.) et de precio diversorum granorum et brasiorum de exitibus molendinorum de Dee per Willelmum Marshal clericum et appruatorem ibidem sibi venditorum (4s) et per manus Brescy solventibus sibi denariis in pecunia iminata' (3s. 9d.). Hence Robert Whitlegh had in fact received only 3s. 9d. in cash; the remainder he received by being allowed to keep money owed for various purchases. The money due from these purchases was still accounted on the front of the roll 'in the hands of Whitlegh as for his wages … held in his hands for the price [of goods] purchased by him from Roger and William'. Many other wages were paid in this indirect way.[63] This generated an accounting fiction but one so well recorded that errors could not take place, although it must have required a very competent clerk to account these sums in their proper places. In this case, the payment of Whitlegh's wages would be accounted on the chamberlain's account, the sale of bark on the Delamere Forest account, and the sale of grain on the Dee Mills account. Again, it reflects the tendency for little cash to remain in the hands of local officials.

The clerk's account may also provide another piece of evidence in a general argument that at this time the onus of accounting was being shifted to the higher echelons of the financial administration.[64] Several of the local units were no

63 At Delamere the seller of moss was due a wage of £1 per annum. In practice he kept back £1 out of the issues he had raised. In 1407 for instance, he raised £14 10s. 0d. but liveried £13 10s. 0d. (SC 6/792/2, m 2).

64 This suggestion was made as a result of personal discussion with Dr Oschinsky.

longer money accounting units at all. At the Dee Mills for instance, toll was paid in kind, millstones newly purchased were accounted by the chamberlain, and the cost of repairs was transferred wholly to the chamberlain from 1414.[65] Other expenses were 'foreign' – such as annuities and payment of the auditors' wages – and were probably not actually paid out at the mills at all. A similar move is seen at Macclesfield Park where repairs for the park began to be accounted on the forest account, facilitated by the fact that John Savage was both bailiff of the forest and parker. At Drakelow, there were, by the nature of the manor and its income, few demesne expenses. The discharge was finely tuned to meet the charge as closely as possible by the granting of annuities. These annuities never lapsed; as one annuitant died, another tended to be granted exactly the same sum. The income, mainly rents, was fossilised so that the discharge could be likewise. The manor was not expected to have any current arrears, although it might have contumacious arrears from the past. If there was a current remainder, then it was supposed to be livered to the chamberlain.[66] This system was only possible where income was relatively static and not diversified. It could not be used at Frodsham, for instance, where there were still many categories of income and expenditure.

All the Cheshire accounts, including those of the chamberlain,[67] were audited at Chester each year by auditors sent out from the prince's household, or from the royal exchequer, depending upon whether the prince or king was earl. This was instead of an itinerant audit being held by the same

65 SC 6/793/1, m 3d.

66 This may explain the frequent commitments to prison of the Drakelow bailiffs. See below pp. 101–3.

67 The accounts of the chamberlain of North Wales were audited at Caernarvon. He was usually the same person as the chamberlain of Chester and Flint. By contrast, in South Wales the chamberlain's account was audited at Westminster, not locally (R. A. Griffiths, *The Principality of Wales in the Later Middle Ages: The Structure and Personnel of Government*, 1: *South Wales 1277–1536*, Board of Celtic Studies, University of Wales, History and Law Ser., 26 (Cardiff: University of Wales Press, 1972), p. 42).

auditors across all of the prince's estates. Generally, the audit at Chester took place between the January and April following the Michaelmas at which the accounts terminated.[68] It was conducted in the presence of the justiciar, chamberlain and, occasionally, the earl's councillors. The escheator attended as an accounting official in his own right, and sometimes as steward of certain of the demesnes. All local accounting officials had to be present. They would be called upon to show their subsidiary documents and swear to certain revenues and statements. It appears, for instance, that John Savage was not present at the audit of the 1422 account.[69] As a result, his repairs in the forest of Macclesfield were disallowed 'because the aforesaid bailiff did not appear nor did anyone wish to appear in his name before the auditors to render account on oath' ('quia prefatus ballivus non apparuit nec aliquis nomine suo coram auditoribus pro compoto reddendo in sacrum prestare voluit quoquemodo pro reparaciones infrascriptas disallocatus').[70] If rolls and other documents were not shown, the accounting officials would be charged whatever sum the auditors thought fit.[71] After the audit, the auditors took the duplicate rolls back to London with them. In 1414, a chest was purchased for the royal exchequer at Westminster in which the rolls of the time when Henry V had been prince of Wales and earl of Chester were to be kept, so that they could be consulted when necessary by the council. Its cost was charged to the Chester chamberlain.[72]

68 For fourteenth-century practice see Booth, *Financial Admin.*, p. 16.

69 SC 6/807/3, m 2d.

70 In South Wales, non-appearance at the audit could give trigger a fine of between 20 and 40 shillings (Griffiths, *Principality*, i. 41).

71 In 1399 the officials of Macclesfield *burgus* had been charged £4 9s. 3½d. for the market tolls of that year because they did not show the *parcella* of such tolls. In 1406 they did show the records and it was found that they only owned £1 6s. 8d., so £3 2s. 7½d. was allowed to them on that year's account (SC 6/805/16, m 1).

72 SC 6/1302/15, m 1d.

## Accountability of officials and the collection of arrears

Medieval accounts were not so much a method of calculating profit but rather of keeping a check on manorial officials to avoid fraud.[73] Officials were bound by law to account.[74] The first stage in their accountability was that they should present an account. Officials were often appointed subject to their accounting for their profits. This requirement would be included in the terms of appointment, as was the case for the chamberlain.[75] But other officials were also bound to render account.[76] On 16 September 1406, for instance, John Mainwaring and William Venables of Kinderton entered into a recognizance of £200 that Matthew del Mere should render a reasonable account of his escheatorship.[77]

The second stage of accountability was the examination of the account rolls presented and the striking of an agreed balance.[78] It was the officer himself who was accountable rather than the unit. When officials left office, any debts from their period of control were still accounted to them, the distribution of responsibility for arrears being specified by person in both the arrears section of the accounts and after the remainder. In addition to the accountant, people leasing manorial properties

73 Oschinsky, 'Notes', p. 144; R. R. Davies, 'Baronial Accounts, Incomes, and Arrears in the Later Middle Ages', *Economic History Review*, 2nd ser., 21 (1968), 211–29, at p. 221.

74 J. Sabapathy, *Officers and Accountability in Medieval England 1170–1300* (Oxford: Oxford University Press, 2014), pp. 47–52.

75 As in the appointment of John Trevor, bishop of St Asaph, on 16 Aug 1399 (CHES 2/73, m 9(4), *36 DKR*, p. 99; *CPR 1396–9*, p. 591) which includes the condition that he account for all that relates to this office as other previous chamberlains have done.

76 See in general T. F. T. Plucknett, *The Medieval Bailiff* (London: Athlone Press, 1954), p. 18.

77 CHES 2/78, m 6 (3), DKR, 36, p. 318. Mere was appointed escheator on 18 Sept 1403 and was in office from Michaelmas 1403 to 31 Mar 1407. Richard de Manley was appointed on 4 Mar 1407 and began to account from 31 Mar (Appendix I (d)). The date of the appointment suggests it was already known at the beginning of the accounting year that Mere was poised to step down during the year.

78 Plucknett, *Medieval Bailiff*, p. 27.

were made personally responsible for their debts. This was the case in Delamere Forest, for instance, where various sources of income were leased out and the liveries and arrears of each lessee were itemised on the relevant account in detail. If an accounting official died within his term of office, then his executors became responsible for any outstanding sums[79] although, as we have seen, John Savage took over responsibility for the debts of John de Mottram as bailiff of Macclesfield Forest, by means of a private agreement whilst the latter was still alive. When accounting officials changed annually, as at the Wiches and Macclesfield *burgus*, then personal responsibility was still maintained and recorded.

In general, on all the demesnes in Cheshire an accounting official entered office completely free of any inherited debt because his predecessor continued to be held personally responsible for his own debts and arrears.[80] There are some examples of exceptions to this rule. The first occurs with regard to the accountability of the Chester chamberlain, but as we shall see, this was rather a special case. At the change of chamberlain on 16 August 1399 – within the reign of Richard II but with Henry Bolingbroke already effectively in control of such appointments – the usual method was followed whereby the debt of outgoing chamberlain, Robert Parys, was transferred to the Great Roll of Debts, where it remained his responsibility.[81] The incoming chamberlain, John Trevor, bishop of St Asaph, began his first account with a clean sheet.[82] However, when Trevor himself

79 For instance, SC 6/793/11, m 4, 791/1, m 1d, 791/7, m 5. See also Somerville, *History of the Duchy of Lancaster*, p. 109.

80 'If a change of reeve had occurred some estates demanded that the newly appointed officer took over the debt and accounted for it, while others held the reeve responsible during whose office the debt was incurred' (Oschinsky, 'Notes', p. 146). In the duchy of Cornwall each newly elected reeve took office completely free of debt (Hatcher, *Rural Economy*, p. 51). A similar situation existed on the estates of Ramsey Abbey where the new reeve began with no arrears and the outgoing reeve paid his debt to the abbot in instalments (Oschinsky, *Walter of Henley*, pp. 218–19).

81 SC 6/774/10, m 2d.

82 SC 6/774/11.

ceased accounting in 1404 following his defection to Glyndŵr, arrears owed by him remained on the chamberlain's account and were transferred to the charge of his successor, Thomas Barneby.[83] At the time, Trevor could not be communicated with and made to pay his arrears. This presumably explains the transfer of the debt to his successor in office rather than its reflecting any change of attitude towards the personal and official accountability of the chamberlain. There may also be some connection with the change in accounting methods around this time. All arrears now needed to be collected, so it was now more acceptable for them to remain accounted as part of the charge, rather than being transferred to the Great Roll of Debts. At the next change of chamberlain in December 1412, Barneby left office owing only a farthing which was consequently written off, so that William Troutbeck began his period as accounting official with no outstanding arrears.[84]

It was one thing to force an official to account and quite another to make him pay up his arrears or even issues.[85] We have already witnessed the control over officials in general. Attention will be turned specifically to the control exercised with regard to accountability and the collection of arrears. If officials defaulted, in the last resort they could be committed to prison.[86] In Cheshire, the only examples of officials

83 SC 6/775/4.

84 SC 6/775/14 and SC 6/775/15.

85 See, for instance, Barbara J. Harris, 'Landlords and Tenants in England in the Later Middle Ages: The Buckingham Estates', *Past and Present*, 43 (1969), 146–50, at p. 149, where the author claims that the duke of Buckingham in the 1490s never solved the problem of forcing officials to account for all the money they had collected owing to two conflicting aims as landlord, the first to raise as much income as possible, the second to use his estates as a means of extending his political and social influence, an example of this being the appointment of prominent men as receivers and bailiffs.

86 See also Somerville, *History of the Duchy of Lancaster*, p. 109; Hatcher, *Rural Economy*, p. 51; Levi Fox, *The Administration of the Honour of Leicester in the Fourteenth Century* (Leicester: Edgar Backus, 1940), p. 58; T. B. Pugh, *The Marcher Lordships of South Wales, 1415–1536: Select Documents* (Cardiff: University of Wales Press, 1963), p. 158. In

being arrested and placed in custody are indeed for offences concerned with accounting. We have discovered eight instances of committal to prison, which seems quite a substantial number over a sample of only twenty-three years.

**Table I. The imprisonment of officials for debt**

| | | | |
|---|---|---|---|
| Bailiff of Drakelow and Rudheath | 1404 | debt of £1 11s. 11d. | SC 6/791/7 m. 1d |
| Bailiff of Drakelow and Rudheath | 1408 | debt of £1 6s. 10d. | SC 6/792/3 m. 1d |
| Bailiff of Drakelow and Rudheath | 1413 | debt of £9 14s. 0d. | SC 6/791/10 m. 1d |
| Sheriff of the county | 1405 | debt of £147 17s.10½d. | SC 6/791/10 m. 5d |
| Sheriff of the county | 1406 | debt of £92 10s. 6½d. | SC 6/792/1 m. 6d |
| Sheriff of Chester city | 1415 | debt of £44 3s. 11¼d. | SC 6/793/2 m. 1 |
| Catchpole of Macclesfield *burgus* | 1408 | debt of £6 14s. 5¾d. | SC 6/806/3 m. 1d |
| Deputy bailiff of the escheatries, Macclesfield hundred | 1404 | debt of £8 5s. 6½d. | SC 6/805/14 m. 1 |

Save for the sums owed by both sheriffs, none of the amounts for which officials were arrested was large. Indeed, it is true throughout all instances where any kind of action was being instituted over arrears that the sums involved were often small and seemingly insignificant. The cause for concern was not, then, the size of revenue lost, but rather the principle that

all these areas where such drastic action was taken over contumacious arrears, offenders seem to have been released quickly, either on payment of their debts or upon finding adequate security for them.

any should be outstanding at all. We can also detect ongoing monitoring and comparison with earlier patterns of income. In the case of the imprisonment of the sheriff in 1405, for instance, he had only managed to hand over 40% of revenues due after a considerably better performance in previous years.

The Drakelow examples are the most revealing since three imprisonments in twenty-three years is remarkably high compared with elsewhere. Yet here no attention was paid to contumacious arrears, for instance £10 5s. 10d. which had been incurred by 1407 and which remained outstanding in 1422. It has already been noted that the attitude as regards this unit was that all the current remainder should be paid off within the year in question. If there were any current arrears, it was therefore wholly apparent that the bailiff had not worked the system efficiently. The ideal was obviously reached in those years, ever frequent under Henry V, where there were no current arrears at all. It is interesting to note the definite drop in arrears over the period as a whole, especially when it is remembered that Drakelow had a bad reputation for revenue collection in the fourteenth century because the earl's rights there had never been well established. Larger arrears were also permissible in years when the size of annuity payments did not meet the size of the charge. This explains why the bailiff was not chastised in years when, from the size of the remainder, one might have expected him to be. It is significant, too, that after two imprisonments, Ralph Pope was replaced as bailiff by Ralph Leycester in 1409. By contrast, none of the other officials imprisoned lost his post as a result.

The following table (Table II) demonstrates the payment of arrears at Drakelow. The remainder in any year is in the first column; after current liveries have been subtracted, the sum owing for that particular year is entered in the column marked 'year one'. Subsequent columns record the reducing size of the particular debt until it is paid off. Unfortunately, in some years, liveries of arrears and of current issues are not differentiated. As a result, the reduction of debts in the early years of the period has proved difficult to trace. Imprisonments occurred in those years in bold.

## Table II. The payment of arrears at Drakelow and Rudheath

| Account | Year | Balance excl. arrears (i.e. net charge) | Current liveries | Year 1 | Year 2 | Year 3 |
|---|---|---|---|---|---|---|
| SC6 791/1 m. 1d | 1400 | £24 9s. 2d. | £2 13s. 4d. | £21 15s. 10d. | nil | |
| SC6 791/3 m. 1 | 1401 | £28 6s. 1d. | £10 0s. 0d. | £18 6s. 1d. | nil | |
| SC6 791/5 m. 1 | 1402 | £36 14s. 9d. | £16 13s. 4d. | £20 1s. 5d. | £10 1s. 5d. | nil |
| SC6 791/6 m. 1 | **1403** | £17 0s. 2d. | £12 1s. 7d. | £4 18s. 7d. | ? | |
| SC6 791/7 m. 1 | 1404 | £1 11s. 11d. | nil | £1 11s. 11d. | ? | |
| SC6 791/10 m. 1 | 1405 | £11 2s. 5d. | ? | ? | ? | |
| SC6 792/1 m. 1 | 1406 | £17 9s. 1d. | £12 16s. 8½d. | £4 12s. 3½d. | ? | |
| SC6 792/2 m. 1 | 1407 | £16 8s. 10d. | £1 1s. 8d. | £13 7s. 2d. | £4 4s. 1½d. | |
| SC6 792/3 m. 1d | **1408** | £10 9s. 9¼d. | £9 2s. 11¾d. | £1 6s. 10d. | nil | |
| SC6 792/5 m. 1d | 1409 | £11 17s. 0½d. | £11 17 0½d. | nil | | |
| SC6 792/6 m. 1d | 1410 | £16 5s. 8d. | £16 5s. 8d. | nil | | |
| SC6 792/8 m. 1d | 1411 | £21 3s. 8¼d. | £11 3s. 8¼d. | £10 0s. 0d. | £8 11s. 11d. | nil |
| SC6 792/9 m. 1d | 1412 | -£1 8s. 1d. | nil | nil | | |
| SC6 792/10 m. 2 | **1413** | £29 4s. 3d. | £19 8s. 8d. | £9 14s. 7d. | nil | |
| SC6 793/1 m. 2 | 1414 | -£1 14s. 9d. | nil | nil | | |

| Account | Year | Balance excl. arrears (i.e. net charge) | Current liveries | Year 1 | Year 2 | Year 3 |
|---|---|---|---|---|---|---|
| SC6 793/4 m. 2 | 1416 | £19 14s. 6d. | £19 4s. 5½d. | ½d. | ½d. | ½d. (still outstanding 1422) |
| SC6 793/5 m. 2 | 1417 | £29 7s. 5¾d. | £18 7s. 11d. | £10 9s. 6¾d. | £3 15s.1¾d. | £3 15s. 1¾d. (still outstanding 1422) |
| SC6 793/7 m. 2 | 1418 | -£6 14s. 5d. | nil | nil | | |
| SC6 793/9 m. 2 | 1419 | £1 12s. 0d. | nil | £1 12s. 0d. | £1 12s. 0d. | £1 12s. 0d. |
| SC6 793/11 m.2 | 1420 | £23 5s. 7d. | £16 5s. 7d. | £7 0s. 0d. | £6 9s. 11d. | £2 3s. 2d. |
| SC6 794/1 m.2 | 1421 | £5 4s. 11d. | £5 4s. 11d. | nil | | |
| SC6 794/2 m.2 | 1422 | £11 2s. 4d. | £7 8s. 4½d. | £3 13s. 11½d. | | |

Such drastic action as imprisonment was not always necessary because of the pre-existing channels of general administrative control and surveillance,[87] the generally healthy position of the majority of manors,[88] and the other less hard-hitting methods of collecting debts or enforcing their collection. Distraint for the debt could be taken but there are few examples of this over estates as a whole, and none in the Cheshire accounts save for that of John de Mottram, where his debts as bailiff of the forest were to be taken out of the value of his lands and tenements. Removal from office was also possible, as in the cases of Mottram and Roger Torfot.[89] The most common method

87 As Davies notes ('Baronial Accounts', p. 221), 'the wiles of the local accountants were matched by the constant supervision of central officials'.

88 See pp. 181–2 and Hatcher, *Rural Economy*, p. 51 note 2.

89 See pp. 75, 77.

of ensuring future payment of arrears was the demanding of pledges to guarantee such payment. This could also be used as the first stage in recovering debts before recourse was made to more stringent or more magnanimous action, but pledges would also be demanded in the case of commitment to prison.[90] The order to find pledges was generally entered after the remainder on the accounts.[91] It was occasionally formalised by a recognizance for the debt, entered into by the debtor and his guarantors. These recognizances bound officials to pay the debt on a future specified date,[92] or in instalments, or that the guarantors would have the debtor at the next county court, or before the chamberlain and auditors for a discussion of the debt. John Done of Utkinton, for instance, came in to the Chester exchequer before the auditors in July 1404 and said that he would be before them at the next audit to carry out what the prince's council should decide upon the matter of his debt.[93]

Promises to pay sums due did not always necessitate a formal recognizance. For instance, John Brounwynd, farmer of the escheatries at Macclesfield in 1401 and 1402, owed £1 6s. 8d. He made a surety, which was not enrolled, to pay off these

90 John Hope, sheriff of Chester city owed £44 3s. 11¼d. in 1415 'for which sum he be committed to prison and find debtors for the sum under the security of the chamberlain of Chester for which sum the chamberlain is charged and obliged to respond to the king in his next account' ('pro qua summa committitur prisoni et inveniet debitores eiusdem summe securitate camerario cestrie pro qua summa idem camerarius in proximo compoto regi reddendo respondere valdit et ideo oneretur') (SC 6/793/2, m 1).

91 For instance, see SC 6/806/6, m 4d: 'for which sum he will find pledges', 'the security of the chamberlain' ('pro qua summa inveniet plegios', 'securitatem camerario').

92 On 7 Apr 1407, Robert Hickson, the catchpole of Northwich, acknowledged a debt of £10 to be paid off within 15 days following. He was also to be present at the exchequer at the next audit to render to the prince his account of moneys arising from his office (CHES 2/79, m 3 (7), *36 DKR*, p. 365). Other examples of recognizances in this context are to be found in *36 DKR* and *37 DKR* under the names of the relevant officials.

93 CHES 2/77, m 8 (11), *36 DKR*, pp. 446–7.

arrears within one week of the termination of the account.[94] Arrangements for payments in instalments could also be carried out informally. In 1421, the sheriff of the city of Chester, Stephen Belleyester, was allowed to pay off the £24 15s. 0d. remaining in his hands in two instalments on 24 June and 25 December 1422, on account of his poverty.[95] In 1422, Robert Castell's deputy at the Dee Mills owed £45 15s. 0d. in arrears which he was allowed to pay off over six years from February 1423.[96] Other debts were exonerated, either as a mark of favour – Robert Legh's arrears as sheriff before the time of Henry IV were pardoned in 1404 by the prince's special grace[97] – or because it was realised that their collection was impossible.

Often a combination of several methods was used to collect debts. This can be seen if we consider a particular debt, that of Catherine Page at Drakelow. In 1399 she owed £3 13s. 4d. for the farm of the turbary, and £22 9s. 10d. arrears with John Rose as bailiff for the general issues of the manor.[98] In that same year, she paid off £4 9s. 10d. of the larger debt. The remaining £18 was to be paid in biannual instalments of £3, the first payment being at Easter 1401. By 1404, the larger debt had been reduced to £6; half of this was pardoned by the prince in 1405,[99] and the remaining £3 was paid off in 1406.[100] The smaller debt of £3 13s. 4d. was respited each year until 1410 when it was removed from the charge of the bailiff of the manor and transferred to the Great Roll of Debts, to be paid off in the following year.[101] By 14 January 1411, Catherine had paid off £6 8s. 0d. of this. The remaining £3 6s. 8d. was respited to be paid off in instalments over the following ten years.[102] This agreement was formalised

94 SC 6/805/11, m 1. His arrears were noted as being paid off in the next year's account (SC 6/805/13, m 1).
95 SC 6/794/1, m 1.
96 SC 6/794/2, m 7d.
97 SC 6/791/7, m 5.
98 SC 6/791/1, m 1d.
99 SC 6/791/10, m 1d.
100 SC 6/792/1, m 1.
101 SC 6/792/6, m 1d.
102 SC 6/792/7, m 10.

by a recognizance entered into by herself and four guarantors.[103] How the prince fared in the recovery of the rest of this sum is uncertain. No payment was made in 1411,[104] and thereafter there are no surviving Great Rolls of Debts.

A further method of dealing with contumacious arrears – the establishment and use of the Great Roll of Debts – deserves more detailed consideration. This roll had appeared from 1352 onwards,[105] and was regularly appended to the ministers' accounts in this period until 1412. Even after this date, liveries from the Great Roll of Debts continued to be accounted by the chamberlain until 1420. From 1414 to 1420 these were very small, at under £1 per annum. This implies that the roll was continued but that copies are no longer extant. Several of the debts on the 1412 roll were still not cleared at that date.[106] However, it is perhaps significant that there were no transfers of arrears from the ministers' accounts to the Great Roll of Debts during the reign of Henry V. This may mark a change in policy towards arrears, with a preference then for arrears to be settled upon the individual accounts, or else to be retained on the accounts as another element in the need to assess the cumulative total resources of the units. After the end of the Welsh wars there was certainly less need for the collection of arrears. This can be taken to explain the marked drop in interest in the use of the Great Roll of Debts, reflected by the small amounts paid off under Henry V and the non-survival of the roll after 1412.

The idea of the Great Roll of Debts was that specific arrears should be transferred to it from the individual ministers' accounts, on the one hand to remove contumacious arrears from the total charge of the unit where they could be misleading in an assessment of its value and efficiency, and on the other to

103 CHES 2/83, m 2 (3), *36 DKR*, p. 271.

104 SC 6/792/8, m 9.

105 Booth, *Financial Admin.*, p. 37; Sharp, 'Earldom and County of Chester', p. 148. The prince's estates in Cornwall had a similar roll compiled by the receiver (Hatcher, *Rural Economy*, p. 51). Desperate arrears were classified separately on the estates of the Staffords later in the century (Davies, 'Baronial Accounts', p. 221).

106 SC 6/792/8, m 9. £292 8s. 2¼d. remained owing.

facilitate collection of such specific arrears. Transfer to the roll was not equivalent to the debts being written off. Often debts so transferred were to be paid in instalments which provided a better chance that they would be collected; substantial liveries were made to the chamberlain at least up to 1412, up to £66 per annum, although there was a tailing off after 1403 down to around £13 in later years.

The Great Roll of Debts was thus quite a successful method of ensuring the payment of contumacious arrears, although it must be pointed out that some entries at the head of the roll, dating back to the 1380s, were unlikely ever to be paid off. The roll further demonstrates the enhanced importance of arrears in the years of the Welsh wars. From 1405, certain debts were singled out for investigation, and attempts made to speed up collection.[107] By 1412, eighteen of the thirty-two debts on the roll in 1400 had been cleared. Fourteen new debts had been transferred during the reign of Henry IV, and by 1412 all but three of these had been paid off, and two of these three had been added to the roll only in the previous two years. Thus it would be fair to say that those remaining on the roll after 1412 were unlikely ever to be paid off.

Some general considerations of the importance of arrears in medieval financial administration, as well as an assessment of the Cheshire evidence in comparison with elsewhere, would not be amiss here. The question of revenue collection and of arrears is important because of its potential use as a test of administrative efficiency. High arrears were accepted by Rees Davies as the most pressing problem for medieval estate administrators, although the role of arrears may not have been as important in baronial fortunes in this period once demesne farming had been abandoned.[108] His views have been challenged by individual estate studies. Pollard, in his study of the Talbot estates at Whitchurch, came to the conclusion that failure to collect arrears was not necessarily a sure measuring rod of inefficiency in baronial administration: on these estates, as in

107 SC 6/791/10, m 9.

108 Davies, 'Baronial Accounts', p. 220.

Cheshire, there can be no doubt that the collection of arrears was in the hands of efficient and effective administrators.[109] Ministers' debts were exacted to the last possible penny even if it took several years; the irrevocable debt may only have been 1% of the total income.[110] Of this, loss through ministerial efficiency was minimal; failure to collect in specific years was more likely due to economic fluctuations.

In the earldom of Chester, there is no doubt that a great deal of attention was paid towards arrears and their recovery. Medieval officials showed far greater tenacity in pursuit of arrears than we give them credit for, by a continually present surveillance which could be stepped up in certain years if necessary, as, for instance in 1413, when the officials of Macclesfield hundred, *burgus* and park all had to find pledges for debts outstanding.[111] A considerable backlog of debt was cleared up at Delamere in 1404.[112]

However, it is difficult to see arrears in the county as arising from economic fluctuations; as we shall see in Chapter 3, there was relatively little scope for either an increase or decrease in yield. When revenues were as appertained to a rentier economy, any major arrears can only have been due to failure of collection by dishonesty or inefficiency. Tenants were prepared to pay higher rents to sub lessees of the earl's lands, such as John de Macclesfield,[113] so it is hardly likely that they were unable to pay the rents due to the earl. Profits of justice may have proved more difficult to collect, or so it might seem from the frequently high remainders on the sheriff of the county's account. Overall, however, the majority of issues were paid in the year in question, or else very soon afterwards.

109 A. J. Pollard, 'Estate Management in the Later Middle Ages: The Talbots and Whitchurch, 1383–1525', *EcHR*, 2nd ser., 25 (1972), 559–66, at pp. 564–5.

110 A. J. Pollard, 'The Family of Talbot, Lords Talbot and Earls of Shrewsbury in the Fifteenth Century', unpublished PhD thesis (University of Bristol, 1968), p. 389.

111 SC 6/806/6, m 1, 2 and 4d.

112 SC 6/791/7, m 2.

113 See below pp. 133–4.

Many sources of income may not have been expected to be paid off in the year they were due. This could be especially true of judicial income. Paul Booth arrived at the conclusion for Macclesfield *burgus* in the fourteenth century – where there was much income from courts and seigneurial monopolies – that revenue was collected over a two-year period, with the result that a standard amount of arrears was carried over each year. This is also true for the *burgus* of Macclesfield in the fifteenth century where, if all issues were not rendered in the year due, they were most certainly paid off in the following year or, at the very least, in the year after. Arrears were thus seen here, as elsewhere, as a postponement of payment, not an abandonment of revenue. They were not regarded as a problem unless either they failed to maintain a steady and expected norm, or else measures had been taken, as at Drakelow, to ensure that there would be no arrears. The size of arrears is not important in itself. It is the rate of change which is significant, although it must also be noted that often it was only differences in the size of arrears which created any fluctuations in the accounts at all. Liveries, and hence arrears, rose and fell without explanation and without any discoverable correlation to economic or administrative factors.

Here it is worth making a brief excursus into the early years of the reign of Henry VI in order to discuss a useful case study in the collection of arrears. The lordship of Macclesfield was granted to Queen Catherine in dower after the death of Henry V. Although the first extant account of her administrators is for 1425–6 they had assumed responsibility from 1 September 1422.[114] However, there were certain arrears upon the last account of her husband's reign which were not the responsibility of the queen's officials in the lordship.[115] Such arrears could not be written off, so the solution was to transfer them to a separate account as contumacious arrears. I have traced these arrears and how they were reduced or dealt with until the account

114 SC 6/807/5.
115 SC 6/807/3.

ending at Michaelmas 1439,[116] by which time the lordship had passed back into direct royal/comital control after the death of Catherine in 1437. The following Tables III (a) and (b) summarise these debts and attempts to pay them off. Liveries of the arrears are given in bold italics.

## Table III. Arrears at Macclesfield 1422–9

### *(a) Macclesfield Hundred*

| **SC 6** | **794/3<br>m.15<br>1423** | **794/4<br>m.14d<br>1424** | **794/5<br>m.15d<br>1425** | |
|---|---|---|---|---|
| Fine of Robert Legh, Laurence Fitton, Oliver de Staveley, Hugh and Robert Davenport, John Arderne – £5 each | £30 | £30 | £30 | Remained a debt to 1427 when £5 for arrears of Laurence Fitton pardoned by letters patent 5 May 1437 (SC 6/796/1 m.17) |
| Arrears of Thomas Swetenham bailiff<br>1417 | £1 4s. 10d. | £1 4s. 10d. | £1 4s. 10d. | Remained debt to 1439 (SC 6/796/4 m. 18d) |
| Arrears of William Honford and James Fitton, bailiffs<br>1421 | £20 0s. 6d.<br>***£3 10s. 0d.*** | £16 10s. 6d. | £16 10s. 6d.<br>***£6 0s. 0d.*** | *In 1427 Honford and Fitton's total debt of £19 4s. 3d. agreed to be paid over the next two years in instalments |
| Arrears of Honford and Fitton as bailiffs<br>1422 | £15 13s. 9d.<br>***£7 0s. 0d.*** | £8 13s. 9d. | £8 13s. 9d. | |
| Total | £66 19s. 1d.<br>***£10 10s. 0d.*** | £56 9s. 1d. | £56 9s. 1d.<br>***£6 0s. 0d.*** | |

116 SC 6/796/4, m 18d.

| SC 6 | 794/7 m.15d 1426 | 794/9 m.16d 1427 | 795/3 m.15d 1429 | |
|---|---|---|---|---|
| Fine of Robert de Legh, Laurence Fitton, Oliver de Staveley, Hugh and Robert Davenport, John Arderne – £5 each | £30 | £30 | £30 | Remained a debt to 1427 when £5 for arrears of Laurence Fitton pardoned by letters patent 5 May 1437 (SC 6/796/1 m.17) |
| Arrears of Thomas Swetenham bailiff 1417 | £1 4s. 10d. | £1 4s. 10d. | £1 4s. 10d. | Remained debt to 1439 (SC 6/796/4 m. 18d) |
| Arrears of William Honford and James Fitton, bailiffs 1421 | £10 10s. 6d. | £10 10s. 6d.* | | *In 1427 Honford and Fitton's total debt of £19 4s. 3d. agreed to be paid over the next two years in instalments |
| Arrears of Honford and Fitton as bailiffs 1422 | £8 13s. 9d. | £8 13s. 9d.* | | |
| Total | £50 9s. 1d. | £50 9s. 1d. ***£19 4s. 3d.*** | £31 4s. 10d. | |

## *(b) Macclesfield burgus*

| SC 6 | 794/3 m.15 1423 | 794/4 m.14d 1424 | 794/5 m.15d 1425 | |
|---|---|---|---|---|
| Richard Honne and John Glaskurion, accounting officials in 1422 | £3 19s. 9¼d. + 34 arrowheads ***£3 0s. 0d.*** | 19s. 9¼d. | 19s. 9¼d. | remained debt in 1439 (SC 6/796/4 m. 18d.) |

| SC 6 | 794/7 m.15d 1426 | 794/9 m.16d 1427 | 795/3 m.15d 1429 | |
|---|---|---|---|---|
| Richard Honne and John Glaskurion, accounting officials in 1422 | 19s. 9¼d. | 19s. 9¼d. | 19s. 9¼d. | remained debt in 1439 (SC 6/796/4 m. 18d.) |

Some points arising from the tables are worthy of further discussion. Some arrears were already worthy of the title 'contumacious' in 1422. The £30 fine in the hundred had been owing since 1412, when it was temporarily respited because its debtors claimed they had letters of pardon from the prince.[117] These were never shown, and the chamberlain William Troutbeck was, after the accession of Henry as king, ordered to levy this fine within one year from 1414.[118] This proved impossible, presumably because the group of local gentry simply refused to pay. It was similarly difficult to collect the sum due from William Sherd for the farm of Whaley Mill; in 1422 the mill was completely broken up and Sherd had left the county.[119]

Other debts were of a rather different kind. We should expect perhaps arrears in the first years of Queen Catherine's holding of Macclesfield dating back to the last years of Henry V's reign, if we accept the view that there was an average possible delay of two years in collecting issues. This seems to be validated by the fact that Honford and Fitton as bailiffs of the hundred were able to halve their debt within three years of 1422. Savage's debts as parker and forester were more serious, if only for their size. Certainly the size of the remainder in the forest had been rising considerably since 1420, possibly because Savage's absence overseas had led to a lack of surveillance. Of the balance of 1422 (£41 0s. 0¾d.) nothing had been delivered to the chamberlain.[120]

117 SC 6/806/5, m 1.
118 SC 6/806/8, m 1.
119 SC 6/807/3, m 2.
120 SC 6/807/3, m 3.

Possibly the transfer of the lordship to Catherine so shortly before the end of the accounting year – Henry V died on 31 August – had caused dislocation in the administration of the lordship. It is a salient comment upon Savage (or his deputies) that he could only raise another £20 within four years. Is it possible that these Macclesfield officials felt no compunction to deal with their arrears from the time of Henry V, despite the fact that several saw office again under Catherine?[121]

In 1427, or slightly earlier, the royal council had decided to do something about these arrears now that it was clear that they were not going to be cleared without interference.[122] John Fray, a baron of the royal Exchequer, and John Geryn, an auditor, were assigned to hear and terminate the accounts of the ministers of the palatinate, with specific powers to settle debts.[123] Several of the Macclesfield arrears were dealt with at this point. Honford and Fitton's debt was to be paid over the next two years. Savage's cumulative debt of £133 15s. 3¼d. was transferred to the escheator's account where Savage already owed some money for the farm of the manor of Adlington. Obviously it was deemed easier to deal with his debts in one account and it was arranged that they should be paid off over the next three-and-a-half years. The worst arrears were dealt with in 1427. The remainder were either too small to bother with or so decidedly contumacious that they were unlikely to be collected no matter what measures were applied. The only solution under such circumstances was exoneration, as happened in 1437 to Laurence Fitton for his share of a fine which dated back to the first decade of the century.

121 Thomas Swetenham and James Fitton were bailiffs of the hundred in 1431 (SC 6/795/5, m 16), Fitton also in 1427 (SC 6/794/9, m 16d).

122 Note that there is a possibility that the years 1425–7 saw a full examination of the Cheshire financial system, as suggested by the survival of several subsidiary documents for these years. See above pp. 92–3.

123 SC 6/794/9, m 15.

## The calculation of value

The calculation of value can be carried out in two main ways; the first is by using values from the period, as given in 'valors', the second is by modern calculation from the surviving account rolls. Valors are informative on the aims of baronial accounting and the question of the approach to profit. It has been claimed that they provide an impersonal assessment of economic yields rather than of the liability, honesty and efficiency of officials.[124] This is, of course, true if the figures given as the value of the individual units are of potential value (i.e. arrears and receipts minus expenses) rather than of actual value (i.e. liveries).

There are only two extant valors for this period which concern Cheshire revenues. The first is a valor of the issues and revenues of all the possessions of the prince of Wales which probably dates to 1403. The method used to arrive at the final Cheshire figure here (£425 1s. 4d.) is puzzling.[125] The second valor concerns only the prince's estates in the county itself and was undoubtedly compiled from the accounts of the various ministers of the county of the year 1402–3 since its heading reads 'according to the reply made there by the officials of the lord in the county' ('secundum quod responsum erat inde per ministros domini in eodem comitatu').[126] For most units, the value stated in this second valor is the net charge, i.e. current

124 *The Grey of Ruthin Valor: The Valor of the English Lands of Edmund Grey, Earl of Kent, Drawn up from the Ministers' Accounts of 1467–8*, ed. R. I. Jack (Sydney: Sydney University Press, 1965), pp. 80–9. See also C. D. Ross and T. B. Pugh, 'Materials for the Study of Baronial Incomes in the Fifteenth Century', *EcHR*, 2nd ser., 6 (1953–4), 185–94, at pp. 191–2, and R. R. Davies, 'Baronial Accounts', p. 214. On calculations of profit in general, see Oschinsky, *Walter of Henley*, p. 220 sq, and E. Stone, 'Profit and Loss Accounting at Norwich Cathedral Priory', *Transactions of the Royal Historical Society*, 5th ser., 12 (1962), 25–48, at p. 28.

125 SC 11/862, transcribed in Appendix VI and discussed below pp. 311–16. The county is given a total value of £824 14s. 10d. but £399 13s. 4d. is deducted for manors alienated and annuities and fees granted out.

126 SC 11/904, transcribed in Appendix V.

receipts minus current expenses, where there are any. These figures are thus the same as those given as the balance excluding arrears in the accounts of the year ending at Michaelmas 1403.[127] There are, however, some exceptions to this method of calculation. At Middlewich, the value given is of receipts alone; expenses of £4 10s. 9d. have not been deducted despite the fact that the Middlewich entry is supposedly 'beyond declared expenses' ('ultra reprisas declaro').[128] The sums stated in this second valor for the sheriff and escheator of the county are, in fact, actual value rather than potential. For the sheriff, the sum given is the liveries of issues;[129] for the escheator, the liveries of issues and arrears.[130] In the case of the Dee grinding mills, repairs and purchase of millstones accounted by the chamberlain in this year 1402–3 had been subtracted from the net charge to provide the figure entered on the valor,[131] despite the fact that £5 was allocated for the purchase of millstones on the expense side of the valor.[132] In the case of the Dee fulling mills, repairs accounted by the chamberlain had also been subtracted from the farm. For the most part, then, the sums stated on the second valor were the potential rather than the actual values of the units. Only in the case of the sheriff and escheator were actual values stated. The sums for each unit are then totalled to give the value of the county. The discharge is made up of potential rather than actual expenses.[133]

There are further casual references in other sources to the supposed value of certain of the demesnes. For instance, it was said in 1406 that Shotwick, although farmed for £10, was in

127 The relevant accounts are SC 6/774/15, 791/6 and 805/11.

128 SC 6/791/6, m 4.

129 SC 6/791/6, m 7.

130 SC 6/791/6, m 8.

131 The net charge was £162 6s. 6d. (SC 6/791/6, m 7) less £4 19s. 6d. for repairs and new millstones (SC 6/774/15, m 2d), to arrive at the valor figure of £157 7s. 0d.

132 SC 11/904 dorse.

133 For instance, £248 11s. 8d. was allowed for wages although only £178 10s. 3½d. was actually paid out. £329 8s. 6d. was allowed for annuities although £393 18s. 7½d. was paid (SC 6/774/15).

fact worth £26 13s. 4d. per annum.[134] This last sum bears a close relationship to both the net current charge and the liveries of the last complete year under direct comital control.[135] Values for Frodsham and Overmarsh were also stated on the valor of all the lands of the prince of Wales: the Frodsham value of £56 3s. 4d. is only 10 shillings less than that given on the Black Prince's valor of 1376,[136] and at the confirmation of the grant to Radegonde Béchet in 1386.[137] How the assessment of the value of Overmarsh was reached is not clear. Macclesfield was valued as £153 19s. 4d. overall in the valor. When it was granted to Queen Catherine in November 1422, it was valued at £66 5s. 4½d. plus £83 0s.10d. granted out in annuities.[138] This is not far off the total for the lordship in terms of the average annual livery from the various elements together (Table IV).

The method of calculation of value is important as regards the reliability of the sums stated. To take the potential value of one year may not have provided particularly illuminating results, although by this period most revenues did not show much fluctuation from one year to the next. It is significant that those revenues which did, such as the issues of the sheriff and escheator, were stated in terms of actual value.

To assess how typical the values stated on the 1403 Cheshire valor were, they have been compared with the 1403 liveries of issues and arrears, and both the average potential and actual values over the whole period. The results are given in Table IV. In general, the potential value of 1403 as expressed in the valor compares favourably with the average potential value over the period. As regards actual value, there could be significant yearly fluctuations, as in 1403, but overall, actual liveries corresponded well with potential value. This is very important as regards both the problem of the efficiency of administration and the collection of arrears. It is the question of the discrepancy

134 SC 6/791/10, m 3.

135 Net charge, £24 11s. 7d., liveries £25 6s. 9d. (SC 6/791/1, m 3).

136 C 47/9/57, m 7, Booth, *Financial Admin.* Appendix III.

137 *CPR 1385–9*, p. 202.

138 *PROME*, x. 46.

between potential and actual yield which takes us to the heart of the problem of the efficiency of seigneurial administration.[139] Actual value included money paid out of current issues as well as out of arrears. Because the annual average actual value compares favourably with the average current charge or potential value, this suggests yet again that little revenue remained uncollectable and that that which was lost in one year would be regained in another with little overall effect upon revenue as a whole. Often, too, annual actual revenue far exceeded annual potential revenue because of the payment of outstanding arrears. This situation parallels that found on other seigneurial estates in the fifteenth century.[140] Fluctuations in revenue from one year to the next were almost solely because of the rise and fall in arrears liveried.[141]

It is interesting that the same method of calculation was not used in the Cheshire valor of 1402–3 as had been in 1376 for a valor of the Black Prince's estates. In the earlier instance, figures from a series of three years were used although, according to Paul Booth, the overall result may have had a margin of error of 66%.[142] The reason for the method of calculation in 1402–3, which stated potential income, is revealed by the function of the valor produced at that point. Both this valor of Cheshire lands and that of all the prince's lands were the result of efforts to assess the maximum possible resources at the prince's disposal, to be expended upon both his regular expenses and the support of the garrisons of Wales in the early stages of the Welsh war, a topic we shall return to in Chapter 7. They were, therefore, an

139 See Jack, *Grey of Ruthin Valor*, p. 9, and Davies, 'Baronial Accounts', p. 219.

140 For instance, on Richard, duke of York's estates later in the century, a large percentage of arrears came from arrears, fluctuating between 16% and 80% and being generally around 30%–40% (J. T. Rosenthal, 'The Estates and Finances of Richard, Duke of York', *Studies in Medieval and Renaissance History*, 2 (1965), 115–204, at p. 152).

141 F. R. H. Du Boulay, 'A Rentier Economy in the Later Middle Ages: The Archbishopric of Canterbury', *EcHR*, 2nd ser., 16 (1964), 427–38, at p. 437.

142 Booth, *Financial Admin.*, pp. 40–1.

attempt to provide a guide to future income and expenditure by means of a full analysis of the sources and character of present potential income.[143]

## Table IV. Calculations of value, 1400–22

| | 1403 valor SC 11/904 (potential value) | 1403 livery to chamberlain SC 6/774/15 (actual value) | Average balance excl. arrears (potential value) | Average livery 1400–22 (actual value) |
|---|---|---|---|---|
| Chester city – sheriff | £102 12s. 4d. | £112 12s. 4d. | £103 13s. 10d. | £96 17s. 9d. |
| Chester city – escheator | 7s. 0d. | 7s. 0d. | £1 12s. 1½d. | 15s. 8d. |
| Dee corn mills | £157 7s. 0d. | £197 17s. 3½d.[a] | £178 6s. 2d.[a] | £172 0s. 9d.[a] |
| Dee fulling mills | £8 11s. 6½d. | £8 9s. 6½d.[b] | £10 10s. 0d.[a] | £10 10s. 0d.[a] |
| Delamere Forest | £44 15s. 8d. | £52 7s. 8½d. | £55 13s. 0d. | £52 7s. 0d. |
| Drakelow and Rudheath | £12 0s. 2d. | £25 1s. 7d. | £15 15s. 10d. | £16 18s. 8d. |
| Frodsham | £56 3s. 4d.[c] | | £41 18s. 5d.[d] | £41 6s. 8d.[d] |
| Middlewich | £43 3s. 9½d. | £49 15s. 5½d. | £48 17s. 2d. | £46 11s. 10d. |
| Northwich | £28 8s. 10d. | £40 11s. 10d. | £26 19s. 9½d.[e] | £27 7s. 5d.[e] |
| Overmarsh | £10 0s. 0d.[c] | | | |
| Shotwick | £10 2s. 3d. | £6 15s. 7d. | £7 19s. 0d.[e] | £7 15s. 2d.[e] |
| Macclesfield hundred | £24 14s. 8d. | £29 1s. 3d. | £30 8s. 5d.[f] | £22 9s. 3d.[f] |
| Macclesfield *burgus* | £23 0s. 7½d. | £38 10s. 10¾d. | £21 19s. 3d.[f] | £20 11s. 0d.[f] |
| Macclesfield Forest | £106 4s. 0½d. | £194 2s. 7d. | £88 8s. 6d.[f] | £83 11s. 3d.[f] |

143 See Ross and Pugh, 'Materials', p. 192.

| | **1403 valor SC 11/904 (potential value)** | **1403 livery to chamberlain SC 6/774/15 (actual value)** | **Average balance excl. arrears (potential value)** | **Average livery 1400–22 (actual value)** |
|---|---|---|---|---|
| Macclesfield park | nil[g] | | £3 2s. 0d.[f] | £3 6s. 0d.[f] |
| Sheriff of county | £180 18s. 8½d. | £216 18s. 3½d. | £196 16s. 5d. | £171 14s. 0d. |
| Escheator of county | £50 1s. 3d. | £50 1s. 3½d. | £220 7s. 9d.[h] | £122 9s. 9d.[h] |

[a] The sums are given without taking into account any deductions for repairs or purchase of millstones. [b] See below p. 163. [c] SC 11/862. [d] Covering 1409–22 only. [e] Covering 1400–10 only. [f] A sample of 19 years as there are no accounts extant for 1400, 1409 and 1411. [g] Nil as the herbage therein had been granted for no render to John Kingsley. [h] A sample of 21 years as there is no account extant for 1415.

## CHAPTER 3

# *The Economy of the Demesne*

### Rents

As demesne leasing became the norm in England after the Black Death, the move was towards a seigneurial economy where tenant rents formed the basis and backbone of income for all kind of lords. Sixty per cent of the manorial revenue of the archbishops of Canterbury, for instance, came from rents collected by their reeves, and tenant rents formed the most important element in the manorial income of the Percy earls of Northumberland.[1] The relative contribution to the earl of Chester of rents varied from manor to manor, depending upon the nature of the rent and indeed of the manor itself, as we shall see in this review of rental income from each location.

Where the earl had largely lost control of tenurial arrangements, rents contributed very little because they were merely token. So at Middlewich and Northwich, a static small rent called 'Kingesmole' was paid on certain properties, but its revenue formed only a small proportion of total income – about 6% at Northwich and 4% at Middlewich.[2] The earl gathered no revenue from arable lands held by the townsmen in neighbouring townships, although certain tenements where 'Kingesmole' was not payable could be leased separately.[3] In the account of the bailiffs of the hundred of Macclesfield, the

1 F. R. H. Du Boulay, 'Who were Farming the English Demesnes at the End of the Middle Ages', *EcHR*, 2nd ser., 17 (1965), 443–55 at p. 446; J., M. W. Bean, *The Estates of the Percy Family 1416–1537* (London: Oxford University Press, 1958), p. 15.

2 Other tolls payable in connection with salt manufacture in the Wiches may also have had some relation with tenure but this is difficult to know for this late period.

3 For instance, from 1420 a 'placea' near to the Moothall in Middlewich was rented out on a 20-year lease at 6s. 8d. per annum (SC 6/793/11, m 4).

only income was from perquisites of justice and rents of some manors held of the manor of Macclesfield in socage.[4] Rents, at £6 6s. 8d. per annum, provided on average 20% of the total income.

In the *burgus* of Macclesfield, however, rents, at slightly over £14 per annum, formed 60% of the charge side of the account up to 1412, thence increasing to 73% for the remainder of the period as income from other sources declined. At Drakelow and Rudheath, tenant rents provided the whole manorial income save for a little from time to time from the perquisites of court. On the other two 'rural' manors, Shotwick and Frodsham, tenant rents contributed 25% and 42% respectively of the total income. Rents were payable by certain townships in Delamere Forest, £17 12s. 4d. from frithmote and £3 8s. 0d. in lieu of a rent, probably for free agistment originally taken in kind. The frithmote and custom had stood at these values in 1398 when granted in their entirely to John Done snr. [5] Together these formed around 40% of the forest income. In Macclesfield Forest, tenant rents were paid as in a normal manorial structure. At £68 per annum or more, they made up 60% to 65% of the total annual charge. The city of Chester paid a fee farm of £100 per annum, in addition to a few miscellaneous rents.

By this period, almost all tenant rents were taken in money, although certain were still taken in kind. The six pounds of pepper due for chamber rents in the city was given to the auditors regularly as a supplement to their fee,[6] or else was sold and the profit accruing accounted by the chamberlain. Arrowheads were due for certain rents in Macclesfield Forest and *burgus*. In some years these appear actually to have been delivered, but often a severe backlog built up which caused concern.[7]

4 Booth, *Financial Admin.*, p. 113.

5 CHES 2/71, m 38 (16, 17), *36 DKR*, p. 154. See also B. M. C. Hussain, 'Delamere Forest in Later Medieval Times', *THSLC*, 107 (1955), 29–39, at p. 38. Done later surrendered this grant and received in lieu an annuity of £10 to be taken from the same source. See below p. 255 n. 72.

6 For instance, SC 6/793/1, m 1.

7 See SC 6/806/1, m 1d and SC 6/806/4, m 1d.

Although rents were clearly important in the context of the earl's demesne revenue, their shortcoming was their static nature. Once settled and recorded in a rental, there was little scope for increasing revenue from this source. Most of these Cheshire demesne rents had been established for a long while as assized rents, and, save for Macclesfield where a new rental had been drawn up in 1383, there was no conscious move in this period to keep rentals up to date.[8] Very little new land was brought into cultivation or formed into new tenant holdings. In addition, there are few instances of an increase in the rent of pre-existing holdings. Where burgage rents were concerned, there was inevitably little scope for increase or indeed for realistic assessment. In the Macclesfield *burgus*, by 1413 only 2s. 9d. worth of rent had been added to the value of the 1383 rental.[9] This was achieved by the renting out of a new shop underneath the hall of pleas, along with some land near the lord's fold recently taken into cultivation. But the increase in revenue from these new rents was somewhat offset by the reduction in rent of two other shops from 9s. 6d. in 1383 to 8s. 0d. in 1413.

Of course, within the town itself there would be little new land available, but we might expect ample scope for the creation of new holdings or the enlargement of existing holdings in Macclesfield Forest. The assized rents of each township in the forest were established by the 1383–4 rental, where they were itemized by tenement.[10] In certain cases, extra income had arisen since 1383 in the form of increased rents, or rents from lands newly taken into cultivation. Table V displays the increase in income from rent in Macclesfield Forest over the period 1383 to 1421. The first column gives the rental of 1383,

8 This contrasts sharply with contemporary policy in the duchy of Lancaster where there was a move to keep rentals up to date because the charges of the ministers' accounts were based on them. Robert Somerville interprets this as true concern for the maintenance and improvement of revenues (*History of the Duchy of Lancaster*, 1: *1265–1603* (London: Duchy of Lancaster, 1953), p. 174).

9 SC 6/806/6, m 1d, compared with SC 11/898, m 1d.

10 SC 11/898, mm 2–5.

the second the total rent of each township in 1421.[11] The third column gives details of any increases in the rents of pre-existing holdings, and the fourth, rents of lands taken into cultivation since 1383. Because of the decrease in rents at Sutton, the increase in income over the period was 16s. 0¾d., although 18s. 7¼d. of new and increased rents had been added.

## Table V. Rents in Macclesfield Forest, 1383–1422

| Township | 1383 | 1421 | incrementum | 'new lands' |
|---|---|---|---|---|
| Sutton | £26 11s. 10¼d. | £26 12s. 6¼d.[12] | 10½d. | 2s. 4d. |
| Astbury | 8s. 4d. | 8s. 4d. | | |
| Rainow | £8 1s. 11¼d. | £8 5s. 3¾d. | 6d. | 2s. 10½d. |
| Hurdsfield | £4 8s. 9½d. | £4 9s. 6d. | | 8½d. |
| Pott Shrigley | £5 19s. 6¼d. | £6 3s. 8¾d. | | 4s. 2½d. |
| Stanley | £1 1s. 10½d. | £1 1s. 10½d. | | |
| Disley | £4 2s. 0d. | £4 5s. 1d. | | 3s. 1d. |
| Yeardsley | £5 11s. 11½d. | £5 11s. 11½d. | | |
| Kettleshulme | £4 4s. 6¼d. | £4 6s. 0¼d. | | 1s. 6d. |
| Upton | 15s. 4d. | 15s. 4d. | | |
| Bollington | £5 3s. 7d. | £5 3s. 7½d. | ½d. | |
| Holyncete in Sutton | 6s. 8d. | 6s. 8d. | | |
| Thorncete in Sutton | 6d. | 6d. | | |
| Wincle in Sutton | 13s. 4d. | 13s. 4d. | | |

11 SC 6/807/2, m 2.

12 Rents in Sutton had been reduced by 2s. 6½d. for no specified reason.

| Township | 1383 | 1421 | incrementum | 'new lands' |
|---|---|---|---|---|
| 'Esynge'[13] | | 3d. | | 3d. |
| Irdswall | | ¾d. | | ¾d. |
| Toddestlick | | 1s. 0d. | | 1s. 0d. |
| Le Fence | | 1d. | | 1d. |
| 1½ acres in the forest, location unspecified | | 1s. 0d. | | 1s. 0d. |
| Total | £78 6s. 5¼d. | £79 2s. 6d. | 1s. 5d. | 17s. 1¼d. |

Most of the new tenements were small plots assarted by various tenants from waste land in the forest. At Pott Shrigley, where the greatest increase took place, eight new plots had been taken into cultivation, ranging in size from one rod to 3½ acres, as outlined in Table VI.

## Table VI. Assarts in Macclesfield Forest

| | | | |
|---|---|---|---|
| Before 1399 | 1 rod | John Togod | 2d. |
| 1393–4 | 1 rod | Geoffrey del Dounes[14] | 2d. |
| 1393–4 | 3½ acres | Geoffrey del Dounes | 2s. 4d. |
| 1393–4 | 3 rods | John Shrigley | 6d. |
| 1393–4 | 1 rod | John Togod | 2d. |
| 1398–9 | 1 acre | John del Dounes[15] | 8d. |
| 1402 | ½ acre | Robert Brocklehurst | 4d.[16] |
| 1415 | a parcel | John Hurle | ½d.[17] |

In general, increases to the area under cultivation were small and were made by tenants who already held land in

13 'A clearing': Dodgson, *Place Names*, i. 119.

14 Geoffrey already held 4 acres and 1 rod in 1383. A William del Dounes held 96½ acres in the same township (SC 11/898, m 4).

15 Son of Geoffrey del Dounes.

16 SC 2/255/4, m 2d.

17 SC 2/255/11, m 5d.

that particular township, possibly to straighten boundaries of their tenements, or to join up strips. Certain assarts elsewhere were taken up as complete holdings.[18] Overall, only about seventeen acres were taken into cultivation in this period. Nor could there be a wholesale increase in the rents of pre-existing tenements. Advantage was taken of some land transfers to increase individual rents,[19] but such cases were very few. In fact, there had been no increase either in individual rents or the area under cultivation since 1417. Many of these new tenements had already been taken into cultivation before 1400. By 1401, 11s. 11½d. had been added to the value of the rental,[20] and after 1401 an additional 6s. 7¾d. An experiment had been made with the township of Bollington. Up to 1393 it had been farmed, together with its mill, for £6 per annum. In this year, Queen Anne's ministers had taken it back in hand, hoping to make a larger profit.[21] This recovery had been a failure in terms of financial benefit. The mill had fallen into decay and so brought in no revenue, and the rents remained at the same level as in the 1383 rental, save for a ½d *incrementum* for permission to enter a parcel of waste in 1411.[22] Admittedly, it was noted in the accounts that the Queen's council had not been adequately informed in 1393.

The scope for increasing income from rent was thus very limited. Possibly, the need to increase the rent of every holding every time it changed hands was deemed unnecessary by the fact that entry fines (*ingressus*) were levied upon such occasions. At Macclesfield, in both the *burgus* and forest, such entry fines were levied at the rate of twice the annual rent of the holding, but profits so raised were accounted under perquisites of justice rather than within the accounting for rents because transactions

18 For instance, 'Esynge' (SC 6/805/7, m 3).

19 For instance, 2½ acres in Rainow, paying a rent of 1s. 8d. in 1383 (SC 11/898, m 3d) were forfeited by their tenant in 1403, William Edmanston, because he had been outlawed for murder. They were taken up in the same year by John Dixon (SC 6/805/11, m 3).

20 SC 6/805/7, m 3.

21 SC 6/805/7, m 3.

22 SC 6/806/5, m 3.

were made in the relevant manorial courts. When new land was taken into cultivation, the entry fine was levied at a higher rate, generally at six times the intended annual rent.[23] However, such entry fines did not offset low and stagnant rents. At Frodsham, for instance, rents had shown little increase since the mid-fourteenth century, and although additional income accrued from possibly both communal and individual entry fines, this was cancelled out by decayed rents.[24]

### *Rents at Drakelow and Shotwick*

The problem of the static nature of rents was offset in the assessionable manors of the duchy of Cornwall by re-leasing tenant holdings on average every seven years. Although rents there also remained fixed, the assession fines, levied at the releasing and payable over the first six years of a seven-year *conventio,* were regularly adjusted according to the valuation of the tenement by Duchy officials, and potential tenants, and according to demand.[25] At both Drakelow and Shotwick, there appears to have been some attempt to create a similar system in order to combat the problem of fixed rents.

As we have noted, tenant rents formed by far the most important element in income at Drakelow. Rents of free tenements, settled in 1371 at £25 8s. 8d., made up slightly under 50% of the rent total. The remaining lands were leased to 'termors' for a certain number of years and so the opportunity for reassessment, and for the imposition of a large communal entry fine, was afforded at the end of the term of the lease.[26] This method had been established by the Black Prince when the manor of Drakelow had been newly created out of the waste of

23 For instance, SC 2/255/11, m 5d.

24 See below p. 131.

25 John Hatcher, *Rural Economy and Society in the Duchy of Cornwall 1300–1500* (Cambridge: Cambridge University Press, 1970), p. 53.

26 Other landlords in the county may have employed a similar system. There are references to 'terminarii' as tenants of Sir Richard Vernon in his manors of Haslington, Minshull, Picton and Hurleston (E 163/6/41, item 24).

Rudheath, although the strategy had not proved as successful as in Cornwall. By the late fourteenth century, the term involved at Drakelow was generally twenty years. The tenements had been leased to tenants in 1388 for this term at a total rent of £19 3s. 9d.[27] Certain lands left in the earl's hands after this lease, presumably for lack of tenants in 1388, were disposed of separately later. The 1388 lease was due to expire in 1407, but in 1402, with no explanation being given, the rent due was reduced to £17 14s. 7d,[28] and remained at this level up to and including the account of 1407.[29] In January 1408, the escheator and two other commissioners came to the manor and reviewed the tenements.[30] They were re-leased in February 1408 again for a term of twenty years.[31] But it had proved impossible to increase the value of the rental. Income from this source remained at £17 14s. 7d. for the rest of the period. However, in conjunction with this re-leasing, a communal entry fine of £16 10s. 7½d. was imposed, to be paid within three years at the same times of the year, Martinmas and the Nativity of Saint John the Baptist (11 November and 24 June), as the rent itself was payable.[32] It had been paid off by 1411 in six instalments of £2 15s. 1¼d. accounted under the perquisites of court.[33]

A similar system of periodic reassessment would appear to have been employed at the manor of Shotwick. Whilst the manor was in the earl's hands, £6 15s. 11d. was received in assized rents. In 1400 and 1401, certain tenements were paying increased rents, to a total of £1 8s. 7d.[34] The manor was leased to Richard Moston from April 1401, but when it was taken back in hand after his death in 1408, opportunity was taken to reassess the rents of certain tenements, some of which had

27 CHES 2/60, m 3 (12), *36 DKR*, p. 413.
28 SC 6/791/5, m 1.
29 SC 6/792/2, m 1d.
30 SC 6/792/3, m 1d.
31 CHES 2/81, m 4 (2), *36 DKR*, p. 413, The calendar inaccurately gives the date of this re-lease as 27 Feb 1407.
32 SC 6/792/3, m 1d.
33 SC 6/792/8, m 1d.
34 SC 6/791/1, m 3, 791/3, m 3.

already been paying an increased rent at the beginning of the period. This provided an *incrementum* of £3 1s. 7d. in 1408 and £3 6s. 9d. in 1409 and 1410.[35] Some of these increases seem to have been implemented by Moston; it was said in 1408 that the increase in rents was as described in a rental made by him. Some of the increases of 1409 were detailed in the court roll of June 1408.[36] Tenants are seen here taking up their tenements for a term of ten years but, unlike Drakelow, certainly not all tenements were being reassessed on such a basis.

Only at Shotwick was there any considerable degree of *incrementum*, suggesting that in the county at this time there was no great demand for tenements, such as might have resulted in higher rents. Rents in the county remained low at between, for instance, 6d. to 1s. per acre in Macclesfield Forest and 6½d. to 2s. per acre at Frodsham. Significantly, at Drakelow, where a favourable assessment for the lord in 1408 had proved impossible, presumably owing to lack of tenant demand, rents were as low as 4d.–6d. per acre,[37] whereas at Shotwick, where there was more pressure on land and hence the possibility of higher rents, between 1s. 4d. and 3s. 0d. per acre was being charged.[38] On the other hand, there is no suggestion that rents were having to be reduced to persuade tenants to take up holdings. On the whole the picture was one of stagnation. In 1422, some land in Rainow had been seized into the lord's hands because it had been forfeited by William Tomlinson. Despite the fact that a public proclamation was made to the effect that it would be given to the highest bidder, it could only be re-let at the same rate as previously.[39] Where lands were seized for non-payment of rent, there appeared no difficulty in finding a new tenant, but only at the same rent. For instance, in the Macclesfield halmote of July 1400, the heirs of Richard

35 Respectively, SC 792/3, m 3, 792/5, m 2, 792/6, m 2.

36 SC 2/156/13, m 2. The demesne and fishery were also leased at this court.

37 SC 6/792/9, m 1d; CHES 2/92, m 5 (7), 37 DKR, p. 167.

38 SC 6/791/1, m 3, SC 2/156/13, mm 2–2d.

39 SC 2/255/19, m 2d.

Rydale of Sutton were ordered to satisfy a debt of rent owed to the earl, under threats that if they did not, then their tenements would be forfeit. Their lands were in fact seized at this halmote, but by November of the same year, they had been taken up by a new tenant, Richard Swytelegh.[40]

## *Decayed rents*

To weigh against the stagnation of rents and the lord's relative inability to increase revenue from this source, we should note there was a very low level of decayed rents. In other words, there was enough demand to ensure the continuing occupation of tenements, and to avoid abandonment of occupancy and cultivation. The lord may have had a limited income from rents but it was a regular and reliable one, assuming at least that such rents were actually collectable. In Macclesfield Forest, twelve individual holdings, ranging in size from a cottage to 20 acres, were at some time in the hands of the lord, to the loss of £2 6s. 0d. per annum. Some of these tenements had already been out of cultivation in 1383. There are, in addition, two examples of rent being reduced to attract tenants, to a further loss of 12s. 8d. per annum.[41] In the halmote of July 1417, the bailiff of the forest was ordered to take in hand two small tenements in Kettleshulme and Disley. The tenants had not put their hands to their tenements, so that now the latter were empty and uncultivated, and no profit could be taken.[42] Such losses were not written off lightly. On four occasions, inquiries were ordered into decayed rents in Macclesfield Forest, but no favourable outcome was evidently possible.[43]

Such decayed rents should not be taken as indicative of economic malaise, however. The sum lost amounted to very little in financial terms – c. 4% of the potential income from rent. Some lands may have fallen into decay because they were

40 SC 2/255/3, m 1d; SC 2/255/4, m 2d.

41 For instance, SC 6/805/7, m 3.

42 SC 2/255/13, m 9.

43 SC 6/805/14, m 2d, 805/16, m 2d, 806/1, m 2d, and 807/1, m 3.

of poor quality. The 1383 rental of Macclesfield, for instance, refers to some tenements where the rocky terrain hampered cultivation.[44] This may explain the fact that once they had fallen out of cultivation they were not taken up again, despite the relative buoyancy, at least in the demand for land. What is significant is that no further tenements fell into decay in Macclesfield Forest after 1399.

Significantly, there is no evidence of decayed rents at Shotwick where the most increase in rent value is seen. The amount lost in decayed rents at Frodsham fluctuated from year to year, but was generally around £2 10s. 0d. per annum, or 9.4% of the value of the rental. 'Decasus' (decayed rents) formed a definite category in the discharge, signifying perhaps that a regular, but small, loss was to be expected. Loss of revenue occurred either through lack of a tenant, the dilapidation of the tenement itself, or by the enforced reduction in the rent charged in order to find a tenant. Only in the township of Mickledale were decayed rents a problem; of a total rental of £1 13s. 0¼d., 19s. 9¼d. was lost in 1409 and 1410.[45] Otherwise, many of the tenements lying unoccupied were smallholdings.

Quite substantial sums were lost in decayed rents at Middlewich in the first five years of the period, indeed at up to 25% of the total rental.[46] However, it was at Drakelow and Rudheath that the problem of decayed rents was at its most intransigent. Difficulties arose when tenements fell vacant after the re-leasing. In 1400, £1 11s. 11¾d. was allowed for tenancies lying in the lord's hands for lack of tenants.[47] Rather than continuing to account this as 'decasus', it is likely that the rental was reduced to take into account such decay as a permanent feature. In 1407, the Merefield had been re-leased at £1 6s. 4d. per annum, but it was lying vacant by 1409, and when leased again in 1410, the rent had to be reduced to £1 4s. 0d. for the

44 SC 11/898, mm 4, 4d.
45 SC 6/792/5, m 10d, SC 6/792/6, m 6d.
46 SC 6/791/1, m 4 to SC 6/791/7, m 4.
47 SC 6/791/1, m 1d.

remaining seventeen years of the twenty year term.[48] Another plot fell into the lord's hands in 1415; no one was willing to pay the accustomed rent or take it into cultivation.[49] By 1422, this plot was still in the lord's hands and the Merefield still had to be leased at the lower rate. In addition, lands in Bradford worth 7s. 0d. per annum were in the lord's hands for lack of a tenant. The justiciar, chamberlain and auditors had carried out an examination of the rental of the lordship in this year, and had acknowledged further decasus of £1 11s. 7d. The total of decayed rents was respited, in the hope that new tenants could be found for these tenements.[50] Tenants could not be found for certain free tenements, also in the earl's hands.[51] Income from rents at Drakelow thus underwent continuous decrease, with more and more lands falling into the lord's hands, which it was not always possible to lease out again. Possibly, tenants were finding cultivation on the heath as unprofitable as the earl now experienced. Other evidence, primarily judicial, points to a small population in this area, and hence perhaps a lack of tenants willing to take up new holdings. The fall in population may in its turn have been caused by migration, if the difficulties in eking out a living there had proved too onerous.

In general, income from rents in the county displays the same tendencies as elsewhere, in that it fluctuated but only slightly as holdings fell vacant or were taken up again.[52] Save for one or two local exceptions, decayed rents were negligible. It is difficult, because of such a tendency, to use rent as an indicator of economic trends. Yet the same trend is not shown in the duchy of Cornwall where the first quarter of the fifteenth century witnessed an exceptional growth in land values,[53] nor

48 SC 6/792/6, m 1d.
49 SC 6/793/1, m 2.
50 SC 6/794/2, m 2d.
51 SC 6/794/2, m 8.
52 F. R. H. Du Boulay, 'A Rentier Economy in the Later Middle Ages: The Archbishopric of Canterbury', *Economic History Review*, 2nd ser., 16 (1964), 427–38, at p. 436.
53 Hatcher, *Rural Economy*, p. 149.

indeed on the estates of Leicester Abbey where there was a 33⅓% fall in income from rents in the period 1341–1477.[54]

## *Evidence of sub-letting*

Furthermore, the rental and income from rents as recorded on the earl's accounts can be proved to be totally misleading. It is clear that the profits he gained from tenant rents were exceeded by the rents which his own tenants could raise from subletting the tenements they rented from him. This is most notably evidenced by the survival of a rental of property in Macclesfield *burgus* and forest held by John de Macclesfield,[55] where we have information on both the rent de Macclesfield paid to the lord, and that which he received from his own subtenants. This rental was drawn up in 1415. At that point, de Macclesfield held a total of 23 burgages in Macclesfield, one fifth of the total of 123 burgages. For these, he paid £1 3s. 0d. to the earl, at the standard rate of 1s. per burgage. He paid a further 17s. 8d. to other tenants from whom he held, as subtenant, three-and-a-half burgages out of his twenty-three. His total outgoing rent was then £2 0s. 8d., but his rental itemises rent received from subtenants occupying these burgages to a total of £8 18s. 0d.. Hence he profited to the tune of £6 17s. 4d. In some cases, the discrepancy between the rent received by the earl and that received by de Macclesfield was strikingly large. A half burgage rendered 6d. to the earl, but 6s. 6d. to de Macclesfield. Three tenements in the market place and two shops below ground level rendered 1s. 4d. in rent to the earl, but £2 6s. 8d. to de Macclesfield. Nor was this his maximum profit: five and three-quarter burgages lay in decay, so that he received no rent for these, although he still had to pay their accustomed rents to the earl.[56] He held further non-burgage tenements in the town.

54 R. H. Hilton, *The Economic Development of some Leicestershire Estates in the Fourteenth and Fifteenth Centuries* (London: Oxford University Press, 1947), p. 86.

55 BL, Cotton MS Cleopatra D VI, f. 196 and following. For more on de Macclesfield see below pp. 225–7.

56 For his principal tenement where he himself lived, he paid one shilling

Taking these and the burgages together, he received £17 17s. 9d. in rents, after expenses and decayed rents had been deducted. Out of the sum, he paid £3 3s. 3d. in rents to the earl and his own chief tenants. His total profit from rents was £14 14s. 6d., more in fact than the earl himself received from rents in the *burgus*. In the town fields and forest, he held further lands which were also sublet at a profit. In the township of Sutton, for instance, he held lands to the value of £4 17s. 6d., yet paid to the earl only £1 4s. 7d. He had recently acquired lands in Mottram, Macclesfield and Sutton, formerly held by John de Mottram, lately bailiff of the forest. For these he paid 16s. 0¼d. to the earl but took in rent himself a further £3 4s. 9½d.

The information provided then by this rental reveals a quite startling state of affairs. The earl's rents bore no relation to the economic, potential and actual value of his tenements. Nor did they reflect the true demand for tenements. If de Macclesfield was able to charge such high rents, then there must surely have been a very high demand for land. It is not surprising, therefore, that the earl experienced little decay in rents in Macclesfield *burgus*, when tenants were prepared to pay the economic rent to de Macclesfield. To some extent, the situation in Macclesfield may have been exceptional, although de Macclesfield was certainly not the only tenant making such vast profits from subletting. Roger Jodrell received £2 15s. 6d. from the rents of his lands in Whaley from his subtenants, but paid only 12s. 0d. to the earl.[57]

The situation in the Wiches must have been very similar, for there the earl's income from rents was totally divorced from the economic value of the tenements, and certainly there was much subleasing at sums far in excess of their render to the lord. Subleasing was also well advanced in Frodsham.[58] Where

to the earl because it contained one burgage, and 3s. 6d. to the heirs of Roger de Bower (BL, Cotton MS Cleopatra D VI, f. 196v). He had a barn converted to his own use which also contained a burgage, so in both cases he received no rent himself (f. 197).

57 JRRIL, Jodrell MS 6. Richard de Morton received rent of £1 0s. 6½d. but unfortunately we do not know how much he paid to the earl (BL, Additional Charter 37,248).

58 See below p. 203.

it was at a reasonably high level, then it is likely that there was a similar situation as regards the uneconomic nature of the earl's income from rents as in Macclesfield. The earl's rentals then, emphasise the fossilised nature of his income from this source, which his enterprising tenants could turn to their own advantage. The profits which de Macclesfield and his kind made were at the earl's expense. Whereas the latter was hidebound by custom, they possessed a much greater freedom of action. Even if theoretically illegal in customary tenure, subletting was on a scale where legal niceties would be completely overwhelmed by economic reality.

## Leases of manors and agricultural profits

The debate over the relative virtues and profitability of direct exploitation (where the lord's officials oversaw the actual cultivation) as opposed to the leasing out of agricultural resources had already been settled in the earl's estates in the county by the late fourteenth century. Experiment in the mid-fourteenth century had proved that competitive leasing was profitable.[59] By the early fifteenth century, there was no direct exploitation, but within the basic policy of leasing there were two broad choices to be made: the first to hold onto the manor and to lease out demesnes and miscellaneous profits individually, the second to farm out manors in their entirety. Clearly, within these alternatives, there lay much room for experiment, displaying the pragmatic nature of medieval estate administration.

The tendency in the early years of our period was to keep manors in hand and to lease the various elements individually. In part, this was a reaction against the policy of Richard II who, in both Cheshire and Cornwall, had sanctioned the alienation

59 P. H. W. Booth, 'The Financial Administration of the Lordship and County of Chester 1272–1377', unpublished MA thesis (University of Liverpool, 1974) pp. 206–8, 220 and following. Other lords in Cheshire had also ended direct exploitation. Sir Richard Vernon, for instance, leased his demesne at Haslington for 10 marks per annum in the early fifteenth century (E 163/6/41 item 24).

of many units, generally for the sake of patronage. In 1399, for example, Frodsham, Middlewich and Northwich were all granted out for no render,[60] although Richard had recently recovered Northwich by exchange with John Holland.[61] After 1399, Frodsham, Shotwick and Northwich were all, at some point, the subject of grants, but only Shotwick and Northwich were ever leased as whole manors. A detailed discussion of these leases is necessary to understand the general estates policy of the Lancastrians.

### *Leases of whole manors*

The lease to Richard Moston of the manor of Shotwick on 27 April 1401 displays more characteristics of an instance of patronage than of profit making.[62] First, it was for life, unlike the Northwich leases which were for a specified term of years, and therefore endured until his death in March 1408. Secondly, the lease, at its rate of £10 per annum, was clearly not economic; in 1406, it was noted that the manor was farmed at this rate despite the fact that it was worth 40 marks (£26 13s. 4d.) or more per annum.[63] Such a tendency for the size of the farm to bear no relation to true market values was typical of the policy towards the lands of the crown in general.[64] Shotwick was considerably more valuable, both in actual and potential terms, in the years in which it was directly controlled. Liveries of £25 6s. 9d. were made in 1400 before the grant was made.[65] After it was taken back in hand in 1408 it rendered £30 16s. 9d., and in the following year £36 12s. 7d..[66]

60 See pp. 13, 16
61 SC 6/790/10, m 2d. The exchange is dated 15 Jan 1398 (*CPR 1396–9*, p. 467).
62 SC 6/791/3, m 3d.
63 SC 6/791/10, m 3.
64 B. B. Wolffe, *The Royal Demesne in English History: The Crown Estate in the Governance of the Realm from the Conquest to 1509* (London: Allen and Unwin, 1971) p. 69.
65 SC 6/791/1, m 3, when its remainder was £20 9s. 4d..
66 SC 6/792/3, m 3 (when its remainder was £37 13s. 4d.); SC 6/792/5, m 2 (when the livery was of the total sum of the remainder).

It is likely that Moston's lease of April 1401 was granted in lieu of an annuity of £10 which had been paid to him out of the issues of Shotwick on the account of 1400–1.[67] He already had a grant of 20 marks from forfeitures in London in 1400,[68] and in February 1404 he was granted the stewardship of the lordship of Dunham for as long as the latter should remain in the prince's hands.[69] In addition, it is highly likely that Moston was an absentee lessee since he held various offices in the household of Henry of Monmouth. As clerk of the prince's pantry and butlery from 1401 to 1404, he was responsible for the payment of wages of certain household officials.[70] Significantly, Moston would be in the county in these years when the prince was using Chester as his headquarters for the conduct of the Welsh War. In 1401, Shotwick Park was used to pasture stock from the Welsh manors of the prince which were to be used for his larder.[71] It is tempting to think that Moston, by virtue of his domestic offices, supervised this pasturing and so became aware of the potential profit to be made from a lease of the manor. Increased revenues from the manor after Moston's death in March 1408 suggest that he had indeed managed to increase issues and so gain some profit from his lease.[72] He may therefore have offered to take the manor to farm because he anticipated financial remuneration. With the lease settled at such an uneconomic rate, he could hardly have failed to make a profit. There is sufficient evidence to demonstrate that Exchequer valuations of the royal demesne allowed financial returns to farmers far beyond what we might regard as reasonable.[73]

Moston's own involvement in Shotwick's manorial administration in these years is difficult to establish but it is

67 SC 6/791/3, m 3d.

68 *CPR 1399–1401*, p. 188.

69 CHES 2/77, m 7 (1, 2), *36 DKR*, p. 354.

70 E 101/404/16, mm 2–4. See also E101/404/23 and E 101/405/26.

71 SC 6/791/3, m 3.

72 SC 6/792/2, m 3. The date of his death halfway through the accounting year meant that Moston's farm was accounted up to Michaelmas 1407.

73 Wolffe, *Royal Demesne*, p. 99.

possible he employed the same officials as the earl. Roger de Ashley made liveries of the farm in 1405 and can be shown to have been reeve after the manor was taken back in hand in 1408.[74] The existing parker, William de Helegh, certainly remained in office until he was replaced by John Brounwynd in September 1403.[75] By the terms of the lease, Moston was responsible for the parker's wages. In addition, Moston was responsible for the cost of repairs in both the manor and the park, and was to prepare the park and hold it freely available should the prince wish to use it. Enough pasture was to be maintained in the park for the prince's beasts. The lease would seem therefore to be pleasing to both parties. The prince's council may have regarded direct control of the manor as irksome, because income arose from divers sources, none of which were especially profitable. The lease to Moston fulfilled two needs, favour and financial return. Significantly too, the manor of Shotwick already had some tradition before 1399 of being released from comital control, and was to be let out again in later decades.[76] It is not surprising that it was granted to William Porter, another close associate of the prince without Cheshire links, in 1410 for no render.[77]

Northwich, too, may be a special case, in that direct control of the town by the prince may have been regarded as a temporary measure until it should be restored to the Hollands. However, his advisors were quite adamant that the town should be kept in the earl's hands, at least in the early years of the period. On 26 March 1403, a lease and accompanying recognizance were enrolled in the Chester exchequer.[78] By the lease, the town with its mills, ovens, courts and all other profits were to be taken to farm by Hugh Winnington for three years at 70 marks per annum. The Winningtons were a Northwich family. Hugh

74 SC 6/791/7, m 3.

75 SC 6/775/9, m 4.

76 See, for instance, CHES 2/57, m 1d. (3, 6), *36 DKR*, p. 80, for 1385, and CHES 2/125, m 4d. (6), *37 DKR*, p. 720, for 1425.

77 See below p. 246.

78 CHES 2/76, m 4 (2, 3), *36 DKR*, p. 532.

Winnington himself was described as constable of the town in 1406.[79] He also held the custody of the heiress of William Bate of Northwich along with her lands in the town, and had married her to his son, Hamo.[80] A John Winnington was steward of Northwich in 1415,[81] and receiver of Kingesmole in the later Holland administration.[82] Richard Winnington had leased the town of Northwich from John Holland snr in 1395,[83] and despite involvement on the Percy side at Shrewsbury in 1403, served in subsequent commissions in the hundred of Eddisbury.[84] He held several *saline* (salt houses) in the town.[85]

Hugh Winnington certainly entered into possession of the town,[86] but by 28 April 1403, the escheator of the county had been commanded to take the town back into the earl's hands because the lease had been granted without the knowledge of the prince and his council.[87] It would seem here that the chamberlain or his lieutenant had made the decision to lease to Winnington on his own initiative, despite the fact that the lease of 26 March was said to be by assent of the council ('per assensum consilii'). Possibly the Cheshire administration had been lured by the substantial sum (£140) which Winnington had offered in advance for the lease, but the prince's council

79 CHES 25/10, m 21d.

80 CHES 2/75, m 5 (9), *36 DKR*, p. 532, for grant of custody; CHES 2/81, m 2d. (5), *36 DKR*, p. 26, for writ *de etate probanda*; CHES 2/81, m 5 (5), *36 DKR*, p. 533 for livery of inheritance to Hamo as Ellen Bate's husband. Other lands of Ellen Bate were held in custody by Peter de Dutton, himself a sometime lessee of the town (CHES 2/80, m 1d. (8), *36 DKR*, p. 26).

81 SC 6/793/2, m 4.

82 SC 6/810/15, m 1.

83 CHES 2/69, m 11d. (9), *36 DKR*, p. 531.

84 For commissions see CHES 2/77, m 4d. (1) and CHES 2/78, m 2 (9), *36 DKR*, p. 532. For this involvement at Shrewsbury see CHES 2/76, m 12 (5), *36 DKR*, p. 532, writ to the escheator to seize his lands as he has been declared a rebel. He had earlier been retained by Richard II and had served in Ireland in 1399 (CHES 2/71, m 19d. (1) and CHES 2/73, m 4d. (2), *36 DKR*, p. 532).

85 JRRIL, Arley Charters Box 28 no. 10.

86 He liveried £1 10s. 11½d. in 1403 (SC 6/791/6, m 2d).

87 CHES 2/76, m 4d. (4), *36 DKR*, p. 532.

obviously had other plans for the town and desired to keep it in hand, especially in this period when there was a need to maintain the level of income for the sake of the Welsh war.[88]

The town was not leased again until 14 January 1411, when Sir Laurence Merbury took up a lease for ten years at £48 per annum, entering into a recognizance of £100 that he would surrender the town when required.[89] In fact, Merbury only held the town from Michaelmas 1410 to Michaelmas 1413,[90] at which point it passed back into direct control until leased out again for six years on 1 October 1415 to Sir Peter de Dutton, again at £48 per annum.[91] He held the town from Michaelmas 1416 until it was restored to the Hollands on 12 May 1418.[92]

Why should a lease of this particular town be so coveted? To the earl, Northwich was by far the less valuable of the two Wiches under his control. Merbury's lease may be directly related to the financial situation in the previous year, when the profit had been severely reduced by the need to rebuild the mill. The cost of the latter had amounted to £34 5s. 10d., hence leaving a current balance of 6s. 6d., a considerable decline from the average current balance of previous years at around £30.[93] The £48 farm would provide a larger income than when the town had been directly controlled, but only marginally so. In fact, in the same year as Merbury's lease, annuities were granted out of the issues of the town which completely annihilated any

88 It is possible that the restoration of the town to Elizabeth, dowager countess of Huntingdon (and Henry IV's sister) had initially been intended. She successfully petitioned for restoration of her dower lands in the duchy of Cornwall in the parliament of Jan 1404 (*PROME*, viii. 248–50).

89 CHES 2/83, m 2 (4, 5), *36 DKR*, p. 366.

90 SC 6/792/8, m 2d. to 792/10, m 3d.

91 CHES 2/89, m 1 (1), *36 DKR*, p. 566.

92 SC 6/793/4, m 4d. to SC 6/793/7, m 4d. Holland had successfully petitioned in the parliament of Oct 1416 for restoration of his lands and title when he came of age on 29 Mar 1417 (*Complete Peerage*, v. 206 note 1).

93 SC 6/792/6, m 3d.

income from the farm.[94] The overall policy regarding Northwich after the Welsh wars seems to have been one of marking time until the town could be restored to the Hollands.

Winnington's abortive lease seems to indicate that pressure and enthusiasm for such leases came from the potential lessees themselves. What attraction did such a lease hold? The leases included a clause that the lessees were granted all profits and issues of the town 'according to the customs used there which belong to us by right' ('secundum consuetudines eiusdem hactenus usitatas de iure nobis spectantes sive pertinentes'). Ostensibly this would not allow the farmer to create new sources of income or to change the organization of the administration and resources of the town, if they did indeed take up such leases for the sake of profit. Certainly Merbury's administration seems to have been very similar to that of the earl; a court held under him in October 1413 was enrolled in the same format as later courts of that year and the next.[95] His bailiff, Thomas le Cariour, remained in office as catchpole for the rest of the year.[96]

Peter de Dutton was possibly an enterprising landlord, with a feeling for such economic expansion. He had already enclosed and emparked Dutton Park, along with 40 acres of arable and 200 acres of meadow and wood nearby, and by his death in 1433, held lands in Dutton, Runcorn, Halton, the Wirral, Aston, Church Minshull and the city of Chester, as well as interests in *saline* in the town of Northwich.[97] Possibly by the lease he aimed to strengthen his control over the salt industry in the town. Laurence Merbury's motives are a little more puzzling. His influence in the county seems to have sprung from

94 See p. 249. In the two years intervening between the end of Merbury's lease and the beginning of Dutton's, the size of the annuity had to be manipulated to fit the current balance.

95 SC 2/156/11, m 1.

96 SC 6/793/1, m 5.

97 CHES 2/84, m 1 (3,4,5), *37 DKR*, p. 229. Dutton had seen service under Richard II as constable of Chirk (CHES 2/81, m 16d. (8, 9), *36 DKR*, p. 161). He supported Hotspur at the battle of Shrewsbury but later played an active role in Cheshire government under the Lancastrians. See the various entries in *36 DKR*, pp. 226, 162, 533.

his connection with the Talbot family, most notably perhaps the justiciar, Gilbert Talbot.[98] Most of his service had been in Ireland, both in the early 1400s and after 1414,[99] but he was sheriff of Chester from January 1411 to Michaelmas 1414, and temporarily constable of Chester Castle. Possibly Northwich provided him with a base in the county whilst sheriff. Certainly the chronology of the appointment and lease would suggest such a connection, although his name suggests that he already held land in Marbury in the south of the county, where the Talbots also held estates. Unfortunately, we cannot ascertain the profits made by either Merbury or Dutton as lessees.[100] Certainly, their farms were placed at an economic level. What is certain, too, is that such leases were attractive to both local men such as the Winningtons and Dutton, and to men introduced through the household or county administration.

### *Leases of demesne lands*

In general, save for these two special cases of Shotwick and Northwich, the earl's administration preferred to keep manors under direct control at least, and to farm out the demesne lands and other profits individually, or occasionally to keep such profits in hand and exploit them directly by means of special officials appointed to the task. This method allowed for more manipulation of revenues.

98 In 1421, for instance, he was nominated by Beatrice, Gilbert's widow, as her attorney in England (*CPR 1416–22*, p. 373). His first known connection with John Talbot is in 1414 (A. J. Pollard, 'The Family of Talbot, Lords Talbot and Earls of Shrewsbury in the Fifteenth Century' (unpublished PhD thesis, University of Bristol, 1968), pp. 214, 249).

99 *CPR 1399–1401*, p. 387 (treasurer), *CPR 1413–16*, p. 163 (chancellor): Pollard, 'Family of Talbot', pp. 125, 249; J. H. Wylie, *History of England under Henry the Fourth*, 4 vols (London: Longmans, Green, 1884–98), ii. 133, iii. 162.

100 Lessees may have been able to take larger profits than the lord due to smaller overheads and by ignoring the need for repairs (Booth, 'Financial Administration', p. 219). There may have been quite a severe backlog of repairs at Shotwick after Moston's lease (SC 6/792/2, m 5).

In the case of Shotwick, Drakelow and Macclesfield Forest, those areas which had in earlier days been directly cultivated by the earl were now leased or approved en bloc. The demesne at Drakelow, which in 1347 formed more than 156 acres of the possible 1287 acres of the whole manor,[101] was leased throughout this period by Ralph Mainwaring, equitator of Delamere Forest, and the brother of John Mainwaring who was sheriff of the county from 1403 to 1408. Ralph himself was prominent in local commissions, and had served with his brother in an expedition to Anglesey in 1405.[102] Ralph had been granted the reversion of the Drakelow demesne in 1398.[103] This grant was confirmed on 20 May 1400.[104] The £5 received for this farm cannot have reflected the true economic value of the demesne land, unless the same malaise had struck these lands and their lessee as seems to have created difficulties for the tenants of Rudheath, as is reflected in the level of decayed rents. Mainwaring's lease of Drakelow was for life, although he may have already occupied the demesnes under the previous lessee.[105] These demesnes had been leased at the slightly higher rate of £6 13s. 4d. in 1356 but the rate of £5 was settled at least by 1391.[106] There was, in fact, no change in render until 1445 when an increase of 6s. 8d. was made.[107] This lease was already rather a dead letter.

About 30 bovates (or 90 acres) was held in demesne at Shotwick.[108] In the early fifteenth century this had been leased out separately from the other issues of the manor in those years when the manor was in the earl's hands. These lessees were local men who took up the lands for a short term or else upon a yearly basis. In 1399, these lands were leased to Roger Simpson,

101 SC 11/900, m 1; Booth, *Financial Admin.*, p. 128.

102 See, for instance various entries in *36 DKR*, pp. 55, 532 and *37 DKR*, pp. 37, 75. For service in 1405 see SC 6/775/4, m 1d.

103 CHES 2/71, m 6 (1), *36 DKR*, p. 317.

104 CHES 2/74, m 16 (12), *36 DKR*, p. 317.

105 SC 6/791/1, m 1d.

106 Sharp, 'Earldom and County of Chester', pp. 395–6.

107 CHES 2/118, m 5 (1), *37 DKR*, p. 104.

108 SC 12/ 6/33 (temp. Edward I).

one of the largest tenant landholders in the manor,[109] and to Hugh Daukyn, for six years at £5 13s. 4d. per annum.[110] When the manor was resumed into the prince's hands after Richard Moston's death, the then reeve, Roger de Ashley, and other tenants (Geront del Wodehouse and John Goldyng) took the demesne lands to farm at £6 per annum, for eight years. The lease was made in the manorial court of June 1408 before the chamberlain of Chester.[111]

There were six areas in the Macclesfield Forest which seem to have formerly comprised the earl's demesne, where in the fourteenth century there had been a cattle farm, until such direct exploitation had proved an economic loss.[112] These were still valuable in the early fifteenth century, being leased to the deputy steward, Reginald del Dounes in 1400 for eight years at £20 per annum, on condition that he was to bear the cost of repairs of all the houses, messuages and pastures therein.[113] In 1409, the farm was increased to £21 and taken up for ten years by John Savage and Reginald del Dounes.[114] At the expiry of this lease, the then steward, John Stanley jnr, took up a new lease at the same rate for six years.[115] By this time, these lands were used solely for pasturing. This was probably a lucrative lease and hence eagerly taken up by those most closely involved in the forest administration.

The former demesne lands at Frodsham were leased in small parcels, generally on a yearly basis, to tenants of the lordship. Some parcels clearly remained in the same hands over a longer period as, for instance, the fifteen acres leased to Geoffrey de Dutton from 1411 to 1418. This demesne, lying in the Seeflats towards the north and north-west of the town, was split into large ditched fields. Under the heading 'issues of the demesne

109 See below p. 220.
110 SC 6/791/1, m 3. This was the second year of their lease.
111 SC 6/792/3, m 3, SC 2/156/13, m 2.
112 Booth, *Financial Admin.*, pp. 93–7.
113 SC 6/805/7, m 2d.
114 SC 6/806/4, m 2d; CHES 2/82, m 1 (3), *36 DKR*, p. 422, dated 21 Oct 1409.
115 CHES 2/94, m 5d. (3), *37 DKR*, p. 66, dated 4 Apr 1422.

land' ('exitus terrarum dominicalium'), arable in le Overheye and le Netherheye was leased and presumably used as arable by the tenant lessees. However, these areas were also used as pasture, and their issues accounted under the heading of 'agistamentum' (pasturage). Indeed, by this period, there was much confusion over where issues from leases should be accounted. If in the past there had been a meaningful distinction between 'exitus terrarum' and 'agistamentum', then this was now lost, and there was a lack of consistency. This makes assessment of the extent, nature and value of these lands more problematical. Descriptions of the areas also vary, sometimes being described in small parcels, and at other times in larger conglomerations. This may reflect changes in the pattern of leasing over the period. This is especially noticeable after 1417, when over 150 acres in le Overheye, le Nethurheye and Reemarsh were leased together for agistment. In 1418, at least 250 acres were leased, 209½ being accounted as demesne and around 42 acres as agistment.[116] In addition, other unmeasured plots, again in the common or Reemarsh, were leased out. In general, lands were leased at around 1s. 0d. per acre.

Changes in land use were probably frequent, although in general less land was used for arable than for pasture, and this may explain the inconsistency in entries. In 1421, there may have been a move towards closer seigneurial surveillance; a new fold was built on land previously leased to tenants for agisting their animals, and a salaried keeper of animals appointed with control over the demesne.[117] If his appointment was made in the hope of increasing revenue from the demesne, then it was a failure, for after 1421 the combined profit of demesne leases and agistment declined rather than increased. Sometimes, the value of the leases in general had to be reduced because a tenant could not be found to take it on at the previous sum. An area called Rushycawen had to be taken in hand in 1422 because it had fallen into decay owing to the poverty of the tenant.[118] It

116 SC 6/793/7, m 5.
117 SC 6/794/1, m 5.
118 SC 6/794/2, m 5.

was possible to increase the rate of the lease of certain lands, but this additional revenue did not compensate for other losses elsewhere. One area, Hopulmeadow, part of le Overheye, fell in value by 5% over two years, 1410 to 1411.[119] Taking the revenues from demesne lease and agistment together to mitigate any inconsistency in methods of entry, the profits raised were generally in the £12–£14 range, with a fall in 1413–14, and after 1418 (see Table VII).

This was an increase in value compared to the late fourteenth century. In 1394 'the lord's land with meadow' ('terra dominicalis cum pratis') was valued at £12.[120] In the accounts of the early fifteenth century, the yearly sale of the ten separately named areas of meadow, totalling 59½ acres, was accounted as another category, bringing in additional revenue of £6–£8 per annum, save towards the end of the period when there was a 50% fall in revenues. This fall was due to a number of factors. Sometimes, as in the arable demesne, a tenant could not be found and the price had to be reduced.[121] These meadows, and indeed the demesne lands as a whole, were especially susceptible to flooding. 'Mukulmeadow' sold at £3 2s. 8d. in 1411, but at only £2 2s. 6d. in 1412, because it had been damaged 'by floods and incursions of the sea' ('per diluvium et cretenam maris').[122] In 1421, no profit was raised from four of the meadows for a similar reason.[123] Any income was thus reduced by the cost of the frequently necessary repairs to the ditches around the demesnes and their sluice gates.[124] Several other factors were blamed for fall in income from the sale of meadows, drought in 1419, 'pestilencia' ('plague') in 1420, and stormy seas and incessant rainfall in 1421 and 1422.[125]

119 SC 6/792/6, m 6, SC 6/792/8, m 5.
120 Ormerod, *Cheshire*, ii. 50.
121 For example, in 1414, SC 6/793/1, m 4.
122 SC 6/792/8, m 5, SC 6/792/9, m 4.
123 SC 6/794/1, m 5.
124 Radegonde Béchet had the manor confiscated in 1406 for failure to maintain these ditches. See below p. 262.
125 Respectively, SC 6/794/1, m 5, SC 6/794/2, m 5, SC 6/793/11, m 5, SC 6/793/9, m 5.

Other areas and perquisites at Frodsham, for example, the orchard, garden of the former manor house and dairy house, formerly directly controlled by the earl, were also leased out to the tenants of the lordship, but it was proving difficult in these times to find tenants. By now, tenants were able, in all leases, to lay down their own conditions, to the detriment of the earl and his profits from such agricultural sources in the lordship. Piecemeal leasing may have been marginally more profitable than leasing en bloc: at least it prevented fossilization of revenue. But it could also be highly erratic, and required a much closer degree of supervision by the lord's officials.

### *Leasing policies and practices*

Other agricultural and non-agricultural revenues were frequently farmed rather than directly exploited. These are considered in greater detail under the relevant sections of this chapter, but it is important here to consider some points concerning leases in general. The first concerns the general motive. Most of the smaller leases, for instance of mills and tolls, were made for the sake of the earl's profit, but this was not necessarily true in leases of whole manors or even demesne lands. Administrative convenience and the demands of good lordship also played a part. A second major point is that such revenues were administered on a very pragmatic basis. It was possible to lease one year, and change lessees or directly control the next, with very little disruption, as, for instance, in the management of the agistment of Delamere Forest, discussed later in this chapter. It is difficult, therefore, to see any overall policy, even in the one unit. Certain issues could be leased and yet others kept in hand in the same year. In Macclesfield Forest, for instance, some mills were directly controlled whilst others were leased. Custom was also an unquestionable pressure upon the lord. Manorial custom, with the force of local law, might tie the lord's hands as to the length and condition of his leases and the amount of his rents.[126]

126 P. Laslett, *The World We Have Lost*, 2nd edition (London: Routledge, 1971), p. 79. Laslett used sixteenth- and seventeenth-century evidence to reach this conclusion, but it holds true for earlier centuries too.

## Table VII. Leases of the demesne and agricultural profits at Frodsham, 1409–22

| Account | Year | Issues of demesne lands | Agistment | Sale of pastures | Issues of the manor |
|---|---|---|---|---|---|
| SC 6/792/5 m. 10 | 1408–9 | £3 14s. 6d. | £8 5s. 9½d. | £8 6s. 0d. | 14s. 2d. |
| SC 6/792/6 m.6 | 1409–0 | £5 18s. 6d. | £7 6s. 6½d. | £8 7s. 0d. | 16s. 3d. |
| SC 6/792/8 m.5 | 1410–11 | £6 17s. 7½d. | £6 7s. 7½d. | £8 7s. 0d. | £1 1s. 10½d. |
| SC 6/792/9 m.4 | 1411–12 | £6 17s. 6d. | £5 19s. 4d. | £6 4s. 4d. | 16s 5½d. |
| SC 6/792/10 m.6 | 1412–13 | £3 1s. 10d. | £7 12s. 4d. | £6 19s. 4d. | 15s. 3d. |
| SC 6/793/1 m.4 | 1413–14 | £1 15s. 0d. | £10 1s. 2d. | £7 17s. 5d. | 18s. 7d. |
| SC 6/793/2 m.6 | 1414–15 | £4 2s. 4d. | £8 4s. 2d. | £8 1s. 10d. | £1 4s. 5d. |
| SC 6/793/4 m.6 | 1415–16 | £4 11s. 1d. | £8 19s. 3d. | £7 1s. 10d. | £1 5s. 0d. |
| SC 6/793/5 m.5 | 1416–17 | £4 9s. 3d. | £9 12s. 5½d. | £7 7s. 8d. | £1 5s. 8d. |
| SC 6/793/7 m.5 | 1417–18 | £11 12s. 2d. | £3 6s. 0d. | £8 3s. 8d. | 19s. 0d. |
| SC 6/793/9 m.5 | 1418–19 | £8 1s. 11½d. | £3 9s. 5d. | £6 6s. 8d. | 19s. 0d. |
| SC 6/793/11 m.5 | 1419–20 | £7 2s. 9d. | £3 7s. 6½d. | £3 10s. 5d. | 16s. 0d. |
| SC 6/794/1 m.5 | 1420–1 | £7 6s. 5d. | £2 15s. 4½d. | £3 4s. 10½d. | 13s. 4d. |
| SC 6/794/2 m.5 | 1421–2 | £6 6s. 0d. | £3 6s. 11½d. | £4 18s. 9½d. | 14s. 2d. |

Those who took up the most important leases were those who might be expected to do so, having some connection with estate administration either by being estate officials in their own right or by having contacts in the right quarters. Laurence Merbury had close connections with Gilbert Talbot; Ralph Mainwaring's brother was sheriff and he himself held local office. Several members of the Done family, whose most senior member was master forester and bailiff of the forest, took up leases in Delamere Forest. In general, tenurial connections with the unit were necessary. Smaller profits in particular were always leased to local men, again predominantly to demesne officials or members of their family. Estate officials were in the best position to assess the potential value of the lease and to suggest that they should take it up. They could easily exercise control of that particular revenue within their other duties. Indeed, they would be responsible in the last resort for its profits, however the revenue was managed. The lord may have thus been more willing to allow officials to take up leases.[127] In addition, it may have been common for officials to be granted leases on more favourable terms. For instance, William Farington, deputy bailiff of Drakelow, leased the Merefield at a cheaper rate in 1410 than it had previously been leased to other tenants.[128] The desire for profit must have been their main consideration, but that of the lord was the ensuring of a regular income from trustworthy officials and lessees. In those units where personnel changed each year (such as the *burgi*), few officials took up leases, probably because of the lack of continuity. In most cases, we can be quite certain that the lessees named were those who actually managed the item, be it land or profit. But sometimes the farmer must have acted merely as a collector of revenue, whilst others managed or perhaps even sublet the commodity. The strongest evidence for this is the sublease of the manor and

127 R. H. Hilton, *The English Peasantry in the Later Middle Ages* (Oxford: Clarendon Press, 1975), p. 42. For the small circle of lessees at Shotwick see pp. 143–4.

128 SC 6/792/6, m 1d.

park of Shotwick by Sir William Porter, the earl's grantee, to Sir William Stanley in 1423.[129]

Leasing implies the alienation of seigneurial control over revenues. Most leases, where relevant, thrust the burden of repairs upon the lessees, although the lord undertook to provide 'grossum maeremium' ('large timber'). Other than that, the lessee had no other responsibility than to pay his farm on the requisite date. The earl's administration still maintained some degree of surveillance, however small, but enough, for instance, to involve forfeiture of the lease in the case of non-payment of the farm due.[130] The earl also retained the right to terminate the lease, although he was to give adequate warning of his intention. A year's warning had to be given in the case of the lease of the agistment of Delamere Forest to Richard de Manley and Richard Done in 1401.[131]

We can note that leases were issued in different ways. The diplomatic (the formulas by which they were conducted and recorded in documents) of leasing in the county falls into three main categories. The first were those made by letters patent of the earl under the Chester seal, and sometimes enrolled in the Chester enrolments. The second were taken out in a similar way to recognizances. In such cases, the lessees, and sometimes their sureties, entered the exchequer upon a certain day, generally before the chamberlain and/or auditors and took the revenue in question to farm. The third category were those made locally, usually under the supervision of the steward of the manor, but sometimes of the chamberlain of Chester. Such leases were sometimes enrolled on the court rolls of the manor in question.

We might expect a hierarchy of leases to correspond with this hierarchy of diplomatic practice. Indeed, all the major leases, of manors and major profits, were made by letters patent, although it is necessary to point out that not all such leases were enrolled. The lease of the manor of Shotwick to Richard Moston in 1401,

129 See below pp. 262, 265.

130 See, for instance, terms of a lease of the mills at Macclesfield in 1402 (CHES 2/76, m 3 (4), *36 DKR*, p. 294).

131 SC 6/791/3, m 2.

despite being made, as it was said, by letters of the prince and assent of the council, was not enrolled on the recognizance rolls.[132] The second category were clearly those leases which could be made without active conciliar involvement, and the third those which could be disposed of by local officials. Yet the leases themselves do not always fit into this pattern. For instance, the mills of Macclesfield were leased in the exchequer of Chester before the chamberlain and auditors in December 1402 and June 1404, but in October 1408 they were leased by letters of the prince issued under his privy seal.[133]

All leases made upon a yearly basis were made locally by the steward or Chester chamberlain, representing the third category of practice. Otherwise, the longest leases were for twenty years (as in the case of the lease of the Macclesfield mills in 1410 and the lease of the herbage of Macclesfield park in 1408), but the majority were for three to six years, with a few in the eight to twelve-year category. This variation seems to suggest that leasing was not yet fossilised in the county. There was enough demand and enthusiasm for leases to keep them, for the most part, short and economical, so that they were acceptable to both the lord and the lessee. There were few long leases in the county at this time, save those for life, which were certainly motivated by patronage rather than economic considerations.

## Forests and Parks

Forests and parks had traditionally close connections with the lord, and both were administered with considerable attention to the enforcement of seigneurial rights.[134] Parks were frequently

132 SC 6/791/3, m 3.

133 Respectively, CHES 2/76, m 3 (4), *36 DKR*, p. 294; CHES 2/77, m 8 (2), *36 DKR*, p. 313; CHES 2/81, m 2 (1), *36 DKR*, p. 422.

134 For surveys see Charles R. Young, *The Royal Forests of Medieval England* (Philadelphia: University of Pennsylvania Press, 1979); John Langton, 'Royal and Non-Royal Forests in England and Wales', *Historical Research* 88 (2015), 381–401, the latter linked to a research project at St John's College Oxford. On parks, see Stephen A. Mileson, *Parks in Medieval England* (Oxford: Oxford University Press, 2009).

kept in hand long after other lands had been leased. Cheshire had an absentee lord, but the management of his forests of Delamere and Macclesfield and parks of Shotwick and Macclesfield display these characteristics.

Royal hunting lodges were maintained in both forests although there is no firm evidence that Prince Henry hunted in either the parks or the forests during his stay in the county. Frequent repairs were carried out to the lodge in Macclesfield Forest and to an enclosure for the game over winter.[135] There was a hunting lodge in Delamere Forest from the thirteenth century although it does not appear in the accounts.[136] The game was to be preserved at all costs. In 1404, the master forester of Delamere was ordered to expel all dogs and pigs from the forest because the game had been much damaged by the coursing of the former and the grubbing of earth by the latter.[137] Some venison was provided from Delamere Forest to the household at Chester in 1403.[138] At Shotwick park, the game and timber of the park were reserved to the prince's use even when the manor was leased to Richard Moston (1401–7) and after it was granted to William Porter in 1410.[139] In Porter's grant, it was specifically stated that the game in the park was to be preserved for the recreation of the prince and his heirs. When Porter himself leased out the manor and park to Sir William Stanley in 1423, again the beasts in the park were reserved to the prince.[140] At Macclesfield park, sufficient pasture for the royal beasts was to be preserved even when the herbage of the park passed out of direct comital control.[141]

Especially strict control was maintained over the park at Shotwick. Rules were laid down regarding access. There was to be only one gate, and people were to enter and exit only

135 SC 6/805/11, m 2d, 806/17, m 3.
136 Dodgson, *Place Names*, iii. 214.
137 CHES 2/77, m 2d. (9), *36 DKR*, p. 142.
138 E 101/404/23.
139 SC 6/791/3, m 3; CHES 2/81, m 5d. (2, 3), *36 DKR*, p. 433.
140 JRRIL, Rylands Charter 1418.
141 SC 6/805/7, m 3d; CHES 2/74, m 6 (9), *36 DKR*, p. 312.

by licence of the lord's ministers. Anyone tarrying in the park without just cause was regarded with suspicion. In October 1406, Ralph Peeket of Chester was indicted in the manorial court for being in the park for four days, for what reason it was not known.[142] We know that in 1401 the park was used to pasture cattle which had been taken from the prince's manors in Wales for his larder at Chester. Hence there was no profit from the pasturing of tenants' cattle in the park that year.[143]

Close control was necessary in order to protect the two most important (and lucrative) commodities to be found in the parks and forests, hunting rights and timber. There were frequent indictments for illegal hunting in Shotwick park.[144] Although there were none in this period in Macclesfield park,[145] there were many in the two forest areas, which was to be expected when many gentry held land in these areas.[146] Fines were large and seem to be punishment for the offence rather than payments for licences to hunt, although that remains a possible interpretation. For example, Laurence Fitton was fined £33 for two offences in 1403 and 1405.[147] Such fines were therefore an important source of revenue, accounted within the perquisites of both manorial, hundred and county courts where such offences were dealt with.[148] There was thus a very strong and well-staffed forest administration in both cases for the regulation of hunting and the detection of offenders.

Timber from the forests and parks was used for repairs and works in the demesnes both by the earl and his lessees, or even

142 SC 6/156/13, m 2.

143 SC 6/791/3, m 3.

144 For instance, CHES 25/10, m 26.

145 There is, however, an indictment for this offence in Le Parkhed next to Macclesfield park, in 1412 (CHES 25/23, m 8).

146 See for instance the 26 presentments by John Done as master forester of Delamere in Jan 1410 (CHES 25/10, m 30). These include a variety of offences committed over the previous 18 months, but are dominated by men letting dogs run at deer in the forest. We also see shooting and killing deer and attacks on the sub-foresters.

147 E 163/6/41 item 19.

148 For indictments see CHES 25/10, 25/11, and 25/23. See also the Macclesfield halmote rolls in SC 2/255.

elsewhere. In 1422, for example, timber from Delamere Forest and Shotwick park was used for repairs at Beaumaris Castle.[149] Leases usually included a proviso that the earl should provide 'large timber' ('grossum maeremium') for repairs. The surplus, along with any dead wood, bark and acorns, was sold, and could bring in as much as £10 per annum in Delamere Forest.[150] In addition, income accrued from fines for those who took timber from the forest without permission.[151] This was on a scale large enough to bring in valuable income, for fines were the equivalent of licences to take the earl's wood. In December 1402, for instance, thirty-seven men were indicted for the offence in Delamere Forest.[152] Both timber and game formed valuable gifts to those whom the administration wished to favour. There were frequent gifts of timber to religious houses, such as those from both Delamere and Shotwick to the dean and chapter of St John's Chester for the repair of the church in 1412.[153] Entries in the Chester enrolments also show that venison was frequently given in gift to the constable of Chester Castle, and as a perquisite of office, the parker and reeve of Shotwick were allowed to take certain quantities of wood free of charge.[154]

In addition to these profits arising from the exercise of the basic, seigneurial rights, the forests and parks were also used in much the same way as the demesnes at Frodsham and Macclesfield, as areas upon which tenants must pay in order to agist their livestock. At Delamere this was an important source of income, and one in which much interest was hence shown, and much experimentation in methods of exploitation carried out. When the period opened, the agistment and pannage were

149 *PPC*, ii. 319.
150 SC 6/792/6, m 3 (1410).
151 For examples of indictments in Shotwick park see SC 2 156/13, m 2, 2d. and 3.
152 CHES 25/10, m 11.
153 CHES 2/86, m 1d. (2, 3), *36 DKR*, p. 104.
154 SC 6/156/3, m 2d; JRRIL, Rylands Charter 1310. Some tenants claimed to have the right to fell wood free of charge in Macclesfield Forest by dint of charters granted by the Norman earls (CHES 2/90, m 3d. (8), *37 DKR*, p. 323).

controlled directly by means of two approvers, and an income of £18 2s. 0d. received,[155] but at the end of the year the two profits were leased for a larger return of £22 per annum[156] This lease was taken up by the then escheator, Richard de Manley, and the master forester's brother, Richard Done of Utkinton. The latter had already farmed this profit in the time of Richard II for we find him paying arrears for it in 1400.[157]

Certainly, leasing proved more profitable than direct control, because the two approvers had been paid a wage of 13s. 4d. which further reduced this profit. This farm was held for its full eight years, but a subsequent lease for a further six years was at a reduced rate of £18 per annum.[158] When this lease terminated in 1416, direct control was again attempted, possibly because the lessees could not be persuaded to take up another lease. Certainly, they had been finding it difficult to pay the full farm, whereas the earlier and larger farm had been paid regularly.[159] However, direct control proved as unprofitable. The £16 18s. 9d. raised by Richard Done as approver in 1417 remained outstanding at the end of the reign.[160] It is not surprising that Done was removed from this function in the following year, but what is puzzling is that the agistment continued to be approved. Profits from the agistment and pannage (separately controlled) were now lower than the £18 farm, and often were paid off over two or three years. By 1426, the agistment was again farmed at £21 per annum.[161] The farming of such issues generally proved more profitable than direct control, especially towards the end of the period; in 1417, pannage in Macclesfield Forest was farmed at 18s. per annum.[162]

155 SC 6/791, m 2.
156 SC 6/791/3, m 2.
157 SC 6/791/1, m 2.
158 SC 6/792/8, m 2; CHES 2/84, m 1 (8), *36 DKR*, p. 324.
159 Of the £18 owed, they paid £12 8s. 4d. in 1411 (SC 6/792/8, m 2), £14 6s. 8d. in 1413 (SC 6/792/10, m 3), £12 14s. 4d. in 1414 (SC 6/793/1, m 2d), £8 7s. 8d. in 1415 (SC 6/793/2, m 3) and as little as £ 4 6s. 8d. in 1416 (SC 6/793/4, m 3).
160 SC 6/793/5, m 3.
161 CHES 2/90, m 1d. (2), *37 DKR*, p. 432.
162 SC 6/806/13, m 2d.

This sum brought in a higher revenue than in the previous four years of direct control, but less than sums received from such in earlier years. On the other hand, direct control of the turbary of Delamere Forest brought in a larger income than the £12 farm taken up in 1411.[163] Not surprisingly then, the farm was allowed to last for only one year of its intended four-year term before a return to direct control.

Manipulation of these profits shows a considerable attention to profit. Clearly they were important enough to merit such attention, by both the earl's administration and the potential lessees. A similar situation is seen at Shotwick park, where much higher profits were achieved in those years when the herbage and agistment were directly controlled. In 1400, £4 was received from the lease of Sir John Massey of Puddington but over £9 was received in 1408 and 1410 when the profits were directly controlled by the reeves.[164] Macclesfield park was exceptional in that, until 1408, very little attention was paid to it as a source of revenue. Managerial control was sadly lacking at the opening of the reign. The park at Macclesfield had been farmed by Sir Peter Legh. He was killed as a Ricardian supporter in 1399 and no one, according to the account roll of 1398–9, knew to whom the evidences concerning his account had devolved.[165] Control was not restored by the appointment under the new regime of an absentee parker (Hugh Hoby), nor by the grant of the herbage of the park to John de Kingsley in April 1400.[166] After the latter's forfeiture of this grant by involvement in Hotspur's rebellion in 1403, the issues of the park ought to have been accounted.[167] Indeed, the parker was called upon to render an account in 1403,[168] but in fact there was a lapse of five years.

163 SC 6/792/8, m 2; CHES 2/83, m 3d. (6), *36 DKR*, p. 66.

164 SC 6/791, m 3; SC 6/792/3, m 3; SC 6/792/5, m 2.

165 SC 6/805/6, m 2d.

166 SC 6/805/7, m 3d.

167 SC 6/791/7, m 2. Kingsley petitioned the king and the prince's council for this grant to be restored (E 163/6/41 item 5). He was compensated for its loss by the grant of an annuity out of the issues of the turbary of Delamere on 1 Oct 1405 (CHES 2/78, m 6d. (2, 3), *36 DKR*, p. 274).

168 SC 6/805/11, m 3.

Some sense had been made of the situation by the appointment of John Savage as parker, but it would appear that some dereliction had occurred in the meantime. Over £23 had to be spent on repairs between 1402 and 1407.[169] The herbage was now farmed, as it had been in 1400, by John de Macclesfield at £6 13s. 4d., but from 28 October 1408, Savage himself agreed to pay an increased farm of £7 per annum.[170] It is interesting to note, however, that de Macclesfield and Savage had already been associated in connection with the park. In 1402, a licence had been granted to them both to raise £2 per annum for twelve years out of the turbary of the park. This sum was to be expended upon the enclosure of the park.[171] There is no evidence that they acted upon this although it would explain why there were no park accounts between 1402 and 1407. The park remained an economic failure, because of the high cost of repairs.

With careful management, then, these traditional revenues could still provide a lucrative and reliable source of income, but this needed a considerable degree of surveillance. It is significant that, in general, such control was maintained and that keener attention was paid to the exploitation of these revenues than to commercial monopolies. Here the earl's administration was working along well tried and reliable lines with sources of revenue that were well understood.

## Mills

Mills were always an important source of revenue in a seigneurial economy. Compulsory use of the manorial corn mills was a general condition of tenure; tenants were liable to be fined if they took their grain elsewhere to be milled, or milled it themselves. In January 1411, for instance, Chester bakers were indicted for not having their corn milled at the earl's Dee Mills.[172] A toll in kind was exacted at each milling, and the grain thus accruing could be sold to the lord's profit.

169 SC 6/806/1, m 3.
170 CHES 2/81, m 2 (2), *36 DKR*, p. 422.
171 CHES 2/75, m 10 (4), *36 DKR*, p. 313.
172 CHES 25/10, m 33.

Such was the profit when the mills were kept in hand, but by the early fifteenth century most of the less important, and presumably less lucrative, mills were put out to farm. The mills of the townships of Rainow, Shrigley and Whaley in Macclesfield Forest were leased by relatively prominent local tenants for terms of up to twenty years for small sums. Rainow was leased to Nicholas Gardiner for 12 years in 1402 for 12s. 0d. per annum.[173] Three years later, Pott Shrigley mill was leased to Robert del Dounes for twenty years for 5s. 0d. per annum.[174] The same rate was kept in 1415 when the mill was leased to William Ashton for twelve years.[175] Whaley Mill was more valuable, attracting a farm of £2 6s. 8d. when it was leased by Roger Jodrell in 1399 for six years, and by William del Sherd in 1411 for thirteen years.[176]

The granting of longer leases demonstrates the trend away from direct control, making a return to the latter less likely. There was no difficulty in finding lessees so long as the mills were in a reasonable state of repair but, clearly, this was not always the case. Sometimes extra encouragement was needed. Sherd had to be allowed three years' free tenure before he was to pay his farm for the Whaley Mill, presumably to compensate him for the repairs which he needed to carry out before he could make any profit from the mill. The earl paid for repairs to the mill at Pott Shrigley in 1405, no doubt to encourage Dounes to take up his twelve-year lease. He also paid for repairs at Rainow in 1419 even though the then lessee, Ellen Gardiner, wife of Nicholas, was held responsible for repairs by the terms of her lease.[177] Disrepair was a major problem. Bollington Mill stood empty and in complete disrepair throughout this period. In 1406 there was discussion on this situation, as there was also two years later upon the possibility of finding someone to lease

173 SC 2/255/5, m 1.
174 SC 6/806/14, m 2.
175 SC 6/806/9, m 2, SC 2/255/11, m 4.
176 CHES 2/74, m 5 (11), *36 DKR*, p. 520 ; CHES 2/84, m 1 (4), *36 DKR*, p. 430; SC 6/806/5, m 2d.
177 SC 6/806/17, m 3.

the mill, but neither brought about any change.[178] By 1422, Whaley Mill too was in the lord's hands and completely broken up. Its lessee, del Sherd, had left the county without paying his farm in the previous two years.[179]

Mills were not only costly to maintain but also to run. Expenses exceeded issues at Northwich in four years out of the fifteen in which the town and the mill were directly controlled, as Table VIII demonstrates. This may have encouraged the council to lease the town in its entirety.

## Table VIII. The cost of maintaining the mill at Northwich, 1400–20

| Year[180] | Issues of the mill | Repairs | Tithe[181] | Wages of miller | Total expenses |
|---|---|---|---|---|---|
| 1400 | £9 1s. 2½d. | £5 12s. 7½d. | 13s. 4d. | 6s. 0d. | £6 11s. 11½d. |
| 1401 | £8 7s. 8d. | £14 14s. 7½d. | 13s. 4d. | 6s. 0d. | £15 13s. 11½d. |
| 1402 | £8 8s. 11d. | £6 7s. 3d. | 13s. 4d. | 6s. 0d. | £7 6s. 7d. |
| 1403 | £7 15s. 0d. | £3 16s. 4d. | 13s. 4d. | 6s. 0d. | £4 15s. 8d. |
| 1404 | £6 6s. 5d. | £2 5s. 7d. | 12s. 0d. | 6s. 0d. | £3 3s. 7d. |
| 1405 | £6 1s. 10d. | £2 10s. 3d. | 12s. 2d. | 6s. 0d. | £3 8s. 5d. |
| 1406 | £4 18s. 8d. | £6 0s. 1d. | 9s. 6d. | 6s. 0d. | £6 15s. 7d. |
| 1407 | £5 6s. 7d. | £1 9s. 4d. | 10s. 7½d. | 6s. 0d. | £2 5s. 11½d. |
| 1408 | £4 13s. 7d. | 11s. 9d. | 9s. 4d. | 6s. 0d. | £1 7s. 1d. |
| 1409 | £3 13s. 3d. | 8s. 8d. | 7s. 3d. | 6s. 0d. | £1 1s. 11d. |
| 1410 | £6 0s. 1d.[182] | £34 5s. 10d. | 6s. 8d. | 6s. 0d. | £34 18s. 6d. |

178 SC 6/806/8, m 3d, SC 6/805/16, m 2, SC 6/806/3, m 2.

179 SC 6/807/3, m 2d.

180 References are to the relevant account for each year, as in Appendix II (g).

181 Payable on the issues of the mill to the vicar of Budworth.

182 There was no more profit as the mill had stood empty for the greater part of the year undergoing rebuilding, which explains the higher cost of repairs this year (SC 6/792/6, m 3d).

| Year | Issues of the mill | Repairs | Tithe | Wages of miller | Total expenses |
|---|---|---|---|---|---|
| 1411 | farm | | | | |
| 1412 | farm | | | | |
| 1413 | farm | | | | |
| 1414 | £4 7s. 2d. | £1 15s. 1d. | 6s. 0d. | 6s. 0d. | £2 7s. 1d. |
| 1415 | £2 4s. 7d. | £2 5s. 9d. | 6s. 0d. | 0d.[183] | 32 11s. 9d. |
| 1416 | farm | | | | |
| 1417 | farm | | | | |
| 1418 | farm | | | | |
| 1419 | £4 13s. 8d. | £13 15s. 4d | | 6s. 0d. | £14 4s. 8d. |
| 1420 | £7 10s. 10½d. | £3 5s. 4½d. | ? | ? | ? |

Both direct control and leasing had their problems. On the whole, a rather ambivalent attitude towards the management of mills was held, and each case decided upon its own merits. Direct control was maintained at Northwich both by the earl and by the Hollands despite frequent financial loss. At Macclesfield, however, the town mills, situated in the township of Sutton,[184] were directly controlled in the first years of the reign of Henry IV, as they had been in the last years of the reign of Richard II. This method of exploitation proved to be grossly uneconomical. Although receipts from toll corn amounted to £13 8s. 8d. and £10 8s. 3d. in 1401 and 1402, respectively,[185] well over half of these sums was consumed by the cost of repairs (£7 12s. 4d. and £5 2s. 3d.) and by tithes. Each year, one pound was paid to the abbot of Chester for tithe due to the church of Prestbury, within which parish Sutton lay. In addition, arrears were a problem, at over £10 in both years. Not surprisingly then, a decision to lease the mills was taken in 1402, most likely at the offer of the

183 In this year the chamberlain and catchpole were held responsible for collecting the issues of the mill and oven (SC 6/793/2, m 4).

184 Dodgson, *Place Names*, i. 150; Ormerod, *Cheshire*, iii. 744.

185 SC 6/805/7, m 2, SC 6/805/9, m 2. John de Legh and Reginald del Dounes held the office of controller in both years.

present controllers and a third individual, John de Newhall.[186] A ten-year farm was set at £10 13s. 4d., less than receipts from the sale of toll corn in certain years, but with no expenses to be deducted; the lessees took on the responsibility for repairs and the purchase of utensils. Initially, however, the lease did not prove as successful as had been hoped, and it was forfeited in 1404 for non-payment. Only £2 of the farm had been paid in the accounting year of 1403–4.[187] A new lease on similar terms was immediately taken out by Robert del Dounes,[188] and the rate increased to £11 13s. 4d. in a twenty-year lease taken out by John Savage and Richard Liversegge in 1410.[189] By this time, the farm of the mills clearly offered the possibility of remuneration for the lessees, and a much more reliable source of income for the earl.

The attraction to the earl of leasing was not so obvious in the case of the mills of Frodsham, until the downward trend in receipts from the sale of toll corn was observed, from over £14 in 1409 to £5 10s. 2d. in 1416, with repairs costing an average £2–£3 per annum.[190] The lease of May 1417 did bring in a larger revenue, being set at £6 per annum for a term of six years, especially as the lessees, Robert Savage and John Triket, undertook to repair the mills at their own expense.[191] However, by 1433 at least, the mills were back under direct control.[192] It was still quite acceptable, for the most part, that mills should be directly controlled, but if anyone was willing to lease them then their offer would be considered and perhaps taken up. Lessees would experience the same problems as the earl, especially as regarded running expenses. It is not surprising, therefore, to note that William del Sherd had failed to maintain the mill of Whaley when in his hands. Under such circumstances, although leases may have brought in a greater financial return

186 CHES 2/76, m 3 (4), *36 DKR*, p. 294.
187 SC 6/805/13, m 2d.
188 CHES 2/77, m 8 (2), *36 DKR*, p. 313.
189 SC 6/806/4, m 2.
190 SC 6/792/5, m 10, SC 6/793/4, m 6.
191 CHES 2/90, m 5d. (10), *37 DKR*, p. 638; SC 6/793/7, m 5d.
192 SC 6/1241/3, SC 6/795/7, m 6.

in the short term, they may not have served to the advantage of the earl in the long term, nor even to the advantage of the lessees themselves.

The fulling mills on the Dee in Chester were leased regularly, generally for a seven-year term at £10 13s. 4d. per annum. William de Wynbunbury leased them on these conditions from March 1395, renewing his lease for a further seven years from Michaelmas 1402.[193] Even so, the cost of repairs still had to be maintained by the earl, which reduced the profit of the farm by up to £8 per annum. After 1409, these mills could only be leased on a yearly basis until, in 1420, they stood empty for four months of the year,[194] and new lessees had to be found in 1421. Later in the 1420s, the fulling mills were once again a viable proposition for lessees and longer leases were taken out.[195]

Administrative as well as financial considerations played their part in the motivation towards leasing. Surveillance over the Macclesfield mills when under direct control was inadequate; there were frequent cases of thefts of grain from them.[196] Once leased, the onus of such surveillance would pass to the lessees. However, the behaviour of the labour force employed at the fulling mills remained a problem, even when lessees were installed.[197] In direct exploitation, the honesty of the officials employed was a problem, which provided further motivation towards leasing. However, at the Dee grinding mills – by far the most profitable of all the mills and possibly of all the sources of revenue belonging to the earl – the obvious dishonesty of the millers was countenanced for the sake of the far greater profits which accrued from direct control. Indeed, the frequent indictments, at specially instituted courts held

193 SC 6/774/11, m 2; *36 DKR*, p. 544, CHES 2/76, m 13 (4).

194 SC 6/1303/3, m 1.

195 For four years from 1425 (CHES 2/90, m 1 (4), *37 DKR*, p. 341), six years from 1435 (CHES 2/107, m 2d. (2), *37 DKR*, p. 547), and ten years from 1447 (CHES 2/121, m 5 (1), *37 DKR*, p. 547).

196 For example, SC 2/255/5, m 2d.

197 Rupert H. Morris, *Chester in the Plantagenet and Tudor Reigns* (Chester: printed for the author, 1893), p. 106. See also CHES 2/67, m 2d. (6), *36 DKR*, p. 41, and CHES 25/10 and 11 passim.

at the mills, of the millers for extortion and other nefarious practices, and of the citizens of Chester for failing to pay suit, and the commission of inquiry of 1400 into complaints of the citizens, are indications of an increasingly rigorous control over this vital source of revenue. For instance, the millers were indicted for charging too high rates for grinding, taking grain to their own use and failing to clean the mills.[198]

The inquiry settled many points in favour of the citizens; the mayor and commonalty of the city had complained about the malpractices of the millers in 1397.[199] But overall, it was the rights and profits of the lord which benefited from the new level of scrutiny. Richard II had abolished tolls on certain types of grain. The keeper, newly appointed by the new regime, was ordered to take tolls 'as of old accustomed' because the issues of the mills were not as large as they had been.[200] In addition, running costs were to be reduced. Millers had been receiving a money fee under Richard II. Following the 1400 inquiry, they were to revert to their old fees (presumably in kind) and were not to receive any other wage. From 5 July 1403, toll was taken on thirteen kinds of grain and grain products instead of only six, and a new keeper, Robert Castell, was installed.[201] In monetary terms, however, this imposition did not, as had been anticipated or hoped by the prince's council, cause a significant rise in revenue, because in fact the additional tolls were on a group of grains less valuable than those upon which tolls were consistently taken. The average livery of the years 1377 to 1399 therefore compares favourably with the equivalent figures for the period from 1400 to 1422 (see Table X).

198 Respectively, CHES 25/10, m 10, CHES 25/11, m 8, CHES 25/11, m 8. See also Richard Bennett and J. Elton, *History of Corn Milling*, vol. 4: *Some Feudal Mills* (London, 1904, repr. Wakefield: EP Publishing, 1975), p. 66. For the inquisition of 1400 see CHES 2/74, m 9 (7), *36 DKR*. p. 454. The results of the inquisition of 1400 are printed in full in Morris, *Chester in the Plantagenet and Tudor Reigns*, pp. 112–14.

199 CHES 2/71, m 9d. (5), *36 DKR*, p. 98.

200 CHES 2/74, m 9 (7), *36 DKR*, p. 454.

201 SC 6/791/1, m 5.

The inquiry of 1400 may have been more important as a reaffirmation of the earl's rights rather than as a move towards raising more revenue. The Dee Mills were especially important as one of the few demonstrations of seigneurial control in the city of Chester.[202] From the very large quantities of toll corn sold, it is clear that it was not only grain grown by the men of the city which was being milled and from which toll was being taken. There was little agricultural land in the city, although the citizens would most certainly have arable lands in the environs. Possibly toll was exacted upon grain housed in the city overnight as well as that grown there (as was the case at Macclesfield). There was most certainly an active trade in grain with the Welsh in which the citizens may have acted as middlemen. In 1402, for instance, bakers of the city were indicted for purchasing grain in Bromfield and having it milled in Wales at their own mills.[203] Grain was also brought in by ship from the Wirral, and much of this was probably sold to the Welsh. In 1400 it was claimed that such grain was paying toll when it should have been exempt.[204] In February 1402, there was a commission to investigate the conduct of certain 'engrossers and regrators' of the hundred of Wirral who had allegedly bought up and hoarded grain for sale in foreign parts to the damage of the poor of the hundred. It was subsequently ordered that the grain was to be sold in the open market and not leave the hundred.[205]

There was some decline in revenue from the sale of toll corn from 1400 to 1405, but prices per quarter were considerably higher in this period,[206] so that the decline occurred because less grain was being milled. This must surely have been due to restrictions upon export of corn from the Wirral and from the banning of the lucrative trade in corn with the Welsh.[207]

202 The king jealously guarded his rights to multure even when a guild of bakers was recognised in the 1460s (Bennett and Elton, *Some Feudal Mills*, pp. 78–80).

203 CHES 25/10, m 10.

204 Morris, *Chester*, p. 113.

205 CHES 2/75, m 3d (8), *36 DKR*, p. 385.

206 See Appendix III.

207 CHES 2/76, m 8d. (4), *36 DKR*, p. 103; CHES 2/78, m 1 (3–5), *36 DKR*, p. 23; *36 DKR*, p. 226 passim; *PROME*, viii. 40.

More grain taken in toll at the mills was being commandeered for the use of the prince's household based in Cheshire and for English armies and garrisons in North Wales. In 1404, grain from the mills was used for the victualling of troops used for the recovery of the castle of Beaumaris.[208] In the following year, William Venables, as constable of Chester Castle, had taken twenty-three pounds of corn from the mills for the provisioning of the castle when Glyndwr was threatening the county.[209] In 1401, corn had been delivered to the treasurer of the prince's household. It is not a coincidence that Robert Castell, who had been appointed keeper of the Dee Mills in June 1401, was also havener (*avenarius*) of the prince's household at this point.[210] Such supplies to the household would decrease the stocks available for sale and so inflate the price of grain in the city. After 1412, profits from the sale fluctuated in accordance with the rise and fall in prices, for quantities milled were relatively constant. As prices were lower in the first half of the period, income from the mills was depleted, but still formed an important contribution to the earl's demesne revenue.

## Fisheries and Ports

Cheshire was well endowed with rivers and had easy access to the sea. Hence the earl might expect a reasonable income from a monopoly of fishing rights in his demesnes. Fish remained an important element in the medieval diet, especially in Lent, when, in Cheshire, it formed the diet on Fridays and Saturdays.[211] The earl's fishery in the River Dee at Chester was kept in hand throughout the period. Profits from the sale of fish were accounted by the keeper of the Dee grinding mills, although a fisherman was employed to administer the fishery. It

208 SC 6/791/7, m 6.

209 SC 6/791/10, m 8d. He did not pay for it but was pardoned the sum in Aug 1413 (*CPR 1413–16*, p. 93).

210 SC 6/791/3, m 5, E 101/406/24, f. 34.

211 C. Anne Wilson, *Food and Drink in Britain: From the Stone Age to Recent Times* (London: Constable, 1973), p. 31. Elsewhere in Britain it was also the sole diet on Wednesdays. For evidence of fish in the diet of the chamberlain of Chester, see E 101/620/24.

would appear from indictments for stealing fish from the fishery that it consisted of an enclosed space of water in which fish were reared. In order to gain access, thieves had to remove stones from the Dee bridge.[212] In 1399–1400, £26 3s. 7d. was spent on repairing the stone of the bridge for the sake of the protection of the mills as well as the defence of the city.[213] There were much larger stocks than were sold, and it is impossible to assess the determinants of sale. For instance, according to an indictment of 1401, 1,200 lampreys were stolen in one night, yet there are no records of profits from the sale of that kind of fish.[214] Some fish would presumably be kept for breeding purposes, others used as victuals at Chester Castle and elsewhere. Certainly, five salmon from the fishery were consumed by the prince's council when it was in Chester in March and April 1408.[215] Salmon were sold in the largest quantities for the largest return, but with wide yearly fluctuations in quantity. In 1415, for instance, 155 were sold but only twenty-six in 1416.[216] Young salmon, kippers (*keperes*), dead fish and lampreys were also sold.

There was an active market for fish in the city of Chester, and not only fish from the Dee fishery was sold there but also fish caught at Shotwick. In 1422, for instance, Richard Wellay of Runcorn was charged with forestalling the market by buying fish at Shotwick which was bound for sale at Chester, and carrying it for sale at Coventry.[217] The fisheries at Shotwick were important items in manorial income, although they were leased to certain tenants for a farm of around £3 per annum when not included in the lease of the whole manor.[218] In addition, small profits were derived from licences to fish on the seashore

212 CHES 25/10, m 7d, CHES 25/11, m 1, m 8.

213 SC 6/774/11, m 6.

214 CHES 25/10, m 7d.

215 SC 6/792/3, m 5d.

216 SC 6/793/2, m 8, SC 6/793/4, m 5. Of the total income of £13 10s. 10d. from the sale of fish in 1409, £11 13s. 0d. came from the sale of 114 salmon. Of £18 7s. 11d. in 1406, £17 13s. 0d. was from the sale of 162 salmon (SC 6/792/5, m 5, SC 6/791/10, m 8).

217 CHES 25/11, m 22d. See also CHES 25/9, m 49.

218 For instance, SC 6/791/1, m 3, SC 2/156/13, m 2.

within the lordship of Shotwick, from a salmon toll, from tidal fish traps and from a freshwater lake in the park.[219] The tenants may have controlled the major fisheries, but the lord's rights over what must have been an extensive activity in the manor were maintained. In April 1409, for instance, a tenant was punished for constructing a fishery on the lord's water without permission.[220] There was similar control at Northwich, where the fishery was leased between 1403 and 1410 at 2s. 6d. per annum,[221] and also over unlicensed fishing in the River Dane in Macclesfield Forest.[222]

When Frodsham was taken back into direct control after the death of Radegonde Béchet in 1408, there was very little profit accruing from the fisheries there, although four were in existence. There was no profit from 'Tursheb' and 'Blyndeb', and only 4s. 0d. to 5s. 0d. from 'Les Warthes', although the first two were said to be worth 10s. 0d. each, and the third £1 4s. 0d.[223] There was some attempt to increase income from these three fisheries and the fourth, 'Inchweir', by means of leases for a term of years. Les Warthes was leased to two tenants for seven years from September 1419 for 13s. 4d. per annum, and Inchweir to Laurence de Aston for two years from April 1414 at 3s. 4d. per annum.[224] Disrepair was a problem, and Inchweir passed back into the lord's hands after its lease for two years in 1414 and could not be leased out again for lack of a tenant.

Income from the customs of the ports of Frodsham and 'Pull' (Overpool and Netherpool) was also disappointing, despite their importance. Frodsham was already an important

219 On tidal traps see Dodgson, *Place Names*, iii. 235.

220 SC 2/156/13, m 3.

221 SC 6/791/6, m 2d. – SC 6/792/6, m 3d. For an example of unlicensed fishing there in 1411 by Robert, son of William Starkey, see CHES 25/9, m 138.

222 SC 2/255/14, m 5, SC 2/255/18, m 3.

223 SC 6/793/2, m 6. Les Warthes were 'places on the shore', and Tursheb 'a pointed tongue of land on the shore' (Dodgson, *Place Names*, iii. 235).

224 CHES 2/92, m 9d. (8), *37 DKR*, p. 297; CHES 2/87, m 5 (6), *37 DKR*, p. 296.

port in the late thirteenth century; in the following century, salt was exported from there.[225] In 1409, the first year of comital control, only 17s. 4d. was raised, and discussion on this source of revenue was ordered.[226] There was an initial increase, but then issues were sadly depleted, falling to as little as 8d. in 1421, the issues of one ship at Frodsham.[227] In 1413, John Willoughby of 'Pull' was ordered to levy the customs for three years in the port of Frodsham from 'Pull' (now Overpool and Netherpool) to Le Wormehole.[228] He raised £1 in 1414 and 1415 but could only raise 5s. 8d. in the following year.[229] In response, the port was farmed to Sir John Pulle for two years from 1416 for 10s. 0d. per annum[230] After his farm, issues fell to 1s. 3d. per annum, suggesting that the port of Frodsham had declined substantially in business and importance in the early fifteenth century.[231] Little profit was received in this period from customs at Chester on wine, iron and leather, indicating perhaps a lack of seigneurial exploitation rather than a lean time for the commercial sector of the city.[232]

## Seigneurial Monopolies

In addition to manorial mills where the paying of suit by tenants was compulsory, and forests and parks where there was a continuing stress upon seigneurial rights, the earl derived

225 Sharp, 'Earldom and County of Chester', pp. 361–2; P. H. W. Booth, *Cheshire Estate Records: Use and Abuse*, University of Liverpool, School of History and Institute of Extension Studies, Medieval Cheshire Seminar (Nov. 1975), privately printed, p. 10.

226 SC 6/792/5, m 10.

227 SC 6/794/1, m 5d.

228 CHES 2/86, m 3d. (2), *37 DKR*, p. 816.

229 SC 6/793/1, m 4, SC 6/793/2, m 6, SC 6/793/4, m 6.

230 SC 6/793/7, m 5.

231 1419, 3 shillings (SC 6/793/9, m 5), 1420 1s. 4d. (SC 6/793/11, m 5d), 1421, 1s. 8d. (SC 6/794/1, m 5d), 1422, 1s. 8d. (SC 6/794/2, m 5d).

232 J. T. Driver, *Cheshire in the Later Middle Ages* (Chester: Cheshire Community Council, 1971), p. 98. See also K. P. Wilson, 'The Port of Chester in the Fifteenth Century', *THSLC*, 117 (1965), 1–15.

profits from the exploitation of other seigneurial monopolies. Tolls connected with merchandising in general were levied at Frodsham, Macclesfield *burgus*, Northwich and Middlewich. With one exception, such tolls (market dues and stallage) were directly controlled and collected by the relevant local official.[233] The exception was stallage at Macclesfield which was leased to a group of tenants from 1413.[234] After 1417, it was leased to Reginald del Dounes at a reduced rate, for six years.[235] At least his farm of £1 per annum ensured a steady income after a rather disastrous year in which only 13s. 7d. had been raised from the tenants. In addition, at the Wiches, there was income from tolls imposed upon certain aspects of the salt industry, customary payments assessed upon the number of leads in each salthouse ('hurdelsalt', and 'stuth' at Middlewich), a charge upon carts bringing wood into the towns for use in boiling ('stuth' at Northwich and Middlewich) and a toll on purchases of salt ('tolstok').[236] A further toll at Middlewich, 'sisebriche', may have had some connection with fines for licences to brew.[237] In addition, fines for licences to boil salt were paid by non-burgesses in both Wiches, and accounted within the perquisites of courts.[238] Such categories of income were extremely important; at Middlewich, salt and market tolls provided 70–75% of the total income.[239]

233 Profits of the market tolls at Macclesfield were accounted 'beyond the fees of the officials of the lord king' ('ultra feoda officiarii domini regis') (SC 2/255/17, m 4d). The catchpole was at one time called 'approver of the tolls and stallage' (SC 2/255/12, m 5d).
234 SC 6/806/6, m 1d.
235 SC 6/806/13, m 1d; CHES 2/90, m 9 (2), *37 DKR*, p. 219.
236 The nature of these tolls is discussed in detail in *A Middlewich Chartulary*, ed. Joan Varley, 2 vols, Chetham Society, 105, 108 (with James Tait) (1941–4), i. 43 onwards.
237 SC 2/156/3, m 3.
238 SC 2/156/11, m 1, SC 2/156/3, m 1d; *Middlewich Cartulary*, i. 23.
239 References to the accounts of each year are as in Appendix II (e), (f), (g), and (i).

## Table IX (a) Tolls at Frodsham, 1400–22

| Year | Small tolls and tallage |
|---|---|
| 1409 | 4s. 10d. |
| 1410 | 2s. 4½d. |
| 1411 | 1s. 11d. |
| 1412 | 3s. 10½d. |
| 1413 | 3s. 2d. |
| 1414 | 3s. 7d. |
| 1415 | 1s. 4d. |
| 1416 | 1s. 8d. |
| 1417 | damaged. |
| 1418 | 1s. 6d. |
| 1419 | 1s. 6d. |
| 1420 | 1s. 2d. |
| 1421 | 1s. 1d. |
| 1422 | 1s. 0d. |
| | |

## (b) Tolls at Macclesfield *burgus*, 1400–22

| Year | Market tolls | Small tolls and stallage | Total |
|---|---|---|---|
| 1401 | £2 13s. 7d. | £1 14s. 2d. | £4 7s. 9d. |
| 1402 | £3 17s. 7d. | £1 11s. 7d. | £5 9s. 2d. |
| 1403 | £ 1 18s. 9½d. | £1 3s. 4d. | £3 2s. 1½d. |
| 1404 | £2 5s. 7d. | £1 3s. 4d. | £3 8s. 11d. |
| 1405 | £1 14s. 8d. | £1 6s. 4d. | £3 0s. 0d. |
| 1406 | £1 2s. 10d. | £1 6s. 9d. | £2 9s. 7d. |
| 1407 | £ 12s. 6d. | £1 7s. 0d. | £2 19s. 6d. |
| 1408 | 18s. 11d. | £1 7s. 0d. | £2 5s. 11d. |
| 1409 | | | |
| 1410 | £3 4s. 4d. | £1 7s. 0d. | £4 11s. 6d. |
| 1411 | | | |

| Year | Market tolls | Small tolls and stallage | Total |
|---|---|---|---|
| 1412 | £2 3s. 1d. | £1 7s. 0d. | £3 10s. 0d. |
| 1413 | 17s. 10d. | £1 7s. 0d. | £2 4s. 10d. |
| 1414 | 10s. 5d. | £1 7s. 0d. | £1 17s. 5d. |
| 1415 | £1 8s. 0d. | £1 7s. 0d. | £2 15s. 0d. |
| 1416 | 12s. 5d. | 13s. 7d. | £1 6s. 0d. |
| 1417 | 9s. 4½d. | £1 | £1 9s. 4½d. |
| 1418 | 12s. 6d. | £1 | £ 1 12s. 6d. |
| 1419 | nil | £1 | £1 |
| 1420 | 11½d. | £1 | £1 0s. 11½d. |
| 1421 | 5½d. | £1 | £1 0s. 5½d. |
| 1422 | 6d. | £1 | £1 0s. 6d. |

## (c) Tolls at Northwich, 1400–22

| Year | Market tolls | Stuth and Hacstuth | Total |
|---|---|---|---|
| 1400 | £18 19s. 1d. | 18s. 6d. | £19 7s. 7d. |
| 1401 | £13 14s. 9d. | 9s. 0d. | £13 13s. 9d. |
| 1402 | £23 0s. 11d. | 13s. 4d. | £23 14s. 3d. |
| 1403 | £23 14s. 0d. | 13s. 4d. | £24 7s. 4d. |
| 1404 | £27 17s. 4d. | 13s. 4d. | £28 10s. 8d. |
| 1405 | £26 10s. 2d. | 13s. 4d. | £27 3s. 6d. |
| 1406 | £26 16s. 6d. | 13s. 4d. | £27 9s. 10d. |
| 1407 | £29 2s. 0d. | 13s. 4d. | £29 15s. 4d. |
| 1408 | £20 4s. 4d. | 13s. 4d. | £20 17s. 8d. |
| 1409 | £21 19s. 6d. | 13s. 4d. | £22 12s. 10s. |
| 1410 | £25 16s. 11d. | 13s. 4d. | £26 10s. 3d. |
| 1411 | farm | farm | farm |
| 1412 | farm | farm | farm |
| 1413 | farm | farm | farm |
| 1414 | £19 7s. 9d. | 13s. 4d. | £20 1s. 1d. |
| 1415 | £22 13s. 6d. | 13s. 4d. | £23 6s. 10d. |

| Year | Market tolls | Stuth and Hacstuth | Total |
|---|---|---|---|
| 1416 | farm | farm | farm |
| 1417 | farm | farm | farm |
| 1418 | farm | farm | farm |
| 1419 | £21 5s. 9d. | 13s. 4d. | £22 9s. 1d. |
| 1420 | c. £16 14s. 10½d. | 13s. 4d. | £17 8s. 2½d. |

## (d) Tolls at Middlewich, 1400–22

| Year | Fairs | Farms of shops and stallage | Issues of the hall | Sisebriche |
|---|---|---|---|---|
| 1400 | 8s. 3d. | £1 8s. 8d. | 10s. 10½d. | £7 12s. 7d. |
| 1401 | £1 2s. 7d. | 5s. 8d. | 7s. 7½d. | £7 10s. 7d. |
| 1402 | 7s. 8d. | 19s. 0d. | 10s. 5½d. | £5 9s. 7d. |
| 1403 | 12s. 2d. | 18s. 0d. | 10s. 2d. | £7 12s. 9d. |
| 1404 | 14s. 3d. | £1 1s. 4d. | 14s. 4½d. | £9 11s. 6d. |
| 1405 | 14s. 11d. | £1 4s. 8d. | 15s. 3½d. | £8 11s. 7d. |
| 1406 | £1 0s. 6d. | £1 7s. 4d. | 14s. 0d. | £5 9s. 0d. |
| 1407 | 15s. 9d. | £1 7s. 4d. | 9s. 8½d. | £8 10s. 2d. |
| 1408 | £2 3s. | £ 1 12s. 0d. | 5s. 3d. | £7 1s. 3d. |
| 1409 | 10s. 4d. | £1 13s. 10d. | 3s. 3½d. | £6 14s. 6d. |
| 1410 | £1 0s. 0d. | £1 7s. 4d. | 14s. 0d. | £5 2s. 0d. |
| 1411 | 9s. 2d. | £1 6s. 8d. | 3s. 5d. | £6 4s. 4d. |
| 1412 | 11s. 7½d. | £1 3s. 4d. | 3s. 6½d. | £6 7s. 11d. |
| 1413 | 5s. 8d. | £1 3s. 4d. | 3s. 9½d. | £6 1s. 5d. |
| 1414 | £1 7s. 9½d. | £1 0s. 0d. | 3s. 5½d. | £4 15s. 1d. |
| 1415 | 6s. 6d. | £1 4s. 8d. | 11½d. | £6 3s. 5d. |
| 1416 | 9s. 0d. | £1 3s. 5d. | 2s. 9½d. | £5 1s. 0d. |
| 1417 | 5s. 11d. | £1 4s. 0d. | 2s. 6½d. | £6 5s. 0d. |
| 1418 | 5s. 11d. | £1 4s. 0d. | 2s. 6½d. | £6 5s. 0d. |
| 1419 | 8s. 8d. | £1. 0s. 0½d. | 1s. 3d. | £3 11s. 1d. |

| Year | Fairs | Farms of shops and stallage | Issues of the hall | Sisebriche |
|---|---|---|---|---|
| 1420 | 3s. 3½d. | £1 3s. 4d. | with fairs | £5 8s. 1d. |
| 1421 | 2s. 8d. | £1 0s. 0d. | with fairs | £4 8s. 3d. |
| 1422 | 3s. 0d. | £1 0s. 0d. | with fairs | £4 0s. 9d. |

| Year | Tolstock | Stuth | Hurdelsalt |
|---|---|---|---|
| 1400 | £15 19s. 0d. | £2 4s. 7d. | £6 11s. 8½d. |
| 1401 | £16 5s. 5d. | £2 2s. 8d. | £6 19s. 7½d. |
| 1402 | £22 0s. 0d. | £2 3s. 1d. | £7 15s. 9½d. |
| 1403 | £15 3s. 0d. | £2 3s. 11d. | £6 6s. 0½d. |
| 1404 | £21 17s. 0d. | £2 2s. 11d. | £7 11s. 11d. |
| 1405 | £22 9s. 10d. | £2 0s. 8d. | £7 10s. 3½d. |
| 1406 | £24 12s. 8d. | £2 2s. 0d. | £8 15s. 10d. |
| 1407 | £20 5s. 5d. | £2 4s. 4d. | £8 19s. 10d. |
| 1408 | £15 11s. 0d. | £2 6s. 1d. | £5 7s. 0½d. |
| 1409 | £22 19s. 2d. | £2 5s. 9d. | £7 15s. 6½d. |
| 1410 | £20 0s. 0d. | £2 6s. 0d. | £6 0s. 0d. |
| 1411 | £14 15s. 9d. | £2 0s. 0d. | £7 0s. 10d. |
| 1412 | £15 1s. 2d. | £2 4s. 4½d. | £6 12s. 10½d. |
| 1413 | £19 4s. 11d. | £2 0s. 11d. | £7 3s. 1½d. |
| 1414 | £15 16s. 5d. | £2 2s. 0½d. | £7 6s. 3½d. |
| 1415 | £17 17s. 4d. | £2 1s. 8½d. | £6 11s. 0d. |
| 1416 | £16 19s. 0d. | £1 18s. 2½d. | £5 19s. 11d. |
| 1417 | £15 18s. 7d. | £2 1s. 4½d. | £6 19s. 11d. |
| 1418 | £15 18s. 7½d. | £2 1s. 7½d. | £6 19s. 11d. |
| 1419 | £14 13s. 2d. | £1 17s. 7½d. | £5 16s. 0d. |
| 1420 | £10 16s. 3½d. | £2 2s. 1½d. | £6 16s. 6½d. |
| 1421 | £12 9s. 1d. | £1 19s. 4½d. | £5 15s. 3d. |
| 1422 | £14 14s. 7d. | £1 18s. 3½d. | £6 7s. 0d. |

| Year | Total | Year | Total |
|---|---|---|---|
| 1400 | £34 15s. 8d. | 1412 | £32 4s. 10d. |
| 1401 | £34 12s. 2d. | 1413 | £36 3s. 1½d. |
| 1402 | £39 5s. 9d. | 1414 | £32 11s. 1d. |
| 1403 | £33 6s. 0½d. | 1415 | £34 5s. 7d. |
| 1404 | £43 14s. 3½d. | 1416 | £32 13s. 4½d. |
| 1405 | £43 7s. 3d. | 1417 | £32 17s. 4d. |
| 1406 | £43 11s. 4d. | 1418 | £32 18s. 5½d. |
| 1407 | £42 12s. 6½d. | 1419 | £290 7s. 10d. |
| 1408 | £34 16s. 11½d. | 1420 | £26 9s. 8d. |
| 1409 | £42 2s. 5d. | 1421 | £26 4s. 7½d. |
| 1410 | £36 9s. 4d. | 1422 | £28 3s. 7½d. |
| 1411 | £32 0s. 2½d. | | |

Income from all such tolls is stated in Table IX (a-d). With the exception of Northwich, all units display a considerable decline towards the end of the period in income received from market and allied tolls. This is especially noticeable in the level of market tolls at Macclesfield, where they fell from £2–£3 at the opening of the period to a few pence in the last years of Henry V. Possibly market dues remained more buoyant at the Wiches, especially Northwich, owing to the salt market in the town which would attract much custom. There was also a fall in income from salt tolls, but this was not as marked as with the general market tolls, save in certain bad years. In 1420 for instance, Tolstock received at Middlewich was half what it had been ten years previously. Considering total income from all tolls, the decline over the period is very noticeable. This may have been due to economic trends affecting market sales and salt prices, or to the falling off of comital exploitation.

The earl had little means, despite these salt tolls, to exploit the already highly important Cheshire industry of salt production. He had little control over the tenure of salthouses (*saline*). He was not himself directly involved in production, for he did not possess any salthouses under his direct control. This may have been true of the lords of Nantwich also; in the early part of the fifteenth century, the total profits of mills, perquisites of court, market and salt tolls there were estimated at £12 per annum.[240]

There was little comital exploitation of industry elsewhere in the county. As discussed earlier in this chapter, the Dee fulling mills were leased regularly. The two iron forges in Macclesfield Forest, located at 'Rudyng', contributed no revenue. This was not a new problem by any means. They had been intended to yield over £17 in 1349, but by 1351 only one was operative and by 1354 none at all, 'for lack of farmers'.[241] The accounts for 1399–1422 explain year-on-year that no one could be found to take them to farm, yet an entry for them was retained. There was some small income from coal mining in the forest in certain years, rights being leased for 8s. 0d. per annum.[242] Ancillary industries must have existed, especially in the forest areas, but the earl did not participate nor exploit them, save by controlling the supply and sale of wood.

It might have been expected that the earl should have a stranglehold over the economy of the *burgi* especially by virtue of the exercise of his seigneurial rights, yet he did not. This is further displayed by the small income he was able to raise from the communal ovens. At Northwich, Middlewich, Frodsham and Macclesfield *burgus*, all tenants owed to suit at the oven. At Macclesfield, burgesses and residents in the *burgus* were to pay suit at the lord's oven no matter what kind of bread was to be baked there and were to pay the accustomed fee.[243] In fact, all ovens were leased; that at Frodsham to the community as

240 E 163/6/41 item 24. For an assessment of Cheshire salt production in general, see A. F. Calvert, *Salt in Cheshire* (London: Spon; New York: Spon and Chamberlain, 1915) and A. R. Bridbury, *England and the Salt Trade in the Later Middle Ages* (Oxford: Clarendon Press, 1955).

241 Booth, *Financial Admin.*, p. 97. For other forges in the forest in the late fourteenth century see A. M. Tonkinson, *Macclesfield in the Later Fourteenth Century: Communities of Town and Forest*, Chetham Society, 3rd ser., 42 (1999), pp. 21–2.

242 SC 2/255/5, m 5, SC 2/255/6, m 4d, SC 2/255/7, m 2d.

243 SC 11/898, m 2. The common oven in the town remained crown property until the nineteenth century (Dodgson, *Place Names*, i. 113).

a whole, the other three to local tenants. It is hard to believe that the small farms (£1 10s. 0d. at Frodsham, Middlewich and Northwich and £2 per annum at Macclesfield) were the maximum profits which could be raised when every tenant had to bake his bread there. Farming the ovens was probably preferred because of the high costs of repairs. At Middlewich, a new oven was built at the earl's expense in 1415 at a cost which exceeded the income from the farm in that year. Over the whole period, the farm brought in a revenue of £30 10s. 0d. but repairs cost a total of £7 6s. 4d.[244] It is interesting to observe that, in the first year of the tenure of Northwich by the Hollands, the oven was directly exploited and a special official installed. But, in fact, he raised only 9 shillings compared with the previous income from the farm of £1 10s. 0d. Blame was placed upon the state of disrepair of the oven. In the subsequent year, the oven was leased to a local baker but at a much reduced rate of 10s. 0d. per annum.[245]

Whatever the disadvantages of direct control, it is clear, both from the examples quoted here and from the further evidence of other sources of income arising out of the exercise of lordship, that seigneurial monopolies and rights were not being exploited to the full. In general, the lord's control over revenue and commercial organisation was becoming more nominal and anachronistic, especially in the *burgi*. The decline in revenue from such sources was symptomatic of a continuing and unremitting ossification and stagnation. Such a phenomenon has been seen on the other estates in the period. On the Talbot estates at Whitchurch, there was a sharp drop in income from courts, mills and markets (especially when in hand) in the early fifteenth century.[246] There, too, the fall in income was not just

244 SC 6/793/2, m 5. Over the whole period the farm brought in a revenue of £30 10s. 0d. but repairs cost a total of £7 6s. 4d.

245 SC 6/810/15, m 1, m 3; SC 6/810/15, m 2.

246 A. J. Pollard, 'The Family of Talbot, Lords Talbot and Earls of Shrewsbury in the Fifteenth Century', unpublished PhD thesis (University of Bristol, 1968), pp. 373–5, 380; A. J. Pollard, 'Estate Management in the Later Middle Ages: The Talbots and Whitchurch 1383–1525', *EcHR*, 2nd ser., 25 (1972), 553–66, p. 558. A similar

due to a decline in the prosperity of the manor, but also to the failure of the lord to tap the actual sources of mercantile and commercial income, and to a slackening intensity of exploitation. It is perhaps in this phenomenon, rather than in economic trends, that we must seek evidence for and causes of the malaise of the seigneurial economy in this period.

## Judicial Income

All tenants of the demesnes owed suit at the manorial courts, so that the latter were an important demonstration and reaffirmation of continuing seigneurial control when other categories of income were gradually being alienated from such control. They were also a valuable source of income. Indeed, as in the duchy of Cornwall, such courts were probably geared more towards the raising of money than to the enforcement of manorial discipline.[247] Income from such a source was highly irregular, however, varying from year to year according to the amount of business put before the court, and to any supplementary, perhaps casual, sources of income which were accounted within the total of perquisites of court.[248] Communal and individual entry fines at Macclesfield and Drakelow were so accounted. Judicial income was not a source of revenue which allowed much scope for intentioned increase or decrease, yet often the sum raised in a particularly remunerative year was quoted as a model to be emulated in subsequent years.

Judicial income in the demesnes arose from many sources. In addition to manorial courts held at Drakelow, Frodsham, Shotwick, Northwich, Middlewich, Macclesfield Forest and Macclesfield *burgus*, where the major income arose from fines imposed for misdemeanours, there was miscellaneous casual

situation existed regarding the mills of the earls of Northumberland at Cockermouth and Topcliffe (Bean, *Estates of the Percy Family*, pp. 19, 25 and 39).

247 Hatcher, *Rural Economy*, p. 193.

248 Full details on the income of courts at various locations is given in Appendix II.

income from strays, the sale of chattels of felons, and death duties. In the city of Chester, for instance, the citizens were allowed to keep the profits of goods and chattels of felons to the value of £30, so that the earl received £5 only in 1421 when Thomas Haune had forfeits worth £35.[249] The regard of the forest was never held in this period; it was noted on the accounts that it was due to be held every three years, and the council certainly discussed the possibility of holding it in 1407.[250]

Even so, much income arose in both Delamere and Macclesfield Forest from fines connected with forest rights – fines for illegal hunting, cutting wood, forfeits, etc. Judicial income from such offences, as from many other cases arising in the demesnes, which were dealt with in the eyre or county court were accounted by the sheriff, save in the case of Macclesfield and Frodsham where they were accounted on the relevant demesne accounts. The burgesses of Macclesfield were not bound to appear at the county court at Chester so a special eyre was held in the lordship.[251] Judicial income formed all the revenue accruing in the hundred of Macclesfield, save for £6 6s. 8d. in rents.

Where there were few other sources of income, perquisites of court formed an important contribution. Such was the case at Middlewich and Northwich where they formed 25% and 20%, respectively, of the total income. Only around 5% of the total income came from such a source at Shotwick and Drakelow, and 10–25% at Frodsham. All three Macclesfield accounting units where judicial income was raised experienced a decline in this source over this period, and hence a decline in total revenues. This is especially marked in the case of Macclesfield hundred where so much of the income came from courts. In the *burgus*, c. 16% of total income arose from judicial income during the reign of Henry IV. In the reign of his son, this fell to 7½%, with a corresponding fall in real money value.

A decline in judicial income in the fifteenth century was seen on the estates of the Talbots in North Shropshire and also on

249 SC 6/794/1, m 1.
250 SC 6/792/2, m 2.
251 Sharp, 'Earldom and County of Chester', p. 329.

the prince's estates in the duchy of Cornwall.[252] In the second case, this was seen as a result of the combined influence of many factors, amongst which was the slow fall in the numbers of the unfree, for previously many perquisites had arisen from various tenurial obligations. In Cheshire, too, a multiplicity of factors is seen, although income connected with tenurial obligation was already minimal. In general, the decline in income from courts was yet another indication of the malaise of the seigneurial economy.

## Conclusions on expenditure and profitability on the demesnes

An examination of the size and nature of demesne expenses is necessary in order to assess the cost of direct control in relation to farming out, and to consider the question of capital investment as a reflection of estate policy. Some general observations might be made initially. The first is that administrative costs were not always the prime factor in the minds of policy makers; efficiency and the need for good lordship were more important than their price. The concept of profit in medieval terms was multi-faceted and did not comprise solely financial return. The second was related to Cheshire in particular, where there was a conscious move in this period to keep expenses charged on the demesne accounts as low as possible, sometimes artificially so by transferring their cost to the chamberlain's accounts. Before the motivation behind this policy, and also general economic trends in the county are discussed, it is necessary to pay some attention to the size and nature of demesne expenses.

In general, demesnes had very low running costs even without this move towards bearing them out of county revenues. Wages were usually at the rate of 1d.–3d. per day, or even lower. A few shillings would be expended upon parchment, or paid in tithe, on the issues of the mills or, as at Shotwick, on the herbage of the park.[253] Repairs of capital equipment were the

252 Pollard, 'Family of Talbot', p. 376; Hatcher, *Rural Economy*, p. 196.
253 SC 6/792/3, m 3d.

largest and most troublesome expense on almost all demesnes. At Macclesfield park, for instance, their cost could consume half or more of the current issues; in 1410, for instance, repairs cost £7 7s. 8d. whilst receipts were £8 10s. 10d.[254] Although repairs in the forest and *burgus* were not so significant in relation to current issues, in some years they could be very expensive. In the *burgus* they were certainly increasing towards the end of the period.[255] All mills were costly to maintain, as we have seen. At Frodsham, there was always the problem of encroachment by the sea on the demesne lands. The sea ditch had to be repaired and strengthened against the tides almost every year, but floods could still cause much damage in this area. It was owing to the neglect of repairs to the ditch that the manor had been temporarily seized back into the hands of the prince in 1406, and much had to be spent on repairs after the death of Radegonde Béchet when the manor passed back into the permanent control of the earl.[256] In most cases, repairs cannot be seen as capital investment, but rather as attention necessarily paid to the preservation and maintenance of pre-existing sources of income. In Macclesfield Forest there was possibly capital investment in the erection of new fencing and enclosures.[257] The building of a new mill at Northwich might also be interpreted in such a light.

Overall, little money was invested in the demesnes, and there was a conscious policy to run them on a shoestring. Demesne expenses were sometimes kept low by artificial means. Several demesne officials were paid out of county revenues. These included the stewards of Macclesfield. Demesne issues would have been sadly depleted if their fee of 100 marks per annum had to be paid out of them.[258] Those demesne officials

254 SC 6/806/4, m 3.

255 See Appendix II (i) and (k).

256 Their total cost amounted to £58 7s. 2½d. in 1409 and £47 5s. 6d. in 1410 (SC 6/792/5, m 10, SC 6/792/6, m 6).

257 SC 6/807/2, m 3.

258 On the last account of the reign of Henry V, however, the steward was paid out of Macclesfield revenues for the Michaelmas term of 1422 when the manor was in the hands of Queen Catherine (SC 6/807/3, m 2d).

who no longer fulfilled any active function were also paid out of county revenues, their wages being equivalent to annuities. The equitators of Delamere and Macclesfield forests were so paid, as was the keeper of Chester Castle garden. Certain officials who performed their duties in person were also paid out of county revenues, such as the sellers of crops in Delamere Forest and the parkers of Macclesfield and Shotwick. After 1414, all repairs to the Dee corn mills were transferred to the cost of the chamberlain.[259] Those of the fulling mills were already accounted there.

There are two reasons behind this treatment of demesne expenses, both embodying phenomena only possible in a rentier economy. First, there was the development of the idea of a non-accounting unit, such as already noted at Drakelow, and, as we shall see, at Northwich, where the discharge was intended to consume the charge completely. Secondly, it was already realised that demesne income was relatively static. There was a desire to keep it as such, without the fluctuations which an increase or decrease in expenses could create, so that the revenue arising from the demesne could be accurately anticipated. This was important once a commitment had been made, based upon such knowledge, to pay foreign expenses out of demesne issues. Annuities were therefore granted according to revenues available. After 1411, those at Northwich were adjusted to consume the entire charge. By 1415, with the exception of the wages of the fisherman, only foreign expenses were paid out of the revenues of the Dee Mills, namely wages of 6d. per day to the absentee keeper, annuities to the value of £20 per annum, and the daily expenses of the auditors whilst in the county. Fossilization of income was thus an integral part of this rentier economy.

The Cheshire demesne economy of this period demonstrates two main trends –fossilization and/or decline of revenues. Where income was chiefly from rents, then income was fossilised. Although there is little evidence of decayed tenements

259 See Appendix I (b).

on a large scale, there was little scope for increasing rents, so that those received by the earl were grossly uneconomic. Forests and parks provided a steady but traditional income. The leasing of lands still had some vitality, but overall there was little increase or decrease in income. Where there was fluctuation in income, the trend was downwards. There was, for instance, a considerable decline in income from seigneurial monopolies for two basic reasons. First, the revenue of a borough, comprised largely of such monopolies, was less susceptible to control than a manorial type of lordship. Secondly, there was a slackening intensity of exploitation of commercial activities by the earl, possibly based upon ignorance of such untraditional sources of seigneurial income. This was crucial as regards the overall trends of demesnes revenues. As there was little chance of an increase in income from agricultural sources, or rents, the only opportunities for such lay in the exercise of seigneurial monopolies and jurisdiction, the profits of which were declining.

These trends are demonstrated in the following table of comparative values over a period of almost eighty years (Table X). Where values for this period were not roughly the same as in the 1376 valor of the Black Prince's lands in the county,[260] then in almost every case they were lower, the exceptions being Delamere Forest and, more significantly perhaps, the revenues of the sheriff and escheator of the county, which are considered in Chapter 6.

Significant declines are seen in the *burgi* of Middlewich, Northwich and, to a lesser extent, Macclesfield, where revenue was chiefly from seigneurial monopolies and the profits of justice. It seems from the cursory glance at statistics for the reign of Richard II that a decline in income occurred in the decades after 1376, with perhaps a slight recovery in this period. After this period, there was a more substantial decline towards the valor of the estates of Edward, prince of Wales, in Cheshire in 1454,[261] although to assess this fully one would need to examine all the intervening accounts. A foreboding of this decline in

260 C 47/9/57, m, given in Booth, *Financial Admin.* Appendix VII.
261 SC 11/868.

demesne revenues is reflected in trends from about 1409 onwards. Income from the Cheshire demesnes, including the revenues from the sheriff and escheator of the county, shows a downward trend from nearly £700 in 1409 to £500 in 1422, with a similar fall in Macclesfield revenues of over 50% in these years. When these revenues are split into their constituent parts, then the decline in revenue from landed as opposed to non-landed income is clearly demonstrated.

## Table X. Comparative values 1376–1454

| | 1376 valor | Average livery 1377–99[a] | Average balance excl. arrears 1400–22 | Average livery 1400–22 | 1454 valor |
|---|---|---|---|---|---|
| Chester city – sheriffs | £104 0s. 0d. | £59 9s. 4d. | £103 13s. 10d. | £96 17s. 9d. | £20 7s. 2½d. |
| Chester city – escheator | | 6s. 8d. | £1 12s. 1½d. | 15s. 8d. | 7s. 0d. |
| Dee corn mills | £240 0s. 0d. | £174 7s. 4d.[b] | £178 6s. 2d.[b] | £172 0s. 9d.[b] | £68 6s. 4d. |
| Dee fulling mills | | £7 7s. 2d.[b] | £10 10s. 0d.[b] | £10 10s. 0d.[b] | |
| Delamere Forest | £51 7s. 0d. | £38 9s. 10d. | £55 13s. 0d. | £52 7s. 0d. | £27 11s. 1½d. |
| Drakelow and Rudheath | £50 0s. 0d. | £19 9s. 11d. | £15 15s. 10d. | £16 18s. 8d. | £37 5s. 0d. |
| Frodsham | £56 13s. 4d. | | £41 18s. 5d.[c] | £41 6s. 8d.[c] | |
| Middlewich | £64 0s. 0d. | £18 9s. 8d.[d] | £48 17s. 2d. | £346 11s. 10d. | £15 9s. 2d. |
| Northwich | £66 0s. 0d. | £2 8s. 7d.[e] | £26 19s. 9½d.[f] | £27 7s. 5d.[f] | |
| Overmarsh | £15 0s. 0d. | £9 18s. 8d.[g] | | | £2 15s. 4d. |

| | 1376 valor | Average livery 1377–99[a] | Average balance excl. arrears 1400–22 | Average livery 1400–22 | 1454 valor |
|---|---|---|---|---|---|
| Shotwick | £30 14s. 1d. | £5 17s. 2d.[h] | | | |
| | £7 19s. 0d.[f] | £7 15s. 2d.[f] | nil | | |
| Macclesfield hundred | £31 14s. 0d. | | £30 8s. 5d.[i] | £22 9s. 3d.[i] | |
| Macclesfield *burgus* | £31 0s. 0d. | | £21 19 3d.[i] | £20 11s. 0d.[i] | |
| Macclesfield Forest | £88 0s. 0d. | | £88 8s. 6d.[i] | £83 11s. 3d.[i] | |
| Macclesfield park | £6 0s. 0d. | | £3 2s. 0d.[i] | £3 6s. 0d.[i] | |
| Sheriff of county | £124 7s. 4d. | £186 15s. 7d. | £196 16s. 5d. | £171 14s. 0d. | £23 19s. 3½d. |
| Escheator of county | £100 0s. 0d. | £57 10s. 8d. | £220 7s. 9d.[j] | £122 9s. 9d.[j] | £19 19s. 10d. |

## *Notes on Table X*

[a] A random sample of accounts has been taken: SC 6/772/11, 772/16, 772/17, 773/1, 773/6, 773/10, 774/4, 774/6, 774/8, and 774/10.

[b] The sums are given without taking into account any deductions for repairs or purchase of millstones.

[c] Covering 1409–22 only.

[d] 1387 only (SC 6/773/1 m. 1).

[e] 1399 only (SC 6/774/10 m. 1).

[f] Covering 1400–10 only.

[g] Five years only: 1378 (SC 6/772/11 m. 3), 1382 (SC 6/772/16 m. 1), 1384 (SC 6/772/17 m. 1), 1393 (SC 6/773/10 m. 1), and 1399 (SC 6/774/10 m. 1).

[h] Three years only, 1378, 1382 and 1399.

[i] A sample of 19 years as there are no accounts extant for 1400, 1409 and 1411.

[j] A sample of 21 years as there is no account extant for 1415.

A glance at Table XI (in Chapter 6 where there is fuller discussion), showing demesne revenues against total palatinate revenues, indicates another trend earlier in the period worthy of note. From c.1403 to 1408, there was a substantial increase in actual demesne revenues as a whole. This increase clearly arose within landed rather than non-landed sources. It is possible to detect a conscious move towards increasing demesne revenues in these years, it being necessary to do so in order to meet the additional costs of the Welsh wars. The valor of 1403 had demonstrated how inadequate current Cheshire revenues would be in the face of these new financial burdens.[262] The policy towards the demesnes in these six years, then, is closely linked with the use of Cheshire revenues as a whole.

Our attention focuses especially around the years 1403 to 1405 when increasing attention was being paid to demesne revenues. This shows itself in the commending of certain categories of income for attention by the council, presumably with a view towards increasing revenue from that particular source. This was especially common with tolls arising from seigneurial monopolies. For instance, the stallage and market tolls of Macclesfield *burgus* were singled out for such attention in 1404–5.[263] The success of this kind of policy is perhaps revealed by the increase in income from tolls in the Wiches from 1404 to 1410, as noted in the relevant parts of Table IX. Such attention was also paid to judicial income at Macclesfield.[264] Certain similar moves have already been referred to in passing and fit in with this general trend. For instance, the prince's council refused to lease the town of Northwich in 1403 even though a lessee had been found. In 1405, John de Legh was forced to account for his debts as receiver of Macclesfield under Richard II.[265] Greater attention was being paid to the collection of arrears, and the payment of debts was now enrolled on the great roll of debts. The parker of Macclesfield was eventually cajoled into presenting his account.

262 Appendix V.
263 SC 6/805/13, m 1d, SC 6/805/14, m 1d.
264 SC 6/805/13, m 2, SC 6/805/14, m 2.
265 SC 6/805/14, m 3.

Most significant, perhaps, was the change in accounting techniques, geared towards assessing the maximum revenue available for disbursement in North Wales. The pressure placed upon demesne revenues in these years paid off in the short term with increased revenues. When the pressure fell off later in the reign, and even more so in the reign of Henry V, then the decline in both issues and liveries continued apace. Although interest could still be paid to certain sources of income in this later period, the overall trend was one of alienation of interests, with more leases and grants of demesnes.

Save for the brief interlude of the Welsh wars, therefore, economic trends in these demesnes parallel those witnessed elsewhere.[266] An especially useful comparison can be drawn with the Whitchurch estates of the Talbot family, geographically close to the Cheshire demesnes. Although a much longer period was considered there, there were several trends which were echoed in Cheshire in these years. At Whitchurch, too, there was no continuous rise in the number of vacant holdings, nor a continuous fall in the value of rents and farms, but there was a slackening intensity of exploitation which led to a severe decline in profits from seigneurial monopolies, justice and commerce.[267] Overall, revenues were fossilised, although the first four decades of the fifteenth century also marked a crucial period of decline.[268] There, as elsewhere, however, much of this decline was due to the impact of the Welsh war. The raid of 1404 on Whitchurch reduced revenue by 58% in the four years following. Damage in Denbigh caused a decline of 33% to 50%, and in Newport of 25%. There was also a drastic collapse in judicial revenue in the lordships of the earldom of March.[269] It is difficult to detect

266 On the Percy estates, for instance, there was a decline of about 25% in revenues between 1416 and 1461 (Bean, *Estates of the Percy Family*, pp. 24, 44). See also Hatcher, *Rural Economy*, p. 148.

267 Pollard, 'Family of Talbot', pp. 380, 409.

268 Pollard, 'Estate Management', pp. 566, 559.

269 Pollard, 'Family of Talbot', pp. 359–60; G. A. Holmes, *The Estates of the Higher Nobility in Fourteenth Century England* (Cambridge: Cambridge University Press, 1957), p. 101; T. B. Pugh, *The Marcher Lordships of South Wales, 1415–1536: Select Documents* (Cardiff:

a similar phenomenon in Cheshire as a result of war. Certainly, no raid took place as at Whitchurch; most of the demesnes, save perhaps Overmarsh, Chester and Shotwick, were far distant from spheres of Welsh influence. Grain prices may have been affected by the wars and accompanying trading regulations, but there was none of the opposition to such restrictions on the demesnes as seen in the Wirral and around Malpas.[270]

Little interest was placed in demesne revenues after c.1408 because there was no need to. Kenneth McFarlane, justifiably it would seem, saw the improving landlord in this period as 'only too often the one whose assets were in danger of shrinking and whose other traditional outlets were barred'.[271] The opposite was also true, that there was no need to pay attention to the increase of landed revenue if other sources of income were available. The earl of Chester was fortunate that he had other, profitable, sources of income to tap, independent of his landed resources, including taxation. As in the fourteenth century, landed revenue did not provide a conspicuously large part of the earl's total revenue from the county, as will be further elucidated in Chapter 6. The availability of these alternative sources of income diverted his attention further away from his landed estate.

University of Wales Press, 1963), p. 152; C. D. Ross, 'The Estates and Finances of Richard, Duke of York', *Welsh Historical Review*, 3 (1966–7), 29–32.

270 For disregard of the regulations in the Wirral see above p. 167. For action at Malpas below pp. 291–2. On prices and wages see Appendix III.

271 K. B. McFarlane, *The Nobility of Later Medieval England* (Oxford: Clarendon Press, 1973), p. 10.

CHAPTER 4

# The Tenants of the Earl's Demesne

Because most of the surviving documentation emanates from the earl's financial administration, it provides little information on the tenants of the demesne save in their interactions with that administration. In the previous chapter we have seen the importance to the lord of income from rents of tenants, and also how some of these tenants were involved in leasing various kinds of resources. But fleshing out our information on the tenants, or coming to valid conclusions on population size, is much more difficult. In this period, no rental or survey was made on any of the demesne manors which might have listed all tenants with the size and location of their tenements. The best we can do is look back to a rental of the lordship of Macclesfield drawn up in 1383–4.[1]

We can also deploy court rolls in order to consider not only interactions between tenants and their lord but also between tenants themselves. Macclesfield has a good run of surviving court rolls covering seventeen of the twenty-two years of our period, which give insights into interactions between the inhabitants of the lordship.[2] For the manors of Frodsham, Middlewich, Northwich and Shotwick, only one manorial court roll is extant in this period.[3] In the case of Frodsham, only the

1 SC 11/898.

2 The long and continuous run of court rolls for Macclesfield (from the mid-fourteenth century to the abolition of manorial authority in 1925) would be eminently suitable for detailed analysis along the lines of Zvi Razi's study, *Life, Marriage and Death in a Medieval Parish: Economy, Society and Demography in Halesowen, 1270–1400* (Cambridge: Cambridge University Press, 1980). Such a project lies beyond the scope of this book, but Andrew Tonkinson has shown the value of the approach in his study of an earlier period (A. M. Tonkinson, *Macclesfield in the Later Fourteenth Century: Communities of Town and Forest*, Chetham Society, 3rd ser., 42 (1999), especially Chapter 2).

3 Shotwick 9–11 Henry IV (SC 2/156/13); Frodsham 1–2 Henry V (SC 2/155/83); Middlewich 1–2 Henry V (SC 2/156/3); Northwich

halmote roll and extract of eyre survive – tenurial arrangements would have been recorded on the roll of the manorial court – but Macclesfield and Shotwick court rolls provide useful information on tenure. At Middlewich and Northwich, the rolls are mainly taken up by litigation between tenants, which is also amply evidenced at Macclesfield.[4] The different kinds of evidence afforded by the court rolls is, of course, significant in revealing the differences between the various places held by the earl. Those manors where the rolls are dominated by inter-tenant litigation demonstrate a highly developed society and community largely independent of seigneurial control. By contrast, those where tenurial obligations to the lord and inter-tenant land transactions form the main business demonstrate greater seigneurial control over tenure and peasant activity in general.

Where tenure was by copy of court roll, the relative entries of surrender, note of inheritance, etc. on the manorial court rolls themselves are complemented in some cases by survival of the copy of the entry which was given to the individual or family it concerned. Such copies survive in private collections, a number of which have been drawn on in this study.[5] Of course, it must be remembered that the copies which survive are but a random selection, preserved owing to the interest of a particular family in certain tenements, although this in itself can be significant in revealing those leading tenants of the manor who were the most precocious in record keeping and emphasizing their rights.

Considering all of these sources together enables us to focus on four major topics: tenure; the community of the vill; social structure; and law and order.

1–2 Henry V (SC 2/156/11). The Middlewich roll in the TNA is incomplete. The missing membrane which covers June to Aug 1414 is abstracted in *A Middlewich Chartulary*, ed. Joan Varley, 2 vols, Chetham Society, 105, 108 (with James Tait) (1941–4), i. 209.

4 For a breakdown of court business at Macclesfield between 1349 and 1396 see Tonkinson, *Macclesfield*, p. 52, Table 5.

5 See above p. 23.

## Tenure

Although we can ascertain conditions of tenure, there are some problems of interpretation. The documents at our disposal tend to present a static picture of tenure and disguise any changes which might have been occurring. A good example is vestiges of servile tenure. Such tenure still existed in principle on certain of the demesne lands but was most likely a dead letter in reality. More significantly, the records of the earl's demesne disguise the extent of subleasing, which would most certainly have had an effect upon tenurial conditions, leading to a weakening of seigneurial control. Subleasing was well advanced even where technically disallowed or made difficult by tenure. It has been noted in our discussion of rental income in Chapter 3 that such subleasing was often motivated by a desire for profit, but at the lord's expense, much as it was within the duchy of Cornwall.[6] In short, therefore, although we can examine the theoretical conditions of tenure as indicated in the accounts and rentals, we know less about conditions in practice.

Types of tenure were diversified across the earl's demesnes, with examples of customary, copyhold and burgage (or quasi burgage) tenure. Certain characteristics, however, appear overall in terms of the obligations of tenants to their lord. The most common obligation, irrespective of the kind of tenure, was compulsory suit for one's tenement at the lord's court. This is often evidenced by fines for non-appearance. At Northwich, for instance, tenants were indicted for not appearing for their fee tenements at the eyre held at Middlewich, and customary/copyhold tenants in Macclesfield Forest were fined for non-attendance at the halmote.[7]

The second common obligation was suit at the lord's mills and oven, as is found at the Dee Mills, Northwich, Middlewich (oven only) and Macclesfield *burgus* and forest.[8] The rental of the

6 John Hatcher, *Rural Economy and Society in the Duchy of Cornwall 1300–1500* (Cambridge: Cambridge University Press, 1970), pp. 232–4.

7 Respectively, CHES 25/9, m 40 and SC 2/255/3, m 1.

8 See above p. 157. Multure payment for grinding at the lord's mill and

lordship of Macclesfield of 1383–4 exemplifies such obligations. The burgesses and others resident in the *burgus* owed suit at the Macclesfield mills (located at Sutton) both for grain grown on their own lands and for grain which they had purchased elsewhere but which had been housed in the *burgus* overnight. A toll of the twentieth grain was to be taken. In addition, the burgesses owed suit at the common oven.[9] The tenants of various townships in the forest also owed suit at the various mills of the lordship.[10] The tenants of Sutton owed similar suit to the burgesses, save that their toll was taken at the sixteenth grain. In addition, the tenants of certain lands – a specified five bovates in Sutton and one bovate in Hurdsfield to the immediate south of the mill – were theoretically held responsible for cleaning out a certain part of the mill pond. Each of the relevant tenants was to clean out 15 feet of the pond, along with a similar length of the watercourse running beneath the mill. They were also to carry, or else pay half the cost of carriage of, millstones to the mill when such were required.[11] There is no record in the period of them ever carrying out any such duties. We can wonder whether they were still obliged to perform them after the mills were leased and, most especially, when they were put to lease for extended periods of time as they were in 1410 for twenty

prohibition from grinding elsewhere were especially common in the north of England. The former was paid as a percentage of the corn which had been ground, at the tenth, thirteenth, sixteenth or twentieth grain (N. Neilson, 'Customary Rents', in Paul Vinogradoff (ed.), *Oxford Studies in Social and Legal History*, vol. 2 (Oxford: Clarendon Press, 1910), pp. 98–9).

9 SC 11/898, m 2.

10 The tenants of Astbury and Rainow owed suit at Macclesfield mills (SC 11/898, m 3d) as did those of Hurdsfield, Upton and Fallibroome (SC 11/898, m 4d). The tenants of Pott Shrigley owed suit at the mill of their township (SC 11/898, m 4). The tenants of Stanley, Disley, Yeardsley, Whaley and Kettleshulme owed suit at Whaley Mill (SC 11/898, m 4d), and the tenants of Bollington at the mill of that township (SC 11/898, m 5), although this last mill did not function in this period. For discussion of the services in this rental see Tonkinson, *Macclesfield*, p. 8 n. 32.

11 SC 11/898, m 3.

years.[12] Further written responsibilities of the tenants of Sutton in the rental of 1383–4 were to transport any game caught in the lord's hunt to the manor of Macclesfield using their own oxen and horses, and to make a stall in the market at All Saints (1 November) where the market tolls were to be collected. They were also responsible for building the lord's fold in Macclesfield, save for its gate.[13]

There are other examples, both in Macclesfield Forest and elsewhere, of tenure by performance of a particular service. The manor of Bradshaw in the city of Chester was held in socage by the service of 1d. per annum and the finding of a bailiff for the office of bailiff of Eastgate Forestreet.[14] Certain townships in the hundred of Macclesfield were to find men to make 'stabilitates' during the lord's hunt.[15] Certain lands in the forest were also responsible for finding hunters to follow the lord's dogs in his hunt in Le Combes.[16] There were nine 'forestaria' in the forest, dating back to the time of the Norman earls, which were held in fee by the service of providing foresters and performing certain duties in return for certain perquisites in the form of the right to game and to be quit of pannage.[17] Whether these duties were actually performed in the early fifteenth century is uncertain. The 'forestaria' still existed but had been much subdivided.[18]

Tenure in Macclesfield Forest was highly diverse. The rental of 1383–4 lists only customary tenants, not all tenants holding land of the earl in the forest. Much more extensive lands were

12 SC 6/806/4, m 2.

13 SC 11/898, m 3.

14 SC 6/791/1, m 1. The sergeant at Frodsham probably held a bovate in Overton by service of grand sergeanty (Ormerod, *Cheshire*, ii. 51).

15 SC 11/898, m 1. 'Stabilitates' were large nets placed between trees to help entrap deer.

16 SC 11/898, m 3. The Coombes were one of three separate woodland areas in Macclesfield Forest (Tonkinson, *Macclesfield*, p. 2).

17 Ormerod, *Cheshire*, iii. 538. Their duties and perquisites are cited in Earwaker, *East Cheshire*, ii. 7. They are also listed in the chartulary of John de Macclesfield (BL, Cotton MS Cleopatra D VI, f. 4).

18 For instance, in 1389 John del Sherd had held a ninth part of a 'forestaria' at Disley by right of his wife (CHES 2/61, m 4 (6), *36 DKR*, pp. 429–30).

held by knight's service or in socage. If we take the township of Disley, for example, the total acreage in the hand of nine tenants in 1383–4 was about 120 acres.[19] Yet, when John de Sutton of Sutton snr died in 1428, he held three messuages, 100 acres of land, four acres of meadow and two acres of wood in Disley, of Queen Catherine in chief by knight's service as of the manor of Macclesfield and by the service of finding one forester.[20] The tenurial structure in the forest is complicated by the fact that such holdings as Sutton could be subleased to tenants who already held lands directly from the earl by customary tenure. John Sutton's father himself held lands in Sutton in socage which were listed on the rental.[21] Some lands in the forest were held in ancient demesne but had been alienated over the years, with only some vestiges remaining in the mid-fourteenth century.[22] By that time some were held by custom of the manor. That was the most predominant tenure in the early fifteenth century.

At this time, customary tenure in Macclesfield Forest was displaying the same tendencies as elsewhere, where it had become free from the taint of servility and had become copyhold by custom of the manor.[23] The entry on a court roll gave a feeling of freedom as well as security by making tenure a contractual relationship with the lord. In strict law, the copyholder remained a tenant at will, but by custom he was allowed inheritance, as was the case with freeholders. The method by which copyhold lands were conveyed reflected the theoretical continuance of the lord's authority. In any transaction or inheritance, the land was surrendered to the lord who admitted the grantee. Such a transaction was performed in the manorial court at which all

19 SC 11/898, m 4.

20 CHES 2/98, m 5 (4), *37 DKR*, p. 695.

21 SC 11/898, m 2d. See also CHES 2/83, m 5 (4), *36 DKR*, p. 460.

22 Sharp, 'Earldom and County of Chester', p. 317.

23 R. H. Hilton, *The Decline of Serfdom in Medieval England* (London: Macmillan, 1969), p. 44. The copy holder was still at the mercy of the lord by his common right to eject a tenant but the latter's security was improving in the fifteenth century (A. W. B. Simpson, *An Introduction to the History of Land Law*, 2nd edition (Oxford: Oxford University Press, 1967), p. 152).

tenants were bound to attend as suitors.[24] At Macclesfield such surrenders were made in full halmote before the steward or his deputy and the other tenants, of whom the most prominent were usually named in the court roll entry. Usually the grantor came into court in his own person, although attorneys were used on occasions.[25] The grant was said to be performed via the lord's ministers. The steward attached his seal to the copy.

In these transactions, it would appear that tenants were still burdened by some of the customary tenurial exactions, for instance, heriot and entry fine (*ingressus*). Entry fines for tenements were payable at Macclesfield at twice the annual rent of the tenement in question, but payments of heriot there seem to have been the exception rather than the rule.[26] For instance, when Margery Alan died in October 1418, she had amongst her possessions one cow worth 6s. 8d. Of this sum, half went to the church as a mortuary payment, the other half to the lord as heriot. In the next halmote, her son took up her lands, one messuage and three acres, in the usual way.[27] Although there are some further examples, it is clear that not every tenant paid heriot.[28] A possibility is that those who were obliged to do so held the lands described in the Macclesfield rental as 'terra nativa'.[29] However, Margery's lands in Sutton do not appear to have been thus described,[30] nor were the lands of William del Cloghes in Sutton who paid heriot in 1420.[31]

24 Ibid., p. 160.

25 See, for instance, CALS, Cholmondeley MSS, DCH R6 (Halmote of June 1432, where John Plot junior acts as attorney of Ralph Odam).

26 Tonkinson, *Macclesfield*, p. 28 notes that payment of merchet for the right to marry, often a test of servile status, was levied on the manor ten times between 1350 and 1371 but not thereafter. There are no mentions of its payment in our period.

27 SC 2/255/16, m 3.

28 For instance, SC 2/255/3, m 1. In this example the wife of the dead man purchased the beast paid as heriot, 255/11, m 4, 255/14, m 4d, 255/18, m 2d.

29 SC 11/898, m 2.

30 Margery Alan's lands are difficult to ascertain. They were possibly those of Margery, daughter of Richard, son of John, described in SC 11/898, m 2.

31 SC 2/255/18, m 2d; SC 11/898, m 2d.

Sometimes it is possible to trace the descent of certain holdings and to assess the extent to which they passed within or outside a family. For instance, in 1383–4 lands in Rainow were held by Richard, son of Alexander le Taylor, having formerly belonged to Nicholas Slegh.[32] In May 1396, Richard, son of Roger le Taylor, presumably a kinsman although his exact relationship is not known, came into the halmote and surrendered these lands to the lord, who then granted them out to Ralph Odam, who paid a one shilling entry fine. In 1432, Ralph Odam senior surrendered these lands to Queen Catherine via his attorney John Plont, along with another messuage and lands adjoining, also in Rainow, formerly belonging to John Knokke. The lands were then granted to Ralph Odam junior for a total rent of 2s. 4½d. and an *ingressus* of 5s. 9d.[33] In these transactions, therefore, we see a tenement held by, and purchased by, three different families – Slegh, Taylor and Odam – although the nature of the records may disguise any blood relationships between them.

It is clear that not all transactions were inter-familial but a rough estimation is that 80% were. Particularly notable are the transactions between generations, even during the lifetime of a father or brother as well as at death.[34] In copyhold, a transaction was technically a surrender into the lord's hands to the use of the recipient, but it appears that in practice the lord always accepted the alienator's choice of recipient.[35] In the case of surrenders during the lifetime of the present holder, it was common for anyone with an interest to give quitclaim. In the case of a surrender by a father to his son, the mother

32 SC 11/898, m 3d. The lands consisted of a message with undefined adjacent lands. The rent was 6d. per annum.

33 For all these transactions, see CALS, Cholmondeley MSS, DCH R6.

34 For an example of succession post mortem, see SC 2/255/3, m 1. For transactions 'inter vivos' ('between the living'), Robert del Dounes surrendered his lands in Rainow, Pott Shrigley, Sutton and Bollington, which were due to devolve to his son (SC 2/255/11, m 4). See also surrenders by Roger Jodrell to his son George in June 1418 (SC 2/255/14, m 4).

35 Simpson, *Introduction to the History of Land Law*, p. 158.

could be called upon to make a public quitclaim, saying that she had not been coerced into acceptance by her husband.[36] If the holder was dead, however, then his heir simply came to the halmote and paid for licence to enter the tenement,[37] implying that the standard inter-generational right of inheritance was acknowledged and accepted by the lord.

The evidence of the court rolls suggests tenancies changed hands frequently. Scarcely a halmote went by without transactions. The fluidity of tenure between families is shown in the Rainow example given above. In another example in the same township, Margery, wife of Richard Watson, and Alice, wife of Richard del Enese, held one messuage and two-and-a-half acres in 1383–4 which had previously been in the hands of Hugh Pymeson.[38] In 1403, the current holder of these lands, William Edmanston, who appears to have been no relation to the two women, forfeited the holding due to being outlawed for murder. The lands were taken up by John Dixon at an increased rent.[39]

The control of the lord over transactions would thus appear to have passed out of his hands since, in practice, the holder of a tenement could nominate his heir, despite the fact that at each transaction the system of surrender emphasised that all land appertained to the lord and was held by his grant. The lord's position was maintained by the fact that such transactions had to take place in the manorial court where attendance and suit were enforced. The copyholder had no customary right to

36 For instance, in Nov 1405 in the case of the surrender by John Togod of a tenement in Pott Shrigley in favour of his son Reginald, where Agnes, wife of John, was examined that she had not been compelled by her husband. Once this had been done, the court declared that she should be excluded in perpetuity from any rights she might have had (SC 2/255/6, m 4).

37 As in the case of Richard, son and heir of John de Liversegge, for lands of his father in Hurdsfield in Nov 1399, with the added observation that he was represented in the court by his attorney Robert le Baker rather than being there in person (SC 2/255/3, m 1).

38 SC 11/898, m 3d.

39 SC 6/805/11, m 3.

sublease his land for more than a year; if he wished a longer term, he had to have the licence of the lord.[40] At Macclesfield, it would seem that there was a considerable degree of subletting which is not recorded at the halmote. A lease by John Slegh of Macclesfield to Stephen del Rowe in June 1417, for instance, is known through a surviving document in private hands, but was not enrolled at the halmote.[41] Where tenants did sublease, they could lay down their own conditions of tenure. Thurstan del Wood leased a messuage and eight acres of land and meadow in the township of Disley from Roger Jodrell. The lease was for twenty years at 13s. 4d. per annum. Wood had to provide a hayward (*messor*) in the autumn, two geese and 3d. worth of bread at Christmas, and to bear the cost of repairs himself. In addition, he could not cut any wood without Jodrell's permission. These were much more stringent conditions of tenure than the earl ever laid down in Macclesfield.[42]

Turning our attention to labour services owed by tenants to their lord, the county as a whole had never experienced large scale labour services.[43] The relatively small size of the lord's demesne in Cheshire made labour services unimportant. Commutation mainly took place after the Black Death, as we see in Macclesfield Forest,[44] but there were already many money rents in existence which had never been exacted in labour. Vestiges of villain tenure lingered longest on the earl's demesnes where the lord's income remained primarily from agricultural sources, despite the fact that direct exploitation had ceased, and despite the dominance of copyhold tenure by custom of the manor.[45]

Some small-scale ploughing and carrying services were ascribed to the category of bondmen in an extent of the manor

40 Simpson, *Introduction to the History of Land Law*, p. 158.
41 JRRIL, Tatton of Wythenshawe Muniments TW/160.
42 JRRIL, Rylands Charter 806 (Nov 1416). See also SC 11/898, m 4.
43 D. Kenyon, 'Rural Settlement Patterns in Medieval Cheshire', unpublished MA thesis (University of Manchester, 1974), p. 58.
44 Sharp, 'Earldom and County of Chester', p. 318.
45 For examples of uneven survival of naifty elsewhere, see Hilton, *Decline of Serfdom*, p. 49.

of Shotwick of 1280.[46] Labour services at Shotwick were ostensibly commuted after the Black Death.[47] In the court of April 1409, however, it was noted that Thomas Wilcockson, William Hugson and John Fox ought, and were accustomed, to be with the lord in Lent, each of them with his plough for one day, for his conditions of tenure (*tenure*) of the lord in the vill. It was claimed that they had withdrawn this service and concealed it, to the detriment of the lord, with the result that the bailiff, Hugh Daukyn, was ordered to distrain them to perform this ploughing.[48] The ministers' accounts do not contain any references to such services nor to the commutation of the same. However, it is unlikely that these were the only tenants of the earl who owed such services, especially when we have several further examples of villein tenure and its consequent obligations at Shotwick, other than labour services.

Chevage (a payment for licence to live outside the manor) was paid at Shotwick by two *nativi*, a common word used for unfree tenants, in 1409 and 1410.[49] Furthermore, it is clear that the performance of the office of reeve was regarded as an obligation of the *nativi* of the manor, such a requirement being a common characteristic of unfree status. Ironically, however, we know this as a result of payments of 13s. 4d. to Shotwick reeves for the exercise of their office because they were of free status, as in the case of Simon le Shepherd in 1400.[50] Indeed, there are no examples of *nativi* holding the office in this period. Heriots on the death of *nativi* were paid regularly. In 1409,

46 SC 12/6/33, transcribed in R. Stewart-Brown, 'The Royal Manor and Park of Shotwick', *THSLC*, 64 (1912), 82–142, at pp. 138–40.

47 H. J. Hewitt, *Medieval Cheshire*, Chetham Society, new ser., 88 (1929), p. 165.

48 SC 2/156/13, m 3. John Fox had himself been bailiff in the previous year.

49 One shilling was paid by John Craddock, and 6d. by Thomas Craddock (SC 6/792/5, m 2, 792/6, m 2, SC 2/156/13, m 3). Chevage was still paid by the *nativi* on the assessionable manors of the duchy of Cornwall. If they moved away from their manor, their new location was stated. In each case a marked urban bias is seen (Hatcher, *Rural Economy*, p. 221).

50 SC 6/791/1, m 3.

Roger Simpson, *nativus*, died. The court roll noted that after every such death the lord had the right to take the most valuable possession of the deceased. In this case, a money payment of 8s. 8d. was made.[51] In the court of May 1408, there arose an interesting and significant case. When Agnes, wife of Geront de Wodehouse, died in 1408, she held in villeinage three messuages and three bovates in Saughall, but no heriot was payable as her husband was a free man and was still alive. Indeed he was one of the tenants who had leased the lord's demesne lands and fishery in 1407–8.[52] But Agnes's son by a previous marriage, Hugh Barb, was a *nativus*. As her nearest heir, he was to pay the lord a fine to enter into her tenements; the fine was to be agreed between him and the lord's council.[53] At the court of June 1408, Hugh paid a fine of £1 6s. 8d. described as a 'relief'. As we do not know the rent payable, we cannot ascertain how the relief was calculated and whether it followed the standard practice of entry fines being twice the annual rent. His status did not affect Barb's prominence in the manor. He frequently served as a juror and was constable in 1409.[54]

Assized rents at Shotwick were said to be of *nativi* and free men, of whom one was named as Richard, son of Henry.[55] Why he should be singled out is puzzling. Elsewhere in the accounts, in the section concerning increased rents, we find references to messuagers and cottagers but whether these were free or unfree is unspecified.[56] Free men at Shotwick owed suit of court.[57] Some tenants also seem to have had the responsibility of carrying out repairs to their tenements, but it is not clear whether these were free or unfree, or both. In May 1408, Roger de Ashley, Roger Simpson and Simon le Shepherd were liable to repair two

51 SC 2/156/13, m 3.
52 SC 6/792/3, m 2, SC 2/156/13, m 2.
53 SC 2/156/13, m 2.
54 Respectively, SC 2/156/13, m 3, 2d.
55 See, for instance, SC 6/791/1, m 3.
56 SC 6/791/1, m 3.
57 Some were named and fined for non-attendance at 3d. each or pardoned when they had licence to absent themselves (SC 2/156/13, mm 1, 2d, and 3).

houses, three houses and one house and one barn, respectively, but had not done so.[58] Ashley and Shepherd had both served as reeves where it was noted that they were free. Simpson (if he was the same man who died in 1409) was a *nativus*.

From the evidence of the Shotwick court roll of May 1408, it is clear that tenements were taken up there for a term of ten years at a time.[59] Again, it is not clear whether these were free or unfree (*nativi*) tenements. No specification is given, and it was certainly possible for free men to hold villein land. Nor do the tenements listed in the roll constitute every tenement within the manor. These ten-year tenements were not held by copyhold. The court roll entry concerning them is basically a rental giving details of increased rents which were to be applied to them. Most of these holdings had already been held by the tenants for a previous term, and were taken up for an annual rent, above other due and customary services. This system gave the lord, as in the assessionable manors in Cornwall, a chance to reassess rents every so often and to raise additional cash from entry fines.[60] In the Shotwick case, the lord enjoyed an opportunity of revision every ten years. On the assessionable manors of the duchy of Cornwall, it was every seven years.

At Drakelow, the tenurial structure was similar to that of Shotwick. When the manor was newly created in 1347, some tenancies (possibly those which had been held by hereditary right before the recovery) were held in fee by charter with hereditary succession.[61] These included lands held by the abbots of Chester and Dieulacres, who contributed £13 9s. 0d. of a total of £25 8s. 8d. free rent. Free tenants owed suit to the manorial court and paid reliefs of two years rent upon inheritance.[62] The

58 SC 2/156/13, m 2.

59 See above p. 128.

60 The assession rolls in the duchy give the names of all tenants as well as the size, location and rent of each holding. Being drawn up every seven years with few exceptions, they can also give an impression of fluidity or permanence within the ranks of the tenants (Hatcher, *Rural Economy*, p. 3).

61 Booth, *Financial Admin.*, p. 4.

62 For example, SC 6/793/7, m 13d.

second category was of 'termors', a less secure tenure for a term of years, the length of which was initially unspecified.[63] By the late fourteenth century, these lands were released to the tenants every twenty years when a new rental was drawn up. At such a point, they paid a communal entry fine (*ingressus*).[64] The earl was responsible for repairs to the tenements of the 'termors'.[65]

At Frodsham (setting aside burgage tenure for the present), there were both free tenants, who owed suit to the halmote court, and customary tenants. Certain of the latter, described generally as *nativi*, owed heriot[66] and chevage. The last named obligation was noted as a category of income in the accounts but no money was received from this source in this period, which may suggest that the requirement of such licences to live away from the manor was not imposed in practice. We know that a Walter Stone had left the lordship but still kept the responsibility for repairs of his tenement, even when non-resident,[67] yet there is no record that he paid chevage. The lord carried out repairs to tenant houses, receiving a small income from tenants for this,[68] although the sums paid did not meet the cost of repairs. In 1412, for instance, the tenants paid the lord 13s. 4d. but he paid out £5 8s. 9d. for repairs of their houses.[69]

Entry fines were also payable at Frodsham. In the account for 1418–19, *ingressus* was placed under the title of 'perquisites of court' – 'for which entry fine each tenant of the lord is obliged to pay each tenth year, which will be in the year following' ('pro quo quidem ingressu quilibet tenens domini ibidem

63 SC 6/801/3, cited in Booth, 'Financial Administration', p. 203. Michael J. Bennett, *Community, Class and Careerism: Cheshire and Lancashire Society in the Age of Sir Gawain and the Green Knight* (Cambridge: Cambridge University Press, 1983), p. 96, also discusses those tenants on a number of non-royal manors, as well as Frodsham and Drakelow, who held for a number of years ('terminarii').

64 SC 6/792/3, m 1d.

65 CHES 2/119, m 9 (11), *37 DKR*, p. 221.

66 For example, SC 6/793/9, m 5.

67 SC 6/793/2, m 6d.

68 SC 6/793/2, m 6d; CHES 2/92, m 8 (6), *37 DKR*, p. 297.

69 SC 6/792/9, m 4d.

tenetur solvere quelibet decimo anno qui erit in anno proximo futuro').[70] Indeed, in 1421, £1 14s. 8d. was accounted for the *ingressus* of divers tenants who took up their land anew at the end of twelve years, this year being the first of a new term.[71] This, then, was similar to the system at Shotwick, save for a difference in the number of years involved, and had similarities with the assessionable manors in the duchy of Cornwall. In 1410, £4 19s. 8d. had been received from divers tenants.[72] This was, of course, ten (financial) years before 1421, and the size of the sum would suggest that this was a communal *ingressus*, despite the fact that it was not noted as such.

In other years, however, entry fines were paid by individual tenants upon entry to a tenement.[73] It seems likely, therefore, that both individual and communal fines were payable, presumably on the same tenements, in a similar manner to that operated on the Cornish assessionable manors, although not as sophisticated as on the latter.[74] A seven shilling payment of *egressus* was also noted in 1410–11, but with no explanation. No such payment is found in any other year.[75] According to Neilson, this was a payment made to enable the tenant to depart from his land or to take up other land.[76]

On the whole, tenurial conditions were unrestricted. The vestiges of a previous more rigorous control were, by the fifteenth century, rather meaningless. At Frodsham, seigneurial control was probably rendered even less rigorous by the existence of a *burgus* which had distinct characteristics of urban tenure, although we know little of who the burgesses were. Only a few

70 SC 6/793/9, m 5.

71 SC 6/794/1, m 5.

72 SC 6/792/6, m 6d.

73 For instance, in 1409 two shillings was received from Richard le Sumnour for a parcel of land (SC 6/792/5, m 5d).

74 Hatcher, *Rural Economy*, p. 58.

75 SC 6/792/8, m 5d. This totalled seven shillings.

76 At Ely, if a free tenant had sold all his land and did not wish to remain on the demesne he could pay 2s. 8d. to the bishop for 'egressus'. 'Ingressus' was payable at the same rate. See Neilson, 'Customary Rents', p. 88.

names are known from fines for non-appearance at the eyre, but £6 11s. 3d. was received in burgage rents,[77] and burgage tenure would appear equivalent to that found elsewhere. The *burgus* at Frodsham had had its charter of liberties confirmed by Richard II but some payments for this confirmation were still outstanding in 1404.[78] There are several extant deeds concerning both the *burgus* and the remaining lands of the lordship.[79] These are mainly dating to the fourteenth century, but of the fifteenth-century deeds which survive, most are grants of burgages with appurtenant lands in the fields.[80] As with the Middlewich deeds to be discussed later, these show a highly developed system of land transfers and enfeoffments. The charter of 1209–28 gave burgesses one free burgage in the *burgus* and one acre in the fields,[81] and even in the fifteenth century the position of holdings in the fields corresponded to that in the *burgus*. Non-burgage tenements in the township also had appurtenant strips in the fields. A messuage in 'Le shepestrete', for instance, was the subject of a transaction, together with one acre of land in the 'Longefield'. Burgages could be sold,[82] as it seems could lands in the fields, but probably only those connected with burgage tenements.[83]

Margaret Sharp stated that there was no sign of burgage tenure at Middlewich and Northwich.[84] Varley, on the other hand, saw some traces of burgage rents in the rent called Kingesmole, and suggested further that the burgage, as the basis of burgage right, had been replaced by a different sort

77 SC 2/155/83, m 1d.

78 CHES 25/10, m 15d. In 1402 £5 was noted as due to William de Frodsham senior, now deceased (his lands were in the hands of the prince) from the borough for this confirmation (CHES 2/75, m 7d (7), *36 DKR*, p. 193).

79 CALS, Cholmondeley MSS DCH Box F.

80 For instance, CALS, DCH F123, 773 (14th Century).

81 Ormerod, *Cheshire*, ii. 46.

82 CALS, DCH F5, F119.

83 CALS, DCH F112, F124.

84 Sharp, 'Earldom and County of Chester', p. 377.

of qualification.[85] In the earliest grants and references, the burgesses of both places claimed that the brine and saltsprings were their tenements, and that non-burgesses had no right to the brine with which to make salt, and therefore had to pay annually for licences to boil. There are certainly references to burgesses at Middlewich who formed a sort of guild, the membership of which was not tied to land. It would seem that they had the right to appoint new burgesses, although burgess-ships could be inherited. The earl could also grant burgess-ships. On the chamberlain's account of 1399, Richard Crowther paid 16s. 4d. as the fee of the seal for letters patent whereby the king granted that he should be a burgess in the town of Middlewich.[86] In 1414, we find him as chamberlain of Middlewich. Prince Henry granted a burgess-ship to Roger Green of Middlewich and his heirs in 1406 in recompense for his services in the prince's Welsh expeditions.[87]

Although the earl held these two Wiches as part of his demesne, tenurial arrangements had passed out of his hands and he received but token rents. In both places, there is much evidence of subleasing, especially of *saline* (salt houses), and little mention by this stage of a chief lord. For Middlewich there is ample evidence of land transactions, exchanges, surrenders and sales, dating from the thirteenth to the seventeenth century, in a seventeenth-century compilation.[88] These documents further demonstrate that tenure of salt houses and messuages in the town was freehold, usually described as socage, if not burgage.

85 For what follows, see *Middlewich Chartulary*, i. 21–5, 28, 208.

86 SC 6/774/10, m 2.

87 CHES 2/79, m 1 (8) (9) (10), *36 DKR*, p. 203. This enrolment was an order to the bailiff to receive Roger into the 'burgensis ville'. Roger is described there as a 'valettus', which could suggest he served as an archer under the prince in Wales. So far his name has not been found in musters or pay records for the Welsh campaigns. A Roger Grenhalgh served in Ireland under Sir John Stanley and Nicholas Orell in 1389 (E 101/41/18, m 25 and, m 14). A Roger Grenam served as a man-at-arms under Sir William Porter in 1415 (E 101/44/30/4 part 4/5). In 1409 he was pardoned for the murder of Matthew Hardyng at Bostock (CHES 2/81, m 2d (1), *36 DKR*, p. 203).

88 For an example of a sale in 1403, see *Middlewich Chartulary*, i. 32.

Salt houses were held by burgesses, other townsmen and men from neighbouring townships, even some from further afield, but the lord appears to have had no control over their tenure at all.[89] Even where the lord did have some control, for instance over non-burgage tenements, leases tended to be long.[90] There is much less evidence concerning Northwich, but even isolated survivals are enough to suggest a similar state of affairs. *Saline* were heavily sublet,[91] as were other tenements in the town. For instance, Amice Stratchart leased a chamber in the *burgus* from Joanna, wife of Thomas Starkey, for 1s. 6d..[92] In August 1422, William de Bulkeley of Eton leased two messuages in the township of Northwich to Alan Tomkynson and Hugh Draper for life, although these were in fact to be held by a third party, Edmund Starkey.[93]

At Macclesfield, the tenurial structure in the *burgus* was more complicated than the accounts would lead us to believe. There were ostensibly 123 burgages, 120 paying one shilling each in burgage rent, and one each appertaining to the three accounting officials of the *burgus* who otherwise received no remuneration for their services. It is known that the burgages and other lands in the town had been subdivided and subleased. At this time, it is highly unlikely that there were 120 burgesses, if burgess-ship still depended upon the holding of a burgage: John de Macclesfield, for instance, held twenty-three burgages.[94] Licences to enter the liberty of the lordship, as recorded on the roll of the mayor's court, were probably equivalent to admission to burgess-ships.[95] However, there appears to have been a

89 *Middlewich Chartulary*, i. 38–9. There was much mobility in the ranks of salt house holders (p. 40).

90 For instance, in 1444 a messuage was leased out by the king for 34 years at one shilling per annum (*Middlewich Chartulary*, i, item 70C).

91 JRRIL, Arley Charters Box 28 no.10 (receipt by Robert Abbot of Hulton to Sir Richard Winnington of 10s. for the rent of two salt houses in Northwich, July 1410).

92 SC 2/156/11, m 1d.

93 HMC, Leicester of Tabley Charters and Deeds, Northwich B12.

94 See above p. 133.

95 JRRIL, Tatton of Wythenshawe Muniments TW/1184.

greater degree of seigneurial control over land transactions in the Macclesfield *burgus* than at the Wiches. Transactions were carried out in the portmote before the steward or his lieutenant, the mayor, the clerk of the courts and others there present. Most of the transactions recorded, including those involving burgage tenements, were petitions for private charters to be enrolled.[96] Surrenders and regrants were made along the same lines as for the customary tenements in the forest. The lord issued licences to enclose,[97] and granted out lands which had fallen into his hands.[98] As in the forest, too, tenements frequently changed hands, but on the initiative of the tenants themselves. The lord provided a means of registration and enrolment. Disputes over tenure were also dealt with in the portmote at Macclesfield. For instance, in March 1426 Stephen del Rowe and Philip Massey were involved in a dispute over a burgage which dated back to the days of the last non-royal earl, John the Scot. [99]

## The community of the vill

Whilst the tenants of the earl's demesnes had a direct relationship with him through his officials, we should not forget the communities which those living on the earl's lands generated themselves.[100] The development of a village economy is

96 SC 2/255/4, m 4d.

97 As in licence given to Richard le Harper in Oct 1415 to newly enclose a *parcella* of land containing one rood by estimation adjoining the field called Le Haleghe (SC 2/255/12, m 5d).

98 SC 2/255/9, m 2d.

99 JRRIL, Tatton of Wythenshawe Muniments TW/161.

100 Here inspiration is taken from the research of the Toronto school into peasant communities, drawing largely on the archives of Ramsey Abbey, first represented by J. A. Raftis, *Tenure and Mobility* (Toronto: Pontifical Institute of Mediaeval Studies, 1964) and developed by E. B. DeWindt, *Land and People in Holywell-cum-Needingworth* (Toronto: Pontifical Institute of Mediaeval Studies, 1972), Edward Britton, *The Community of the Vill: A Study in the History of the Family and Village Life in Fourteenth-Century England* (Toronto: Macmillan of Canada, 1977). The study of agricultural by-laws generated largely by the inhabitants of villages although within the manorial court has also

important as far as the question of economic and social freedom is concerned – as important perhaps, although interrelated with, the decline in stronger manorial authority.[101] In Cheshire, the latter appears as weak as the former is strong, reflected also in the close check upon the lord's officials maintained by the tenants, as well as their attitude towards the preservation of their rights. In this section, the development of the community of the vill on the earl's manors is looked at from two directions, the first concerning the degree and function of communal organization and administration, the second specifically from the perspective of communal agriculture in the demesnes.

All communities were capable of controlling their own inhabitants and especially those coming in from the outside, something which tended to be done by the people rather than the lord.[102] Such a situation was to be expected in places with aspirations towards, and genuine claims to, borough status. In general, it has been said that Cheshire saw an absence of aspirations towards borough autonomy and of an emergence of an urban middle class. Jenny Kermode interprets the reason for this as being the complex effect of palatinate status and military exploitation of the county and its economy.[103] At Macclesfield, for instance, she suggests that the administration of the borough was closely supervised by the overlord. It was called a free borough and could elect a mayor, but only under the supervision of the lord's steward. The same degree of supervision is seen over all the earl's demesnes, be they borough or manor.

Nevertheless, although nominal self-government might be lacking, this was adequately compensated for in practice.

been much supported by the work of W. O. Ault, culminating in his *Open Field Farming in Medieval England* (London: Allen & Unwin, 1972).

101 R. H. Hilton, *The English Peasantry in the Later Middle Ages* (Oxford: Clarendon Press, 1975), pp. 18–19.

102 Hilton, *English Peasantry*, pp. 55–6.

103 J. Kermode, *Medieval Cheshire Boroughs: Some Preliminary Observations*, University of Liverpool, School of History and Institute of Extension Studies, Medieval Cheshire Seminar (Sept 1975), privately printed, pp. 3–4.

The burgesses at Middlewich existed with some control over the town, which varied in accordance with the closeness of supervision by the earl.[104] The latter was slackening rather than tightening at this time.[105] With regard to small towns (of which these Cheshire demesne 'boroughs' are good examples) and their courts, Rodney Hilton noted that these did develop under the lord's bailiff but were dominated by their own jury of notables, which formed a shadow government behind the official screen of the portmote.[106] Such was the case in Cheshire, although there was an obvious overlap in personnel and families. The earl's steward was in charge of holding courts at Middlewich and Northwich, but juries were made up of the locally prominent. At the great court held each June at Northwich, a panel of burgesses dealt with a larger than usual amount of violations of local by-laws.[107] A similar court existed at Middlewich.[108] At Frodsham halmote, a panel, presumably of burgesses, elected sergeants of the peace,[109] two jurors, and three *prepositi* (reeves).[110]

Developments at Macclesfield are probably the most significant. The mayor of the town was not, as Stella Davies thought,[111] the equivalent of the reeve (*prepositus*) who was one

104 *Middlewich Chartulary*, i. 21.

105 Stella Davies, for instance, claims that the direct influence of the crown in Macclesfield was declining in the fifteenth century (*A History of Macclesfield*, ed. C. Stella Davies (Manchester: Manchester University Press, 1961), p. 43).

106 Hilton, *English Peasantry*, p. 88. See also R. H. Hilton, 'Small Town Society in England Before the Black Death', *Past & Present*, 105 (1984), 53–78.

107 SC 2/156/11, mm 3d–4.

108 *Middlewich Chartulary*, i. 23.

109 Beamont, *An Account of the Ancient Town of Frodsham*, p. 71. These were 'satellites, probably sergeants or people who were to present for certain offences.

110 SC 2/155/83, m 2. 'Tassatores' are also found in office at Frodsham. Beamont (p. 70) interpreted these as haywards, from the term 'tasatus' meaning a hayrick, or overseers of the harvest, from 'tasagium', the service of stacking.

111 *History of Macclesfield*, p. 10.

of the accounting officials in the town. For some years we know the names of both mayor and *prepositus*.[112] The mayor seems to have had no function within the structure of comital demesne administration. He was presumably elected annually, although he appears to have held office for several years running. He held his own court which appears, from its surviving roll for 1404–5, not to have been under the scrutiny of the steward.[113] The court is recorded here as being held before the mayor of the time, Roger Alcock, with no reference to the steward's presence. The mayor's court was generally held on Fridays, whilst the portmote, over which the steward did preside, was held on Tuesdays.

In the surviving roll recording the business of the mayor's court in 1404–5, we see that, at the first meeting of Friday 10 October 1404, the names of officials for the following year were stated. These were officials of the town itself, not of the earl. The officials of the earl elected at the portmote were the catchpole, *prepositus* and the keepers of the assizes of ale, bread and meat.[114] In the roll of the mayor's court, Roger Alcock was named as mayor, John Scribons as serjeant of the peace, John Falibrome and another man named William, whose surname is not clear in the record, as 'custodes'. From evidence elsewhere in the document, this is clearly a judicial office of some description. In addition, six keepers of the pavement were named: Stephen del Rowe and William de Haynel of Insgate, John le Slegh, William le Lemmeson of le Wanegate, Thomas del Sherd and John de Harstanley of Churchgate. Only John de Falibrome had served as one of the earl's officials in the years 1399 to 1422, being *prepositus* in the following year, 1405–6, and again in 1411–12. Previous decisions taken by the twelve *electi* (we can assume, but cannot be certain, that they were the same jury of burgesses who acted in the earl's portmote) were confirmed concerning the various assizes, but not those commonly stated in the portmotes (which were usually ale only). Further by-laws formulated by this mayor's court are stated. Pigs were not

112 See appendix I (n) ii.

113 JRRIL, Tatton of Wythenshawe Muniments TW/1184.

114 See, for instance, SC 6/255/12, m 5.

to be allowed in the town field ('campum burgi'); any found there would be fined at 1d. each and this income accounted under the market tolls. Tranters (who carried out small-scale transportation and peddling with a horse and cart) were to pay two shillings for the common pyx ('ad communem pixidem'), the expression suggesting that the money went into the town's own funds. Tenant litigation in the mayor's court was much the same as at the portmote, although licences to enter the liberty of the *burgus* were only recorded in the mayor's court.

In addition to the records of this court for 1404–5, a book of orders of the mayor for the reign of Henry IV survives in a later fifteenth-century transcript.[115] This includes administrative arrangements as well as commercial ones, reflecting a considerable degree of self-government in both respects. There was to be a communal chest in which the records of the *burgus* were to be kept. This was to have two locks; the mayor was to keep one key and another official the other.[116] The chest was to be opened only when both officials were present, a common practice across Western Europe to avoid fraud. The mayor was to have a servant who was allocated certain duties. In addition, the book contains ordinances limiting the sale and purchase of victuals to the vicinity of the market cross or at properly constructed stalls.

Later in the fifteenth century, communal organization at Macclesfield developed further. By 1462, there was a mayor, alderman, bailey and recorder in the *burgus*. They, in conjunction with a John Savage and four burgesses, are found certifying the right to an inheritance.[117] Savage was probably steward at this time, but it is interesting to see these town officials acting in conjunction with him. Such elected town officials represented the interests of the community. Officials such as catchpole, chamberlain and *prepositus*, although elected from the same ranks, were forced to carry out the dictates of the lord.

115 SC 2/315/6.

116 Unfortunately, the name of this official cannot be ascertained. The record, being of paper rather than parchment, has deteriorated badly.

117 JRRIL, Tatton of Wythenshawe MS 784.

All the *burgi*, indeed all the manors of the earl, demonstrate regulation of inter-tenant activity through by-laws enforced and created at the local courts. These concern the blocking of highways, encroaching, breaking the assizes, and other generally anti-social behaviour. Emphasis was placed upon preserving the rights of the commercial sector, with controls over production and marketing. For instance, in 1401 the wife of Nicholas Ravenowe in Macclesfield was brought to task for refusing to sell ale to her neighbours (i.e. the burgesses) and yet later selling it to others.[118] At Middlewich, it was reaffirmed at the eyre in 1410 that the men of the town were to sell their meat only in the market place, and then only if they had a licence to have a stall there.[119] William de Hasuldere, a butcher, had broken this law, it was said, by selling his meat within the free tenements of the town. He was the catchpole of the town in 1409 and is recorded as breaking the assize of meat on more than one occasion.[120] Forestalling the market was regarded as a particularly heinous crime, as was selling wine at extortionate prices.[121]

Even in manors where activities were primarily agricultural, there was a great degree of self-government within the structure of comital government. At Shotwick, for instance, general surveillance of activity was not in the hands of a steward but of the chamberlain or his lieutenant who held the courts of the manor.[122] It could hardly be expected that the chamberlain would be available for day-to-day control. The reeve was chosen from amongst the tenants, as appear to be also the bailiff, two constables and two ale tasters, who administered the lord's resources as well as representing and furthering the interests of the community as a whole. Many offences mentioned in the court rolls also reflect communal organization, being offences against the community as a whole, such as blocking up roads, failure to repair ditches, etc..[123]

118 SC 2/255/4, m 5.
119 CHES 25/9, m 125.
120 *Middlewich Chartulary*, i, item 100.
121 CHES 25/11, m 6d.
122 SC 2/156/13 passim.
123 At the court at Shotwick in 1409, Thomas Craddock was charged

In general, it can be said that the tenants organised their own activity and commercial organization, no doubt to an even greater extent than the surviving judicial records suggest. The earl was involved only in so far as providing, in most cases, the courts by which such activities were regulated and, via such courts, adding his own sanction to such regulation; and thirdly and most importantly, the profits from such regulation largely went into his pocket.

Little mention has been made here of the citizens of Chester city. The economic and social development of the city is a vast subject in itself and cannot sensibly be included here.[124] As a fully corporate town, it was very different in nature from the other demesne *burgi* we have been considering. However, we can see similar traits, not least the consistent emphasis upon rights and their preservation. In the time of Henry IV, the mayor and sheriff of the city complained to the prince's council because the sheriff of the county had involved himself in a case which they claimed was within their own and the city's jurisdiction. The decision given seems to have favoured the city, but rather craftily, because the chamberlain of the county was to supervise the case to ensure that the mayor could proceed in the accustomed way.[125]

The earl had ceased direct exploitation, with the result that the accounts furnish little evidence upon agriculture in the demesnes. However, we have some evidence of peasant agriculture from a variety of sources. This enables us to

with blocking the road from Saughall to the water of Dee so that no men or animals could pass that way to the harm of his neighbours and all travellers. At the same court Richard (no surname is given) was charged with blocking a highway leading from Saughall to Shotwick by failing to repair a ditch belonging to him (SC 2156/13, m 3).

124 For full discussion of the city see C. P. Lewis and A. T. Thacker (eds), *The Victoria History of the Counties of England: A History of the County of Chester*, v/i: *The City of Chester: General History and Topography* (London: Boydell and Brewer for the Institute of Historical Research, 2003). See also Bennett, *Community*, pp. 117–21 for occupational structures in the city.

125 E 163/6/41, item 20.

explore the subject in general before focusing in more detail on communal organization in farming. At most manors it is clear that tenants held their arable lands in strips in the open fields, although there is no evidence that there was an equal distribution of strips of one person's holding throughout all the fields of the township.[126] This was certainly the case at Frodsham. For instance, two-and-a-half rods granted by Thomas Hall to William Bredbury were made up of four strips, three of half a rod and one of one rod, each described by reference to holders of neighbouring strips.[127] Tenants of the *burgi* commonly held agricultural land elsewhere, such as in neighbouring townships. The burgesses of Middlewich held farming land in the neighbouring townships of Newton and Kinderton,[128] and those of Northwich in Witton.[129] At Macclesfield, land was held in the town fields. We find many references to land held in the fields ('in campis') both in the court rolls and in the cartulary of John de Macclesfield.[130] Many of the Macclesfield burgesses also held land in the forest townships. It is clear from the descriptions of holdings in the 1383–4 rental that these were in strips.[131]

More is known of agriculture at Frodsham than elsewhere. Here the arable lands and meadows lay to the north and north-west of the settlement towards the Weaver and the sea.[132] Being less than 50 feet above sea level, they were subject to frequent flooding.[133] This has been a problem in more recent times as

126 Kenyon, 'Rural Settlement in Medieval Cheshire', pp. 44, 47.
127 CALS, Cholmondeley MSS DCH F123.
128 *Middlewich Chartulary*, i. 333, and item 41a.
129 Dodgson, *Place Names*, ii. 192–3
130 For instance, SC 2/255/4, m 5; BL, Cotton MS Cleopatra D VI.
131 SC 11/898. The same is true of lands held by the burgesses and townsmen in Rowood (Dodgson, *Place Names*, i. 120, temp. Ed. III, the 'rough woods' implying recent clearing).
132 As indicated on the Ordnance Survey of Cheshire, first edition 6" map 1875, sheet XXIV.
133 This is reflected in the field names (Dodgson, *Place Names*, iii. 224): 'le ferrundyngs' – a rushy clearing; 'dychedeze' – ditched meadows. Field names at Drakelowe and Rudheath also suggest a boggy area (ibid., ii. 200–2).

well as in the fourteenth century. The dykes to the north broke frequently, causing much destruction, and were a constant source of expense.[134] Nevertheless, this area must have provided fertile land, which was split into strips of tenant land and demesne land, which was readily leased by the tenants. The ministers' accounts of the earl show that the major crops at Frodsham were mixed grain (rye and wheat) and oats. At Macclesfield we know that oats, barley and mixed grain were grown.[135] It has been argued wheat had never been very common in medieval Cheshire, spring crops of barley and oats being far more usual but coroners' valuations of property of fugitive felons as well as fourteenth-century demesne corn and stock accounts show ample wheat production.[136]

The demesnes at Frodsham appear to have been leased more for pasturing, the water meadows being ideal for such a purpose, although the peasant economy in Frodsham was based upon mixed farming, as elsewhere. Sheep were especially important. There had been a marked increase in the number of sheep kept by the earl at Frodsham in the fourteenth century, from 15 in 1315–16 to 598 in 1357–8.[137] Sheep were pastured in the common marsh (i.e. Remershe), and part of the demesne land was leased to tenants specifically for this function.[138] In 1403, we see an inter-tenant purchase of twenty sheep.[139] Driver claims that sheep were also found in large numbers in the clearing of

134 See above p. 180 and Sharp, 'Earldom and County of Chester', p. 180. Flooding was a problem elsewhere in the Wirral (see CHES 25/9, m 35).

135 SC 6/805/7, m 2; SC 6/805/9, m 2.

136 Kenyon, 'Rural Settlement Patterns', p. 50, where the author also notes that chroniclers stressed its unsuitability for wheat growing. According to Driver (J. T. Driver, *Cheshire in the Later Middle Ages* (Chester: Cheshire Community Council, 1971), p. 93), barley and oats were grown throughout the county, peas and beans were concentrated in the north, and rye in the south. I am grateful to Dr Booth for his advice on fourteenth-century trends.

137 Hewitt, *Medieval Cheshire*, p. 45.

138 See above p. 145. There are also field names such as 'le shepefeld' and 'Eucroft' (meadow where ewes kept) (Dodgson, *Place Names*, iii. 234).

139 CHES 2/76, m 8d (4), *36 DKR*, p. 343.

Delamere Forest and the upland areas of Macclesfield Forest, although between 1399 and 1422 only one reference has been found to sheep in the latter area, and that is only to four sheep in 1402.[140] Pigs are found in large quantities at Frodsham, the remainder of Delamere Forest (where goats were also kept) and in Macclesfield Forest. With regard to the last, we have the only surviving indication of the numbers of animals kept by individual tenants. Most tenants had only one or two pigs each. Very few had more than this, although numbers were increasing. In 1402, 64 had one pig, 58 two, 18 three, 4 four, and two six, but in 1407 we find 25 with one pig, 53 two, 23 three, 20 four, 5 five and 5 six.[141]

There are few examples in the records of clearing and assarting in this period, although small intakes were made from the waste in Macclesfield Forest.[142] Nor was there any detectable widespread movement towards enclosure of land in the common fields as opposed to individual *placea*.[143] In some cases, field names do suggest a degree of enclosure,[144] and there are some references to enclosures made in the demesnes. In August 1415, tenants in the lordship of Frodsham were prosecuted for making enclosures.[145] A year later a gang from Manchester destroyed enclosures made by tenants at Macclesfield.[146] Moves towards enclosure might be expected in the *burgi* if the contemporary experience of Coventry is anything to go by.[147]

140 Driver, *Cheshire in the Later Middle Ages*, pp. 93–4. SC 2/255/5, m 7.

141 SC 2/255/5, m 6.

142 See above pp. 125–6. Most references to clearing are thirteenth and fourteenth century. (For the late fourteenth century see Tonkinson, *Macclesfield*, p. 29.) During the next two centuries, mention of clearing is much more sporadic and is often obviously a reference to land cleared much earlier (Kenyon, 'Rural Settlement Patterns', p. 40).

143 For enclosure of *placea* in the late fourteenth century, see Tonkinson, *Macclesfield*, p. 30.

144 Dodgson, *Place Names*, ii. 201 ('Hulkoeshy' at Rudheath); iii. 232, 234, 225 ('Botheyworde', 'Cawanmedow', 'Crosseyord' – newly enclosed land – at Frodsham), iii. 227, 234 (other lands ending in -hey at Frodsham).

145 SC 2/155/83, m 3d.

146 CHES 25/11, m 8.

147 On the suburban manors of Coventry Priory, the tendency towards

Tenant prosperity is difficult to comment upon owing to lack of information. Perhaps more important than the lack of new land was the fact that there was no widespread decay or abandonment. We cannot know whether the tenants of the demesne were harshly affected by the anti-Welsh statutes of the early fifteenth century, which severely restricted trade in corn and livestock between Cheshire and Wales, but presumably some tenant cattle were amongst the seven hundred carried off by raiders from Derbyshire and Staffordshire from Macclesfield Forest in 1399.[148] There is reference to a plague (*pestilencia*) in Macclesfield in 1416, severe enough to prevent the holding of the eyre there, but with no other noted effects.[149]

Ostensibly the earl maintained control over agriculture in the demesne lands through his officials, but in fact this control was nominal and peripheral, focusing on the seizure of strays and such like.[150] Although agricultural offences were said to be committed against the lord, it is clear that it was usually the tenants interests which were threatened. But this was not always the case. The courts were used to preserve the lord's interests too. Richard de Sumnour was indicted at Frodsham in October 1414 for occupying the lord's pasture with his animals.[151] Presumably he had not paid for the right to do so. It is unlikely, however, that the lord had much control over the choices behind land use, although tenants were likely to follow well-worn paths of cultivation. It is obvious that there would be need for some collective controls: diversion of a stream for one's

enclosure, originating from the wooded nature of the terrain, was reinforced by the urban investors who had the capital available for enclosing and for independent cultivation (D. Greenblatt, 'The Suburban Manors of Coventry 1279–1411', unpublished PhD thesis (Cornell University, 1967), p. 110).

148 *CPR 1399–1401*, p. 83.

149 SC 6/1303/1, m 1d.

150 A similar position is found at this time in Leicestershire where the tenants paid money rents and attended courts but were otherwise comparatively independent of seigneurial agriculture (R. H. Hilton, *The Economic Development of Some Leicestershire Estates in the 14th & 15th Centuries* (London: Oxford University Press, 1947), p. 15).

151 SC 2/155/83, m 3.

own use at a mill, for instance, could flood a neighbour's lands. The indictment roll tells us that in Nantwich hundred in 1409, David le Seintpierre diverted the River Weaver for a mill to the detriment of lands which were at the time in the lord's hands by escheat.[152] In most manors there were common pastures, as we find for the earl's tenants in Sutton in Macclesfield Forest, and the tenants of Rainow. [153] A resident of Overhouse was fined for pasturing his beasts on the common pasture of the latter; it was clearly intended for the use of the local tenants alone.[154] At Frodsham, tenants pastured their animals on the common marsh, but the lord gained profits from strays which he impounded in a fold built upon one of the burgage plots. By 1422 this structure was in decay, suggesting a lack of maintenance by the lord's officials.[155] There was a common fold at Macclesfield town where the tenants could fold their beasts. For this privilege the mayor and community paid the earl a rent of 4d. per annum.[156]

Common rights were jealously guarded and any assaults upon them punished rigorously. In 1408, John Gardiner, a tenant of the Abbot of Chester in Little Saughall, had asserted 200 square feet of land in the earl's common at Saughall. This was not so much an attack upon the earl's rights as against the earl's tenants there, by a tenant of another manor.[157] Others were prosecuted for trespassing in the common crops,[158] or for encroaching upon the common pasture. For instance, in 1417 Richard Titherington encroached upon two acres of common pasture in Bollington 'to the serious harm of his neighbours' ('in grave nocumento viciniorum suorum').[159] In 1420, William de Lonesdale, a tailor of Macclesfield, was indicted for devastating

152 CHES 25/9, m 109.
153 SC 6/807/1, m 3.
154 SC 2/255/19, m 2.
155 SC 6/794/2, m 5d.
156 SC 11/898, m 1d, SC 6/806/6, m 2.
157 SC 2/156/13, m 2d.
158 As in the case of Richard Rodour at Frodsham in 1414 (SC 2/155/83, m 2).
159 SC 2/255/14, m 4.

the common turbary in the town as well as for digging up his neighbour's moss and selling it.[160] Three such offences were recorded at a Macclesfield portmote in 1402. Ellen Massey cut herbage belonging to John Walkeden; John Clapham and his son fished in the marl pit (*cretum*) of John de Falibrome in the fields of the town; and Cecilia de Bromley took peat belonging to Stephen del Rowe.[161] There are several examples of inter-tenant service. For example, at Shotwick in 1408, Hugh Daukyn claimed that Adam Belewe owed him 7 shillings for ploughing certain lands for him.[162] At Shotwick too, as on most other manors, there was an active peasant market in agricultural produce, revealed by pleas of debt involving the sale of peas, corn, stock, etc.[163]

There is little information in the demesne records about industry in the county at this time, even on the salt industry in Northwich and Middlewich over which there was little control by the earl's officials and little comital income.[164] Yet many in these locations were involved in salt production, presumably supplementing their income from landholdings, or even perhaps deriving their whole income from it. Such activity also required communal regulation such as is described in the Middlewich Chartulary. There were frequent fines for blocking the streets with timber, for instance, vast quantities being needed for boiling salt.[165] The salt industry stimulated ancillary industries in these towns, such as smithies where lead pans for boiling were made.[166] These urban centres would offer a growing market for

160 CHES 25/23, m 44. See also SC 2/255/16, m 3, 255/17, m 3.
161 SC 2/255/5, m 2d.
162 SC 2/156/13, m 2. See also my comments on pleas of trespass, below pp. 233–4.
163 SC 2/156/13 passim. See also cases of theft of crops elsewhere, such as oats at Frodsham in 1417 (CHES 25/11, m 13).
164 See above pp. 174–5 for seigneurial profits from industry. On the salt industry in general see A. F. Calvert, *Salt in Cheshire* (London: Spon; New York: Spon and Chamberlain, 1915) and A. R. Bridbury, *England and the Salt Trade in the Later Middle Ages* (Oxford: Clarendon Press, 1955).
165 *Middlewich Chartulary*, i. 211.
166 Dodgson, *Place Names*, ii. 192–3, 241, on the pace names thus associated.

agricultural produce, especially the Wiches, whence came many merchants involved in the salt trade. The demesne tenants may also have found forests a source of income and employment.[167] Overall, tenants would combine agricultural with industrial and commercial functions. The indictment rolls give some ideas on occupations, mentioning coopers and mercers in each township.[168] The tenants of the demesnes were still agriculturally based, but might have had opportunities to earn cash from other sources. Certainly there is nothing to suggest that their economy was anything but flourishing, although we can say so little upon standards of living and on all the many aspects of peasant life we should wish to elucidate.

## Social Structure

The later Middle Ages display certain phenomena in social developments. One of the most notable, perhaps, was the growth of a peasant 'aristocracy'. With the increasing availability of land after the Black Death, enterprising tenants were able to accumulate larger and more compact holdings. Such became the most prominent families of the manor. Aided often by the prestige and advantages of office-holding, both as demesne officials and representatives of the community of the vill, they in turn developed responsibilities in relation to their wealth and standing.[169] In these 'official families' we see offices handed over from father to son, or families producing several leading men at any one time.[170] We also find a high degree of intermarriage

167 In the duchy of Cornwall the manorial court rolls were littered with references to tenants cutting down trees for timber, collecting fuel and acorns, making charcoal, etc., without the leave or the lord, sometimes on a commercial basis (Hatcher, *Rural Economy*, p. 223).

168 See, for instance, CHES 25/9, m 28 (Middlewich), and CHES 25/10, m 5 (Frodsham).

169 A particularly lucid assessment of this phenomenon is to be found in J. A. Raftis, 'The Concentration of Responsibility in Five Villages', *Medieval Studies*, 28 (1966), 92–118.

170 For the similar elite at Macclesfield in the second half of the previous century, see Tonkinson, *Macclesfield*, pp. 101–2, 109–14.

between such families. These families also tended to provide the majority of lessees of the lord's demesnes, mills and miscellaneous profits. Movement took place in the other direction too; local officials took up leases and perhaps accumulated enough cash and standing to purchase or marry into land.

The identification of the leading tenants and families in the earl's demesnes is easy. Evidence suggests that social structure in these manors parallels the general pattern of developments of this period. At Shotwick, for instance, there appears a distinct group of tenants as office holders and lessees. Roger de Ashley and Richard Gille were both reeves on several occasions, and both were in the group of tenants who leased the small fisheries and sluice gates in 1408; Ashley and two others, Geront de Wodehouse and John Goldyng, leased the demesnes in the same year, with Richard Gille, Hugh Jackson and John Fox standing as their pledges.[171] John Fox was bailiff in the same year, and he, Jackson and Hugh Gille leased the main fishery.[172] The same small group often appear as jurors at the manorial court.[173] At the same time they were those most frequently indicted for pleas of debt, which suggests they were involved in many transactions and deals with fellow villagers.

In the absence of a rental for Shotwick, it is difficult to say whether these same men were the largest landholders in the manor. Ashley held at least two messuages and two bovates, Hugh Jackson one messuage and two bovates, Richard Gille one messuage and 6 selions in Saughall.[174] One of the tenants with the largest holdings, Roger Simpson, does not appear in any office in this period, although he did lease the demesne lands in 1399.[175] He held at least four messuages, four bovates, two acres, six selions and a cottage, and may already have been advanced in years since he died in 1409.[176] It is also difficult

171 SC 6/792/3, m 3, SC 2/156/13, m 2.
172 SC 6/792/3, m 3.
173 SC 2/156/13, mm 2, 2d, 3.
174 SC 2/156/13, mm 2–2d.
175 SC 6/791/1, m 3.
176 SC 6/791/1, m 3, SC 2/156/13, m 2d.

to tell whether all these men were freemen. Villein tenure did not prevent office holding. Hugh Barb was a *nativus* but was catchpole at Shotwick in 1408.[177] Simpson also may have been a *nativus* although he held more land than many a freeman in the manor.

A glance at the lists of office holders at the Wiches shows the predominance of certain families. At Middlewich, the Hicksons and Hickocksons (possibly the same family or closely related), the Wilsons and Crowthers all had several members in office. William Swetenham, who was chamberlain in 1419 and 1420, was a burgess in 1414,[178] and a collector of the subsidy in the hundred of Northwich in June 1418.[179] He and his wife Joanna had considerable holdings in the town.[180] The Middlewich Chartulary gives evidence upon holdings in the town, but unfortunately there are few early fifteenth-century examples and the entries are selective, so it is not possible to reconstruct the pattern of landholding in the town completely. Certainly some men seem to be more active in the land market than others, although we must bear in mind that some families preserved their muniments and others did not. An urge towards preservation, however, may in its turn indicate an active and zealous interest in increasing and consolidating one's holding, so the selective nature of survival is not altogether accidental nor misleading in the context of the present study, and of the specific point in question here. Richard Hickockson, for instance, seems to have been interested in increasing the size of his holding.[181] In addition, he frequently acted as a feoffee for the Swetenhams. In 1392, Thomas Swetenham granted him all his lands and tenements in Middlewich, Newton and Kinderton, which were of his wife, Mary's, inheritance.[182] In 1404, Hickockson regranted these estates to Thomas's son,

177 SC 2 156/13, m 2d.

178 *Middlewich Chartulary*, i, item 76a.

179 CHES 2/91, m 6 (9), *37 DKR*, p. 103.

180 *Middlewich Chartulary*, i, items 138 a–i.

181 *Middlewich Chartulary*, i, items 9a–111a, 146d, 147c.

182 *Middlewich Chartulary*, i, item 138a.

William.[183] There was also much intermarriage between these most prominent families. Agnes, daughter of Roger de Hulme, a burgess in 1414,[184] was to marry William Swetenham's own son, Thomas, in 1419. If Thomas died, she was to marry his brother Hugh.[185]

This group of prominent tenants does not seem to have been restricted solely to those who were burgesses. If it still holds true in this period that non-burgesses had to pay fines for licences to boil salt, then Ralph Coventry and John Bermond, who paid for such a licence in 1379, were not burgesses.[186] Yet Bermond (or perhaps his son – the use of the same name over generations makes firm identification difficult) was catchpole in 1418, and lessee of the lord's oven in 1405 and 1411.[187] The leading men also provided the majority of litigants on the court rolls. For instance, at the first court of the year 1413–14, the Hicksons figure prominently. Richard was the plaintiff in two pleas of trespass and one of debt, Hugh in one plea of a broken agreement, and he and Thomas leased one shop each.[188] They also often appear as pledges in other cases. This reflects the importance and full involvement of such men in the commercial and social life of the *burgus*, and the complex web of inter-pledging and interdependence. At Northwich, too, we find the same small circle of 'trustworthy men' ('probi homines'). The Starkeys, who saw office as both steward and chamberlain, held burgages and other land in the *burgus* itself and in the neighbouring township of Plumley.[189] This kind of man was also able to use the lord's courts as an organ for his own litigation. We see a particularly good example of this at Macclesfield, where John de Macclesfield was able to use the lord's portmote of the *burgus* of October 1415 to sanction his

183 *Middlewich Chartulary*, i, items 138b–d, 146d, 147c.

184 *Middlewich Chartulary*, i, item 76a. He also held lands in Knutsford (items 206c and 139c).

185 *Middlewich Chartulary*, i, item 206b.

186 SC 6/772/15, m 2.

187 SC 6/791/10, m 4, 792/8, m 3.

188 SC 2/156/3, m 1.

189 HMC, Leicester of Tabley Deeds, Northwich B12 and B13.

attempts to recover three shillings' rent for a burgage sublet to Margery Burgeys, for which he himself only paid one shilling to the earl.[190]

Deeds which survive concerning landholding in Frodsham do not provide any evidence of the accumulation of vast holdings by any one individual or family, but they do offer a rare opportunity to study the role and position of one family, the Torfots, over a period of time.[191] This is unusual on two counts: the first is the aspect of continuity of the family's prominence over a century.[192] The second is the early establishment of a distinctive family name. Frodsham seems to have lagged behind the other demesne manors in the development of surnames: before the late fourteenth century, most tenants there used an occupational name (but with few detectable family connections), or else took their name from the vill in which they lived. At Frodsham, too, the lord's officials and village officials are most frequently found as witnesses to private deeds, especially, for instance, the bailiff and coroners.[193]

The Torfots emerged as a distinct group (at least according to the evidence provided in the aforementioned deeds) in the 1340s, although there are some earlier references to them in the manor.[194] The last references to them in these deeds date from the 1440s. From the deeds, I have drawn up a possible genealogy (Fig. 1). The earlier generations are incomplete. There are several other Torfots referred to in the 1340s and 50s whom I have not been able to relate to those who relationships are certain. One of the Torfots regularly occupied the office of bailiff of Frodsham from 1351 to 1420 at least, save in the years

190 SC 2/225/12, m 5.

191 CALS, Cholmondeley MSS DCH Box F.

192 Raftis noted a considerable fluidity in these prominent families, with a 50% turnover in a sample period of 70 years. It was rare, then, for one family to remain prominent for more than two generations.

193 CALS, Cholmondeley MSS DCH Box F.

194 A Henry Torfot may have been bailiff in 1318 although there is some dispute over the dating of this particular deed (CALS, MSS F12). The family is also discussed by Ormerod, *Cheshire*, ii. 47.

when the manor was not in the hands of the earl.[195] Holders of the office are indicated on the genealogy which follows.[196] Other members of the family are also seen frequently in other local offices. In 1414, Robert, Ralph and John Torfot were on the panel of jurors who elected the village officials.[197] A William Torfot was serjeant in the 1440s.[198] Members of the family are also found frequently as lessees of demesne lands, etc..[199] In this period alone, Roger leased the Eucroft and other lands in the demesne. John (possibly his son) leased Bruggehouse marsh from 1412.[200] Despite running into conflict with the authorities in 1416 over an indictment for trespass (he was outlawed but soon pardoned),[201] Ralph Torfot leased the orchard,[202] as well as the Eucroft and other demesne lands after Roger had given up this lease.[203]

The family held several burgages in the town in the mid-fourteenth century.[204] In the 1360s and 1370s, several other burgages came into the hands of Henry Torfot, then obviously the leading member of the family.[205] They also had considerable holdings in the fields of the township.[206] Again, the 1360s

195 These were 1357 and 1369 (bailiff Henry de Frodsham; Booth, *Financial Admin.*, pp. 19, 22); 1384 (bailiff John de Frodsham; CALS, Cholmondelely MS F108); 1388 (Richard de Manley, ibid., F109); 1397 (Peter de Quitlegh, ibid., F116).

196 Note also that Roger may have been bailiff in 1406 when the manor was still in the hands of Radegonde Béchet (CALS, Cholmondelely MS F121).

197 SC 2/155/83, m 2.

198 CALS, Cholmondeley MSS F 132.

199 For instance, SC 6/793/4, m 6.

200 SC 6/792/9, m 4.

201 CHES 2/91, m 3 (11), *37 DKR*, p. 713.

202 SC 6/793/7, m 5 to SC 6/793/11, m 5.

203 From 1421, SC 6/794/1, m 5.

204 For instance, CALS, Cholmondeley MSS F61.

205 For instance, CALS, Cholmondeley MSS F72, 83, 85, 93, 100. In 1365 Henry had been granted a burgage which had escheated to the earl for lack of an heir (F82). Thomas, his son, was leasing a burgage from the prior of Norton in 1390 which he had granted to the use of his daughter, Margery (F110).

206 CALS, Cholmondeley MSS F40, 61. 63.

and 1370s mark a period of accumulation.[207] The Torfots also appear as 'improving' tenants: they took in several assarts from the waste at this time.[208] They also held land in Bradley and Overton.[209] The late fourteenth and fifteenth century saw a period of consolidation, and the increase of family interest in the holding.[210] It is interesting to speculate upon criticism of Roger Torfot during his term as bailiff as an expression of animosity towards this family, which must have so dominated the town in all its aspects.

According to Stella Davies, the fourteenth century had seen the beginnings of consolidation in burgess holdings in Macclesfield: a number of deeds dating from 1363 to 1389 show exchanges going on, presumably in order to get contiguous land.[211] Certain men of the town appear most often in transactions in this period, such as Stephen del Rowe in the early 1400s and, later, Roger Jodrell and Richard Liversegge.[212] But by far the most prominent was John de Macclesfield, clerk, senior, whose interest in his accumulated holdings was enough to prompt him to record the various deeds and transactions in a cartulary, now BL Cleopatra D VI.[213] We have already witnessed the extent of his holdings in the *burgus* of Macclesfield, and the profits made by him in his subletting activities. His is the clearest cut example of the accumulation of large and compact holdings. Most of his property seems to have been accumulated after 1383. Many transactions concerning burgages occur in

207 CALS, Cholmondeley MSS F78, 88, 93, 99. In the seventeenth and eighteenth centuries one field was still called the 'Torfotheys' (Dodgson, *Place Names*, iii. 235).

208 CALS, Cholmondeley MSS F82.

209 CALS, Cholmondeley MSS F814, 816 (Bradley), F375, F132 (Overton).

210 This is witnessed by an increasing number of enfeoffments to use (for instance, CALS, Cholmondeley MSS F125, 128).

211 Davies, *History of Macclesfield*, p. 12.

212 Respectively SC 2/255/4, 255/5, 255/6; JRRIL Jodrell 6, SC 2/255/14, m 4; SC 2/255/10, m 2d.

213 See also J. L. C. Bruel, 'An Edition of the John de Macclesfield Cartulary', unpublished PhD thesis (University of London, 1969); Tonkinson, *Macclesfield*, p. 108.

the 1390s shortly before the petition in 1398 to crenellate his house, which appears to have been quite an impressive building containing a chapel.[214] At this time, he appears to have been acquiring a block of burgages at the junction of Godisslane, Wallgate and Souters Lane, in the area where his house is likely to have been. He was still buying plots in 1416 in the vicinity of this house.[215]

De Macclesfield is significant in that he achieved a position of considerable standing in the town by means of landholding rather than office holding. He is only mentioned in the earl's accounts as some time lessee of the herbage of the park.[216] This is a most revealing example of how the accounts can fail to give a picture of the actual situation of landholding and social control. De Macclesfield thus remains a shadowy figure, but one whose presence looms large over tenurial arrangements in the town and forest, whose interests were large enough to warrant the employment of his own bailiff for the collection of rents due to him.[217]

De Macclesfield had achieved early prominence by his service at a national level to Richard II, becoming keeper of the Great Wardrobe in November 1397.[218] But his prominence in Macclesfield arose from his probable membership of the Alcock family[219] and his desire to provide for his own family

214 CHES 2/72, m 37d (3), *36 DKR*, p. 312. For the crenellation see BL, Cotton MS Cleopatra D VI, f. 196v and for the chapel, f. 92r. See also D. K. Maxfield, 'Pardoners and Property: John Macclesfield 1351–1422, Builder of Macclesfield Castle', *Journal of the Chester Archaeological Society*, 69 (1986), 79–95.

215 BL, Cotton MS Cleopatra D VI, ff. 83, 215, 217.

216 See above p. 157.

217 SC 2/255/12, m 5.

218 *CPR 1396–9*, p. 266. John de Macclesfield was named 'king's clerk' in 1384 (*CPR 1381–8*, p. 379). He was rewarded by numerous clerical preferments. In 1397 he held the rectory or wardenship of the free chapel of 'Barwe' in Cheshire (*CPR 1396–9*, p. 44), the provostship of Wells Cathedral (p. 154), and was vicar of St Giles without the bar of Old Temple, London (p. 162). He also held the rectory of Denham (p. 429).

219 His father, John Alcock, was stock keeper in Macclesfield for the Black

by his mistress, Katherine de Kingsley. He appears on several occasions in collusion with John Savage, such as in the leasing of the herbage of Macclesfield park. His eldest (illegitimate) son, John, married Savage's daughter. Both fathers settled property in Wallgate on the couple on their marriage.[220] Both Savage and de Macclesfield benefited from the disgrace of John de Mottram, Savage by succeeding to his office as bailiff of the forest, and de Macclesfield by acquiring lands formerly held by him.[221]

The higher echelons of society, represented by such as the Torfots and John de Macclesfield, are easy to define and distinguish. At the other end of the social scale, the smallholders, cottagers, servants, etc. are also relatively well recorded. There are references to at least nine cottagers at Frodsham, found mainly in lists of decayed rents in the bailiff's accounts. In addition, twenty-one tenants on the manor probably held only one bovate, which seems to have been equivalent to three Cheshire acres (seven statute acres). There are also references to cottagers at Shotwick. In the thirteenth and fourteenth century, the usual holding there had been one bovate.[222] In the court of May 1408, some tenancies were re-leased. One cannot be sure whether these were the total holdings of the tenants named therein but, on the whole, holdings were still on the small side at this time, although larger than in the previous centuries. Of the ten tenants named at this court, three held one bovate, two held four acres, two held two bovates, one held four bovates, one six

Prince (*Accounts of the Chamberlain and Other Officers of the County of Chester 1301–1360*, ed. R. Stewart-Brown, RSLC, 59 (1910), pp. 242, 246, 260). He was probably a member of the cadet line of the Alcock family whose senior members included Roger Alcock, sometime mayor of Macclesfield, who died in 1412. Roger acted as trustee and factor for John de Macclesfield on several occasions (see, for instance, BL, Cotton MS Cleopatra D VI, f. 23). This probable family relationship was pointed out to me by Professor Michael Bennett.

220 BL, Cotton MS Cleopatra D VI, f. 150 sq.

221 BL, Cotton MS Cleopatra D VI, ff. 201r–v. De Macclesfield was also involved in other transactions with John Savage concerning lands in Sutton (ff. 162–3).

222 Stewart-Brown, 'Manor and Park of Shotwick', p. 138.

selions and one a butt of land.[223] At Drakelow, what evidence we have suggests that tenements were small. William Bothe, for instance, held five acres in 1412. On another occasion, Henry de Whitlegh, a free tenant, is recorded as holding a messuage and two acres.[224] In Macclesfield Forest, the average holding was c. 15 acres, although there was a wide variation in the size of holdings. In Disley in 1383–4, for instance, Robert Stykull held three-and-a-half acres, but Roger Jodrell more than 60 acres.[225] Generally, the holdings are not large, except perhaps in Macclesfield Forest where, along with Delamere Forest, many of the Cheshire gentry held land.

Servants and labourers, to a large extent landless, occupied an important role in village society.[226] Most of the wage labour at Shotwick appears to have been provided by men and women of Welsh origin. Agnes, daughter of one Bellyn ap Eign, had supposedly contracted to serve Roger Ashley for one year from Michaelmas 1408 for 5 shillings. Roger claimed that she had broken this agreement, but the jury on this occasion decided in her favour.[227] Not all these servants were necessarily landless. Some certainly subleased property from manorial tenants. Wirmill ugh Glevuelot leased a house from John le Carter but fell into arrears with his rent in October 1409.[228] Some were able to rise in the social scale: a Conus le Welshman appears on the panel of jurors at Shotwick in February 1408.[229] Several Welshmen provided unskilled labour in repairs in Macclesfield park in 1414.[230] At Middlewich yet another servant of obviously Welsh extraction, Alice ap Atha, was charged with breaking a spinning wheel belonging to Katherine de Halton.[231]

223 SC 2/156/13, mm. 2–2d.
224 Respectively, SC 6/792/9, m 1d; SC 6/792/10, m 9, CHES 2/98, m 1 (5), *37 DKR*, p. 582.
225 SC 11/898, m 4.
226 Hilton, *English Peasantry*, pp. 30–1.
227 SC 2/156/1, m 3. There are several similar cases on m 2d.
228 SC 2/156/13, m 3.
229 SC 2/156/13, m 1.
230 SC 2/155/88, m 8d.
231 SC 2/156/3, m 4d.

There are several cases on the indictment rolls of violations of the Statute of Labourers, but very few occur on the demesne lands. Most examples arise in the hundred of Wirral, especially at the time of the autumn harvest, since this area was an important grain producing area.[232] There are one or two examples at Northwich, where, because of the salt industry, one might expect a large number of those who made their living from service.[233] In 1402, for instance, John Leftwich was fined for 'kidnapping' Eleanor Orell, the servant of William Starkey, from the latter's service. Judging from references to poaching servants in this way, labour would seem to be at a premium throughout the county. The miller of Henry Marshall of Offerton was threatened with physical violence by Robert Coterell if he did not leave his present master's service immediately.[234] Men were frequently prosecuted in the bailiff of Macclesfield hundred's tourn for leaving their area in the time of the autumn harvest.[235] Yet wages do not appear to have been any higher in the county, at least not as regards employment on the earl's demesnes is concerned, as Appendix IIIc shows.

With so little information on the size of tenements in the demesne, it is difficult to trace the typical: we can only see the extremes of the social scale. It is the ill-defined, middling ranks which escape our notice. Possibly some of those discussed in the category of the 'peasant aristocracy' really belong to these middling ranks, but survival of evidence makes them artificially prominent.[236] We can only name and trace those who held office, leased lands, etc.: for the rest, we suffer from a lack of rentals. Only in the case of Macclesfield Forest do we have a comprehensive list of manorial tenants, and even this dates from almost twenty years before our period.[237] One of the first points

232 See, for instance, CHES 25/9, m 1.
233 CHES 25/9, m 18.
234 SC 2/255/6, m 1.
235 SC 2/255/5, m 8.
236 Bennett, *Community*, p. 105, gives examples of peasants within the county who were 'able to achieve modest capital accumulation'.
237 SC 11/898.

which this rental demonstrates is the wide diversity in the social status of tenants in this lordship. In both this forest and that of Delamere, much land was held by the gentry, generally by knight service. For instance, Sir Thomas Grosvenor held land in Kettleshulme in Macclesfield Forest.[238] Sir Peter de Dutton held the manor of Dutton as well as 200 acres of meadow and wood in Acton within the forest of Delamere, which he was allowed to impark in 1410.[239] Little land in the other demesnes was held by this social group, although there are exceptions. John Done of Utkinton held land and burgages in Frodsham.[240] Several members of the Cheshire gentry held saline in the two demesne Wiches, such as John Done and Robert Legh of Adlington, in Northwich.[241] Office holding and leasing of the earl's profits by such men was concentrated in the forest areas where they were substantial landholders, although in general few gentry were involved in demesne administration proper. Like the peasant aristocracy, the gentry were involved in much subleasing and many tenurial arrangements amongst themselves.[242]

## Law and Order

The demesne lands appear to have had their fair share of cases involving violence. Certainly there are many cases of assault, armed robbery, etc., although relatively few of murder. There were few prolonged and vicious quarrels, such as that pursued between John de Macclesfield snr and John Kingsley, where each appears to have launched organised attacks on each other's houses.[243] Kingsley was quite a scoundrel: contemporary court rolls abound with references to his felonies and treasons, including an alleged conspiracy to murder Henry IV and the

238 SC 6/806/11, m 2.

239 CHES 2/82, m 3d (9), *36 DKR*, p. 162.

240 CHES 2/106, m 8d, *37 DKR*, p. 211.

241 Respectively, CHES 2/106, m 8d, *37 DKR*, p. 211; CHES 2/81, m 2 (17), *36 DKR*, pp. 295–6.

242 For a full study see Bennett, *Community*, chapter 5.

243 CHES 25/11, m 12.

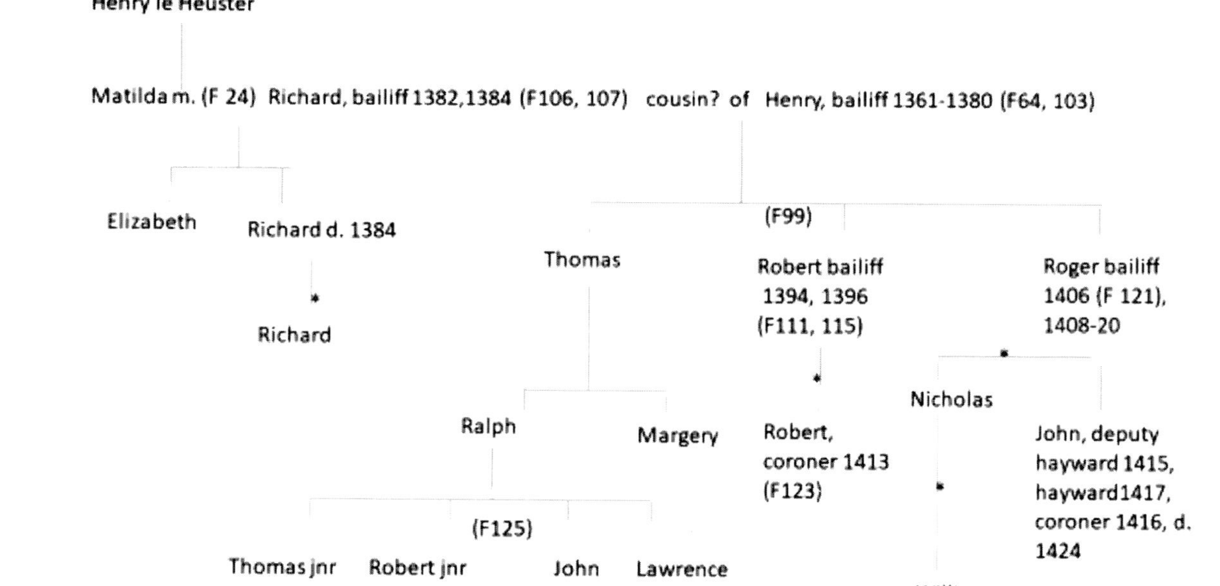


**Fig 1. Possible genealogy of the Torfot family at Frodsham.**

* indicates a possible rather than certain relationship

F: refers to the relevant document in CALS, Cholmondeley MSS DCH Box F

For the offices held by John, son of Roger, see SC6 793/2 m. 6, deputy hayward 1415; SC6 793/5 m.5, hayward 1417; CHES 25/11 m. 8, coroner 1416. For his death in 1424 see CHES 2/95 m.1d(2), *37 DKR*, p. 713.

For the service of Roger as bailiff from 1408 to 1420 see Appendix I (j).

prince of Wales.[244] His quarrel with de Macclesfield, possibly concerned with family honour – his sister Katherine was de Macclesfield's mistress and bore him six children – as well as material concerns, was eventually settled by both parties agreeing to abide by the arbitration of Sir John Stanley.[245]

The county had a reputation for being 'one of the last law-abiding parts of the country'.[246] Where court rolls survive, there is inevitably more evidence of bad behaviour, which may make the tenants seem less law-abiding than they really were. This judgement may also arise from the fact that misdemeanours in the demesne lands could be dealt with in the manorial courts, hundred courts, by the justiciar in eyre in the hundreds and in the county court. For instance, at the eyre held in the hundred of Eddisbury on 17 September 1403, Henry Wetour and his brother Robert, lessees of the meadow 'Rushycawan' at Frodsham, were fined for attacking John Warde of Frodsham.[247] Many cases remained unsettled from one court to the next, either because of legal technicalities or because the felons could not be made to appear. Another problem was keeping felons in custody whilst awaiting trial. Both John de Mottram at Macclesfield and William Venables, constable of Chester Castle, suffered for allowing such to escape. Henry de Galway, sergeant at Frodsham, let a felon escape in 1410 and was fined £8, although half of this fine was later pardoned.[248] Thus any

244 CHES 25/10, m 34. See also CHES 29/128, m 19–19d. See also D. K. Maxfield, 'Was John Macclesfield a Scoundrel?', *Cheshire History*, 28 (1991), 19–20.

245 Lancashire County Record Office, DDK 456/1. I am grateful to Professor M J. Bennett for this reference.

246 B. Hanawalt, 'Economic Influences on the Pattern of Crime in England, 1300–1348', *American Journal of Legal History*, 18 (1974), 297, cited in Tonkinson, *Macclesfield*, p. 138. In his fourth chapter, Tonkinson also provides extensive discussion on crime and disorder in the late fourteenth century. See also for the period 1354–1377, *Chester County Court Indictment Roll 1354–1377: Dealing with Serious Crime in later Fourteenth-Century Cheshire*, ed. Phyllis Hill and Paul Booth, Chetham Society, 3rd ser., 53 (2019).

247 CHES 25/9, m 27.

248 SC 6/792/6, m 6.

conclusions we can draw from the records must be qualitative rather than quantitative.

The very fact that offences were recorded implies that they were detectable, that offenders could be brought to task and punishments meted out. Such punishments were usually small scale, and cases were often difficult to prove. Frequently the plaintiff was unable to proceed with his claim: juries could often decide in favour of the defendant. This may imply that many pleas were unjustified and were occasioned by personal vindictiveness. This is potentially demonstrated by the frequently retaliatory nature of offences. At Shotwick in April 1409, for instance, John le Carter charged John Goldyng with damaging his crops with his pigs and geese: Goldyng in his turn charged Carter with destroying his corn and cutting down a tree on his land.[249] Of course this 'eye-for-an-eye' behaviour may also reflect the inadequacy of the judicial system, when men found it necessary, or more effective, to take the law into their own hands rather than relying on punishment through more formal channels.

Were most crimes detected? A definite, unequivocal answer cannot, of course, be made. Certainly the courts never suffered from a lack of business! Society was litigious if not law abiding, and clearly these two characteristics are not incompatible. Another consideration which must be borne in mind is the definition of 'crime'. Many cases brought before the courts do not merit such a description. Pleas of debt, trespass and the breaking of by-laws which formed the majority of cases did not often include violence. Many pleas of debt and trespass conceal inter-peasant commercial and agricultural agreements which misfired: a plea of debt, for instance, might be merely a haggling over the price which was to be paid, or even a way of registering a transaction in the court in order to record it to the benefit of both parties. Many suits for trespass were claims for payment of arrears for rent for pasture,[250] or else reflect problems in subletting. This would seem to be behind the

249 SC 2/156/13, m 3.

250 Hatcher, *Rural Economy*, p. 234.

strange case at Northwich in 1413 where Ralph Leicester and Nicholas le Baker brought a plea of trespass against Matilda le Draper. They had demolished a house belonging to her, but she claimed they had no right to its tenancy.[251] Inter-family pleas of trespass may reveal problems in apportioning out inheritances. This can explain such cases as that at Middlewich where John Bermond, son of the man of the same name who was catchpole in 1418, stole silver and lead from his father.[252]

In Barbara Westman's study of the peasant family and crime, cases of trespass and land disputes were the most numerous internecine crimes, after assault. Such clashes occurred primarily between brothers and over widow's dower lands. Many cases of violence also arose out of property disputes within families.[253] As Westman puts it, 'Suing over debt, trespass, and ownership of goods could not unreasonably be considered a peasant pastime and perhaps also as a vital way to earn a little extra income. By indulging in property suits, families were practising on each other what was done by the whole community'. Many fines ostensibly for breaking village by-laws were, in reality, payments for licences to break them: fines for breaking the assize of ale, which have long been recognised as payments for the right to brew, fall into such a category.[254] At Macclesfield *burgus* and the Wiches, there was much more litigation of this nature than at the rural manors, a reflection yet again of the intensive 'commercial' activity in these units.

One point which does emerge from a study of the legal records of the demesnes during this period, if not the whole county, is that crime was not confined to any specific social groups. In the demesne manors, the most prominent tenants, those who appeared most frequently in office, also appeared most frequently in court cases, both in criminal and civil cases.

251 SC 2/156/11, m 2d.

252 CHES 25/9, m 28.

253 Barbara Hanawalt Westman, 'The Peasant Family and Crime in Fourteenth Century England', *Journal of British Studies*, 13 (1974), 1–18, at pp. 5–6, with the following quote at p. 8.

254 Neilson, 'Customary Rents', ii. 35.

This reflects their involvement in all aspects of the community, subletting, money lending, etc. Certain families appeared in court more frequently than others, but again these tend to be the more prominent.[255] The gentry as much as the peasantry involved themselves in what we would consider nefarious undertakings. There were problems even with those whom we would assume to be upright servants of the Crown. Roger Alcock, mayor of the Macclesfield *burgus*, for instance, refused to pay the money he had collected as subsidy in Macclesfield hundred to Thomas le Wodeward, bailiff itinerant, nor even to give guarantee for future payment. Wodeward claimed that he had to flee for fear of assault.[256] In July 1411, Robert Legh of Adlington seized a distraint from Thomas Chedle as bailiff of the hundred of Macclesfield, which the latter had a mandate to take from the lands of Richard de Clitheroe as a forfeit imposed in the third hundred after Eyre.[257] Officials were frequently subject to violence or to the impeding of the performance of their duties. There was trouble in 1404 at Frodsham when Thomas le Wodeward and Ralph Sparke, bailiff of the hundred of Eddisbury, came to take distraint in the *burgus* for the money owed by the burgesses to the prince for a confirmation of their charter of liberties. In three cases where they took goods in distraint, the burgesses stole them back from where they were being stored.[258]

Indeed, the gentry and upper ranks of the peasantry seem to have committed more offences involving violence than men of

255 This possibly contradicts Raftis's conclusion in his *Warboys: Two Hundred Years in the Life of an English Mediaeval Village* (Toronto: Pontifical Institute of Mediaeval Studies, 1974), p. 235, that the families which were excessively aggressive tended to be the poorer ones; they could be residents of the village for a long time and yet still be always getting into trouble. However, there are plenty of cases on the Cheshire demesnes of servants involved in brawling and petty theft, which fits with Westman's conclusion that, in general, the tendency was for families to group together in committing crime rather than turning on one another ('Peasant Family', p. 14).

256 CHES 25/10, m 15d (Sept 1404).

257 CHES 25/10, m 34d.

258 CHES 25/10, m 15d.

lesser social status, at least according to the evidence provided by the indictment rolls. Possibly gentry offences could not escape detection and the misdoers could be more easily brought to justice than an insignificant, nameless peasant. The gentry of the county were an extremely litigious group.[259] Bennett argues for the inadequacies of the law courts of the county, yet the gentry did not seek protection in the retinue of a private patron, retaining their direct link with the crown. Rather, their system seems to have been one of mutual credit and collective security in which no one family predominated. A particular problem in the county seems to have been the degree to which people, even the most prominent, were prepared to conceal others who had committed crimes. To cite but one example linked to the prominent Torfot family in Frodsham: in 1400, John de Barton of Frodsham was indicted for the death of Thomas Torfot, possibly the brother of the late bailiff, Roger. Barton had been harboured by John Triket, himself later bailiff and John Spark of Frodsham.[260]

The waste of Rudheath traditionally had a reputation as a sanctuary for criminals, along with Hoole Heath and Overmarsh.[261] Unfortunately, no court rolls survive for the manor of Drakelow and lordship of Rudheath, but we know from the perquisites of courts which were accounted by the bailiff that few courts were held there in this period. I have found only one reference to Rudheath on the indictment rolls; in 1405, John le Wright was fined for stopping up the water of Hobbelake on Rudheath on the highway between Lancashire and London, in the which lake many horses had perished and their loads been lost due to this action.[262] This hardly seems a criminal offence unless it conceals undertones of intentional highway robbery. Of course, it is possible that Rudheath was

259 M. J. Bennett, 'A County Community: Social Cohesion Amongst the Cheshire Gentry 1400–1425', *Northern History*, 8 (1973), 24–44, at p. 35.

260 CHES 25/10, m 5d.

261 Sharp, 'Earldom and County of Chester', p. 398.

262 CHES 25/9, m 59.

so lawless that courts could not be held nor culprits detected, but surely such a grave state of affairs would not have gone uncommented. It is likely that the reason for so little judicial activity here was that there were so few inhabitants.[263] The same was probably true for Overmarsh, where there are no offences recorded for this period.

As we have seen, there are many cases involving violence. At the county court of 1406, contestants in a case even began fighting in the hall of pleas before the justiciar and all those present 'to the great affray of those present and to the hindering of the hearing of the pleas'.[264] Without more detailed study, however, it would be difficult to claim that lawlessness here was a greater problem than in any other county, or that the courts and machinery of law enforcement were inadequate overall. That said, violence was sometimes political in nature, as in the case of the Cheshire response to taxation in 1416.[265]

263 The first edition 6" OS map XXXIV indicates a similar situation in the mid-nineteenth century. There were scattered farmsteads on the heath but no nucleated settlements. Sharp, 'Earldom and County of Chester' (p. 398) found little sign of the presence of criminals in the period she studied.

264 CHES 25/10, m 21.

265 Michael J. Bennett, 'Henry V and the Cheshire Tax Revolt of 1416', in Gwilym Dodd (ed.), *Henry V: New Interpretations* (Woodbridge: York Medieval Press, 2013), pp. 171–86. See also the second part of Chapter 6 below.

# CHAPTER 5

# *Patronage and the Demesne*

There can be no doubt that the dictates of 'good lordship' played an important role in estate management in the medieval period. This was no less the case for the royal demesne. In the lands of the crown, patronage was often the most influential determinant of policy, at least until the later fifteenth century. As Jack Lander put it, 'Desirable though their cash revenues might be, the crown lands could never be run exclusively from the point of view of profit. Patronage above all kept the body politic in harmony'.[1] Bertram Wolfe provided a comprehensive assessment of this function of crown lands.[2] Outlining a hierarchy of priorities, he considered the first to be that crown lands should be used to support the royal family – hence the whole concept and practice of a landed appanage were for the heir to the throne, the prince of Wales, which included the earldom of Chester, as also for the queen and queen dowager, as we see in the grant of Macclesfield to Queen Catherine after Henry V's death. The next most important function of crown lands was patronage, not only the temporary alienation of manors to others but also the granting of annuities (annual payments) from the income of royal lands. Only after these considerations was the royal demesne seen as the provider of an intermittent and fluctuating contribution to crown revenue. Indeed, Lander even goes so far as to suggest that 'good lordship and efficient royal finance would seem to have been incompatible'.[3]

Throughout England, the king dispensed the greatest patronage of anyone but, as Ralph Griffiths pointed out, 'this patronage was often shared with, and therefore limited

1 J. R. Lander, *Crown and Nobility, 1450–1509* (London: Edward Arnold, 1976), p. 44.

2 B. P. Wolffe, *The Royal Demesne in English History: The Crown Estate in the Governance of the Realm from the Conquest to 1509* (London: Allen and Unwin, 1971) especially p. 65.

3 Lander, *Crown and Nobility*, p. 48.

by, several of their subjects', not least by the prince of Wales when in possession of his appanage. The study of Cheshire in the period from 1399 to 1422 usefully allows us to investigate potential contrasts between the period of princely control and that of the king. As Griffiths reminds us, 'in the palatinates of Chester and Lancaster, in the duchy of Cornwall, and the principality of Wales, the Lancastrians were exclusive, direct lords. There, their patronage was rarely curtailed, and hence the impact of their appointments and grants on government, society and the practice of kingship can be clearly observed'.[4] In other words, when Henry V was king, he had the whole of the royal demesne at his disposal as well as the entire patrimony of the prince of Wales and the duchy of Lancaster, inherited from his patrilineal line. Such an assemblage of lands in the hands of a king was unprecedented. We can therefore justifiably assess whether, when Cheshire was in the hands of the king himself, the county demonstrated the same application and experience of policies as the rest of the royal demesne.

In addition to these general considerations, there are certain specific events in this period which may have had an effect upon the attitude towards and application of patronage. We would expect, for instance, that the change of dynasty in 1399 would lead to a purge of the holders of Ricardian patronage and their replacement by Lancastrian feedmen, all the more so as, in Chapter 1, we have already identified such a trend in administrative personnel in the first years of the reign of Henry IV. Furthermore, the reign of Henry IV saw the crown in financial difficulties and under pressure from critics.[5] In 1404, the Commons in parliament urged for the resumption of crown lands into royal hands.[6] It was considered that the royal

4 R. A. Griffiths, 'Patronage, Politics and the Principality of Wales 1413–61', in H. Hearder and H. R. Loyn (eds), *British Government and Administration: Studies Presented to S. B. Chrimes* (Cardiff University of Wales Press, 1974), pp. 69–86, at pp. 69–70.

5 Christopher Given-Wilson, *Henry IV* (New Haven CT and London: Yale University Press, 2016), especially Chapter 10, The Search for Solvency (1404–1406).

6 *PROME*, viii. 291–4; Wolffe, *Royal Demesne*, p. 77 sq.

demesne had been wantonly misused as a result of the many alienations made for the sake of patronage. The Commons wanted to force the king to 'live of his own' by virtue of higher income from his own lands, which would take the pressure off the rest of the population forced to contribute to repeated requests for taxation.

Technically Cheshire lay outside the remit of the Commons' petition and royal response. It was held directly by the prince of Wales as his appanage. It did not return members to parliament. Nonetheless, it is relevant to explore whether contemporary opinion on the use of the royal demesne, as reflected in the petition of 1404, had any effect upon policies pursued by the prince in the county. Furthermore, the prince held other lands within his appanage. Whilst Wales similarly lay outside the remit of the petition, the duchy of Cornwall, with its lands in Devon and Cornwall as well as its foreign manors, did not. The exercise of patronage in Cheshire therefore needs to be set within the wider context of the prince's lands as a whole.

It is impossible in this present study to discuss all aspects of royal and princely patronage in the county. We shall concentrate primarily upon the use of the demesne for patronage purposes under three headings: the alienation of manors for no render; the payment of annuities out of demesne issues (as well as those paid out of county revenues as a whole); and the appointment of officials. Since officers were paid an annual wage, it was possible for an appointment to be made for the purposes of patronage alone, the officeholder collecting the wages but never exercising the office in person. He might appoint a deputy at a lower cost, or else the office itself may have been honorific without any actual function.

The administration of the demesne often demonstrated further instances of patronage. This is reflected, for instance, in leases made upon favourable terms to household men as well as local officials, as we saw in Chapter 3. A further demonstration of patronage – the granting and selling of feudal incidents such as wardships and custody of manors falling to the crown by escheat – cannot reasonably be studied here as it is a huge topic in its own right, covering much land within the county beyond the earl's demesne lands. It is enough to say that local officials and members of Prince Henry's household figure prominently as beneficiaries in such a context. For instance, in 1408, Roger Leche, steward of the prince's household, was granted the custody of lands formerly of Richard Vernon.[7] Thirteen years later, William Troutbeck, the chamberlain of Chester, was able to purchase the custody of the lands and heiress of Thomas Holes.[8]

Of course, the use of demesne as a source of patronage was not an innovation. The Black Prince's involvement in foreign wars, and his desire to reward his military retinue, had helped to inaugurate a policy in the county of granting lands and offices for life as well as the increasing direction of income towards the payment of annuities. In 1371, out of approximately £2,500 revenue chargeable in Cheshire and Flintshire, over £1,800 was assigned to be paid in annuities to the prince's followers.[9] Increasing 'damage' was done in the reign of Richard II, especially with regard to the alienation of whole manors. Until her death in 1385, his mother, Joan, princess of Wales, held Middlewich as part of her dower lands.[10] From 1389, Richard's favourite, Sir William Bagot, held the place for life.[11] In 1385, Frodsham, also held by princess Joan to her death, was granted to Radegonde Béchet, dame de Morthemer, who hailed from Gascony but whose third husband was the Flintshire knight, Gregory Sais (d. 1390), who had had an extensive military career in France under the Black Prince.[12] After Richard's marriage, Anne of Bohemia

7 CHES 2/81, m 1d (2), *36 DKR*, p. 284. On this aspect of patronage in general, see J. A. Tuck, 'Richard II's System of Patronage', in F. R. H. Du Boulay and C. M. Barron (eds), *The Reign of Richard II: Essays in Honour of May McKisack* (London: Athlone Press, 1971), pp. 1–20.
8 SC 6/794/1, m 1d.
9 SC 6/772/7, m 5.
10 SC 6/788/10, m 3.
11 CHES 2/61, m 3d (4), *36 DKR*, p. 17.
12 The original grant made to Radegonde in Sept 1385 insisted that she account for any issues above 100 marks per annum (*CPR 1381–8*, p. 36). Subsequent grants in 1386 and 1391 dropped this and other conditions (*CPR 1381–8*, p. 202; Sharp, 'Earldom and County of Chester', appendix IV, pp. 174–8). Radegonde was the daughter of

held Macclesfield, which was often used as part of the landed resources of the queen.[13] The king's half-brother, John Holland, earl of Huntingdon, and later duke of Exeter, had been granted Northwich and revenues from Overmarsh in 1380 'in aid of the maintenance of his estate'.[14] A similar phenomenon has been observed in the duchy of Cornwall. As Hatcher observes, 'Richard showed no desire to retain any of the assessionable manors in his possession, and with the exception of a number of deer parks and castles, the manorial estates were dispersed far and wide … effecting the most serious disruption of the duchy ever made without legal sanction'.[15]

## Alienation of manors

From the accession of Henry IV, there was a move to curtail alienation and to restore those units which Richard II had granted to his favourites to royal/princely control. There was only one initial exception. Frodsham was left in the hands of Richard's donee, Radegonde Béchet. Presumably she was not considered a political threat to the new regime, either in the county or in the kingdom as a whole.[16] On 16 October 1399, the king confirmed the full grant of the manor to her.[17] She held Frodsham until her death in the autumn of 1408, although it would seem she was never in residence on the manor.[18]

Aiméry Béchet, seigneur des Landes. Her second husband was Guy Sénéchal, lord of Morthemer in Poitou, which explains her description as Dame de Morthemer. There is extensive consideration of both Radegonde and her husbands in Guilhem, Pépin, 'Towards a New Assessment of the Black Prince's Principality of Aquitaine: A Study of the Last Years (1369–72)', *Nottingham Medieval Studies*, 50 (2006), 59–114. For her last marriage see A. D. Carr, 'A Welsh Knight in the Hundred Years War: Sir Gregory Sais', *Transactions of the Honourable Society of Cymmrodorion* (1977), 40–53, at p. 47.

13 See, for instance, SC 6/804/13, the accounts for 1391–2.

14 CHES 2/53, m 1d (9), *36 DKR*, p. 241.

15 Hatcher, *Rural Economy*, p. 7.

16 Her state of impoverishment is seen in her petition to the king in 1404 concerning her lands in France (SC 8/230/11 491).

17 *CPR 1399–1401*, p. 22; SC 6/792/5, m 10.

18 She was, however, living in England, probably in London, given that

By contrast, Middlewich was immediately resumed into royal hands by Henry IV from Sir William Bagot, Richard's favourite, who had managed to escape to Ireland in July 1399 but was brought back for trial in October.[19] In 1380, Northwich had been granted to the king's half-brother, John Holland, earl of Huntingdon and subsequently duke of Exeter (c. 1352–1400).[20] But it had already passed back into royal hands by virtue of an exchange of lands between Holland and Richard II in 1398.[21] Any chance of an immediate regrant by the new regime was removed by Holland's involvement in the Epiphany plot of 1400, which led to his execution.

Richard Colfox, had been granted the moor of Overmarsh for life, free of rent, in 1395.[22] He seems to have hailed from Nantwich.[23] On 4 March 1400, he had the grant confirmed by Prince Henry, and on 22 May, livery of the marsh to Colfox was ordered.[24] But this did not happen in full until February

she made her will there on 23 Oct 1408 (*Calendar of Wills Proved and Enrolled in the Court of Husting, London. Part 2, 1358–1688*, ed. R. R. Sharp (London: Corporation of the City of London, 1890), pp. 30–3).

19 Bagot, a Warwickshire knight, was only imprisoned briefly and released in the autumn of 1400. Whilst his lands were restored to him and he served as an MP for Warwickshire in 1402 he did not have Middlewich regranted to him. He died in 1407. J. S. Roskell, Linda Clark, and Carole Rawcliffe (eds), *The House of Commons 1386–1421*, 4 vols (Stroud: Alan Sutton for the History of Parliament Trust, 1993), i. 99–103.

20 *CPR 1377–81*, p. 539.

21 SC 6/790/10, m 2d. The exchange was dated 15 Jan 1398 (*CPR 1396–9*, p. 467.)

22 CHES 2/69, m 2 (7), m 3d (1), *36 DKR*, p. 117.

23 He was perhaps the son of the William Colfox who, in 1384, took to farm the office of beadle of the hundred of Nantwich for 3 years a £12 per annum (CHES 2/56, m 1 (3), *36 DKR*, p. 117), but it is not clear if he was related to Nicholas Colfox believed to be involved in the murder of Thomas of Woodstock, duke of Gloucester, in 1397, and to be the 'col-fox' of Chaucer's Nun's Priest's Tale (J. L. Hotson, 'Colfox v. Chauntecleer', *Proceedings of the Modern Language Association of America*, 39 (1924), 762–81).

24 CHES 2/74, m 5 (8), m 8 (7) (8), *36 DKR*, p. 117. Colfox had actually put the marsh to farm on 8 May 1399 to John de Pulford and John Kettull of Stretton for three years at £14 per annum (CHES 2/73

1402 when he was again granted the moor for life, with an annual rent of £7 6s. 8d. arising out of it.[25] In the interim, he accounted as if a tenant of the marsh,[26] but in April 1402 he was accorded arrears from the previous year.[27] Although on 4 July 1404 the escheator was ordered to seize the moor,[28] Colfox was holding it again at least by 1407, with all arrears.[29] Early in the reign of Henry V, he was suspected of Lollard sympathies but, after examination, was pardoned on 23 May 1415 and restored to his holdings, including the grant of Overmarsh with arrears (but not, it seems, the full annual rent).[30] He went on participate in the 1415 expedition to France.[31] He died in 1434 and held the grant until then.[32]

In some cases, as we have seen, the resumption of manors in 1399 was occasioned by political exigencies. This was so for Bagot's tenure of Middlewich, and for Northwich too, after the execution of John Holland. However, there was also a financial imperative. The Commons in the first parliament of the reign of Henry IV had petitioned for the resumption of all grants made by Richard II, whether for a term of years or in fee,

n. 6d (7), *36 DKR*, p. 394). The first minister's account of the reign of Henry IV notes that it was farmed by Richard Pulford (SC 6/791/1, m 3d).

25 CHES 2/75, m 3d (1) (2), *36 DKR*, p. 272.

26 SC 6/791, m 3d, SC 6/791/3, m 4.

27 SC 6/774/14, m 2d.

28 CHES 2/77, m 8 (12), *36 DKR*, p. 272.

29 SC 6/792/3, m 3d.

30 CHES 2/88, m 5 (5), *37 DKR*, p. 159; J. H. Wylie and W. T. Waugh, *The Reign of Henry the Fifth*, 3 vols (Cambridge: Cambridge University Press, 1914–29), i. 272. With Sir John Oldcastle, Colfox was an executor of the will of the Lollard knight Sir Lewis Clifford (*Issues of the Exchequer: Being a Collection of Payments made out of His Majesty's Revenue, from King Henry III to King Henry VI. Inclusive*, ed. Frederick Devon, Record Commission (London: John Murray, 1837), p. 323). In 1413, Oldcastle, Colfox and three others sold a clasp to the king for a large sum of money, suggesting he was connected with Henry's household (*CPR 1413–16*, p. 73).

31 BL, Harley MS 782, f. 72v.

32 He was dead by 5 Feb 1434 when the escheator was ordered to find what lands he had held (CHES 2/105, m 4 (10), *37 DKR*, p. 159).

from the lands of the principality of Wales and the earldom of Chester. Such grants, the petition recounts, had been made 'to various unworthy persons so that little or nothing remained of the principality and earldom out of which the most honourable prince can support his estate as is proper' ('as diverses personnes nient dignes que poy ou riens remaynt des dits principalitee et countee dont le dit tres honore seigneur le prince puisse sustenir son tres honore estat come affiert').[33] Even though these lands were under direct royal control, it was nonetheless feasible for the Commons to express a view. Their fear was that the newly installed prince would have to be subsidised out of national funds if he did not have full control of his whole patrimony. The royal reply – 'with regard to unworthy persons once known their letters should be annulled' ('quant as persones nient dignes après ceo qu'ils soient conuz lour letters serront repelles') – was highly politic. It suited the new regime to end patronage to Richard's erstwhile supporters. The desire of the Commons was thereby fulfilled in practice in the earldom. This helps to explain why there was no Commons' pressure for further resumption in 1404. Furthermore, the chances of any additional alienations of manors were considerably lessened by the necessary deployment of Cheshire revenues for the cost of Welsh defences once the prince's income from his Welsh domains proved impossible to collect. This matter will be discussed more fully in Chapter 7.

Even in later years, there were few wholesale alienations in the earldom, in keeping with Lancastrian policy towards the royal demesne in general. Between 1404 and 1437 there was little alienation of crown lands outside the immediate royal family.[34] The granting of Macclesfield to Queen Catherine in 1422, after Henry's death, should therefore be seen in this light, especially when the lordship already had a tradition of being granted in dower to the queens of England and when there was

33 *PROME*, viii. 68–9. There is an interesting parallel here with the first parliament of the reign of Richard II when a request was made that the issues of the patrimony of the heir to the throne should in the meantime be devoted to the Exchequer (Wolffe, *Royal Demesne*, p. 57).

34 Wolffe, *Royal Demesne*, p. 87.

an obvious need for the queen to have lands to support her household.

There was however one alienation of a Cheshire manor made during the reign of Henry IV. This was made in April 1410, when the prince's Welsh revenues were once more being collected. William Porter, a close associate of the prince, was granted the manor of Shotwick for life, free of any charge in lieu of a £20 annuity from the fee farm of the town of Coventry, which the prince held within the foreign manors of the duchy of Cornwall.[35] In April 1412, Porter was also granted an annuity of 50 marks from Cheshire revenues,[36] and his wife Agnes was granted the reversion of the manor of Shotwick.[37] Porter, from an obscure Rutland family, first served Sir Hugh Despencer but was in the household of Prince Henry in Wales by 1403,[38] the annuity from Coventry being granted in 1404 as a result of good service to the prince. Porter also enjoyed the patronage of Queen Joan and was a king's esquire by 1409. In 1411, he served in a force which Prince Henry sent under the earl of Arundel to support the duke of Burgundy, which was partly funded from Cheshire revenues.[39] Porter was very close to Henry as king, undertaking special diplomatic missions and serving on the French campaigns. He seems to have been knighted during or after the 1415 expedition. In June 1421, Henry named him as an executor as well as administrator of his will. In this context, Porter continued to serve the king even after his death, as well as crossing to France with his young son on the coronation campaign of 1430–2.

It was not until 1418, however, that Northwich was regranted to the Hollands. The widow of John Holland, earl of

35 CHES 2/82, m 5d (2, 3), *36 DKR*, p. 386. For a full biography see Roskell, Clark, and Rawcliffe, *House of Commons 1386–1421*, iv. 118–21.

36 CHES 2/84, m 4d (7), *36 DKR*, p. 387.

37 *CPR 1408–13*, p. 235. This reversion also included the annuity which Porter was granted out of Cheshire revenues at this point, and a grant of wine from the port of London.

38 E 101/404/24, f. 4v.

39 SC 6/775/12, m 2d.

Huntingdon and duke of Exeter, was Elizabeth (1363–1426), sister of Henry IV. After her husband's execution in January 1400, she married Sir John Cornwall (1364–1443). Although this was without royal permission, the couple were pardoned and Sir John went on to have a successful career in Lancastrian service, both in England and in France. In 1404, Elizabeth was allowed to recover lands in the duchy of Cornwall previously granted to her Holland husband.[40] Their eldest son, John Holland jnr (1395–1447), served on the 1415 campaign to France where he distinguished himself in dangerous activities at the siege of Harfleur. He petitioned for the restoration of his father's lands in the parliament of October 1416 and gained the livery of those lands at his coming of age in March 1417.[41] He was then formally recognised as earl of Huntingdon, although he had, in practice, already been known by that title earlier. In August 1417, he crossed to Normandy with Henry V and thereafter was almost continuously involved in the wars in France, although he was in French captivity for four years after the battle of Baugé in March 1421.

The accounts of the chamberlain of Chester show Holland and his mother enjoying the profits of Northwich from 12 May 1418, together with £7 6s. 8d. annual rent from Overmarsh.[42] In order for this to happen, Peter de Dutton had to be compensated for the early termination of a lease of the *burgus* of Northwich, which he had taken up in 1416 for six years. Instead, he was granted custody of the lands of Hugh Venables.[43] The Hollands remained in possession of Northwich thenceforward for the rest of the period under consideration and beyond.

The restoration of the Hollands to their interest in Northwich involves certain peculiarities. It was made by a royal warrant issued under the great seal of Chester, dated 14 December 1418 and addressed to the escheator.[44] But Henry V made no

40 *Complete Peerage*, v. 199; *PROME*, viii. 248–9.
41 *Complete Peerage*, v. 205; *PROME*, ix. 190–2.
42 SC 6/793/7, m 4d.
43 CHES 2/92, m 5d (1), *37 DKR*, p. 227.
44 SC 6793/7, mm. 4d, 12.

new grant of Northwich to the Hollands. The warrant to the escheator ignored the fact that the manor had passed back into royal hands by exchange before Richard's reign had ended. It also ignored the Holland forfeiture of 1400, for John Holland snr's inquisition post mortem implied that he had died still holding Northwich in fee tail. In practice, therefore, in 1418 Henry V was simply restoring John Holland jnr to what was deemed to be the totality of the lands held by his father. The exchange of 1398 was conveniently overlooked in the desire to reward the young earl for his loyal and brave service to date, and to encourage his continuing participation in the French wars.

The nature of the restoration of the Hollands confused Ormerod. As he summarised, 'The quality of Holland's estate (i.e. fee tail) is clear from this finding and there is no evidence here of the forfeiture'.[45] He saw a possible solution in the fact that the treason of 1400 had been against the king and not directly against the grantee's lord in Cheshire, i.e. the earl. It may therefore be a question of how far an estate tail in the Palatinate might strictly have been affected by treason when the eldest son of the king was earl, remembering that this county was virtually a distinct sovereignty and, logically, a blood attainder such as Hollands could not reach it except indirectly. In the present case, the reversal of the attainder or the restoration in blood soon after the beheading of Holland, would perhaps explain the finding of the inquisition referred to.

Ormerod was ignorant of the fact that Richard II had exchanged the town with the Hollands in 1398. He raises interesting points but, in short, both Henry IV and V, to varying degrees, were keen to restore Elizabeth Holland and her son to their landed wealth. Henry IV's interest in the position of his sister could explain why a lease of Northwich to Hugh Winnington in 1403 was prevented on the grounds that it had been granted without the knowledge of the prince and his council.[46] At that point, the prince's rule of the county was still very much under the purview of the king. It was not until 1411 that Northwich

45 Ormerod, *Cheshire*, iii. 159.
46 CHES 2/76, m 4d (4), *36 DKR*, p. 532.

was leased out again. Significantly, the terms of the lease to Sir Lawrence Merbury included a clause that he must surrender the town if and when required.[47] Henry V took Northwich back under direct control at Michaelmas 1413, shortly after his accession, despite the fact that Merbury's lease still had over seven years to run.[48] On 1 October 1415, Northwich was leased to Sir Peter de Dutton for six years,[49] a rare example, perhaps, of an effort to ensure every last ounce of revenue was derived for the benefit of the king, as earl of Chester. But by 1418, the king considered that the young earl of Huntingdon had redeemed his family's reputation and so could be restored to the act of patronage first begun by Richard II back in 1380.

## Annuities

If alienation of manors were no longer favoured by the first Lancastrian kings, the payment of annuities and the granting of life offices were. In effect, this was a return to the policy of the Black Prince. His period had seen the increase of assignment of revenues in annuities, which at the time was an innovation, since previously the expedient had been the granting of manors for life.[50] The granting of annuities and offices for life enabled attention to be paid to patronage but also allowed the earl to keep the majority of his patrimony in his own hands. The granting of annuities had a further advantage in allowing the resources of patronage to be more widely spread. Admittedly, they entailed a loss of revenue but not of seigneurial rights, to which territorial grants for life threatened to lead.

There were basically two methods of paying annuities from county revenues.[51] The majority were paid out of the overall

47 CHES 2/83, m 2 (4) (5), *36 DKR*, p. 366.

48 SC 6/792/10, m 3d.

49 CHES 2/89, m 1 (1), *36 DKR*, p. 566.

50 Booth, *Financial Admin.*, p. 67.

51 In the discussion which follows I have excluded annual payments which were made for the holding of a particular office, such as equitator of the forests, even though it appears that many such offices were purely nominal.

receipts of the chamberlain: fifty-six different annuities were paid out of this source in the period 1399 to 1422. Some were said to be taken out of demesne revenues but were still accounted by the chamberlain.[52] This was therefore little more than an accounting fiction.[53] Annuities, often of smaller amounts than those paid directly from county revenues, were paid directly from demesne resources and accounted by the relevant local officials: twenty-three were paid in this manner paid over the period as a whole. Annuities of this kind were disbursed regularly at the Dee Mills, Northwich and Drakelow, and occasionally at Delamere Forest and Shotwick.

Regular payment out of annuities could only be made where income was relatively static and demesne expenses small or non-existent. Both at Drakelow and Northwich we can detect an attempt to manipulate the size of annuities to completely consume the charge. Soon after Northwich was leased to Laurence Merbury in 1411 for £43 per annum, an annuity of the same amount was granted out of the issues of the town to John Grey and Thomas Dutton.[54] Since an annuity of £10 was already payable there to Robert Castell, issues of the town had been over-assigned.[55] As a result, the actual payment of the annuity to Grey and Dutton had to be adjusted each year to the amount of revenue actually available. This was also the case in 1414 and 1415 when Northwich was again in royal hands. Thus the system here was for all manorial income to be assigned at source, considerably simplifying the financial administration of such units. Amounts spent upon annuities on the demesne accounts remained relatively static because income was itself static. Grants accordingly operated in a vacancy system. For

52 Such as the grant in 1403 to Nicholas Burcestre of 5 marks for life from the issue of a fishery on the Dee but payable at the Chester Exchequer by the chamberlain (SC 6/775/15, m 5). See Appendix IV for a list of annuities granted in 1399–1422.

53 For parallels see J. T. Rosenthal, 'The Estates and Finances of Richard, Duke of York', *Studies in Medieval and Renaissance History*, 2 (1965), 115–204, at p. 188.

54 CHES 2/83, m 4 (10), *36 DKR*, p. 202.

55 For the original grant to Castell in 1400, see SC 6/791/3, m 2d.

instance, when Robert Sandbache died in 1416, his annuity of £5, payable from Drakelow, was granted to Charles de Holland. On the latter's death in 1419, the same amount was granted to William Goolde.[56]

Resources were equally limited on the chamberlain's account, but in general the amount due to be spent on annuities lay between £300 and £400. In 1403, for instance, annuities on the chamberlain's account were assessed at £329 8s. 6d. Actual payments, however, varied substantially from year to year, as can be seen from the summary of the chamberlain's accounts in Appendix II (m). Less was paid out in the first year of the reign of Henry IV. The reason for this is simple: several of the annuities granted by Richard II were no longer being paid as a result of political changes, and new grants were still to be effected and existing ones confirmed. It was necessary for grants to be confirmed at the accession of Henry IV, as later at the accession of Henry VI, but this was not required when Henry V came to the throne; the grants he had made as prince were automatically continued. During the Welsh wars of Henry IV's reign, annuities were allowed to fall into arrears because the first priority for the use of the chamberlain's revenues was the defence of North Wales. In subsequent years it was possible to apply more funds to annuities. In 1408, three new and substantial annuities were accorded, the first, in February, of 250 marks per annum (£166 13s. 4d.) to the king's close friend, Thomas Fitzalan, earl of Arundel (1381–1415), the second, in May, of £50 to William, Lord Zouche of Harringworth (1373–1415), and third, in October, of £50 to Sir Thomas Grey of Heton (1384–1415). In return, all three entered into a formal indenture to serve the prince for life, in peace and war.[57] By 1412, it was also possible to clear the backlog of arrears of annuity payments which the diversion of funds to Wales had generated. The chamberlain's account for 1412 shows an

56 Holland: SC 6/793/4, m 1d, CHES 2/90, m 4d, *37 DKR*, p. 374. Goolde: SC 6/793/9, m 1d; CHES 2/92, m 10 (2), *37 DKR*, p. 315.

57 Respectively, CHES 2/80, m 3 (2), *36 DKR*, p. 9; SC 6/775/9, m 6; SC 6/775/11, m 6.

expenditure of £808 13s. 4d. on annuities that year in contrast to around £380 in the two previous years.

Towards the end of the reign of Henry V, there was some falling off in terms of annuities granted from the chamberlain's revenues as recipients died and were not replaced. After the earl of Arundel died at the siege of Harfleur in 1415, for instance, his large annuity was not regranted.[58] By contrast, there was no parallel falling off in payments made directly from demesne revenues, although the alienation of Northwich to John Holland, earl of Huntingdon in 1418 blocked off that source of revenue for new annuities, but existing ones, we must assume, continued to be honoured by the Hollands.

Over the whole period, annuities made up 31.5% of the actual discharge of the chamberlain's account. For the reign of Henry IV, the annual average was 24.8%. From 1404 to 1406 – in the face of the need to use Cheshire revenues in Wales – the proportion spent on annuities fell to 10–11%. From 1412 to 1415, when the backlog of arrears was being cleared, annuities consumed 50% of expenses. The average proportion for the reign of Henry V was 38.6%.

Most annuities, lands, offices, wardships and such like were granted as the result of a petition to the earl. A copy survives of John Kingsley's petition to the prince's council for the restoration of his annuity which he had forfeited by his support of Hotspur in 1403. On the dorse it is clearly indicated that he invoked the support of the king in the matter.[59] In 1405, Robert Stokely gained new letters for his annuity at the instance of Thomas Arundel, archbishop of Canterbury.[60] This system of

58 SC 6/775/9, m 6.

59 E 163/6/41, item 5. On 7 Oct 1403 the escheator had been ordered to confiscate his lands (CHES 2/76, m 12 (9), *36 DKR*, p. 273). He was pardoned on 20 Jan 1404 (CHES 2/77, m 4d (10), *36 DKR*, p. 273) and an annuity of £10 per annum for life from the turbary of Delamere Forest granted on 1 Oct 1405 on surrender of an earlier grant of 1401 (CHES 2/78, m 6d (2) (3), *36 DKR*, p. 274).

60 SC 6/791/7, m 6. For the system of petitioning in general, see Wolffe, *Royal Demesne,* p. 99, and Tuck, 'Richard II's System of Patronage', pp. 4–8.

petitioning may explain the preponderance of royal household officials and others of the 'court circle' within the ranks of those receiving annuities from Cheshire revenues. Such men would be in the best position to gain the royal, and subsequently the princely, ear. It would be an advantage to be able to supplement their small wages or annuities from sources other than the already over-subscribed household funds. A substantial portion of annuities paid by the chamberlain of North Wales at the Caernarvon exchequer in the reigns of Henry V and VI was also to royal household officials, esquires and servants.[61]

The predominance of such recipients also raises an interesting point concerning the actual mechanics of payments of annuities to their grantees. Under Richard II, it seems to have been general practice for the chamberlain of Chester to distribute the cash during his visit to the royal Exchequer in Westminster. During one such visit in 1396, the chamberlain made payments out of Cheshire revenues to knights, esquires and yeomen for their fees and annuities, as well as his other liveries to the royal treasurer.[62] For South Wales, however, Ralph Griffiths considered that payments were made at the local exchequer: as he notes, there were amongst Henry V's annuitants there three Herefordshire esquires 'who could seek assistance from friends in the administration to collect their cash'.[63] There is some evidence that proxies were used by annuitants to collect their payments at the Chester exchequer. All save one of the extant acquittances for 1425–6, for instance, are dated at Chester, but that of Sir Richard Redmayne is dated at his own seat of Harewood (Yorkshire, West Riding), implying that the money was taken to him there.[64]

61 Griffiths, 'Patronage, Politics and the Principality of Wales', pp. 78–9.
62 SC 6/774/7, m 2d.
63 Griffiths, 'Patronage, Politics and the Principality of Wales', p. 78.
64 SC 6/1268/4 file 4. Although his hereditary seat was at Levens in Westmorland, Sir Richard Redmayne (d. 1426) came into possession of one half of the manor of Harewood through marriage to Elizabeth, elder sister and co-heir of William, Lord Aldeburgh, and sat as MP for Yorkshire in five parliaments. He had been granted the annuity from Cheshire revenues in Oct 1397 (CHES 2/74, m 14 (5), *36 DKR*,

Having made general comments regarding the recipients of annuities at Chester, this is a good point at which to consider this in more detail. The type of recipient fits into distinctive chronological divisions. It must be observed first of all that Richard II had made most of his grants out of Cheshire revenues to local men in order to bolster up his already substantial support in the county. Indeed, after the creation of his principality in 1397, there had been a stepping up of local patronage. Some who received annuities at this point had already served as officials in the palatinate, but the majority had taken no previous part in the affairs of the county and had no particular claim to enjoy the king's favour there.[65]

In 1399, at least sixteen of Richard's annuities granted from Cheshire revenues were suppressed. This was to be expected in the case of Richard's household officials. Richard and Margaret Long, for instance, ceased to receive their payment out of the revenues of Drakelow. She had been one of the women of the chamber of Anne of Bohemia.[66] That said, despite his service as a yeoman of Richard II's household, Robert Compnour soon had his annuity from the revenues of the Dee Mills confirmed.[67] Cheshire archers in Richard's bodyguard, such as Thomas Becheton, found their annuity ended by the new regime.[68]

Twenty-five of Richard II's annuities from Cheshire revenues, which included four dating back to the time of his

p. 400). He was speaker in the parliament held in Nov 1415. For a full biography see Roskell, Clark, and Rawcliffe, *House of Commons 1386–1421*, iv. 183–7.

65 P. McNiven, 'Rebellion and Disaffection in the North of England 1403–1408', unpublished MA thesis (University of Manchester, 1967), pp. 39–40.

66 SC 6/790/10, m 1d.

67 CHES 2/64, m 8 (8) *36 DKR*, p. 120; SC 6/774/14, m 6.

68 Gillespie comments that although half of the group of Richard II's bodyguard of archers with an English patent had their grants confirmed by Henry IV, only one archer with a Cheshire patent ever had his grant ratified and that ratification was delayed until 1450. James L. Gillespie, 'Richard II's Cheshire Archers', *THSLC*, 125 (1974), 1–39, at p. 7. Gillespie's view may be over-negative as there are other examples of Richard's Cheshire archers who served the new regime. A detailed study of their fates is needed.

father, the Black Prince,[69] were confirmed by the Lancastrians. On the whole, it seems that local men were more likely to keep their annuity than those from outside the county, although we can also see confirmations for men such as Richard's surgeon, John Leche, and his door keeper (janitor), Robert Stokely.[70] As Appendix IV shows, those with confirmations included key local players such as Sir Peter Dutton, Sir John Stanley snr, John Done of Utkinton, Roger Brescy, Sir Robert Legh and John de Legh of Booths.[71] Done kept his annuity, paid from the revenues of Delamere Forest, despite his involvement in rebellions in 1400 and 1403.[72] Dutton and Robert de Legh likewise kept theirs, despite his support for Hotspur in 1403.[73]

Eighteen new annuities were granted between 1399 and 1403. The majority went to members of the royal household, such as John Attelbrigg, doorkeeper of Henry IV's hall.[74] Only six went to men we might call 'of Cheshire' although it must be remembered that there was an overlap between the categories, as

69 John le Clerk of Tutbury; Richard Filongley; Sir John Massey of Tatton (who was killed at the battle of Shrewsbury fighting for Hotspur); Ralph Roberdson.

70 *CPR 1399–1401*, p. 203; CHES 2/74, *36 DKR*, p. 454.

71 The others were William de Frodsham, Sir John de Calverley (whose annuity under Richard had replaced an earlier life grant to him of Shotwick, SC 6/774/10, m 5, and who died at Shrewsbury fighting for Henry IV), Richard le Wodeward and Nicholas Orell whose service had been largely outside the county.

72 On 14 July 1401, Done surrendered his original grant made by Richard II and was made a new grant of £10 per annum along with confirmation of expenses as forester (CHES 2/75, m 3 (9), *36 DKR*, p. 154). Although there was an order to the escheator to seize his lands as a rebel, by Jan 1404 he was trusted enough to play a role in administration and had been fully pardoned by 1406 on payment of recognizance (*36 DKR*, pp. 155, 532 passim).

73 For Dutton's confirmation of 1404, see SC 6/775/6, m 6. See also Peter McNiven, 'The Men of Cheshire and the Rebellion of 1403', *Transactions of the Historic Society of Lancashire and Cheshire*, 129 (1979), 1–29, at pp. 4–5, 24. Although Sir Robert de Legh was pardoned (McNiven, 'Men of Cheshire', p. 23) his annuity never seems to have been withdrawn.

74 SC 6/774/13, m 7; E 101/404/16, m 3.

in the case of the lawyer Hugh Holes. In these years, the choice was clearly being made by the king rather than the prince, as for instance in an annuity granted to the Derbyshire knight, Sir Thomas Wendesley, who, on 13 October 1399, the king had appointed steward of Maccesfield for life.[75] But we can also see rewards for Cheshire loyalty in the face of Hotspur's rebellion in 1403.[76]

Grants made between 1405 (none were made in 1404) and 1410 again show more Cheshire recipients, most notably those who had given valuable service under the prince in Wales, for instance the Mainwaring brothers, John and Ralph.[77] John Stanley jnr and John Savage also appear in the list of annuitants for the first time in 1407, along with other demesne officials, such as Ralph Pope, bailiff of Drakelow. But the emphasis was on members of the prince's close circle, which was developing as he grew older and more in control of his own affairs. So we see annuities in 1406 to the Lancashire knights, Sir William Harington of Hornby (d. 1440) and Sir Thomas Tunstall of Thurland (d. 1415), who had headed a joint retinue under the prince in Wales.[78] Three major annuities – to the earl of Arundel, William, Lord Zouche, and Sir Thomas Grey of Heton – were granted in 1408 but backdated to the end of the previous year, all linked to indentures to serve the king in peace and war. All three men were very closely connected with the prince.

A study of the other parts of the prince's lands indicates that it was from the autumn of 1407 that Henry began to spend distinctly more on patronage. Whilst between 1401 and 1407 fewer than ten annuities had been issued in any one year across

75 *CPR 1399–1401*, p. 31. Sir Thomas was killed at the battle of Shrewsbury fighting for the king.

76 Morgan, *War and Society*, p. 206.

77 Ralph had served in a Cheshire contingent in Henry IV's army taken to Scotland in 1400. If he can be identified with a Randal Mainwaring then he had previously been a member of Richard II's Cheshire archer bodyguard (CHES 2/71, m 35 (7), *36 DKR*, p. 317) and served on Richard's Irish campaign in 1399 (CHES 2/72, m 4 (5), *36 DKR*, p. 317), as had his brother (ibid.).

78 E 101/404/24, f. 12.

all his lands, in the year following Michaelmas 1407, fifty-one new grants were made.[79] Cheshire shared in this expansion, testimony not only to the end of pressure on its finances from the costs of the Welsh wars but also to the establishment of the prince's own party as he sought to play a larger role in national and international politics. From 1411 to 1413, ten annuities were granted, including to John Grey of Heton, younger brother of Thomas Grey, Lewis Robessart and William Porter, who were close to the prince and were to become prominent members of Henry's inner circle after his accession as king.[80] Only two men with largely local links – Thomas Dutton and Hugh Venables – received annuities in those years.[81]

As king, Henry was distinctly careful in his largesse, as he prepared to devote so much resource to war with France. No annuity was granted between 1413 and 1416. After 1416, only two grants were made from county revenues through the chamberlain – to John Dedwode, the deputy chamberlain, and Walter Goolde, Henry V's doorkeeper.[82] Nine new annuities were paid out of demesne revenues. Almost all were to royal household officials, with the exception of two to William Troutbeck, the chamberlain of Chester.[83] In Wales too, Henry

79 Anne Curry, 'The Making of a Prince: The Finances of "the Young Lord Henry", 1386–1400', in Gwilym Dodd (ed.), *Henry V: New Interpretations* (Woodbridge: York Medieval Press, 2013), pp. 11–33, at p. 33.

80 Grey, along with Thomas Dutton, from Northwich revenues, 23 June 1411 (CHES 2/104, m 4 (10), *36 DKR*, p. 202); Robessart, Oct 1412 (SC 6/775/15, m 7); Porter, Apr 1412 (CHES 2/84, m 4d (7), *36 DKR*, p. 387).

81 Dutton and Grey shared the annuity, implying they were linked by service to the prince; Venables of Kinderton, Oct 1412, SC 6/775/15, m 7. It is notable that in these years some grants, as that to Robessart and Venables were made by direct order of the prince and were not enrolled in the Chester enrolments (CHES 2).

82 Dedwode: CHES 2/89, m 5 (7), *37 DKR*, p. 196, SC 6/1303/1, m 5; Goolde: CHES 2/92, m 10 (2), *37 DKR*, p. 315 (from a rent payable at the Chester Exchequer by the abbot and convent of St Werburgh's).

83 Examples from the revenues of Drakelow are John Yarondale, yeoman of the king's pantry, and Robert Castleton, yeoman of the ewery (SC 6/793/11, m 2). Troutbeck had £10 from Drakelow and £10 from the Dee Mills (CHES 2/92, m 6 (4), *37 DKR*, p. 717).

V, as king, dug deep into his coffers for annuities for his personal servants.[84]

All of this reflects the extent to which the county was becoming increasingly assimilated into the royal demesne. This tendency can be seen in the reign of Richard II where a good number of annuities went to household officers and other associates, much as happened from other royal lands. The special relationship at the end of the reign had perhaps boosted local patronage for a short while, especially for the royal bodyguard. Under the Lancastrians, however, recipients of annuities and grants of land in Cheshire were predominantly non-Cheshire men. They were royal household servants and members of the close circles of the prince. Some already held annuities from royal or princely funds elsewhere, again indicating that there was no special targeting of Cheshire funds. For example, in 1417 John de la Rys, valet of the king's chamber, received £10 per annum from the issues of Cheshire alongside 6d. per day from the shrievalty of Huntingdonshire and Cambridgeshire.[85] The people who the prince and king wished to reward were supported from whatever revenues were available. In many cases it was a case of dead men's shoes: since annuities lasted for life (save in the case of rebellion), opportunities arose when existing holders passed away. Grants often note the previous holders and that the new grant is made on identical terms. It would appear in some cases that grants were made in anticipation of a 'vacancy' arising in an annuity.

Cheshire annuities were sometimes granted in lieu of annuities previously taken elsewhere, as in the case of William Porter, whose life grant of the manor of Shotwick was made on his surrendering an annuity of £20 which he held from the fee farm of Coventry.[86] Such swopping of the source of payment also demonstrates how the county was regarded in the same light as the rest of the royal demesne. Its patronage could be used indiscriminately and not solely or predominantly to favour

84 Griffiths, 'Patronage, Politics and the Principality of Wales', pp. 78–9.

85 CHES 2/90, m 5 (6), *37 DKR*, p. 633.

86 CHES 2/82, m 5d (2, 3), *36 DKR*, p. 433.

its inhabitants. Cheshire resources were thus being used along the same lines as elsewhere. This situation was given further permanence by the long period after 1413 of royal rather than princely control, both under Henry V and subsequently Henry VI. Nowhere is this clearer than in an order to the chamberlain William Troutbeck in November 1428, that he should send to the barons of the royal Exchequer a list of annuitants and office holders, together with details of warrants for appointment and payment.[87]

A study of annuities tells us much about the practices of royal patronage but it also provides insights into how people in Cheshire faced the challenge of regime change in these turbulent times. A strong example is found in Robert Sandbache. By September 1398, he was a member of Richard II's special Cheshire archer bodyguard, in the company of Adam Bostok.[88] As such, he saw which way the wind was blowing in the summer of 1399. At Chester on 20 August, along with a fellow archer, Thomas Haslington, he submitted 'to the mercy of Henry, duke of Lancaster, steward of England', then in the city, with Sir John Stanley and Sir Robert de Legh giving securities for his good behaviour.[89] On 22 July 1401, he was granted an annuity of £5 out of the revenues of Drakelow.[90] Two years later he was serving Prince Henry in Wales.[91] By 1409 he was a yeoman of the chamber (and so a bodyguard much as he had been for Richard) for Prince Henry, and given a one-off gift of 10 marks from Cheshire revenues.[92] He was still in Henry's close service after his accession as king.[93] As a trusted and effective close servant, he was treated to a further annuity of 6d. per day from the issues of Shropshire in October 1413.[94] He served as an archer in the 1415 campaign and we have no reason to think he

87 E 163/6/44.
88 E 101/42/10, m 4.
89 CHES 2/73, m 7 (4), *36 DKR*, p. 222.
90 SC 6/792/9, m 2.
91 E 101/404/24, f. 7v.
92 SC 6/775/9, m 1d.
93 E 101/406/21, f. 28.
94 *CPR 1413–16*, p. 172.

was not with the king at Agincourt.[95] Perhaps he was wounded at the battle since he died on 9 January 1416.[96]

## Appointments

The role of patronage in appointments is rather more complex. Certainly there were instances of sinecure holders. Indeed, there is evidence to suggest that there was an increasing number of such 'officials' under the Lancastrians. Overall, however, there were few officials appointed in name only or for life, a contrast with the position under the Black Prince where there were many such appointments.[97] The major executive officials of the county (chamberlain, sheriff and escheator) were appointed during pleasure or during good behaviour, the standard format for royal officials. Hotspur held the justiciarship for life but that had not turned out to be a happy experience. It is therefore significant that his successors were appointed during pleasure. Parkers, bailiffs of the forest and stewards of Macclesfield, as well as keepers of the Dee Mills, were generally appointed for life or in fee, although this did not rule out the possibility of removal from office if discovered to be inefficient, as we saw in the case of John Mottram as bailiff of the forest of Macclesfield.[98] That there were few purely nominal officials may have been due to the continuing separateness and independent nature of the county's administration. It is impossible to state categorically to what extent any officer holder could hope to gain further favour and exercise greater local influence by means of his office, although clearly this was an important incentive towards office holding, as in the case of the career of John Savage.[99]

95 A Robert Sonbage, archer, is listed in the muster of the royal household contingent taken at Swanwick Heath on 14 July 1415 (E 101/45/18, m 8). A Robert Sonbache is listed as a man-at-arms on the so-called Agincourt roll (BL, Harley MS 782, f. 81v).

96 SC 6/793/4, m 2.

97 Booth, *Financial Admin.*, p. 136.

98 See p. 77.

99 See pp. 77–8 and index sub Savage, John. See also Griffiths, 'Patronage, Politics and the Principality of Wales', pp. 70–1.

Several criticisms of such a system of patronage have been voiced. These have taken two principal forms: first that such patronage weakened the authority of the government, and secondly that it proved a serious drain upon financial resources. Booth argued for the validity of the first criticism, basing his conclusions upon a study of the financial administration of Cheshire under the Black Prince. As county administration had to be heavily geared to raising the maximum revenue, many of the prince's rights of lordship and administrative control were gradually alienated. It is clear that every time an office was granted away for life or an important manor was leased out to a syndicate of local men, the government's authority was weakened.[100] Booth further argued that patronage was detrimental to the maintenance of law and order in the county. Assignment of revenue in annuities and the alienation of manors for no render inevitably meant that less money was available for local expenditure, for instance, on law keeping.[101]

Can such a judgement also be applied to patronage in the county in the early fifteenth century? In some respects, it cannot. As we have seen, the payment of annuities was preferred to the alienation of manors in gift, a policy pursued to avoid the loss of seigneurial control rather than income, perhaps. Only in the case of Northwich was a manor alienated in fee. Otherwise, the royal earl maintained at least a reversionary interest in the property. Indeed, in practice there was a considerable degree of comital surveillance over those manors granted out, despite the fact that the terms of the alienations implied a redirection to the recipient, not only of revenues but also of seigneurial control. Judicial rights and profits did not pass completely out of the hands of the earl. During William Porter's tenure of the manor of Shotwick, for instance, the earl retained the right to prosecute

100 P. H. W. Booth, 'Taxation and Public Order: Cheshire in 1353', *Northern History*, 12 (1976), 16–31, at p. 29.

101 P. H. W. Booth, 'The Financial Administration of the Lordship and County of Chester 1272–1377', unpublished MA thesis (University of Liverpool, 1974), p. 156.

those found hunting illegally in the park.[102] Crimes committed at Frodsham during the tenure of Radegonde Béchet were dealt with by the justiciar, or by a special eyre held in the town by justices commissioned by the prince.[103] The earl's influence at Shotwick was also maintained by the continuing presence of the parker, since the right to appoint to this office was retained even when the manor was in the hands of another.[104] In leases of the parks of Shotwick and Macclesfield, the earl retained hunting rights; this proviso was maintained when, in his turn, William Porter leased Shotwick to William Stanley in 1423.[105]

Moreover, a grant for life could be revoked if the necessary conditions were not fulfilled. The manor of Frodsham was indeed temporarily resumed by the prince in 1405–6. It was claimed that Radegonde Béchet had failed to carry out the necessary repairs to the sea ditch, and that the resulting encroachment by the sea had caused much damage to the manor. The prince appointed a receiver of issues who accounted for £20 income from the manor in this year, this sum being accounted under the foreign receipts on the chamberlain's account.[106] The seizure was but a temporary measure, for in the following year the manor was returned to Radegonde, along with the £20 received by the prince.[107] This restoration was made only upon her agreement to carry out the necessary repairs under the supervision of the chamberlain of Chester.[108] A similar control was exercised over the grant of rents from Sutton in Macclesfield Forest to John de Legh of Booths, initially made in 1397, lost temporarily after his involvement in the Cheshire revolt of 1400 but regranted

102 CHES 25/11, m 8. Other offences committed at Shotwick were also dealt with in the county court (CHES 25/11, m 22d).

103 CHES 25/9, m 27.

104 Sharp, 'Earldom and County of Chester', p. 355.

105 JRRIL, Rylands Charter 1418.

106 SC 6/775/4, m 2.

107 SC 6/775/5, m 2d.

108 CHES 2/78, m 5 (1, 2, 3), *36 DKR*, p. 28; W. Beamont, *An Account of the Ancient Town of Frodsham, in Cheshire* (Warrington: Percival Pearse, 1881), p. 67.

in July 1401, although under less generous conditions.[109] This second grant was dependent upon his paying any surplus revenue from the town above £13 6s. 8d. to the earl. When he failed to do this in 1419, the annuity was forfeited, although it began to be paid again in 1423.[110]

There is much to suggest that a change in the holder of a manor did not always affect local administrative personnel. Roger Torfot, bailiff of Frodsham from 1408 to 1420, may also have served as bailiff under Radegonde Béchet.[111] The Torfots were certainly involved in the administration of the manor when it was not in direct royal hands: Robert Torfot was described in 1396 as formerly bailiff of William de Frodsham as farmer of the manor.[112]

A comparison between the administration of the king and of the Hollands in the first two years of their tenure of Northwich, 1418 to 1420, reveals a mixture of innovation and continuity.[113] The Holland's local officials were drawn from the same families which had earlier provided the steward, chamberlain and catchpole, although none had themselves previously served under the royal earl. John Triket, clerk of the courts in 1419 and 1420, had served as receiver of Frodsham in 1405, and as bailiff of the same manor from 1420. He also leased the mills there in 1418 and part of the demesne arable in 1422.[114] He later served as deputy steward in Queen Catherine's administration

109 The grant of 1397 was for all profits of the rents as well as an annuity of 100s, but the regrant in July 1401 was for rents up to 20 marks (£13 6s. 8d.) per annum, his being required to answer to the earl for any rent income above this (CHES 2/75, m 3 (10), *36 DKR*, p. 293. See also Keele University Library, Legh of Booths Charters 265, 266; SC 6/805/11, m 2d, /16, m 2d.

110 SC 6/807/3, m 3d. Legh fell into arrears on other occasions, in 1401 (SC 6/805/7, m 3) and 1413 (SC 6/806/6, m 2d). By 1419 he was also badly in debt in his function as sheriff (see p. 276).

111 CALS, Cholmondeley MSS DCH F 12.

112 CHES 2/70, m 4 (11), *36 DKR*, p. 473.

113 SC 6/810/15.

114 SC 6/793/7, m 5d, and SC 6/794/2, m 5 respectively.

at Macclesfield.[115] These first two years of Holland control were clearly a transitional period in administrative terms, but the transfer of control was achieved without difficulty. William Troutbeck, chamberlain of the county, acted as receiver for both Elizabeth and John Holland, earl of Huntingdon, in 1419, but he was being used only as a temporary measure, for already part of Earl John's revenues were being paid directly to William Yerd, his own receiver-general.[116] In the following October, Earl John appointed John Mason as receiver of all his lands, including Northwich.[117] Holland's council, too, soon began to play the role expected of them. In 1419 and 1420 they ordered and supervised repairs to the mill and the payment of John Triket's fee.[118] Payments out of the issues of the town began to be made to Holland's nominees in place of those annuities previously paid by the king to John Grey and Thomas Dutton. William Chauntrell was paid a small fee in 1420. He may have performed some services in the transfer of administration to Holland. He had already served as a justice in eyre in the county and continued to do so.[119] In 1432, he was appointed by Queen Catherine as justiciar of Flintshire.[120]

The administration of the revenues of Northwich under the Hollands again reflects this mixture of preservation and change. Most items of revenue were administered in exactly the same way and for about the same return as under royal control. The mills in the town continued to be directly controlled, but additional income was now derived from the issues of the bushel. The Hollands chose to control the oven directly rather than continuing the king's policy of leasing it, but in fact they received a much lower return. Fees of local officials were paid

115 CALS, Cholmondeley MS DCH R6 (1432). He died in 1442 (CHES 2/115, m 7d (3), *36 DKR*, p. 717).

116 SC 6/810/15, m 3.

117 CHES 2/92, m 2 (2), *37 DKR*, p. 514. Mason had been described as clerk of the lord's receipt in 1419 (SC 6/810/15, m 3).

118 SC 6/810/15, mm 1, 2.

119 SC 6/810/15, m 2; *37 DKR*, p. 668 passim.

120 CHES 2/102, m 1 (10), *37 DKR*, p. 668. At his death in 1439 he held no lands in Northwich (CHES 2/113, m 1 (14)).

at the same rate, with the exception of the steward who was paid half as much as in the royal administration. A comparison between the efficiency of the two administrations is not possible because of the survival of the accounts for only two years of Holland control. Little can be said, for instance, on the relative success in the collection of arrears, for royal policy had been to avoid such arrears by consuming the whole charge in annuities. Only 50% of the balance was paid to the Hollands in the first year of their tenure, but this may have been due to the problems caused by their recent assumption of control. The grant of Northwich in fee to the Hollands cannot have had any effect other than the weakening of royal control over the town. As we have seen, the royal earl had but little control over tenure and salt production in the town even before this alienation.

Despite examples of continuing royal control, there is no evidence of surveillance as rigorous as that in the duchy of Lancaster, where, in July 1419, the two chief stewards were ordered to enquire into waste and dilapidation on fees and lands held of the duchy for life.[121] What also calls into question the maintenance of royal control is evidence that the actual grantees rarely exploited their acquisitions, and that the reality of this situation was not always noted on the royal earl's accounts. As far as one can tell, John Goodfelowe directly administered the properties he had been granted in Little Saughall. Overmarsh, however, was occupied and farmed, at least initially, not by its grantee, Richard Colfox, but by Richard de Pulford.[122] The Hollands directly controlled Northwich in the last years of the reign of Henry V, but John Holland snr had leased the town in 1395 to a local man, Sir Richard Winnington, for eight years.[123] William Porter appears to have directly administered Shotwick from 1410 to 1423 but on 6 May 1423, he leased out the manor and park for seven years at £30 per annum to Sir William Stanley of Hooton snr. Stanley was to hold the manor

121 Robert Somerville, *History of the Duchy of Lancaster*, 1: *1265–1603* (London: Duchy of Lancaster, 1953), p. 189.

122 SC 6/791/1, m 3d.

123 CHES 2/69, m 11d (9), *36 DKR*, p. 531.

under the same conditions as Richard Moston had done earlier as lessee of the prince, being responsible for all maintenance and also for the accounting of the profits of sales of wood still due to the king. The farm was to be paid to Porter at Colyweston in Northamptonshire.[124]

The ministers' accounts refer to Radegonde Béchet as holder of the manor of Frodsham, but there is much to suggest that she delegated control to others. In 1396, William de Frodsham snr was described as farmer of the manor, and at his death in 1398 he held lands in the town and its environs from Radegonde.[125] An undated memorandum of the time of John Trevor as chamberlain of Chester stated that William Mainwaring had leased the manor of Frodsham from Radegonde Béchet for the previous five years.[126] It is likely, therefore, that William de Frodsham snr leased the manor until his death, and that the farm was then taken up by William Mainwaring. An enrolment of 1398 seems to confirm this. In this, Robert Torfot, formerly bailiff of William de Frodsham snr, late farmer of the manor of Frodsham, acknowledged that he owed £87 17s. 7½d. but petitioned that allowance should be given for payments he had made to Radegonde Béchet, William Mainwaring and the abbot of Basingwerk.[127] Such subleasing by Radegonde should be judged, perhaps, in the light of the evident neglect of repairs to the sea ditch in the manor in 1405.

124 JRRIL, Rylands Charter 1418.

125 CHES 2/70, m 4 (11), *36 DKR*, p. 473; CHES 2/71, m 6 (4), and CHES 2/74, m 4 (3), *36 DKR*, p. 193. See also Ormerod, *Cheshire*, ii. 49. In 1405, £5 was deemed as owing at his death from the burgesses of Frodsham for confirmation of their charter (CHES 2/88, m 7d (7), *36 DKR*, p. 193) Arrears of rent due to him from tenants of the manor were paid to the prince after the death of Radegonde Béchet (SC 6/792/5, m 2d). Beamont (*Account of the Ancient Town of Frodsham*, p. 64) claimed that his nephew, William de Frodsham jnr, was sometime lessee of the manor but I have found no evidence of this.

126 JRRIL, Arley Charter Box 25 no. 6. Ormerod, *Cheshire* (ii. 49) had it that William, John and Ralph Mainwaring, Sir Robert Grosvenor and Sir Richard Winnington all farmed the manor, but this memorandum states clearly that the sole farmer was William. The others were probably his guarantors.

127 CHES 2/70, m 4 (11), *36 DKR*, p. 473.

The case of Frodsham may lead us to believe that alienation could lead to a deterioration in the state and value of a manor due to neglect by the grantee. The manor of Frodsham had been valued at £56 3s. 4d. in the early years of the reign of Henry IV, the same value as it had been assigned in 1376.[128] However, during the fourteen years of comital control between 1409 and 1422, both its potential and actual value were about £15 lower. Certainly the prince had to make a considerable outlay on repairs in the first two years of his renewed control. In 1409, these expenses reduced the potential value of the manor to as little as £5 19s. 1d. The value of Northwich had also declined considerably since the valor of 1376. Then it was valued at £66, but in 1403 at only £28 8s. 10d., a figure close to the average potential and actual values for those years which we have accounts. The chronology of this decline in value suggests that the worst loss must have occurred during the first period of tenure by the Hollands, between 1380 and 1398. However, there is no suggestion of subsequent decline in value under the Hollands from 1418 onwards, although it must be remembered that income may have been suffering from the general fall in revenue from seigneurial monopolies within this period.

Such cases would suggest that alienation of manors was detrimental to the future income of the royal demesne. In this respect, Booth may have been correct in seeing patronage as a drain upon resources, and a self-defeating policy in that it limited the possibility of raising revenue further. However, those units granted out for no render were often those which were financially unrewarding or administratively demanding. Little Saughall, for instance, was worth £4 at most, and Overmarsh only £7 6s. 8d., when in the hands of an occupier.[129] The prince's policy towards Shotwick and Northwich already demonstrated a preference for indirect control. Patronage may therefore have provided a useful method of removing the burden of relatively unprofitable units.

128 SC 11/862. For 1376 see C 47/9/57, m 7.
129 SC 6/791, m 3d.

Were annuities a drain upon resources? Taking into consideration those paid on the demesne as well as the chamberlain's accounts, they consumed around 40%–50% of Cheshire revenues over the whole period. Yet the percentage of income disbursed in annuities could be purposefully lowered when revenue was required for other expenses, as for instance, during the Welsh wars, and after 1416 for the French wars. There is no parallel, however, with the drastic pruning of annuities in the duchy of Lancaster under Henry IV.[130] In comparison with elsewhere, the amount expended in annuities in the county was not excessive. In 1406–7, annuities paid in the northern part of the duchy of Lancaster constituted two-thirds of the total discharge, and on the estates of the earls of Northumberland, ordinary and extraordinary fees consumed between one-third and one-half of total income.[131]

Expensive though such a system of patronage might be, it is difficult to see how the situation could be remedied considering the need of the royal earls for political and military support. Such needs led to the viewing of land resources not simply in financial terms but as a valuable element in reward and patronage. In the eyes of contemporaries, alienations of land and revenue to supporters constituted a legitimate charge upon the crown estate. As Wolffe observed, if used wisely, they could produce a much more valuable dividend in service and support than any lost potential contribution to ordinary expenses.[132] Although several annuities, lands and offices were undoubtedly granted as a reward for past service, for instance by Cheshire men in county administration, and in the Welsh wars, the enjoyment of annuities committed men to future service too.

In certain cases, Cheshire annuities were granted in conjunction with a formal indenture for military service. There are four such examples in this period. John de Legh of Booths

130 Somerville, *History of the Duchy of Lancaster*, p. 187.

131 Somerville, *History of the Duchy of Lancaster*, p. 166; J. M. W. Bean, *The Estates of the Percy Family 1416–1537* (Oxford: Oxford University Press, 1958), p. 91.

132 Wolffe, *Royal Demesne,* p. 60.

secured the restoration of an annuity of 20 marks from the issues of Sutton in October 1404 in return for an indenture for life, promising service in peace and war.[133] William, Lord Zouche and Sir Thomas Grey of Heton were similarly retained in 1408.[134] The earl of Arundel's annuity of 250 marks was granted in February 1408 in return for an indenture to serve the prince in peace and war. He was to provide four esquires and six valets at his own cost: any further troops raised by him would be paid in the usual way by the prince.[135] Indentures of this kind were not wholly necessary: the mere taking of the fee or annuity made the recipient liable to service when called upon. Certainly some receiving annuities from county revenues served in the campaign to recover Harlech in 1403.[136] In that year, the prince seems to have issued a summons in Cheshire to all those holding lands, fees and wages, using similar wording to that of the crown in 1400 and on later occasions.[137] Many later served in France under Henry V.[138]

Patronage undoubtedly played its part in reconciling the inhabitants of the county to the Lancastrian regime, although this did not prevent Sir John Massey of Tatton from dying for Hotspur at Shrewsbury in 1403, or Griffith ap Owen ap David joining Glyndŵr's rebellion.[139] That said, the desire of Henry

133 CHES 2/78, m 3 (1–3), *36 DKR*, p. 295.

134 SC 6/775/11, m 6, /9, m 6)

135 CHES 2/80, m 3 (2), *36 DKR*, p. 9.

136 E 101/404/24, ff. 11–12v.

137 CHES 2/76, m 11 (2), *36 DKR*, p. 102. In 1407, for example, all those holding lands, fees and wages by royal gift were ordered, under threat of forfeiture of the same, to join the king at Evesham for service at the siege of Aberystwyth (*CPR 1405–8*, pp. 362–3). See also Somerville, *History of the Duchy of Lancaster*, p. 165.

138 SC 6/776/4, m 3d–4d. See also Somerville, *History of the Duchy of Lancaster*, p. 183.

139 On 3 Aug 1403, the escheator was ordered to seize Sir John's lands and a writ diem clausit extremum noting his death was issued on 3 Oct 1403 (CHES 2/76, m 9d (5), m 11d (7), *36 DKR*, pp. 333–4). In the chamberlain's account of 1403–4, SC 6/775/3, m 6, it was noted that Griffith had been paid only the first instalment of his annuity 'and no more because he is a rebel' ('et non plus quia rebellis est').

IV and his son to conciliate is clearly revealed in the fact that the other six annuitants who fought for Hotspur (John Done of Utkinton, Sir Peter Dutton, John Kingsley, Sir Robert Legh, Sir John de Legh of Booths and Peter Warburton) were pardoned and thus able to continue to enjoy their annuities or else had them regranted after a temporary loss.

What conclusions, then, can we draw from this study of patronage? First, it is clear that good lordship was given a greater importance than financial return from the county. That said, the system was not so inflexible as to prevent its temporary curtailment when the cost of Welsh defences became the first priority. The county also shared in the contemporary move away from the wholesale alienation of royal lands, but remained an important source of financial resources which could be used to engage and reward financial and military support.

Perhaps the most important observation which can be made is that the patronage resources of the county were being used in this period in much the same way as in other areas of the royal demesne, even during the principate of Henry of Monmouth. They were regarded principally as part of the general funds at royal disposal not as a means of favouring and buying the support of local men. This is a further demonstration of the extent to which the county was increasingly assimilated into the royal demesne as a whole.

## CHAPTER 6

# *The Demesne and Palatinate Revenues*

Until the later part of the fifteenth century, income from the royal demesne of the kings of England, considered in its entirety, made only a minor contribution to the finances of the crown.[1] Much more significant was income from direct taxation (the lay subsidy) and indirect taxation (customs duties and other levies linked to commerce), although both required the approval of the Commons in parliament.[2] It is important, therefore, to consider the royal earl's demesne revenues in Cheshire in the context of his palatinate revenues as a whole, to see whether this conclusion applies to the income from the earldom of Chester in the time of Henry V as both prince and king. Cheshire did not contribute to the tax grants made to the king in parliament, since its status meant that it was not represented in parliament. Instead, it made its own tax grants (called the mise) to its earl under procedures established in previous centuries.[3] It is therefore relevant, when considering the relative contribution of demesne and other income, to consider also income from taxation which was collected in the county on four occasions between 1399 and 1422, three times as the mise (1401, 1416 and 1419) and once as a collective fine for rebellion (1403).

1 B. P. Wolffe, *The Royal Demesne in English History: The Crown Estate in the Governance of the Realm from the Conquest to 1509* (London: Allen and Unwin, 1971), pp. 10, 30.

2 For a succinct discussion see W. Mark Ormrod, 'The Domestic Response', in A. Curry and, m Hughes (eds), *Arms, Armies and Fortifications in the Hundred Years War* (Woodbridge: Boydell Press, 1994), pp. 83–101, at pp. 87–94, and, specifically for the reign of Henry V, W. Mark Ormrod, 'Henry V and the English Taxpayer', in Gwilym Dodd (ed.), *Henry V: New Interpretations* (Woodbridge: York Medieval Press, 2013), pp. 187–216.

3 Tim Thornton, 'Taxing the King's Dominions: The Subject Territories of the English Crown in the Later Middle Ages', in W. Mark Ormrod, Margaret Bonney and Richard Bonney (eds), *Crises, Revolutions and Self-Sustained Growth: Essays in European Fiscal History, 1130–1830* (Stamford: Shaun Tyas, 1999), pp. 97–109.

## Landed revenue and other sources of income

The trends in demesne revenue have already been discussed under each type of income in Chapter 3, but the importance of such revenue to the earl's overall income is emphasised by Table XI. This table displays demesne, or landed, income, based on liveries to the chamberlain, as a percentage of total revenue for each year between 1399 and 1422, save for 1408–9 where there is no surviving chamberlain's account. In order to place such demesne revenues in context, they have been expressed as a percentage of regular palatinate income, which included monies from the functions of the sheriff and escheator, as well as of total palatinate income, which included revenue from taxation.

Taken over the whole period, we can see that landed income produced an annual average of 42.3% of regular income and 31.3% of total income. It will be noted that there was a sharp increase in both real and relative terms between 1403 and 1407, when pressure was being placed on the county for higher revenues in order to meet the costs of the Welsh wars, which were being met directly out of Cheshire income. Even in years of taxation in this first decade (1401 and 1403), the demesne still produced well over one-third of the total income, and over 40% in one year (1403–4). In the later years of taxation, 1417 to 1421, the contribution of the demesne fell to less than one-third and, in some years, to less than one-quarter. This decline was caused not by an increase in the contribution of taxation but a decline in the real, and therefore also the relative, contribution of the demesne. It must be pointed out, however, that even after this downturn, demesne revenue still formed the largest *regular* contribution to palatinate revenues.

## Table XI. The contribution of the Cheshire demesne to palatinate revenues 1400–22

| Year | Demesne revenues | % of total income (including income from mise) | % of regular income |
|---|---|---|---|
| 1400 | £562 3s. 10d. | 42.6 | 42.6 |
| 1401 | £521 18s. 1½d. | 31.8 | 39.9 |
| 1402 | £486 17s. 4¼d. | 25.8 | 40.0 |
| 1403 | £757 16s. 10¼d. | 33.3 | 45.7 |
| 1404 | £611 16s. 8¼d. | 44.1 | 45.2 |
| 1405 | £598 17s. 9¼d. | 26.4 | 46.3 |
| 1406 | £672 12s. 3½d. | 36.7 | 56.3 |
| 1407 | £651 13s. 11¼d. | 36.8 | 45.6 |
| 1408 | £539 7s. 9¼d. | 38.7 | 38.7 |
| 1409 | not known | not known | not known |
| 1410 | £594 14s. 1¼d. | 51.8 | 51.8 |
| 1411 | £500 6s. 6¼d. | 42.3 | 42.3 |
| 1412 | £555 9s. 0½d. | 37.5 | 37.5 |
| 1413 | £563 8s. 1d. | 47.0 | 47.0 |
| 1414 | £544 1s. 11¼d. | 45.6 | 45.6 |
| 1415 | £545 4s. 1¼d. | 44.4 | 44.4 |
| 1416 | £487 6s. 9½d. | 39.2 | 39.2 |
| 1417 | £561 2s. 7d. | 22.6 | 22.6 |
| 1418 | £461 5s. 2d. | 23.1 | 34.7 |
| 1419 | £461 3s. 4¾d. | 30.6 | 39.3 |
| 1420 | £408 5s. 4d. | 30.9 | 30.9 |
| 1421 | £433 0s. 5d. | 27.5 | 34.9 |
| 1422 | £390 15s. 6¼d. | 34.7 | 34.7 |
| | | | |

In any year, an additional 10% to 25% was contributed by the demesne in Flintshire (Table XII). It is noticeable that the latter was so much more valuable after the Welsh wars. In 1401 it was already the case that certain areas of Flintshire had been totally depredated by Welsh rebels and had to be excused payment.[4] It was impossible to collect any revenues in Flintshire between 1404 and 1406 and revenues were still depleted in 1407 and 1408. By 1411, however, income was surpassing even the value of £342 19s. 5d. ascribed to Flintshire in the undated valor of the lands of the prince of Wales.[5] In addition, income from the Flintshire *donum* and from fines for involvement in the Welsh rebellion were accounted alongside Cheshire revenues. A *donum* (literally, gift) of £100 had been 'granted' by the community of Flintshire for a respite of execution of punishment for rebellion; the sum was to be paid at the Chester exchequer in the fifth year of Henry IV (1403–4). In addition, £20 was granted from Flintshire in 1405 for the same reason.[6]

## Table XII. The contribution of the Flintshire demesnes to palatinate revenues, 1400–22

| Year | Demesne revenue | % of total income | % of regular income |
|---|---|---|---|
| 1400 | £287 18s. 10d. | 21.8 | 21.8 |
| 1401 | £263 18s. 6d. | 16.1 | 20.2 |
| 1402 | £269 8s. 8½d. | 14.2 | 22.1 |
| 1403 | £221 4s. 9d. | 9.7 | 13.3 |
| 1404 | Nil due to rebellion | | |
| 1405 | Nil due to rebellion | | |
| 1406 | Nil due to rebellion | | |
| 1407 | £150 13s. 5d. | 8.5 | 10.3 |
| 1408 | £149 14s. 5d. | 10.7 | |

4 SC 6/774/13, m 5d.

5 SC 11/862, in Appendix VI.

6 J. E. Messham, 'The County of Flint and the Rebellion of Owen Glyndwr in the Records of the Earldom of Chester', *Journal of the Flintshire Historical Society*, 23 (1967–8), 1–34, at p. 20. The £20 had been agreed before William de Leysongly and others of the council of the prince in Chester on 3 Mar 1405.

| Year | Demesne revenue | % of total income | % of regular income |
|---|---|---|---|
| 1409 | Not known | Not known | Not known |
| 1410 | £298 4s. 4d. | 25.9 | |
| 1411 | £375 5s. 8d. | 31.7 | |
| 1412 | £506 9s. 0¼d. | 34.2 | |
| 1413 | £287 14s. 0d. | 23.9 | |
| 1414 | £348 5s. 4¾d. | 29.2 | |
| 1415 | £333 8s. 3d. | 27.1 | |
| 1416 | £303 3s. 0¾d. | 24.4 | |
| 1417 | £302 4s. 9¼d. | 12.1 | 20.4 |
| 1418 | £320 15s. 7¾d. | 16.1 | 19.3 |
| 1419 | £252 18s. 2½d. | 16.8 | 21.5 |
| 1420 | £272 4s. 2d. | 20.6 | 27.5 |
| 1421 | £281 2s. 3½d. | 17.8 | 22.6 |
| 1422 | £372 0s. 2¼d. | 33.1 | |

Even though demesne income from both Cheshire and Flint was the largest regular contribution to overall revenues, it was always inadequate by itself to meet the charges upon Cheshire resources. Non-landed revenue was increasingly important in what was, by the early fifteenth century, largely a rentier economy, where many elements of demesne income were fixed. The manipulation and administration of revenues can shed light upon estate policy as a whole, but we should remember that little distinction would have been drawn by contemporaries between landed and non-landed income.

Certain small categories of income were accounted directly by the chamberlain of Chester. These included profits from the prise of wine and from the chancery functions of the Chester exchequer. Apart from taxation, which will be discussed separately in the second half of this chapter, the other major sources of income were accounted by the sheriff and escheator, both of whom made a substantial contribution to county revenues, as can be seen in Tables XIII and XIV. In Table

XIII, the non-landed income from the sheriff and escheator is tabulated and compared with demesne income, so that the relative contribution to regular total income can be seen. Table XIV separates out the income from the sheriff and escheator and calculates the contribution of each to total income.

In general, we can see that the sheriff was financially the more important official in terms of the earl's income although inevitable there were yearly fluctuations in his issues. As on the demesnes, profits of justice could not be increased artificially although a rise could be achieved by more efficient collection. The sheriff's actual income was showing much the same trend as demesne revenues, with a marked decline towards the end of the period. Less of the revenue was being collected in the year due, or even in the following year, since it was common practice for fines imposed in one year to be collected in the next.

Current issues of the sheriff were declining from an annual average of £239 15s. 0d. in the reign of Henry IV to £167 13s. 11d. under his son, but the major problem was proving to be one of collectability. This may have been because of the generally decreasing pressure on income after the Welsh wars which, as we have seen, were also a major factor in the decline of demesne revenues. It may also have its cause in the personal incompetence of John de Legh of Booths, sheriff from 1411 to 1421. He had already run into difficulties over the non-payment of the surplus of rent of the township of Sutton which he had held as an annuity to the value of 20 marks per annum. In 1419 this annuity had been terminated owing to default of payment.[7] After rendering no issues at all from the current profits of the shrievalty in 1420 and 1421, and thereby accumulating arrears totalling £400, Legh was, not surprisingly, removed from office in October 1421.[8] By contrast, there were high liveries in the years 1406 to 1408, no doubt in response to the move to increasing county revenues to meet Welsh expenses.

7 SC 6/806/17, m 3.

8 SC 6/793/11, m 6, 794/1, m 6.

## Table XIII. The relative contribution of landed and non-landed income to palatinate revenues, 1400–22

| Year | Total income (demesne, sheriff, escheator, tax) | Demesne revenues | % of total | Non-landed income (sheriff and escheator) | % of total |
|---|---|---|---|---|---|
| 1400 | £829 1s. 11¾d. | £562 3s. 10d. | 67.7 | £266 18s. 1¾d. | 32.3 |
| 1401 | £850 4s. 9d. | £521 18s. 1½d. | 61.2 | £328 6s. 7½d. | 39.8 |
| 1402 | £707 14s. 5½d. | £486 17s. 4¼d. | 68.8 | £220 17s. 1d. | 31.2 |
| 1403 | £1035 19s. 7d. | £757 16s. 10¼d. | 73.1 | £278 2s. 8¾d. | 26.9 |
| 1404 | £888 15s. 8d. | £611 16s. 8¼d. | 68.8 | £276 18s. 11¾d. | 31.2 |
| 1405 | £902 12s. 7¾d. | £598 17s. 9¼d. | 66.2 | £303 14s. 10¾d. | 33.8 |
| 1406 | £1023 2s. 8¾d. | £672 12s. 3½d. | 65.6 | £350 10s. 5½d. | 34.4 |
| 1407 | £1094 7s. 8½d. | £651 13s. 11¼d. | 59.5 | £442 14s. 9d. | 40.5 |
| 1408 | £966 11s. 0d. | £539 7s. 9¼d. | 72.9 | £261 1s. 7¾d. | 27.1 |
| 1409 | Not known | Not known | Not known | Not known | Not known |
| 1410 | £783 11s. 5d. | £594 14s. 1¼d. | 75.8 | £188 17s. 3¾d. | 24.2 |
| 1411 | £813 7s. 7¾d. | £500 6s. 6¼d. | 72.3 | £224 17s. 5d. | 27.7 |
| 1412 | £860 7s. 7¾d. | £555 9s. 0½d. | 64.5 | £304 18s. 9¾d. | 35.5 |
| 1413 | £655 19s. 0d. | £563 8s. 1d. | 85.9 | £92 10s. 11d. | 14.1 |
| 1414 | £809 19s. 3d. | £544 1s. 11¼d. | 67.2 | £265 17s. 3¾d. | 32.8 |
| 1415 | £829 10s. 2¼d. | £545 4s. 1¼d. | 65.7 | £284 6s. 1d. | 34.3 |
| 1416 | £749 16s. 7d. | £487 6s. 9½d. | 65.0 | £262 9s. 9½d. | 35.0 |
| 1417 | £812 14s. 4½d. | £561 2s. 7d. | 69.0 | £251 11s. 9½d. | 31.0 |
| 1418 | £688 3s. 3½d. | £461 5s. 2d. | 67.0 | £226 18s. 1½d. | 33.0 |
| 1419 | £643 19s. 11¾d. | £461 3s. 4¾d. | 71.6 | £182 16s. 7d. | 29.4 |
| 1420 | £541 13s. 5d. | £408 5s. 4d. | 75.4 | £133 8s. 1d. | 25.6 |
| 1421 | £701 12s. 4d. | £433 0s. 5d. | 61.7 | £268 11s. 11d. | 29.3 |
| 1422 | £552 19s. 0¾d. | £390 15s. 6¼d. | 70.6 | £162 3s. 6½d. | 29.4 |

## Table XIV. The contribution of the revenues of the sheriff and escheator to palatinate revenues, 1400–22

| Year | sheriff | % of total income | escheator | % of total issues |
|---|---|---|---|---|
| 1400 | £185 0s. 6¾d. | 14.0 | £86 11s. 8d. | 6.5 |
| 1401 | £222 16s. 0½d. | 13.5 | £104 17s. 4d. | 6.3 |
| 1402 | £115 13s. 6½d. | 6.1 | £88 12s. 5d. | 4.7 |
| 1403 | £216 18s. 3½d. | 9.5 | £50 1s. 3½d. | 2.2 |
| 1404 | £162 3s. 7¾d. | 14.3 | £74 2s. 9d. | 5.3 |
| 1405 | £133 15s. 3½d. | 5.9 | £157 17s. 2½d. | 6.9 |
| 1406 | £239 5s. 8d. | 13.0 | £109 7s. 0¼d. | 5.9 |
| 1407 | £276 3s. 7d. | 15.6 | £82 6s. 7¾d. | 9.1 |
| 1408 | £234 4s. 6d. | 16.7 | £22 12s. 6d. | 1.6 |
| 1409 | £172 19s. 1d. | Not known | £14 19s. 2d. | Not known |
| 1410 | £166 12s. 9½d. | 14.6 | £16 0s. 0d. | 1.4 |
| 1411 | £149 12s. 5d. | 12.6 | £68 13s. 4d. | 5.8 |
| 1412 | £360 19s. 6¼d. | 18.5 | £24 16s. 8d. | 1.6 |
| 1413 | £104 19s. 4d. | 13.5 | £146 17s. 2½d. | 15.9 |
| 1414 | £186 3s. 8¼d. | 15.6 | £74 4s. 2d. | 6.2 |
| 1415 | £195 14s. 8d. | 15.9 | £83 3s. 4½d. | 6.8 |
| 1416 | £82 4s. 0d. | 6.7 | £180 5s. 9½d. | 14.5 |
| 1417 | £86 14s. 4d. | 3.4 | £166 17s. 5½d. | 6.7 |
| 1418 | £91 11s. 9d. | 6.7 | £135 6s. 4½d. | 6.8 |
| 1419 | £92 2s. 5d. | 6.1 | £90 14s. 2d. | 6.0 |
| 1420 | £91 8s. 8d. | 6.9 | £40 19s. 5d. | 3.1 |
| 1421 | £135 10s. 3d. | 8.6 | £133 1s. 8d. | 8.4 |
| 1422 | £75 3s. 6½d. | 6.6 | £87 0s. 0d. | 7.7 |

More attention seems to have been paid to revenues from escheats. In the early fourteenth century, receipts from escheats had been very small, at £54 in 1350 and only £21 in 1351.[9] Later in the century, when it was already proving difficult to increase

9 *Accounts of the Chamberlain and Other Officers of the County of Chester 1301–1360*, ed. R. Stewart-Brown, RSLC, 59 (1910), pp. 156, 205.

revenue from traditional sources in the county, additional emphasis had been directed towards increasing revenues from judicial activity and escheats as well as from taxation: income from escheats increased nine-fold between 1349 and 1373.[10] Under Richard II also, all wardships and marriages were sold for the best price possible whilst escheated lands were let for a good rent.[11] Such was the policy in the early fifteenth century too, at least towards lands newly escheated, although valuable farms of escheated lands and wardships were also used as instruments of patronage. In 1409, for instance, Hugh Holes was granted the fee farm of certain lands which had formerly belonged to Sir Richard Vernon, as well as the custody of his heir for no charge.[12]

The most valuable escheats and wardships were accounted at Westminster rather than in Cheshire so that the escheator's accounts do not give the full value of total income in the county. For example, after the death of Thomas Holes in November 1420, the chamberlain William Troutbeck was granted custody of his lands as well as wardship of Margery, his heiress. A payment of 350 marks had been agreed between Troutbeck and the treasurer of England with the proviso that it should be paid directly at Westminster.[13] In addition, especially large or important lands which escheated to the earl could be given their own account within the ministers' accounts. From 1398 to 1415, the lands formerly of William de Frodsham (d. 1398), previously chamberlain of North Wales, were separately accounted to pay off the debts of his office. In most years these were farmed to his son for a farm of slightly over £6 per annum, until the debt was satisfied in 1415.[14] In the years of increased exploitation, several escheats were not farmed out by the earl's

10 Booth, *Financial Admin.*, pp. 120–5, 140.
11 Sharp, 'Earldom and County of Chester', p. 455.
12 SC 6/792/5, m 9d.
13 SC 6/794/1, m 1d. There are other examples of this during the principality of Henry, when the money was paid to the prince's exchequer at Westminster by the hands of his receiver-general (e.g. SC 6/791/10, m 6d).
14 SC 6/793/2, m 3d.

administration but, rather, a salaried bailiff was installed who was made responsible for manorial profits.[15] One such example concerns the manor of Malpas in 1405.[16] It is interesting to speculate that this experience of direct comital control might have caused antagonism and contributed to the later opposition of the inhabitants of the areas to the *mise*, to which we shall return in the following section of this chapter.

Overall we can see a distinct trend towards boosting revenue from escheated lands. Certainly current issues from 1404 to 1406 were considerably increased and more of them were being liveried, as the summary of the escheator's accounts demonstrates (Table XV). The year 1404 marked the beginning of payments from the issues of escheats directly to the prince's central financial officials, by-passing the chamberlain of Chester. From 1404 to 1406, such payments were made out of specific escheats, noticeably those which had been directly controlled by the earl's officials. In these years, £43 13s. 4d., £66 13s. 4d. and £33 6s. 8d. were paid out, respectively, from the issues of lands formerly of Thomas de Beeston and Richard Massey, and from the manors of Dunham and Ashton, directly to John Wynter, the prince's receiver-general by the hands of Hugh Mortimer, his chamberlain.[17] In 1404, a further £66 13s. 4d. was paid out of the issues of the lands of Thomas Beeston to Martin de Killom, a merchant of London, as payment for purchases already made by the prince.[18]

From 1408 to 1413, a clear-cut system evolved whereby the escheator regularly made liveries in person to the prince's chamberlain, but this was from the escheator's total revenues rather than out of specific escheats. In 1408, £84 19s. 6½d. was so delivered, but we see lower sums in 1409 (£71 3s. 9d.), 1410 (£48 12s. 9d.), 1412 (£37 6s. 8d.) and 1413 (£46 11s.

15 See, for instance, SC 6/79/7, m 7 (1404), 791/10, m 6 (1405).

16 SC 6/791/10, m 6. See also SC 6/791/7, m 7.

17 SC 6/791/7, m 7; SC 6/791/10, m 6d; SC 6/792/1, m 7d. An indenture witnessing receipt of the first sum by Mortimer survives, dated at Lichfield on 31 Aug 1404 (E 101/405/1, m 9).

18 SC 6/791/7, m 7.

## Table XV. Summary of the accounts of the escheator, 1400–22

| | **1400** | **1401** | **1402** |
|---|---|---|---|
| Arrears | £151 1s. 3¼d. | £166 16s. 8¾d. | £141 8s. 10¾d. |
| Issues | £119 17s. 3d. | £125 1s. 9d. | £101 8s. ½d. |
| Issues and Arrears | £270 18s. 6¼d. | £291 18s. 3¾d. | £242 16s. 11¼d. |
| Liveries of arrears | £8 10s. 8d. | £2 13s. 4d. | £67 6s. 8d. |
| Liveries issues | £78 1s. 0d. | £102 4s. 0d. | £21 5s. 9d. |
| Total liveries | £86 11s. 8d. | £102 17s. 4d. | £88 12s. 5d. |
| | **1403** | **1404** | **1405** |
| Arrears | £137 11s. 2¼d. | 143 16s. 2¾d. | £154 3s. 4½d. |
| Issues | £68 3s. 0d. | £256 2s. 7¼d. | £392 18s. 4½d. |
| Issues and Arrears | £205 14s. 2¼d. | £399 18s. 10d. | £447 1s. 9d. |
| Liveries of arrears | | £1 0s. 0d. | £22 3s. 10¾d. |
| Liveries issues | £50 1s. 3½d. | £183 9s. 5d. | £202 6s. 7¾d. |
| Total liveries | £50 1s. 3½d. | £184 9s. 5d. | £224 10s. 6½d. |
| | **1406** | **1407** | **1408** |
| Arrears | £185 3s. 2d. | £171 15s. 1d. | £69 5s. 0½d. |
| Issues | £245 9s. 0¼d. | £143 15s. 10d. | £206 9s. 1¼d. |
| Issues and Arrears | £330 12s. 2¼d. | £315 10s. 11d. | £275 14s. 1¾d. |
| Liveries of arrears | £4 1s. 9½d. | ? | £13 10s. 3¼d. |
| Liveries issues | £138 11s. 11¾d. | ? | £94 2s. 9d. |
| Total liveries | £142 13s 9¼d. | £162 5s. 6¼d. | £107 13s. 0¼d. |
| | **1409** | **1410** | **1411** |
| Arrears | £77 19s. 7½d. | £70 7s. 9d. | £619 14s. 11½d. |
| Issues | £168 16s. 5¼d. | £626 19s. 6d. | £243 17s. 7½d. |
| Issues and Arrears | £276 16s. 0¾d. | £697 7s. 3d. | £863 12s. 7d. |
| Liveries of arrears | £14 19s. 2d. | £6 0s. 0d. | ? |
| Liveries issues | £71 3s. 9d. | £58 12s. 9d. | ? |
| Total liveries | £86 2s. 11d. | £64 12s. 9d. | £68 13s. 4d. |

8d.).[19] On the first three occasions, the escheator was paid expenses for taking the money in person – to London in 1408 and 1409, and to Leicester in 1410. This emphasises once again the importance of the escheator's income. Not only was he contributing directly to the prince's personal resources but he was continuing to render further sums to the chamberlain of Chester as part of the general fund of county resources.

The direct liveries to Henry from the escheator ceased once the prince became king, although in 1416 and 1422 issues from specific escheats were paid to the royal exchequer by the chamberlain.[20] Such activity again reflects the interest in exploitation of non-demesne revenues and also its vital contribution to palatinate revenues.

## Taxation

Taxation in medieval Cheshire is an intrinsically fascinating subject. There was no taxation imposed from Westminster after 1292 yet it was only in 1379–80 that we find a clear statement that the county was not bound to contribute to lay subsidies with the rest of the kingdom because it did not send representatives to the English parliament. Instead, the county contributed in its own peculiar way until standard lay subsidies were imposed from 1534.[21] That said, we should not assume that Cheshire was more lightly taxed because of its special position. As Paul Booth has shown, the various efforts of the Black Prince, based both on a fine levied in the county for confirmation of privileges or pardon for offences, and on a *subsidium* or *donum* (often described as a 'mise'), brought in substantial sums of money for

19 Respectively, SC 6/792/3, m 8d; SC 6/792/5, m 9; SC 6/792/7, m 9d; SC 6/792/9, m 7d; SC 6/792/10, m 9d.

20 In 1416, £50 (SC 6/776/4, m 4d), and in 1422 £36 13s 4d (SC 6/1303/5, m 4d).

21 Tim Thornton, *Cheshire and the Tudor State, 1480–1560* (Woodbridge: Boydell, 2000), pp. 76–7; W. H. B. Bird, 'Taxation and Representation in the County Palatine of Chester', *English Historical Review*, 30 (1915), 303; Booth, *Financial Admin.*, pp. 116–17.

the earl.[22] A subsidy was levied in 1346 (£1,000), 1353 (5,000 marks),[23] and 1368 (2,500 marks).[24] The same form of grant, this time of 3,000 marks, was made once in the reign of Richard II in 1389, apparently in return for confirmation of the charters of liberty of the county, although it is uncertain whether it was ever collected.[25]

We can ascertain much about the mechanics of Cheshire taxation, yet certain important aspects still elude us. It is hoped here to shed a little more light on the subject by discussing instances of taxation between 1399 and 1422. The contribution of taxation to county revenues was important, all the more so in the latter half of this period when landed revenues were declining.

There were four grants made to the earl in this period which can be described as taxation. Three of these – namely the payments of 1401, 1416 and 1419 – were described as a 'mise'.[26] The first two granted 3,000 marks (i.e. £2,000), and the third 1,000 marks (£666 6s. 8d.). The fourth payment was a fine of 3,000 marks imposed in November 1403 to be paid to the king in return for a pardon for the county's involvement

22 Booth, *Financial Admin.*, p. 118.

23 On this occasion in return for the prince aborting a general eyre. See B. E. Harris, 'The Palatinate 1301–1547', in B. E. Harris (ed.), *The Victoria History of the Counties of England: A History of the County of Chester*, ii (Oxford: Oxford University Press for the University of London Institute of Historical Research, 1979), p. 23; P. H. W. Booth, 'Taxation and Public Order: Cheshire in 1353', *Northern History*, 12 (1976), 16–31.

24 In addition, in 1347 and 1357 a communal fine was raised by implementation of the forest eyre. On the second occasion very heavy fines were raised, 2,000 marks in the case of Delamere (*Cheshire Forest Eyre Rolls 1357. Part One: The Forest of Wirral*, ed. Phyllis M. Hill, J. Heery and members of the Ranulf Higden Society, Record Society of Lancashire and Cheshire, 2015)).

25 Harris, 'The Palatinate', p. 24; Michael J. Bennett, *Community, Class and Careerism: Cheshire and Lancashire Society in the Age of Sir Gawain and the Green Knight* (Cambridge: Cambridge University Press, 1983), pp. 219–22.

26 See, respectively, SC 6/774/13, m 2, SC 6/776/4, m 2 and SC 6/1303/3, m 2 for first notice of these payments.

in Hotspur's rebellion.[27] The city of Chester was excluded from this pardon but had its own granted in return for either its own contribution of 300 marks (£200) or else to find, at the citizen's own expense, shipping and victuals for the proposed attempt to rescue Beaumaris Castle; they chose the latter method of payment.[28] In August 1404, Henry IV granted the revenues of this 1403 fine to the prince of Wales, to be spent upon the defence of Denbigh and other castles in North Wales.[29] As a result, it was accounted in the usual way by the chamberlain of Chester as part of Cheshire revenues and directed immediately to the costs of the defence of North Wales.[30] The grants of 3,000 marks, whether in the form of mise or fine, were in all cases to be paid in three instalments over three years, in other words at 1,000 marks each year. That of 1416, for instance, was intended for payment on 3 May 1416, 10 November 1416 and 24 June 1417.[31] This use of instalments paralleled similar practice in the administration of the fourteenth-century mise.[32]

It would seem that the grant of the mise was customarily associated with a particular event, such as the creation of a new earl or at the confirmation of the county's liberties. To

27 *CPR 1401–5*, p. 331; CHES 2/77, m 3 (1), *36 DKR*, p. 103. The charters of pardon for both the county and city were kept in the custody of the vice chamberlain Roger Brescy until fulfilment of the conditions. The documents had been delivered to him by Ralph Pope, Sir John Pulle and Richard de Manley to be read to the people of the county and the mayor and commonalty of the city (CHES 2/77, m 3 (3)).

28 CHES 2/77, m 3 (2), *36 DKR*, p. 103. On 31 Dec 1403 Robert Castell appeared before the vice chamberlain Roger Brescy to testify to the fulfilment of the conditions of the charter for Chester touching the rescue of Beaumaris, after which the charter was delivered to the mayor, the city sheriffs and John de Eulowe, citizen of Chester (CHES 2/77, m 3 (4), *36 DKR*, p. 103). See also CALS, Chester Corporation Charters CH 24 cited in P. J. Morgan, *War and Society in Medieval Cheshire, 1277–1403*, Chetham Society, 3rd ser., 34 (1987), p. 225 n. 183.

29 *CPR 1401–5*, p. 412, *PPC*, i. 236.

30 SC 6/775/4, m 2.

31 CHES 2/89, m 6.

32 Booth, *Financial Admin.*, p. 124.

circumvent such limitations, the Black Prince had been forced to resort to profitable judicial proceedings instead, out of which the community of the county could buy themselves.[33] The 1403 grant is a clear manifestation of this strategy in action again in the early fifteenth century. The first grant of our period in 1401 had been made as a result of the creation of Prince Henry as earl. Arguably, we could interpret the grant of April 1416 as a payment made upon Henry's accession as king, although it was made three years into his reign and he had already received a mise at his initial creation as earl in 1401. There appear to be no special circumstances surrounding the grant of 1419. It seems apparent, therefore, that both the 1416 and 1419 grants were made as contributions towards the financing of the wars with France. These Cheshire grants therefore parallel the enthusiastic financial support of the rest of the kingdom at this stage of the war. The Commons in the parliament of October 1416 had granted two tenths and fifteenths to be collected in two instalments by 11 November 1417. In the parliament of October 1419, they had granted one and a third tenths and fifteenths to be collected in two instalments by 11 November 1420.[34]

It is of considerable significance that revenue from the first instalment of the Cheshire mise in 1416 contributed to the cost of the force of Cheshire archers and their captains who had served on the first French campaign of 1415.[35] A further instalment of the mise of 1416 was assigned to the Cheshire knight, Sir John Savage, for the defence of Calais.[36] It is clear, therefore, that Cheshire could be expected to contribute to national revenues at times of need along the same lines and on the same scale as the rest of the country, despite the continuing existence

33 Ormerod, *Cheshire*, iii. 883–4. See also Booth, *Financial Admin.*, pp. 119–24.

34 M. Jurkowski, C. L. Smith and D. Crook, *Lay Taxes in England and Wales 1188–1688* (Kew: PRO Publications, 1998), pp. 81, 82–3. The parliament of Mar 1416 had also agreed to bring forward, from Nov to June 1416, the tenth and fifteenth granted in the parliament of Nov 1415 (p. 80).

35 SC 6/776/4, mm 3d–4d.

36 SC 6/1303/2, m 4d.

of its system of non-parliamentary taxation. Such a situation demonstrates the high degree of assimilation with the rest of the royal demesne and with the kingdom as a whole, especially once Henry V acceded to the throne. This assimilation continued under the infant king/earl Henry VI. In February 1430, a baron and auditor of the royal exchequer were appointed by the king to treat with the people of the palatinate concerning a grant of a subsidy in aid of the expedition which the king intended to lead in person to France, with a view to effecting his coronation there.[37] A mise of 1,000 marks was subsequently granted.[38]

The system of granting and collecting the various payments in this period appears to be the same as in previous centuries. It was 'voted' by an assembly, most probably the county court which seems to have been regarded as the quasi-parliament of the palatinate. In 1389, the sheriff had been paid expenses for acting on behalf of the community in the matter of the grant of the subsidy.[39] All three mises of our period were said to have been granted by the community of the county, but beyond this, the specific instances offer few further details. The chamberlain's account of 1417 speaks of the subsidy as being granted by the laity ('laici') of the county, but the various appointments of the collectors refer to a unanimous and voluntary grant by the 'prelates, magnates, nobles and the whole community of our county' ('prelati, magnates, procures et tota communitas comitatus nostri').[40] A further reference to the subsidy adds the gloss 'both lesser and greater' ('tam minores quam maiores').[41]

Generally, five collectors for each of the seven hundreds of the county were appointed, responsible for each instalment, or for more if two instalments were due within one year. Not

37 CHES 2/100, m 4 (12), *37 DKR*, p. 610. On the expedition, see Anne Curry, 'The "Coronation Expedition" and Henry VI's Court in France, 1430–1432', in J. Stratford (ed.), *The Lancastrian Court* (Stamford: Paul Watkins Press, 2003), pp. 30–54. There is no evidence of a special archer company being raised in Cheshire for this army.

38 Thornton, 'Taxing the King's Dominions', table 4.1, p. 102.

39 CHES 2/62, m 6 (8), *36 DKR*, p. 95.

40 SC 6/776/4, m 4d, CHES 2/90, m 6 (1–7), *37 DKR*, passim.

41 CHES 25/11, m 9d.

all appointments of collectors were enrolled on the Chester enrolments. For the collection of the fine of 1404, for instance, there is only one set of extant enrolled appointments dated to 18 June 1406. These are for the collectors responsible for the third instalment of the mise due on 24 June 1406.[42] Whether the collectors were nominated by the hundreds, offered themselves for the office, or were appointed by the earl's administration is unclear. It would seem that they had to be resident in the hundred for which they were responsible: in January 1421 new collectors had to be appointed for the hundred of Northwich in place of two original appointees who were now dwelling outside the hundred and therefore could not attend to the collection of the subsidy.[43]

It was usual for completely different collectors to be appointed for each instalment. In the complete set of enrolled appointments for the 1416 mise, it is interesting to note that those appointed to collect the first instalment were predominantly gentry and certainly the leading members of the county community.[44] In the two subsequent appointments, collectors were drawn from lower strata of county society.[45] It is possible that the first group of collectors represented those who had voted the subsidy in the first place.[46] They were certainly those whom we should most expect to be included in the 'whole community' which was deemed to represent the county. We can compare here with the situation in 1436, when 29 gentlemen were summoned to the royal council at Chester to discuss

42 CHES 2/78, m 4 (1–7), *36 DKR*, pp. 411–12.

43 CHES 2/93, m 2d (8), *37 DKR*, p. 168.

44 CHES 2/89, m 6 (1–7), *37 DKR*, passim. For instance, Sir John Savage, Sir Laurence Fitton and John de Legh were amongst the collectors in Macclesfield hundred. Michael Bennett ('Henry V and the Cheshire Tax Revolt', p. 173) suggests that Henry had travelled north in Mar 1416 to meet leading lords and knights of Cheshire, possibly at Nantwich, at which meeting the taxation grant was agreed, but the king's presence in the county at this point is not certain

45 CHES 2/90, m 6 (1–7), and 2/91, m 5 (6–12).

46 Unfortunately it is not possible to check my hypothesis for other subsidies because the first sets of appointments have not been enrolled.

various matters including the granting of a subsidy in the name of the whole community of the county.[47] In 1404, Ralph Pope, sometime bailiff of Drakelow, Richard de Manley, sometime escheator of the county, and Sir John Pulle had been involved in negotiations with the council concerning the fine.[48] The collectors were not remunerated for their labours, which must surely have been onerous especially in the face of any reluctance to contribute. They certainly had aid from men described as 'servants' and possibly also from local officials.[49]

The method of assessment presents us with the most complex problem. To assist in analysis we can draw on a surviving collectors' book preserved in the Tatton of Wythenshawe manuscripts at the John Rylands Research Institute and Library.[50] Whilst this is dated 1405 in pencil on its back cover, it belongs largely to collection of the mise of 1416.[51] In five of the hundreds, the names listed for the collectors are those appointed in April 1416, indicating that the book relates to the payment of the first instalment of the 1416 mise. For the hundreds of Eddisbury and Macclesfield, however, reference is made to the instalment of the 1403 fine paid in June 1405.[52]

Within the book, the hundreds appear in the same order as they do in enrolments of the appointments of collectors. The constituent townships are also listed in an order which suggests various routes taken around the county by the collectors, although it is possible that these 'circuits' had been established in earlier collections, presumably those taken in the collection of

47 Michael J. Bennett, 'A County Community: Social Cohesion amongst the Cheshire Gentry 1400–1425', *Northern History*, 8 (1973), 24_44, at p. 39.

48 CHES 2/77, m 3 (3), *36 DKR*, p. 103.

49 Respectively, SC 2/255/6, m 1d, JRRIL, Rylands Charter 798.

50 JRRIL, Tatton of Wythenshawe Muniments TW/345.

51 Bennett, 'Henry V and the Cheshire Tax Revolt', p. 172. In my MA thesis of 1977, I followed the customary assumption that the book related to the 1405–6 instalment of the 1403 fine, as did Brian Harris in his chapter on the Palatinate in volume 2 of the Victoria County History, published in 1979.

52 JRRIL, Tatton of Wythenshawe Muniments TW/345, mm 1, 7, 8.

earlier mises. For some hundreds we also see names or initials of collectors against the townships for which they were responsible. For each township an assessment is given indicating the sum expected. The figures given for the Bucklow and Northwich hundreds appear to be the same as in 1353. It could be, therefore, that the assessments fixed under the Black Prince had changed little, or not at all, since his period as earl.[53] Furthermore, an indenture of receipt dated to 1401 for an instalment of the first mise levied in the period records the same sums as were paid forty years later.[54] The likelihood of fossilisation of assessments – paralleling the lay subsidy within the rest of the realm which was still based on assessments laid down in 1334[55] – makes it dangerous to try to link expected contributions with the value or income prevailing in 1416. That said, for the earl's demesnes the hierarchy of assessments matches the hierarchy of values save for one difference. Middlewich and Northwich are assessed at similar rates (respectively £3 16s. 10d. and £3 7s. 2d.)[56] even though in terms of actual and potential value, Middlewich was by far the more profitable in the early fifteenth century.

The collectors' book also shows that the expected contribution for each township was split into two parts, one part being paid by the lord of the manor and the other by the tenants in varying proportions, but we do not know when or how these distributions were imposed or negotiated. References in the indictment roll could be taken to imply that the 1416 mise was assessed and collected on moveable property of the residents and tenants in each township ('de bonis et catallis hominum residencium et tenentium in eadem villa').[57] On the following membrane, the scribe has substituted the word 'dwellers'

53 More research on the township payments across the fourteenth and fifteenth centuries would no doubt be useful to confirm or modify this conclusion.

54 JRRIL, Rylands Charter 798.

55 For full discussion see *The Lay Subsidy of 1334*, ed. Robin E. Glasscock, Records of Social and Economic History (Oxford: Oxford University Press and British Academy, 1975).

56 JRRIL, Tatton of Wythenshawe Muniments TW/345, m 4.

57 CHES 25/11, m 10d.

('commorantium') for tenants ('tenentium') suggesting that the landless might also be expected to contribute to the subsidy. But again we find a parallel with the lay subsidy elsewhere in the realm where the fixed assessments of 1334, which were still in use, had been based on evaluations of moveable goods in 1332.

The division in responsibility for payment between lord and tenant was also established practice before 1416. It is evidenced, for instance, in the fact that, in the escheator's account for 1405, 14s. 8d. was allowed for divers townships which were in the hands of the earl on account of his custody of the lands of Sir Walter Cokesey.[58] In the surviving collectors' book for 1416, however, only Shotwick, out of all of the demesne lands of the earl, had the proportions of contributions between lord and inhabitants stated.[59] At this point, the manor of Shotwick was held in grant by Sir William Porter. It would seem therefore, that in other cases of the earl's demesne, no levy was expected from the earl himself as landlord.

The indictment roll indicates that there was opposition to the 1416 mise, which we shall consider shortly. There had certainly been some small-scale opposition earlier in the period. This is revealed by efforts to recover chattels by force which had been taken by the collectors as destraints because of failure to pay sums due: we find examples of this in 1405 concerning the third instalment of the fine.[60] There are also cases of local collectors refusing to hand over what they had collected. In 1404, for instance, Roger Alcock, a collector in the hundred of Macclesfield, refused to hand over his receipts to the bailiff itinerant and even threatened violence against him.[61] What is most interesting is the suggestion of opposition to the mise on a larger scale even in the early days of the Lancastrians. The Dieulacres chronicle contains an enigmatic reference concerning the first year of the reign of Henry IV: 'the commons

58 SC 6/791/10, m 6.

59 JRRIL, Tatton of Wythenshawe Muniments TW/345, f.3.

60 CHES 25/10, m 21d (Northwich, Sept. 1405). The situation is seen again in 1417 (CHES 25/11, m 9, Eddisbury hundred, Jan. 1417).

61 CHES 25/10, m 15d.

rising against the magnates because of taxation' ('communibus insurgentibus contra magnates propter tallagium').[62] This cannot be a reference to the Cheshire rising of 1400, for the first mise was not granted until after this event, nor is there any other evidence of widespread opposition to taxation at the beginning of the reign.

The situation was quite different in 1416, where we find substantial evidence in the indictment rolls of opposition to the mise.[63] An increasing number of goods which had been taken as distraints were being stolen back, and in some cases collectors were prevented by violence from taking distraints in the first place.[64] In some areas there were also organised acts of opposition. A crowd of around 300 gathered in Malpas in the autumn of 1416 and refused to disband, despite the fact that the chamberlain and leading men of the county had promised them that the subsidy would not be demanded of them until the king's will was known as to whether they should pay it or not. If the subsidy was to be levied from them, then they were to be asked whether they would be willing to contribute voluntarily. It would seem that the crowd did disperse, but they were probably compelled to do so by force since several arrests were made.[65]

Whilst there is no evidence of opposition from the inhabitants of the manors of the earl, there was some armed resistance in Macclesfield hundred involving men of the townships of Northenden, Stanley and Hollingworth. Their reasons for opposition to the subsidy, as stated in the indictment roll, are extremely interesting. These *valetti* gathered together on 14

62 Cited in Peter McNiven, 'The Cheshire Rising in 1400', *Bulletin of the John Rylands Library*, 52 (1969–70), 375–96, at p. 376. He also notes that the subsidy of 3,000 marks granted in 1389 had still not been collected two years later, and that in the interim, the sheriff had not only been obstructed in his duties but had been robbed of such money as he had managed to collect (p. 379).

63 For a fuller discussion see Bennett, 'Henry V and the Cheshire Tax Revolt', pp. 178–83.

64 CHES 25/11, m 9–10.

65 CHES 25/11, m 9d–10.

October 1416, armed themselves and prevented the collectors from performing their duties 'saying that the sum should not be levied on them because the sum had not been granted by the assent of the whole community of the county' ('dicendo quod summa predicta super eos fieri et levari non deberent eo quod summa illa ex assensu totius communitatis comitatus predicti concessa non fuit)'. They also wished to know whether it was the king's will that they should be taxed.[66] This seems a clear cut example of 'no taxation without representation', or at least without some form of consent. There can be no doubt that the mise was voted by the leading men of the county not by the community in any wider sense. In that context it is interesting that the indictment went to great lengths to suggest that consent had been forthcoming from the lower ranks of society: it goes much further than any other official document in saying that the subsidy had been granted 'both by the lower and upper ranks of the county of Chester from the goods and chattels of all men' ('tam minores quam maiores comitatus Cestrie concessa fuit levandum de bonis et catallis omnium hominum').

To some degree it might seem odd that resistance was concentrated in 1416, the first year of taxation under Henry V, given that there had been no taxation of the county since 1407. It may be that inhabitants of the county felt that they had suffered enough in the Welsh wars. Between 1405 and 1407, certain townships in the county beyond the River Dee had been pardoned their contribution to the fine because the Welsh had laid the area waste: even so, the earl's auditors were not satisfied that all methods of collection had been attempted.[67] This reflects a relentless attitude of exploitation of the county at this time, ignoring the sufferings that its inhabitants were experiencing. It is significant, therefore, that much of the opposition in 1416 was concentrated in an area which had been badly hit by the parliamentary statutes against trade with the Welsh earlier in the period and which had been accused of disregarding

66 CHES 25/11, m 9d.

67 CHES 2/78, m 1 (3–5), *36 DKR*, p. 23. For the comments of auditors see SC 6/775/4, m 2, 775/5, m 2, 775/6, m 2.

such prohibitions. There was perhaps a continuing feeling of disgruntlement against the earl's administration because of this? The earl had prevented Cheshire men from taking their usual profits and yet was demanding further financial sacrifice. There may also have been antagonism caused by the treatment of the manor of Malpas when it was escheated to the crown in 1404 and 1405 and a bailiff installed.[68]

Another reason why there was resistance in 1416 may have been affront at what was an irregular grant, occasioned by none of the usual justifications for taxation in Cheshire. But it is certain that the king had in mind not only plans for further action in France in 1416 – 400 Cheshire archers served in the campaign of that year aimed at the rescue of Harfleur – as well as the need to pay outstanding wages from the 1415 campaign, including the Cheshire archers who had served.[69] In that context, it is significant that the first instalment of the 1416 mise was assigned to the chamberlain towards the 1415 wages.[70] We also see a response to resistance by the postponing of payment of half the subsidy to 1418, and also that only 1,000 marks was granted in 1419. We know, too, that collectors were fined for non-payment of the first instalment of the 1419 grant due in November 1420, but were later pardoned because it was claimed that they had not been able to collect the subsidy because of popular unrest, although no specific details of the nature of this unrest have been uncovered.[71] At this point, the reaction to taxation in Cheshire was much the same as elsewhere. In the parliaments of December 1420 and May 1421, the Commons were not asked for a tax grant. The king and his advisors thought it preferable to use other means of raising revenue, notably loans. Cheshiremen contributed

68 See above p. 280.

69 Bennett, 'Henry V and the Cheshire Tax Revolt', p. 178; Anne Curry, 'After Agincourt, What Next? Henry V and the Campaign of 1416', in Linda Clark (ed.), *Conflicts, Consequences and the Crown in the Late Middle Ages*, The Fifteenth Century, 7 (Woodbridge: Boydell Press, 2007), pp. 23–51.

70 SC 6/776/4, mm 3d–4d.

71 SC 6/794/1, m 12d.

to the loan campaign of May–June 1421 to fund the king's return to France with an army, although the county, with loans totalling only £60, was not particularly generous. Lancashire, by contrast, raised up to £400.[72]

Despite opposition to the collection of the mise, further evidence suggests that the collectors were, in the long term, successful in gathering the requisite sums. The 1419 subsidy was due in two instalments, both of £333 6s. 8d., the first due on 24 June 1420, the second on 11 November 1420.[73] These sums were paid to the exchequer at Westminster on 17 February and 9 May respectively.[74] There was a collection period of eight months in the first case and six in the second, but the exact expected sums were delivered. This would suggest that taxation was a more reliable source of income to the earl than demesne revenues, despite the relatively good performance in the collectability of the latter. But the limitation of taxation, and hence the advantage of landed income, was that the former could never be a regular source of revenue. That said, of the 22 years of this study, revenue from taxation was received in at least 12 of them. Such taxation provided a large and necessary contribution to county revenues. Table XVI, with figures drawn from the chamberlain's accounts, demonstrates how valuable the mise was as a contribution to the overall receipts of the county.

72 Anthony Steel, *The Receipt of the Exchequer, 1377–1485* (Cambridge: Cambridge University Press, 1954), p. 191.

73 SC 6/1303/3, m 2, 1303/4, m 2. The second payment date paralleled that for the final part of the parliamentary subsidy – another example of assimilation with the rest of the kingdom – but the first instalment of that grant of the 1419 parliament had been due by 2 Feb 1420.

74 SC 6/1303/3, m 4d, 1303/4, m 4d.

## Table XVI. The contribution of the mise to palatinate revenues, 1400–22

| Year | Taxation sum due | Percentage of total receipts |
|---|---|---|
| 1401 | £333 6s. 8d. | 20.3 |
| 1402 | £666 13s. 4d. | 35.4 |
| 1403 | £618 18s. 3d. (£666 13s. 4d.)[75] | 27.2 |
| 1404 | £332 6s. 10½d. (£333 6s. 8d.) | 24.0 |
| 1405 | £971 17s. 9d. (£1000) | 42.9 |
| 1406 | £647 18s. 6d. (£666 13 s. 4d.) | 35.4 |
| 1407 | £323 19s. 3d. (£333 6s. 8d.) | 18.3 |
| Total temp. H IV | £3,895 0s. 7½d. (£4000) | |
| 1417 | £1000 0s. 0d. | 40.3 |
| 1418 | £666 13s. 4d. | 33.5 |
| 1419 | £333 6s. 8d. | 22.1 |
| 1420 | £333 6s. 8d. | 25.2 |
| 1421 | £333 6s. 8d. | 21.2 |
| Total temp. H V | £2,666 13s. 4d. | |

The contribution of taxation can also be viewed in the wider context of the palatinate's contribution to the prince's household and, after 1413, to the royal exchequer. During the reign of Henry V, Cheshire made very little contribution to the latter but such contribution as it did make came chiefly from taxation. In fact, there were no payments made under Henry V until 1417 when the first payments of the mise of 1416 were received. If we compare total liveries from the chamberlain of Chester to the exchequer in this and subsequent years with the liveries of taxation (Table XVII), we can see that 71% of the

75 Between 1403 and 1407 some of the mise was assigned at source to Cheshire captains for their troops serving in Wales. The percentage contribution has been calculated therefore from the lower figure.

revenue received from Cheshire sources at the exchequer in the reign of Henry V came from taxation.

## Table XVII. Liveries to the royal exchequer and liveries of taxation 1417–22

| Year | Total liveries | Liveries of taxation | Non taxation liveries |
|---|---|---|---|
| 1417 | £940 0s. 0d. | £833 6s. 8d. | £106 13s. 4d. |
| 1418 | £731 16s. 8d. | £666 13s. 4d. | £65 4s. 8d. |
| 1419 | £596 18s. 10d. | £333 6s. 8d. | £263 12s. 2d. |
| 1420 | £375 0s. 0d. | £333 6s. 8d. | £41 13s. 4d. |
| 1421 | £731 13s. 4d. | £333 6s. 8d. | £398 6s. 8d. |
| 1422 | £113 12s. 9d. | nil | £113 12s. 9d. |
| Total | £3489 1s. 7d. | £2500 0s. 0d. | £989 3s. 11d. |

Such revenues were ploughed into royal revenues as a whole for a multitude of uses. In 1419, however, it was specifically stated that the instalment of £333 6s. 8d. due on 11 November 1419 was to be paid to Sir John Savage for the wages of troops in his service as garrison at Calais.[76] In other words, as with the 1415 archer contingent from the county, revenues from Cheshire taxation were assigned directly to a captain from Cheshire. There is a precedent for this in the reign of Henry IV. From 1403 to 1408, part of the income from the fine was assigned before delivery into the prince's coffers. Contributions from certain townships were retained by those Cheshire captains involved in the Welsh wars to be used for payment of their troops. In 1403, for instance, Sir William Stanley and Sir John Pulle were paid £44 9s. 11d. out of the contribution of the hundred of Wirral for the wages of troops raised within that hundred for the recovery of Harlech.[77] It is likely that this use of Cheshire revenues was initiated, or at least encouraged,

76 SC 6/1303/2, m 4d. Sir John indented in Mar 1419 to serve at Calais for one year (E 101/70/3/631; E101/49/23, m 1).

77 SC 6/774/15, m 2.

by the king's grant of the revenues of the fine of 1403 to the prince, on condition that it should be spent on the defence of North Wales. Otherwise, save for one year, revenue from the 1401 mise and 1403 fine was not paid to the prince's receiver or household but rather ploughed back into Cheshire resources. This was necessary in those years when Cheshire revenues were being directed to the costs of defence of North Wales since regular Cheshire income was totally inadequate to cover such costs. The exceptional year was 1402, when a large total of £855 8s. 8d. was delivered by the chamberlain of Chester to the prince's central administration, although it is impossible to know exactly how much of this sum had been derived from the revenue of the first mise of 1401.[78]

Income from taxation therefore formed a crucial part of Cheshire revenues throughout the period. Its role, especially towards the end of the period, reflects a continuation of the use of the royal demesne before 1399, whereby the king and government concentrated their financial energies on the exploitation and development of rights of taxation rather than of landed revenues.[79] The success of such a policy in Cheshire, especially in the reign of Henry V, was another nail in the coffin of the demesne economy within the county.

78 SC 6/774/14, m 5d.

79 Wolffe, *Royal Demesne*, p. 70.

## CHAPTER 7

# *The Wider Context*

The demesne of the earl of Chester in the reigns of Henry IV and V cannot be viewed in isolation. The administration of the earl's lands was closely interwoven with the government of the county as a whole, as in the previous century.[1] In addition, the lands and revenues of the earldom were part of a much larger whole – the patrimony of the prince of Wales, or the royal demesne as a whole when there was no prince. The policies of prince and king towards their resources influenced the financial administration of their lands in Cheshire. The clearest expression was the use made of Cheshire revenues outside the county. The period from 1399 to 1422 was much affected by war, initially against the Welsh who rose up under Owain Glyndŵr, but also against Henry Hotspur, erstwhile justiciar of the county, who challenged the Lancastrian usurpation. Subsequently, the focus became France after the reopening of the Hundred Years War in the 1410s.

The crown's military demands were experienced by the whole realm but the impact on Cheshire was distinctive. The earldom already had a well-established tradition of military service at home and abroad, given its direct relationship with the crown. Furthermore, its geographical position gave it a special importance in any conflict with the Welsh. By examining the policies of prince and king towards the financial administration of the county, we can also learn much from how its resources, both money and men, were deployed in the military activities of the period. We can also see how war affected the relative importance of Cheshire within the princely or royal lands as a whole.

1 Sharp, 'Earldom and County of Chester', p. 302.

## Prelude

During the rule of the Black Prince receipts and expenses in the county both increased but so too did liveries of cash to his central officials. The chamberlain's accounts reveal that six or seven payments were generally made each year to the receiver-general of the prince at Westminster. The county was therefore making a larger contribution to the prince's revenues than it had been earlier in the fourteenth century. In 1302, liveries from Cheshire and Flintshire had totalled £1,000. In 1325–6 they reached £1,470, but in 1359–60, they had increased to £2,600.[2] The raising of troops in the county is in evidence from the reign of Edward I onwards.[3] In the early phases of the Hundred Years War, archer companies were raised, costs being supported out of both county and royal revenues.[4] Once the Black Prince was fully active in the wars, Cheshire began to play a notable role, as witnessed by entries in his Register. In 1346–7, for example, arrayed archers from Cheshire, clothed and equipped by the prince, received wages from the chamberlain up to the official muster centre or port of embarkation, from which point the crown took over responsibility for wages.[5] This continued to be

2 Sharp, 'Earldom and County of Chester', p. 146; B. E. Harris, 'The Palatinate 1301–1547', in B. E. Harris (ed.), *The Victoria History of the Counties of England: A History of the County of Chester*, ii (Oxford: Oxford University Press for the University of London Institute of Historical Research, 1979), p. 23. Even so, large amounts were paid out in annuities, fees and wages to the Black Prince's retinue, not all of whom had links with the county. £1,537 7s. 6d. was so dispersed in 1369 (P. J. Morgan, *War and Society in Medieval Cheshire, 1277–1403*, Chetham Society, 3rd ser., 34 (1987), p. 70).

3 Michael Prestwich, *Armies and Warfare in the Middle Ages: The English Experience* (New Haven CT and London: Yale University Press, 1996), pp. 127, 133–5.

4 Morgan, *War and Society*, pp. 45–7. In the 1330s and early 1340s, payments for their service in Scotland and France are included in the Wardrobe records, along with the rest of the king's armies. I am grateful for discussion with Dr Andrew Ayton on this and following points.

5 *Register of Edward the Black Prince Preserved in the Public Record Office*, 4 vols (London: HMSO, 1930–3), i. 13–14.

the case into the 1350s where the Black Prince deployed some local resources for the payment and clothing of his Cheshire troops.[6]

When the earldom was held by Richard II as king, little income came into central royal coffers from it. Cheshire revenues were largely dissipated at source in the payment of annuities and other ad-hoc rewards for faithful service. In the chamberlain's accounts which Margaret Sharp examined, liveries of money to the royal exchequer were generally low and, on occasion, non-existent (Table XVIII).[7]

### Table XVIII. Payments to the royal exchequer for a selection of years under Richard II

| Year | Amount | Reference |
|---|---|---|
| 1378 | nil | SC 6/772/11 |
| 1382 | £33 6s. 8d. | SC 6/772/16 |
| 1384 | £13 6s. 8d. | SC 6/772/17 |
| 1387 | £116 13s. 4d. | SC 6/773/1 |
| 1390 | £40 0s. 0d. | SC 6/773/6 |
| 1393 | nil | SC 6/773/10 |
| 1396 | £574 16s. 8d. | SC 6/774/4 |
| 1397 | £192 12s. 6d. | SC 6/774/6 |
| 1399 | £23 6s. 8d. | SC 6/774/10 |

The tendency towards the assignment of large sums of county revenues at source during Richard's reign undoubtedly extended the importance of the Chester exchequer as a spending rather than revenue-collecting department. Indeed, in two years of Richard's reign, expenses exceeded receipts. In 1384, there had been a 'superplusagium' (deficit) of £460 17s. 8¾d.[8]

6 H. J. Hewitt, *The Black Prince's Expedition of 1355–1357* (Manchester: Manchester University Press, 1958), p. 18.

7 Sharp, 'Earldom and County of Chester', p. 141. When they were made, they were generally paid to the Lower Exchequer.

8 SC 6/773/12 (1384), SC 6/774/10 (1399).

In 1399 the deficit was £143 12s. 11¾d. In the last years of the reign such liveries that were made to the royal exchequer were from arrears rather than current issues. It is important to note, however, especially in the context of a similar situation under Henry V, that income from the mise was sometimes paid directly into central royal coffers. In 1392, for instance, 1,000 marks (£666 13s. 4d.) from the mise was paid directly to the royal household to cover household expenses.[9]

Whilst Cheshire men, including Richard's famous bodyguard, were given annuities from the revenues of the county, their military service was funded by royal revenues as a whole. Although they were to be paid by the hands of the chamberlain of Chester, the sums involved were not to come from Cheshire revenues.[10] Similarly, when Richard took a company of 10 knights, 110 men-at-arms and 900 archers from the county to Ireland in 1399, they were paid by the royal exchequer in the same way as troops raised elsewhere in England, with moneys being paid to Robert Parys, the chamberlain.[11]

9 CHES 2/64, m 8 (8), *36 DKR*, p. 120. The payment was received by Robert Compnour, yeoman of the chamber, from Roger de Brescy, clerk of the then chamberlain John de Wodehouse.

10 J. L. Gillespie, 'Richard II's Cheshire Archers', *THSLC*, 125 (1974), 1–39, at p. 8.

11 E 403/562, m 16 (12 July 1399). For the names of some participants based on the evidence of protections in the Chester enrolments, see D. Biggs, *Three Armies in Britain: The Irish Campaign of Richard II and the Usurpation of Henry IV, 1397–99* (Leiden and Boston: Brill, 2006), pp. 69–71. For use of Cheshire troops under the duke of Surrey in advance of preparations for the king's Irish campaign, see Biggs, *Three Armies*, p. 41. Commissions of array for the recruitment of archers in the county were appointed on 24 Feb 1399 with a plan that the men should cross to Ireland from ports in the Wirral on 17 May (CHES 2/73, m 2 (10–15), *36 DKR*, p. 491). Richard had Cheshire troops in his company in his first expedition to Ireland in 1394 but details of numbers and payment have not been found (J. F. Lydon, 'Richard II's Expeditions to Ireland', *Journal of the Royal Society of Antiquaries of Ireland*, 93 (1963), 135–49, at p. 142).

## The new dynasty

At the accession of Henry IV, a reversion to the policy of the Black Prince might have been expected. Prince Henry needed to be provided with his own sources of income rather than be dependent upon the revenues of the crown as a whole.[12] Indeed, the Commons in Henry IV's first parliament petitioned for this very policy. They deplored the excessive and importunate alienations made by Richard II from the revenues of the earldom, claiming that if these were maintained, it could force the prince to be a burden on the revenues of the kingdom.[13] They petitioned that such alienations should be declared null and void so that the prince could enjoy the full benefit of his patrimony. The king agreed that if any unworthy recipients were identified, their grants should be annulled. Yet, as we saw in Chapter 5, whilst some Ricardian supporters lost their grants and annuities from Cheshire revenues, the deployment of county income for the purposes of patronage was continued. The new dynasty remained committed to the payment of some existing annuities as well as new ones, with the result that annuities continued to consume 40 to 50% of county revenues.

The Commons of Henry IV's first parliament had also petitioned that the 'great sums of gold and silver' doled out by Richard to the captains of his Cheshire bodyguard should be repaid. Henry's reply was that he understood they would not be able to repay the money given to them and that his will was therefore that they should 'do him service for a certain time at their own cost'.[14] This may be what happened in the summer of 1400 when Henry raised a large army of 1,771 men-at-arms and 11,314 archers for a short campaign into Scotland.[15] Before

12 Anne Curry, 'The Making of a Prince: The Finances of "the Young Lord Henry", 1386–1400', in Gwilym Dodd (ed.), *Henry V: New Interpretations* (Woodbridge: York Medieval Press, 2013), pp. 25–31.

13 *PROME*, viii. 68–9.

14 *PROME*, viii. 63.

15 Anne Curry, Adrian R. Bell, Andy King and David Simpkin, 'New Regime, New Army? Henry IV's Scottish Expedition of 1400', *English Historical Review*, 125 (2010), 1382–1413.

the end of June, there had been discussion between the king and the sheriff, Sir John Massey, about the provision of troops from the county. On 25 June, the king wrote from Pontefract to order Massey to send 60 men-at-arms and 500 archers to Newcastle to arrive on 12 July.[16] An enumeration of the companies sent from each of the hundreds of the county is extant, giving the names of 61 men-at-arms and the number of archers in each company, to a total of 488 archers.[17]

Although the royal letter of 25 June ended with the comment that when the Cheshire troops arrived in Newcastle, the king would arrange such wages as would content them, there is no record of any payment made to the Cheshire troops, either in the chamberlain's accounts or in the records of John Curson, treasurer of the royal household, who was otherwise responsible for campaign wages. It is therefore possible that the Cheshire troops represented the fulfilment of the king's will as expressed in response to the Commons' petition. This could also explain why in two cases within the list, a man-at-arms is noted as serving in the stead of another unable to participate, such a comment suggesting there was an obligation incumbent upon them to offer military service.

It is apparent that the king was keen to conciliate with the inhabitants of the county despite the involvement of some of them in a rising against him early in 1400. As the king began the preparations for his Scottish campaign, he had ordered a proclamation in the county that there should be a suspension in the execution of justice against those who had rebelled and that they would be treated according to how they conducted themselves in the meantime.[18] The success of this policy is

16 *Calendar of Signet Letters of Henry IV and Henry* V, ed. J. L. Kirby (London: HMSO, 1978), no. 9; CHES 2/74, m 9 (3), *36 DKR*, p. 332 (this calendar gives the figure erroneously as 300 archers).

17 E 101/42/29, printed in Morgan, *War and Society*, pp. 209–10. The distribution by hundred is as follows: Macclesfield 11 men-at-arms and 100 archers; Northwich 8+60; Nantwich 8+60; Bucklow 13+103; Broxton 8+60; Eddisbury 8+65; Wirral 6+40. There were two men-at-arms serving for themselves and in the name of another.

18 *PPC*, ii. 42, from BL, Cotton MS Vespasian F VII, f. 92.

revealed by the fact that eight of the men-at-arms had been amongst those excluded from the general pardon to Cheshire men implicated in the rising. That five of those who had been captains of Richard's Cheshire bodyguard participated in Henry IV's 1400 campaign is also a clear sign that the Lancastrians had been able to win over, or perhaps compel, the gentry of the county.

The Chester exchequer remained important, primarily as a spending department during the rule of Prince Henry. Expenses absorbed almost all income and remainders on the chamberlain's account were small. There were years, however, when moneys were transferred to the prince's central officials (Table XIX) and a distinct pattern can be detected.

With the exception of income received directly from the escheator for specific escheats, receipts from Cheshire were concentrated at the beginning of Henry's principate. Seventy per cent of the total which the earldom paid over the whole period was delivered to central officials between 1400 and 1403.[19] One single financial year, 1402–3, saw 32% of the total for the whole period so delivered. After this year, only 1408–9 saw a notable payment, constituting of 13% of the total render. Even the largest payment of the last years of the principate in 1412–13 constituted only 5% of the total paid over the whole period.

Although the amounts delivered from general county issues to the prince's central financial administration between 1400 and 1403 were higher than those paid to the exchequer under Richard II, they were considerably depleted when compared with liveries during the first half of the fourteenth century. The liveries of 1401 and 1402 included an unspecified amount from the first mise. Even though the first years of the principate saw the largest liveries from Cheshire, the contribution of the county to the prince's total revenues in this period was small

19 Note also payments in the 1400–1 account for the carriage of money from Chester to London, Tutbury (Staffs), Eccleshall (Staffs), Blakemere and elsewhere where the household of the lord is to be found (SC 6 774/13, m 7).

## Table XIX. The contribution of the county to the revenues of Prince Henry, 1399–1413

| Year | Account | Source | Destination | Amount |
|---|---|---|---|---|
| 1402 | SC 6/774/14 m. 5d | Chamberlain | John Attelbrigg (role unspecified) in London | £246 6s. 8d. |
| 1402 | SC 6/774/14 m. 5d | Chamberlain | John Spenser, prince's receiver-general | £3 6s. 8d. |
| 1404 | SC 6/791/7 m. 7 | Escheator (specific escheats) | John Wynter, prince's receiver-general | £43 13s. 4d. |
| 1405 | SC 6/791/10 m. 6d | Escheator (specific escheats) | John Wynter, prince's receiver-general | £66 13s. 4d. |
| 1406 | SC 6/792/1 m. 7d | Escheator (specific escheats) | John Wynter, prince's receiver-general | £33 6s. 8d. |
| 1408 | SC 6/792/3 m. 8d | Escheator (general issues) | Hugh Mortimer, prince's chamberlain | £84 19s. 6½d. |
| 1408 | SC 6/775/8 m. 1 | Chamberlain (fines in Flint for rebellion) | John Wodehouse, keeper of the prince's secret treasury | £266 13s. 4d. |
| 1409 | SC 6/792/5 m. 9 | Escheator (general issues) | Hugh Mortimer, prince's chamberlain | £71 3s. 9d. |
| 1402 | SC 6/774/14 m. 5d | Chamberlain | John Attelbrigg (role unspecified) in London | £246 6s. 8d. |
| 1402 | SC 6/774/14 m. 5d | Chamberlain | John Spenser, prince's receiver-general | £3 6s. 8d. |
| 1404 | SC 6/791/7 m. 7 | Escheator (specific escheats) | John Wynter, prince's receiver-general | £43 13s. 4d. |

| Year | Account | Source | Destination | Amount |
|---|---|---|---|---|
| 1405 | SC 6/791/10 m. 6d | Escheator (specific escheats) | John Wynter, prince's receiver-general | £66 13s. 4d. |
| 1406 | SC 6/792/1 m. 7d | Escheator (specific escheats) | John Wynter, prince's receiver-general | £33 6s. 8d. |
| 1408 | SC 6/792/3 m. 8d | Escheator (general issues) | Hugh Mortimer, prince's chamberlain | £84 19s. 6½d. |
| 1408 | SC 6/775/8 m. 1 | Chamberlain (fines in Flint for rebellion) | John Wodehouse, keeper of the prince's secret treasury | £266 13s. 4d. |
| 1409 | SC 6/792/5 m. 9 | Escheator (general issues) | Hugh Mortimer, prince's chamberlain | £71 3s. 9d. |
| 1410 | SC 6/792/7 m. 9d | Escheator (general issues) | Hugh Mortimer, prince's chamberlain | £48 12s. 9d. |
| 1411 | SC 6/775/12 m. 2d | Chamberlain (foreign expenses – fine of Welsh rebel) | Thomas Carnyka, prince's receiver-general | £40 0s. 0d. |
| 1412 | SC 6/792/9 m. 7d | Escheator (general issues) | Hugh Mortimer, prince's chamberlain | £37 6s. 8d. |
| 1412 | SC 6/775/14 m. 2d | Chamberlain (foreign expenses – fine for misjudgement) | Thomas Carnyka, keeper of the prince's wardrobe | £100 0s. 0d. |
| 1413 | SC6 792/10 m. 9d | Escheator (general issues) | Hugh Mortimer, prince's chamberlain | £46 11s. 8d. |

when compared with his other estates. For instance, John Waterton, the prince's receiver in the duchy of Cornwall, paid £2,720 between November 1402 and February 1404 to Simon Bache, treasurer of the prince's household. Waterton made a further payment of £200 between 20 July and 21 November 1403 to John Spenser as controller of the prince's household.[20]

The financing of the prince's involvement in the war in Wales proved a difficult problem. He could hardly be expected to 'live of his own' for the support of his military activities and payment of his retinues in this war, although that was what his father seems to have expected at the outset of the Welsh wars. In 1401, the prince was reminded that 'the onus of payment for the siege of Conway lay on him because he held the castle and lordship in fee'.[21] The prince's household accounts in these years undoubtedly reveal a very narrow margin between his receipts and expenses. Between April and July 1403, his income totalled £7,174 6s. 8d. but out of this he had to meet expenses totalling £7,153 5s. 3¾d.[22] Not surprisingly, royal revenues had to be increasingly directed to his use. For instance, between 17 April and 18 July 1403, the royal treasurer contributed £5,323 6s. 8d., significantly more than the £1,851 from the prince's own resources.[23] That said, the prince's complaints of being kept short of money were frequent.[24]

The prince's own revenues, especially of areas as close to Wales as Cheshire, might be expected to play a major part in the financing of his war effort. Yet, as we have seen from

20 E 101/404/23.

21 W. R. M. Griffiths, 'Prince Henry, Wales, and the Royal Exchequer, 1400–14', *Bulletin of the Board of Celtic Studies*, 32 (1985), 202–15, at p. 204.

22 E 101/404/24, ff. 2, 12v.

23 E 101/404/24, f. 2. See also *PPC* ii. 96–7, *Issues of the Exchequer: Being a Collection of Payments made out of His Majesty's Revenue, from King Henry III to King Henry VI Inclusive*, ed. Frederick Devon, Record Commission (London: John Murray, 1837), pp. 283, 314, 374.

24 In May 1403 he wrote to his father, revealing how he had been forced to pawn his 'petits joyaulx' to pay his troops in Wales, and also how food for horses was in short supply in Wales, forcing him to order his men to carry oats with them (*PPC*, ii. 62–3).

Table XIX, the chamberlain made no direct contribution from general county revenues to the prince's central financial officers after 1402–3. All payments from 1404 onwards were from specific sources of income, such as specific escheats or fines. The lack of liveries from general county revenues is explained by the decision of the prince's council to tap county revenues at source and redirect them to the financing of the defence of North Wales without the need for them to pass through Prince Henry's central financial organisation. Behind this decision, as we shall see, lay the total collapse of the prince's revenues in his principality of Wales.

The first years of the reign of Henry IV had already witnessed a multiplicity of foreign expenses taken out of county revenues.[25] The Chester exchequer already bore the cost of works and victualling at the castles of Chester, Flint and Rhuddlan and also the garrisons held at Chester and Flint.[26] The impact of rebellion against Henry IV in 1400 is immediately apparent in the chamberlain's account for the first year of the new reign. After the balance of the account had been struck, a further allowance of £15 8s. 7d., was made to the sheriff, Sir John Massey of Puddington and other troops in Chester Castle during January 1400 because of fears of the action of rebels in North Wales and Cheshire.[27]

The growing restlessness in Wales even before the formal revolt of Glyndŵr is also in evidence. At Chester, we see the garrison of eight men-at-arms and 35 archers boosted by a further 26 men 'during the time of the insurrection of the Welsh'.[28] Sir John Massey was also recompensed out of Cheshire revenues for victuals he purchased for the castle of

25 The term 'expensa forinseca' ('foreign expenses') was used on account rolls to indicate expenses other than those incurred in running a particular unit or organisation.

26 SC 6/774/11, mm 2d, 6. We also see a very small expenditure on works at Beeston but no victualling is in evidence for that castle.

27 SC 6/774/11, m 3d.

28 SC 6/774/11, m 2d. Flint's company of 24 archers under Robert de Massey was boosted by 4 men-at-arms and eight archers.

Conway.[29] Six quarters of wheat were purchased by the order of the prince's council at Chester to be milled and made into bread to be sent to the king and his army in North Wales.[30] Cheshire revenues were used to cover the costs of wine sent to Prince Henry when he was in North Wales in October 1400.[31] They were even deployed for the costs of the audit of ministers' accounts in South Wales in February 1401, a sign that collection of revenues from the principality were already in jeopardy.[32] It is clear, too, that there was much ongoing discussion by the officers of the prince concerning his financial position. An allowance of £30 0s. 11½d. from Cheshire revenues was made for the costs of Master William Feriby, chancellor of the prince, and to Robert Parys, his chamberlain in North Wales, whilst they pursued with the king the expenses of the prince in the autumn of 1400 concerning the governance of the principality of Wales.[33]

Chester was well placed for receiving reports on what was happening in Wales. The chamberlain's accounts record expenditure on messengers sent to the king and prince, in

29 SC 6/774/11, m 4d. Sir John Massey did not succeed in holding Conway and gave himself up to the king's mercy for its loss, but Cheshire knights and gentry came to the prince to act as guarantors (see also the various letters of the prince in *Anglo-Norman Letters and Petitions from All Souls' MS 182*, ed. M. Dominica Legge, Anglo-Norman Text Society, 3 (Oxford, 1941), no. 247). It was presumably as a result of this failure that he lost his post as sheriff. Chester was used for provisioning castles in North Wales from Flint to Aberystwyth, Bristol for provisioning from Aberystwyth to Kidwelly, and border towns such as Worcester for the castles of east Wales (R. R. Davies, *The Revolt of Owain Glyn Dŵr* (Oxford: Oxford University Press, 1995), p. 255).

30 SC 6/774, m 3d. This sum was disallowed for defect of a warrant.

31 SC 6/774/11, m 4d. There are various other entries which suggest that, at this point, Chester Castle had quite a wine cellar, in part because of the prise of wine coming into the port of Chester, although a half cask had 'gone off' ('putrefactum est') and a full barrel had been damaged in storage.

32 SC 6/774/11, m 3d.

33 SC 6/774/11, m 3d.

London and elsewhere, with news.[34] We can also see small payments made to individuals going to Machynlleth and Harlech in the service of the prince who were probably acting as spies: all have names indicating they were Welsh speakers.[35] Chester was also a base from which supplies could be sent to Wales. In 1401, victuals were sent by sea from Chester both to Caernarvon and Harlech.[36] Victuals were also purchased in Chester and sent to Bala for the prince and his army for a summer campaign.[37] Hotspur, as justiciar of Chester and North Wales, was funded out of Cheshire revenues to buy victuals for himself and his company whilst holding sessions in North Wales in April and May.[38] In the following year, 1402, we see further payments from Cheshire revenues for munitions (including guns) and food sent to Conway, Harlech and Criccieth castles.[39] Troops in Conway Castle and town as well as Harlech were already receiving some pay from the chamberlain of Chester.[40] In May, a naval force of over 70 left from Cheshire to the North Welsh castles and in June a force of Cheshire archers and men at arms were sent to Denbigh.[41] Tents were carried from Chester to Bridgnorth in June 1402 as the prince made his way

34 See, for instance, SC 6/774/13, m 7.
35 SC 6/774/14, m 5d.
36 SC 6/774/13, m 3d. The delivery at Harlech gave rise to a marginal note by the auditors to enquire whether the grain had been received by William Curteys, one of the prince's yeomen.
37 SC 6 774/13, m 3d. A force of over 500 was organised at Chester and sent via Bala to relieve Harlech (Davies, *Revolt of Owain Glyndŵr*, p. 105). It was not always easy for the prince's officers to gain supplies. An undated letter from the prince orders the arrest of R. Huls and his imprisonment in Chester Castle for having incited people not to sell to the prince's purveyors because they offered less than the market price (*Anglo-Norman Letters and Petitions*, no. 258).
38 SC 6/774/13, m 4d.
39 This is also seen from a stock account at the end of the chamberlain's account for 1401–2 which shows receipts of munitions from London for sending on into Wales (SC 6/774/14, m 6d).
40 SC 6/774/14, mm 2d–5d. The chamberlain had distributed 16 bows and two sheaves of arrows to members of the prince's household.
41 Davies, *Revolt of Owain Glyn Dŵr*, p. 108, citing SC 6/1185/4, E 101/43/9.

through Shropshire into Wales for an action against Glyndŵr.[42] Significantly, disruption in North Wales had left Robert Parys unable to pay officials and the captain of Caernarvon, and he was given a payment of £81 14s. 9d. to support his costs.[43]

By the summer of 1402, therefore, Cheshire revenues were subsidising the cost of victuals and munitions in several North Welsh castles, with Chester Castle being used to store provisions for campaigns in North Wales.[44] Such payments for the castles were generally accounted as allowances, deducted after the balance of the account had been calculated rather than as a distinct category in the discharge. However, these small casual payments may have encouraged the decision to use Cheshire revenues further.

An undated ordinance of the royal council, drawn up sometime between 1401 and 1403, demonstrates the initial intention regarding the financing of Welsh defences.[45] Here the total cost of the garrisons of the Welsh castles was estimated at £2,421 3s. 4d. per annum, whilst the sole available revenue amounted to only £1,333 6s. 8d. per annum, leaving a deficit of £1,087 16s. 8d. under this head alone. In this ordinance, only the costs of the defence of the castles of Flint and Rhuddlan were to be borne by the issues of Cheshire and Flintshire. It was presumably hoped that the cost of the remaining castles could continue to be met out of the revenues of their locality. Denbigh and Beaumaris was maintained by Henry Percy (Hotspur) until he rebelled.[46] However, as the rebels gained ground in Wales, the prince's administrative structure therein collapsed and such charges could not be met out of local revenues. The financial situation now appeared desperate. This is made clear in a valor which covered all of the prince's lands, and which is given in

42 SC 6/774/14, m 3d.

43 SC 6/774/14, m 4d.

44 SC 6/774/14, m 3d–4d; James Hamilton Wylie, *History of England under Henry the Fourth*, 4 vols (London: Longmans, Green, 1884–98), i. 284.

45 *PPC*, ii. 64–7; Wylie, *Henry IV*, i. 341. The prince was appointed as royal lieutenant in the Welsh marches on 7 Mar 1403.

46 Wylie, *Henry IV*, i. 342–3.

Appendix VI.[47] This valor is undated but, as we shall see, seems to post-date the rebellion of Hotspur.

Although it was calculated in the valor that the prince held lands with a maximum annual gross value of £10,758 12s. 9¼d., administrative costs and annuities immediately consumed £2,742 10s. 1¾d. In addition, the prince could no longer command any income whatsoever from his lands in North Wales, South Wales and Flintshire. This reduced his total potential annual income by a further £5,613 17s. 6d. Only £2,402 7s. 1½d. remained, out of which he was expected to meet the usual expenses of his household and wardrobe and the maintenance of his castles and manors in England, as well as ensure the adequate defence of his castles and towns in the principality of Wales. This would clearly be impossible. The same valor stated that the cost of garrisoning and victualling these same castles was at least £2,903 per annum. Thus the prince was already £500 12s. 10½d. in the red before he even began to meet his regular expenses. His estate revenues alone, therefore, could not meet the charges incumbent upon him in these years.

With the net value of Cheshire given on this valor as £425 1s. 5d., it would seem ridiculous that any attempt should be made to meet these Welsh expenses out of county revenues. Yet another valor of the county alone did precisely that. This valor was compiled from the accounts of the various accounting officials within the county for the financial year 1402–3 and is given below as Appendix V.[48] In this valor, the net value of Cheshire revenues was totalled (using potential values for the accounting year ending at Michaelmas 1403), this time at £798 4s. 0d. Then followed detail of expenses intended to be met out of this sum. Significantly, the first item placed on the discharge side of this valor was the wages of the garrisons of certain towns and castles in North Wales at the same daily, weekly and annual rates as in the valor of all of the prince's lands. On the Cheshire valor, the costs of the garrisons of Chester, Rhuddlan, Flint,

47 SC 11/862.

48 SC 11/904. For further discussion see pp. 87, 115.

Beaumaris, Caernarvon town and castle, and Conway town and castle were itemised. The valor of the whole of the prince's lands omitted Chester but also included the castles of Harlech, Aberystwyth and Cardigan.

In addition, the Cheshire valor notes that the usual county expenses had to be met as well as the fees of the constables of Caernarvon, Beaumaris and Rhuddlan at £40 per annum each, and the cost of munitions at £10 per annum. Such fees were said to be 'newly assigned on the issues of the receipt of the Chester exchequer' ('super exitum recepte scaccarii Cestrie de novo assignata'), and munitions were to be purchased 'during the time of the war' ('durantibus guerris'). On the Cheshire valor, expenses directly related to the Welsh wars came to £1,553 7s. 4d. of a total discharge of £2,284 7s. 4d. which was described as 'the total burden falling on the Chester exchequer per annum during the wars and the payments of wages of men-at-arms and archers' ('summa totalis oneris scaccario Cestrie incumbentis per annum durantibus guerris et solucionibus vadiorum hominum ad arma et sagittariorum'). If all these expenses were met out of demesne revenues alone, then the Cheshire exchequer would be seriously in the red to the extent of £1,486 3s. 4d. per annum. Yet Welsh expenses to a total of £1,342 0s. 6¾d. had ostensibly been paid out by the Chester exchequer during the accounting year of 1402 to 1403.[49]

How, then, did this use of Cheshire revenues come about and how was it possible to meet such expenses when demesne revenues were so inadequate? The first question would be easier to answer if the valor of the whole of the prince's lands was dated, in order to establish its relationship with the Cheshire valor. The general valor was certainly drawn up sometime between October 1403 and September 1406, the period when we know from the chamberlain of Chester's accounts that no income was received from the prince's demesnes in Flintshire due to rebellion.[50] It was certainly drawn up after the death of Hotspur at the battle of Shrewsbury on 21 July 1403 since

49 SC 6/774/15.
50 SC 6/775/3, m 1; SC 6/775/4, m 1; SC 6/775/5, m 1.

he had previously been held responsible for the defence of Beaumaris and Denbigh. Prince Henry had been appointed royal lieutenant in Wales from 1 April 1403, but his wounding at Shrewsbury put him out of action until the summer of 1404.[51] In the meantime, Edward, duke of York, was appointed to South Wales and the earl of Warwick to Brecon.[52]

We might expect some connection between the general valor and the Cheshire valor which was drawn up after the end of the accounting year 1402–3, after, or at the same time, as the writing up of that year's account, which we would expect to have occurred between December 1403 and March 1404. However, there seems to be no connection between the different net values of Cheshire given on these two valors. I have been unable to ascertain how the values for Cheshire in the general valor were calculated. It is possible, in the light of our knowledge of the size and use of Cheshire resources, that the general valor was drawn up during the first months of the accounting year of 1403–4 (i.e. October 1403 to December 1403), but taking Cheshire values from the account of 1401–2, since the 1402–3 account would still be in the process of compilation. At the point – perhaps at the end of 1403 – that it was decided to meet at least half of Welsh military expenses out of Cheshire funds, a new up-to-date county valor was therefore drawn up.

What can have occasioned this decision? The idea of diverting such large amounts out of Cheshire revenues was only made feasible by the availability of additional revenue in the form of taxation. There was still some anticipated income from the mise of 1401 which had granted 3,000 marks to be collected by the end of 1404. This brought in over £600 in 1403 and an anticipated £300 in 1404. But more significant was the knowledge of new income from a fine of 3,000 marks, collectable from the inhabitants of the county over the next years in return for a pardon for their involvement in Hotspur's rebellion. This fine was announced on 3 November

51 Griffiths, 'Prince Henry, Wales, and the Royal Exchequer', p. 203.

52 Davies, *Revolt of Owain Glyn Dŵr*, pp. 113–14.

1403,[53] although it was not until August 1404 that Henry IV formally granted the revenue of this fine to the prince of Wales, specifically to spend upon the defence of Denbigh and other castles in North Wales.[54] The citizens of Chester were given the choice in November 1403 of whether to pay their share of the fine in cash or instead to supply shipping and victuals for the proposed attempt to recover Beaumaris.[55] By the end of the year they had decided to go for the second option. On 31 December 1403, Robert Castell appeared before the vice chamberlain, Roger Brescy, to testify to the fulfilment of the conditions of the charter for Chester touching the rescue of Beaumaris, after which the charter was delivered to the mayor, the city sheriffs and John Eulowe, citizen.[56]

This is another indication of discussions going on in the last months of 1403 and into 1404, adding to the likelihood that the general valor belongs to that period, with the Cheshire valor being made soon after.[57] In this scenario, Henry IV's decision in August 1404 to grant the fine for the 1403 revolt to his son was made in the light of the Cheshire valor, where it had been clearly demonstrated that the prince's landed resources in the county were inadequate to support such costs.[58] Given

53 *CPR 1401–5*, p. 331; CHES 2/77, m 3 (1), *36 DKR*, p. 103.

54 *CPR 1401–5*, p. 412; *PPC*, i. 236. For its first accounting by the chamberlains see SC 6/775/4, m 2.

55 CHES 2/77, m 3 (2), *36 DKR*, p. 103. In Oct 1403, a barge manned with 60 men had been sent to patrol the coastline of Anglesey and support the castle of Beaumaris (SC 6/774/15, m 4, cited in Davies, *Revolt of Owain Glyndŵr*, p. 254).

56 CHES 2/77, m 3 (4), *36 DKR*, p. 103. See also CALS, Chester Corporation Charters CH 24 cited in Morgan, *War and Society*, p. 225 n. 183.

57 Rhyddian Griffiths also argued for a date of around Feb 1404 for the general valor ('Prince Henry, Wales, and the Royal Exchequer, 1400–14', p. 205).

58 *CPR 1401–5*, p. 412, *PPC*, ii. 236. There is an outside possibility that the general valor, SC 11/862, was drawn up as late as 1406, in the last year before Flintshire demesne revenue became collectable once more. On this valor, there was no charge for the victualling of the castles of Flint and Rhuddlan on the grounds that their neighbourhood was in peace although this was described as being 'late in the day'. Doubtless

that the prince was out of action for around a year after being wounded at Shrewsbury, the suggestions on the dating of the valors would suppose that they were created at the order of the king, or at least the council of the prince, and that the latter's own involvement in discussions may have been minimal. In the summer of 1404, the chamberlain, John Trevor, decided to defect to Glyndŵr. These were most challenging times but there were real efforts towards a solution, but perhaps one with which Trevor did not agree.

The contribution of the fine, however, enabled the wages of the garrisons of Chester, Flint, Rhuddlan, Caernarvon town and castle, and Conway town and castle to be met regularly out of Chester revenues. In some years, the wages of the garrisons of Harlech, Denbigh and Beaumaris were also so paid. By 1405, the fees of the constables of the castles of Caernarvon, Beaumaris, Conway, Rhuddlan and Flint were also being met out of Cheshire revenues.[59] Officials responsible for the victualling and supervision of repairs in the North Welsh castles and towns were paid out of Cheshire revenues between the accounting years 1403–4 and 1406–7.[60] Many miscellaneous payments were also made, such as those to the master gunners in the expedition to recover Beaumaris in 1406.[61]

The move was financial as well as administrative. Cheshire revenues were not simply fulfilling the previous function of North Welsh revenues. The Chester exchequer was also taking over the function of the Caernarvon exchequer and of various receiverships in North Wales, even if only during the temporary collapse of authority in the principality. It was stated even in the account for 1402–3, for instance, that the fee of the constable of Beaumaris was generally paid by the receiver of Anglesey but

the date of the valor could be established more firmly by a study of the accounts of the other lordships held by Prince Henry.

59 SC 6/775/4, m 3d. For general discussion on the garrisons in Wales in these years, see W. R. M. Griffiths, 'Prince Henry's War: Armies, Garrisons and Supply during the Glyndwr Rising', *Bulletin of the Board of Celtic Studies*, 34 (1987), 165–73.

60 SC 6/774/15, m 4 to SC 6/775/5, m 4.

61 SC 6/774/15, mm 3d–4d.

that, owing to the rebellion, it had to be paid by the chamberlain of Chester.[62] As we have seen, in 1402 £81 14s. 9d. had already been paid by the chamberlain of Chester to Robert Parys, previously chamberlain of North Wales, to cover the costs of arrears and current issues of the fees of officers and to wipe off the deficit ('superplusagium') of his last account.[63] However, in the following year, it was seen that Parys owed money from the last years of the fourteenth century when he had been the receiver of Bromfield. The council therefore advised that his 'superplusagium' as chamberlain of North Wales should be deducted from this debt in preference to more money being paid to him out of Cheshire revenues.[64]

To divert Cheshire revenues to the costs of the Welsh wars was a sensible and convenient system. It would have wasted valuable time and effort to have sent Cheshire issues to London only to have them redirected to North Wales. It was a natural development out of the fact that Chester was the military headquarters of Prince Henry.[65] The system can only have increased the standing of the Chester exchequer now that it was directly involved, indeed was indispensable, in the prince's war effort.

The demands of the Welsh wars, however, placed a considerable burden upon the finances of the county. Without the contribution of the mise and fine, expenses would have exceeded receipts in four years between 1401 and 1407. But with the mise, this was only the case in two years, 1404 and 1406. Taxation was not the only means by which the prince and his council hoped to meet such high expenses out of Cheshire receipts. From 1403 to 1408 there was a substantial increase in demesne revenues occasioned by a conscious move towards the goal of meeting Welsh costs. In addition, greater attention was paid to the collection of arrears. The latter had to be collected to help meet the increased expenses. If they were not met, then

62 SC 6/774/15, m 4d.

63 SC 6/774/14, mm 3d–4d.

64 SC 6/774/15, m 5d, 791/6, m 10.

65 See Wylie, *Henry IV*, i. 285.

the county would be running at an even greater loss. It is no coincidence, therefore, that the method of accounting in the county underwent change between 1402 and 1405, as we saw in Chapter 2. The newly adopted Westminster form regarded arrears as cash in hand, thereby providing a clear picture of the cumulative total of resources available for disbursement in Wales.

Despite such provision, there was still not enough revenue to meet the Welsh costs. Cheshire revenues alone were inadequate. We know that the constables of Caernarvon paid £561 1s. 2½d. to their captains and archers between 1405 and 1407. They recovered £478 18s. 3½d. from Chester, leaving £82 12s. 11d. still to be found.[66] In 1405, £133 6s. 8d. was paid into the Chester exchequer by John Waterton, keeper of the prince's secret treasury. This sum was to be used to help with the payment of garrisons in North Wales and was paid into the Chester exchequer by Robert Castell, who appears to have been acting as paymaster for the prince's troops.[67] In 1409, Gilbert Talbot, who had been appointed justiciar of the county after Hotspur's death and who was much involved in the Welsh wars, borrowed £60 from the sheriffs of the city of Chester to pay for the victualling of Harlech.[68]

Cheshire revenues were rarely used, it would seem, to pay the wages of those Cheshire men involved in the Welsh wars, presumably because it was realised that they would be totally inadequate if this charge was made. In an expedition to North Wales in the spring of 1403, Cheshire captains and their retinues were paid out of the prince's household funds by John Spenser, its controller.[69] Cheshire men, and especially annuitants, were prominent in the expedition later in the same year to Harlech: their wages were paid in the same way as earlier.[70] An exception

66 E 101/43/39. See also Wylie, *Henry IV*, ii. 172.

67 SC 6/775/4, m 2.

68 SC 6/792/5, m 1.

69 E 101/404/24, f. 2 sq. For use of Cheshire men see Griffiths, 'Prince Henry's War: Armies, Garrisons and Supply', p. 167.

70 E 101/404/24, ff. 11–12v. See also E 101/405/1.

was the part financing in January 1406 of the sheriff, John Mainwaring's expedition to reduce Anglesey to royal obedience when £290 11s. 0d. was given from Cheshire revenues alongside £450 9s. 0d. already given to them by the prince.[71] Mainwaring was subsequently appointed captain of the island.[72] Sir John Pulle was also paid out of Cheshire revenues to keep the sea between Anglesey and Ireland.[73]

The diversion of Cheshire revenues to the costs of Welsh defences was regarded as only a temporary measure. The prince's council hoped to meet the expenses for the defence of North Wales out of Welsh revenues as soon as possible. In the audit of the account for the 1404–5 financial year, when an increasing number of constables of Welsh castles were taking their fees from Cheshire revenues, we find a marginal note on the chamberlain's account recommending 'to speak about these fees as they should be assigned on divers lordships in Wales for their safe keeping' ('loquendum pro istis feodis quia assignanda super diversa dominia infra Wallia pro salva custodia ibidem').[74] In the following year we should note that part of the money for the expedition to Anglesey, including the £100 paid to Mainwaring as captain of the island, was initially disallowed on the chamberlain's account as it was hoped to meet such costs out of the revenues of Anglesey once royal control had been established therein.[75]

By the financial year 1406–7 assignment of Cheshire revenues to Welsh expenses was declining. Sir John Bolde, as constable of Conway, continued to received part of his fee from the chamberlain of Chester but a further £60 due to him was paid by the bailiff of the town of Conway from the latter's issues.[76] From Michaelmas 1411, Bolde was ordered to take

71 SC 6/775/4, m 3d; Davies, *Revolt of Owain Glyn Dŵr*, p. 123. See also Glyn Roberts, 'The Anglesey Submissions of 1406', *Bulletin of the Board of Celtic Studies*, 15 (1952–4), 39–61.

72 SC 6/1216/2, m 6.

73 SC 6/775/5, m 3d.

74 SC 6/775/5 m 3d.

75 SC 6/ 775/5, m 4d.

76 SC 6/775/9, m 3d.

all of his fee from the issues of the town of Conway.[77] In the Chester chamberlain's account of 1409–10, only the garrison of Conway town and of the castles of Rhuddlan and Flint were being paid out of Cheshire revenues.[78] At the beginning of the new reign only the regular expenses of the garrisons of Chester, Flint and Rhuddlan were being so met, a return to the situation in 1399–1400.[79]

Cheshire revenues were severely over-assigned, especially once there was no further income from the fine. Indeed, expenses exceeded receipts in three, and possibly four, of the last years of the reign of Henry IV, although this was not simply due to Welsh expenses. By 1406–7, demesne revenues had been exploited as far as they could be. From 1407 there was a sharp decline in Macclesfield demesne revenues. From 1409 the revenues of the Cheshire demesnes as well as of the sheriff and escheator also began to decline. This could also be interpreted as the result of a lower level of pressure on and interest in the finances of the county as the prince's revenues in Wales were recovered.

The payment of regular expenses had also suffered in the years when the Welsh expenses were high. As we saw in Chapter 5, from 1404 to 1406, payments of annuities were allowed to fall into arrears to help keep higher levels of funds which could be applied to the war. Although there was some recovery in subsequent years, the backlog was not cleared until 1412 when the Welsh crisis was virtually at an end. Had the grave situation in Wales persisted for any longer than it did, more serious problems would surely have arisen for Cheshire finances.

From 1407, income was once more received from the prince's demesne in Flintshire. In the last three years of the reign of Henry IV such income increased substantially and helped towards a partial recuperation of finances now that income from the Cheshire demesnes was falling. In addition, further income was received from the inhabitants of Flintshire in fines

77 SC 6/775/14, m 2d.
78 SC 6/775/11, m 2d.
79 SC 6/775/15, m 2d.

for their participation in Glyndŵr's rebellion although much of the amount so received was assigned to other outlets. In 1407, Gilbert Talbot and his troops were paid £1,179 7s. 3d. for holding sessions in Flint and Denbigh.[80] In the following year, £266 13s. 4d. of the fines collected in Flintshire were paid directly to John Wodehouse, keeper of the prince's secret treasury, and a further £229 assigned to the defence of Denbigh castle.[81] In fact only £115 2s. 1d. was ever paid into the Chester exchequer from the Flintshire fines.[82]

Payments to the prince's household could be recommenced in the last years of the reign of his father although they were much smaller than at the opening of the reign. It is perhaps surprising that receipts by the prince from the palatinate were so small in these later years. We might have expected that as Prince Henry involved himself further in central government, especially from December 1409 to November 1411 when he held control of the royal council, that he might have found it necessary to lean more heavily on his landed resources to finance his political and military activities. Whilst in control of the government he most certainly wished to appear as a reformer in terms of royal finances which were in a bad state, proposing cuts to the costs of the royal household but also raising loans at a higher level.[83]

The possible redirection of county revenues back to the prince's household may have been the purpose behind the proposed visit of his council to Chester in August 1410, led by

80 SC 6/775/7m. 2. In addition, £33 6s. 8d. was paid to Elizabeth, countess of Salisbury, from the fines of rebels in her lordships in Flintshire.

81 SC 6/775/8, m 1.

82 SC 6/775/12, m 1. Wylie, *Henry IV*, ii. 421, refers to similar fines in Anglesey levied in Nov 1406. He claims that £537 7s. 0d. was paid from this source to the needy treasury of the prince at Chester. I have found no record of this sum being received in the Chester exchequer.

83 Anne Curry, *Henry V: Playboy Prince to Warrior King* (London: Allen Lane, 2015), pp. 22–3; Anthony Steel, *The Receipt of the Exchequer 1377–1485* (Cambridge: Cambridge University Press, 1954), pp. 100–1.

Thomas Tykhull, the steward of the prince's lands.[84] However, it is clear that Cheshire revenues were not in an adequately healthy state to bear further exploitation, and it was thought preferable first to clear up the backlog of regular Cheshire expenses once the county's revenues ceased to be needed to support the Welsh wars.

In the autumn of 1411, however, the prince chose to support some of the costs of sending troops to France under his friend Thomas Fitzalan, earl of Arundel from Cheshire-accounted revenues.[85] The earl already held a large annuity from county revenues which had been granted to him in February 1408 in return for an indenture for service of the prince in peace and war.[86] The expedition, which arrived in France in early October 1411, was sent to support Duke John the Fearless at the behest of the prince, who saw a Burgundian alliance as the best means of advancing English interests in France. In the following year, the king was to turn instead to supporting the Armagnac party. It may therefore have been politic, if not essential, for Prince Henry to use his own landed resources to pay the initial wages of Arundel's troops, who are thought to have numbered 200 men-at-arms and 800 archers, although Duke John is also known to have paid for part of their service.[87] The chamberlain's account suggests that loans from the bishop of Coventry and Lichfield (100 marks) and the abbot of Chester (£50), made in late August 1411, now repaid to their lenders at the Chester exchequer, had offered a way of finding cash to pay Arundel's troops.

The prince was in the political wilderness from November 1411 to his father's death. This forced him to rely more upon income from his own estates. More money was delivered from

84 SC 6/775/11, m 2d.

85 SC 6/775/12, m 2d; J. A. Tuck, 'The Earl of Arundel's Expedition to France, 1411', in Gwilym Dodd and Douglas Biggs (eds), *The Reign of Henry IV: Rebellion and Survival, 1403–1413* (Woodbridge: York Medieval Press, 2008), pp. 228–40.

86 CHES 2/80, m 3 (2), *36 DKR*, p. 9.

87 Tuck, 'Earl of Arundel's Expedition', pp. 232, 234.

Cheshire revenues to his central officials in the last year of Henry IV's reign than between 1409 and 1412, although the sums were small, and as noted earlier, constituted only 5% of the revenue sent to the prince over the whole period of his rule.

Overall, therefore, save for a brief interlude occasioned by the loss of income in the principality of Wales, the trend between 1399 and 1422 as a whole was to re-establish the Chester exchequer primarily as a spending department, creating little surplus. Save for the first years of the reign, there was relatively little direct financial return from the county to the prince, and a growing indifference towards the exploitation of demesne revenues. Significantly large and direct financial return from the county had only proved possible in the years of irregular income, especially that generated by taxation.

## The reign of Henry V

Although the structure of the financial administration of the earldom was not affected by the accession of Henry V, it would be a mistake not to expect changes in the importance of the palatinate and its revenues. As king, Henry had all of the resources of the crown at his disposal, including the vast Lancastrian inheritance, alongside the lands he had held as prince. Any revenues which Cheshire could provide would constitute a much smaller proportion of his assets as a whole. Whilst the revenues and importance of the county had been temporarily boosted during the Welsh wars, the financial significance of the county was eroded once it was part of a much greater whole.

With respect to administrative changes after Henry's accession, we have seen that the tendency was for the county to be left to its own devices under the firm hand of an able chamberlain. During Henry V's reign, relatively little contact occurred between the royal and Chester exchequers. As we shall see, such payments that were made from county revenues to the royal exchequer were limited almost completely to the years in which there was irregular income from taxation.

As the annual summaries of the chamberlain's accounts in Appendix II (m) show, for the first four years of the reign no payment was made to the royal exchequer. The preference was to assign Cheshire revenues at source. In these years, the balance at the end of the chamberlain's account was kept small not only because of a decline in demesne revenues but also because of an intentional increase in the discharge so that it consumed all of the charge. This increase was generated by paying the arrears of annuities. The chamberlain's account thus began to reflect the same tendency towards the simplification in financial administration as seen in some of the manorial units, such as Northwich, Drakelow and the Dee Mills, where the discharge was designed to consume the entire charge.[88] The Chester exchequer was once again important as a spending department since most revenues were disbursed in fees, annuities and foreign expenses. For instance, in 1413 £20 was paid to Thomas Marchant, receiver of Dover Castle, in compensation for the money he had paid to a group which had included the chamberlain William Troutbeck on its way to Sandwich to escort an esquire of the duke of Burgundy.[89]

Such assignment was only possible when, as now, revenues and demesne expenses were fossilised. The balance of each year's account, at least if arrears were not taken into consideration, would be reasonably constant and could be assigned to annuities and foreign expenses in advance and on a regular basis. If in any year there was irregular income then it would be more likely for such to be delivered to the central financial organisation for disbursement, as in the case of taxation. We can see that this is precisely what happened in the case of Cheshire revenues. Between 1417 and 1422, money was transferred to the royal exchequer every year. The change was caused by the collection of the mise granted in 1416.

Overall, 71% of Cheshire's contribution to royal revenues between 1417 and 1422 came from taxation, although the proportion varied year on year (Table VII). As this table

88 See above p. 181.
89 SC 6/775/15, m 2d.

also shows, between 1417 to 1420 demesne revenues only contributed 20% to 30% of the annual render to the royal exchequer but in 1421 this proportion increased to 55%. In 1422, a delivery of £113 12s. 9d. was made to royal funds out of demesne revenues alone. Such a payment in a year when there was no regular income from taxation in the county may imply a change in policy towards the end of Henry's reign. It is possible also that there was a conscious policy to increase the revenues by decreasing the discharge side of the account. There is some suggestion, for instance, that annuities were being allowed to decline by not making a new grant after the death of their holder.

All of the issues delivered to the royal exchequer in 1422 were immediately paid out in fees and pensions.[90] Payments from this source were most frequently made to men who had held household offices under Henry as prince of Wales, as for instance to John Spenser in 1417, 1419 and 1421.[91] Further payments were made to men with Cheshire connections, often as supplements to their regular fees. Roger Horton, justice of the king's bench, received various additional sums from the Chester exchequer for the performance of this office.[92] He had served as sergeant-at-law in Chester and Flint between 1399 and 1419, when his fee for this office had been disallowed because he was a justice ('quia justiciarius est'), and because he was 'occupied in the service of the king' ('pro eo quod occupatus in servicio regis').[93] Isabella, widow of William le Scrope, received £12 from Cheshire revenues paid to the king in 1418.[94]

The use of Cheshire revenues in this way indicates a high degree of assimilation of the county into the royal demesne and royal financial organisation during the reign of Henry V.

90 SC 6/1303/5, m 4d.

91 SC 6/776/4, m 4d, 1303/2, m 4d, 1303/4, m 4d.

92 1419: SC 6/1303/2, m 4d (£33 6s. 8d.); 1421: SC 6/1303/4, m 4d (£33 6s. 8d.); 1422: SC 6/1303/5, m 4d (£40).

93 SC 6/774/11, m 4 to SC 6/1303/2, m 3.

94 SC 6/776/5, m 4d. In the parliament of Oct 1404, in response to her petition, she had been granted £100 per annum to be taken at the exchequer (*PROME*, viii. 317; *CPR 1401–5*, p. 466; TNA SC 8/22/1076).

The assignment of Cheshire revenues was to increase further in the reign of his son and especially in the 1430s.[95] This was a development paralleled in other areas of the royal demesne but most notably in those lands which otherwise formed the patrimony of the prince of Wales.[96] After 1413, we enter a long period where there was no prince of Wales and therefore where all of the customary lands held by the heir to the throne, Cheshire included, were held by the king.

## Cheshire troops in France 1415–21

On a couple of occasions during the reign of Henry V, we can see that Cheshire revenues were used at source for costs which the crown wished to cover. Both concerned the wars in France. The first related to the service of the contingent of Cheshire archers on the 1415 campaign and the second to reinforcements sent to Calais in 1419. On other occasions, however, Cheshire men served in France, paid by the royal exchequer out of the general revenues of the crown.

In 1415, Henry made every effort to raise as large an army as possible for his campaign which culminated in victory at Agincourt. An archer company was raised from Cheshire as it was also from Lancashire and South Wales, both areas which had a special relationship with the crown. From Lancashire, 500 archers were raised, grouped into companies of 50 each under the command of a knight or esquire.[97] In South Wales, the chamberlain, John Merbury, raised a total of 500 archers from the counties of Camarthen and Cardigan and the lordship of Brecon.[98]

95 Steel, *Receipt of the Exchequer*, p. 175.

96 For this development with regard to South Wales see Griffiths, *Principality of Wales*, i. 43.

97 E 101/46/36, the account of the sheriff, Sir Robert Urswyk, which details all of the companies. A reference in a post-campaign account suggests that at least some of these Lancashire archers were used by Henry as his personal bodyguard (E 358/6 rot. 4). Some of the knights and gentry leading these archer groups also served on the campaign with their own small retinues.

98 E 101/46/20. For discussion see Adam Chapman, *Welsh Soldiers in the*

The size of the Cheshire contingent is more complex. The accounts of the chamberlain William Troutbeck for 1416–17 note payments of arrears to 182 archers of the county who had served at the siege of Harfleur and battle of Agincourt, each archer still being owed 25s. 6d. for their service.[99] The entry notes that letters under the privy seal had been issued to Troutbeck on 11 December 1415 to authorise payment on his account, and that further royal letters of 7 April 1416 had ordered the payments to come from the taxation of the county of Chester granted to the king, as well as from other revenues, farms and profits coming from the same county. The entry on his account is followed by a list of archers grouped by the 16 captains to whom they were assigned. The entry also mentions that the names are to be found in a roll. Such a contemporary roll has come to light in the Shropshire Archives, giving the same names and groupings.[100]

Troutbeck paid out a total of £232 1s. 0d. to these archers. But he made further payments on his account to 14 other captains, five of whom had also been recorded as leading archer contingents for the second quarter of the campaign.[101]

*Later Middle Ages 1282–1422* (Woodbridge: Boydell Press, 2015), pp. 133–41.

99 SC 6/776/4, mm 3d–4d. The 16 company leaders were Sir Philip Leche, Sir Thomas Grosvenor, Sir Ralph Bostock, John Manley, Thomas de Dutton, Robert de Davenport, William Cholmondeley (now deceased), Peter de Legh, Sir William Stanley, John Done, Sir William Stanley junior, John Hondford, John Kingsley, Sir John Savage, Ralph Davenport and Richard de Legh.

100 Shropshire Archives 6000/48. This is headed 'Here follow the names of certain archers under certain knights and esquires written below lately assigned for the last campaign of the king to each of these archers there being due and applied 25s. 6d. for the campaign' ('Censuivent les noms de certeins archers a certeins chevaliers et escuiers desouz escrits iatarde assignez pour le darrein viage notre seigneur le roy a chescun des queuex archers sont dues et adereres xxvs. vid. pour mesme le viage'). I am grateful to Tony Carr for this reference as well as for photographs and a transcript. Tony and I share the same great grandfather and hence the same pupil teacher great aunt whom I mentioned in my foreword. It is a remarkably small world!

101 SC 6/776/4, m 4d. Sir John Savage, himself, four other men-at-arms

Together, these totalled 79 men (made up of three knights, 16 men-at-arms and 60 archers). Within the entry we read that the king had learned that their wages for the second quarter had not been paid and so had ordered the chamberlain to remedy this out of the revenues of the county of Chester and North Wales. These men, it was added, had been listed in the book of the controller of the household of the king, suggesting that these Cheshire troops had, like their Lancashire counterparts, served as a bodyguard to the king.

In total then we see 251 Cheshire men paid for their service in the second quarter. But what had been the number recruited in Cheshire in the first place? An initial order had gone out on 28 May 1415 to the justiciar, chamberlain and sheriff to array men-at-arms and archers in the county to accompany the king on his expedition to France.[102] The sheriff was ordered on 12 July to instruct those who had received wages to assemble at Newcastle-under-Lyme en route to joining the king, who was then at Southampton.[103] Transcripts made in the early eighteenth century of royal exchequer records of the period, which no longer appear to survive, suggest that a company of 50 men-at-arms and 650 archers had been anticipated from the county.[104] Since the payments made by the chamberlain related only to the second quarter after Harfleur had been captured, it may be that the Cheshire company had been larger but had

and 15 archers; Sir William Stanley self, one other man-at-arms and 11 archers; Sir Peter Leigh self plus three archers; John Kingsley self plus three archers; Robert Orell self plus three archers; Hugh Orell self plus three archers; John Done self plus three archers; John Pygot self plus three archers; George de Asshleyam self plus four archers; Christopher del Hogh self plus three archers; Roger de Middleton self plus three archers; John Massey self plus three archers; William Massey self plus three archers; Jacob de Chatterton self plus three archers.

102 CHES 2/88, m 5 (6), *37 DKR*, p. 703. A similar order was made for Flintshire on the same day (m. 5 (7).

103 CHES 2/88, m 6 (8), DKR, 37, p. 132.

104 N. H. Nicolas, *History of the Battle of Agincourt* (3rd edn, London: Johnson & Co., 1833), p. 385, from BL, Sloane MS 4600, a listing made from original documents by Ralph Sanderson in the preparation of Thomas Rymer's *Foedera*.

suffered attrition during the first stages of the expedition. After all, the size of the Cheshire contingent in 1400 had totalled 549 men.

For the campaign to rescue Harfleur in the early summer of 1416, Troutbeck received money from the royal exchequer which he paid out to a company of 400 archers.[105] He also received pay for the wages of a further group of eight knights, 32 men-at-arms and 80 archers from the county who were retained by the king for the expedition.[106] Such arrangements reflect the make-up of the troops serving in 1415, but we do not know any names from the financial records and there is no surviving muster roll, although a handful of those who participated can be identified from the letters of protection enrolled in the Chester enrolments.[107]

Archers from Cheshire were also sought for the king's second major invasion of France which began with a landing in Lower Normandy on 1 August 1417. The names of 405 archers, grouped by hundred, are listed on the last membrane of a muster roll made as the army prepared to depart from the Southampton area.[108] These may not reflect the whole Cheshire contingent since the figure is lower than the 500 men for whom Troutbeck received pay from the treasurer of the household, Sir

105 E 403/624, m 4 under 3 Jun. See also E 101/328/6. J. H. Wylie and W. T. Waugh, *The Reign of Henry the Fifth*, 3 vols (Cambridge: Cambridge University Press, 1914–29), ii. 354 n. 8. A contingent of 400 archers was also provided from Lancashire for the campaign as a whole, for whom Ralph Radcliffe received pay. See Anne Curry, 'After Agincourt, What Next? Henry V and the Campaign of 1416', in Linda Clark (ed.), *Conflicts, Consequences and the Crown in the Late Middle Ages*, The Fifteenth Century, 7 (Woodbridge: Boydell Press, 2007), pp. 23–51.

106 E 403/624, m 4 under 3 Jun.

107 These have been included in the database www.medievalsoldier.org from the Appendix to *37 DKR*.

108 E 101/51/2, mm. 42–3. The location given for the muster of the Cheshire men is the unidentified 'Caudernerdowne'. See Anne Curry and David Cleverly, 'Henry V's Army of 1417', in Linda Clark (ed.), *Enmity and Amity*, The Fifteenth Century, 19 (2022 for 2021), pp. 35–67, at p. 41.

John Rothenale, as recorded on the issue roll.[109] A comparison of the names of those in this muster roll with those in the lists for 1415 shows very little commonality: only 20 of the Cheshire archers seem to have served on both occasions, a lower rate of continuity than for archers across the royal armies of 1415 and 1417 as a whole.[110]

Some of the Cheshire and Lancashire archers crossing in 1417 can be shown to have continued in service in France after the expiry of their initial twelve-month contract. This is revealed by orders in the Norman rolls to muster the archers of these counties on various occasions from December 1418 through to December 1420. We find them at the siege of Rouen in December 1418, distributed across nine different divisions of the army.[111] Some at least continued in service at the siege into January 1419.[112] They are also found at the sieges of Evreux, Vernon and Pontoise in March, May and July 1419, respectively.[113] They are found at Pontoise in May 1420, the siege of Sens in June and that of Melun in November, and with the king at the entry to Paris in early December 1420.[114]

Preparations for a new royal expedition in the summer of 1421 included the raising of archers in Cheshire. On 13 May, a commission of array for 200 archers was ordered, the troops to be at Dover by the end of the month.[115] On 17 May, the treasurer of war, Sir Walter Beauchamp, paid the chamberlain, William Troutbeck, and John Kingsley the wages of the 200

109 E 403/627 under 11 Mar. On the same day Troutbeck received money for the wages of 400 archers from Lancashire. No muster survives for this group but we know that these Lancashire troops were raised by Sir William and Sir James Harrington, with two-thirds to be mounted and one-third on foot, and were to be brought to Southampton by 10 May 1417 (DL 42/17, f. 112, cited in Robert Somerville, *History of the Duchy of Lancaster*, 1: *1265–1603* (London: Duchy of Lancaster, 1953), p. 184).

110 Curry and Cleverly, 'Henry V's Army of 1417', p. 59.

111 C 64/9, m 6d.

112 C 64/10, m 30d, 41d.

113 Respectively, C 64/11, mm 78d, 72d, 31d, 29d, 20d.

114 Respectively, C 64/13, m 9d; C 64/14, mm 29d, 15d, 12d.

115 CHES 2/93, m 7 (7), *37 DKR*, p. 133.

archers who had been chosen from the county and retained with the king for his expedition.[116] No muster roll survives for these troops.

Only once, however, were Cheshire revenues used at source to pay the wages of Cheshire troops serving in armies which Henry V led to France. Otherwise they were paid out of royal revenues as a whole, as was the case for the rest of the army. The exception was the payment which chamberlain Troutbeck was ordered to make to cover arrears due to archers who had served in 1415. As we have seen, this was paid several months after the end of the campaign. Such an arrangement was only feasible in anticipation of the first instalment of the mise which was due on 3 May 1416.[117] The relevant entry in the chamberlain's account for 1416–17 shows that a payment from Cheshire revenues had been authorised in December 1415 but could not be effected until money was known to be forthcoming. At that point troops were being raised in the county for another campaign to rescue Harfleur. We can suggest that it was necessary to pay the arrears for the 1415 campaign to encourage service again in 1416.

A small payment of £19 16s. 8d. was made out of the mise to John Rothenale, royal treasurer of war, on 25 May 1418, but its purpose was not explained.[118] In the following year, Cheshire revenues were used to pay the wages of Cheshire troops in the garrison of Calais. On 16 January 1419, a payment from the Cheshire exchequer was made to Sir John Savage for the wages of 59 men-at-arms and 180 archers ordered to go with him to Calais and to remain there for the defence of the place.[119] This

116 E 403/649 under 17 May. The wording 'capiendum et eligendum ('taking and choosing') as the means of selection is interesting and suggests similarities with commissions of array as ordered in the county in 1400 and 1415.

117 CHES 2/89, m 6. A further two instalments were due on 10 Nov 1416 and 24 June 1417.

118 SC 6/776/5, m 4d.

119 SC 6/1303/2, m 4d. The name of one of his soldiers, Laurence del Rythyn, is known through a protection in the Chester enrolments on 17 Feb 1419 (CHES 2/92, m 4d (5), *37 DKR*, p. 633). Rythyn also appears on the muster roll E 101/49/23, m 4d. John de Macclesfield,

payment is explicitly stated on the chamberlain's account for 1418–19, as deriving from revenues of the royal exchequer as well as from the Cheshire mise granted in 1416 and from the general receipts of the chamberlain of the county, and the entry shows that further instalments were paid to Savage on 13 May and 1 June 1419. The reinforcements Savage led to Calais were mustered on 7 and 8 March 1419.[120]

## The relative value of the earldom of Chester

The county palatine was undoubtedly the least valuable part of the patrimony of a prince of Wales. This was already the case in 1376. A valor drawn up shortly after the death of the Black Prince gave the total value of his lands as £9,982 12s. 8¾d. As prince of Wales, his lands in North Wales were valued at £3,041 7s. 6¼d. and in South Wales at £1,850 4s. 11¼d.[121] The duchy of Cornwall generated three sources of income: that from Cornwall was given as £2,219 7s. 9½d., of which slightly less than half was for coinage of tin. The income from Devon was given as £273 19s. 5¾d., and from the foreign manors of the duchy £922 11s. 2s. The value of Cheshire was given as £1,082 1s. 9d., Flintshire as £442 19s. 5d., and the lordship of Macclesfield as £170. Translating this into proportions, we can

clerk, also took out a protection to cross with the troops (C 76/101, m 2). John Savage is a name found on three musters for the 1400 campaign: a man-at-arms in the contingent from Bucklow hundred under Sir William Legh (E101/42/29, m 1), leading his own company (E 101/42/16, m 45d) and within the royal contingent (E101/42/16, m 27). He led troops to France on the 1415 campaign (BL, Harley MS 782D VI 83 v, SC 6/774 m 2d, and Shropshire Archives 6000/48). He seems to have been knighted on the campaign since in July 1415. He was not a knight but by 2 Nov 1415 was so described (*37 DKR*, p. 667)

120 E 101/49/23, mm 1–4d, E 101/49/22, m 2. His son also served. We can also see the presence of Cheshire captains such as Adam Edgeworth, Ralph de Beeston, and Adam Hesketh. There was also an archer called John Savage serving in Harfleur and various other garrisons in this period. For references see www.medievalsoldier.org.

121 C 47/9/57, translated in Booth, *Financial Admin.*, pp. 173–5.

see that the Welsh lands plus Flintshire constituted 53%, the duchy of Cornwall 34% and Cheshire 13%.

We see a similar hierarchy of values in the valor made of Prince Henry's lands during the Welsh wars.[122] Here the total potential value was given as £10,758 12s. 9¼d. Of this, the gross value of revenues in Devon and Cornwall was £2,493 7s. 3¼d. and (by calculation) of the foreign manors of the duchy of Cornwall £1,182 15s. 2d. The gross value of Cheshire (which we must take to include Macclesfield for which no separate entry was given) was given as £913 18s. 6d. The prince's Welsh lands including Flintshire were given a total value of £5,513 17s. 6d. Expressing these as proportions, Welsh lands constituted 51%, the duchy of Cornwall 23% and Cheshire only 8%. In comparison with the proportions for 1376, we can see that both the proportionate and real value of the Welsh lands and the duchy of Cornwall were quite consistent, but those of Cheshire were lower. The value of Cheshire was 16% lower than it had been 27 years before.

This valor of the lands of Prince Henry, however, noted that there was no revenue at all forthcoming from the prince's lands in North and South Wales and in Flintshire because of the rebellion of the Welsh. As a result, the actual total gross value was £4,245 of which Cheshire therefore provided 21.5% rather than 8%, and the duchy almost all of the rest. Although Cheshire was the least valuable of Prince Henry's estates, the importance of even its small revenues during the Welsh wars should not be underestimated. As we have seen, the prince's income from Cheshire proved vital in sustaining his military activity in Wales. Furthermore, the valors do not include revenue from taxation. The Cheshire mise made a vital contribution to the prince's income and to the pursuit of war in Wales, and subsequently helped to fund Henry's wars in France when king, as well as supporting Cheshire's military involvement directly on two occasions.

122 SC 11/862, Appendix VI. The dating is discussed in Chapter 2. There has been no effort here to deal with discrepancies in the figures cited.

At the accession of Henry V, all his princely lands were united with those of the crown. The contribution of Cheshire continued to be less significant than that of elsewhere. An estimate of revenues and expenditure of the kingdom from June 1415 to June 1416 gave total income as £56,966 13s. 4d.[123] Income from South Wales was given as 2,000 marks (£1,333 6s. 8d.), from North Wales as 1,000 marks (£666 13s. 4d.), and from the duchy of Cornwall as 4,000 marks (£2,666 6s. 8d.). No mention is made of Cheshire, presumably because it was expected to contribute nothing in that year to royal finances, at least from its demesne revenues. We have seen that no liveries were made to the royal exchequer for the first four years of the reign.

Even with the mise of 1416, the contribution which Cheshire made to the finances of Henry V as king was a mere drop in the ocean of royal receipts – only £3489 1s. 7d. between 1417 and 1422. The inhabitants of the county also seem to have contributed very little to the loans raised by Henry V when compared with elsewhere. Anthony Steel identified only £60 loaned from Cheshire during the whole of the reign, making it the second lowest contributor of any English county.[124]

The county declined further in terms of financial importance to the crown, given that the king controlled the whole of the duchy of Lancaster. All of the Lancastrian kings kept this vast estate separate from other royal resources for it proved more easily controllable and accessible than the royal exchequer. Compared with the earldom of Chester which was part of the royal demesne, the duchy of Lancaster remained the personal property of the Lancastrian kings with potential annexation to the crown only in the failure of heirs. It had already proved valuable in financial terms to Henry IV, and it is significant that he continued to hold its assets even though he had created his son duke of Lancaster in 1399.[125] In comparison with

123 *PPC*, ii. 172–80. None of these areas are mentioned in a similar document dated 6 May 1421 although this is fragmentary (*PPC*, ii. 312–15).

124 Steel, *Receipt of the Exchequer*, p. 191. Only Cumberland, at £10, was lower.

125 Somerville, *History of the Duchy of Lancaster*, pp. 160–2.

the paucity of interchange between Cheshire and the crown's resources, Henry V used duchy of Lancaster revenues to the fullest extent. It has been calculated that they contributed over £14,000 to the king over the whole reign. Money from the duchy was even conveyed to the king's use in France.[126]

Differences in attitude are also reflected in Henry V's emphasis on the efficient exploitation of duchy of Lancaster lands. This culminated in a series of ordinances for the governance of the duchy drafted in February 1417 at a special meeting in the king's presence. Such ordinances brought duchy finances under the control of the royal household: money for the king's use was given priority over the payment of annuities.[127] This contrasts sharply with the indifference shown towards Cheshire revenues after the Welsh wars, save in years when taxation was raised from the county. Not surprisingly, we see increasing commonality in the policies deployed towards former patrimony of the prince of Wales as part of the royal demesne as a whole. Such a unity of approach is revealed by the fact that the areas were seen as sources of indirect financial return and were exploited largely for the purposes of royal patronage.

In the estimates put forward by Ralph, Lord Cromwell, as treasurer of England in 1433, we see that the relative hierarchy of values remained much the same as earlier.[128] At this point, however, the revenues of Cheshire and Cornwall were much more heavily assigned at source, largely in annuities (Table XXI). As can be seen, virtually the whole of the Cheshire revenues were assigned. In addition, the manor of Shotwick

126 Somerville, *History of the Duchy of Lancaster*, pp. 164, 186.

127 Ibid., pp. 187–9; R. R. Davies, 'Baronial Accounts, Incomes and Arrears in the Later Middle Ages', *EcHR*, 2nd ser., 21 (1968), 211–29, at p. 223.

128 *PROME*, xi. 104–13. See B. P. Wolffe, *The Royal Demesne in English History: The Crown Estate in the Governance of the Realm from the Conquest to 1509* (London: Allen and Unwin, 1971), p. 92, and J. L. Kirby, 'The Issues of the Lancastrian Exchequer and Lord Cromwell's Estimates of 1433', *Bulletin of the Institute of Historical Research*, 24 (1951), 121–51. There seems to be no income given for the foreign manors of the duchy of Cornwall.

was listed separately but no income was received from it as it was still in the hands of William Porter, to whom it had been granted in 1410. By contrast, in the valor of Prince Henry's lands, we see the gross value of Cheshire as £824 13s. 10d., charges at £399 13s. 4d. (48.4%) and a net value of £425 1s. 5d. The respective figures for the duchy of Cornwall in Devon and Cornwall are £2,493 7s. 3¼d., £1,200 6s. 3¾d. (48.1%) and £1,242 1s. 9½d. If we compare the gross value of Cheshire in the valor for Prince Henry and the estimates of 1433, we see a decline of 16% over a thirty-year period, the same rate of decrease as between 1376 and the early fifteenth century.

Detailed discussion on the impact of the princely lands remaining for over 40 years within the royal demesne is beyond the scope of this book. It can already be seen from Table XXI that the value of Cheshire was continuing to decrease. A valor for the next prince of Wales, Edward, son of Henry VI, in 1454 also shows clearly the decline in the value and hence significance of most of the elements of the demesne within the earldom of Chester.[129] The gross value of the county is given there as £667 4s. 3½d.. This demonstrates a decrease in gross value since 1433 of 13%, of 27% since the early fifteenth century and of 39% since 1376. Table X in Chapter 2 provides further evidence of the pattern of decrease at the level of the individual accounting unit within the county.

By the mid-fifteenth century, therefore, it is clear that Cheshire had been fully assimilated into the royal demesne – for better or for worse. The level of integration is reflected by the fact that the county felt the impact of the Act of Resumption of 1457, even when there was a prince of Wales and earl of Chester in the shape of Prince Edward, the son of Henry VI, born in 1453. This is particularly revealing when we remember that a similar act in 1404 had not been applicable within Prince Henry's lands in Cheshire. The process of assimilation with the royal lands as a whole began under Richard II and had only been temporarily halted during the principate of Prince Henry

129 SC 11/868.

because of the Welsh wars. Assimilation continued without interruption from 1413 onwards for 41 years, the longest period without a prince of Wales across the whole of the later middle ages.

### Table XX. The estimates of 1433

| 1433 | Area | Gross value | Charges | Charges as % of gross value | Net value |
|---|---|---|---|---|---|
| | Cheshire | £764 10s. 2¾d. | £719 19s. 6¾d. | 94.2% | £44 10s. 8d. |
| | Cornwall | £2,788 12s. 3¾d. | £2,637 12s. 6½d. | 94.5% | £151 0s. 9¼d. |
| | North Wales | £1,097 17s. 3d. | £506 18s. 11½d. | 46.2% | £590 18s. 3½d. |
| | South Wales | £1,139 13s. 11d. | £669 8s. 6½d. | 58.7% | £470 5s. 4½d. |

# *Conclusion*

The years from 1399 to 1422 formed a very special and significant period in the development of Cheshire. This significance is revealed in two seemingly disparate respects. First, we can observe certain trends in the financial administration of the earl's lands and resources which are unique to the county. Yet in so many other aspects it is clear that this period witnessed the ever increasing degree of 'normalisation' of the county within the royal demesne.

Many of the peculiarities for which the county was renowned were maintained throughout and after these years. Its palatinate status remained unimpaired and its local administrative structure was preserved. However, such developments as made the county unique in the early fifteenth century were in addition to these pre-existing peculiarities. Each part of this present study has pointed to the years from 1403 to 1408 as a significant period in the history of the county. The demands of the war in Wales had not only re-established the strategic importance of the county as a border area but had also enhanced its administrative and financial functions, through payment for and direction of the defence of North Wales from the Chester exchequer. This had led to an increased exploitation of demesne revenues, to a new enthusiasm for the collection of arrears, accompanied by a change in accounting techniques which demonstrated the full significance of arrears as potential income, and to a temporary curtailment of the payment of regular county expenses. Overall then, the county, and in particular its demesne resources, were indispensable in the Lancastrian war effort in Wales.

It is also clear from this study, however, that this indispensability was short lived. Hence the period of 1403 to 1408 was merely an 'interlude' between two periods in which the principal direction of royal policy was towards the absorption of the county more completely within the national infrastructure. The direct effect of this mainstream royal policy was the decline in importance of demesne revenues as a regular source of princely or royal income. From 1399 to 1403 and after c. 1412, these revenues were assigned, for the most part at source, in patronage. In these years there was an inevitable lack of interest in the exploitation of the Cheshire demesne. An interesting parallel can be drawn between trends in the early fifteenth century and those in the period from 1272 to 1377, as elucidated by Paul Booth.[1] Between 1272 and 1340, financial administration in Cheshire was subordinate to political considerations, especially patronage and the military and political aspects of the conquest of Wales, a situation paralleled in mainstream royal policy for most of period from 1399 to 1422. From 1346 to 1377, financial considerations were uppermost when the Black Prince needed Cheshire revenues to subsidise his campaigns in France. Such considerations were given priority again between 1403 and 1408 when money was needed in Wales, the prince having found it impossible to collect his revenues within the principality.

In 1399, it was certain that the events of the recent past would assure Cheshire of a prominent, if equivocal, position under the first Lancastrian. Richard II's attempt to create a personal power bloc based upon the county by elevating it into a principality and annexing to it the Fitzalan inheritance in North Wales created an initial problem for Henry IV, a problem further aggravated by the fact that the county remained, at least until the battle of Shrewsbury in July 1403, the centre of opposition to the new dynasty. Henry IV's subsequent attitude towards the leading Cheshire rebels may have been one of personal reconciliation, but his policy towards the county as a whole, best reflected in changes in demesne personnel and annuitants, was one of infiltration and absorption.

The policies of both Richard II and Henry IV were aimed at bending the county to the royal will. The former, however, relied upon personal charisma and the exploitation of the naive and anachronistic desires of certain leading gentry for increased local independence. Here they were perhaps reacting against the

1 Booth, *Financial Admin.*, pp. 133–41.

obvious and already well advanced 'normalisation' of the county under the Black Prince. Henry IV and his son relied upon slower but surer means – the gradual imposition on the county of such royal control as was familiar in other areas of the royal demesne. The county maintained its integrity as part, if now a lesser part, of the patrimony of the heir apparent but there are clear signs that this integrity was noticeably eroded in the long period after 1413 when the county was in the hands of the king. From 1413, periods of tenure by princes of Wales were brief and ineffectual until the turn of the century. By 1422, Cheshire revenues were being used along the same lines as royal demesne revenues elsewhere, principally for patronage. The county could by then be expected to contribute taxation at much the same time and same scale as the rest of the kingdom, whilst maintaining its own system of granting such sums. Admittedly, the independent action of local administrators appears to have been enhanced under Henry V but, when the most important offices were held by such Lancastrian feedmen as William Troutbeck, there could be little fear of any administration which went against the interests of the Lancastrian kings.

In the policy of absorption, the Lancastrians were aided by three contemporary developments. The first was the fact that after 1399 problems needing national resolution, such as the Welsh and French wars, inevitably brought the county into line with the rest of the kingdom. The second was the fact that the county had already undergone considerable 'normalisation' in the fourteenth century, principally by means of the growth of the royal earl's central authority under the Black Prince.[2] The rule of Richard II may have witnessed a temporary reversal of this trend. Certainly this appears to be the case when we study the recipients of annuities. The Black Prince used county revenues primarily to reward those who had afforded him military support in France. Richard II, on the other hand, had granted annuities for the most part to Cheshire men in order to build up local support. The Lancastrians returned to rewarding

2 Sharp, 'Earldom and County of Chester', pp. 44–5.

principally non-local men, or else those whom they themselves had introduced and brought to power in the locality. Although it is true that, by the mid-fourteenth century, Cheshire had become more important through its connection with the royal house rather than through its peculiar privileges, developments in this direction in the early fifteenth century were at a much greater scale than before. Whereas in the fourteenth century the county's importance was by connection with the prince or king, in the next century it was by virtue of being an integral part of the royal demesne as a whole.

A third development which aided absorption was the growth of the rentier economy. Since demesne revenues and expenses were already fossilised, income was regular and uncomplicated. As a result, it could be administered without difficulty and assigned regularly and completely at source. Such assignment did not need to take into consideration local vagaries but could be made along the lines of the rest of the royal demesne. Now that it was impossible to increase or manipulate income from landed sources, the earl, in common with many other lords, was forced to rely upon non-landed income, in the case of the earldom of Chester principally taxation and escheats. The availability of such alternatives to direct cultivation was yet another nail in the coffin of the Cheshire demesne economy.

The slackening of demesne exploitation had inevitably led, and was still leading, to a weakening of seigneurial control over the tenants. Administrative control, however, had not disappeared completely and there is little to suggest that the demesne was not administered efficiently, when it was required to be administered at all in a rentier economy. There is little to suggest that demands for revenues in this period had a similar effect as in the mid-fourteenth century. Then, Booth claimed, the Black Prince, in his need for money, found it necessary to delegate authority locally and in so doing encouraged lawlessness and the downfall of good government.[3] The exploitation of landed resources in the early fifteenth century was much less

3 Booth, *Financial Admin.*, pp. 137–8.

rigorous than in the fourteenth, save for the brief interlude when money was required in Wales. There is no sign of such rampant lawlessness: arguably, political animosity to the new dynasty and subsequent military involvement in Wales and France absorbed local aggression.

Royal policy in the years from 1403 to 1408 may have been detrimental to Cheshire interests. Certainly, there was a sharp decline in revenues after 1408 but this was largely due to the end of the need for serious exploitation rather than, or in addition to, such revenues ceasing to be available. Values of Cheshire resources had declined since 1376 and continued to do so. Where there was any sign of fluctuation in demesne revenues the trend was downwards. This was caused by the gradual weakening and disintegration of the structure of seigneurial monopolies and private jurisdiction, which was experienced by the prince of Wales and by many of his contemporaries. It cannot be denied that, after 1408, the financial importance of the county declined substantially and, with it, its standing as an independent unit within the prince's appanage. With such a consideration, the subsequent development and success of a royal policy of absorption into the royal demesne appears likely, if not inevitable.

If the fourteenth century saw the absorption of the Cheshire demesne within the patrimony of the prince of Wales, then the fifteenth century saw its assimilation into the royal demesne as a whole. The sixteenth century was to witness its final inclusion in the kingdom by the erosion of its palatinate status.[4] This last move was a direct, even if gradual, result of the two earlier developments.

4 Although the results of Thomas Cromwell's decision in 1536 'to sweep away much of the previous structure of government in Wales and Cheshire' did not prevent the continuing strength of the palatinate. See Tim Thornton, *Cheshire and the Tudor State, 1480–1560* (Woodbridge: Boydell, 2000), p. 213.

APPENDIX I

# *Lists of officials*

(a) Chamberlain

(b) Justiciar

(c) Sheriff of the county

(d) Escheator of the county

(e) Auditors

(f) Officials in Chester city

(g) Keeper of the Dee corn mills and fishery

(h) Officials in Delamere forest

(i) Bailiff of Drakelow and Rudheath

(j) Bailiff of Frodsham

(k) Officials at Middlewich

(l) Officials at Northwich

(m) Officials at Shotwick

(n) Officials at Macclesfield

- (i) steward
- (ii) burgus
- (iii) hundred
- (iv) forest
- (v) park

## (a) Chamberlain

**Holder of post under Richard II: Robert Parys**

| | |
|---|---|
| **John Trevor, bishop of St. Asaph** | |
| appointed 16 August 1399 | *36 DKR*, p. 99; CHES 2/73 m. 9 (4) |
| during pleasure[1] | |
| reappointed 1 Nov. 1399 | *36 DKR*, p. 100; CHES 2/74 m. 1 (1), 16 (5) |
| during pleasure | |
| in office from 16 Aug. 1399 | SC 6/774/11 m. 3 |
| to Mich. 1404[2] | SC 6/775/3 m. 3 |
| **Thomas Barneby** | |
| in office from Mich. 1404 | SC 6/775/4 m. 1, 3 |
| to 16 Dec. 1412 | SC 6/775/14 m. 3 |
| **William Troutbeck** | |
| appointed 1 Nov. 1412 | *36 DKR*, p. 476; CHES 2/86 m. 1 (1) |
| during pleasure[3] | |
| in office from 16 Dec. 1412 | SC 6/775/15 m. 1 |
| still in office at Mich. 1422 | SC 6/1303/5 m. 1 |
| confirmed in office 4 October 1423 | SC 6/1303/5 m. 1 |

1 Appointed simultaneously as chamberlain of Chester, Flintshire and North Wales in both August and November.

2 Payment of his fee for this year was erased 'as it is said he is a rebel' ('quia rebellis est ut dicitur').

3 This appointment is for Chester only.

## (b) Justiciar

**Holder of post under Richard II: William le Scrope, earl of Wiltshire**

**Henry Percy ('Hotspur') appointed for life by the King**

| | |
|---|---|
| 29 Oct. 1399 | *36 DKR*, p. 379;<br>CHES 2/74 m. 7 (4) |
| confirmed by prince | |
| 14 May 1400 | SC 6/774/11 m. 3 |
| in office from 13 Oct.1399 | SC 6/774/11 m. 3 |
| to 1 July 1403 | SC 6/774/15 m. 3 |
| **deputies: William Swinburne and John Knyghtley** | *36 DKR*, p. 379;<br>CHES 2/74 m. 7d (4) |
| | |
| **Gilbert, Lord Talbot** | |
| appointed during pleasure | |
| 24 July 1403 | *36 DKR*, p. 464;<br>CHES 2/77 m. 1d (1) |
| in office from 24 July 1403 | SC 6/774/15 m. 3 |
| to 19 Oct. 1418 (death) | SC 6/1303/2 m. 3 |
| **deputy: John Knyghtley** | *36 DKR*, p. 464;<br>CHES 2/77 m. 1d (2) |
| **James del Holt in office from** | SC 6/1303/2 m. 3<br>19 Oct. 1418 |
| to 10 Feb. 1421 | SC 6/1303/4 m. 3 |
| **Thomas Beaufort, duke of Exeter** | |
| appointed at pleasure | SC 6/1303/4 m. 3 |
| 10 Feb. 1421 | |
| still in office at 1422 | SC 6/1303/5 m. 3 |
| confirmed in office 21 Nov. 1422 | SC 6/1303/5 m. 3 |
| **(deputy: Peter del Pole** | SC 6/1303/4 m. 3<br>SC 6/1303/5 m. 3) |

## (c) Sheriff of the county

| | |
|---|---|
| **Holder under Richard II: Sir Robert Legh** | |
| **John Massey of Puddington Kt** | |
| in office from Mich. 1399 | SC 6/791/1 m. 7 |
| to during 1401 | SC 6/791/3 m. 7 |
| **Henry de Ravenscroft**[4] | |
| in office during 1401 | SC 6/791/3 m. 7 |
| to Mich. 1403 | SC 6/791/6 m. 5 |
| **John Mainwaring** | |
| appointed 18 Sept. 1403 | *36 DKR*, p. 318; CHES 2 /76 m. 12 (1)(2) |
| in office from Mich. 1403 | SC 6/791/7 m. 5 |
| to 8 Dec. 1408 | SC 6/792/5 m. 6 |
| **William Brereton Kt** | |
| appointed 6 Dec. 1408 | *36 DKR*, p. 55; CHES 2/81 m. 2d (3) |
| in office from 8 Dec. 1408 | SC 6/792/5 m. 6 |
| to 13 Jan. 1411 | SC 6/792/9 m. 8 |
| **(deputy and attorney: Hugh Knutsford** | SC 6/792/9 m. 8) |
| **Laurence Merbury** | |
| appointed 14 Jan. 1411 | *36 DKR*, p. 324; CHES 2/84 m. 1d (2)(3) |
| in office from 14 Jan. 1411 | SC 6/792/9 m. 9 |
| to Mich. 1414 | SC 6/793/1 m. 7 |
| **John de Legh of Booths** | |
| appointed 12 Sept. 1414 | *37 DKR*, p. 446; CHES 2/87 m. 3d (5) |
| in office from Mich. 1414 | SC 6/793/2 m. 7 |
| to Mich. 1421 | SC 6/794/1 m. 12 |

4 Previously appointed sheriff in 1396 (CHES 2/70 m. 1 (9), *36 DKR*, p. 399. Massey seems to have surrendered his office because he failed to hold Conway of which he was constable (*Anglo-Norman Letters and Petitions from All Souls' MS 182*, ed. M. Dominica Legge, Anglo-Norman Text Society, 3 (Oxford, 1941), no. 247).

| | |
|---|---|
| **(deputy: Thomas Haslington** | SC 6/793/2 m. 7) |
| **Hugh Dutton** | |
| appointed 2 Oct. 1421 | *37 DKR*, p. 227; CHES 2/94 m. 1 (4)(5) |
| in office from Mich. 1421 | SC 6/794/2 m. 13 |

## (d) Escheator of the county

| | |
|---|---|
| **Holder under Richard II: Adam Kingsley** | |
| **Richard de Manley** | |
| appointed 10 Nov. 1399 | *36 DKR*, p. 323; CHES 2/74 m. 1 (7) |
| in office from 7 Nov. 1399 | SC 6/791/1 m. 9 |
| to 19 Sept. 1403 | SC 6/791/6 m. 8 |
| **Matthew del Mere** | |
| appointed 18 Sept. 1403 | *36 DKR*, p. 340 |
| in office from Mich. 1403 | SC 6/791/7 m. 7 |
| to 31 March 1407 | SC 6/792/2 m. 7 |
| **Richard de Manley** | |
| appointed 4 March 1407 | *36 DKR*, p. 324; CHES 2/79 m. 2 (6) |
| in office from 31 Mar. 1407 | SC 6/792/2 m. 10 |
| to 11 April 1412 | SC 6/792/9 m. 6 |
| **Henry Ravenscroft** | |
| appointed 8 April 1412 | *36 DKR*, p. 399; CHES 2/84 m. 2 (8) |
| in office from 11 April 1412 | SC 6/792/9 m. 6 |
| to Mich. 1421 | SC 6/794/1 m. 8 |
| **Richard Done of Cronton** | |
| appointed 1 Oct. 1421 | *36 DKR*, p. 210; CHES 2/94 m. 1 (2) |
| **John Whetenhale of Nantwich** | |
| appointed 26 April 1422 | *37 DK*,782; CHES 2/94 m. 3 (10) |
| both in office from Mich. 1421 | SC 6/794/2 m. 8 |

## (e) Auditors

| | | |
|---|---|---|
| **Richard Stokes** | | *CPR 1399-1401*, p. 33 |
| **William Spridlington** | appointed 5 Dec. 1399 | *36 DKR*, p. 453; CHES 2/74 m. 4 (4)(5) |
| **Nicholas Burdon** | | |
| **John Bonyngton** | | |
| | appointed 17 May 1404 | *36 DKR*, p. 453; CHES 2/77 m. 7d |
| | in office from Mich. 1403 | SC 6/774/15 m. 4 |
| | to Mich. 1411 (at least) | SC 6/775/12 m. 4 |
| **Richard Appleton** | | |
| | appointed 1 Dec. 1413 | *CPR 1413-16*, p. 139 |
| | | *37 DKR*, p. 132; CHES 2/87 m. 1d (9) |
| **Roger Westwood** | | |
| **William Ryman** | | |
| | appointed 16 July 1414 | *CPR 1413-16*, p. 228 |
| **Richard Appleton** | | |
| **William Ryman** | | |
| | appointed 27 Oct. 1414 | *CPR 1413-16*, p. 247 |
| **Roger Appleton** | | |
| | | *37 DKR*, p. 632; CHES 2/88 m. 3 (12) |
| | in office from Mich. 1414 | SC 6/1302/15 m. 2d |

## (f) Officials in Chester city

### *(ii) Sheriff*

| | | | |
|---|---|---|---|
| John de Hawardyn | Robert de Bradley | 1399-1400 | SC 6/791/1 m. 1 |
| Richard Stalmyn | William del Heth | 1400-1401 | SC 6/791/3 m. 1 |
| John de Hawardyn | Thomas de Acton<br>John de Arwe | 1401-1402 | SC 6/791/5 m. 1 |
| Innocent de Chesterfield | William Kemp | 1402-1403 | SC 6/791/6 m. 1 |
| John de Halle | John de Arwe | 1403-1404 | SC 6/791/7 m. 1 |
| Thomas Aleyn | William de Rochdale | 1404-1405 | SC 6/791/10 m. 1 |
| Robert Chamberlain | John Hatton | 1405-1406 | SC 6/792/1 m. 1 |
| Thomas de Cotingham | John Hatton | 1406-1407 | SC 6/792/2 m. 1 |
| John Walsh | Elie Trevor | 1407-1408 | SC 6/792/3 m. 1 |
| John Walsh | Hugh de Multon | 1408-1409 | SC 6/792/5 m. 1 |
| John Torporlegh | Hugh de Multon | 1409-1410 | SC 6/792/6 m. 1 |
| John Trevor | John Brom | 1410-1411 | SC 6/792/8 m. 1 |
| Richard de Hatton | William del Hope | 1411-1412 | SC 6/792/9 m. 1 |
| John Hope | Hugh de Multon | 1412-1413 | SC 6/792/10 m. 1 |
| John Hope | Richard Spicer | 1413-1414 | SC 6/793/1 m. 1 |
| John Hope | John Overton | 1414-1415 | SC 6/793/2 m. 1 |
| John de Hatton | Robert del Hope | 1415-1416 | SC 6/793/4 m. 1 |
| John de Hatton | Richard Spicer | 1416-1417 | SC 6/793/5 m. 1 |
| Robert Hale | Thomas del Cliff | 1417-1418 | SC 6/793/7 m. 1 |
| Alexander Henbury | John Bradley | 1418-1419 | SC 6/793/9 m. 1 |
| Robert Hale | Stephen le Belleyester | 1419-1420 | SC 6/793/11 m. 1 |
| William Malpas | Nicholas Wirvyn | 1420-1421 | SC 6/794/1 m. 1 |
| William Malpas | Richard Massey | 1421-1422 | SC 6/794/2 m. 1 |

### *(ii) Mayor and Escheator*

| | | |
|---|---|---|
| John Capenhurst | 1399-1400 | SC 6/791/1 m. 1 |
| John de Bebington | 1400-1401 | SC 6/791/3 m. 1 |
| John de Bebington, Robert Marshall | 1401-1402 | SC 6/791/5 m. 1 |
| Roger le Potter | 1402-1403 | SC 6/791/6 m. 1 |
| Richard de Hatton | 1403-1404 | SC 6/791/7 m. 1 |
| John de Preston | 1404-1405 | SC 6/791/10 m. 1 |
| John Eulowe | 1405-1406 | SC 6/792/1 m. 1 |
| John Eulowe | 1406-1407 | SC 6/792/2 m. 1 |
| John Eulowe | 1407-1408 | SC 6/792/3 m. 1 |
| John Eulowe (William Brereton)[5] | 1408-1409 | SC 6/792/5 m. 1 |
| John Eulowe | 1409-1410 | SC 6/792/6 m. 1 |
| Roger le Potter | 1410-1411 | SC 6/792/8 m. 1 |
| John Walsh | 1411-1412 | SC 6/792/9 m. 1 |
| John de Whitmore | 1412-1413 | SC 6/792/10 m. 1d |
| John de Whitmore | 1413-1414 | SC 6/793/1 m. 1d |
| John de Whitmore | 1414-1415 | SC 6/793/2 m. 1d |
| John Walsh | 1415-1416 | SC 6/793/4 m. 1d |
| William de Hawardyn | 1416-1417 | SC 6/793/5 m. 1d |
| John Overton | 1417-1418 | SC 6/793/7 m. 1d |
| John Overton, William de Hawardyn | 1418-1419 | SC 6/793/9 m. 1d |
| John Hope | 1419-1420 | SC 6/793/11 m. 1d |
| John Hope | 1420-1421 | SC 6/794/1 m. 1d |
| John Hope | 1421-1422 | SC 6/794/2 m. 1d |

5 Commission of William Brereton temporarily, the prince having exonerated John Eulowe for a time: 6 August 1409; *36 DKR*, p. 104, CHES 2/81 m. 6 (8).

## (g) Keeper of the Dee corn mills and fishery

**Holder under Richard II: William Marsham**

**Henry Strangeways**

| | |
|---|---|
| appointed 16 Oct. 1399 | *CPR 1399-1401*, p. 11 |
| for life | *36 DKR*, p. 454; CHES 2/74 m. 1d (3)(4)(5) |
| accounting from Mich. 1399 | SC 6/791/1 m. 5 |
| to 5 July 1401 | SC 6/791/3 m. 5 |

**Robert Castell**

| | |
|---|---|
| appointed 6 June 1401 for life | SC 6/791/3 m. 6 |
| accounting from 5 July 1401 | SC 6/791/3 m. 6 |
| to end of reign | |
| confirmed in office 8 Dec. 1422 | SC 6/794/2 m. 7 |

*Deputy*

**John Hatton**

| | |
|---|---|
| in office from Mich. 1399 | SC 6/791/1 m. 5 |
| to 5 July 1401 | SC 6/791/3 m. 5 |

**Thomas Overton**

| | |
|---|---|
| in office from 5 July 1401 | SC 6/791/3 m. 6 |
| to Mich. 1406 | SC 6/792/1 m. 5 |

**John del Lowe**

| | |
|---|---|
| appointed 3 Feb. 1407 | *36 DKR*6, p. 201: CHES 2/79 m. 3d (5) |
| in office at Mich. 1407 | SC 6/792/2 m. 5 |
| to Mich. 1409 | SC 6/792/5 m. 5 |

**Robert del Hope**

| | |
|---|---|
| appointed 23 Oct. 1409 | *36 DKR*, p. 504: CHES 2/82 m. 1 (5) |
| in office from Mich. 1409 | SC 6/792/6 m. 5 |
| to Mich. 1421 | SC 6/794/1 m. 7 |

**William Foster**

| | |
|---|---|
| in office from Mich. 1421 | SC 6/794/2 m. 7 |
| in office 29 Jan. 1422 | *37 DKR*, p. 516; CHES 2/94 m. 4d (7) |

## (h) Officials in Delamere Forest

*Master forester and bailiff of the forest*

**John Done of Utkinton snr.**

| | |
|---|---|
| in office at Mich. 1399 | SC 6/791/1 m. 2 |
| still in office at Mich. 1422 | SC 6/794/2 m. 3 |

*Seller of moss – (in Delamere Forest and Frodsham)*

**Richard del Dedwood**

| | |
|---|---|
| appointed 24 April 1406 | *36 DKR*, p. 140; CHES 2/78 m. 2(16) |
| in office from Mich. 1405 | SC 6/792/1 m. 2 |
| still in office at Mich. 1422 | SC 6/794/2 m. 3 |

*Seller of wood*

**Roger del Dedwood**

| | |
|---|---|
| in office 1399-1400 | SC 6/791/1 m. 2 |

**William Hare**

| | |
|---|---|
| appointed 4 Feb. 1401 | SC 6/774/15 m. 4 |
| in office from Mich. 1400 | SC 6/791/3 m. 2 |
| still in office at Mich. 1422 | SC 6/794/2 m. 3 |

*Equitator*

**Equitator under Richard II: William de Becheton**[6]

**John Kingsley**

| | |
|---|---|
| appointed 16 June 1401 | SC 6/774/13 m. 6 |
| Forfeit July 1403 | SC 6/775/3 m. 6<br>E 163/6/41 item 5 |

6 William le Scrope, earl of Wiltshire had been surveyor of all of the forests of the county/principality under Richard II.

**Ralph Mainwaring**

| | |
|---|---|
| appointed 16 July 1405 | SC 6/775/15 m. 5 |
| Confirmed 1 Feb. 1423 | SC 6/1303/5 m. 5 |

***Surveyor, master forester and equitator of Delamere Forest***

| | |
|---|---|
| See below, Appendix I(n)(i) | Macclesfield, stewards of the lordship |

## (i) Bailiff of Drakelow and Rudheath

**Holder under Richard II: John Rose**[7]

**Richard de Manley (receiver of issues)**

| | |
|---|---|
| appointed 5 Feb. 1400 | SC 6/791/1 m. 1d |
| in office from Mich. 1400 | SC 6/791/1 m. 1d |
| to 20 June 1401 | SC.6 791/3 m. 1 |

**Ralph Pope** *(bailiff)*

| | |
|---|---|
| appointed 20 June 1401 | SC 6/791/3 m. 1 |
| in office from 20 June 1401 | SC 6/791/3 m. 1 |
| to Mich. 1409 | SC 6/792/5 m. 1 |
| surrenders letters of appointment 26 Nov. 1408 | SC 6/792/5 m. 1 |

**Ralph Leycester** *(bailiff)*

| | |
|---|---|
| appointed 11 Feb. 1409 | SC 6/792/6 m. 1d |
| in office from Mich. 1409 | SC 6/792/6 m. 1d |
| still in office at Mich. 1422 | SC 6/794/2 m. 2 |
| confirmed in office 27 Jan. 1423 | SC 6/794/2 m. 2 |

***Deputy bailiff***

**Hugh Knutsford**

| | |
|---|---|
| in office 1403-1404 | SC 6/791/7 m. 1d |

**William Farington**

| | |
|---|---|
| in office 1406-1407 | SC 6/792/2 m. 1d |

7 Rose had been granted the bailiwick for life in 1378, and although the grant was confirmed by Henry IV on 4 Nov. 1399 (CHES 2/51 m. 1 (4,5), *36 DKR*, p. 413; *CPR 1399-1401*, p. 129). Rose was replaced by Richard de Manley from 5 Feb. 1400.

| | | |
|---|---|---|
| **Thomas Balle** | | |
| | in office 1406-1407 | SC 6/792/2 m. 1d |
| **William Farington** | | |
| | in office from Mich. 1407 | SC 6/792/3 m. 1d |
| | to Mich. 1410 | SC 6/792/6 m. 1d |
| **John Laurenson** | | |
| | in office from Mich. 1410 | SC 6/792/8 m. 1d |
| | to Mich. 1415 | SC 6/793/2 m. 2 |
| **Hugh Knutsford** | | |
| | in office from Mich. 1415 | SC 6/793/4 m. 2 |
| | to Mich. 1418 | SC 6/793/7 m. 2 |
| **John Done** | | |
| | in office 1418-1419 | SC 6/793/9 m. 2 |
| **John Bailly** | | |
| | in office from Mich. 1419 | SC 6/793/11 m. 2 |
| | to Mich. 1422 | SC 6/794/2 m. 2 |

## (j) Bailiff of Frodsham

| | | |
|---|---|---|
| **Roger Torfot** | | |
| | in office from Mich. 1408[8] | SC 6/792/5 m. 10 |
| | to Mich. 1420 | SC 6/793/11 m. 8 |
| **John Triket** | | |
| | appointed 30 Sept. 1420 | *37 DKR*, p. 717; CHES 2/93 m. 1(1) |
| | in office from Mich. 1420 | SC 6/794/1 m. 5 |
| | still in office Mich. 1422[9] | SC 6/794/2 m. 5 |

8 Radegonde Béchet, the holder of the manor since 1385, died around 13 Oct. 1408 (SC 6/792/5 m. 10).

9 He was replaced by Henry de Gartside on 1 Oct. 1423 (*37 DKR*, p. 300, CHES 2/95 m. 1d (5)).

## (k) Officials at Middlewich

**Holder under Richard II: granted to Sir William Bagot**

*Steward*

**Henry Ravenscroft**

| | |
|---|---|
| appointed 3 June 1400 | *36 DKR*, p. 345; |
| during pleasure | CHES 2/74 m. 7d (8) |
| in office from Mich. 1399 | SC 6/791/1 m. 4 |
| still in office at Mich. 1422 | SC 6/794/2 m. 4 |

| *Chamberlain* | *Catchpole* | | |
|---|---|---|---|
| William Warihull | William Burgess<br>Robert Ruskyn | 1399-1400 | SC 6/791/1 m. 4 |
| John del Lowe | Henry Vernon<br>William Vernon | 1400-1401 | SC 6/791/3 m. 4d |
| Richard Hicockson | Richard Russell Ralph de Wever | 1401-1402 | SC 6/791/5 m. 3d |
| Thomas Dun | John del Heth<br>William Ebbington | 1402-1403 | SC 6/791/6 m. 4 |
| Thomas Hickson | Hugh Hickson Hugh Coventry | 1403-1404 | SC 6/791/7 m. 4 |
| Richard Hargreve<br>Thomas Hickson | John Hicockson<br>William de Toft | 1404-1405 | SC 6/791/10 m. 4 |
| Hugh le Clerk | William le Smith<br>William le Mason | 1405-1406 | SC 6/792/1 m. 4 |
| Hugh le Clerk | Hugh Bradwall<br>Richard Trumpson | 1406-1407 | SC 6/792/2 m. 3 |
| Thomas Folville | Hugh Legh Thomas Bateson | 1407-1408 | SC 6/792/3 m. 4 |
| Henry Vernon<br><br>Thomas Hickson | William de Hasuldere<br>Thomas Balle | 1408-1409 | SC 6/792/5 m. 4 |
| Thomas Dunn | Robert Ruskin<br>John Weleson | 1409-1410 | SC 6/792/6 m. 4 |

| | | | |
|---|---|---|---|
| William Swetenham | William Dickey<br>Henry Rusky | 1410-1411 | SC 6/792/8 m. 3 |
| William Swetenham | William Bateson<br>Reginald Heyneson | 1411-1412 | SC 6/792/9 m. 3 |
| Hugh Coventry | Roger Ruskin<br>John Bailly | 1412-1413 | SC 6/792/10 m. 4 |
| Richard Crowther | Thomas Hodgkinson<br>Edmund del Crue | 1413-1414 | SC 6/793/1 m. 6 |
| Thomas Bateson | John Mynour John Warihull | 1414-1415 | SC 6/793/2 m. 5 |
| John del Lowe | John Perkinson<br>Thomas Weleson | 1415-1416 | SC 6/793/4 m. 4 |
| Hugh le Clerk | Robert Spencer<br>Hugh Weleson | 1416-1417 | SC 6/793/5 m. 4 |
| Hugh le Clerk | Richard Claytford<br>John Bermond | 1417-1418 | SC 6/793/7 m. 4 |
| William de Swetenham | Richard Erdeley<br>Richard Rownall | 1418-1419 | SC 6/793/9 m. 4 |
| William de Swetenham[10] | Thomas Walsh<br>William Heyneson | 1419-1420 | SC 6/793/11 m. 4 |
| Henry Vernon | William de Erdeley<br>William Weleson | 1420-1421 | SC 6/794/1 m. 4 |
| William Crowther | William Crowther<br>Ralph Spencer | 1421-1422 | SC 6/794/2 m. 4 |

10 He died during this last year of office. His wife Joanna paid off his arrears (SC 6/793/11 m. 4).

## (I) Officials at Northwich

*Steward*

| | |
|---|---|
| **William, son of Roger Starkey** | |
| appointed 24 June 1399 | *36 DKR*, p. 365; |
| | CHES 2/73 m. 6(4) |
| in office from Mich. 1399 to 25 March 1400 | SC 6/791/1 m. 2d |
| **Richard de Manley** | |
| in office from 25 March 1400 | SC 6/791/1 m. 2d |
| until 6 August 1401 | SC 6/791/3 m. 2d |
| also in office 1409-1410 | SC 6/792/6 m. 3d |
| **John de Legh** | |
| in office from 6 August 1401 | SC 6/791/3 m. 2d |
| to Mich. 1403[11]1 | SC 6/791/1 m. 2d |
| **Robert Castell** | |
| appointed 18 Sept. 1403 | *36 DKR*, p. 87: |
| | CHES 2/76 m. 12(4) |
| in office from Mich. 1403 | SC 6/791/7 m. 2d |
| to Mich. 1409 | SC 6/792/5 m. 3d |
| (town leased to Laurence Merbury from Mich. 1410 to Mich. 1413) | |
| **Henry Ravenscroft** | |
| appointed during pleasure | *37 DKR*, p. 610; |
| 10 Oct. 1413[12]2 | CHES 2/87 m. 1(7) |
| in office 1413-1414 | SC 6/793/1 m. 5 |
| **John Winnington** | |
| in office 1414-1415 | SC 6/793/2 m. 4 |
| (town leased to Peter de Dutton from Mich. 1415 to 21 May 1418) | |
| **John Starkey** | |
| in office 1418-1419 | SC 6/810/15 m. 1 |
| (clerk: **John Triket**) | |
| and 1419-1420 | SC 6/810/15 m. 2 |

11 He forfeited the Michaelmas payment of 1403 due to his support of Hotspur at Shrewsbury.

12 There is a previous appointment enrolled on 29 September 1406; *36 DKR*, p. 399, CHES 2/78 m. 6(9).

| *Chamberlain* | *Catchpole* | | |
|---|---|---|---|
| **William, son of Peter Starkey** | | | |
| | John Bradshawe | 1401-1402 | SC 6/791/5 m. 2d131 |
| **William, son of Peter Starkey** | | | |
| | John Nicholson | 1402-1403 | SC 6/791/6 m. 2d |
| **(John del Lowe and William Bate)**[14] | | | |
| | | 1403-1404 | SC 6/791/7 m. 2d |
| Thomas Paver[15] | Robert Hickson | 1405-1406 | SC 6/792/1 m. 2d |
| Thomas Paver | Robert Hickson | 1406-1407 | SC 6/792/2 m. 2d |
| Thomas Paver | John Snelleston | 1407-1408 | SC 6/792/3 m. 2d |
| Thomas Paver | John Vernon | 1408-1409 | SC 6/792/5 m. 3d |
| **(town leased to Laurence Merbury from Mich. 1410 to Mich. 1413)** | | | |
| Thomas Paver | Thomas Cariour | 1413-1414 | SC 6/793/1 m. 5 |
| John Bradshawe | John Brace | 1414-1415 | SC 6/793/2 m. 4 |
| **(town leased to Peter de Dutton from Mich. 1415 to 21 May 1418)** | | | |
| John Norley[16] | John Prince | 1418-1419 | SC 6/810/15 m. 1 |
| John Norley | William Jallock | 1419-1420 | SC 6/810/15 m. 2 |
| William Paver | | 1419-1420 | SC 6/810/15 m. 2 |

## (m) Officials at Shotwick

| *Reeves of the manor* | | |
|---|---|---|
| Simon le Shepherd[17] | in office from Mich. 1399 | SC 6/791/1 m. 3 |
| Richard Gille | to Mich. 1400 | |
| Richard Gille | in office from Mich. 1400 | SC 6/791/3 m. 3 |
| | to 27 April 1401 | |

(Manor leased by Richard Moston from 27 April 1401 to Mich. 1407.

13 William Anderton was named as collector of tolls in this year and the following year.
14 Described as deputies of Robert Castell as Steward.
15 Also described on all occasions of service as Castell's deputy as Steward.
16 Officials from this point were of Elizabeth, Dowager countess of Huntingdon and John Holland, earl of Huntingdon.
17 Already in office temp. Richard II.

Richard Moston died on 1 March 1408 (SC 6/792/3 m. 3))

| | | |
|---|---|---|
| Richard Gille) | in office from Mich. 1407 | SC 6/792/3 m. 3 |
| Roger de Ashley) | to Mich. 1408[18] | |
| Richard Gille | in office from Mich. 1408 to Mich. 1409 | SC 6/792/5 m. 2 |
| Richard Gille | in office from Mich. 1409 to 28 April 1410[19] | SC 6/792/6 m. 2 |

Manor granted to William Porter on 28 April 1410: SC 6/792/6 m. 2). Porter was still in possession in 1423 (JRRIL Rylands Charter 1418).

***Parker of Shotwick***

| | | |
|---|---|---|
| William de Helegh granted reversion of office 1 Oct. 1397 | | *36 DKR*, p. 229; CHES 2/71 m. 14(3)(4) |
| | Confirmed in office 16 Nov. 1399 | *36 DKR*, p. 229; CHES 2/74 m. 5(3) |
| | 20 Dec. 1400 | JRRIL Rylands Charter 1309, 1310 |
| | in office to 27 April 1401 | SC 6/774/13 m. 4 |
| John Brounwynd | in office from 15 Sept. 1403 | SC 6/775/9 m. 4 |
| | appointment enrolled 4 August 1410 | *36 DKR*, p. 433; CHES 2/82 m. 5d (1) |
| | still in office at Mich. 1422 | SC 6/794/2 m. 4d |
| | confirmed in office 13 Feb. 1423 | SC 6/1303/5 m. 4 |

18 John Fox described as bailiff (SC 2 156/13 m. 1, 2).

19 Hugh Daukyn described as bailiff (SC 2 156/13 m. 2d).

## (n) Officials at Macclesfield

### *(i) Stewards of the lordship*[20]

**Holder under Richard II: Sir Robert Legh**

| | |
|---|---|
| **Thomas de Wendesley Kt** | |
| appointed by King for life 13 Oct. 1399 | *CPR 1399-1401*, p. 31 |
| confirmed by Prince | SC 2/255/3 m. 2 |
| 20 Jan. 1400 | *36 DKR*, p. 312; CHES 2/74 m. 2d (6) |
| **Hugh le Despencer Kt** | |
| appointed 8 Oct. 1401 | *36 DKR*, p. 145; CHES 2/75 m. 1 (4)(5) |
| **John Stanley Kt** | |
| appointed 13 Sept. 1403 | *36 DKR*, p. 446; CHES 2/77 m. 2d (3) |
| confirmed by King 21 July 1404 | *CPR 1401-5*, p. 400 |
| **John Stanley jnr.** | |
| appointed 1 Feb. 1414 | *37 DKR*, p. 666; CHES 2/87 m. 2d (5)(6) |
| *Deputy* | |
| **Robert Staveley** | |
| appointed to hold courts during pleasure 2 Dec. 1399 | *36 DKR*, p. 312; CHES 2/74 m. 2d (6) |
| **Reginald del Dounes** | |
| **Robert del Dounes** | |
| late deputies of Thomas de Wensley | *36 DKR*, p. 145; CHES 2/75 m. 1(7) |
| 9 Oct. 1401 | SC 2/255/4 m. 4d |
| **Robert Legh Kt** | |
| appointed deputy by Hugh le Despencer | |

20 Appointed as steward of Macclesfield and as master forester, equitator and surveyor of the forests of Macclesfield and Delamere.

| | |
|---|---|
| 9 Oct. 1401 | *36 DKR*, p. 145; CHES 2/75 m. 1 (6) |
| still in office 1406 | SC 2/255/6 m. 1 |
| 1407 | SC 6/806/1 m. 2d |
| 1409 | SC 2/255/7 m. 1 |

**John Savage**

lieutenant of John Stanley snr.

| | |
|---|---|
| 1411-1412 | SC 2 255/8 m. 1 |
| 1412-1413 | SC 2 255/9 m. 1 |
| 1413-1414 | SC 2 255/10 m. 1 |

## *(ii) Burgus*

| *Catchpole* | *Prepositus* | | |
|---|---|---|---|
| Stephen Blag | Nicholas Ravenowe | 1399-1400 | SC 2/255/4 m. 5d |
| Thomas de Bowe | Henry de Prestbury | 1400-1401 | SC 6/805/7 m. 1 |
| John Hurdsfield | Robert Thorbalde | 1401-1402 | SC 6/805/9 m. 1d |
| John del Lowe | John del Lowe | 1402-1403 | SC 6/805/11 m. 1d |
| John del Stubbes | John del Stubbes | 1403-1404 | SC 6/805/13 m. 1d |
| Thomas del Lowe | Richard Davy | 1404-1405 | SC 6/805/16 m. 1d |
| John Rossyndale | John de Falibrome[21] | 1405-1406 | SC 6/805/16 m. 1d |
| Roger Rossyndale | Thomas del Lowe | 1406-1407 | SC 6/806/1 m. 1d |
| Robert Cartwright | Edmund Holyncete[22] | 1407-1408 | SC 6/806/3 m. 1d |
| John Hurdesfield | John de Newhall | 1408-1409 | SC 6/806/4 m. 1d |
| John del Lowe | Reginald Lowe | 1409-1410 | SC 6/806/4 m. 1d |
| John de Falibrome | William Billing | 1411-1412 | SC 6/806/5 m. 1d |
| John de Newhall | John Bedlem | 1412-1413 | SC 6/806/6 m. 1d |
| Ralph le Fletcher | Thomas Beek | 1413-1414 | SC 6/806/8 m. 1d |
| James Boulond | John del Lowe | 1414-1415 | SC 6/806/9 m. 1d |
| John Hurdesfield[23] | Reginald Lowe | 1415-1416 | SC 6/806/11 m. 1d |

21 SC 2/255/6 m. 2.

22 SC 2/255/7 m. 3.

23 At the portmote of October 1415, Reginald del Lowe was elected

| | | | |
|---|---|---|---|
| Thomas Beek | Richard Honde | 1416-1417 | SC 6/806/13 m. 1d |
| Richard Phelip | Geoffrey de Lowe | 1417-1418 | SC 6/806/16 m. 1d |
| Adam Okeden | John Billing | 1418-1419 | SC 6/806/17 m. 1d |
| John Bagueley[24] | Thomas Okedene | 1419-1420 | SC 6/807/1 m. 1d |
| Laurence Blag | Thomas Blag | 1420-1421 | SC 6/807/2 m. 1d |
| Richard Honne | John Glaskurion | 1420-31 Aug. 1422 | SC 6/807/3 m. 1d |
| ***Mayor*** | | | |
| Roger Alcock | in office | 1400-1401 | SC 2 255/4 m. 4d |
| | | 1404-1405 | JRRIL Tatton MS 1184 |
| | | 1405-1406 | SC 2/255/6 m. 2d |
| Reginald del Dounes | in office | 1406-1407 | SC 2/315/16 |
| | | 1412-1413 | SC 2/255/9 m. 3d |
| | | 1413-1414 | SC 2/255/10 m. 2; CHES 25/23 m. 42 |

## *(iii) Bailiffs of the hundred*

**Thomas Chedle**

**John Brounwynd**

| | |
|---|---|
| in office from Mich. 1400 | SC 6/805/7 m. 1 |
| to Mich. 1402 | SC 6/805/9 m. 1 |

**(deputy of John de Legh)**

**Thomas Chedle**

**William Grene**

| | |
|---|---|
| in office from Mich. 1402 | SC 6/805/11 m. 1 |
| to Mich. 1405 | SC 6/805/14 m. 1 |

catchpole and Thomas le Wright *prepositus*: it was announced that the latter had died, so Richard le Clerk was appointed in his place (SC 2/255/12 m. 5). However, Lowe accounted as *prepositus*, and Hurdesfield, who had been on the jury which elected these officials, as catchpole.

24 He served in place of Geoffrey de Lowe (SC 2/255/17 m. 4).

**(deputy of John Legh)**

**Thomas Chedle**

**Roger Alderley**

| | |
|---|---|
| in office from Mich. 1405 | SC 6/805/16 m. 1 |
| to Mich. 1408 | SC 6/806/3 m. 1 |

**(deputy of John Legh)**

**Thomas Chedle**[25]

**Thomas Swetenham**

| | |
|---|---|
| in office from Mich. 1408 | SC 6/806/4 m. 1 |
| to Mich. 1414 | SC 6/806/8 m. 1 |

**James Fitton**

**Thomas Swetenham**

| | |
|---|---|
| in office from Mich. 1414 | SC 6/806/9 m. 1 |
| to Mich. 1417 | SC 6/806/13 m. 1 |

**James Fitton**

**William Honford**

| | |
|---|---|
| in office from Mich. 1417 | SC 6/806/16 m. 1 |
| to 31 Aug. 1422 | SC 6/807/3 m. 1 |

## *(iv) Bailiff of the forest in fee and collector of revenues*

**John de Mottram**

| | |
|---|---|
| in office Mich. 1400 | SC 6/805/7 m. 2 |
| removed from office Mich. 1413 | SC 6/806/6 m. 3 |

*deputy*

**Reginald del Dounes**

| | |
|---|---|
| until 1408 | SC 6/806/3 m. 2 |

**John Savage**

| | |
|---|---|
| in office from Mich. 1409 | SC 6/806/4 m. 2 |
| to Mich. 1413 | SC 6/806/6 m. 3 |

25 Chedle died within the term of the account of 1414 (SC 6/806/8 m. 1). James Fitton was described as his deputy and accounted on the dead man's behalf. (Writ *diem clausit extremum* on the death of Chedle (*37 DKR*, p. 130; CHES 2/88 m. 2d (12)).

| | |
|---|---|
| **John Savage** | |
| in office from Mich. 1413 | SC 6/806/8 m. 3 |
| still in office 31 Aug. 1422 | SC 6/807/3 m. 2 |

## *(v) Park*

| | |
|---|---|
| *Parker* | |
| **Hugh Hoby** | |
| appointed by the King for | *CPR 1399-1401*, p. 41 |
| life 29 Oct. 1399 | *36 DKR*, p. 235; |
| | CHES 2/74 m. 8d (1) |
| confirmed in office by prince | *36 DKR*, p. 235; |
| 4 Dec. 1399[26] | CHES 2/74 m. 8d (2) |
| in office from Mich. 1400 | SC 6/805/7 m. 3d |
| to Mich. 1403 | SC 6/805/11 m. 3 |
| **John Savage** | |
| in office from Mich. 1403[27] | SC 6/805/16 m. 3 |
| still in office 31 Aug. 1422 | SC 6/807/3 m. 3d |
| *Sellers of peat* | |
| **Robert Parker** | |
| in office from Mich. 1412 | SC 6/806/6 m. 4d |
| to Mich. 1419 | SC 6/806/17 m. 3d |
| **Thomas Overhand** | |
| in office from Mich. 1419 | SC 6/807/1 m. 3d |
| to 31 Aug. 1422 | SC 6/807/3 m. 3d |

26 Licence to appoint a deputy whilst engaged in the wars in Scotland or overseas, 5 Dec. 1399 (*36 DKR*, p. 235; CHES 2/74 m. 8d (3). John Savage acted as his deputy.

27 He did not account, however, until Michaelmas 1406, when he accounted for the past five years. He had already been granted the office of park keeper for life in January 1398 (*36 DKR*, p. 292; CHES 2/71 m. 25 (15) (16)). New letters had been granted on 2 Jan. 1400, but he did not 'recover' the office from Hoby until 8 Dec. 1405, from which date he was deemed accountable (SC 6/775/6 m. 4).

APPENDIX II

# *Abstracts of accounts*

## Appendix II (a): Sheriff of Chester city

| SC 6 | 791/1 m.1 1400 | 791/3 m.1 1401 | 791/5 m.1 1402 | 791/6 m.1 1403 | 791/7 m.1 1404 |
|---|---|---|---|---|---|
| Rents | 103.13.10 | 103.13.10 | 103.13.10 | 103.13.10 | 103.13.10 |
| Goods & Chattels | - | - | - | - | - |
| Receipts | 103.13.10 | 103.13.10 | 103.13.10 | 103.13.10 | 103.13.10 |
| Arrears | 8.0.6 | 3.13.10 | - | 10.0.0 | - |
| Receipts & Arrears | 114.14.4 | 107.7.8 | 103.13.10 | 113.13.10 | 103.13.10 |
| Liveries | 108.0.6 | 106.6.2 | 55.19.0 | 112.12.4 | 102.12.4 |
| Allowances | | 1.1.6[1] | 37.14.10[2] | 1.1.6 | 1.1.6 |
| Remainder | 3.13.10 | - | 10.0.0 | - | - |

| SC 6 | 791/10 m.1 1405 | 792/1 m.1 1406 | 792/2 m.1 1407 | 792/3 m.1 1408 | 792/5 m.1 1409 |
|---|---|---|---|---|---|
| Rents | 103.13.10 | 103.13.10 | 103.13.10 | 103.13.10 | 103.13.10 |
| Goods & Chattels | - | - | - | - | - |
| Receipts | 103.13.10 | 103.13.10 | 103.13.10 | 103.13.10 | 103.13.10 |
| Arrears | - | - | - | - | - |
| Receipts & Arrears | 103.13.10 | 103.13.10 | 103.13.10 | 103.13.10 | 103.13.10 |
| Liveries | 102.12.4 | 103.13.10 | 102.12.4 | 102.12.4 | 102.12.4 |
| Allowances | 1.1.6 | - | 1.1.6 | 1.1.6 | 61.1.6[3] |
| Remainder | - | - | - | - | - |

1 Allowed almost every year to the prioress and convent of the Blessed Virgin Mary of Chester for the manor of Newerk.

2 Includes £36.13.4 allowed to the sheriffs for the payment of the fee farm of the city due at Easter 1402.

3 £60 allowed to sheriffs for money borrowed from them by Gilbert Talbot for victualling of Harlech castle.

| SC 6 | 792/6 m.1 1410 | 792/8 m.1 1411 | 792/9 m.1 1412 | 792/10 m.1 1413 | 793/1 m.1 1414 |
|---|---|---|---|---|---|
| Rents | 103.13.10 | 103.13.10 | 103.13.10 | 103.13.10½ | 103.13.10½ |
| Goods & Chattels | - | - | - | - | - |
| Receipts | 103.13.10 | 103.13.10 | 103.13.10 | 103.13.10½ | 103.13.10½ |
| Arrears | - | - | -- | 7.10.0½ | 22.19.0½ |
| Receipts & Arrears | 103.13.10 | 103.13.10 | 103.13.10 | 111.3.11 | 126.12.11 |
| Liveries | 42.12.4 | 102.12.4 | 95.2.4 | 87.3.4½ | 70.6.8 |
| Allowances | 1.1.6 | 1.1.6 | 1.1.6 | 1.1.6 | 1.1.6 |
| Remainder | - | - | 7.10.0½ | 22.10.0½ | 55.4.9 |

| SC 6 | 793/2 m.1 1415 | 793/4 m.1 1416 | 793/5 m. 1 1417 | 793/7 m.1 1418 | 793/9 m.1 1419 |
|---|---|---|---|---|---|
| Rents | 103.13.10½ | 103.13.10½ | 103.13.10½ | 103.13.10½ | 103.13.10½ |
| Goods & Chattels | - | - | - | - | - |
| Receipts | 103.13.10½ | 103.13.10½ | 103.13.10½ | 103.13.10½ | 103.13.10½ |
| Arrears | 55.4.9 | 44.3.11¼ | 52.17.5¼ | 52.3.7½ | 38.13.10½ |
| Receipts & Arrears | 158.18.7½ | 147.17.9¾ | 156.11.3¾ | 155.17.6 | 142.7.9 |
| Liveries | 113.12.2¼ | 93.18.10½ | 103.6.2 | 116.2.1½ | 83.13.4 |
| Allowances | 1.1.6 | 1.1.6 | 1.1.6 | 1.1.6 | 19.15.4½[4] |
| Remainder | 44.3.11¼ | 52.17.5¼ | 52.3.7 | 38.13.10½ | 38.19.0½ |

4 Of this, £18.13.10½, being the arrears of John Hope as sheriff in 1413 and 1414 was transferred to the roll of contumacious arrears of Flintshire this year.

| SC 6 | 793/11 m.1 1420 | 794/1 m.1 1421 | 794/2 m.1 1422 |
|---|---|---|---|
| Rents | 103.13.10½ | 103.13.10½ | 103.13.10½ |
| Goods & Chattels | - | 5.0.5[5] | - |
| Receipts | 103.13.10½ | 108.13.10½ | 103.13.10½ |
| Arrears | 38.19.0½ | 52.12.4½ | 69.18.1 |
| Receipts & Arrears | 142.12.11 | 161.6.3 | 173.11.11½ |
| Liveries | 88.19.0½ | 80.6.8 | 64.3.1 |
| Allowances | 1.1.6 | 1.1.6 | 1.1.6 |
| Remainder | 52.12.4½ | 69.18.1 | 108.7.4½ |

## Appendix II (b): Dee Corn Mills and Fishery

NB Miscellaneous sales are made up of sales of wood and old mill stones

| SC 6 | 791/1, m.5 1400 | 791/3, m.5&6 1401[6] | 791/5, m. 4 1402 | 791/6, m. 7 1403 | 791/7, m. 6 1404 |
|---|---|---|---|---|---|
| Sales of grain | 194.7.9 | 216.4.10 | 234.16.5½ | 192.19.1 | 1193.6.2 |
| Sales of fish | 6.6.3 | 8.18.11 | 12.0.8 | 7.0.10 | 11.0.4 |
| Misc sales | 5.8 | 8.8. | 8.0 | 4.0 | - |
| Receipts | 200.19.8 | 225.12.5 | 247.5.1½ | 200.4.9 | 204.6.6 |
| Arrears | 39.16.11½ | 52.17.7½ | 76.5.11½ | 46.17.3 | 11.6.5½ |
| Receipts & Arrears | 240.16.7¼ | 278.10.0½ | 323.11.1 | 247.2.0 | 215.12.11½ |
| Wages | 30.8.6 | 9.2.0 | 9.2.6 | 9.2.6 | 9.2.6 |

5 Due from the forfeiture of Thomas Hanne, 2 October 1421. In fact, this sum together with £24.15.0 (the arrears of Stephen Belleyeter as sheriff in 1420) was respited, the former to be paid in the next year, the second in instalments over the next two years.

6 An amalgamation of the two accounts for this year: Mich. 1400 to 5 July 1401 of Henry Strangeways (m. 5), and 5 July 1401 to Mich. 1401 of Robert Castell (m. 6).

| SC 6 | 791/1, m.5 1400 | 791/3, m.5&6 1401[7] | 791/5, m. 4 1402 | 791/6, m. 7 1403 | 791/7, m. 6 1404 |
|---|---|---|---|---|---|
| Repairs | 10.5.5½ | 9.7.1½ | 8.3.1 | 9.3.0½ | 8.11.1 |
| Annuities | 25.0.0 | 20.0.0 | 20.0.0 | 20.0.0 | 20.0.0 |
| Total expen. | 63.13.11½ | 38.9.1½ | 37.5.7 | 38.5.6½ | 37.13.7 |
| Balance inc arrears | 185.2.7¾ | 240.0.11 | 286.5.6 | 208.16.5½ | 177.19.4½ |
| Balance exc arrears | 135.5.8½ | 187.3.3½ | 209.19.6½ | 161.19.2½ | 166.12.11 |
| Liveries | 122.5.0¼ | 148.0.9 | 202.11.0½ | 197.17.3½ | 132. 16. 11½ |
| Allowances | - | 15.14.2 | - | 36.17.2 | - |
| Remainder | 52.17.7½ | 76.5.11½ | 46.17.3½ | 11.6.5½[8] | 10.19.5 |

| SC 6 | 791/10, m.8 1405 | 792/1, m. 5 1406 | 792/2, m. 5 1407 | 792/3, m.5 1408 | 792/5, m.5 1409 |
|---|---|---|---|---|---|
| Sales of grain | 200.18.1½ | 223. 19.1 | 309.5.6 | 253.7.7½ | 292.1.1½ |
| Sales of fish | 8.12.9 | 18.7.11 | 13.2.7 | 16.3.1 | 13.10.10 |
| Misc sales | 4.0 | 8.0 | 10.4 | 1.14.3 | 8 |
| Receipts | 209.14.10½ | 242.15.00 | 322.18.5 | 271.4.11½ | 305.12.7½ |
| Arrears | 10.19.5 | 33.19.4 | 33.19.4 | 59.17.7 | 38.9.9 |
| Receipts & Arrears | 220.14.3½ | 276.14.4 | 356.17.9 | 331.2.6½ | 344.2.4½ |
| Wages | 10.15.10 | 10.15.10 | 10.15.10 | 10.15.10 | 10.15.10 |
| Repairs | 8.6.6½ | 8.2.8 | 12.3.0 | 9.8.8½ | 9.3.5½ |
| Annuities | 20.0.0 | 20.0.0 | 20.0.0 | 20.0.0 | 20.0.0 |
| Total expen. | 39.2.4½ | 38.18.6 | 42.18.10 | 40.4.6½ | 39.19.3½ |

7 An amalgamation of the two accounts for this year: Mich. 1400 to 5 July 1401 of Henry Strangeways (m. 5), and 5 July 1401 to Mich. 1401 of Robert Castell (m. 6).

8 Including 7s. 9½d. charged after the account settled.

| SC 6 | 791/10, m.8 1405 | 792/1, m. 5 1406 | 792/2, m. 5 1407 | 792/3, m.5 1408 | 792/5, m.5 1409 |
|---|---|---|---|---|---|
| Balance incl arrears | 181.11.11 | 237.15.10 | 313.18.11 | 290.18.0 | 294.3.1 |
| Balance excl arrears | 170.12.6 | 203.16.6 | 79.19.7 | 231.0.5 | 265.13.4 |
| Liveries | 142.12.7 | 203.16.11 | 255.1.4 | 243.13.3 | 254.14.6½ |
| Allowances | 34.3.0 | - | - | 8.15.0 | 6.13.4 |
| Remainder | 33.19.4 | 33.19.4 | 59.17.7 | 38.9.9 | 42.15.2½ |
| Payment to auditors | | | | - | - |

| SC 6 | 792/6, m.5 1410 | 792/8, m. 1d 1411 | 792/9, m.4 1412 | 792/10, m.5 1413 | 793/1, m.3 1414 |
|---|---|---|---|---|---|
| Sales of grain | 277.19.0½ | 224.13.7 | 118.5.7½ | 149.2.7½ | 185.8.1¼ |
| Sales of fish | 11.14.4 | 15.0.8 | 9.4.8 | 6.2.9 | 12.1.9 |
| Misc sales | 1.6.0 | 7.4 | 4.8 | 1.2.0 | - |
| Receipts | 280.19.4½ | 240.2.3 | 127.14.5½ | 156.7.4½ | 197.19.10½ |
| Arrears | 42.15.2½ | 63.18.4½ | 82.1.4 | - | 19.18.4½ |
| Receipts & Arrears | 323.14.7 | 304.0.7½ | 209.15.9½ | 156.7.4½ | 217.8.3 |
| Wages | 10.15.10 | 10.15.10 | 10.15.10 | 10.15.10 | 10.15.10 |
| Repairs | 8.14.6½ | 10.13.0 | 10.15.1½ | 10.19.10 | - |
| Annuities | 15.0.0 | 5.0.0 | 15.0.0 | 10.0.0 | 10.0.0 |
| Total expen. | 34.10.4½ | 26.8.10 | 36.10.11 | 31.15.8 | 20.15.10 |
| Balance incl. arrears | 289.3.1 | 277.11.9½ | 173.4.10½ | 124.11.8½ | 196.12.5 |
| Balance excl. arrears | 246.9.0 | 213.13.5 | 91.3.6½ | 124.11.8½ | 177.4.0½ |
| Liveries | 218.5.10 | 167.13.8 | 173.4.10½ | 104.13.4 | 164.6.10½ |
| Allowances | 7.0.0 | 27.16.9½ | - | - | - |

| SC 6 | 792/6, m.5 1410 | 792/8, m. 1d 1411 | 792/9, m.4 1412 | 792/10, m.5 1413 | 793/1, m.3 1414 |
|---|---|---|---|---|---|
| Remainder | 63.18.4½ | 82.1.4 | - | 19.18.4½ | 32.5.6½ |
| Payment to auditors | - | - | - | - | - |

| SC 6 | 793/2, m.8 1415 | 793/4, m. 2 1416 | 793/5, m. 2 1417 | 793/7, m. 2 1418 | 793/9, m. 2 1419 |
|---|---|---|---|---|---|
| Sales of grain | 191.16.11½ | 194.13.8½ | 178.19.10½ | 174.0.8½ | 177.10.10 |
| Sales of fish | 11.12.4 | 4.12.7 | 9.2.5½ | 5.7.2 | 7.1.4 |
| Misc sales | - | 17.8 | 4 | 5.0 | 1.3.4 |
| Receipts | 203.8.3½ | 200.3.10½ | 188.2.9½ | 179.12.10½ | 185.15.6 |
| Arrears | 32.5.6½ | 51.8.0 | 83.10.8½ | 61.17.9½ | 54.8.10 |
| Receipts & Arrears | 235.14.10 | 251.11.10½ | 271.13.6 | 241.10.8 | 240.4.4 |
| Wages | 10.15.10 | 10.15.10 | 10.15.10 | 10.15.10 | 10.15.10 |
| Repairs | 3.4[9] | 3.4 | 3.4 | 3.4 | 3.4 |
| Annuities | 5.0.0 | - | 8.12.0½ | 45.0.0 | 19.7.10 |
| Total expen. | 15.19.2 | 10.19.2 | 19.11.2½ | 55.19.2 | 30.7.0 |
| Balance incl. arrears | 219.15.8 | 240.12.8 | 252.2.3½ | 185.11.6 | 209.17.4 |
| Balance excl. arrears | 187.9.1½ | 189.4.8½ | 168.11.7 | 123.13.8½ | 155.8.6 |
| Liveries | 146.7.8 | 136.8.8 | 168.17.10 | 109.160.0 | 124.8.5½ |
| Allowances | - | - | - | - | - |
| Remainder | 51.8.0 | 83.10.5½ | 61.17.9½ | 54.8.10 | 64.2.2½ |
| Payment to auditors | 22.0.0[10] | 20.13.4 | 21.6.8 | 21.6.8 | 21.6.8 |

9 Repairs now accounted by the chamberlain of Chester. Henceforward only miscellaneous expenses charged here such as a parchment for the records of the mill.

10 Auditor's wages were charged here but most likely actually paid to them by the chamberlain.

| SC 6 | 793/11, m.2 1420 | 794/1, m. 2 1421 | 794/2, m. 2 1422 |
|---|---|---|---|
| Sales of grain | 173.18.11½ | 144.3.9 | 181.9.5 |
| Sales of fish | 6.10.3 | 8.16.8 | 9.7.6 |
| Misc sales | - | 1.1.8 | 13.6 |
| Receipts | 180.9.2½ | 154.2.1 | 191.10.5 |
| Arrears | 64.2.2½ | 84.4.8½ | 79.4.6½ |
| Receipts & Arrears | 244.11.5 | 238.6.9½ | 270.14.11½ |
| Wages | 10.15.10 | 10.15.10 | 10.15.10 |
| Repairs | 3.4 | 3.4 | 3.4 |
| Annuities | 20.0.0 | 20.0.0 | 20.00.00 |
| Total expen. | 30.19.2 | 30.19.2 | 31.2.6 |
| Balance incl. arrears | 213.12.3 | 207.7.7½ | 239.12.5½ |
| Balance excl. arrears | 149.10.0½ | 123.2.11 | 160.7.11 |
| Liveries | 106.14.2½ | 107.9.9 | 148.18.10½ |
| Allowances | - | - | - |
| Remainder | 84.4.8½ | 79.4.6½ | 74.3.7 |
| Payment to auditors | 22.13.4 | 20.13.4 | 16.10.0 |

## Appendix II (c). Delamere Forest

| SC 6 | 791/1 m.2 1400 | 791/3 m.2 1401 | 791/5 m.1d 1402 | 791/6 m.2 1403 | 791/7 m.2 1404 |
|---|---|---|---|---|---|
| Rents | 21.0.4 | 21.0.4 | 21.0.4 | 21.0.4 | 21.0.4 |
| Agistment | 18.2.0 | 22.0.0 | 22.0.0 | 22.0.0 | 22.0.0 |
| Sale of moss | 9.0.0. | 7.10.10 | 2.6.8 | 2.6.8 | 15.13.4 |
| Sale of wood | 3.2.7 | 4.16.2 | 13.18.2 | 4.5.4 | 4.12.4 |

| SC 6 | 791/1 m.2 1400 | 791/3 m.2 1401 | 791/5 m.1d 1402 | 791/6 m.2 1403 | 791/7 m.2 1404 |
|---|---|---|---|---|---|
| Fines and forfeits | 14.5 | 1.7.0 | 1.6.1½ | 3.4 | 1.1.4 |
| Receipts | 51.19.4 | 56.19.4 | 50.11.3½ | 49.15.8 | 64.7.4 |
| Arrears | 112.11.10½ | 119.18.6½ | 118.10.6 | 115.14.5½ | 105.11.5½ |
| Receipts & Arrears | 174.11.2½ | 176.12.10½ | 169.1.9½ | 165.10.1½ | 169.18.9½ |
| Wages | 1.0.0 | - | - | - | - |
| Annuities | - | 2.2.2 | 10.0.0 | 5.0.0 | - |
| Balance incl. arrears | 173.11.2½ | 174.10.8½ | 159.1.9½ | 160.10.1½ | 169.18.9½ |
| Balance excl. arrears | 50.19.4 | 54.12.2 | 40.11.3½ | 44.15.8 | 64.7.4 |
| Liveries | 53.12.8 | 42.19.1 | 54.7.11 | 50.3.10 | 117.3.1 |
| Allowances | - | 13.1.1½ | - | 2.10.11½ | - |
| Respites | 45.0.0 | 64.14.0 | 48.2.0½ | - | 20.0.0 |
| Remainder | 74.18.6½ | 53.16.6 | 67.16.5 | 105.11.5½ | 32.15.8½ |

| SC 6 | 791/10 m.2 1405 | 792/1 m.2 1406 | 792/2 m.2 1407 | 792/3 m.2 1408 | 792/5 m.3 1409 |
|---|---|---|---|---|---|
| Rents | 21.0.4 | 21.0.4 | 21.0.4 | 21.0.4 | 21.0.4 |
| Agistment | 22.0.0 | 22.0.0 | 22.0.0 | 22.0.0 | 22.0.0 |
| Sale of moss | 15.13.4 | 14.17.0 | 14.10.0 | 14.1.4 | 12.14.0 |
| Sale of wood | 6.18.6 | 7.1.4 | 6.7.1 | 6.13.0 | 6.3.7 |
| Fines and forfeits | 4.18. | 2.8.0½ | 1.12.1 | 1.13.4 | 3.4 |
| Receipts | 70.10.6 | 67.6.8½ | 65.9.6 | 65.8.0 | 67.1.3 |
| Arrears | 52.15.8½ | 69.9.3 | 41.10.11½ | 29.9.5½ | 29.12.5½ |
| Receipts & Arrears | 123.6.2½ | 136.15.11½ | 107.0.5½ | 94.17.5½ | 91.13.8½ |
| Wages | - | 1.0.0 | - | 2.0.0 | 1.0.0 |
| Annuities | - | - | - | 10.0.0 | 10.0.0 |

| SC 6 | 791/10 m.2 1405 | 792/1 m.2 1406 | 792/2 m.2 1407 | 792/3 m.2 1408 | 792/5 m.3 1409 |
|---|---|---|---|---|---|
| Balance incl. arrears | 123.6.2½ | 135.15.11½ | 107.0.5½ | 92.17.5½ | 90.13.8½ |
| Balance excl. arrears | 70.10.6 | 66.6.8½ | 65.9.6 | 63.8.0 | 66.1.3 |
| Liveries | 53.16.11½ | 76.5.0 | 59.6.0 | 63.5.0 | 59.1.7 |
| Allowances | - | 18.0.0 | 18.5.0 | - | - |
| Respites | - | 32.4.4 | - | 5.8.1 | 8.18.9 |
| Remainder | 69.9.3 | 9.6.7½ | 29.9.5½ | 24.4.4½ | 22.13.4½ |

| SC 6 | 792/6 m.3 1410 | 792/8 m.3 1411 | 792/9 m.2 1412 | 792/10 m.3 1413 | 793/1 m.2d 1414 |
|---|---|---|---|---|---|
| Rents | 21.0.4 | 21.0.4 | 21.0.4 | 21.0.4 | 21.0.4 |
| Agistment | 22.0.0 | 18.0.0 | 18.0.0 | 18.0.0 | 18.0.0 |
| Sale of moss | 13.11.2½ | 12.0.0 | 13.0.10 | 13.5.1 | 13.0.1 |
| Sale of wood | 9.15.10 | 5.1.5 | 5.13.2 | 2.5.3 | 4.9.3 |
| Fines and forfeits | 3.4 | 16.0 | 6.8 | 6.8 | 1.16.8 |
| Receipts | 66.10.8½ | 56.17.9 | 58.1.0 | 54.17.4 | 58.6.4 |
| Arrears | 31.12.1½ | 43.9.7½ | 70.1.3½ | 48.12.1½ | 63.12.5½ |
| Receipts & Arrears | 98.2.10 | 100.7.4½ | 128.2.3½ | 103.9.5½ | 121.18.9½ |
| Wages | 1.0.0 | - | 1.0.0 | 1.0.0 | 1.0.0 |
| Annuities | 10.0.0 | 10.0.0 | 10.0.0 | 10.0.0 | 10.0.0 |
| Balance incl. arrears | 97.2.10 | 110.7.4½ | 124.4.7½ | 92.9.5½ | 110.18.9½ |
| Balance excl. arrears | 65.10.8½ | 56.17.9 | 54.3.4 | 43.17.4 | 47.6.4 |
| Liveries | 53.13.2½ | 30.4.5 | 67.12.6 | 28.17.0 | 49.11.6 |
| Allowances | - | 1.8 | 7.0.0 | - | - |
| Respites | 8.18.9 | 8.18.9 | 23.10.8 | 17.17.4 | 15.12.1 |
| Remainder | 34.10.10½ | 61.2.6½ | 25.1.5½ | 46.15.1½ | 45.15.2½ |

| SC 6 | 793/2 m.3 1415 | 793/4 m.3 1416 | 793/5 m.3 1417 | 793/7 m.3 1418 | 793/9 m. 2 1419 |
|---|---|---|---|---|---|
| Rents | 21.0.4 | 21.0.4 | 21.0.4 | 21.0.4 | 21.0.4 |
| Agistment | 18.0.0 | 18.0.0 | 16.18.9 | 15.10.7 | 16.7.10 |
| Sale of moss | 12.0.7 | .9.7 | 9.2.4 | 9.6.10 | 8.8.5 |
| Sale of wood | 3.3.6 | 2.12.8 | 4.6.10 | 2.13.4 | 3.7.7 |
| Fines and forfeits | 6.8 | 3.19.2 | 6.8 | 1.16.0 | 1.4.0 |
| Receipts | 54.11.1 | 55.1.9 | 51.14.11 | 50.7.1 | 50.8.2 |
| Arrears | 61.7.3½ | 66.11.6½ | 73.11.0½ | 46.5.7 | 46.19.4 |
| Receipts & Arrears | 115.18.4½ | 121.13.3½ | 125.5.11½ | 96.12.8 | 97.7.6 |
| Wages | 1.0.0 | 1.0.0 | 1.0.0 | 1.0.0 | 1.0.0 |
| Annuities | 10.0.0 | 10.0.0 | 10.0.0 | 10.0.0 | 10.0.0 |
| Balance incl. arrears | 104.18.4½ | 110.13.3½ | 114.5.11½ | 85.12.8 | 86.7.6 |
| Balance excl. arrears | 43.11.1 | 44.1.9 | 40.14.11 | 39.7.1 | 39.8.2 |
| Liveries | 38.6.10 | 37.2.2 | 31.3.6 | 38.13.4 | 39.4.4 |
| Allowances | - | - | 36.16.10½ | - | - |
| Respites | 46.5.1 | 8.18.9 | 11.18.9½ | 12.16.9 | 12.16.9 |
| Remainder | 20.6.5½ | 64.12.3½ | 34.6.10 | 34.2.7 | 34.6.4 |

| SC 6 | 793/11 m.3 1420 | 794/1 m.3 1421 | 794/2 m. 3 1422 |
|---|---|---|---|
| Rents | 21.0.4 | 21.0.4 | 21.0.4 |
| Agistment | 17.7.9 | 16.7.9 | 14.1.4 |
| Sale of moss | 8.10.0 | 6.11.7 | 4.13.6 |
| Sale of wood | 4.18.3 | 3.4.0 | 4.3.3 |
| Fines and forfeits | 6.0 | 16.2½ | - |

| SC 6 | 793/11 m.3 1420 | 794/1 m.3 1421 | 794/2 m. 3 1422 |
|---|---|---|---|
| Receipts | 52.2.4 | 48.9.10½ | 43.18.5 |
| Arrears | 47,3,1 | 48.7.4 | 51.16.6½ |
| Receipts & Arrears | 99.5.5 | 96.17.2½ | 95.14.11½ |
| Wages | - | 1.0.0 | 1.0.0 |
| Annuities | 10.0.0 | 10.0.0 | 10.0.0 |
| Balance incl. arrears | 89.5.5 | 85.17.2½ | 85.1.7½ |
| Balance excl. arrears | 42.2.4 | 37.9.10½ | 33.5.1 |
| Liveries | 40.18.1 | 34.0.8 | 31.19.8 |
| Allowances | - | - | - |
| Respites | 7.8.8 | 7.8.8 | 7.8.8 |
| Remainder | 40.18.8 | 44.7.10½ | 45.3.3½ |

## Appendix II(d): Drakelow and Rudheath

(NB Income from courts includes communal ingressus, reliefs, forfeits).

| SC6 | 791/1 m.1d 1400 | 791/3 m.1 1401 | 791/5 m.1 1402 | 791/6 m.1 1403 | 791/7 m.1 1404 |
|---|---|---|---|---|---|
| Rents | 50.12.5 | 50.12.5 | 49.3.3 | 49.3.3 | 49.3.3 |
| Turbary | 2.0.10 | 1.0.0 | Nil | Nil | Nil |
| Courts etc. | 12.10¾ | 1.11 | 12.4 | 17.9 | 9.6 |
| Total Receipts | 53.6.1¾ | 51.14.4 | 49.15.7 | 50.1.0 | 49.12.9 |
| Arrears | 75.13.2 | 85.19.2 | 68.8.10 | 55.14.9 | 32.13.4 |
| Receipts & Arrears | 128.19.3¾ | 137.13.6 | 116.4.5 | 105.15.9 | 82.6.1 |
| Wages | Nil | 3.8.3 | 3.0.10 | 3.0.10 | 3.0.10 |
| Annuities | 27.5.0 | 20.0.0 | 10.0.0 | 30.0.0 | 45.0.0 |
| Discharge | 27.5.0 | 23.8.3 | 13.0.10 | 33.0.10 | 48.0.10 |

| SC6 | 791/1 m.1d 1400 | 791/3 m.1 1401 | 791/5 m.1 1402 | 791/6 m.1 1403 | 791/7 m.1 1404 |
|---|---|---|---|---|---|
| Balance incl. arrears | 101.14.3¾ | 114.5.3 | 105.3.7 | 72.14.11 | 34.5.3 |
| Balance excl. arrears | 26.1.1¾ | 28.6.1 | 36.14.9 | 17.0.2 | 1.11.11 |
| Liveries | 14.3.2 | 43.15.5 | 49.8.10 | 25.1.7 | 3.0.0 |
| Allowances | 1.11.11¾ | Nil | Nil | 15.0.0 | Nil |
| Respites | 61.13.4 | 4.13.4 | 40.13.4 | Nil | Nil |
| Remainder | 24.5.10 | 19.19.6 | 19.1.5 | 32.13.4 | 31.5.3 |

| SC6 | 791/10 m.1 1405 | 792/11 1406 | 792/2 m.1 1407 | 792/3 m.1d 1408 | 792/5 m.1d 1409 |
|---|---|---|---|---|---|
| Rents | 49.3.3 | 52.5.3 | 51.2.9 | 51.2.9 | 51.2.9 |
| Turbary | Nil | Nil | Nil | Nil | Nil |
| Courts etc. | Nil | 3.4.3 | 3.6.11 | 3.1.2¼ | 5.15.1½ |
| Total Receipts | 49.3.3 | 55.9.11 | 54.9.6 | 54.3.11 | 56.17.10½ |
| Arrears | 31.5.3 | 17.7.6 | 10.9.10½ | 23.17.0½ | 15.6.0 |
| Receipts & Arrears | 80.8.6 | 72.17.5 | 64.19.6½ | 78.0.11¾ | 72.3.10½ |
| Wages | 3.0.10 | 3.0.10 | 3.0.10 | 3.0.10 | 3.0.10 |
| Annuities | 35.0.0 | 35.0.0 | 35.0.0 | 39.13.4 | 42.0.0 |
| Discharge | 38.0.10 | 38.0.10 | 38.0.10 | 42.14.2 | 45.0.10 |
| Balance incl. arrears | 48.7.8 | 34.16.7 | 26.18.8½ | 35.6.9¾ | 27.3.0½ |
| Balance excl. arrears | 11.2.5 | 17.9.1 | 16.8.10 | 11.9.9½ | 11.17.0½ |
| Liveries | 22.0.2 | 24.6.8½ | 3.1.8 | 18.6.0 | 13.3.10½ |
| Allowances | 3.0.0 | Nil | Nil | 1.14.9½ | Nil |
| Respites | Nil | 3.13.4 | 3.13.4 | 3.13.4 | 3.13.4 |
| Remainder | 17.7.6 | 6.16.6½ | 20.3.8½ | 11.12.8 | 10.5.10 |

| SC6 | 792/6 m.1d 1410 | 792/8 m.1d 1411 | 792/9 m.1d 1412 | 792/10 m.2 1413 | 793/1 m.2 1414 |
|---|---|---|---|---|---|
| Rents | 51.2.9 | 51.2.9 | 51.2.9 | 51.2.9 | 51.2.9 |
| Turbary | Nil | Nil | Nil | Nil | Nil |
| Courts etc. | 8.1.9 | 2.5.1¼ | 3.4 | Nil | Nil |
| Total Receipts | 59.4.6 | 53.17.10¼ | 51.6.1 | 51.2.9 | 51.2.9 |
| Arrears | 13.19.2 | 10.5.10 | 20.5.10 | 18.17.9 | 20.0.5 |
| Receipts & Arrears | 73.3.8 | 64.3.8¾ | 71.11.11 | 70.0.6 | 71.3.2 |
| Wages | 3.0.10 | 3.0.10 | 3.0.10 | 3.0.10 | 3.0.10 |
| Annuities | 39.13.4 | 29.13.4 | 49.13.4 | 18.13.0 | 49.13.4 |
| Discharge | 42.14.2 | 32.14.2 | 52.14.2 | 21.13.10 | 52.14.2 |
| Balance incl. arrears | 30.9.6 | 31.9.6 | 18.17.9 | 48.6.8 | 18.9.0 |
| Balance excl. arrears | 16.10.4 | 21.3.8 | -1.8.1 | 29.8.11 | -1.11.7 |
| Liveries | 16.5.8 | 11.3.8 | Nil | 28.1.7 | 7.19.10 |
| Allowances | 3.18.0 | Nil | Nil | 4.8 | 3.4 |
| Respites | Nil | Nil | Nil | Nil | Nil |
| Remainder | 10.5.10 | 20.5.10 | 18.7.9 | 20.0.5 | 10.5.10 |

| SC6 | 793/2 m.2 1415 | 793/4 m.2 1416 | 793/5 m.2 1417 | 793/7 m.2 1418 | 793/9 m.2 1419 |
|---|---|---|---|---|---|
| Rents | 51.2.9 | Nil | Nil | Nil | Nil |
| Turbary | Nil | Nil | 1.8.4¾ | Nil | 16.5 |
| Courts etc. | Nil | 51.2.9 | 52.11.1¾ | 51.2.9 | 51.19.2 |
| Total Receipts | 51.2.9 | 10.5.10 | 10.5.10½ | 20.15.5 | 14.1.0½ |
| Arrears | 10.5.10 | 61.8.7 | 62.17.0¼ | 71.18.2¼ | 66.0.2¼ |
| Receipts & Arrears | 61.8.7 | 3.0.10 | 3.0.10 | 3.0.10 | 3.0.10 |
| Wages | 3.0.10 | 28.4.5 | 19.19.10 | 54.13.4 | 47.3.4 |
| Annuities | 29.13.4 | 31.5.3 | 23.0.8 | 57.14.2 | 50.4.2 |
| Discharge | 32.14.2 | 30.3.4 | 39.16.4¼ | 14.4.0¼ | 15.16.0¼ |

| SC6 | 793/2 m.2 1415 | 793/4 m.2 1416 | 793/5 m.2 1417 | 793/7 m.2 1418 | 793/9 m.2 1419 |
|---|---|---|---|---|---|
| Balance incl. arrears | 28.14.5 | 19.17.6 | 29.10.5¾ | -6.11.5 | 1.15.0 |
| Balance excl. arrears | 18.8.7 | 19.14.5½ | 18.17.11 | Nil | Nil |
| Liveries | 16.5.7 | 3.0 | 3.0 | 3.0 | 3.0 |
| Allowances | 3.0 | Nil | Nil | Nil | Nil |
| Respites | Nil | 10.5.10½ | 20.15.5¼ | 14.1.0 | 15.13.0¼ |
| Remainder | 10.5.10 | | | | |

| SC6 | 793/11 m.2 1420 | 794/1 m.2 1421 | 794/2 m.2 1422 |
|---|---|---|---|
| Turbary | Nil | Nil | Nil |
| Courts etc. | Nil | 1.2.2½ | Nil |
| Total Receipts | 51.2.9 | 52.4.11½ | 51.2.9 |
| Arrears | 15.13.0 | 22.13.0 | 22.3.11¼ |
| Receipts & Arrears | 66.13.9¼ | 74.17.11¾ | 73.6.8¾ |
| Wages | 3.0.10 | 3.0.10 | 3.0.10 |
| Annuities | 24.13.4 | 43.16.2½ | 34.13.4 |
| Discharge | 27.14.2 | 46.17.0½ | 37.14.2 |
| Balance incl. arrears | 39.1.7¼ | 28.0.11¾ | 35.12.6¼ |
| Balance excl. arrears | 23.8.7 | 5.7.11 | 13.8.7 |
| Liveries | 16.5.7 | 5.15.0 | 11.15.1½ |
| Allowances | 3.0 | 3.0 | 3.0 |
| Respites | Nil | Nil | 2.3.3 |
| Remainder | 22.13.0¼ | 22.03.11¼ | 21.11.1¼ |

# Appendix II(e) Frodsham

| SC6 | 792/5m.10 1409 | 792/6m.6 1410 | 792/8m.5 1411 | 792/9m.4 1412 | 792/10m.6 1413 |
|---|---|---|---|---|---|
| Rents[11] | 26.10.2¾ | 26.10.2¾ | 26.10.2¾ | 26.10.2¾ | 26.10.2¾ |
| Demesne etc[12] | 23.9.9 | 23.10.2½ | 24.14.11½ | 22.1.11½ | 21.4.3 |
| Courts[13] | 4.3.9 | 20.9.6 | 4.12.8 | 7.12.11 | 5.4.9 |
| Sales of corn & wood | 14.0.6½ | 12.1.6 | 10.9.3½ | 6.19.8½ | 5.9.10½ |
| Seigneurial profits[14] | 2.6.2 | 5.10.4½ | 1.14.11 | 2.6.10½ | 2.9.0 |
| Receipts | 70.10.5¼ | 87.17.9¼ | 68.2.0¾ | 64.6.0¼ | 60.18.1¼ |
| Arrears | - | 4.10.5 | 14.2.8 | 14.4.0 | 2.18.9 |
| Receipts & Arrears | 70.10.5¼ | 92.8.2¼ | 82.4.9¼ | 78.10.0¼ | 63.16.10¼ |
| Decasus | 2.9.4¼ | 2.12.9¼ | 1.15.9¼ | 1.16.9¼ | 2.7.7¾ |
| Wages | 3.7.10 | 3.8.6 | 3.8.6 | 3.8.6 | 3.8.6 |
| Repairs | 58.7.2½ | 47.5.6 | 17.15.7½ | 13.8.0 | 23.16.1 |
| Misc. Exp. | 7.0 | 8.4 | 6.4 | 7.4 | 8.4 |
| Total Exp. | 64.11.4½ | 53.15.1¼ | 23.6.2¾ | 19.0.7 | 30.0.6¾ |
| Balance incl. arrears | 5.19.1 | 38.13.1½ | 58.18.6 | 59.9.5 | 33.15.3½ |
| Balance excl. arrears | 5.19.1 | 34.2.8½ | 44.16.10 | 45.5.5 | 30.17.6½ |
| Liveries | 1.6.8 | 20.10.5 | 42.11.6½ | 51.10.8 | 31.16.9½ |
| Allowances | 2.0 | 4.0.0 | 2.3.0 | 5.0.0 | - |
| Remainder | 4.10.5 | 14.2.6½ | 14.4.0 | 2.18.9 | 1.19.6 |

11 Free rents, assized rents, new and increased rents.

12 Leases of demesne lands, agistment, sale of pastures, pannage and issues of the manor.

13 Perquisites of eyre, halmote, court of Frodsham, strays, chattels of felons, heriot, escheats, ingressus and egressus.

14 Fisheries, oven, ports, stallage, market tolls, the office of hayward.

| SC6 | 793/1m.4<br>1414 | 793/2m.6<br>1415 | 792/4m.1<br>1416 | 793/5m.5<br>1417 | 793/7m.5<br>1418 |
|---|---|---|---|---|---|
| Rents[15] | 26.10.2¾ | 26.10.2¾ | 26.10.2¾ | 26.10.2¾ | 26.10.2¾ |
| Demesne etc[16] | 23.10.8 | 24.3.1 | 24.13.2 | 25.9.0½ | 25.16.1 |
| Courts[17] | 7.0.11 | 3.0.1 | 2.0.9 | [5] | 5.11.8 |
| Sales of corn & wood | 9.13.1 | 5.3.10 | 5.14.0 | 2.10[5] | 6.1.4 |
| Seigneurial profits[18] | 2.18.7 | 4.6.2 | 3.7.2 | 5 | 3.6.6 |
| Receipts | 65.13.5¾ | 63.3.4¾ | 62.5.3¾ | 65.10.7¼ | 67.5.8¾ |
| Arrears | 1.19.6 | 5.17.0 | 5.1.4 | 2.0.0 | 4.17.4½ |
| Receipts & Arrears | 67.12.11¾ | 69.0.4¾ | 67.6.7¾ | 67.10.7¾ | 72.3.1½ |
| Decasus | 2.3.6¼ | 2.5.7¼ | 2.16.9¾ | 2.12.8¼ | 2.12.8¼ |
| Wages | 3.8.6 | 3.1.10 | 3.1.10 | 3.1.10 | 3.1.10 |
| Repairs | 17.14.11½ | 10.12.9½ | 13.0.9 | 8.13.4½ | 13.17.0 |
| Misc. Exp. | 10.0 | 13.4 | 13.4 | 18.8 | 18.8 |
| Total Exp. | 23.16.11¾ | 16.13.6¾ | 19.12.8¼ | 15.6.6¾ | 20.10.2¼ |
| Balance incl. arrears | 43.16.0 | 52.6.10 | 47.13.11 | 52.4.0½ | 51.12.11 |
| Balance excl. arrears | 41.16.6 | 46.9.10 | 42.12.7 | 50.4.0½ | 46.15.6½ |
| Liveries | 37.19.0 | 47.5.6 | 45.11.11 | 47.6 | 47.9.11½ |
| Allowances | - | - | 2.0 | - | - |
| Remainder | 5.17.0 | 5.1.4 | 2.0.0 | 4.17.4½ | 4.2.11½ |

15 Free rents, assized rents, new and increased rents.

16 Leases of demesne lands, agistment, sale of pastures, pannage and issues of the manor.

17 Perquisites of eyre, halmote, court of Frodsham, strays, chattels of felons, heriot, escheats, ingressus and egressus.

18 Fisheries, oven, ports, stallage, market tolls, the office of hayward.

| SC6 | 793/9m.5 1419 | 792/11m.5 1420 | 794/1m.5 1421 | 794/2m.5 1422 |
|---|---|---|---|---|
| Rents | 26.10.2¾ | 26.10.2¾ | 26.10.2¾ | 26.10.2¾ |
| Demesne etc | 21.1.2¼ | 16.19.9¼ | 15.18.4 | 17.7.11 |
| Court[s] | 3.11.0¼ | 1.15.10 | 4.8.6 | 4.2.0 |
| Sales of corn & wood | 6.1.4 | 6.0.0 | 6.0.0 | 6.1.0 |
| Seigneurial profits | 2.19.2 | 3.15.8 | 4.7.9 | 3.17.0 |
| Receipts | 60.2.11½ | 55.1.6¼ | 57.4.9¾ | 57.18.1¾ |
| Arrears | 4.2.11½ | 6.9.3½ | 23.14.2 | 25.19.11 |
| Receipts & Arrears | 64.5.11 | 61.10.9¾ | 80.10.11¾ | 83.18.0¾ |
| Decasus | 2.2.1 | 2.11.1¼ | 2.11.1¼ | 2.6.11¼ |
| Wages | 3.1.10 | 3.1.10 | 3.1.10 | 3.1.10 |
| Repairs | 16.13.5 | 8.7.11 | 11.7.5¼ | 16.19.8½ |
| Misc. Exp. | 16.8 | 11.2 | 6.8 | 6.8 |
| Total Exp. | 22.14.0 | 14.12.0 | 17.7.0¾ | 22.15.1¾ |
| Balance incl. arrears | 41.11.11 | 46.18.9¼ | 63.11.11 | 61.2.11 |
| Balance excl. arrears | 36.8.11½ | 40.9.6 | 39.17.9 | 35.3.0 |
| Liveries | 35.2.7½ | 23.4.7½ | 37.12.0 | 39.5.6½ |
| Allowances | - | - | - | - |
| Remainder | 6.9.3½ | 23.14.2 | 25.19.11 | 21.17.4¾ |

## Appendix II (f) Middlewich

NB The rent payment is known as Kingesmole. From 1420 onwards miscellaneous rents are added.

Tolls include ovens, market tolls and salt tolls.

| SC 6 | 791/1 m. 4 1400 | 791/6 m. 4 1401 | 791/5 m. 3 1402 | 791/6 m. 4 1403 | 791/7 m. 4 1404 |
|---|---|---|---|---|---|
| Rents | 2.2.5 | 2.2.5 | 2.2.5 | 2.2.5 | 2.2.5 |
| Tolls | 36.5.8 | 36.2.2 | 40.15.9 | 34.16.0½ | 45.4.3½ |

| **SC 6** | **791/1 m. 4 1400** | **791/6 m. 4 1401** | **791/5 m. 3 1402** | **791/6 m. 4 1403** | **791/7 m. 4 1404** |
|---|---|---|---|---|---|
| Courts | 9.10.3 | 12.6.10½ | 10.18.0 | 6.5.4 | 12.14.3 |
| Receipts | 47.184 | 50.13.5¼ | 53.16.0 | 43.3.9 | 59.18.11½ |
| Arrears | - | 13.13.10 | 12.4.8 | 11.11.10 | |
| Receipts & Arrears | 47.18.4 | 64.7.3¼ | 66.0.8 | 54.15.7½ | 59.18.11½ |
| Expenses | 3.0.0 | 3.0.0 | 3.0.0 | 4.10.9 | 3.0.0 |
| Balance inc arrears | 44.18.4 | 61.7.3½ | 63.0.8 | 50.4.10 | 56.18.11½ |
| Balance exc arrears | 44.18.4 | 47.13.5½ | 50.16.0 | 38.13.0½ | 56.18.11½ |
| Liveries | 30.13.4 | 48.5.6½ | 50.12.1 | 49.15.5½ | 54.10.3¼ |
| Allowances | 11.2 | 17.1 | 16.9 | 9.5 | 12.4 |
| Remainder | 13.13.10 | 12.4.8 | 11.11.10 | - | 1.16.4 |

| **SC 6** | **791/10 m. 4 1405** | **792/1 m. 4 1406** | **792/2 m. 3 1407** | **792/3 m. 4 1408** | **792/5 m. 4 1409** |
|---|---|---|---|---|---|
| Rents | 2.2.5 | 2.2.5 | 2.2.5 | 2.2.5 | 2.2.5 |
| Tolls | 44.10.3 | 45.1.4 | 44.2.6½ | 36.6.11½ | 43.12.5 |
| Courts | 11.10.3½ | 15.11.9½ | 13.9.9¼ | 15.6.11 | 15.19.5½ |
| Receipts | 58.10.9½ | 62.15.6½ | 59.14.9 | 53.16.3½ | 61.14.3½ |
| Arrears | 1.16.4 | - | 13.8 | 13.8 | - |
| Receipts & Arrears | 60.7.1½ | 62.15.6½ | 60.8.5 | 54.9.11½ | 61.14.3½ |
| Expenses | 3.9.11 | 3.4.8 | 3.0.0 | 3.19.2 | 3.3.4 |
| Balance inc arrears | 56.17.2¼ | 59.10.10¼ | 57.8.5 | 50.10.9½ | 58.10.11½ |
| Balance exc arrears | 55.0.10½ | 59.10.10¼ | 56.14.9 | 49.17.1½ | 58.10.11½ |
| Liveries | 56.17.2½ | 58.17.2½ | 56.14.9 | 50.10.9½ | 49.1.10½ |
| Allowances | - | - | - | - | - |
| Remainder | - | 13.8 | 13.8 | - | 9.9.1 |

| SC 6 | 792/6 m. 4 1410 | 792/?? m. 3 1411 | 792/9 m. 3 1412 | 792/10 m. 4 1413 | 793/1 m. ?? 1414 |
|---|---|---|---|---|---|
| Rents | 2.2.5 | 2.2.5 | 2.2.5 | 2.2.5 | 2.2.5 |
| Tolls | 37.19.4 | 33.10.2½ | 33.4.10 | 37.3.1½ | 33.11.1 |
| Courts | 13.1.8½ | 8.12.3 | 9.7.3 | 11.13.10 | 10.19.2½ |
| Receipts | 53.3.5½ | 44.4.10 | 44.14.2½ | 50.19.4? | 46.12.9 |
| Arrears | 9.9.1 | 4.9.6½ | 13.9 | 14.8 | 7.3.10½ |
| Receipts & Arrears | 62.12.6½ | 48.14.5 | 45.7.11½ | 51.14.0½ | 53.16.7½ |
| Expenses | 3.0.7 | 3.0.0 | 3.0.0 | 3.0.0 | 3.0.0 |
| Balance inc arrears | 59.11.11½ | 45.14.5 | 42.7.11½ | 48.14.0½ | 50.16.7½ |
| Balance exc arrears | 50.2.10½ | 41.4.10½ | 41.14.2½ | 47.19.4½ | 43.12.9 |
| Liveries | 55.2.5 | 45.0.8 | 41.13.3½ | 41.10.2 | 46.2.10½ |
| Allowances | - | - | - | - | - |
| Remainder | 4.9.6½ | 13.9 | 14.8 | 7.3.10½ | 4.13.9 |

| SC 6 | 793/2 m. 5 1415 | 793/4 m. 4 1416 | 793/5 m. 4 1417 | 793/7 m. 4 1418 | 793/9 m. 4 1419 |
|---|---|---|---|---|---|
| Rents | 2.2.5 | 2.2.5 | 2.2.5 | 2.2.5 | 2.2.5 |
| Tolls | 35.5.7 | 32.13.4½ | 33.17.4 | 33.18.5½ | 30.7.10 |
| Courts | 10.7.3 | 11.15.3 | 8.10.5 | 9.10.5 | 11.3.10½ |
| Receipts | 47.15.3 | 46.11.0½ | 45.10.2 | 45.10.5½ | 43.14.1½ |
| Arrears | 4.13.9 | 7.12.3½ | 9.7.0 | 20.8.1½ | 28.17.8 |
| Receipts & Arrears | 52.9.0 | 54.3.4 | 54.17.2 | 65.18.7 | 72.11.9½ |
| Expenses | 6.14.0 | 3.0.0 | 4.14.6 | 3.0.0 | 4.18.0 |
| Balance inc arrears | 45.14.2 | 51.3.4 | 50.2.8 | 62.18.7 | 67.13.9½ |
| Balance exc arrears | 41.0.5 | 43.11.0½ | 40.15.8 | 42.10.5½ | 38.16.1½ |
| Liveries | 38.1.10½ | 41.14.1 | 29.14.6 | 33.19.8 | 42.16.6½ |
| Allowances | - | 2.3 | - | 1.3 | 1.3 |
| Remainder | 7.12.3½ | 9.7.0 | 20.8.1½ | 28.17.8 | 24.16.0 |

| SC 6 | 793/11 m. 4<br>1420 | 794/1 m. 4<br>1421 | 794/2 m. 4<br>1422 |
|---|---|---|---|
| Rents | 2.5.9 | 2.7.7 | 2.9.1 |
| Tolls | 27.9.8 | 27.4.7½ | 29.3.7½ |
| Courts[19] | 10.2.5 | 10.12.11 | 13.6.3 |
| Receipts | 41.3.10 | 40.6.1½ | 44.18.11½ |
| Arrears | 24.16.0 | 34.5.11½ | 26.7.0 |
| Receipts & Arrears | 65.19.10 | 74.12.1 | 71.5.11½ |
| Expenses | 3.0.0 | 3.4.6 | 5.4.5 |
| Balance inc arrears | 62.19.10 | 71.7.7 | 66.1.6½ |
| Balance exc arrears | 38.3.10 | 37.1.7½ | 39.14.6½ |
| Liveries | 28.13.10½ | 44.19.4 | 29.18.11½ |
| Allowances | - | 1.3 | 1.3 |
| Remainder | 34.5.11½ | 26.7.0 | 36.1.4 |

## Appendix II (g) Northwich

Tolls include market tolls, oven and fishery.

| SC 6 | 791/1<br>m.2d<br>1400 | 791/3<br>m.2d<br>1401 | 791/5<br>m.2d<br>1402 | 791/6<br>m.2d<br>1403 | 791/7<br>m.2d<br>1404 |
|---|---|---|---|---|---|
| Rents | 2. 18. 7 | 2. 18. 7 | 2. 18. 7 | 2. 18. 7 | 2. 18. 7 |
| Tolls | 21. 7. 7 | 15. 3. 9 | 25. 6. 9 | 25.19.10 | 30. 3. 2 |
| Courts | 7.18. 7 | 13. 9. 2 | 10.11. 8 | 10.14. 9 | 12.12. 7 |
| Mills | 9. 4. 6½ | 8.10. 8 | 8.11.11 | 7.18. 0 | 6. 9. 5 |
| Receipts | 41. 9. 3½ | 40. 2. 3 | 47. 6. 5 | 47.11. 2 | 52. 3. 9 |
| Arrears | 8. 6.11¾ | 9. 4. 0 | 12. 8. 7 | 15. 9. 8 | 3. 6. 8 |
| Receipts & Arrears | 49.16.3¼ | 49. 6. 3 | 59.15. 0 | 63. 0.10 | 55.10. 5 |

19

| SC 6 | 791/1 m.2d 1400 | 791/3 m.2d 1401 | 791/5 m.2d 1402 | 791/6 m.2d 1403 | 791/7 m.2d 1404 |
|---|---|---|---|---|---|
| Expenses (wages, repairs, tithe) | 7.11.11½ | 20. 7. 8 | 14.19.11 | 9. 2. 4 | 12.13. 7 |
| Annuities | - | 5. 0. 0 | 15. 0. 0 | 10. 0. 0 | 10. 0. 0 |
| Balance inc arrears | 42. 4. 3¾ | 23. 18. 7 | 29.15. 1 | 43.18. 6 | 32.16.10 |
| Balance exc arrears | 33.17. 4 | 14. 4. 7 | 17. 6. 6 | 28. 8.10 | 29.10. 2 |
| Liveries | 32. 0. 3¾ | 11.10. 0 | 14. 5. 5 | 40.11.10 | 29. 7. 2 |
| Allowances | 1. 0. 0 | - | - | - | 3. 0 |
| Remainder | 9. 4. 0 | 12. 8. 7 | 15. 9. 8 | 3. 6. 8 | 3. 6. 8 |

| SC 6 | 791/10 m.2d 1405 | 792/1 m.2d 1406 | 792/2 m.2d 1407 | 792/3 m.2d 1408 | 792/5 m.3d 1409 |
|---|---|---|---|---|---|
| Rents | 2. 18. 7 | 2. 18. 7 | 2. 18. 7 | 2. 18. 7 | 2. 18. 7 |
| Tolls | 28.16. 0 | 29. 2. 4 | 31. 7. 10 | 22.10. 2 | 24. 5. 4 |
| Courts | 11.10. 8 | 14.14. 6 | 14. 5. 4 | 14.12. 4 | 12.11. 9 |
| Mills | 6. 4.10 | 5. 1. 8 | 5. 9. 7 | 4.16. 7 | 3.16. 3 |
| Receipts | 49.10. 1 | 51. 7. 1 | 54. 1. 4 | 44.17. 8 | 43.11.11 |
| Arrears | 3. 6. 8 | 3.16. 8 | 3. 6. 8 | 5.16. 8 | 7. 7. 3 |
| Receipts & Arrears | 52.16. 9 | 55.13. 9 | 57. 8. 0 | 50.14. 4 | 50.19. 2 |
| Expenses (wages, repairs, tithe) | 4. 8. 5 | 8. 9.11 | 3.19. 5¼ | 3. 8. 8½ | 2. 1.11 |
| Annuities | 10. 0. 0 | 10. 0. 0 | 10. 0. 0 | 10. 0. 0 | 10. 0. 0 |
| Balance inc arrears | 38. 8. 4 | 37. 7.10 | 43. 8. 6½ | 37. 5. 7½ | 38.17. 3 |
| Balance exc arrears | 35. 1.8 | 33.11. 2 | 40. 1.10½ | 31. 8 .11½ | 31.10. 0 |

| SC 6 | 791/10 m.2d 1405 | 792/1 m.2d 1406 | 792/2 m.2d 1407 | 792/3 m.2d 1408 | 792/5 m.3d 1409 |
|---|---|---|---|---|---|
| Liveries | 34.11. 8 | 34. 1. 2 | 37.11.10½ | 29.13. 4½ | 35.10. 7 |
| Allowances | - | - | - | 5. 0 | - |
| Remainder | 3. 16. 8 | 3. 6. 8 | 5.16. 8 | 7. 7. 3 | 3. 6. 8 |

| SC 6 | 792/6 m.3d 1410 | 792/8 m.2d 1411 | 792/9 m.2d 1412 | 792/10 m.3d 1413 | 793/1 m.5 1414 |
|---|---|---|---|---|---|
| Rents | 2. 18. 7 | farm | farm | farm | 2. 18. 7 |
| Tolls[1] | 28. 2. 9 | £48 | £48 | £48 | 21.11. 1 |
| Courts | 12. 0. 7 | | | | 10. 7. 2 |
| Mills | 6. 3. 1 | | | | 4. 7. 2 |
| Receipts | 49. 5. 0 | 48. 0. 0 | 48. 0. 0 | 48. 0. 0 | 39. 4. 0 |
| Arrears | 3. 6. 8 | 3. 6. 8 | 10.12.10 | 10.12.10 | 10.12.10 |
| Receipts & Arrears | 52.11. 8 | 51. 6. 8 | 58.12.10 | 58.12.10 | 49.16.103. |
| Expenses (wages, repairs, tithe) | 35.18. 6 | - | - | - | 3.13. 9 |
| Annuities | 10. 0. 0 | 21.10. 0 | 48. 0. 0 | 48. 0. 0 | 35.10. 3 |
| Balance inc arrears | 6.13. 2 | 29.15.10 | 10.12.10 | 10.12.10 | 10.12.10 |
| Balance exc arrears | 2. 6. 6 | 26. 9. 2 | - | - | - |
| Liveries | 2. 6. 6 | 19. 3. 0 | - | - | - |
| Allowances | - | - | - | - | - |
| Remainder | 3. 6. 8 | 10.12.10 | 10.12.10 | 10.12.10 | 10.12.10 |

| SC 6 | 793/2 m.4 1415 | 793/4 m.4 1416 | 793/5 m.4d 1417 | 793/7 m.4d 1418 | 810/15 m.1 & 3 1419[20] |
|---|---|---|---|---|---|
| Rents | 2. 18. 7 | farm | farm | farm | 2. 18. 7 |
| Tolls | 24.16.10 | £48 | £48 | 30. 1. 8½ | 23. 8. 1 |
| Courts | 11. 0. 3 | | | | 10. 6. 2½ |
| Mills | 3. 4. 7 | | | | 3.14 |
| Receipts | 42. 0. 3 | 48. 0. 0 | 48. 0. 0 | 30. 1. 8½ | 40. 7. 6½ |
| Arrears | 10.12.10 | - | - | - | - |
| Receipts & Arrears | 52.13. 1 | 48. 0. 0 | 48. 0. 0 | 30. 1. 8½ | 40. 7. 6½ |
| Expenses (wages, repairs, tithe) | 4.17. 1 | - | - | - | 15.11.10 |
| Annuities | 37. 3. 2 | 48. 0. 0 | 48. 0. 0 | 26.10. 0 | - |
| Balance inc arrears | 10.12.10 | - | - | 3.11. 8½ | 24.15. 8½ |
| Balance exc arrears | - | - | - | 3.11. 8½ | 24.15. 8½ |
| Liveries | - | - | - | - | 12.13. 4 |
| Allowances | - | - | - | - | - |
| Remainder | 10.12.10 | - | - | 3.11. 8½ | 12. 2. 4½ |

| SC 6 | 810/15 m.2 1420[21] |
|---|---|
| Rents | 2. 18. 7 |
| Tolls | 17.18. 2½ |
| Courts | c. 7.14. 7½ |
| Mills | c. 7.12.10½ |
| Receipts | c. 36. 4. 3½ |

20 Total revenues calculated by the amalgamation of the accounts of Elizabeth, dowager countess of Huntingdon (m. 1) and of John Holland, earl of Huntingdon (m. 3).

21 Total revenues calculated from the one surviving account of the year stating the third part of revenues held by the dowager countess.

| SC 6 | 810/15 m.2 1420[22] |
|---|---|
| Arrears | c. 12. 2. 4½ |
| Receipts & Arrears | c. 4. 6. 8 |
| Expenses (wages, repairs, tithe) | c. 5.15. 4½ |
| Annuities | - |
| Balance inc arrears | c. 43.11. 3½ |
| Balance exc arrears | c. 30. 8. 11 |
| Liveries | ? |
| Allowances | ? |
| Remainder | ? |

## Appendix II (h) Shotwick Manor and Park

Rents include leases of demesne lands.

From 1411, Park only as manor granted to William Porter for no render on 18 April 1410. There is no information for 1420.

| SC 6 | 791/1 m.3 1400 | 791/3 m.3 1401 | 791/3 m.3 1401 | 791/5 m.3 1402 | 791/6m. 3 1403 |
|---|---|---|---|---|---|
| Rents | 19.6.2 | 6.9.6 | farm | farm | farm |
| Courts | 1.8.7 | - | £5 | £10 | £10 |
| Agistment | 4.3.4 | 6.8 | | | |
| Sale of wood | 1.9.0 | 1.8.0 | | - | 2.3 |
| Fisheries | 1.7.0 | 5.6 | | | |
| Receipts | 26.7.1 | 7.19.8 | 5.0.0 | 10.0.0 | 10.2.3 |
| Arrears | 4.17.9 | 2.8.7 | - | 9.14.4¾ | 9.14.4¾ |

22 Total revenues calculated from the one surviving account of the year stating the third part of revenues held by the dowager countess.

| SC 6 | 791/1 m.3 1400 | 791/3 m.3 1401 | 791/3 m.3 1401 | 791/5 m.3 1402 | 791/6m. 3 1403 |
|---|---|---|---|---|---|
| Receipts & Arrears | 31.4.10 | 10.8.3 | 5.0.0 | 19.14.4¾ | 19.14.4¾ |
| Expenses | 1.15.6 | 4.7.2 | - | 3.6.8 | - |
| Balance incl. arrears | 29.9.4 | 6.1.1 | 5.0.0 | 16.7.8¾ | 19.16.7¾ |
| Balance excl. arrears | 24.11.7 | 3.12.6 | 5.0.0 | 6.13.4 | 10.2.3 |
| Liveries | 25.6.9 | 1.6.4 | - | 6.13.4 | 6.15.7 |
| Allowances | 1.14.0 | - | - | - | - |
| Remainder | 2.8.7 | 4.14.4¾ | 5.0.0 | 9.14.4¾ | 13.1.0¾ |

| SC 6 | 791/7 m.3 1404 | 791/10 m.3 1405 | 792/1 m.3 1406 | 792/2 m.4 1407 | 792/3 m.3 1408 |
|---|---|---|---|---|---|
| Rents | farm | farm | farm | farm | 19.18.10 |
| Courts | £10 | £10 | £10 | £10 | 3.17.0 |
| Agistment | | | | | 10.8.0 |
| Sale of wood | 2.2.3 | 4.8 | 1.13.8 | 1.0.2 | 1.10.9 |
| Fisheries | | | | | 3.8.6 |
| Receipts | 12.2.3 | 10.4.8 | 11.13.8 | 11.0.2 | 39.3.1 |
| Arrears | 13.1.0¾ | 8.6.8 | 5.6.8 | 5.6.8 | 6.3 |
| Receipts & Arrears | 13.1.0¾ | 18.6.8 | 18.11.4 | 15.6.8 | 39.9.9 |
| Expenses | - | - | - | - | 1.9.9 |
| Balance incl. arrears | 25.3.3¾ | 18.11.4 | 17.0.0 | 16.6.10 | 38.0.0 |
| Balance excl. arrears | 12.2.3 | 10.4.8 | 11.13.4 | 11.0.2 | 37.13.4 |
| Liveries | 15.4.4¾ | 13.4.8 | 11.14.8 (sic) | 16.0.2 | 30.16.9 |
| Allowances | 1.12.3 | - | - | - | - |
| Remainder | 8.6.8 | 5.6.8 | 5.6.8 | 6.8 | 7.3.3 |

| **SC 6** | **792/5 m.2<br>1409** | **792/6 m.2<br>1410** |
|---|---|---|
| Rents | 20.4.0 | 3.10.0 |
| Courts | 1.4.4 | 1.0.11 |
| Agistment | 9.13.2 | 2.6.2 |
| Sale of Wood | 2.2.6 | 4.0 |
| Fisheries | 3.15.0 | 8.6 |
| Receipts | 36.19.10 | 7.9.7 |
| Arrears | 7.7.3 | 3.3.9 |
| Receipts & Arrears | 44.7.1 | 10.13.4 |
| Expenses | 1.14.9 | 9.5 |
| Balance incl. arrears | 42.12.4 | 10.3.11 |
| Balance excl. arrears | 35.8.1 | 7.0.2 |
| Liveries | 36.12.7 | 7.0.2 |
| Allowances | 2.16.0 | - |
| Remainder | 3.3.9 | 3.3.9 |

| **SC 6** | **792/8 m.2d<br>1411** | **792/9 m.2d<br>1412** | **792/10 m. 3d<br>1413** | **793/1 m.6<br>1414** | **793/2 m.3d<br>1415** |
|---|---|---|---|---|---|
| Sale of wood | 1.0.4 | 13.11 | - | 9.8 | 1.11.4 |
| Arrears | - | - | - | - | - |
| Receipts & Arrears | 1. 0. 4 | 13.11 | - | 9. 8 | 1.11.4 |
| Liveries | 1. 0. 4 | 13.11 | - | 9. 8 | - |
| Et debet incl. arrears | - | - | - | - | 1.11.4 |

| SC 6 | 793/4 m.3d 1416 | 793/5 m.3d 1417 | 793/7 m.3d 1418 | 793/9 m.3d 1419 | 793/11 m.2d 1420 | 794/1 m.4d 1421 |
|---|---|---|---|---|---|---|
| Sale of wood | 16.2 | 4.10 | 13.10 | 1.19.6 | 18.4 | 6.11 |
| Arrears | 1.11. 4 | 16. 2 | - | - | 1.19. 6 | - |
| Receipts & Arrears | 2.17. 6 | 1. 1. 0 | 13.10 | 1.19. 6 | 2.17.10 | 6.11 |
| Liveries | 1.11. 4 | 1. 1. 0 | 13.10 | - | 2.17.10 | 6.11 |
| Et debet incl. arrears | 16. 2 | - | - | 1.19. 6 | - | - |

## Appendix II (i) Macclesfield Burgus

Tolls include farm of the oven, stallage and market tolls.

Courts are portmote, eyre, hundred held after the eyre, forest fines.

| SC 6 | 805/7 m.1 1401 | 805/9 m.1d 1402 | 805/11 m.1d 1403 | 805/13 m.1d 1404 | 805/14 m.1d 1405 |
|---|---|---|---|---|---|
| Rents | 14.0.6¾ | 14.0.6¾ | 14.0.6¾ | 14.0.6¾ | 14.0.6¾ |
| Tolls | 6.7.9 | 7.9.2 | 5.2.1½ | 5.8.9 | 5.1.0 |
| Courts | 2.9.5. | 14.5.10 | 3.17.11 | 3.12.10 | 7.14.10 |
| Receipts | 23.17.9 | 35.15.7¾ | 23.0.7¼ | 23.2.1¾ | 25.16.4¾ |
| Arrears | 32.2.5 | 14.17.3¾ | 33.12.3¾ | 18.1.11¾ (sic) | 12.3.2 |
| Receipts & Arrears | 56.0.2¾ | 50.12.11 | 56.12.10½ | 41.4.2 | 38.19.6¾ |
| Repairs | 7.6 | - | - | - | - |
| Balance incl. arrears | 55.128¾ | 50.12.11 | 56.12.10½ | 41.4.2 | 38.19.6¾ |
| Balance excl. arrears | 23.10.3¾ | 35.15.7¾ | 23.0.7½ | 23.2.1¾ | 26.16.4¾ |
| Liveries | 37.12.9½ | 16.17.1¾ | 38.10.10¾ | 29.1.0 | 26.4.2¼ |
| Allowances | 3.2.7½ | 3.6 | - | - | 12.3.2 |
| Respites | 4.3.2 | - | - | - | - |
| Remainder | 10.14.1¾ | 33.12.3 | 18.1.11¾ | 12.3.2 | 12.2 |

| SC 6 | 805/16 m.1d 1406 | 806/1 m.1d 1407 | 806/3 m.1d 1408 | 806/4 m.1d 1410 | 806/5 m.1d 1412 |
|---|---|---|---|---|---|
| Rents | 14.0.6¾ | 14.0.6¾ | 14.0.6¾ | 14.0.6¾ | 14.0.6¾ |
| Tolls | 4.9.7 | 4.19.6 | 4.5.11 | 6.11.4 | 5.10.1 |
| Courts | 6.17.8 | 5.17.4 | 5.7.8 | 5.1.8 | 7.5.3 |
| Receipts | 25.7.9¾ | 24.17.4¾ | 23.14.1¾ | 25.12.6¾ | 26.15.10¾ |
| Arrears | 12.2 | 12.2 | 5.7.1¾ | 7.19.3¼ | 18.5.11½ |
| Receipts & Arrears | 25.19.11¾ | 25.9.6¾ | 29.1.3½ | 33.12.10 | 45.1.10¾ |
| Repairs | - | 3.5.3 | 1.1.0 | - | - |
| Balance incl. arrears | 25.19.11¾ | 22.4.3¾ | 28.0.3½ | 33.12.10 | 45.1.10¼ |
| Balance excl. arrears | 25.7.9¾ | 21.12.1¾ | 22.13.1¾ | 25.12.6¾ | 26.15.10¾ |
| Liveries | 25.5.3¼ | 16.17.2 | 21.5.9¾ | 24.4.8 | 41.2.3½ |
| Allowances | 2.6 | - | - | - | - |
| Respites | - | - | - | - | 17.10 |
| Remainder | 12.2 | 5.7.1¾ | 6.14.5¾ | 9.8.2 | 3.1.8¾ |

| SC 6 | 806/6 m.1d 1413 | 806/8 m.1d 1414 | 806/9 m.1d 1415 | 806/11 m.1d 1416 | 806/13 m.1d 1417 |
|---|---|---|---|---|---|
| Rents | 14.0.6¾ | 14.0.6¾ | 14.0.6¾ | 14.0.6¾ | 14.0.6¾ |
| Tolls | 4.4.10 | 3.17.5 | 4.15.0 | 3.5.9 | 3.9.4½ |
| Courts | 2.12.5 | 2.8.9 | 2.1.4 | 1.0.6 | 3.9.2 |
| Receipts | 20.17.9¾ | 20.6.8¾ | 20.16.10¾ | 18.6.10¾ | 20.19.1¼ |
| Arrears | 3.19.6¾ | 8.16.9½ | 5.12.10½ | 5.8.2¾ | 3.0.10 |
| Receipts & Arrears | 22.17.7½ | 27.19.6¾ | 25.19.11¼ | 23.15.0½ | 23.19.11¼ |
| Repairs | 1.19.9 | 1.3.11½ | 9.10 | - | 14.3.0 |
| Balance incl. arrears | 22.17.7½ | 27.19.6¾ | 25.19.11¼ | 23.15.0½ | 9.6.11¼ |
| Balance excl. arrears | 18.18.0¾ | 19.2.9¼ | 20.7.0¾ | 18.6.10¾ | 6.16.1¼ |

| SC 6 | 806/6 m.1d 1413 | 806/8 m.1d 1414 | 806/9 m.1d 1415 | 806/11 m.1d 1416 | 806/13 m.1d 1417 |
|---|---|---|---|---|---|
| Liveries | 14.0.10 | 22.6.8¼ | 20.11.8½ | 20.14.2½ | 7.3.0 |
| Allowances | - | - | - | - | - |
| Respites | 17.10 | - | - | - | - |
| Remainder | 7.18.11½ | 5.12.10½ | 5.8.2¾ | 3.0.10 | 2.13.11¼ |

| SC 6 | 806/16 m.1d 1418 | 806/17 m.1d 1419 | 807/1 m.1d 1420 | 807/2 m.1d 1421 | 807/3 m.1d 1422 |
|---|---|---|---|---|---|
| Rents | 14.0.6¾ | 14.0.6¾ | 14.0.6¾ | 14.0.6¾ | 4.18.0¾ |
| Tolls | 3.12.6 | 3.0.0 | 3.0.11½ | 3.0.5½ | 2.15.9¼ |
| Courts | 1.6.0 | 1.0.6 | 1.3.2 | 1.10.1 | 19.3 |
| Receipts | 18.19.0¾ | 18.1.0¾ | 18.4.8¼ | 18.11.1 | 8.13.1¼ |
| Arrears | 2.13.11¼ | 3.7.5 | 17.10 | 4.11.5¼ | 8.1.11½ |
| Receipts & Arrears | 21.13.0 | 21.8.5¾ | 19.2.6 | 23.2.6½ | 16.15.0¾ |
| Repairs | 10.5 | 2.10.10½ | 16.1 | - | - |
| Balance incl. arrears | 21.2.7 | 18.17.7¼ | 18.6.5¼ | 23.2.6½ | 16.15.0¾ |
| Balance excl. arrears | 18.8.7¾ | 15.10.2½ | 17.8.7¼ | 18.11.1¾ | 8.13.1¼ |
| Liveries | 17.15.2 | 17.19.9¼ | 13.15.0 | 15.0.7 | 12.15.3½ |
| Allowances | - | - | - | - | - |
| Respites | - | - | - | - | - |
| Remainder | 3.7.5 | 17.10 | 4.11.5¼ | 8.1.11½ | 3.19.9¼ |

## Appendix II (j) Macclesfield Hundred

| SC 6 | 805/7 m.1 1401 | 805/9 m.1 1402 | 805/11 m.1 1403 | 805/13 m.1 1404 | 805/14 m.1 1405 |
|---|---|---|---|---|---|
| Rents | 6.6.8 | 6.6.8 | 6.6.8 | 6.6.8 | 6.6.8 |
| Courts | 19.3.2 | 15.15.11 | 17.14.8 | 30.14.3 | 61.2.9 |
| Receipts | 25.19.10 | 22.2.7 | 24.1.4 | 37.0.11 | 67.9.5 |
| Arrears | 17.4.8 | 15.14.0 | 18.9.9 | 14.16.6 | 22.8.3½ |
| Receipts & Arrears | 43.4.5 | 37.16.7 | 42.11.1 | 51.17.5 | 89.17.8½ |
| Liveries | 20.17.1 | 19.2.10 | 27.14.7 | 29.3.1½ | 31.8.10½ |
| Allowances | 6.13.4 | 4.0 | - | 6.0 | - |
| Respites | - | 6.19.10 | 4.7.9 | 14.6.1 | 53.11.1 |
| Remainder | 15.14.0 | 15.9.11 | 10.8.9 | 8.2.2½ | 4.17.9 |

| SC 6 | 805/16 m.1 1406 | 806/1 m.1 1407 | 806/3 m.1 1408 | 806/4 m.1 1410 | 806/5 m.1 1412 |
|---|---|---|---|---|---|
| Rents | 6.6.8 | 6.6.8 | 6.6.8 | 6.6.8 | 6.6.8 |
| Courts | 18.4.2 | 28.3.1 | 16.13.1 | 33.8.6 | 37.12.1 |
| Receipts | 24.10.10 | 34.9.9 | 22.19.9 | 39.15.2 | 43.18.9 |
| Arrears | 5.8.10 | 11.16.1 | 24.8.1 | 3.18.2 | 20.10.5 |
| Receipts & Arrears | 82.19.8 | 49.5.10 | 47.7.10 | 43.13.4 | 65.10.3 |
| Liveries | 24.15.11 | 17.19.1 | 16.0.3 | 20.18..2 | 28.19.8 |
| Allowances | 46.7.8 | 2.18.8 | - | - | - |
| Respites | 5.18.4 | - | - | 13.15.2 | 30.0.0 |
| Remainder | 5.17.9 | 24.8.1 | 31.7.7 | 9.0.0 | 6.10.6 |

| SC6 | 806/6 m.1 1413 | 806/8 m.1 1414 | 806/9 m.1 1415 | 806/11 m.1 1416 | 806/13 m.1 1417 |
|---|---|---|---|---|---|
| Rents | 6.6.8 | 6.6.8 | 6.6.8 | 6.6.8 | 6.6.8 |
| Courts | 15.13.9 | 18.9.10 | 23.1.8 | 17.8.7 | 18.5.9 |
| Receipts | 22.0.5 | 24.16.6 | 29.8.4 | 23.15.3 | 24.12.5 |
| Arrears | 36.10.6 | 48.3.1 | 44.15.8 | 36.8.10 | 48.18.7 |
| Receipts & Arrears | 58.10.11 | 72.19.7 | 74.4.0 | 60.4.1 | 73.11.0 |
| Liveries | 10.7.10 | 2?.3.11 | 37.15.2 | 10.18.10 | 24.7.10 |
| Allowances | - | - | - | 6.8 | - |
| Respites | 34.12.2 | 30.0.0 | 10.0 | - | - |
| Remainder | 13.10.11 | 14.15.8 | 35.18.10 | 4?18.7 | 49.3.2 |

| SC6 | 806/16 m.1 1418 | 806/17 m.1 1419 | 807/1 m.1 1420 | 807/2 m.1 1421 | 807/3 m.1 1422 |
|---|---|---|---|---|---|
| Rents | 6.6.8 | 6.6.8 | 6.6.8 | 6.6.8 | 6.6.8 |
| Courts | 26.18.5 | 11.17.9 | 23.2.11 | 11.3.4 | 10.15.9 |
| Receipts | 18.4.5 | 18.4.5 | 29.9.7 | 17.10.0 | 15.0.5 |
| Arrears | 51.16.7 | 51.16.7 | 52.6.9½ | 69.19.8½ | 67.7.4 |
| Receipts & Arrears | 82.8.3 | 70.1.0 | 81.16.4½ | 87.9.8½ | 82.7.9 |
| Liveries | 29.18.4 | 17.7.6½ | 11.10.0 | 13.2.5½ | 7.10.0 |
| Allowances | 13.4 | 6.8 | 6.8 | 16.19.11 | 6.8 |
| Respites | 11.2.2½ | 6.13.3½ | 2.4.5¼ | 8.12.0 | 7.12.0 |
| Remainder | 40.14.4½ | 45.13.6 | 67.15.3¼ | 58.15.4 | 66.19.1 |

## Appendix II (k) Macclesfield Forest

| SC 6 | 805/7 m.2 1401 | 805/9 m.2 1402 | 805/11 m.2 1403 | 805/13 m.2 1404 | 805/14 m.2 1405 |
|---|---|---|---|---|---|
| Rents | 68.1.0 | 68.3.4 | 68.3.9¾ | 68.3.9¾ | 68.3.9¾ |
| Mills[1] | 3.3.8 | 3.3.8 | 13.17.0 | 13.17.0 | 13.17.0 |
| Agistment etc[2] | 21.3.0 | 20.19.7 | 20.19.4 | 21.4.2 | 21.5.7 |
| Courts | 6.1.3 | 7.3.4 | 11.9.5 | 17.1.5½ | 16.15. 1 |
| Receipts | 98.8.11 | 99.9.11 | 114.9.7 | 120.6.5¼ | 120.1.5½ |
| Arrears | 121.0.7 | 92.19.9¾ | 154.11.10½ | 62.17.2 | 73.14.11½ |
| Receipts & Arrears | 219.9.6 | 192.9.8¾ | 269.1.5½ | 183.3.7 | 193.16.5¼ |
| Repairs | - | - | 2.6.6½ | 1.16.5 | 1.2.1½ |
| Decasus | 3.2.6 | 3.0.2¼ | 3.0.2 | 3.0.2 | 3.0.2 |
| Annuity | 6.13.4 | 13.6.8 | 6.13.4 | 13.6.8 | - |
| Misc.Exp. | 2.4.0 | 2.17.4 | 9.16.0 | 2.17.4 | 10.17.4 |
| Total Exp. | 11.19.0 | 20.4.2¼ | 21.16.0½ | 21.0.7 | 14.19.7½ |
| Balance incl. arrears | 207.9.7 | 172.5.6½ | 247.5.5 | 162.3.0¼ | 178.16.9¾ |
| Balance excl. arrears | 86.9.0 | 79.5.8½ | 92.13.6½ | 99.5.10¼ | 105.1.10¼ |
| Liveries | 45.8.0 | 18.13 8 | 194.2.7 | 85.18.0¾ | 100.9.5 |
| Allowances | 69.1.10¼ | - | 4.0.0 | 2.10.0 | 12.14.5 |
| Remainder | 92.19.9¾ | 154.11.10½ | 62.17.2 | 73.14.11½ | 81.2.11¾ |

1 From 1403 including Macclesfield mills. Previously these had been accounted separately.

2 Agistment, pannage, herbage and sale of wood.

| SC 6 | 805/16 m.2 1406 | 806/1 m.2 1407 | 806/3 m.2 1408 | 806/4 m.2 1410 | 806/5 m.2 1412 |
|---|---|---|---|---|---|
| Rents | 68.4.9½ | 68.8.0¼ | 68.5.0¼ | 68.5.9¾ | 68.5.10¾ |
| Mills | 13.17.0 | 13.17.0 | 13.17.0 | 14.17.0 | 14.17.0 |
| Agistment etc. | 21.5.4 | 21.7.3 | 21.3.6 | 20.13.6 | 20.15.8 |
| Courts | 8.2.2 | 9.17.8 | 19.14.7½ | 13.17.8 | 18.2.7 |
| Receipts | 111.9.3¾ | 113.6.11¼ | 113.0.1¾ | 117.13.11¼ | 122.0.1¾ |
| Arrears | 81.2.11¾ | 51.16.6 | 61.8.4¾ | 53.7.0¾ | 143.12.11¼ |
| Receipts & Arrears | 192.12.3½ | 165.5.3½ | 174.8.6½ | 171.1.0 | 255.13.1 |
| Repairs | 3.15.8½ | 3.7.8 | - | 21.13.4 | 3.19.1 |
| Decasus | 3.0.2 | 3.0.2 | 3.0.2 | 3.0.2 | 3.0.2 |
| Annuity | 33.6.8 | 13.6.8 | 13.6.8 | 13.6.8 | 13.6.8 |
| Misc. Exp. | 2.4.0 | 3.10.8 | 2.17.4 | 2.17.4 | 2.17.4 |
| Total Exp. | 42.6.6½ | 23.5.2 | 19.4.2 | 40.17.6 | 30.9.4½ |
| Balance incl. arrears | 150.5.9 | 141.18.3½ | 155.6.4½ | 130.3.6 | 225.3.8½ |
| Balance excl. arrears | 69.2.10¼ | 90.1.9¼ | 93.17.11¾ | 76.16.5¼ | 81.10.9¼ |
| Liveries | 98.9.2¾ | 75.3.2¾ | 117.15.9¼ | 62.4.4¾ | 159.5.8½ |
| Allowances | - | - | - | - | - |
| Remainder | 51.16.6¼ | 61.8.4¾ | 34.15.3¾ | 67.19.1¼ | 73.4.1½ |

| SC 6 | 806/6 m.2 1413 | 806/8 m.2 1414 | 806/9 m.2 1415 | 806/11 m.2 1416 | 806/13 m.2 1417 |
|---|---|---|---|---|---|
| Rents | 68.5.10¾ | 68.5.10¾ | 68.5.11¾ | 68.6.5¾ | 68.6.7¾ |
| Mills | 14.17.0 | 12.10.4 | 14.17.0 | 14.17.0 | 14.17.0 |
| Agistment etc. | 21.15.1 | 21.15.4 | 21.18.6 | 21.18.6 | 21.18.6 |
| Courts | 11.19.7 | 9.16.3 | 14.2.11 | 1.16.5½ | 3.12.2 |

| SC 6 | 806/6 m.2 1413 | 806/8 m.2 1414 | 806/9 m.2 1415 | 806/11 m.2 1416 | 806/13 m.2 1417 |
|---|---|---|---|---|---|
| Receipts | 116.17.6¾ | 112.7.9¾ | 119.4.4¼ | 106.18.5¾ | 108.14.3¾ |
| Arrears | 73.4.1½ | 78.8.5¾ | 48.49.2 | 76.16.8¼ | 75.5.2½ |
| Receipts & Arrears | 190.1.8¼ | 190.16.3½ | 168.3.6¼ | 183.15.1½ | 183.19 .6¼ |
| Repairs | 11.5.2½ | 17.8.4½ | 1.17.3 | 6.14.8 | 14.8.0 |
| Decasus | 3.0.2 | 3.0.2 | 3.0.2 | 3.0.2 | 3.0.2 |
| Annuity | 13.6.8 | 13.6.8 | 13.6.8 | 13.6.8 | 13.6.8 |
| Misc. Exp. | 2.17.4 | 2.17.4 | 2.17.4 | 2.17.4 | 2.17.4 |
| Total Exp. | 36.12.6½ | 21.1.5 | 25.18.10 | 25.18.10 | 33.12.2 |
| Balance incl. arrears | 159.12.3¾ | 154.3.9 | 147.2.1 | 157.16.3½ | 150.7.4¼ |
| Balance excl. arrears | 86.6.2¼ | 75.15.3¼ | 98.2.11¾ | 80.19.7¼ | 75.2.1¾ |
| Liveries | 81.3.8 | 105.4.7 | 70. 5.5 | 66.1.1 | 83.2.10¾ |
| Allowances | - | - | - | 16.10.0 | - |
| Remainder | 78.8.5¾ | 48.19.2 | 76.16.8¼ | 75.5.2½ | 57.4.5½ |

| SC 6 | 806/16 m.2 1418 | 806/17 m.2 1419 | 807/1 m.2 1420 | 807/2 m.2 1421 | 807/3 m.2 1422 |
|---|---|---|---|---|---|
| Rents | 68.6.7¾ | 68.6.7¾ | 68.6.7¾ | 68.6.7¾ | 7.7.4 |
| Mills | 14.17.0 | 14.17.0 | 14.17.0 | 14.17.0 | 11.10.11½ |
| Agistment etc. | 21.18.6 | 21.18.6 | 22.5.2 | 22.5.2 | 20.12.5¼ |
| Courts | 7.8.3 | 3.3.2 | 2.8.10 | 7.6.8 | 4.2.8 |
| Receipts | 112.10.4¾ | 188.5.3¾ | 107.17.7¾ | 112.15.5¾ | 43.12.4¾ |
| Arrears | 57.4.5½ | 79.19.10¾ | 72.16.0 | 108.18.9¾ | 144.7.3½ |
| Receipts & Arrears | 169.14.10¼ | 188.5.2½ | 180.13.7¾ | 221.14.3½ | 187.19.8¼ |
| Repairs | 15.10.4½ | 9.12.5 | 9.17.4 | 7.13.5½ | - |
| Decasus | 3.0.2 | 3.0.2 | 3.0.2 | 3.0.2 | - |

| SC 6 | 806/16 m.2 1418 | 806/17 m.2 1419 | 807/1 m.2 1420 | 807/2 m.2 1421 | 807/3 m.2 1422 |
|---|---|---|---|---|---|
| Annuity | 13.6.8 | 13.6.8 | - | - | - |
| Misc. Exp. | 2.17.4 | 2.17.4 | 2.17.4 | 2.17.4 | 2.12.4 |
| Total Exp. | 34.14.6½ | 28.16.7 | 15.14.10 | 13.10.11½ | 2.12.4 |
| Balance incl. arrears | 135.0.3¾ | 155.8.7¼ | 164.18.9¾ | 208. 3.4 | 185.7.4¼ |
| Balance excl. arrears | 77.15.10 | 79.8.8¾ | 92.2.9¾ | 99.4.6¼ | 41.0.0¾ |
| Liveries | 55.0.5 | 86.12.7½ | 56.0.0 | 63.16.0½ | 32.6.8 |
| Allowances | - | - | - | - | - |
| Remainder | 79.19.10¾ | 72.16.0 | 10.18.9¼ | 144.7.3½ | 153.0.8¼[3] |

## Appendix II (l) Macclesfield Park

| SC 6 | 805/7 m.3d 1401 | 805/9 m.3d 1402 | 805/11 m.3 1403 | 805/16 m.3 1406 | 806/1 m.3 1407[4] |
|---|---|---|---|---|---|
| Herbage | 5.14.3 | nil | nil | nil | 13.6.8 |
| Turbary | - | - | - | - | 11.12.1 |
| Sale of wood | - | - | - | - | - |
| Receipts | 5.14.3 | - | - | - | 24.18.9 |
| Arrears | nil | nil | nil | nil | nil |
| Receipts & Arrears | 5.14.3 | - | - | - | 24.18.9 |
| Repairs | - | - | - | - | 23.6.2½ |
| Balance incl. arrears | 5.14.3 | - | - | - | 1.12.6½ |
| Balance excl. arrears | 5.14.3 | - | - | - | 1.12.6½ |

3 Plus £33.6.8 extra charge.

4 Account of John Savage as Parker from Michaelmas 1402 to Michaelmas 1407, i.e. for five complete years.

| SC 6 | 805/7 m.3d 1401 | 805/9 m.3d 1402 | 805/11 m.3 1403 | 805/16 m.3 1406 | 806/1 m.3 1407[5] |
|---|---|---|---|---|---|
| Liveries | 5.14.3 | - | - | - | 6.8[6] |
| Remainder | nil | - | - | - | 1.5.10 [sic] |

| SC 6 | 806/3 m.3 1408 | 806/4 m.3 1410 | 806/5 m.4 1412 | 806/6 m.4d 1413 | 806/8 m.2 1414 |
|---|---|---|---|---|---|
| Herbage | 6.13.4 | 6.13.4 | 7.0.0 | 7.0.0 | 7.0.0 |
| Turbary | nil | 1.17.6 | 1.12.0 | 1.9.0 | 1.12.0 |
| Sale of wood | - | - | - | - | nil |
| Receipts | 6.13.4 | 8.10.10 | 8.12.0 | 8.9.0 | 8.12.0 |
| Arrears | 1.5.10 | 11.0.5 | 18.5.6 | 4.17.10 | 4.8.8 |
| Receipts & Arrears | 7.19.2 | 19.11.3 | 26.17.6 | 13.6.10 | 13.6.8 |
| Repairs | No figures entered | 7.7.8 | 5.18.0 | 5.17.4 | 4.16.7½ |
| Balance incl. arrears | | 12.3.7 | 20.19.6 | 7.9.6 | 8.4.4½ |
| Balance excl. arrears | | 1.3.2 | 2.4.0 | 3.11.8 | 3.15.8½ |
| Liveries | | 13.4[7] | 16.1.8 | 3.0.10 | nil |
| Remainder | | 12.16.11 | 4.17.10 | 4.8.8 | 8.4.4½ |

5 Account of John Savage as Parker from Michaelmas 1402 to Michaelmas 1407, i.e. for five complete years.

6 Allowed 6.8 paid to the clerk for supervising the account.

7 Additional charge of 13.4 (6.8 for this year and previous year) as park now leased to parker at £7 per annum.

| SC 6 | 806/9 m.3d 1415 | 806/11 m.3 1416 | 806/13 m.4 1417 | 806/16 m.3d 1418 | 806/17 m.3d 1419 |
|---|---|---|---|---|---|
| Herbage | 7.0.0 | 7.0.0 | 7.0.0 | 7.0.0 | 7.0.0 |
| Turbary | 1.12.0 | 1.5.0 | 1.2.1 | 1.0.10 | 18.6 |
| Sale of wood | nil | nil | nil | nil | nil |
| Receipts | 8.12.0 | 8.5.0 | 8.2.1 | 8.0.10 | 7.18.6 |
| Arrears | 8.4.4½ | 9.17.7½ | 15.1.9½ | nil | 8.0.10 |
| Receipts & Arrears | 16.16.4½ | 18.2.7½ | 23.3.10½ | 8.0.10 | 15.19.4 |
| Repairs | 3.17.11 | nil | nil | nil | 4.16.0 |
| Balance incl. arrears | 12.18.5½ | 18.2.7½ | 23.3.10½ | 8.0.10 | 11.3.4 |
| Balance excl. arrears | 4.14.1 | 8.5.0 | 8.2.1 | 8.0.10 | 3.2.6 |
| Liveries | 3.0.10l | 3.0.10 | 23.3.10½ | nil | 3.0.10 |
| Remainder | 9.17.7½ | 15.1.9½ | nil | 8.0.10 | 8.2.6 |

| SC 6 | 807/1 m.3d 1420 | 807/2 m.3d 1421 | 807/3 m.3 1422 |
|---|---|---|---|
| Herbage | 7.0.0 | 7.0.0. | 3.10.0 |
| Turbary | 17.1 | 13.9 | 17.1 |
| Sale of wood | nil | nil | nil |
| Receipts | 7.17.1 | 7.13.9 | 4.7.1 |
| Arrears | 8.2.6 | 8.1.1 | 6.19.10 |
| Receipts & Arrears | 15.19.17 | 15.14.10 | 11.6.11 |
| Repairs | 6.8.6 | 5.14.2 | 5.14.6[8] |
| Balance incl. arrears | 9.11.1 | 10.0.8 | 11.6.11 |

8 Disallowed, although respited at the foot of the account.

| SC 6 | 807/1<br>m.3d<br>1420 | 807/2<br>m.3d<br>1421 | 807/3<br>m.3<br>1422 |
|---|---|---|---|
| Balance excl. arrears | 1.19.7 | 1.19.7 | 4.7.1 |
| Liveries | 1.10.0 | 3.0.10 | nil |
| Remainder | 8.1.1 | 6.19.10 | 5.8.5 |

## Appendix II(m) Chamberlain's Account – Revenues of the County[9]

| SC 6 | 774/11<br>1400 | 774/13<br>1401 | 774/14<br>1402 | 774/15<br>1403 | 775/3<br>1404 |
|---|---|---|---|---|---|
| Cheshire Demesnes[10] | 753.0.1¾ | 743.9.3½ | 644.10.5½ | 764.4.10¼ | 742.13.6¼ |
| Macclesfield | 148.1.9 | 106.14.5½ | 63.3.11¾ | 261.14.8¾ | 146.2.1¼ |
| Flintshire Demesnes | 287.18.10 | 263.18.6 | 269.8.8½ | 221.4.9 | -[11] |
| Taxation in Cheshire | - | 333.6.8 | 666.13.4 | 618.18.3 | 332.6.10½ |
| Total Receipts | 1319.3.7 | 1640.5.0 | 1881.19.8¾ | 2268.1.1¾ | 1383.13.5½ |
| Arrears | - | 102.4.8 | 214.17.6½ | 105.18.10½ | 383.17.5½ |
| Receipts & Arrears | 1319.3.7 | 1742.9.8 | 2096.17.3¼ | 2374.0.0¼ | 1767.11.1¼ |
| Alms | 71.10.3 | 54.6.6 | 42.6.6 | 42.6.6 | 42.6.6 |
| Wages & Fees | 213.12.1½ | 189.7.5 | 244.6.6 | 178.10.3½ | 190.4.2 |
| Annuities | 162.5.1 | 226.7.7½ | 273.12.8 | 383.18.7½ | 164.0.10 |
| Works | 109.13.3 | 76.5.5 | 86.7.0¼ | 28.5.4 | 29.13.3¾ |

9 Details of the same sources of income and expenditure have been omitted although they are included in the totals of receipts and expenses, e.g. the donum and fines in Flintshire, payments of instalments on the Great Roll of Debts. Details of allowances and receipts are also omitted, although allowances are deducted from the remainder.

10 Including Dee Fulling Mills.

11 Nil due to the rebellion.

| SC 6 | 774/11 1400 | 774/13 1401 | 774/14 1402 | 774/15 1403 | 775/3 1404 |
|---|---|---|---|---|---|
| Men-at-arms' etc wages | 147.8.4 | 86.4.4 | in Welsh expen. | 1103.13.10 ¾ | 1131.7.1 |
| Welsh expenditure | - | 99.2.3½ | 302.6.9 | 238.6.8[12] | - |
| Total expenditure | 788.16.1½ | 886.18.9½ | 1137.13.3 ¾ | 1990.2.6¾ | 1612.9.11 |
| Balance incl. arrears | 530.7.5½ | 955.10.10½ | 859.3.11½ | 383.17.5½ | 155.1.2 |
| Balance excl. arrears | 530.7.5½ | 853.6.2½ | 844.6.5 | 277.18.7 | -228.16.3¾ |
| Liveries | 353.6.8 | 590.0.0 | 854.18.8 | - | - |
| Remainder | 102.4.8 | 214.17.6½ | 105.18.10½ | 383.17.5½ | 155.1.2 |

| SC 6 | 775/4 1405 | 775/5 1406 | 775/6 1407 | 775/9 1408 | (792/5) 1409 |
|---|---|---|---|---|---|
| Cheshire Demesnes | 743.16.9½ | 874.12.3 | 985.8.2½ | 811.9.2 | 689.4.7½ |
| Macclesfield | 158.15.10¼ | 148.10.5¼ | 109.19.5¾ | 155.1.10 | ? |
| Flintshire Demesnes | -[3] | -[3] | 150.13.5 | 149.14.5 | ? |
| Taxation in Cheshire | 971.17.9 | 647.18.6 | 323.19.3 | - | - |
| Total Receipts | 2263.2.7¾ | 1831.6.4¾ | 1768.7.11¾ | 1395.5.8 | ? |
| Arrears | 155.1.2 | 446.13.1¾ | 231.18.0 | 573.18.6½ | ? |
| Receipts & Arrears | 2418.3.9¾ | 2277.19.6½ | 2020.5.11¾ | 1869.4.2½ | ? |
| Alms | 42.6.6 | 42.6.6 | 42.6.6 | 61.6.6 | ? |
| Wages & Fees | 234.6.8 | 251.18.0 | 250.2.3 | 239.9.8 | ? |

12 This does not represent the total paid out of Cheshire revenues for the way effort: the wages paid to Welsh garrisons are included in the total of wages of men-at-arms' and archers. The sums noted here were for victuals for troops in North Wales.

| SC 6 | 775/4 1405 | 775/5 1406 | 775/6 1407 | 775/9 1408 | (792/5) 1409 |
|---|---|---|---|---|---|
| Annuities | 221.19.7 | 230.15.0 | 422.11.8 | 514.7.1 | ? |
| Works | 26.12.5½ | 40.8.3½ | 67.4.0¾ | 50.8.9¼ | ? |
| Men-at-arms' etc wages | 1228.2.6½ | 1310.3.8 | 501.8.0 | 699.1.4 | ? |
| Welsh expenditure | 53.6.8[13] | 101.13.4 | 48.6.8 | 30.0.0 | ? |
| Total expenditure | 1971.10.8 | 2046.18.0½ | 1446.7.5¼ | 1711.2.9¾ | ? |
| Balance incl. arrears | 446.13.1¾ | 231.18.0 | 573.18.6½ | 158.1.4¾ | ? |
| Balance excl. arrears | 291.11.11¾ | -241.15.1¾ | 342.0.6½ | -415.17.1½ | ? |
| Liveries | - | - | - | - | - |
| Remainder | 446.13.1¾ | 231.18.0 | 573.18.6½ | 158.1.4¾ | 20.11.1¼ |

| SC 6 | 775/11 1410 | 775/12 1411 | 775/14 1412 | 775/15 1413 | 1302/15 1414 |
|---|---|---|---|---|---|
| Cheshire Demesnes | 676.4.2¼ | 649.2.7¾ | 637.18.8 ¾ | 850.5.0½ | 654.4.0¾ |
| Macclesfield | 107.7.2¾ | 77.11.4½ | 222.1.9½ | 131.13.6½ | 155.15.2¼ |
| Flintshire Demesnes | 29.4.4 | 375.5.8 | 506.9.0½ | 287.14.0 | 348.5.4¾ |
| Taxation in Cheshire | - | - | - | - | - |
| Total Receipts | 1146.18.10 ¾ | 1182.5.10¼ | 1478.7.5½ | 1197.4.11 | 1191.14.0½ |
| Arrears | 20.11.1 ¾ | 214.14.11 | 96.4.7¼ | - | 20.6.8½ |
| Receipts & Arrears | 1167.10.0 | 1396.10.9¾ | 1574.12.0 | 1197.4.11 | 1212.4.1 |
| Alms | 61.6.6 | 42.6.6 | 61.6.6 | 10.16.6 | 42.16.6 |
| Wages & Fees | 260.7.4 | 252.7.7 | 290.2.6 | 254.4.8 | 251.0.9 |

13 Payments of the fees of the constables of the castles of North Wales.

| SC 6 | 775/11 1410 | 775/12 1411 | 775/14 1412 | 775/15 1413 | 1302/15 1414 |
|---|---|---|---|---|---|
| Annuities | 383.1.4 | 387.19.4 | 808.13.4 | 586.16.4½ | 580.4.7 |
| Works | 66.10.2 ½ | 55.2.1 | 48.5.4¾ | 77.14.4 | 54.8.2¼ |
| Men-at-arms' etc wages | 168.13.4 | 232.13.0 | 148.19.4 | 49.15.6 | 49.16.8 |
| Welsh expenditure | 30.0.0 | 40.0.0 | 20.0.0 | - | - |
| Total expenditure | 1068.7.2 | 1300.6.2 | 1574.12.0½ | 1172.8.2½ | 1127.4.3½ |
| Balance incl. arrears | 99.2.10 | 96.4.7¼ | ¼ | 24.16.8½ | 84.19.9½ |
| Balance excl. arrears | 78.11.8 ¾ | -118.0.3¾ | -96.4.7 | 24.16.8½ | 64.9.9 |
| Liveries | - | - | - | - | - |
| Remainder | 214.14.11 | 96.4.7¼ | ¼ | 20.6.8½ | 89.19.9 ½ |

| SC 6 | 776/1 1415 | 1303/1 1416 | 766/4 1417 | 766/5 1418 | 1303/2 1419 |
|---|---|---|---|---|---|
| Cheshire Demesnes | 697.17.0¾ | 649.1.7 ½ | 664.16.9 ¼ | 585.9.4 ½ | 518.19.2½ |
| Macclesfield | 131.12.1 ½ | 100.14.11¼ | 147.17.7 ¼ | 102.13.11 | 125.0.9¼ |
| Flintshire Demesnes | 333.8.3 | 303.3.0 ¾ | 320.4.9 ¼ | 320.15.7¾ | 252.18.2½ |
| Taxation in Cheshire | - | - | 1000.0.0 | 666.13.4 | 333.6.8 |
| Total Receipts | 1226.19.4 ¾ | 1259.15.1¾ | 2478.1.2 ¾ | 1991.18.3 ¼ | 1505.5.11 ¾ |
| Arrears | 89.19.9 ½ | 35.12.6 ½ | 123.7.6 | 173.15.10 ¾ | 377.14.1 |
| Receipts & Arrears | 1316.192 ¾ | 1275.7.8 ¼ | 2601.8.8¾ | 2165.14.2 | 1883.3.4 ¾ |
| Alms | 82.6.6 | 211.6.6 | 61.6.6 | 61.6.6 | 61.6.6 |
| Wages & Fees | 261.10.10 | 256.19.7 | 249.13.6 | 285.16.1 | 180.13.4 |
| Annuities | 581.14.7 | 453.18.11 | 385.19.7 | 349.6.3 | 344.6.3 |

| SC 6 | 776/1 1415 | 1303/1 1416 | 766/4 1417 | 766/5 1418 | 1303/2 1419 |
|---|---|---|---|---|---|
| Works | 115.19.6 ¾ | 90.5.10¼ | 98.14.2 | 68.7.2 | 87.15.5 |
| Men-at-arms' etc wages | 63.15.8 | 65.6.10 | 481.15.9½ | 109.12.10 | 141.3.8 |
| Welsh expenditure | - | - | - | - | - |
| Total expenditure | 1281.6.8 ¼ | 1152.0.2 ¼ | 1487.12.10 | 1056.3.5 | 1151.4.5 |
| Balance incl. arrears | 35.12.6 ½ | 123.7.6 | 1113.15.10¾ | 1109.10.9 | 731.18.11¾ |
| Balance excl. arrears | -54.13.11 | 87.8.3 ½ | 990.8.4¾ | 935.1.6¼ | 354.1.6¾ |
| Liveries | - | - | 940.0.0 | 731.16.8 | 596.18.10 |
| Remainder | 35.12.6 | 123.7.6 | 173.15.10¾ | 377.14.1 | 135.0.1¾ |

| SC 6 | 1303/3 1420 | 1303/4 1421 | 1303/5 1422 |
|---|---|---|---|
| Cheshire Demesnes | 458.18.0 | 606.12.5 | 500.7.1¼ |
| Macclesfield | 82.18.1 | 94.19.11 | 52.11.11½ |
| Flintshire Demesnes | 272.4.2 | 281.2.3½ | 372.0.2½ |
| Taxation in Cheshire | 333.6.8 | 333.6.8 | - |
| Total Receipts | 1320.10.8 | 1571.10.10½ | 1122.7.10 |
| Arrears | 135.0.1¾ | 238.3.4 | 119.10.0¾ |
| Receipts & Arrears | 1456.0.9¾ | 1809.14.2½ | 1241.17.10¾ |
| Alms | 61.6.6 | 61.6.6 | 61.6.6 |
| Wages & Fees | 200.4.11 | 234.19.2½ | 249.9.8½ |
| Annuities | 335.19.7 | 345.19.7 | 300.15.4¼ |
| Works | 51.14.1¾ | 61.13.11¼ | 78.10.8½ |

| **SC 6** | **1303/3 1420** | **1303/4 1421** | **1303/5 1422** |
|---|---|---|---|
| Men-at-arms' etc wages | 34.5.6 | 60.0.0 | 197.2.2 |
| Welsh expenditure | - | - | - |
| Total expenditure | 842.17.5¾ | 963.10.9¾ | 992.5.9 |
| Balance incl. arrears | 613.3.4 | 851.3.4¾ | 249.12.1¾ |
| Balance excl. arrears | 477.16.6¾ | 613.0.0 ¾ | 130.2.1 |
| Liveries | 375.0.0 | 731.13.4 | 113.12.9 |
| Remainder | 238.3.4 | 119.10.0¾ | 135.19.4¾ |

## APPENDIX III

# *Prices and Wages*

### Grain

The major source of information on prices of grain are the accounts of the keeper of the Dee mills. From the figures of the quantity of each type of grain sold and the total income received from the sale of each type, we can calculate the average price per quarter. This was grain, of course, which had been taken in toll for milling at the earl's mills. It was then sold 'to divers men at divers prices'.[1] Some sales of grain taken in toll were also accounted at Frodsham until the mills there were put to farm in 1418.[2] In both cases the London measure was used. There are also figures of profits arising from the sale of toll-corn during two years when the mills of Macclesfield were kept in hand.[3] Here the Macclesfield measure was used, which, by comparison of wheat prices for the relevant years, appears to be around four times the size of the London Measure. In order to allow comparison, the annual prices per quarter given for Macclesfield on the following table are a fourth of those actually stated on the accounts themselves. In order to compare these

1 The accounts of the Dee mills used are, in chronological order from 1399-1400 as follows: SC 6 791/1 m. 5; SC 6 791/3 m. 5; SC 6 791/5 m. 7; SC 6 791/6 m. 7; SC 6 791/7 m. 6; SC 6 791/10 m. 8; SC 6 792/1 m. 5; SC 6 792/2 m. 5; SC 6 792/3 m. 5; SC 6 792/5 m. 5; SC 6 792/6 m. 5; SC 6 792/8 m. 4; SC 6 792/9 m. 5; SC 6 792/10 m. 5; SC 6 793/1 m. 3; SC 6 793/2 m. 8; SC 6 793/4 m. 5; SC 6 793/5 m. 6; SC 6 793/9 m. 7; SC 6 793/11 m. 7; SC 6 794/1 m. 7; SC 6 794/2 m. 7.

2 SC 6 793/7 m. 5. See above p. 161. The Frodsham accounts used are, in chronological order from 1408-9, SC 6 792/5 m. 10; SC 6 792/6 m. 6d; SC 6 792/8 m. 5d; SC 6 792/9 m. 4d; SC 6 792/10 m. 6d; SC 6 793/1 m. 4d; SC 6 793/2 m. 6d; SC 6 793/4 m. 6. Sale of grain was also made in 1417 (SC 6 793/5 m. 5d) but this account is damaged and the quantities sold and sums received are illegible.

3 1400-1401 (SC 6/805/7 m. 2); 1401-1402 SC 6 805/9 m. 2).

Cheshire prices with those elsewhere, I have used the averages for grain prices for this period furnished by Thorold Rogers.[4]

I have chosen the major categories of grain although details on the prices of lesser types can be proved by the Dee mill accounts, such as various kinds of flours. The figures given for malt may not be completely comparable. Thorold Rogers does not distinguish the precise kind of malt but in the Cheshire accounts, barley malt, corn malt and malt of milled and unmilled malt are found. Thorold Rogers does not give figures for one of the most important categories in Cheshire, that of mixed grain (principally rye and wheat).

Two striking observations can be made from the table. The first is that in the first half of the period prices of corn and malt in Cheshire were up to twice as high as the national average. The price of peas was also higher in Cheshire but the discrepancy with the national average was not so marked. The second point is the sharp drop in Cheshire prices of corn and mixed grain from 1412. In the first category Cheshire prices fell below the national average until rising sharply again from 1416. This sharp rise is also seen in the prices of oat malt. Barley malt prices in the county remained high, sometimes up to three times the national average, throughout the period, echoing fluctuations in corn prices by showing a sharp decline in 1412 and a correspondingly sharp rise by the end of the decade. The reason for the discrepancy between Cheshire and national prices must be the effect of the Welsh wars. The chronology of the first period of high prices and the sharp decline in 1412 aligns with the period during which the county was feeling the general impact of the war. The phenomenon of Cheshire prices being so inflated may also owe something to restrictions placed upon trade with the Welsh and upon the market in grain in particular.[5] Certainly prices were at the highest from 1401 to 1403 in the initial stages of the Welsh rebellion.

4 James E. Thorold Rogers, *A History of Agriculture and Prices in England*, 6 vols in 8 (Oxford: Clarendon Press, 1866-1902), ii p. 328, iv pp. 282-3.

5 See above p. 164.

## Grain prices per quarter (given in shillings and pence)

Abbreviations: TR: Thorold Rogers, *History of Agriculture and Prices in England*

DM: Dee Mills Macc: Macclesfield mills Frod: Frodsham mills

| | Corn | | | | Barley Malt | | | Oatmalt - milled | | |
|---|---|---|---|---|---|---|---|---|---|---|
| **Year** | ***TR*** | ***DM*** | ***Macc*** | ***Frod*** | ***TR*** | ***DM*** | ***Macc*** | ***DM*** | ***Macc*** | ***Frod*** |
| 1400 | 5.6¾ | 8.7 | - | - | 4.2 | 9.5 | - | 7.5 | - | - |
| 1401 | 7.11¼ | 9.11 | 10.0 | - | 6.11 | 9.8 | 2.4 | 7.7 | 5.6 | - |
| 1402 | 7.5¾ | 11.6 | 8.0 | - | 5.4 | 12.1 | - | 8.1 | 6.0 | - |
| 1403 | 6.8¾ | 9.10 | - | - | 4.9½ | 11.7 | - | 7.2 | - | - |
| 1404 | 4.11¼ | 6.5 | - | - | 3.6 | 7.8 | - | 6.2 | - | - |
| 1405 | 4.0 | 6.11 | - | - | 3.9¾ | 7.3 | - | 6.0 | - | - |
| 1406 | 3.9¾ | 6.2 | - | - | 3.3¼ | 7.9 | - | 6.2 | - | - |
| 1407 | 4.4 | 8.3 | - | - | 3.6¾ | 8.5 | - | 6.8 | - | - |
| 1408 | 4.6¾ | 8.4 | - | - | 4.10 | 8.8 | - | 6.8 | - | - |
| 1409 | 7.3¼ | 8.3 | - | 6.10 | 5.1¾ | 9.1 | - | 7.6 | - | 5.4 |
| 1410 | 8.11½ | 9/10 | - | 9.3 | 4.8½ | 10.3 | - | 8.0 | - | 5.0 |
| 1411 | 4.10½ | 9.2 | - | 7.1 | 4.0½ | 11.6 | - | 7.9 | - | 4.7 |
| 1412 | 4.10 | 3.11 | - | 4.0 | 3.11½ | 5.9 | - | 4.9 | - | - |
| 1413 | 4.10¾ | 4.7 | - | 5.4 | 4.3¾ | 7.5 | - | 5.3 | - | 3.1 |

DM: Dee Mills Macc: Macclesfield mills Frod: Frodsham mills

| | | | | | | | | | | |
|---|---|---|---|---|---|---|---|---|---|---|
| 1414 | 4.3½ | 5.9½ | - | 5.3 | 4.0 | 8.1 | - | 6.11 | - | 3.3 |
| 1415 | 4.3¾ | 4.5 | - | 4.0 | 5.0¼ | 8.0 | - | 6.8 | - | 2.11 |
| 1416 | 6.3½ | 8.9 | - | 5.3 | 5.1½ | 8.0 | - | 6.5 | - | 3.3 |
| 1417 | 7.11¾ | 7.7 | - | - | 5.7¾ | 8.0 | - | 6.5 | - | - |
| 1418 | 5.3½ | 6.2 | - | - | 4.6 | 8.0 | - | 9.4 | - | - |
| 1419 | 6.11½ | 8.0 | - | - | 3.3 | 8.11 | - | 7.1 | - | - |
| 1420 | 4.9¼ | 7.4 | - | - | 4.2½ | 12.0 | - | 9.8 | - | - |
| 1421 | 6.3 | 6.3 | - | - | 4.1½ | 11.9 | - | 6.11 | - | - |
| 1422 | 5.2¾ | 6.10 | - | - | 3.7½ | 10.9 | - | 6.8 | - | - |

| | Oatmalt - unmilled | Peas | | Mixed grain | | |
|---|---|---|---|---|---|---|
| ***Year*** | ***DM*** | ***TR*** | ***DM*** | ***DM*** | ***Macc*** | ***Frod*** |
| 1400 | 8.1 | 2.11 | 5.3 | 6.8 | - | - |
| 1401 | 8.0 | 4.6 | 5.9 | 7.3 | 2.3 | - |
| 1402 | 8.8 | 4.1½ | 5.10 | 8.4 | 5.0 | - |
| 1403 | 7.6 | 3.2 | 4.1 | 6.4 | - | - |
| 1404 | 6.1 | 3.1 | 3.7 | 4.3 | - | - |
| 1405 | 6.0 | 2.8¾ | 3.5 | 4.6 | - | - |
| 1406 | 6.2 | 2.7¾ | 4.9 | 5.1 | - | - |
| 1407 | 6.8 | 2.9½ | 5.2 | 5.11 | - | - |
| 1408 | 6.8 | 3.8½ | 5.6 | 5.7 | - | - |
| 1409 | 7.6 | 4.8 | 6.2 | 6.2 | - | 4.8 |
| 1410 | 9.3 | 3.1½ | 6.4 | 7.3 | - | 4.11 |
| 1411 | 7.5 | 3.0 | 5.0 | 6.10 | - | 5.3 |
| 1412 | 4.4 | 2.10½ | 2.10 | 2.10 | - | 2.2 |
| 1413 | 5.1 | 2.9 | 2.4 | 3.9 | - | 2.3 |
| 1414 | 6.9 | 3.9¼ | 3.0 | 4.7 | - | 2.7 |
| 1415 | 6.8 | 4.11¼ | 3.0 | 3.7 | - | 2.7 |
| 1416 | 6.8 | 3.4 | 3.4 | 4.11½ | - | 2.9 |
| 1417 | 6.2 | 2.9¼ | 2.10 | 4.5 | -- | - |
| 1418 | 6.7 | 2.11 | 2.8 | 4.8 | | - |
| 1419 | 7.2 | 3.6½ | 3.4 | 5.10 | - | - |
| 1420 | 9.8 | 3.3 | 8.0 | 7.1 | - | - |
| 1421 | 13.1 | 2.11 | 5.6 | 4.11½ | - | - |
| 1422 | 6.4 | 3.8 | 6.0 | 5.0 | - | - |

## *Fish*

A considerable quantity of fish from the earl's fishery in the River Dee at Chester was sold. As with grain prices, the figures quoted here are arrived at by dividing the total revenue received for each category by the total of each category sold. The accounts used are the same as those for prices of grain at the Dee mills. Unfortunately, comparative national prices are not available. Thorold Rogers notes that it was difficult to provide accurate figures for lampreys, since the variation in local prices was so extraordinary that there were possibly many different species sold.[6] For instance, he records that 80 lampreys were sold for a total of 1s. 10d. in 1404 but in 1431 they were being retailed at 5d. each.[7] Salmon prices are also difficult to assess. They were usually sold salted and by the barrel, generally at 1s. to 1s. 10d. each, although the price in Canterbury in 1404 was 7s. per fish.[8] We may be seeing here different sizes of fish which are not specified. Cheshire fish prices seem to fit with the general trend although there is no indication whether the salmon were being sold fresh or salted. In 1408 and 1409, salmon were sold at Shotwick at 2s. each,[9] again a price highly comparable with that received at the Dee fishery. Young salmon (*samunculi*) and dead fish (*mortes*) were also sold. These smaller fish sold very cheaply although not as cheaply as eels at Canterbury which in 1404 sold at £2 for 600 fish.[10]

## Fish prices (given in shillings and pence)

| *Year* | *Salmon* | *'Keperes'* | *Lampreys* |
|---|---|---|---|
| 1400 | 1.9 | - | - |
| 1401 | 1.9 | 6 | - |
| 1402 | 2.7 | 7 | 1.0 |
| 1403 | 2.3 | 8 | 1.4 |
| 1404 | 2.3 | 4 | 1.0 |
| 1405 | 1.9 | 1.4 | - |
| 1406 | 2.2 | 6½ | 6 |

6 Thorold Rogers, *History of Agriculture and Prices,* vol. 4, p. 538.
7 Thorold Rogers, *History of Agricu1lture and Prices,* vol. 4, p. 539.
8 Thorold Rogers, *History of Agriculture and Prices,* vol. 4, pp. 528-9.
9 SC 6 792/3 m. 3, SC 6/792/5 m. 3. The fisheries at Frodsham were farmed so we have no figures for prices there.
10 Thorold Rogers, *History of Agriculture and Prices,* vol. 4, p. 230.

| | | | |
|---|---|---|---|
| 1407 | 2.5 | 7 | 3 |
| 1408 | 2.6 | 7 | - |
| 1409 | 2.1 | 7 | - |
| 1410 | 1.8 | 7 | 3 |
| 1411 | 1.5 | 7½ | - |
| 1412 | 1.8 | - | - |
| 1413 | 1.5 | - | 2 |
| 1414 | 1.5 | 6 | 1½ |
| 1415 | 1.5 | 5 | 3½ |
| 1416 | 2.6 | 8 | 2¼ |
| 1417 | 1.6 | 1.4½ | 2¼ |
| 1418 | 1.5 | 9 | 2 |
| 1419 | 2.0 | 6 | 1¾ |
| 1420 | 1.11 | - | 1 |
| 1421 | 1.6 | 5½ | 1¼ |
| 1422 | 1.11 | 9 | 1¾ |

## Wages

Evidence on wage rates in the county derives primarily from the repair accounts at Macclesfield although all too often the costs are expressed as a lump sum. Some supplementary information has been derived from the Statute of Labourers cases on the Indictment rolls, although these are not figures of wages paid on the earl's demesnes. In comparison with Cheshire daily rates I have drawn upon national averages as given by Thorold Rogers.[11] In the table which follows the first column in each category of employment is the national figure and the second any Cheshire examples which have been found.

In general (although any conclusions are weakened bv the lack of a representative sample of Cheshire evidence) wages rates in the county are comparable with national rates. Where there is a discrepancy the Cheshire rate is lower, which is perhaps

11 Thorold Rogers, *History of Agriculture and Prices,* iv 514-15, i, 319; ii 328.

surprising in the light of other litigation which suggests that labour could be at a premium.[12] It may be possible that the rates paid by the earl on demesne repairs were lower than the norm for the county although it must be remembered that there was no tenurial condition at Macclesfield which involved obligation to work for the lord.

## Daily wage rates (given in pence)

| Year | carpenter | mason | tiler | thatcher | unskilled labourer | 'argillatus'[13] |
|---|---|---|---|---|---|---|
| 1400 | 5 – | 8– | 8 | | 3 – 3½ | |
| 1401 | 5 – | 4¼ | 1-1½ | 4¼ | | |
| 1402 | 4¾ – | 6 | 8 | 4½ | | |
| 1403 | 5¼ – 5[14] | 5 | 8 – 4 | | 3 – 2 to 4 | 4 |
| 1404 | 6 – | 8 | 8 | | 4 – 2 | |
| 1405 | 4 – 4[15] | 4¾ | 4¾ | 4½ | | |
| 1406 | 5 – | 8 | 5 | | | |
| 1407 | 5 – 4[16] | 6 | 8 – 4 | | 4 – 3 | |
| 1408 | 4¼ | - | 5 | | 3 – 3 to 4 | |
| 1409 | 5¾ | 5 | 5 | 5¼ | | |
| 1410 | 6 | 6 | 5½ | | | |
| 1411 | 6 | 6 | 8 | | | |
| 1412 | 6 | 6 | 6 | 4¼ | 3½–3 | |
| 1413 | 4½ | - | 8 | | | |
| 1414 | 5 ¼ – 5 to 6[17] | 5 – 5 | 6 – 5 | 4½.– 4 to 5 | 3¼ – 3 to 4 | 4 |

12 See above p. 229.
13 Worker in clay. These are found working on infilling in the construction of timber-framed buildings in Macclesfield. There are no comparative wages given by Thorold Rogers.
14 SC 6/805/11 m 2d.
15 SC 6/805/14 m. 2d.
16 SC 6/806/1 m. 2d.
17 SC 2/155/88 mm. 7, 8. The higher rate was paid in the summer (m. 7).

| 1415 | 4½ | - | 5 | | | |
|---|---|---|---|---|---|---|
| 1416 | 5¼ | 6 | - | | | |
| 1417 | 5 | 6¼ | 5½ | 4½ | | |
| 1418 | 6 – 4[18] | 6 | 6 – 4 | 4¾ | 3 – 1 | |
| 1419 | 5½ | 6 | 6 | 4½ | | |
| 1420 | 5½ | 6¼ | 6 | 4½ | 2½ | |
| 1421 | 5 | 6½ | - | | 3½ | |
| 1422 | 5¼ | 6 | 6 | | 3 | |

18 SC 6/806/16 m. 1d.

APPENDIX IV

# *Annuities taken from Cheshire Revenues 1399-1422*

| Name | First name | Dates | Source | Amount |
|---|---|---|---|---|
| Aldelyn | John | 1397, 1400 | Chamberlain | £20 |
| ap David | Griffith ap Owen | 1402 | Chamberlain | 40 shillings |
| Arundel | Thomas, earl of | 1408 | Chamberlain | 250 marks |
| Atherton | William | 1412 | Chamberlain | 20 marks |
| Attelbrigg | John | 1401 | Chamberlain | 100 shillings |
| Audlem | John | 1400 | Chamberlain | £20 |
| Brescy | Roger | 1397, 1400 | Dee mills | 8d. per day |
| Burcestre | Nicholas | 1402 | Dee fishery | 5 marks |
| Byron | John | 1412 | Chamberlain | £10 |
| Calverley | John kt snr | 1398, 1400 | Chamberlain | £30 |
| Castell | Robert | 1400 | Northwich | £5 |
| Castleton | Robert | 1419 | Chamberlain | £10 w. J. Yarondale |
| Chambre | Nicholas de la | 1399 | Chamberlain | £5 |
| Clerk | John le | 1363, 1401 | Chamberlain | 2d. per day |
| Clifford | William kt | | Chamberlain (issues of Eulowe) | £20 |
| Compnour | Robert | 1387, 1400 | Dee fishery | 5 marks |
| Dedwode | John del | 1416 | Chamberlain | 8d. per day |
| Done | John | 1398, 1401 | Delamere | £10 |
| Draycote | Roger | 1410 | Chamberlain (lands of John Leche in Flints) | 5 marks |
| Dutton | Peter de kt | 1397, 1404 | Chamberlain | £20 |

| Name | First name | Dates | Source | Amount |
|---|---|---|---|---|
| Dutton | Thomas | 1411 | Northwich | £43 with J. Grey |
| Filongley | Richard | BP, 1400 | Chamberlain | £10 |
| Frodsham | William de | 1397, 1400 | Chamberlain | 4d. per day |
| Goolde | Walter | 1419 | Chamberlain | £5 |
| Grey | Thomas kt | 1408 | Chamberlain | £40 |
| Grey | John | 1411 | Northwich | £43 with T. Dutton |
| Haregrove | John | 1410 | Chamberlain (lands of John Leche in Flints) | £10 |
| Harrington | William | 1406 | Chamberlain | 40 marks |
| Hawarden | John | 1403 | Chamberlain | 10 marks |
| Helyon | Robert | 1416 | Dee Mills | £10 |
| Holes | Hugh | 1400 | Chamberlain | 20 marks |
| Holland | Charles de | 1416 | Rudheath | £5 |
| Holland | Nicholas | 1412 | Rudheath | 7 marks |
| Kingsley | John | 1401 | Chamberlain | 20 marks |
| Kingsley | John | 1405 | Delamere | £10 |
| Leche | John (surgeon) | 1382, 1400 | Dee Mills | £10 |
| Legh | Robert de kt | 1387, 1400 | Chamberlain | £40 |
| Legh | John de Booths kt | 1397, 1401, 1406 | Chamberlain/ | |
| Macclesfield | 20 marks | | | |
| Legh | John of Wythenshawe | 1417 | Drakelow | £10 |
| Mainwaring | Ralph | 1405 | Chamberlain | 10 marks |
| Mainwaring | John | 1406 | Chamberlain | 20 marks (aborted.) |
| Massey | Richard | 1377, 1403 | Chamberlain | 40 marks (repl. BP Harlech) |
| Massey | John of Tatton kt | BP, 1400 | Chamberlain | 50 marks |

| Name | First name | Dates | Source | Amount |
|---|---|---|---|---|
| Massey | John of Puddington | 1401 | Chamberlain | 40 marks |
| Menston | William | 1418 | Dee Mills | 10 (w. Thomas Pope) |
| Moston | Richard | 1400 | Shotwick | £10 |
| Norreys | John | 1399 | Chamberlain | 12d. per day |
| Orell | Nicholas | 1398, 1400 | Chamberlain | 12d. per day |
| Pope | Ralph | 1409 | Chamberlain | 10 marks |
| Pope | Thomas | 1418 | Dee Mills | £10, w. Wm Menston |
| Pope | William | 1409 | Chamberlain | £10 |
| Porter | William | 1412 | Chamberlain | £10 |
| Redmayne | Richard | 1397, 1400 | Chamberlain | 40 marks |
| Roberdson | Ralph | BP, 1400 | Chamberlain | £6 |
| Robessart | Lewis | 1412 | Chamberlain | £20 |
| Roteur | Richard | 1404 | Chamberlain | 100s |
| Rys | John de la | 1417 | Drakelow | £10 |
| Sandbache | Robert | 1401 | Drakelow | 100s |
| Savage | John | 1407 | Chamberlain | £20 |
| Stanley | John kt snr | 1397, 1400 | Chamberlain | 40 marks |
| Stanley | John | 1407 | Chamberlain | £20 |
| Stokes | Roger | 1379, 1400 | Chamberlain | £10 |
| Stokely | Robert | 1394, 1399 | Drakelow | £10 |
| Stokely | Robert | 1394, 1400 | Dee Mills | £10 |
| Swetenham | Matthew | 1391, 1399 | Drakelow | £20 |
| Trevour | Edward | 1401 | Chamberlain | 10 marks |
| Troutbeck | William | 1418 | Dee Mills | £10 |
| Troutbeck | William | 1418 | Drakelow | £10 |
| Tunstall | Thomas kt | 1406 | Chamberlain | 40 marks |
| Upton | John | 1407 | Rudheath | 7 marks |
| Vaughan | David | 1387, 1400 | Chamberlain | £10 |
| Venables | Hugh | 1412 | Chamberlain | 20 marks |

| Name | First name | Dates | Source | Amount |
|---|---|---|---|---|
| Venables | William | 1401 | Chamberlain | £10 |
| Warburton | Peter | 1407 | Chamberlain | 10 marks |
| Wendesley | Thomas kt | 1400 | Chamberlain | 100 marks |
| Wodeward | Richard le | 1397, 1400 | Chamberlain | 4d. per day |
| Yarondale | John | 1419 | Chamberlain | £10, with Robert Castleton |
| Yonge | Thomas | 1400 | Chamberlain | 5 marks |
| Zouche | William, lord | 1408 | Chamberlain | £50 |

APPENDIX V

# *Valor of the county 1403 (TNA SC 11/904)*

The annual value of the county of Chester according to the response of officials of the lord in that county from Michaelmas in the third year of the reign of King Henry the Fourth to Michaelmas in year four (1402-1403)

| | | |
|---|---|---|
| The city of Chester | the fee farm of the city | £100 |
| | rent of the chamber | 52s. 4d. |
| | escheats in the city | 7s. |
| | Total | £102 19s. 4d. |

| | | |
|---|---|---|
| Drakelow manor | beyond fees and annuities | £12 0s. 2d. |

Delamere forest beyond the 100s. allocated to John Done of his annuity of £10 per annum for the Easter term in year 4 allocated to him £44 15s. 8d.

| | | |
|---|---|---|
| Northwich | clear, after outgoings | £28 8s. 10d. |
| Shotwick manor | | |
| | farm of that manor | £10 |
| | sale of divers roots of oak trees felled in the past in Saughall wood | 2s. 3d. |
| | Total | £10 2s. 3d. |

| | | |
|---|---|---|
| Lands which were of William de Frodsham snr | | |
| | farm of these lands beyond 15s. paid annually to Anilla who was the wife of Richard de Frodsham for her dower | 116s. 1½d. |

Middlewich clear,
beyond outgoings £43 3s. 9½d.

Office of sheriff of Chester with judicial issues
clear, beyond outgoings £180 18s. 8½d.

Office of escheator of Chester clear, after outgoings
£50 1s. 3d.

Mills for grain and malt of Dee with the fisheries there

beyond annuities and expenses coming out [of issues] there, clear after outgoings £157 7s.

Fulling mill on the Dee, clear after outgoings £8 11s. 6½d.

Lordship of Macclesfield

hundred with escheats, clear £24 14s. 8d.

*burgus* there with issues of the markets and justices itinerant £23 0s. 7½d.

forest beyond unpaid rents, decayed rents and repairs to houses £106 3s. 0½d.

Total: £153 19s. 4d.

Total value of the county of Chester for
this period £798 4s.

Macclesfield park nothing because the herbage there has been granted by the lord to John Kingsley

The wages of men-at-arms and archers in the castles and towns of North Wales staying there for their defence[1]

1 This section between asterisks is in Anglo-Norman.

*Caernarvon castle 1 lance, 12 archers

by the day 7s., the week 49s., the quarter £31 17s., the year £127 8s.

the town of Caernarvon 2 lances and 24 archers

by the day 13s., the week £4 17s., the quarter £63 14s., the year £254 16s.

Beaumaris castle 2 lances and 30 archers

by the day 7s., the week 49s., the quarter £31 17s., the year £127 8s.

Conway castle 1 lance, 12 archers

by the day 7s., the week 49s., the quarter £31 17s., the year £127 8s.

Rhuddlan castle 1 lance 19 archers

by the day 7s., the week 49s., the quarter £31 17s., the year £127 8s.

Flint castle 18 archers

by the day 7s., the week 49s., the quarter £31 17s., the year £127 8s.
Chester castle 8 archers

Total sum for the year £1423 7s. 4d.*

## Alms

The abbot and convent of the monastery of Saint Werburgh of Chester for the finding of a light in the chapel of St Hildeburgh each year 10s.

The same abbot and convent for the tithes of the issues of the city of Chester to be paid each year in equal portions at Easter and Michaelmas £10

The same abbot and convent for the tithes for the ninth part of the fishery of the Dee bridge to be paid each year in equal portions at Easter and Michaelmas 100s.

The same abbot and convent in compensation for the tithes which belonged to the abbot of Chester at Frodsham and which the abbot of Chester at the request of Edward I, former king of England and earl of Chester resigned to the use of the abbot of Vale Royal to be paid each year equally at the same terms £4

The prioress and nuns of Chester for alms granted to them of old to be paid each year equally at the same terms £26 12s. 2d.

The Friars Preacher of Chester for alms granted to them of old to be paid each year equally at the same terms £8 13s. 4d.

The brothers and sisters of the Hospital of St John the Baptist outside the north gate of the city of Chester for alms granted to them of old to be paid at Michaelmas for the whole year £4 11s.

The lepers of St Giles of Boughton for alms granted to them of old to be paid at Michaelmas for the whole year 20s.

The abbot and convent of the monastery of Our Lady of Whalley for alms granted to them of old to be paid at Christmas for the whole year 20s.

Total: £61 6s. 6d.

## Wages and fees of officials

Gilbert Talbot justiciar of Chester, yearly
£100

The chamberlain of Chester yearly
£20

the same from the receipt at Macclesfield
10 marks (£6 13s. 4d.)

William Venables constable of Chester castle, yearly
£18 5s.

Hugh Holes knight keeper of the garden in the ditch of Chester castle, yearly £4 11s. 3d.

William Newehall master carpenter of the lord in the counties of Chester and Flint for his wages, yearly
£9 2s. 6d.

he same for a robe 10s.

the same for a fee called chirp and old timber, yearly 20s.

Thomas Swetenham seller of goods and chattels of felons and fugitives in the counties of Chester and Flint yearly
60s.

William de Wode door keeper of Chester castle, yearly 60s. 10d.

Henry de Birteles sergeant at law of the lord in the counties of Chester and Flint yearly 5 marks (£3 6s. 8d)

Roger de Horton another sergeant at law of the lord in the said counties, yearly 100s.

John Pygot the third sergeant at law of the lord in the said counties yearly 100s.

Nicholas Hauberk knight constable of the castle of Flint yearly £20

Robert Fagan master mason of the lord, yearly
£12 3s. 4d.

William de Hampton master plumber of the lord, yearly
£12 3s. 4d.

William Moresone keeper of the armour of the lord, yearly
£12 3s. 4d.

Hugh le Fletcher keeper of the artillery of the lord, yearly
£4 11s. 3d.

Matthew del Mere attorney of the lord yearly
100s.

Total: £248 11s. 8d.

## Annuities

| | |
|---|---|
| William Clifford knight, yearly | £20 |
| John de Stanley knight, yearly | 30 marks (£26 13s. 4d.) |
| John de Aldelyn snr, esquire, yearly | £20 |
| Richard le Wodeward, yearly | £6 1s. 8d. |
| Richard Redmayne knight, yearly | 40 marks (£26 13s. 4d.) |
| John Norreys esquire, yearly | £18 5s. |
| Nicholas Orell esquire, yearly | £18 5s. |

David Vaughan esquire, yearly £10

Nicholas de la Chambre yearly 100s.

Roger Stokes esquire, yearly £10

Nicholas Bircestre, yearly 5 marks (£3 6s. 8d.)

Ralph Robertson of Norley, yearly 6s.

Roger Brescy, yearly £12 3s. 4d.

Robert Legh knight, yearly £40

William de Frodsham, yearly £6 1s. 8d.

John le Clerk of Tutbury, yearly 60s. 10d.

William Hare, seller of dead wood, roots and cropping of trees in Delamere forest, yearly 30s. 5d.

John de Kingsley esquire, rider (equitator) of Delamere forest, yearly £4 11s. 3d.

John Attelbrigg yeoman of the doors of the lord's hall, yearly 100s.

William Venables of Kinderton esquire, yearly £10

Griffith ap Owen ap David esquire, yearly 40s.

John Defford keeper and supervisor of victuals of the lord in the castles of Conway, Beaumaris and Caernarvon, yearly £9 2s. 6d.

John de Stanley knight steward of Macclesfield and supervisor and rider of the forests of Macclesfield and Delamere, yearly
100 marks (£66 13s. 4d.)

John de Hawardyn esquire, yearly 10 marks (£6 13s. 4d.)

Richard Roteur esquire, yearly 100s.

Thomas le Wodeward bailiff itinerant in the counties of Chester and Flint, yearly 66s. 10d.

Total: £339 8s. 6d.

***Dorse***

Fees of the constables of castles in North Wales newly assigned out of the issues of the receipt of the Chester Exchequer

Robert Parys constable of the castle of Carnarvon yearly
£40

Thomas Bolde esquire constable of the castle of Beaumaris, yearly £40

Henry de Coneway knight constable of the castle of Rhuddlan, yearly £40

Total: £120

Costs of the exchequer and messengers of the county, yearly 20 marks (£13 6s. 8d.)

Total: 20 marks (£13 6s. 8d.)

Various works and repairs to houses, carriage of timber and other necessary items for these works in the county, yearly
£40

Total: £40

Purchase of iron for keys, lead for locks and keys, yearly £10

Total: £10

Gifs and rewards made by the lord earl, yearly
20 marks (£13 6s. 8d.)

Total: 20 marks (£13 6s. 8d.)

Purchase of millstones for the mills of the lord earl, yearly
100s.

Purchase of bows, arrows, arrow heads, gunpowder and other necessities during the time of war £10

Total: £40

Total sum of the charge falling yearly on the Chester exchequer during the wars and the payments of wages to men-at-arms and archers £2284 7s. 4d.

APPENDIX VI

# *Valor of the lands of the Prince of Wales temp. Henry IV (TNA SC 11/862)*

## m. 1

View of the value, issues and revenues of all the lands, lordships and possessions of the lord prince of Wales and [...] and the shortfall (*decasus*) therein

| | | |
|---|---|---|
| North Wales | £3079 | nothing left |
| South Wales | £2091 18s. 1d. | because of |
| Flintshire | £342 19s. 5d. | the rebellion |
| Cheshire | £824 14s. 10d. | |
| of which in manors, annuities and fees granted | £399 13s. 4d. | |
| remainder | £425 1s. 5d. | |
| The counties of Cornwall and Devon | £2493 7s. 3¼d. | |
| of which in manors, annuities and fees granted | £1200 6s. 3¾d. | |
| remainder | £1242 [1s. 9½d.][1] | |

1 illegible

| | |
|---|---|
| The castle and honour of Wallingford | £203 |
| of which in annuities and fees granted | £149 14s. 0d. |
| remainder | £53 6s. 0d. |
| The castle and honour of Berkhamsted | £90 |
| of which in annuities and fees granted | £45 0s. 8d. |
| remainder | £44 19s. 4d. |
| Manor of Beckley | £33 6s. 8d. |
| of which in annuities and fees granted | £20 |
| remainder | £13 6s. 8d. |
| Manor of Kirton in Lindsey | £300 |
| Remainder | £300 |
| Manor of Rising with the Tollbooth in (King's) Lynn | £116 13s. 4d., which is the remainder |
| Manor of Isleworth | £66 13s. 4d., which is the remainder |
| Manor of Newport | £20, which is the remainder |
| Manor of Shoreham | £10, which is the remainder |

| | | |
|---|---|---|
| Manor of Rockingham | £4 2s. 0d., which is the remainder | |
| Manor of Kennington | £13 6s. 8d. | |
| of which in annuities and fees granted | £12 0s. 8d. | |
| remainder | 26s. | |
| Manor of Knaresborough with its appurtenances | £500 | |

in the hands of the king as of the duchy of Lancaster

| | | |
|---|---|---|
| The castle and lordship of Mere £40<br>Manor of Risborough £83 | in the hands of Lewis Clifford | no remainder |
| Manor of Watlington £50<br>Manor of Fordington £80 | in the hands of Baldwin Beresford | no remainder |
| Manor of Whitchurch £23 | in the hands of Thomas Gloucester granted by the present king | no remainder |
| Manor of Little Weldon £16 | in the hands of William Corby | no remainder |
| Manor of Byfleet £37 15s. 2d. | in the hands of Francis Court granted by the present king | no remainder |

Total value £10,758 12s. 9¼d.

| | | |
|---|---|---|
| Manor of Overmarsh £10 | in the hands of Richard Colfox granted by the present king | no remainder |
| Manor of Frodsham £66 3s. 4d. | in the hands of Radegonde Béchet | no remainder |
| Manor of Moston £13 0s. 4d. | in the hands of John Leche | no remainder |
| Castle and manor of Trematon | £48 11s. 9½d | |
| Manor of Calstock | £48 12s. 11d. | in fee |
| Manor and borough (*burgus*) of *Asshe* (Saltash?) | £24 0s. 3d. | |

[The following entries from Tewington to Camelford are given individual values but bracketed in right hand margin and noted as being 'in the hands of the countess of Huntingdon, total with reversions £419 9s. 8¾d., no remainder']

| | |
|---|---|
| Manor of Tewington | £58 7s. 11d. |
| Manor of Moresk | £41 13s. 5d. |
| Manor of Tintagel | £44 |
| Reversion of the manor and borough (*burgus*) of Helston-in-Kerrier | £66 13s. 4d. |
| Reversion of the manor of Bossiney and Trevena | £10 |
| Manor of Restormel | £10 6s. 0½d. |
| Castle and park of Restormel | £22 3s. 6d. |

Manor of Penlyne £6 13s. 4½d

Manor of Penketh 102s. 4½d.

Borough (*burgus*) and township (*villa*) of Lostwithiel
£25 1s. 1d.

Borough (*burgus*) and township (*villa*) of Camelford
£8 18s. 7d.

Manor and borough (*burgus*) of Helston-in-Kerrier
£66 13s. 4d. In the hands of Margaret Sharnefield

Borough (*burgus*) of Bossiney and Trevena no remainder
£10

Fee farm of the borough (*burgus*) of Grampound

£12 11s. 4d. in the hands of John Chaucy, no remainder

Office of the havener with sea wrecks and other profits £100, in the hands of John Norbury, no remainder

[The following three entries have individual values but are bracketed in the right hand margin and noted as being 'in the hands of Philip Courtenay and Agnes his wife, no remainder']

Manor and borough (*burgus*) of Bradninch
£67 13s. 4d.

Manor of Dartmoor £11

Chase of Dartmoor £66 13s. 4d.

| | | |
|---|---|---|
| Bailiff of the water of Dartmouth | £10 | in the hands of John Corp, no remainder |
| Fee farm of Liskeard | £18 1s. 6d., | in the hands of Roger Gate, no remainder |

Total value: £10758 12s. 9¼d.

Total outgoings: £2742 10s. 1¾d.

Total of the shortfall (*decasus*) from North Wales because of the rebellion, as above
£5613 17s. 6d.

Sum remaining for the sustaining of the necessities of the household of the lord and his Wardrobe and other fees arising both within and without the household for the sustaining and safe-keeping of his castles in Wales, and for the repair of all his other castles and manors in England £2402 7s. 1½d.

## **m. 2** (fastened to the foot of m.1)

The charge which my lord the prince has sustained and still sustains on the safeguard and victualling of the castles in his hands in North and South Wales[2]

Flint castle – constable £40 p.a. fee, 18 archers at 4d. per day; nil for victualling as the area is in peace, albeit tardily: total £149 10s.

2 This membrane is in Anglo-Norman.

Rhuddlan castle – constable £40 p.a. fee, one companion at 1s. per day, 13 archers at 6d. per day; nil for victualling for the reason given above: total £277 5s.

Castle and town of Conway – constable £40 p.a. fee, one companion at 1s. per day, 12 archers in his company at 6d. per day; £40 for victualling but not more as adjoining areas are in peace: total £463 5s.

Beaumaris castle – constable £40 p.a. fee, two of his companions at 1s. per day, 30 archers at 6d. per day; £20 for victualling at the time of the rescue to Candlemas last £20: total £370 5s.

Castle and town of Caernarvon – constable £40 p.a. fee, one companion at 1s. per day, and 12 archers at 6d. per day; town, two men-at-arms at 1s. per day, 26 archers at 6d. per day; £100 for the victualling and costs of the same: total £541 10s.

Harlech castle – constable £40 p.a. fee, three companions at 1s. per day, 24 archers at 6d. per day; £100 for victualling not including costs incurred during visits of the prince in person on divers occasions with royal troops and the said castle victualled by land; total £413 15s.

Aberystwyth ('Lampadarn') castle – constable and 2 companions at 1s. per day, 30 archers at 6d. per day; £100 for the victualling not including costs incurred during visits of the prince in person on divers occasions with his troops, the said castle being rescued and victualled on several occasions by land: total £428 10s.

Cardigan castle – constable £20 p.a. fee, three men-at-arms at 1s. per day, 18 archers at 6d. per day; victuals £20, but not more since the inhabitants of the town help with the victualling and also that the area of Carmarthen has been in peace, albeit tardily: total £259

Total £2903

# *Bibliography*


## Manuscript Sources

### *Chester, Cheshire Archives and Local Studies*

| | |
|---|---|
| DCH | Cholmondeley Manuscripts |
| DLT | Leicester of Tabley Charters and Deeds (consulted through the Historical Manuscripts Commission typescript calendar) |

Ordnance Survey, Cheshire First Edition 6" 1875

### *Keele, Keele University Library*

Legh of Booths Charters

### *Kew, The National Archives of the United Kingdom*

| | |
|---|---|
| CHES 2 | Enrolments (commonly called recognizance rolls) |
| CHES 3 | Inquisitions post mortem |
| CHES 17 | Eyre rolls |
| CHES 19 | Sheriffs' tourn rolls |
| CHES 20 | Calendar rolls |
| CHES 23 | Essoin rolls |
| CHES 24 | Gaol files, writs, etc. |
| CHES 25 | Indictment rolls |
| CHES 26 | Mainprise rolls |
| CHES 29 | Plea rolls |
| CHES 31 | Fines and recoveries |
| CHES 37 | Warrants of attorney rolls |
| CHES 38 | Miscellanea |
| E 101 | Exchequer, King's Remembrancer, Accounts Various |
| E 163 | Exchequer Miscellanea |
| E 364 | Exchequer, Foreign Accounts, Enrolled |
| SC 2 | Court rolls |

SC 6 Ministers' and Receivers' accounts
SC 11 Rentals and Surveys (rolls)
SC 12 Rentals and Surveys (portfolios)

The following table displays the survival of accounts for this period.

| Regnal Year | Period | Chamberlain's Account TNA SC 6 | Ministers' Accounts TNA SC 6 | Lordship of Macclesfield TNA SC 6 |
|---|---|---|---|---|
| 23 Richard II – 1 Henry IV | Michaelmas 1399–1400 | 774/11 | 791/1 | - |
| 1–2 Henry IV | 1400–1 | 774/13 | 791/3 | 805/7 |
| 2–3 Henry IV | 1401–2 | 774/14 | 791/5 | 805/9 |
| 3–4 Henry IV | 1402–3 | 774/15 | 791/6 | 805/11 |
| 4–5 Henry IV | 1403–4 | 775/3 | 791/7 | 805/13 |
| 5–6 Henry IV | 1404–5 | 775/4 | 791/10 | 805/14 |
| 6–7 Henry IV | 1405–6 | 775/5 | 792/1 | 805/16 |
| 7–8 Henry IV | 1406–7 | 775/6 | 792/2 | 806/1 |
| 8–9 Henry IV | 1407–8 | 775/9 | 792/3 | 806/3 |
| 9–10 Henry IV | 1408–9 | - | 792/5 | - |
| 10–11 Henry IV | 1409–10 | 775/11 | 792/6 | 806/4 |
| 11–12 Henry IV | 1410–11 | 775/12 | 792/8 | - |
| 12–13 Henry IV | 1411–12 | - | 792/9 | 806/5 |
| 12–14 Henry IV | 1411–13 | 775/14 | - | - |
| 13 Henry IV – 1 Henry V | 1412–13 | 775/15 | 792/10 | 806/6 |
| 1–2 Henry V | 1413–14 | 1302/15 | 793/1 | 806/8 |
| 2–3 Henry V | 1414–15 | 776/1 | 793/2 | 806/9 |
| 3–4 Henry V | 1415–16 | 1303/1 | 793/4 | 806/11 |
| 4–5 Henry V | 1416–17 | 776/4 | 793/5 | 806/13 |
| 5–6 Henry V | 1417–18 | 776/5 | 793/7 | 806/16 |
| 6–7 Henry V | 1418–19 | 1303/2 | 793/9 | 806/17 |

| Regnal Year | Period | Chamberlain's Account TNA SC 6 | Ministers' Accounts TNA SC 6 | Lordship of Macclesfield TNA SC 6 |
|---|---|---|---|---|
| 7–8 Henry V | 1419–20 | 1303/3 | 793/11 | 807/1 |
| 8–9 Henry V | 1420–1 | 1303/4 | 794/1 | 807/2 |
| 9–10 Henry V | 1421-2 | 1303/5 | 794/2 | 807/3 |

### *London, British Library*

Cotton MS Cleopatra D VI — Cartulary of the de Macclesfield family

### *Manchester, John Rylands Research Institute and Library, University of Manchester*

Arley Charters

Jodrell Manuscripts

Mainwaring Manuscripts

Rylands Charters

Tatton of Wythenshawe Muniments

### *Shrewsbury, Shropshire Archives*

6000/48

## Printed Sources

*Accounts of the Chamberlain and Other Officers of the County of Chester 1301–1360*, ed. R. Stewart-Brown, Record Society of Lancashire and Cheshire, 59 (1910).

*Account of Master John de Burnham the Younger, Chamberlain of Chester, of the Revenues of the Counties of Chester and Flint,*

*Michaelmas 1361 to Michaelmas 1362*, ed. P. H. W. Booth and A. D. Carr, Record Society of Lancashire and Cheshire, 125 (1991).

*Accounts of the Manor and Hundred of Macclesfield Cheshire, Michaelmas 1361 to Michaelmas 1362*, ed. P. H. W. Booth, Record Society of Lancashire and Cheshire, 138 (2003).

*Anglo-Norman Letters and Petitions from All Souls' MS 182*, ed. M. Dominica Legge, Anglo-Norman Text Society, 3 (Oxford: Blackwell, 1941).

*Arley Charters: A Calendar of Ancient Family Charters, Preserved at Arley Hall, Cheshire, the Seat of R. E. Egerton-Warburton*, ed. William Beamont (London: McCorquodale and Co., 1866).

*Calendar of Signet Letters of Henry IV and Henry V* (1399–1422), ed. J. L. Kirby (London: HMSO, 1978).

*Calendar of Wills Proved and Enrolled in the Court of Husting, London. Part 2, 1358–1688*, ed. R. R. Sharpe (London: Corporation of the City of London, 1890).

*Calendars of the Charter Rolls.*

*Calendars of the Close Rolls.*

*Calendars of the Fine Rolls.*

*Calendars of the Patent Rolls.*

'Calendars of Recognizance Rolls of the Palatinate of Chester', *Annual Report of the Deputy Keeper of the Public Records*, vols 36 and 37 (London, 1875 and 1876).

*Chester County Court Indictment Roll 1354–1377: Dealing with Serious Crime in later Fourteenth-Century Cheshire*, ed. Phyllis Hill and Paul Booth, Chetham Society, 3rd ser., 53 (2019).

*Chester Forest Eyre Roll 1357*, part one: *The Forest of Wirral*, ed. Phyllis M. Hill, J. Heery and members of the Ranulph Higden Society, Record Society of Lancashire and Cheshire, 151 (2015).

*The Chronicle of Adam Usk, 1377–1421*, ed. C. Given-Wilson (Oxford: Clarendon Press, 1997).

*An Edition of the Accounts of the Manor of Bickley, Cheshire, 1395–1465*, ed. Matt Bazley, Chetham Society, 3rd ser., 56 (2022).

*The Grey of Ruthin Valor: The Valor of the English Lands of Edmund Grey, Earl of Kent, drawn up from the Ministers' Accounts of 1467–8*, ed. R. I. Jack (Sydney: Sydney University Press, 1965).

*Issues of the Exchequer: Being a Collection of Payments made out of His Majesty's Revenue, from King Henry III to King Henry VI Inclusive*, ed. Frederick Devon, Record Commission (London: John Murray, 1837).

*Johannis de Trokelowe et Henrici de Blaneforde, monachorum S. Albani, necnon quorundam anonymorum, chronica et annales*, ed. H. T. Riley, Rolls Ser., 28/iii (London: Longmans, Green, Reader, and Dyer, 1866).

*The Lay Subsidy of 1334*, ed. Robin E. Glasscock, Records of Social and Economic History (Oxford: Oxford University Press and British Academy, 1975).

*The Ledger-Book of Vale Royal Abbey*, ed. John Brownbill, Record Society of Lancashire and Cheshire, 68 (1914).

*A Middlewich Chartulary*, ed. Joan Varley, 2 vols, Chetham Society, 105, 108 (with James Tait) (1941–4).

*Parliament Rolls of Medieval England, 1275–1504*, VIII: *Henry IV, 1399–1413*, ed. Chris Given-Wilson (Woodbridge: Boydell; London: National Archives, 2005).

*Parliament Rolls of Medieval England 1275–1504*, IX: *Henry V, 1413–1422*, ed. Chris Given-Wilson (Woodbridge: Boydell; London: National Archives, 2005).

*La prinse et mort du roy Richart d'Angleterre, based on British Library MS Harley 1319, and Other Works by Jehan Creton*, ed. and trans. Lorna A. Finlay, Camden Society, 5th ser., 65 (2023).

*Proceedings and Ordinances of the Privy Council of England*, ed. N. Harris Nicolas, 7 vols (London: Record Commission, 1834–7).

*Records of Early English Drama: Cheshire, Including Chester*, ed. Elizabeth Baldwin, Lawrence M. Clopper and David Mills, 2 vols (London: British Library; Toronto: University of Toronto Press, 2007).

*Register of Edward the Black Prince Preserved in the Public Record Office*, 4 vols (London: HMSO, 1930–3).

*Reports from Lords Committees touching the Dignity of a Peer*, 5 vols (London: House of Lords, 1829).

*Royal and Historical Letters during the Reign of Henry IV*, ed. F. C. Hingeston, 2 vols (vol. 1, Rolls Ser., 18, London: Longman, Green, Longman, and Roberts, 1860; vol. 2, London: HMSO, 1965).

*St Alban's Chronicle*, vol. II: *1394–1422. The* Chronica Maiora *of Thomas Walsingham*, ed. John Taylor, Wendy R. Childs and Leslie Watkiss (Oxford: Clarendon Press, 2011).

*Walter of Henley and Other Treatises on Estate Management and Accounting*, ed. Dorothea Oschinsky (Oxford: Clarendon Press, 1971).

## Secondary works

Allmand, Christopher, *Henry V* (London: Methuen, 1992).

Ault, W. O., *Open Field Farming in Medieval England* (London: Allen & Unwin 1972).

Barber, Richard, *Edward, Prince of Wales and Aquitaine. A Biography of the Black Prince* (London: Allen Lane, 1978, repr, Woodbridge: Boydell, 1996).

Barraclough, Geoffrey, 'The Earldom and County Palatine of Chester', *Transactions of the Historic Society of Lancashire and Cheshire*, 103 (1951), 23–57.

Beamont, William, *An Account of the Ancient Town of Frodsham, in Cheshire* (Warrington: Percival Pearse, 1881).

Bean, J. M. W., *The Estates of the Percy Family 1416–1537* (Oxford: Oxford University Press, 1958).

Bean, J. M. W., 'Plague, Population and Economic Decline in the Later Middle Ages', *Economic History Review*, 2nd ser., 15 (1962–3), 423–37.

Bennett, Michael J., 'A County Community: Social Cohesion amongst the Cheshire Gentry, 1400–1425', *Northern History*, 8 (1973), 24–44.

Bennett, Michael J., 'Sources and Problems in the Study of Social Mobility: Cheshire in the Later Middle Ages', *Transactions of the Historic Society of Lancashire and Cheshire*, 128 (1979 for 1978), 59–95.

Bennett, Michael J., *Community, Class and Careerism: Cheshire and Lancashire Society in the Age of Sir Gawain and the Green Knight* (Cambridge: Cambridge University Press, 1983).

Bennett, Michael J., 'Henry V and the Cheshire Tax Revolt of 1416', in Gwilym Dodd (ed.), *Henry V: New Interpretations* (Woodbridge: York Medieval Press, 2013), pp. 171–86.

Bennett, Richard and J. Elton, *History of Corn Milling*, vol. 4: *Some Feudal Mills* (London, 1904, repr. Wakefield: EP Publishing, 1975).

Biggs, D., *Three Armies in Britain. The Irish Campaign of Richard II and the Usurpation of Henry IV, 1397–99* (Leiden and Boston: Brill, 2006).

Bird, W. H. B., 'Taxation and Representation in the County Palatine of Chester', *English Historical Review*, 30 (1915), 303.

Booth, P. H. W., 'Taxation and Public Order: Cheshire in 1353', *Northern History*, 12 (1976), 16–31.

Booth, P. H. W., and J. P. Dodd, 'The Manor and Fields of Frodsham', *Transactions of the Historic Society of Lancashire and Cheshire*, 128 (1979 for 1978), 27–57.

Booth, P. H. W., '"Farming for Profit" in the Fourteenth Century: The Cheshire Estates of the Earldom of Chester, *Journal of the Chester Archaeological Society*, 62 (1979), 73–90.

Booth, P. H. W., *The Financial Administration of the Lordship and County of Chester 1272–1377*, Chetham Society, 3rd ser., 28 (1981).

Booth, P. H. W., 'The Last Week of the Life of Edward the Black Prince', in Hannah Skoda, Patrick Lantschner and R. L. J. Shaw (eds), *Contact and Exchange in Later Medieval Europe: Essays in Honour of Malcolm Vale* (Woodbridge: Boydell Press, 2012), pp. 221–45.

Bridbury, A. R., *Economic Growth: England in the Later Middle Ages* (London: George Allen & Unwin, 1962).

Bridbury, A. R., *England and the Salt Trade in the Later Middle Ages* (Oxford: Clarendon Press, 1955).

Britton, Edward, *The Community of the Vill. A Study in the History of the Family and Village Life in Fourteenth-Century England* (Toronto: Macmillan of Canada, 1977).

Brownbill, J., 'The Troutbeck Family', *JCNWAS*, 28 (1929), 149–79.

Burne, R. V. H., 'Richard II and Cheshire', *JCNWAS*, 48 (1961), 27–34.

Calvert, Albert F., *Salt in Cheshire* (London: Spon; New York: Spon and Chamberlain, 1915).

Carr, A. D., 'A Welsh Knight in the Hundred Years War: Sir Gregory Sais', *Transactions of the Honourable Society of Cymmrodorion* (1977), 40–53.

Carus-Wilson, E. M., 'Evidences of Industrial Growth on Some Fifteenth-Century Manors', *Economic History Review*, 2nd ser., 12 (1959–60), 190–205.

Cash, Sarah, 'The Donnes of Utkinton', *Cheshire Notes and Queries*, 2 (1897), 163–8.

Chapman, Adam, *Welsh Soldiers in the Later Middle Ages 1282–1422* (Woodbridge: Boydell Press, 2015).

Clark, Linda (ed.), *The House of Commons 1422–61*, 7 vols (Cambridge: Cambridge University Press, 2020).

Clarke, M. V., and V. H. Galbraith, 'The Deposition of Richard II', *Bulletin of the John Rylands Library*, 14 (1930), 125–81.

Clayton, Dorothy J., *The Administration of the County Palatine of Chester 1442–1485*, Chetham Society, 3rd ser., 28 (1990).

Cokayne, G. E., and Geoffrey H. White (eds), *The Complete Peerage of England, Scotland, Ireland, Great Britain and the United Kingdom, Extant, Extinct and Dormant*, new edn, 12 vols in 13 (London: St Catherine Press, 1910–59).

Colvin, H. M. (ed.), *The History of the King's Works*, 6 vols (London: HMSO, 1963–82).

Curry, Anne, 'Cheshire and the Royal Demesne, 1399–1422', *Transactions of the Historic Society of Lancashire and Cheshire*, 128 (1978), 113–35.

Curry, Anne, 'The Court Rolls of the Lordship of Macclesfield, 1345–1485', *Cheshire History*, 12 (1983), 5–10.

Curry, Anne, 'The "Coronation Expedition" and Henry VI's Court in France, 1430–1432', in J. Stratford (ed.), *The Lancastrian Court* (Stamford: Paul Watkins Press, 2003), pp. 30–54.

Curry, Anne, *Agincourt: A New History* (Stroud: Tempus, 2005).

Curry, Anne, *Henry V: Playboy Prince to Warrior King* (London: Allen Lane, 2015).

Curry, Anne, 'After Agincourt, What Next? Henry V and the Campaign of 1416', in Linda Clark (ed.), *Conflicts, Consequences and the Crown in the Late Middle Ages*, The Fifteenth Century, 7 (Woodbridge: Boydell Press, 2007), pp. 23–51.

Curry, Anne, Adrian R. Bell, Andy King and David Simpkin, 'New Regime, New Army? Henry IV's Scottish Expedition of 1400', *English Historical Review*, 125 (2010), 1382–1413.

Curry, Anne, 'Henry V's Harfleur: A Study in Military Administration, 1415–1422', in L. J. Andrew Villalon and Donald J. Kagay (eds), *The Hundred Years War (Part III): Further Considerations* (Leiden and Boston: Brill, 2013), pp. 259–84.

Curry, Anne, 'The Making of a Prince. The Finances of "the Young Lord Henry", 1386–1400', in Gwilym Dodd (ed.), *Henry V: New Interpretations* (Woodbridge: York Medieval Press, 2013), pp. 11–33.

Curry, Anne, and David Cleverly, 'Henry V's Army of 1417', in Linda Clark (ed.), *Enmity and Amity,* The Fifteenth Century, 19 (2022 for 2021), 35–67.

Davies, C. Stella (ed.), *A History of Macclesfield* (Manchester: Manchester University Press, 1961).

Davies, R. R., 'Baronial Accounts, Incomes, and Arrears in the Later Middle Ages', *Economic History Review*, 2nd ser., 21 (1968), 211–29.

Davies, R. R., 'Richard II and the Principality of Chester, 1397–9', in F. R. H. Du Boulay and Caroline M. Barron (eds), *The Reign of Richard II: Essays in Honour of May McKisack* (London: Athlone Press, 1971), pp. 256–79.

Davies, R. R., *The Revolt of Owain Glyn Dŵr* (Oxford: Oxford University Press, 1995).

Denholm-Young, N., *Seignorial Administration in England* (London: Oxford University Press, 1937).

DeWindt, E. B., *Land and People in Holywell-cum-Needingworth* (Toronto: Pontifical Institute of Mediaeval Studies, 1972).

Dodd, J. Phillip, 'The Growth of a Middle Class in Frodsham Manor 1300–60', *Journal of the Chester Archaeological Society,* 64 (1981), 32–40.

Dodgson, J. McN., *The Place Names of Cheshire*, 4 vols, English Place Name Society, 44, 45, 46 and 47 (Cambridge: Cambridge University Press, 1970–2).

Drew, J. S., 'Manorial Accounts of St. Swithin's Priory, Winchester', *English Historical Review*, 62 (1947), 20–41.

Driver, J. T., *Cheshire in the Later Middle Ages* (Chester: Cheshire Community Council, 1971).

Du Boulay, F. R. H., *An Age of Ambition: English Society in the Late Middle Ages* (London: Nelson, 1970).

Du Boulay, F. R. H., *The Lordship of Canterbury: An Essay in Medieval Society* (London: Nelson, 1966).

Du Boulay, F. R. H., 'A Rentier Economy in the Later Middle Ages: The Archbishopric of Canterbury', *Economic History Review*, 2nd ser., 16 (1964), 427–38.

Du Boulay, F. R. H., 'Who were Farming the English Demesnes at the End of the Middle Ages', *Economic History Review*, 2nd ser., 17 (1965), 443–55.

Earwaker, J. P., *East Cheshire: Past and Present; or A History of the Hundred of Macclesfield, in the County Palatine of Chester*, 2 vols (London: printed for the author, 1877–80).

Fox, Levi, *The Administration of the Honour of Leicester in the Fourteenth Century* (Leicester: Edgar Backus, 1940).

Gillespie, J. L., 'Richard II's Cheshire Archers', *Transactions of the Historic Society of Lancashire and Cheshire*, 125 (1974), 1–39.

Given-Wilson, Christopher, *Henry IV* (New Haven CT and London: Yale University Press, 2016).

Griffiths, R. A., 'The Glyndŵr Rebellion in North Wales through the Eyes of an Englishman', *Bulletin of the Board of Celtic Studies*, 22 (1966–8), 151–68.

Griffiths, R. A., 'Patronage, Politics and the Principality of Wales 1413–61', in H. Hearder and H. R. Loyn (eds), *British Government and Administration: Studies Presented to S. B. Chrimes* (Cardiff: University of Wales Press, 1974), pp. 69–86.

Griffiths, R. A., *The Principality of Wales in the Later Middle Ages: The Structure and Personnel of Government*, 1: *South Wales 1277–1536*, Board of Celtic Studies, University of Wales, History and Law Ser., 26 (Cardiff: University of Wales Press, 1972).

Griffiths, R. A., 'Wales and the Marches', in S. B. Chrimes, C. D. Ross and R. A. Griffiths (eds), *Fifteenth Century England, 1399–1509: Studies in Politics and Society* (Manchester: Manchester University Press, 1972), pp. 145–72.

Griffiths, W. R. M., 'Prince Henry, Wales, and the Royal Exchequer, 1400–14', *Bulletin of the Board of Celtic Studies*, 32 (1985), 202–15.

Griffiths, W. R. M., 'Prince Henry's War: Armies, Garrisons and Supply during the Glyndwr Rising', *Bulletin of the Board of Celtic Studies*, 34 (1987), 165–73.

Harris, B. E., 'The Palatinate 1301–1547', in B. E. Harris (ed.), *The Victoria History of the Counties of England. A History of the County of Chester*, vol. 2 (Oxford: Oxford University Press for the University of London Institute of Historical Research, 1979), pp. 9–35.

Harris, Barbara J., 'Landlords and Tenants in England in the Later Middle Ages: The Buckingham Estates', *Past and Present*, 43 (1969), 146–50.

Harvey, Barbara F., 'The Leasing of the Abbot of Westminster's Demesnes in the Later Middle Ages', *Economic History Review*, 2nd ser., 22 (1969), 17–27.

Harvey, P. D. A., *Manorial Records* (London: British Records Association, 1984).

Hatcher, John, *Rural Economy and Society in the Duchy of Cornwall 1300–1500* (Cambridge: Cambridge University Press, 1970).

Hewitt, H. J., *Medieval Cheshire. An Economic and Social History of Cheshire in the Reigns of the Three Edwards*, Chetham Society, new ser., 88 (1929).

Hewitt, H. J., *The Black Prince's Expedition of 1355–1357* (Manchester: Manchester University Press, 1958).

Hewitt, H. J., *Cheshire under the Three Edwards* (Chester: Cheshire Community Council, 1967).

Hilton, R. H., *The Economic Development of Some Leicestershire Estates in the 14th & 15th Centuries* (London: Oxford University Press, 1947).

Hilton, R. H., *Ministers' Accounts of the Warwickshire Estates of the Duke of Clarence, 1479–80*, Dugdale Society, 21 (1952).

Hilton, R. H., *A Medieval Society: The West Midlands at the End of the Thirteenth Century* (London: Weidenfeld & Nicolson, 1967).

Hilton, R. H., *The Decline of Serfdom in Medieval England* (London: Macmillan, 1969).

Hilton, R. H., *The English Peasantry in the Later Middle Ages* (Oxford: Clarendon Press, 1975).

Hilton, R. H., 'Small Town Society in England Before the Black Death', *Past & Present*, 105 (1984), 53–78.

Holmes, G. A., *The Estates of the Higher Nobility in Fourteenth Century England* (Cambridge: Cambridge University Press, 1957).

Hotson, J. L., 'Colfox v. Chauntecleer', *Proceedings of the Modern Language Association of America*, 39 (1924), 762–81.

Husain, B. M. C., 'Delamere Forest in Later Mediaeval Times', *Transactions of the Historic Society of Lancashire and Cheshire*, 107 (1955), 23–39.

Jacob, E. F., *The Fifteenth Century, 1399 to 1485* (Oxford: Clarendon Press, 1961).

Jones, Francis, *The Princes and Principality of Wales* (Cardiff: University of Wales Press, 1969).

Jones, J. Gwynfor, 'Government and the Welsh Community: The North East Borderland in the Fifteenth Century', in H. Hearder and H. R. Loyn (eds), *British Government and Administration, Studies presented to S. B. Chrimes* (Cardiff: University of Wales Press, 1974), pp. 55–68.

Jurkowski, M., C. L. Smith, and D. Crook, *Lay Taxes in England and Wales 1188–1688* (Kew: PRO Publications, 1998).

Kirby, J. L., 'The Issues of the Lancastrian Exchequer and Lord Cromwell's Estimates of 1433', *Bulletin of the Institute of Historical Research*, 24 (1951), 121–51.

Lander, J. R., *Conflict and Stability in Fifteenth-Century England* (London: Hutchinson & Co., 1969).

Lander, J. R., *Crown and Nobility, 1450–1509* (London: Edward Arnold, 1976).

Langton, John, 'Royal and Non-Royal Forests in England and Wales', *Historical Research*, 88 (2015), 381–401.

Laslett, Peter, *The World We Have Lost* (2nd edn, London: Routledge, 1971).

Lewis, C. P., and A.T. Thacker (eds), *The Victoria History of the Counties of England. A History of the County of Chester, vol. 5, part 1: The City of Chester: General History and Topography* (London: Boydell and Brewer for the Institute of Historical Research, 2003).

*List and Index V. Special Collection 6: Ministers and Receivers' Accounts* (London: HMSO 1894).

*List and Index XXXV. Exchequer Accounts Various* (London: HMSO, 1900).

Lydon, J. F., 'Richard II's Expeditions to Ireland', *Journal of the Royal Society of Antiquaries of Ireland*, 93 (1963), 135–49.

McFarlane, K. B., *The Nobility of Later Medieval England* (Oxford: Clarendon Press, 1973).

McKisack, May, *The Fourteenth Century, 1307–1399* (Oxford: Clarendon Press, 1959).

McNiven, Peter, 'The Cheshire Rising of 1400', *Bulletin of the John Rylands Library*, 52 (1970), 375–96.

McNiven, Peter, 'The Men of Cheshire and the Rebellion of 1403', *Transactions of the Historic Society of Lancashire and Cheshire*, 129 (1979), 1–29

Maxfield, D. K., 'Was John Macclesfield a Scoundrel?', *Cheshire History*, 28 (1991), 19–20.

Maxfield, D. K., 'Pardoners and Property: John Macclesfield 1351–1422, Builder of Macclesfield Castle', *Journal of the Chester Archaeological Society*, 69 (1986), 79–95.

Messham, J. E., 'The County of Flint and the Rebellion of Owen Glyndwr in the Records of the Earldom of Chester', *Journal of the Flintshire Historical Society*, 23 (1967–8), 1–34.

Mileson, Stephen A., *Parks in Medieval England* (Oxford: Oxford University Press, 2009).

Morgan, P. J., 'Cheshire and the Defence of the Principality of Aquitaine', *Transactions of the Historic Society of Lancashire and Cheshire*, 128 (1978), 139–60.

Morgan, P. J., *War and Society in Medieval Cheshire, 1277–1403*, Chetham Society, 3rd ser., 34 (1987).

Morgan, P. J., 'Cheshire and Wales', in Huw Pryce and John Watts (eds), *Power and Identity in the Middle Ages. Essays in Memory of Rees Davies* (Oxford: Oxford University Press, 2007), pp. 195–210.

Morris, Rupert H., *Chester in the Plantagenet and Tudor Reigns* (Chester: printed for the author, 1893).

Neilson, N., 'Customary Rents', in Paul Vinogradoff (ed.), *Oxford Studies in Social and Legal History*, vol. 2 (Oxford: Clarendon Press, 1910).

Nicolas, N. H., *History of the Battle of Agincourt* (3rd edn, London: Johnson & Co., 1833).

Ormerod, George, *History of the County Palatine and City of Chester*, ed. T. Helsby (2nd edition), 3 vols (London: George Routledge & Sons, 1882).

Ormrod, W. Mark, 'The Domestic Response', in A. Curry and M. Hughes (eds), *Arms, Armies and Fortifications in the Hundred Years War* (Woodbridge: Boydell Press, 1994), pp. 83–101.

Ormrod, W. Mark, *Edward III* (New Haven CT and London: Yale University Press, 2011).

Ormrod, W. Mark, 'Henry V and the English Taxpayer', in Gwilym Dodd (ed.) *Henry V: New Interpretations* (Woodbridge: York Medieval Press, 2013), pp. 187–216.

Oschinsky, Dorothea, 'Medieval Treaties on Estate Accounting', *Economic History Review*, 17 (1947), 52–61.

Oschinsky, Dorothea, 'Notes on the Editing and Interpretation of Estate Accounts', parts 1 and 2, *Archives*, 9 (1969–70), 84–9, 142–52.

Pépin, Guilhem, 'Towards a New Assessment of the Black Prince's Principality of Aquitaine: A Study of the Last Years (1369–72)', *Nottingham Medieval Studies*, 50 (2006), 59–114.

Phillips, Seymour, *Edward II* (New Haven CT and London: Yale University Press, 2010).

Plucknett, T. F. T., *The Medieval Bailiff* (London: Athlone Press, 1954).

Pollard, A. J., 'Estate Management in the Later Middle Ages: the Talbots and Whitchurch, 1383–1525', *Economic History Review*, 2nd ser., 25 (1972), 553–66.

Postan, M., 'Some Economic Evidence of Declining Population in the Later Middle Ages', *Economic History Review*, 2nd ser., 2 (1950), 221–46.

Postan, M., 'The Fifteenth Century', *Economic History Review*, 9 (1939), 160–7.

Postan, M. M., *The Medieval Economy and Society: An Economic History of Britain in the Middle Ages* (London: Weidenfeld and Nicolson, 1972).

Powell, E., *Kingship, Law and Society. Criminal Justice in the Reign of Henry V* (Oxford: Clarendon Press, 1989).

Powicke, F. M., and E. B. Fryde (eds), *Handbook of British Chronology* (2nd edn, London: Royal Historical Society, 1961).

Prestwich, Michael, *Edward I* (London: Methuen, 1988).

Prestwich, Michael, *Armies and Warfare in the Middle Ages: The English Experience* (New Haven CT and London: Yale University Press, 1996).

Pugh, T. B., *The Marcher Lordships of South Wales, 1415–1536: Select Documents* (Cardiff: University of Wales Press, 1963).

Raftis, J. A., *Tenure and Mobility* (Toronto: Pontifical Institute of Mediaeval Studies, 1964).

Raftis, J. A., 'The Concentration of Responsibility in Five Villages', *Mediaeval Studies*, 28 (1966), 92–118.

Raftis, J. A., *Warboys: Two Hundred Years in the Life of an English Mediaeval Village*, (Toronto: Pontifical Institute of Mediaeval Studies, 1974).

Roberts, Glyn, 'The Anglesey Submissions of 1406', *Bulletin of the Board of Celtic Studies*, 15 (1952–4), 39–61.

Rogers, James E. Thorold, *A History of Agriculture and Prices in England*, 7 vols in 8 (Oxford: Clarendon Press, 1866–1902).

Rosenthal, J. T., 'The Estates and Finances of Richard Duke of York, 1411–60', *Studies in Medieval and Renaissance History*, 2 (1965), 115–204.

Roskell, J. S., Linda Clark and Carole Rawcliffe (eds), *The House of Commons 1386–1421*, 4 vols (Stroud: Alan Sutton for the History of Parliament Trust, 1993).

Ross, C. D., *The Estates and Finances of Richard Beauchamp, Earl of Warwick*, Dugdale Society Occasional Papers, 12 (1956).

Ross, C. D., 'The Estates and Finances of Richard Duke of York', *Welsh History Review*, 3 (1966–7), 299–302.

Ross, C. D., and T. B. Pugh, 'Materials for the Study of Baronial Incomes in Fifteenth-Century England', *Economic History Review*, 2nd ser., 6 (1953), 185–94.

Sabapathy, John, *Officers and Accountability in Medieval England, 1170–1300* (Oxford: Oxford University Press, 2014).

Saul, Nigel, *Richard II* (New Haven CT and London: Yale University Press, 1997).

Sharp, Tom, 'Reflections on My Grandfather, The Historian T. F. Tout', in Caroline M. Barron and Joel T. Rosenthal (eds), *Thomas Frederick Tout (1855–1929). Refashioning History for the Twentieth Century* (London: University of London Press, 2019), pp. 297–312.

Sharp, M., 'The Central Administrative System of Edward, the Black Prince', in T. F. T. Tout, *Chapters in Medieval Administrative History*, vol. 5 (Manchester, 1930), pp. 289–431.

Simpson, A. W. B., *An Introduction to the History of Land Law* (2nd edn, Oxford: Oxford University Press, 1967).

Smith, J. Beverley, 'The Last Phase of the Glyndŵr Rebellion', *Bulletin of the Board of Celtic Studies*, 22 (1966–8), 250–60.

Somerville, Robert, *History of the Duchy of Lancaster*, vol. 1: *1265–1603* (London: Chancellor and Council of the Duchy of Lancaster, 1953).

Steel, Anthony, *The Receipt of the Exchequer, 1377–1485* (Cambridge: Cambridge University Press, 1954).

Stewart-Brown, Ronald, 'The Royal Manor and Park of Shotwick', *Transactions of the Historic Society of Lancashire and Cheshire*, 64 (1912), 82–142.

Stewart-Brown, Ronald, 'The End of the Norman Earldom of Chester', *English Historical Review*, 35 (1920), 26–54.

Stewart-Brown, Ronald, 'The Exchequer of Chester', *English Historical Review*, 57 (1942), 289–97.

Stone, Eric, 'Profit and Loss Accounting at Norwich Cathedral Priory', *Transactions of the Royal Historical Society*, 5th ser., 12 (1962), 25–48.

Studd, J. R., 'The Lord Edward's Lordship of Chester, 1254–72', *Transactions of the Historic Society of Lancashire and Cheshire*, 128 (1978), 1–25.

Sylvester, Dorothy, 'The Open Fields of Cheshire', *Transactions of the Historic Society of Lancashire and Cheshire*, 108 (1956), 1–33.

Thornton, Tim, 'Taxing the King's Dominions: The Subject Territories of the English Crown in the Later Middle Ages', in W. Mark Ormrod, Margaret Bonney and Richard Bonney (eds), *Crises, Revolutions and Self-Sustained Growth: Essays in European Fiscal History, 1130–1830* (Stamford: Shaun Tyas, 1999), pp. 97–109.

Thornton, Tim, 'Cheshire: The Inner Citadel of Richard II's Kingdom?' in Gwilym Dodd (ed.) *The Reign of Richard II* (Stroud: Tempus, 2000), pp. 85–96.

Thornton, Tim, *Cheshire and the Tudor State, 1480–1560* (Woodbridge: Boydell, 2000).

Titow, J. Z., *English Rural Society, 1200–1350* (London: George Allen and Unwin, 1969).

Tonkinson, A. M., *Macclesfield in the Later Fourteenth Century. Communities of Town and Forest*, Chetham Society, 3rd ser., 42 (1999).

Tuck, J. A., 'Richard II's System of Patronage', in F. R. H. Du Boulay and C. M. Barron (eds), *The Reign of Richard II. Essays in Honour of May McKisack* (London: Athlone Press, 1971), pp. 1–20.

Tuck, J. A., 'The Earl of Arundel's Expedition to France, 1411', in Gwilym Dodd and Douglas Biggs (eds), *The Reign of Henry IV: Rebellion and Survival, 1403–1413* (Woodbridge: York Medieval Press, 2008), pp. 228–40.

Westman, Barbara Hanawalt, 'The Peasant Family and Crime in Fourteenth-Century England', *Journal of British Studies*, 13 (1974), 1–18.

Wilkinson, Bertie, *Constitutional History of England in the Fifteenth Century (1399–1485): With Illustrative Documents* (London: Longmans, 1964).

Wilson, C. Anne, *Food and Drink in Britain: From the Stone Age to Recent Times* (London: Constable, 1973).

Wilson, K. P., 'The Port of Chester in the Fifteenth Century', *Transactions of the Historic Society of Lancashire and Cheshire*, 117 (1965), 1–15.

Wolffe, B. P., 'The Management of English Royal Estates under the Yorkist Kings', *English Historical Review*, 71 (1956), 1–27.

Wolffe, B. P., *The Royal Demesne in English History: The Crown Estate in the Governance of the Realm from the Conquest to 1509* (London: Allen and Unwin, 1971).

Wylie, James Hamilton, *History of England under Henry the Fourth*, 4 vols (London: Longmans, Green, 1884–98).

Wylie, J. H., and W. T. Waugh, *The Reign of Henry the Fifth*, 3 vols (Cambridge: Cambridge University Press, 1914–29).

Young, Charles R., *The Royal Forests of Medieval England* (Philadelphia: University of Pennsylvania Press, 1979).

## Unpublished secondary sources

Booth, P. H. W., *Cheshire Estate Records: Use and Abuse*, University of Liverpool, School of History and Institute of Extension Studies, Medieval Cheshire Seminar (Nov. 1975), privately printed.

Booth, P. H. W., 'The Financial Administration of the Lordship and County of Chester 1272–1377', unpublished MA thesis (University of Liverpool, 1974).

Bruel, J. L. C., 'An Edition of the John de Macclesfield Cartulary', unpublished PhD thesis (University of London, 1969).

Davies, R. G., 'The Episcopate in England and Wales 1375–1443', unpublished PhD thesis, (University of Manchester, 1974).

Greenblatt, D., 'The Surburban Manors of Coventry 1279–1411', unpublished PhD thesis (Cornell University, 1967).

Griffiths, W. R. M., 'The Military Career and Affinity of Henry, Prince of Wales, 1399–1413', unpublished M Litt dissertation (University of Oxford, 1980).

Harris, B. E., *The Chester Recognizance Rolls*, University of Liverpool, School of History and Institute of Extension Studies, Medieval Cheshire Seminar (Aug. 1975), privately printed.

Kenyon, D., 'Rural Settlement Patterns in Medieval Cheshire', unpublished MA thesis (University of Manchester, 1974).

Kermode, J., *Medieval Cheshire Boroughs: Some Preliminary Observations*, University of Liverpool, School of History and

Institute of Extension Studies, Medieval Cheshire Seminar (Sept. 1975), privately printed.

Kirby, J. L., 'The Hungerford Family in the Later Middle Ages', unpublished MA thesis (University of London, 1939).

McNiven, P., 'Rebellion and Disaffection in the North of England 1403–1408', unpublished MA thesis (University of Manchester, 1967).

Pollard, A. J., 'The Family of Talbot, Lords Talbot and Earls of Shrewsbury in the Fifteenth Century', unpublished PhD thesis (University of Bristol, 1968).

Sharp, M., 'Contributions to the History of the Earldom and County of Chester, 1237–1399, Historical, Topographical and Administrative, with a Study of the Household of Edward the Black Prince and its Relations with Cheshire', unpublished PhD thesis (University of Manchester, 1925).

# Index